Religion in Philosophical and Cultural Perspective

A NEW APPROACH TO THE PHILOSOPHY OF RELIGION THROUGH CROSS-DISCIPLINARY STUDIES

Edited by

J. CLAYTON FEAVER
Kingfisher College Professor of the
Philosophy of Religion and Ethics
University of Oklahoma

AND

WILLIAM HOROSZ
Associate Professor of Philosophy
University of Oklahoma

D. VAN NOSTRAND COMPANY, INC.
Princeton, New Jersey   Toronto   London

VAN NOSTRAND REGIONAL OFFICES: *New York, Chicago, San Francisco*

D. VAN NOSTRAND COMPANY, LTD., *London*

D. VAN NOSTRAND COMPANY (Canada), LTD., *Toronto*

PRINTED IN THE UNITED STATES OF AMERICA

Preface

THE PHILOSOPHY OF RELIGION has to steer a course between various extremes of oversimplification. On the one hand, it cannot be simply an echo of traditional religion; if so, it would be futile sound. On the other hand, it cannot become the history of nonconformist religionists, in which philosophers are viewed as dissenting, unaspiring believers; if so, it would be ill-tempered waste or empty fancy. The philosophy of religion is a more legitimate and meaningful enterprise than these and other extremes would indicate. The choice is not between doctrinal regularity and no doctrine at all.

The cross-disciplinary studies of religion in this volume will indicate and feature the more meaningful approach of the philosophy of religion. Moreover, these cross-disciplinary studies will be a healthy antidote to religious sectarianism. New ways of thinking in the area of religion, which do not lose contact with the partnership between education and history, and between education and contemporary ideals, will be found implicit throughout the volume. In Part I several approaches to philosophy of religion will be reviewed with the intention of giving them historical perspective and contemporary relevance. In Part II various contemporary ideals in their interaction with religion will be examined in a cultural context. Taking the two parts together, the reader may gain some appreciation of the comprehensive task of the philosophy of religion and may be motivated to think out the relationship of education to contemporary knowledge, ideals, and aspirations.

Most of the contributors to this volume have some sympathy for the humanist ideal, which is the dominant value of the modern *Zeitgeist*. They are profoundly concerned to avoid the pitfall of an unbalanced culture, but they are also aware of the dangers of conformity and mediocrity which may attend the practice of this ideal.

This venture in cross-disciplinary studies of religion could not have been undertaken except for the premise that religion is a hospitable subject matter, amenable to inquiry. Consequently, the editors of the volume recommend its use not only for the teaching of philosophy of religion in secular colleges and universities, but also in denominational colleges and theological schools. The current disarray of theology in Protestant, Catholic, and Jewish thought, as well as in oriental traditions, is often a cause of consternation to religiously oriented students. A dialogue with cross-disciplinary studies should provide benefits to each partner in the exchange of ideas. Just as religion has become a legitimate topic for philosophical and cultural studies, so must philosophical and cultural aspects of existence be viewed as proper materials for theological studies. John C. Bennett of Union Theological Seminary expresses a similar expectation when he says:

> Today the diversity is greater than ever. No one type of theology connected with one of the great theologians . . . of the recent theological revival has strong influence. . . . There is a definite revival of interest in philosophy [and in culture] as material for the philosophy of religion or philosophical theology. Existential subjectivism is still an important form of religious quest but there is strong countervailing force in the preoccupation with the social and cultural crisis, with the problems of the city and especially with the struggle for civil rights. [From the "President's Column" in *The Tower*, spring 1964, p. 2.]

This volume will have achieved its purpose if it prompts the student to engage in serious, concerned reflection upon religion, both in its historical depth and in its contemporary significance. Such reflection will be serious only on the basis of a vital dialogue among religion, philosophy, and culture.

We are especially grateful to the sixteen contributors to this study in the philosophy of religion—in which the primary concern is for effective communication among the several branches of knowledge. This book is a new venture in cross-disciplinary studies. Each contributor offers a new and original account of the current dialogue between culture and religion, giving sufficient philosophical and historical depth to warrant a new venture in publication.

A word of appreciation is due Mr. Cecil Garlin, Kingfisher College Fellow in the Philosophy of Religion and Ethics at the University of Oklahoma, for his assistance with Chapter 1, and to Mrs. Jerelen Huskey and Mrs. Phyllis Drake for their extensive help with the manuscript.

J. C. F. AND W. H.

Norman, Oklahoma
January 1967

Contents

PART II

RELIGION IN CULTURAL PERSPECTIVE

THE CONTRIBUTORS

GLANVILLE DOWNEY, A.B. and Ph.D. (1934) in classics at Princeton University, has worked in Greece and Syria and has been a member of the Institute for Advanced Study and of the faculty at Yale. Following service in World War II he joined the faculty of the Dumbarton Oaks Center for Byzantine Studies of Harvard University (Washington) and is currently Professor of History and Classics at Indiana University. His books include *A History of Antioch in Syria; Ancient Antioch; Constantinople in the Age of Justinian; Gaza in the Early Sixth Century; Aristotle, Dean of Early Science.*

J. CLAYTON FEAVER, a native of California, is Kingfisher College Professor of the Philosophy of Religion and Ethics and David Ross Boyd Professor of Philosophy. He took an A.B. degree at Fresno State College, a B.D. degree at Pacific School of Religion, and a Ph.D. at Yale. He has taught at Berea College, and in the University of Oklahoma is Chairman of the Executive Committee of the College of Continuing Education, a member of the Founders' Committee and of the Executive Committee of the Southwest Center for Human Relations Studies. He is a past president of the Southwestern Philosophical Society.

CHARLES HARTSHORNE, now Ashbel Smith Professor of Philosophy at the University of Texas, studied at Harvard (A.B., 1922;

Ph.D., 1923) and was a Sheldon Travelling Fellow (Freiburg, Marburg, 1923-25). He has taught at Harvard (1925-28), at the University of Chicago (1928-55), and at Emory University (1955-62). He has served as visiting professor at Stanford, at the New School for Social Research, and at the universities of Melbourne, Frankfurt, Washington, and Kyoto. Past president of several philosophical societies, he is currently President of The Southern Society for Philosophy and Psychology. A distinguished and original writer, Professor Hartshorne's recent books include *The Logic of Perfection* (Open Court, 1962); *The Divine Relativity* (Yale, 1948, 1964); *Philosophers Speak of God* (University of Chicago, 1953, 1963); and in press, *Anselm's Discovery* (Open Court, 1965). His work as editor of *The Collected Papers of Charles S. Peirce* at Harvard is also well known.

PAUL L. HOLMER, a native of Minnesota (B.A., University of Minnesota, 1940; and M.A., 1941; Ph.D., Yale University in philosophy, 1946) has taught at Yale, at Gustavus Adolphus College and at the University of Minnesota. Now teaching at Yale (since 1960) as Professor of Theology and Philosophical Theology, he has also served as visiting professor at Dartmouth College, Northwestern University, Chicago Lutheran Seminary, Moorhead State College, and Sacramento State College. Professor Holmer was a Fulbright Scholar at the University of Copenhagen, and lecturer at Frankfurt-am-Main, Goethe University, in 1953-54. He has recently been a Guggenheim Fellow. Essays from his pen appear in *The Tragic Vision*, ed. by Scott, 1958, in *Christian Ethics*, ed. by Beach and Niebuhr, 1957, in *A Kierkegaard Critique*, ed. by Johnson, 1963, in *Kierkegaardiana*, Copenhagen, 1955, in *Educating for the Ministry*, ed. by Culver and Bridston, 1964, and in other collections and journals. He is also the author of two books, *Philosophy and the Common Life* (Kroler Lectures, University of the Pacific), 1960, and *Theology and the Scientific Study of Religion*, 1961.

WILLIAM HOROSZ is Associate Professor of Philosophy at the University of Oklahoma, and Chairman of the Department 1960-64. His B.A. was received at Elmhurst College, his B.D. degree at Union Theological Seminary in New York City, and the Ph.D. in Philosophy at the State University of New York at Buffalo (1957). Professor Horosz has been writing thematic surveys in contemporary philosophy of religion for the journal *Philosophy and Phenomenological Research* since 1958. He is co-author of the sixth volume of Ueberweg's *Grundriss der Geschichte der Philosophie*, along with Paul Wilpert, and a contributor to the volume of a lengthy essay on "American Philosophy in the Nineteenth Century." He has published articles and reviews in other philosophical journals and is the author of *Escape from Destiny*, published by Charles C Thomas in the American Lecture Series, 1967. He is currently preparing a volume for publication, *The Promise and Peril of Human Purpose*, which attempts to define the ontological dimension of purpose.

BEN F. KIMPEL is a native of Racine, Wisconsin, and received an A.B. in medical science at the University of Wisconsin in 1926. A year as Fellow in Anthropology at the University of Nebraska was followed by studies at Yale, where he received the Tew Prize in Old Testament and a Ph.D. in philosophy. Professor Kimpel taught philosophy at Kansas Wesleyan University, and has been teaching philosophy at Drew University since 1938. A member of honor societies in psychology, sociology, social sciences, biology, art, and philosophy, Dr. Kimpel is also a collector and appraiser of Chinese art. His books include *Religious Faith, Language, and Knowledge; Faith and Moral Authority; Symbols of Religious Faith; Language and Religion; Moral Principles in the Bible; Principles of Moral Philosophy; Hegel's Philosophy of History; Kant's Critical Philosophy; Schopenhauer's Philosophy; Nietzsche's Beyond Good and Evil;* and other books will soon be forthcoming.

PETER KOESTENBAUM, a native of Berlin, Germany, is Associate Professor of Philosophy and Humanities at San Jose State College, San Jose, California. He spent his childhood in Caracas, Venezuela, and has made his residence in the United States since 1945. His degrees (all in philosophy) are from Stanford, Harvard, and Boston University. He has read papers at meetings of professional societies, lectured on the political, religious, and psychiatric implications of existentialism and phenomenology in public, in medical schools, and on television. His publications include articles in *Philosophy and Phenomenological Research, Revue internationale de philosophie, Review of Existential Psychology and Psychiatry,* and the *Journal of Existential Psychiatry*. His book

Edmund Husserl: The Paris Lectures is to be published shortly. He has contributed to several cooperative volumes—*In Quest of Values, The Potential of Woman*, and others—and is the author of a forthcoming introductory philosophy text.

WILBUR LONG is Professor in the School of Philosophy, The University of Southern California, with which he has been associated for many years. Widely traveled, he has been visiting lecturer in several institutions, including the College of Chinese Studies (Peiping), the National University of China (Peiping), and Silliman University (Philippines). He is the author of numerous articles.

O. HOBART MOWRER, Research Professor of Psychology, University of Illinois, has served as President of the American Psychological Association. Currently he is a consultant at the Galesburg (Illinois) State Research Hospital and Director of the Lilly Endowment Fellowship Program at the University of Illinois. He has written numerous technical articles and monographs on the psychology of learning, language, personality theory, and psychotherapy. Among his recent books are *Learning Theory and Behavior, Learning Theory and the Symbolic Processes, The Crisis in Psychiatry and Religion, The New Group Therapy*.

WALTER G. MUELDER has taught at Berea College, Kentucky, the Graduate School of Religion, University of Southern California, and at Boston University School of Theology. He also taught in the Graduate School of the Ecumenical Institute conducted jointly by the World Council of Churches and the University of Geneva. He is currently Chairman of the Board of the Ecumenical Institute. His interests in philosophy, religion, and social ethics are reflected in his major writings. With L. Sears he edited *The Development of American Philosophy* (second edition also with Ann Schlabach). *Religion and Economic Responsibility* appeared in 1953 and *Foundations of the Responsible Society* in 1959. He has analyzed the social ethics of Methodism in *Methodism and Society in the Twentieth Century* (1961) and with Nils Ehrenstrom has edited and contributed a major sociological study of the ecumenical movement, *Institutionalism and Church Unity* (1963). Since 1945 he has been Dean and Professor of Social Ethics at Boston University School of Theology.

GUSTAV EMIL MUELLER was born in 1898, in Bern, Switzerland, where his father was mayor of the city. After taking his Ph.D. in Philosophy in 1923, he combined studies at Heidelberg, Florence and London. Upon his marriage in 1925, he came to the University of Oregon as Instructor and Assistant Professor (1925-1930) and in 1930 became Professor, later Research Professor of Philosophy (1955) at the University of Oklahoma. He is the author of thirty books in philosophy and literature (poetry, plays, stories) both German and English, and some hundred and thirty articles.

EDWARD NORBECK is Professor of Anthropology at Rice University and Dean of the College of Arts and Sciences. He is Non-Resident Associate of Baker College. Dr. Norbeck received his B.A. (1948), M.A. (1949), and Ph.D. (1952) from the University of Michigan. He has done extensive research in religion as an anthropologist and is currently pursuing further studies in Japan. His book, *Religion in Primitive Society*, published by Harper and Brothers in 1961, is a contemporary study and a fine summary statement of what the discipline of anthropology has done with the study of religion in primitive society. He has numerous journal publications to his credit and has also participated in Voice of America programs on scientific topics. His most recent article, "African Rituals of Conflict," is published in the *American Anthropologist*, Vol. 65, No. 6, December, 1963.

FRANCIS H. PARKER is Professor of Philosophy and Chairman of the Department at Purdue University. He has an A.B. from Evansville College, an A.M. from Indiana University, and a Ph.D. from Harvard. President of the Association for Realistic Philosophy 1959-61, member of the Executive Committee of the Eastern Division of the American Philosophical Association 1961-64, and Secretary-Treasurer 1959-62 and President 1964-65 of the Metaphysical Society of America, he was visiting professor at Indiana University 1961, and Fellow of the American Council of Learned Societies and Fulbright Research Professor at the University of Athens, Greece 1962-63. Among his publications (other than those cited in the chapter) are *Logic as a Human Instrument* (with Henry B. Veatch), Harper, 1958; "Realistic Epistemology" in *The Return to Reason* (John Wild, editor), Regnery, 1953; and "Classical Realism and the Integration of Knowledge," *Re-*

view of Metaphysics, Vol. XIV, pp. 543-564 (March 1961). His *The Story of Western Philosophy*, Harper & Row, is to be published shortly.

OLIVER L. REISER (Ph.D., Ohio State University, 1924), is Professor of Philosophy at the University of Pennsylvania. Before going to Pittsburgh, he was Instructor in Psychology and Philosophy at Ohio State University. Dr. Reiser had post-doctoral work at the University of Chicago. He is the author of numerous articles, reviews, and books, including *Integration of Human Knowledge.* His *A New Earth and a New Humanity* was translated into Spanish for Latin American Countries. He is on the Editorial Board of *Darshana International,* the Advisory Board of the "International Institute of Integrative Studies," and Chairman of the "Committee on Scientific Humanism." Dr. Reiser is now at work on a volume, *The Universe: Its Theory.*

PATRICK ROMANELL (Ph.D., Columbia University, 1937) is H.Y. Benedict Professor of Philosophy in the University of Texas at El Paso. He has been teaching and lecturing in this country and abroad since 1936. A member of Phi Beta Kappa, he was President of the Southwestern Philosophical Society in 1961. He was Book Editor, *Journal of Philosophy,* 1939-51; Cutting and Carnegie Fellow in Mexico, 1945-46; Fulbright Lecturer in Italy, 1952-53; Smith-Mundt Lecturer in Ecuador, Panama, and Mexico, 1956; American Philosophical Society Grantee, 1957-58; U.S. Public Health Service Grantee, 1960-63; U.S. Specialist for the State Department in Central and South America, 1961. Dr. Romanell is the author of numerous publications, including nine books in philosophy.

PART I

Religion in Philosophical Perspective

The self-willed solitary glared at the old wretch: 'The mind was not created to grow soft by grinding nor to be bent and yoked like cattle for men's comforts: the more the soul grows old the more it fights its fate!' The old man sighed and answered with great sweetness then: 'The soul was made not to deny or shout in vain but to stoop low and merge with the bread-giving earth. . . . I've seen and taken count: there is no greater good than holy mute obedience to man-eating earth.' Odysseus rose with arrogance and boasted proudly: 'I've also taken count: there is no greater good than when the earth says "Yes" and man with wrath shouts "No!" And I'm acquainted with *one* soul that never deigned to stoop under the yoke of demon, man, or god.' . . .

Nikos Kazantzakis   ⋮   THE ODYSSEY: A MODERN SEQUEL

I J. Clayton Feaver

Philosophy and Religion

Religion, like science or art, is properly brought into philosophical perspective. A statement of this sort suggests some consideration of the nature and function of both philosophy and religion. Both are very old and persistent human ventures; each has a venerable history and a future of promise.

Many definitions come to mind as one considers the meaning of "philosophy." Socrates says philosophy is the love of wisdom. Cicero speaks of it as the pursuit of wisdom—wisdom being "the knowledge of things both divine and human, together with the causes on which they depend. . . ." [1] Philosophy is the knowledge of Reality; it is a concern with rational presentation; it is a discernment of relationships; it is the inquiry into presuppositions. Philosophy is thinking, in its most sophisticated and advanced form; its function is the clarification of meanings. It is a study of the ways of knowing—the manner, possibility, and nature of man's knowledge. Aristotle instructs us that philosophy seeks the cause of perceptible things, and he comments: "It is right also that philosophy should be called knowledge of the truth. For the end of theoretical knowledge is truth, while that of practical knowledge is action. . . ." [2] William James speaks of philosophy as an unusually obstinate endeavor to think clearly; someone else attests, perhaps with tongue in cheek: "Philosophy is the study that enables a person to be unhappy more intelligently." Dubray writes: "Strictly speaking . . . the name philosophy applies to *the science of the higher principles of things*, to the elucidation of

3

those concepts and laws which are common to several sciences and which are used by them without being subjected to any special investigation." [3] And someone, of humane spirit, says the goal of philosophy "is a vision of the Real which will satisfy both head and heart. . . ."

In this chapter we focus on the position that the function of philosophy is to gain as comprehensive a view of human experience and its world as is possible at any particular time of history. In order to do this the philosopher must examine reflectively the concrete aspects of human experience to frame a scheme of general ideas which may serve as a reference to interpret every element of experience. For our day perhaps Alfred North Whitehead has most adequately formulated the requirements of this notion of philosophy. His conception is that such a general scheme of ideas must be coherent, logical, applicable, and adequate.

"Coherent" here means that the fundamental ideas of such a scheme must be interdependent or presuppositions of one another; taken in isolation the fundamental ideas are relatively meaningless. To state the notion differently, philosophical speculation should exhibit the systematic aspects of a human interpretation of reality. This is not to assume that reality or human experience is conceived as a logical straitjacket. There are many areas of human experience that are perhaps irrational, subrational, and even suprarational—as sceptics and mystics, for example, characteristically affirm. It does mean, however, that even these, as legitimate concrete elements of experience, must find a place in the scheme of ideas.

"Logical" here means that the scheme of ideas should be free from inconsistency or contradiction. Again, this is not to assume that concrete human experience is actually free from inconsistencies and irrationalities; but rather to propose that reflection upon these elements and others of a more rationally graspable nature should be developed in a logical manner, whether the structural model is that of mathematics and science or the logic of poetry and aesthetic experience. Philosophers who are closer to being poets than scientists in temperament and method may use a model that portrays the inner consistency of an integral life. This may well be the persistent concern of a man like Gabriel Marcel. Others of poetic disposition, such as Berdyaev and Camus, are concerned to stress at least the honesty of experience as it is felt and lived in its temporal depth.

"Applicable" means simply that specific elements of experience are interpreted by means of the scheme of ideas; and "adequate" means that there are no items incapable of being interpretable; at least there are no ideas that are not amenable to inquiry.

Philosophy, to be comprehensive, includes interpretations of nature. In this aspect it utilizes the knowledge of each science dealing with nature. Philosophy also works out an interpretation of culture; and here it will be noted that philosophy itself, insofar as it is considered historically, is a part of culture and thus is open to continuous reinterpretation and further development. Moreover, philosophy concerns itself with the experiencing human subject. This includes consideration of the modes and validity of the subject's experience and cognition, as well as the structure, validity, and potentiality for human inter- and intrapersonal relationships, which form the matrix or creative source of culture.

When we view philosophy in this manner, it is clearly both a descriptive and a prescriptive enterprise. Philosophy is descriptive insofar as it strives to elucidate the general structure of concrete elements of human experience. Herein it is akin to science and clearly draws upon the sciences. Descriptive philosophy, however, differs from the sciences in that it intends to be more general and comprehensive than the specific sciences. In this sense philosophy is not wholly dependent upon the sciences, nor is its function to be regarded in isolation from them. The descriptive side of philosophy should be interdependent with the sciences.

The prescriptive aspect of philosophy intends to reflect upon, criticize, and establish value judgments. It can do this by making implicit values explicit in propositions or norms which are open to reflective scrutiny to determine their coherence and applicability for possible adoption as guides to living. Here, insofar as religion is concerned with the interpretation and establishment of values, religion and philosophy tend to become interdependent. The religious spirit in his creative surge into the depths of humanity or his loving response to the divine seeks and welcomes participation in value itself, while the philosopher would elucidate the structures and presuppositions of such religious participation.

Particular philosophers (through choice, temperament, limitation) are likely to emphasize one aspect of experience more than another. For example, the linguistic analyst concerns himself with the structures of language as carrier of values and meanings; the idealist tends to uncover the transcendent source of values; the naturalist ponders the immanent source of values and their human meaning. To be sure, the emphasis on one aspect of experience may limit the comprehensiveness of a particular philosopher's view, but there is likely to be a gain in concrete detail and incisive penetration. This multiplicity of approach and interpretation sets the conditions for a fruitful interplay wherein particular philosophers and philosophies are to be seen as complementing each other.

Every philosopher is in interdependent relation to his circumstance, his natural or cultural endowment, and to the language of his particular philosophical heritage. Accordingly he speaks for himself and his time, even though he intends as an ideal to speak for all men. Admittedly, any particular philosopher falls more or less short of this ideal. Nonetheless, the distant ideal acts as a lure for the philosopher's intellectual passion. Even though distant, the goal—the ideal—may be asymmetrically approached and grasped in its spiritual potentiality and meaning. When thus comprehended, the ideal (which may be a good in itself for contemplation) becomes alive as a lure for the continued enhancement of the here and now.

------ ✳ ------

Religion is manifestly a content or element of human experience. The institutions, traditions, convictions, sacred writings, are observables open to inspection. Furthermore, most religions claim to be more than a collection of empirical data; interior dispositions, values, fundamental orientations to life are also religious phenomena. There are special studies calculated to enumerate and interpret these data, each from a particular standpoint—the history, sociology, anthropology, and psychology of religion. But this material, like other materials, calls for philosophical interpretation so as to consider its possible fuller meaning and significance in relation to experience as a whole.

Even more striking: religion claims (or at least many religionists make the claim) to be more than one body of data among others; it claims to be more than a certain kind of experience alongside other experience. Religion claims to be true, and often, in its more developed form, claims ultimate truth—to be in close harmony with ultimate reality. Of course, this does not mean that religion claims to be simply an intellectual attitude toward or grasp of reality. Thought may be secondary to feeling or will, as religious teachers often affirm. But it does mean that religion implies an interpretation of reality. More specifically, it implies an interpretation of the meaning of reality in terms of its value to and for human beings, implies a consideration of the meaning of the universe for human well being, implies reckoning with the possibility that something at the core of reality does respond to and satisfy human demands for life and fulfillment of destiny. The truth claims of religion, every bit as much as the data of its genesis and development, call for careful systematic examination.

The task of the philosophy of religion, which is to examine, criticize, and assess the validity of at least the human elements in religious experience, is thus twofold. On the one hand, it has the function of interpreting, evaluating, and integrating the data of religious experience as these are manifest in human behavior. On the other hand, it must appraise the adequacy of the religious expression as an interpretation of reality.

Religionists should welcome the critical scrutiny of the philosopher of religion; insofar as philosophy and religion are both committed to the pursuit of truth, there can be no ultimate dichotomy in their respective conclusions. To view religion philosophically does not mean prejudgment; ideally, it means free investigation, whether the philosopher is an adherent of a particular faith or not. Again, it is an historic fact that virtually every living religious tradition is permeated from the beginning with philosophical components. To assert this is not necessarily, of course, to claim that religion is wholly dependent upon philosophy or vice versa; it is to note historical interdependence and to suggest that the exchange is of mutual benefit. For example, there is Christianity's involvement with the particular philosophical tradition stemming from the Greeks; and in the Eastern religious traditions, philosophy and religion have characteristically been integrally related. To be sure, there is difference of opinion as to whether a particular religious faith presupposes this or that philosophical position. When philosophy is viewed not simply as a tradition or specific system of interpretation, however, but as an attitude of mind, as an aspect of a person's total response, religion and philosophy are wholly interdependent. For example, the various religious faiths differ in their assumptions and beliefs. There is, also, manifold diversity and disagreement within a particular faith or tradition. Thus it is clear that the language of religious conviction stands in need of clarification as well as interpretation, as is true of all articulate and tacit communication.

The philosophical attitude is particularly apt for the task of clarification and interpretation insofar as philosophy is committed to a type of passionately disinterested inquiry. Disinterested does not mean lack of intellectual commitment or vigor; rather, it means passionate detachment, an attitude in which one is committed to examine all the possible meanings of an element of human experience, within the boundaries of human capacity.

The passionate detachment of the philosophical attitude differentiates it from the religious attitude. The religionist is passionately committed to a tradition and the claim for the divine element which informs and is symbolized by that tradition and its faith. In light of this distinction, however, it should be clear that the respective attitudes of the philosopher and the religionist need not be mutually exclusive, nor need their respective tasks conflict. Were there a necessary conflict, the philosopher would by definition be excluded from religious faith and the religionist would be excluded from the relative detachment that permits him to criticize and interpret his own faith and commitment.

------ ✳ ------

From this preliminary discussion of philosophy and religion we turn to an elaboration of the question, What does it mean to view religion philosophically? Admittedly, we will develop a particular point of view in response to this question, in hopes that the discussion will be faithful to the synoptic concern of philosophy.

The dynamic and fulfillment of philosophical investigation is wisdom in love with itself. If that metaphor seems too poetic, consider Whitehead's statement: "There is an essence to the universe which forbids relationships beyond itself, as a violation of its rationality. Speculative philosophy seeks that essence." [4] The implication of such a view is contrary to a view very much in vogue currently, namely, the one for which "factualistic thinking," whether in philosophy or other disciplines, is featured as the all-inclusive ideal. However important factual or "objective" knowledge is, it is not enough—particularly in philosophy. Understanding is also necessary. Understanding as a cognitive endeavor is akin to the knowing in intimate acquaintance, as, for example, in the intimacy of the lover with the beloved. One can have all sorts of factual information about a person, himself or another, and yet not have an understanding that goes beyond the observables. While including the meaning of descriptive knowledge, understanding is intimate appreciation, guided by the penetrating but never desecrating power of love.

These two modes of knowing—the descriptive and the appreciative—are interdependent. Ideally they should be in harmony with each other, though as a matter of fact they seldom are—a disharmony often decried (for example, by C. P. Snow in his book *The Two Cultures*) between scientific knowledge and aesthetic understanding. Perhaps a viable harmonization is not yet historically possible except in isolated instances; nonetheless, the problem besets us both in its cultural manifestations and in the lives of individuals.

Wisdom in love with itself, as the goal and dynamic of philosophy, seeks the harmonization of the descriptive and the appreciative. Perhaps the elements within the reconciliation sought may be characterized as follows. If by knowledge we mean facts drawn from common sense and the various sciences, then by understanding we mean facts clothed with the living body of imagination, carrier of feeling and emotion, and discerner of intelligible mystery that permeates and feeds creative imagination. If by love we mean that impetus in all things that moves them at once toward differentiation and unitive communication of feeling and characteristics (whether considering electrons, molecules, foxes, or human beings, conscious or unconscious of their activity); and if by human love in particular we mean that impetus that moves us inward to our depths and outward to the core of all things to savor the mysterious kernel of power, feeling, and intelligible spirit that animates us and all beings whose constant perishing in the becoming and dying of all finite entities moves us beyond these contingencies to await the transcendent ever-fulfilling answer of love itself to its own cry in our hearts, then we mean by wisdom the harmonious yet ever-moving union of knowledge, understanding, and love.

Is wisdom humanly possible? Is this personal appropriation and loving integration into the very matrix of our experience and being of the articulated knowledge of the sciences, the arts, philosophy, and religion open

to us in a seemingly fragmented and ever increasingly compartmentalized, mechanized, and specialized world? For a few men in the ancient
world it was more or less possible. Plato, for instance, among the Greeks,
came close; St. Thomas Aquinas in the Middle Ages comes to mind; certainly men generally achieve it in part, at least on occasion. Indeed, wisdom is the very meaning and goal of liberal education, if we do not limit
education to its formal institutionalized aspects. Yet the demands are
overwhelming, full of danger and risk. The *eros* or passion that sends us
upon flights of discovery (whether into outer space, the interior of the
atom, or the recesses of the self) plunges us into depths of meaning or
meaninglessness in our very souls, causes us to thirst after recognition in
the eyes of the beloved, or in the fearful eyes of the resentfully withdrawn, sends us to despair and dissipation in the lust for power, possessions, and self-inflation and to the fleeting but ever alluring oblivion of
sensuality and the flesh.

Is there no fulfillment within the ever increasing scope of the quest?
There is. We may recognize the very source of the passion within our
fully committed and concerned selves in the context of our experience
and pursuits, however limited in scope and intensity, and perhaps we
may open ourselves to the source of wisdom itself which ultimately is
love. If it is the goal of human wisdom, however incomplete in any
instance, to collect, purge, and integrate the various streams of our culture and creativity, then is it not possible that there is a transcendent
source of this impetus that drives and lures us, infinite in its capacity for
receptivity, love, power, and creativity? And, as has been done, may we
not call this infinite capacity for reception, response, and love God? Is
this the reason mystics and saints have called the self-disclosure of this
infinite spiritual capacity the beatific vision? Is this why they have spoken
of its infinite plentude as ineffable—incapable of description? Is this
why they have regarded it as all-fulfilling yet desirous of further creative
act that all might come fully within its light, that its joy may be forever
increased in each renewed response? Is it in some measure this source and
capacity that has sent seers, prophets, and poets screaming from the symbolic or actual mountains of vision to cajole us into action and response,
so that our ears and eyes may be opened to what cannot be heard or seen
but must be felt, intuited, grasped, received dimly or sharply? Is it this
capacity deeply hidden in our souls that has moved the ponderous minds
of metaphysicians up the ladder of abstractions and through the powers
and distractions of the psyche to stretch human consciousness to its outer
limits that it might distantly as through a veil glimpse the glory that
moves within and beyond, and to unite its intimations and permutations
as the Absolute, the Eternal, Thought Thinking Itself, Absolute Self,
Nirvana, The Good?

Is it possible that this infinite capacity has moved within all peoples and nations, eliciting and informing their particular destiny and accepting their creative outpouring while not overstepping their freedom of individual response in particular circumstance and event, even to the extent that their vision of this power and capacity is perverted and turned against its and man's best purposes? Have murder, war, pillage, rape, sacrilege, been done in the name of the divine and with its freely given power which will not coerce nor forcibly restrain once its own limits are broken? Did man's origin in the dim past endow him with a perilous and untamed nature that was inherited from his animal forebears, but which has been determined within broad limits, to a goal and destiny which would include man's bodily and psychic inheritance from his non-human origins and yet purify it, raise it to undreamt heights—even to the extent of eliciting the possibilities of evil that lie buried in the animal inheritance of man? And could this be done by love itself that man may know his own measure in order to rise above it? Is it even possible—this has been the stupendous claim in the Judeo-Christian tradition—that this infinitely informing creative capacity has freely formed a particular people to endow a single individual with a religious culture in whom there is the conscious realization that the culture's depth of meaning is focused upon and located in himself? Did that sudden or gradual realization of the striving, worship, and work of centuries bring forth the blazing transcendent response that transfigured that individual into the God-man capable of pouring forth, concealed yet revealed under human conditions and in human terms, the inner dynamic of the divine-human life itself, with its intimations clothed in events, symbols, and myths of the further destiny and immediate meaning of man and human history? Did the group collected around this person receive intimations and elicitations from their own unlimited depths of soul and feeling, to be clothed with speech and metaphors from their culture that could speak to men throughout history and even consciously and unconsciously form a great part of that history?

Whatever may be said for the particular redemptive history implied in the Judeo-Christian tradition (for that matter, any tradition), it is the concern of wisdom to comprehend this history within a much longer natural history of earth, plants, animals, and men and its relation to cultural redemptive histories and traditions informed by different intimations and insights into the nature of human capacity and divine-human destiny. Man currently is confronted on an unprecedented scale with cultural redemptive histories and traditions wherein presuppositions, insights, and claims about human nature and destiny differ—for example, the striking contrast in the West between Christianity and Communism. While these interpretations differ, they may not be wholly incompatible or mutually exclusive. Each may have its distinctive meaning, and yet be capable of being infused or reconciled with another, even though not on the same level but hierarchically, with exchange and movement within the hierarchy. Philosophy need not speak of an assimilation that does violence to the integrity of any tradition—the identity of traditions is with propriety maintained; but it may seek a reconciliation within a functional hierarchy in which what is higher and what is lower, what is more and what is less complex, are mutually dependent and continuous. Here a contrast may be drawn between a static hierarchy modeled on a governmental structure and a living functional hierarchy of dimensions of the religious life and spiritual potentialities as exemplified in the great living faiths East and West.

Simply stated, the problem of the possibility of wisdom as it is here defined raises a host of questions involving the philosophical scrutiny of religion in its various manifestations. The structure of the inquiry involves us inevitably in the personal pursuit of wisdom.

Historically it has been one of the functions of religion to effect a harmonization of the disparate elements in man's being and in his apprehension of the world. Religion aims at unification, at being all-inclusive and coextensive with the whole of life. With whatever propriety one may speak of a distinction between the secular and the religious, the distinction is relative and provisional. Religion does not mean simply to be one phase of experience among many, existing side by side with others and on equal terms. It means to intensify, vitalize, enhance every human function and activity. It would have man reinterpret and revalue the various phases of life, give depth and meaning to—even transfigure—the commonplace. Accordingly, a central concern of one of the great religious faiths, Christianity, is that life in its ramifications should take on sacramental meaning and be understood in its unification, its wholeness. In order to understand how this unification is brought about, some of the various types of religious experience must be examined.

Insofar as religion aims at the unification of life—perhaps of all being —it is important initially to make a distinction between primary experience and reflective experience. The primary religious experience is in the mode of an encounter. The person is grasped—perhaps even overwhelmed—and shaken by an experience suffused with fear, wonder, awe, reverence. Rudolf Otto refers to this as an encounter with the Holy. Religious writings the world over have recorded types and elements of this experience and have indicated that encounters of this type can take place under various conditions. Sacred rocks, trees, groves, animals, artifacts, and the like, are worshiped because such experiences have occurred in conjunction with or through them; thereby these objects are set apart from what is profane or unholy and are felt to be sacred by the individual or group. Certain acts or rituals are often the carriers of the experience.

Indeed, the central function of the priestly office in most developed religions is calculated to insure that sacrifice and prayer, as the central phases of worship, will either carry or recreate the experience.

Sometimes sex has been worshiped as a symbol of creative power in nature, and its meaning has been expressed in fertility rites or myths of creation. This is one form of religious experience at the primary level. Poetic reflection upon this mode of experience results in mythical accounts where the primary experience is evoked by language which embodies the emotional power of the mythmaker's consciousness of the holy. A further level of articulation is the rationalization of the myth itself. At this level the concern is with language about the holy or the god, rather than with the experience itself or with its mythical embodiment.

Present-day depth psychology, as Carl Jung illustrates, has uncovered the memory traces of these primary experiences which constellate around archetypal structures, forming part of the collective unconscious of man. When these constellations of psychic energy erupt, they may bring about emotional malfunction in the weakly formed or unintegrated psyche; or they may be the very dynamics of spontaneous creative power in the controlled and integrated person.

In Hebrew Scripture there is general condemnation of these sources of religious experience, expressions of which the Hebrew people encountered among the various groups in the Middle East. The Baal cult was such an expression. Another was the institutional practice of prostitution which crept from time to time into Jewish religion, usually provoking fulminations against it from the prophets.

The central meaning of the primary religious experience and its articulation is power. Evidence of this meaning is nowhere more clearly illustrated than in the Hebrew tradition, where there gradually evolved an ethical mode of interpretation of religious inspiration or experience to insure control of the upsurging manifestation of power, whatever its form. It was not enough to have a religious source of power; this power and eventually all human acts must be directed by and oriented to proper ends. Thus, in this context there evolved in the Jewish religion an ethical monotheism which subjugated the source of power in nature to the control of the transcendent holy God, worshiped in ritual and deeds of justice and ethical love. The concept of God which emerged is that of a high God beyond yet involved in nature, who is intimately concerned with the destiny of his people.

Furthermore, in Jewish tradition, the predominant form of religious knowledge became the inspiration of a human intermediary called a lawgiver or a prophet who speaks on behalf of the god. The prophet's laws, historical accounts of religious encounter, with their interpretation and prophetic statements, were recorded and codified for application to daily circumstances by the priesthood.

While it is clear the philosophy of religion is not limited to a particular religious tradition, nonetheless it is appropriate in a chapter devoted to philosophy of religion to speak of a particular religious faith; for philosophy considered under its aspect of critical reflection upon human experience concerns itself with specific manifestations of what are correctly and properly regarded as religious phenomena.

From the cognitive standpoint the major problem that historical religion, at least in Western religious tradition, presents is the problem of revelation. Two aspects of revelation can be distinguished: the original and the dependent. This distinction is comparable to the one made previously in relation to original and dependent religious experience, though viewed in a more restricted sense and with contemporary religious claims in mind.

An original revelation in its phenomenological aspect is analogous to any kind of insight into the nature of reality as grasped and/or received by a human mind and spirit of genius. Paul Tillich aptly describes this experience as reason beyond itself. Another way of characterizing original revelation is that it is creative—it introduces novelty into the life of mankind; new aspects of reality are disclosed and perhaps in a manner created. By "created" we mean at least that something new is actualized in the life of man which by the very nature of being incorporated into the spirit and body of man gives a new configuration to the totality of things, even though the abstract potentiality of this new aspect of things is prefigured in the very nature of the larger world of which man is a part.

Dependent revelation is the creative appropriation of original revelation; it is the incorporation of the insight of the person of genius or spiritual awareness into the matrix of human life. In opening himself to the original insight or revelation as embodied in a scripture, a poem, a philosophy, a person, man participates in the original insight in a way that transforms his being, his outlook, his conceptual heritage: he is even (such is the distinctive claim of many religious faiths) saved, healed, redeemed. This is not to say that religious insight or revelation *is* poetry, art, music, science. It is, rather, to say that the experience is at least analogous. As is always the case, analogy does not mean identity.

At this juncture a major problem arises. It is a common claim that religious revelation is not simply man's creative insight into the structure of his nature and the world in which he is embedded and confronts; it is also the self-giving of God as spirit. Here, of course, the symbol God has been assigned several interpretations. An epistemology or theory of knowledge itself is an interpretation. God can be interpreted as being the spiritual aspect of nature, in which case one speaks only of the "thatness" of God. For example, in the statement "God is that which concerns man ultimately," God is quite devoid of content. From this point of view his "whatness" or attributable nature cannot be spoken of without referring to the totality of nature, culture, and man. Further in this interpretation, God cannot be regarded as a highest being among beings or even as existing, if by existing one means having particularity within the order of being (whether of things, entities, or persons), either actual or potential. In other words, God is the whole of all things rather than a separable existence within or beyond the whole of concrete actuality, whether viewed materially or spiritually.

The most striking conclusion of the interpretation that God is the creative spiritual ground of all things is that there can be no cognitive knowledge of God. Why is this? It is because God has no *existence* apart from the world of things and structures; all knowledge is of these structures and objects, none of which in itself is God, who is beyond the relationship of a knowing self and a known object. It is only when a mysterious depth breaks through into the realm of subject-object that one may speak of God and revelation. Things or persons are capable of pointing to God, not of being God. Clearly from this position there can be no conflict between religious assertions and factual or scientific assertions, because God is not within the order of subject-object knowledge as a possible object. To put this point a bit more technically: God conditions all things; he is not conditioned by them. God is essentially mystery, the unfathomable; he is not a problem that has yet to be worked out nor a puzzle that will one day be resolved with the increase of knowledge.

Further, in this view, God is expressed most adequately through the religious symbol. The symbol is any finite thing or constellation which points beyond itself to a depth dimension; the depth dimension is structured only insofar as it is conjoined to a specific intelligible circumstance in the response of person. To use a simple analogy, a red light at a street corner is a sign to stop. A symbol of this type, a sign-symbol, is wholly arbitrary; it is established by convention or custom or stipulation. A religious symbol, in distinction, participates in that to which it points. It is not wholly arbitrary, like a sign-symbol; it is more like the relationship of smoke and fire: where smoke is seen, the appropriate response is to yell fire. For common sense, there is an essential or intrinsic relationship between smoke and fire; there is no such relationship between a red light and the act of stopping. In the one case the relationship is intrinsic; in the other, extrinsic. Thus, by analogy, the religious symbol God carries with it something of the meaning of an intrinsic relationship between the concrete situation and the depth dimension. Clearly some symbols are more adequate than others to act as carriers of revelation: a human person is more adequate than a rock. At least this is surely true for human religious insight, since human beings are usually more concerned with themselves and their own depth of being than with rocks. This, of course, in no sense means to disparage geologists who happen to be professionally concerned with rocks and their nature. Nor does it mean that rocks do not have religious significance, as they did for the great French paleontologist and theologian Teilhard de Chardin.

In this view the classical characteristics of God—e.g., person or creator—are not attributes of a being among beings; rather, they are symbolic characterizations of God or being itself. It is incorrect to say that God is a person; it is more nearly correct to say that God is personal, meaning that God can be and is related existentially to a human person or persons.

This notion of God and revelation or religious "knowledge" explains many religious phenomena and avoids the conflict that has often arisen between the several branches of humanistic knowledge and religion when religionists assert that their claims have factual and cognitive content not otherwise attainable by means of scientific investigation. Nonetheless, many religionists and philosophers—for example, many Thomists—question the adequacy of this view, contending that it is possible to have rational knowledge of God even though, insofar as this knowledge is expressed in concepts and images derived from human experiences, it can be true only by virtue of an analogous relationship. The assumption that is all-important in the criticism is that God has a nature, essence, or "whatness" that can serve as an "object" of intellection, no matter how much this object in its fullness transcends or goes beyond the limited powers of human intellect. Clearly this conceptualization of God by means of analogous relationship through intellectual abstraction is of the God of the philosopher, if for no other reason than because the process of abstraction is an arduous one requiring long preparation and discipline.

Whatever the difficulties of the noncognitive, highly symbolic approach to knowledge, what difference does it make for man's interpretation of God as a basis for religious knowledge?

One of the merits for the claim of noncognitive apprehension of God is that it undercuts any form of idolatry. By refusing to grant existence to God—that is, by placing him beyond the subject-object relationship —no finite object can ever be confused with the infinite; nor can that which is symbolized be mistaken for the symbol.

A consequence, however, of this view is that two fundamental forms of religious expression are severely (if not wholly) undercut, namely, worship and commitment. The almost universal characteristic expression of religious behavior—worship—tends to be divested of much of its meaning. What does it mean to worship the infinite, which is the creative ground of all that is and can be? Wherein may any one symbol be an adequate pointing beyond for purposes of worship. The very relationship of the finite to the infinite is always self-negating. Likewise, the excessive emphasis on God as symbol involves a difficulty with another manifestation of the religious life, that of commitment. How many people can in a meaningful way say that they are committed to the ground of all that is? Can any? A man might claim that he is committed to creative advance or endeavor. But is not this sort of commitment usually limited to definite and finite occasions—one's profession, personal relationships, social responsibility? To be sure, creative insight of religious significance can be realized in any one of these partial concerns, insofar as they occasion a high degree of involvement. But is it true to ordinary experience to say that we are *ultimately* committed to creative social concerns, scientific advancement, intense personal relationships? And if we do say this, are we not involving ourselves in idolatry?

If idolatry is the peril of finite commitment, how much more is it the peril of worship! Is it not increasingly clear, whether in religion, psychology, or philosophy, that to become involved in the worship of any finite exemplification tends to result in the self-destruction of despair brought about by the inevitable loss of the finite object worshiped? In worship, as in commitment, creativity itself, apart from the concrete circumstances which provide the possibility of its expression, loses any assignable meaning. At this point the notion of religion assimilated to culture breaks down; the religious requirement of an adequate object is attenuated, even lost. Only God in the mode of existence, though not finite existence, can overcome this problem. Only when God is viewed as the unity of existent manifestations of his own creative ground do we meet the religious requirement and at the same time retain the insight of God as ground of being itself. To view God in this manner permits commitment to finite embodiments which are taken up into God's existence and love, thereby freeing the committed person from the perils of idolatry.

To speak of God as that which concerns man ultimately suggests that commitment may be to a universal devoid of content. This is to reduce the religious experience to autonomous subjectivity and thus to render commitment mere appearance. Where ultimately can there be a bridge between the finite and the infinite that does not require the concrete universal, which has the locus of its full expression in history and at the same time points beyond itself to its ground, the eternal? In another language, where may we avoid radical subjectivity except in the God-man which is the dynamic unity of temporal and eternal, finite and infinite, aptly called the everlasting?

By combining the notions of God as creative ground of being and as personal essence, we may resolve the problem of viewing God as a contentless universal, thereby permitting intelligible grasp of God. This allows affective or tacit knowledge of God's essence, capable of rational or conceptual symbolization, as well as symbolic analogy pointing to him as creative ground of being. Further, this combined view does justice to the God of religion and the God of philosophy. There need be no confusion between God as the object of religious commitment and worship and God as the ontological ground of creative cultural expression. In their unity the two may be viewed as the life and dynamic of history, the directive and orientation of history, and the fulfillment and consummation of history. In a strikingly different language, this combined view overcomes the dichotomy between the sacred and the secular and yet maintains the fruitful tension between the two. Participation in the everlasting God-man honors and gives meaning to the ambiguities inherent in the creative cultural process and yet points to the historic overcoming of these ambiguities in the eternal-temporal community.

In considering the notion of the everlasting God-man, two central questions arise. What is the appropriate response to God as the object of religious commitment and worship? And, what view of the world does one take in the light of this response? When God is considered the ground of being and personal essence capable of self-giving, can the response be other than the complete turning of the individual to him? Can it be less than full trust, the giving of oneself in spite of the lack of complete cognitive knowledge? Can it be less than an encounter, an experience that centers the person beyond himself in the full conviction that his commitment is received?

These questions, of course, are rhetorical. Implicit in them is the suggestion that the response is one of complete renunciation of self-centeredness. Love of self is sacrificed for love of God which establishes the self in a new dimension of being. This distinction goes beyond the usual meaning of egoism versus altruism, when egoism means self-concern at the expense of other, altruism concern for other at the expense of self. It also goes beyond concern for other as extension of concern for self to a community or another person, wherein the self attains greater benefit and more power by virtue of being in the relation. Though such concern may have a profound meaning, it may not carry the full meaning of living beyond oneself in encounter with the holy. To give oneself fully in response is to be related to God as essential person and to establish authentic humanness. Herein the interdependent concern for self and other is taken up into the divine life and sanctified. The despair over limitations of human response to situations, institutions, creeds, dogmas—or any particularity—is transcended and justified.

The movement or response is essentially that of love: all communion and union are due to the impetus of love seeking its source. From this fact arise the fervor of faith and its healing power. Insofar as faith and love are orientation of the entire person—a compound of all the elements of man's being: reason, emotion, action—they mean full commitment to and worship of God as person and ground of being.

When the response to God is understood in this manner, body, mind, and spirit are involved in the impetus of faith to fulfill and express itself in ethical action, wisdom, and bodily well-being or joy—all human life. In the full orientation of the whole person to God, head and heart are united. The dichotomies between the world of thought and the world of sense are bridged. Only when a narrow rationalism or a narrow empiricism is adopted does faith become a problem rather than a mystery to be explored. Both the realm of reason and the realm of sense may be suffused with mystery that elicits the impetus of loving quest within us to penetrate into its meaning. Only when the worlds of reason and sense become estranged from our response of loving participation because of undue entanglement in abstraction and partial conceptualizations or unresolved psychic complexes does our natural movement toward faith and its consummation in love become lost or radically questioned. This, of course, does not mean that the elements of tradition which are the concrete embodiments of faith are not open to development and continual questioning and examination; it does mean that they may not become objects of singular devotion.

Here it should become manifestly clear that religion does not purport to make factual claims about the worlds of science, history, psychology, and the like; but it does reserve the right to pass judgment upon these worlds. If we say, however, that religion does not purport to be factual or scientific knowledge, does this mean it has no claim to truth? Manifestly not, when God is understood as being an existent spirit and at the same time the ground of being. As the ground of being, God can be understood as the mystery that penetrates all things, as reason beyond itself. God grounds and fulfills the passion for truth in its manifold aspects, is the impetus in all things and the fulfillment of all things; in a word, God is truth itself. Truth itself does not conflict with truths, nor does it serve as a substitute for the various truths. Truth is the foundation of the truths of existence.

Turning to the other question raised earlier: What are the implications for man's view of the world when God is considered the ground of being and personal essence? Religion characteristically has been man's attempt to relate the disparate elements of his exterior and interior experience into a harmonious vision of the whole that will serve as a guide and a source of meaning for his understanding of himself and his place in the world which enfolds him. World views are made up from all the cultural activities of man—science, art, philosophy, religion. It is not uncommon for them to take on a mythical and sacred status that tends to resist innovation and change. If, however, the component elements of a world view are understood, any radical innovation in man's understanding of the world and of himself must be incorporated. Religion, being the most pervasive element in the changeable, and in one sense the most removed from it (though perhaps the very source of change), provides the matrix for the ever-developing elements in man's experience and projection of himself into a coherent image of his world. If religion is true to its claim, at least in its spiritual genesis, of being able to plumb the depths of man's nature—even of grasping the divine plan—then it will form images that will serve as a guide to man's destiny. It will elaborate man's capacities and limitations, enabling him better to form his life in deference to his inner aim, rather than deny his own essential being by virtue of the primordial capacity for freedom which may result in self-destruction every bit as much as in creative fulfillment.

Who can gainsay that a besetting problem of our distraught age is that current images need to be harmonized and adapted to the proliferating discoveries in every area of human endeavor? The confrontation of age-old world views with one another in a world which is rapidly becoming one world-wide community adds to the problem; it may also be a means of invigoration as each historical view reckons and comes to terms with an opposing view. Indeed, the conflict, or at least tension, within and among opposing views may be singularly fruitful.

Surely an integration of world views in which the authentic elements of each are preserved and placed in proper perspective is the crying need of our time. There is little doubt but that our age is experiencing a crisis brought about by the crumbling of centuries-old systems. We live in an age of transition in which fundamental interpretations of reality involving every aspect of human existence are being radically questioned. Perhaps some of the indications of this changing situation can be given and some sort of guide to answers demanded by it indicated.

The world in which we live is already manifestly dominated by technology, and in all likelihood will become increasingly so. Old cultures which spawned this innovation were oriented to views which featured nature and humanity. The age into which we are now rapidly moving will likely feature a metanatural world, and the old human values will be transformed into metanatural human values. Surely this new world opens tremendous prospects; it will also open potentialities for enormous evil. The natural disasters of floods, earthquakes, and the like, pale beside the potential disaster of world-wide nuclear holocaust; and even this is not the most distressing possibility of evil. The most distressing possibility is that man will acquiesce in his own creations. The machines he invents and the functional principles which pertain to them may well dictate, as it were, his cultural norms. If this be so, man will face the possibility of denying himself in the very act of underestimating himself, thereby jeopardizing if not killing the potentialities of love and spirit which are his destiny. Increasingly the trend is toward humanly created nature which is replacing older organic relationship. For example, there is every possibility of artificial climate; and the felt distinctions of day and night are passing into vague awareness with ever-increasing use of artificial light. These changes will not be merely external; they may very well bring about changes in the deep psychological structure of man, and consequent or subsequent changes in his sensations and sense of bodily awareness. Even today it is virtually impossible for scores of people to work effectively in an un-air-conditioned climate. This is surely a superficial example compared with others likely to come.

Contemplating the remarkable changes taking place and those we might anticipate, we must avoid a number of tempting pitfalls. Surely there may be no hankering for a return to romanticized notions of the past, to nature in the raw, or to a prescientific, pretechnological age. Likewise there may be no hasty a priori limit placed on what the future may hold. For instance, in contemporary discussions of the possibilities of automation and computer function there are those who shrug off possibilities of one kind or another with trite observations about the inherent limitations of machines and human inventiveness. However true these observations may be currently, even now studies are under way which indicate at least the theoretical possibility of constructing an electronic device capable of a form of consciousness and also capable of receiving and integrating direct visual sensations, as well as other types of sensation. There seem to be few intrinsic reasons precluding the actualization of the predictions of the most imaginative science fiction.

From these few remarks it should be clear that the rapid development of the material factor of life with its corresponding emphasis upon function will affect and even set the tempo of human life. To a great extent it has already set the tempo in highly industrialized nations.

One of the major problems that appears concomitant with such a world is that of self-identity. In an older world view with its nature-based organic rhythms, self-identity was achieved through participation in the fruits of work and the natural and conceptual symbols of religious cult. In a technological age of function and process the substantial element in the products of work and in the symbols of religious cult have ceased to be a stabilizing factor in the natural maturation of the human psyche. As a consequence of this de-substantialization of nature and its symbolic extension into human culture, nature is no longer available, at least to the human psyche and mind, as a primary carrier of the divine. In other words, as humanistic and technological man has extended his control over nature, he thereby has gained a controlling knowledge of nature expressed in the conceptual abstractions of the sciences. Nature no longer presents itself to the human mind and imagination as a palpable mystery. This is not an achievement to be regretted, no matter how many problems or how much nostalgia it may present or evoke. Man in freeing himself from subservience to nature may become more responsible and responsive to his own humanity; as a corollary he may become responsible for nature and its uses that his new-found power of control has given him. With the development of his scientific understanding of himself, man may also gain effective control over his own functions and/or dysfunctions. A most cogent example of this possibility is in the field of psychiatry, with its use of tranquilizers and psychic energizers. We do not here even broach the question of psychedelic drugs and their possible effect upon the restructuring of consciousness.

Needless to say, controlling knowledge gained in the area of psychiatry may not only be used to alleviate dysfunction and extend human capacity; conceivably it may also be used to control human function to whatever end the controller or controllers deem expedient. A widely known author (C. W. Ceram) has recently suggested that in time scientific controlling knowledge may make it possible to breed a stable population of mental defectives that could be used for menial chores which frustrate, bore, and consequently render unhappy more highly endowed human beings. Clearly this suggestion raises questions bearing on ethics and religious values. If humanity is self-sufficient and responsible ultimately only to itself, no serious question of ethics need be raised in regard to this proposal, provided such persons are considered human beings rather than slaves. If humanity is not self-sufficient and *is* responsible to value that transcends humanity, the question becomes much more complicated. Can one honor the *sacred* value of human beings by deliberately inducing value regression? If man is responsible for increasing value for himself *and* for the enjoyment of God, would this not logically engender a principle that forbids the eugenic mutilation of the dynamic but structured divine image of man? Even though the controlled breeding of mental defectives might not be a violation of such persons once they were bred, would it not be a violation of the image of man which extols the increase of value for the benefit of mankind as a whole, even at the risk of suffering? The proposed suggestion of eugenically bred mental defectives is, of course, highly hypothetical; but it does bring into sharp relief the sort of problem one may face with advanced technology and clearly indicates the effect this may have on world view and value orientation. And if one contemplates scientific or technological achievement within a totalitarian structure, one's world view and value orientation become manifestly important concerns.

From the foregoing illustrations it should be clear that the problem of self-identity loss brought about by innovation and cultural change, with the consequent breakdown of value-carrying symbols, is currently urgent. It should also be clear that self-identity is not limited to individuals, for individuals need images depicting the identity and integrity of their concept of man or what it means to be human. Indeed the question, What does it mean to be human? is perhaps one of the most distressing in our present age and one capable, certainly, of becoming disastrous with increasing cultural innovation if that innovation is brought about exclusively in the material factors of human culture represented by technology and science. The problem will no doubt be even more distressing should men continue to deny the value-creating potentiality of science and disregard—even disrespect—the value-creating and -conserving function of philosophy and religion.

What contribution may a philosophical and religious orientation to value make in a technological age?

In the ever-growing trend toward highly complex functional organizations with compartmentalized and specialized relationship of the worker and his product or service, there will be as a consequence an increasing demand on interpersonal relations to carry the burden of value orientation. The sense of integrity, of well-being, and of the primary carrier of the holy will be primarily in the area of person rather than in the relationship of producer to product and of man to nature. Rather than being a source of dehumanization, the organization can and should be an opportunity for deepening and widening the scope of interpersonal relations. This should be true almost by definition, since the primary importance of person-to-person relationship replaces the old person-to-object relationship.

To feature the person-to-person relationship is to place a heavy burden upon the need for self-identity and creative individuation; it is also to increase the need for fidelity to other persons within the impersonality of organizational function. This interpersonal orientation will no doubt need to be built into the functional resources of the organization itself; and the requirements of harmonious personal relations will need to be worked out by means of the techniques and resources available in the human sciences. This effort, of course, presupposes that individuals shall be looked upon as persons of sacred worth rather than as so many units fulfilling a delegated function.

Here it is assumed that with increasing demands placed upon the resources immanent in the human person in relation to others, potential energies will be tapped providing a hitherto unrealized source of individuation in collective form. One may even envision a collective mysticism of love, such as has been termed by one author, Herbert Marcuse, erotization.[5] The collective erotized body is a secular analogue of what in religious language and symbol is called the mystical body. Its effect can perhaps be described as a collective "field" with persons as loci providing the condition for a co-uniting of co-inherent persons. While the possibility of refusal is open, the acceptance of such a co-inherence based upon love and responsibility brings about a collective palpable body of energy, communion, and delight. The creation of this field is probably not so much a conscious endeavor, if this at all, as a spontaneous outpouring from the interrelations of persons and their activities in reference to the goals and functions of their cooperative enterprise.

The use of such terms as "erotization" and "energy field of communion" must not be misunderstood. The fidelity and creativity implicit in interpersonal relations mean freedom and self-identity produced by love and responsibility. In no sense is there denial of fidelity or of the structures of conjugal love; rather, only in the full fidelity of person to person may a responsible love do its creative work. Note that this understanding is contrary to some current prognostications of the decline and inadequacy of the traditional family structure, with its supposedly enslaving aspects. Indeed, the traditional family in many cases has been inadequate, having been based primarily upon socioeconomic considerations rather than the complementary meaning of man and woman in interpersonal union grounded in love with its emphasis on the sacred integrity of each. Whatever the problems of the traditional family structure, however, in a highly mobile population with decreasing chances for strong intimate personal ties within the larger community, marriage may be expected to have an increasingly dominant and profound meaning in reference to collectivization and impersonal organization. Indeed, for many couples it has meant the creation of person in the responsible love relationship. With the illustration of marriage and the family in mind, as a unique interpersonal relation wherein each individual is related to each other in the fidelity of responsible love, it will be clear that the loci of the collective field of communion are fed from the intensive field set up by means of the polarity or "fruitful tension" that obtains between individuated or integrated persons in the man-woman relationship. This, it is suggested, is the metaphysical meaning of marriage; it is the metaphysical meaning of interpersonal relationship. As the marriage relationship may be the source of the most creative energies obtainable in the person-to-person realm—aptly symbolized and actualized in its procreative function—so the interpersonal relationship is the source of creative energies. In a different language, the suggestion is this: it is a universal principle that value intensity comes about through polar contrast.

For this reason the collective field of communion is of supreme importance as the source of value for a community of persons. An analysis of interpersonal relations in and of itself is insufficient, unless it is seen that the full meaning of person-to-person relationship is achieved in man beyond himself and caught up within the meaning of God as personal essence and ground of being. Man in exploring the immanent value of the created order exhausts himself in his own activity. In exploring the value of creation in reference to God as personal essence and ground of being he opens inexhaustible possibilities for advance. More specifically, in the intimacy of interpersonal activity in relation to the transcendent, freedom and self-identity are given full ontological status. Only in relationship to the transcendent and everlasting is the infinite yearning for recognition satisfied and full acceptance of self and other possible. The relationship to transcendence in which the drive beyond the self for purposes of self-possession is satisfied is the very ground of the dynamic life of person: transcendence is the source of the power and courage to be in freedom and love. It always acts as a lure and as an informing power which elicits creative endeavor and fulfillment from the person who fully responds, within the measure of his capacity and circumstance. Self-identity and active creative potential are the *sine qua non* of intense value in creative personal relationships. To return to the earlier illustration of marriage: without the transcendent dimension as informing and grounding the man-woman relationship, there is apt to be either superficiality of mutual response or excessive dependence on the part of one partner or both which stultifies the creative potential by breaking the polar energizing reciprocity. Could it be that the potentialities of the man-woman relationship grounded in the divine transcendence will open a source of virtually unimaginable possibilities for the actualization of latent human powers? And could it be that this is the hope for all persons in relations of fidelity? And, of course, what may be commonplace in the future (barring cosmic disaster) can be often joyfully pursued and immanently appreciated even now.

The actualization of religious or ontological self-possession or psychological self-identity creates an immanent personal freedom that means transcending psychological and organismic compulsions and related forms of psychic dysfunction. This achieved personal freedom permits centered self-control. The person is free to act and at the same time free from acting in any particular circumstance. This type of freedom is an intrinsic value and is the presupposition for actualizing all other values. It is the very basis of ethical action or behavior. Behavior brought about by virtue of constraint or inner compulsion *may* result in a good act in itself; but it is short of the goal of free personal choice and decision. Man comes to God *from* a personal freedom and in freely responding creates a further actualization of freedom *for* a particular mode of human and divine fulfillment and value actualization. Man is most himself in free commitment to responsible action at the behest of divine love which would pour itself out and at the same time receive its enjoyment of the divine-human mutual response.

The human process of achieving its highest freedom moves in individuals and in history through the three stages of dependence, independence, and interdependence, where the intrinsic value of dependence and independence are retained and yet taken up into the fruitful tension and harmony of interdependence. This process is as true of more strictly interhuman as of divine-human relationships. It may be an anguish-filled long-drawn-out temporal task; it may be a joyous immanent unfolding of dimensions of interior growth; it may be the cordial achievement of the full consent of all being to all being. Whatever its mode of actualization, it is a task for all men and women here and now; it is the task of history itself; it is the task of the God-man. Its first term is the intrinsic individuation of all being; its final term is free and everlasting creativity and delight within the normatively structural freedom of a transfigured personal cosmos actuated by love and glory.

NOTES FOR CHAPTER 1

1 Charles A. Dubray, *Introduction to Philosophy*, New York, Longmans, Green, and Co., 1912, p. 7. (Writer's translation.)
2 Richard McKeon (ed.), *The Basic Works of Aristotle*, New York, Random House, 1941, p. 712.
3 Dubray, *op. cit.*, p. 8.
4 Alfred North Whitehead, *Process and Reality*, New York, Humanities Press, 1955, p. 6.
5 Herbert Marcuse, *Eros and Civilization*, Boston, Beacon Press, 1955.

QUESTIONS

1 What is the peril and advantage of viewing religion (a) philosophically? (b) phenomenologically?
2 Consider the similarities and differences in the respective modes of response in religion, philosophy, and science.
3 Wherein is the conflict between religious and scientific knowledge legitimately retained? Wherein may it be overcome?
4 What contributions may the social and behavioral sciences make to religious understanding?

SUGGESTED READINGS

Henri Louis Bergson, *The Two Sources of Morality and Religion*, Garden City, N.Y., Doubleday, 1954.
Martin Buber, *I and Thou*, New York, Scribner's, 1957.
Jacques Maritain, *Approaches to God*, New York, Harper, 1954.
Rudolf Otto, *The Idea of the Holy*, London, Oxford University Press, 1'
Michael Polanyi, *Personal Knowledge*, Chicago, University of Chicago J 1958.
Pierre Teilhard de Chardin, *The Phenomenon of Man*, New York, F 1959.
Paul Tillich, *The Dynamics of Faith*, New York, Harper, 1957.

2 *Wilbur Long*

Religion in the Idealistic Tradition

By common agreement *religion, philosophy,* and *idealism* are among the most significant words in the language, because they point to the critical issues of man and his existence, his career, his values, his obligations, his destiny, and his world. At this preliminary point, however, mutual concurrence ends. How these words ought to be defined is widely disputed, and what is equally disconcerting, religions, philosophies, and idealisms exist in bewildering variety. To make sense out of this tangle of terms and standpoints is a difficult and complex business: it is too commonly the case that discussions of them flounder in dogmatic presuppositions and in arbitrary use of language which serve to slant the outcome towards prejudice rather than enlightenment. Even when these hurdles have been surmounted, an intelligent inquiry into their mutual relationships is scarcely to be expected without some background acquaintance with history.

Idealism, as the term is used in contemporary discourse, is not a special school of philosophy but a generic standpoint about things, whose alternative is materialism. This basic distinction can be considered from several modes of subdivision. From that of datum, materialism is the position which accents the spatial and sensuous *as such*. As a speculative standpoint it is pictorialism; that is, it considers the world to be essentially or on the whole the sort of thing we contact in visual or tactual experience, or at least it is to be conceived on the analogy of this experience. Materialism in its original form based its theory of the world on the engineering model, according to which the real is corporeal mass, and process is mechanically controlled motion. All sophisticated refinements of this point of view still hold to it in principle. In the realm of ethics and values, materialism is naked egoism directed to the love of abstract power and animal enjoyments as such. Idealism is, most broadly, the negation of this position. It maintains that the real is, on the whole at least, something nonsensuous and immaterial, and it postulates that process is chiefly nonmechanical; that is, it is purposive or target-directed, organic or holistic. In the realm of ethics and values, idealism is altercentric and holds that the essential and legitimate principles that concern and direct human life are such things as conscience or obligation, justice, "spiritual" values, and the like. From a second standpoint—that of grading—materialism represents the policy of downgrading by emphasizing the "lower" or "inferior"; idealism upgrades by accenting the "higher" or "superior." Ultimately the two standpoints converge.

Idealism, moreover, involves several important distinctions of its own. First, it divides into *Idea-ism and Spiritualism*. Idea-ism is the theory that the predominantly real is what is simply *connate* with man's essential self, that is, what he is peculiarly at home with—intellectual concepts, universals, species, or values such as beauty and goodness. In principle this sort of entity Plato named Form (*eidos*) or Idea (*idea*), and he proposed that "ideas" are not human thoughts, but that which human intellectual thoughts are *of*. (The use of "idea" to mean a human thought as such was introduced into philosophical language in the seventeenth century by Descartes.) Such a view is properly called Idea-ism; but this is awkward in speech, and for the sake of euphony the word has become Idealism.

"Spiritualism" names the class of theories which hold that reality is, at least on the whole, what is *like* ourselves or at least is in some significant respect analogous to the human self, or more broadly, to some aspect of the self (for instance, when reality is characterized as Will). "Spiritualism," however, has an ectoplasmic connotation and consequently is terminologically objectionable; for this reason it is falling into disuse. The upshot is that "Idealism" has come to stand as the name for both types of immaterialism.

Idealism further divides into dominant and pure. From the standpoint of pure idealism, reality is solely ideal or spiritual. In the West this notion did not appear until about the year 1700. Dominant idealism, on the contrary, acknowledges the reality of material or spatial things, or at least a nonideal component in things, but maintains that ideal reality is more powerful and significant. A theory of pure dualism, which claims that the material and the ideal are equally real and have nothing intrinsically to do with one another, is found only in India.

Another division among idealistic positions is that between impersonalism and personalism. Any viewpoint is personalistic so far as it acknowledges the reality of the self-conscious person as an abiding agent-self —that is, a self-active, intelligent being who maintains his identity through change or time—and consequently (as substantival in some manner or other) is not a mere stream of momentary, interlinked states of consciousness passively aware of events, or a mere spectator, without any creative capacity and individual responsibility. Metaphysical personalism is the theory that reality, either predominantly or altogether, is in some degree analogous to the human person, although not, of course, in its physical embodiment. Theism, strictly understood, is personalism with respect to the divine: it postulates that deity is rational, self-conscious, active, and according to conventional doctrine, ethical. Normative or "practical" personalism is the view that human persons are essentially structured or qualified by moral principles and "spiritual" values which are extrapsychological and universally objective; and they share this type of structure or character with persons everywhere, whether supermen, angels, divinities, or the Absolute. A devil, however, would not be a person, strictly speaking, because he is incapable of love, and the capacity to love is an essential quality of persons. Impersonalism is any view, whether idealistic or materialistic, which rejects the personalistic position. The Judeo-Christian tradition is that of dominant personalism. Impersonalistic idealism has been popular in India, China, ancient Greece, and recent Western thought. Whether this kind of idealism provides a satisfactory doctrinal frame for religion depends, of course, on what kind of religion is considered satisfactory. Let us now elaborate on some outstanding expressions of idealism in religion.

IDEALISM IN ASIA

Universal religion, philosophic consciousness, and pure speculative idealism first emerged among the Indo-European peoples of Iran, India, and Greece; and their first flowering was in southern Asia in the lands lying to the east and west of the Indus river.

Iran: Spiritual Dualism West of the Indus, in Iran, Zarathustra (c. 700 B.C.) created the first universal religion, with a theology of spiritual dualism and a humanistic philosophy of man and values. He taught that the physical world is a field of struggle between two personalized spiritual forces, that of good and that of evil. Good is everything of affirmative value—light, truth, health, harmony, beauty, order, and happiness; evil is everything negative and destructive—darkness, untruth, disease, disorder, chaos, disharmony, ugliness, and unhappiness. The world scene is thus historical and eschatological, that is, bent towards the future. Ultimately the spiritual forces of good, identified with Ahura Mazda, the god of goodness, will prevail: the spiritual forces of evil, identified with Angra Mainyu, the god of destructiveness, will be enchained forever. Meanwhile man's vocation is to join up on the side of the good, to aid in establishing the rule of harmony and happiness. Constructive labor of all kinds is a religious service—for instance, for a farmer to make productive a piece of waste land. Religion is, in sum, sturdy yea-saying to the cosmic purpose to goodness and militant loyalty to this enterprise which is the content of the divine will. The practical idealism of this Iranian religion was surprisingly mature: it taught that the material world is a means of serving spiritual ends (humanism). Heaven and hell are self-imposed states of mind, not mere places of reward or punishment: man, in other words, is the creator of his own destiny. Zarathustra's theology or philosophy has its echo in the ethics of the strenuous life, preached by Theodore Roosevelt, and in the contemporary theology of a finite God.

India: Philosophical Idealism　India, lying east of the Indus, is said to be the most religious region on earth; and here, about the time of Zarathustra, began a naissance of religious and intellectual thought that proliferated in all doctrinal directions to make this nation one of the preeminent centers of spiritual and philosophic consciousness. Nearly every conceivable point of view is represented in Indian philosophy and religion, and a cursory account of the total picture is inevitably a distortion. Some Indian philosophies, for example, are theistic; and certain semiphilosophical sects, notably those devoted to Vishnu, which identify piety with *bhakti* or selfless love of God, resemble Christianity. Others to the astonishment of Westerners link religion with atheism (Jainism, Sankhya, Mimamsa) or agnosticism (original Buddhism) or allot to deity a minor role (Yoga). With the sole exception of the minor school of materialism (Carvaka), all Indian philosophies are religions dedicated to the goal of salvation. The "orthodox" schools accept the Vedic scriptures as supernatural revelation (Sankhya, Yoga, Mimamsa, and Vedantism), as orthodox Jews accept the Torah, Christians the Bible, and Mohammedans the Koran. With the exception of the Carvaka and of original Buddhism, which substituted the theory of a stream of consciousness for that of an abiding self or soul, all schools are idealistic in either one of two senses. (1) Those that are ontologically dualistic have recognized that the soul is independent of matter and superior to it in quality. (2) Those that are monistic have maintained that the Self or its equivalent is the sole reality and that the spatial, material world is only a thought-appearance of the mind. Indian tradition shares with Christianity the characteristic of being powerfully eschatological; that is, it looks with hope towards the future for the consummation of man's religious purpose to escape from imperfection and attain eternal security, however this may be described.

In general outlook and development, Indian world views and life views are opposite to those of Zarathustrianism, with which the Western mind and Christianity are more in sympathy. Zarathustrianism was personalistic, humanistic, optimistic, social, militant, and voluntaristic; that is, it implied that will is the center of personality. Indian thought, on the contrary and on the whole, has been impersonalistic (self-consciousness is not an intrinsic or desirable property of the self); pessimistic (personal or individual existence is not desirable); ascetic in varying degrees; individualistic (salvation of the individual is the individual's preoccupation and is attained solely by his autosoteric endeavor); and intellectualistic (evil is ignorance, resulting in bodily infection, not bad will; hence the self is intrinsically innocent).

Indian idealism agrees with other religious philosophies that in this life man should possess a regenerate heart and a spiritual quality of consciousness; but instead of anticipating eternal beatitude within a society of perfected persons in the "kingdom of heaven," it aspires to eventual and permanent release (*mukti, moksha*) from bodily existence and self-conscious individuality. This final state, which is peace akin to that in deep and undisturbed sleep, not annihilation, seems to the Westerner a weird and repulsive sort of ideal good; but considered within a frame of beliefs that are axiomatic in Indian tradition, it is logical rather than fantastic.

The first of these beliefs is the feeling that finitude is spiritually dissatisfying because it involves incompleteness and spiritual loneliness: only the Infinite or Absolute can be perfectly satisfying. As the Vedic writer says, "The Infinite [superlative, supreme] is bliss. There is no bliss in anything finite." [1] But to escape from the fragmentary and from the loneliness of isolation requires an escape from individuality, and this involves release from self-consciousness. A second belief is the doctrine that self-consciousness is not an intrinsic character of soul, but only an accidental consequence of its union with the body. A third is the belief that the soul repeatedly, indeed almost endlessly, is reborn in a body (reincarnation, *samsara*); this is held to be an axiom too obvious to need justification.

The sting of this notion, which gives to the contemplation of human existence an oppressive aura, is, fourthly, a vivid awareness of the immensity of time not shared by any other ethnic people. The Chinese and Greeks, for instance, took the endlessness of time for granted, but they did not contemplate it with imaginative emotion. Peoples whose thought has been Biblical, on the contrary, have supposed that time began with the creation of the world a few thousand years ago. Locke suggested, for instance, that the date of about 4,000 B.C. was as good as any. The imaginative Indian thinker, however, has conceived the universe as indefinitely massive in space, richly peopled with souls of various grades, and an endless succession of worlds, the life of each being a *kalpa* or

4,320,000,000 of our years. According to the Jainas, the founder of their sect lived innumerable trillions of *palyas* ago, and a *palya* is the time it takes to empty a well one mile deep and filled with fine hairs, when one hair is removed from it every century.

In terms of its own postulates, then, the Indian aspiration for mere release from *samsara* is more than reasonable, particularly when we consider the fact that each death and rebirth involves the destruction of memories (at least with rare exception) and the dissolution of all loving ties that bind persons to one another. In this Sisyphus-like situation the project of personal living becomes theoretically, at least, wretched. The individualistic and autosoteric feature of Indian religion follows logically also from its axiomatic doctrine of *karma*, according to which man's destiny is exclusively the consequence of the operation of the spiritual law of cause and effect. No one can save another, because this law operates solely on the individual through his own actions: as we individually sow, we individually reap.

Idealism in the Upanishads The Upanishads or Vedanta (the last of the Vedas, which constitute the authoritative scriptures of Hinduism) are the earliest extant writings that give extensive expression to mature philosophic consciousness, and they are the earliest known depository of a sophisticated kind of monistic idealism. Commonly poetic in form, they are composite in character, unsystematic in arrangement of thought, diverse in specific doctrine, and like the Bible, exhibit various strata of theology and religion. In general they represent a contempt for the popular religion of priestly sacrifice, the way of "beasts," and teach a spiritual method of salvation by knowledge. The dominant theme, though by no means the exclusive one, is that behind and within all things is a spiritual Absolute of which they are manifestations: "As the spider sends forth and draws in its thread, as plants grow on the earth . . . thus does everything arise here from the Indestructible." [2] Or again, things are said to be fulgurations or sparks from the One: "As from a blazing fire sparks, being like unto fire, fly forth a thousand-fold, thus are various beings brought forth from the Imperishable, and return thither also." [3] This is not a statement of pure pantheistic idealism, although on occasion such a notion is perhaps anticipated, as in the paradoxical assertion that "If the killer thinks that he kills, if the killed thinks that he is killed, they do not understand; for this one does not kill, nor is that one killed." [4]

The question of what the Indestructible is was answered diversely by two ancient schools of thought. According to one it is Brahman (cosmic power); according to the other it is Atman (cosmic self or soul). Eventually the two views merged in the formula that Brahman is Atman; that is, the Absolute is Infinite Consciousness without self-consciousness. An occasional passage, however, suggests the personalistic position—for instance, the statement that the One is Purusha (self-conscious self or person), "one eternal thinker, thinking non-eternal thoughts, who, though one, fulfills the desires of many." [5] However described, Brahman-Atman is universal unseen Presence, ruling all thoughts and things and "imagined by the heart, by wisdom, by the [spiritual] mind." [6]

According to the Upanishads the possession of this truth about Brahman-Atman, when it produces a spiritual transformation of the self, releases the individual from rebirth. Salvation is, so to speak, the fruit of divine assimilation, on the principle that we become what we love because to love is to become identified with the loved object. As one writer puts it, "he who knows the oldest and the best, becomes the oldest and the best." [7] According to another passage: "As the flowing rivers disappear in the sea, losing their name and their form [i.e., their individuality], thus a wise man, freed from name and form, goes to the divine Purusha who is greater than the great. He who knows that highest Brahman, becomes even Brahman." [8] This doctrine that the self within the human heart is Brahman suggests a certain feeling of creaturehood and piety. The One is that which is dearer to us than all else: "This, which is nearer to us than anything, this Atman, is dearer than a son, dearer than wealth, dearer than all else." [9] It is that which makes all else dear: only as partaking of it do husband or wife become lovable and loved. As Plato would have said, all good and lovable things are such only because they participate in the Divine. In its final form, however, the Upanishads teach that salvation is exclusively by discernment, not devoted participation. Saving truth, revealed by the "science of Brahman," is this: the essential human self is and always has been, not a manifestation of Brahman-Atman, but the Absolute itself. The formula of salvation is simply, "That art thou" or "Thou art It" or "Thou art Brahman" or "I am God." To be saved from rebirth is simply to discover who we are. This is self-deification, without piety or sense of creaturehood.

All Indian philosophies have held, however, that salvation is not merely a remote achievement: we can participate in it in this life. The regenerate man "fears nothing." All his fetters of sensual and selfish desire fall away, "all the ties of the heart are severed here on earth"; the spiritual man no longer "pines after the body," his "sufferings are destroyed," and he possesses now the foretaste of eternal "bliss." Beyond death, of course, he "does not return": the endless pathos of finite existence is finished. One memorable prayer in the Brihadaranyaka Upanishad, endlessly repeated by generations of spiritually minded philosophers, has universal appeal and expresses the aspiration among earnest men everywhere: "Lead me from the unreal to the real! Lead me from darkness to light! Lead me from death to immortality." [10]

Idealism in Mahayana Buddhism   No clear advance was made beyond the inchoate idealism of the Upanishads until the second century A.D., when two thinkers, converted from Hinduism to Buddhism, established the first recorded philosophy of pure speculative idealism. The Madhyamika school, founded by Nagarjuna and Asvaghosha, was so named to indicate that it was the philosophy of a "middle way" between the logical alternatives proposed in the Upanishads,[11] that the origin of things must be either determinate Being or Nothing. Buddha himself (sixth century B.C.) had similarly proposed a "middle way"; he too had rejected the logical alternative and had taught that salvation is a matter of taking account, not of Being or Nothing, but of Becoming. Man is, so far as we can empirically determine, neither a metaphysical, timeless soul nor a mere vaporish awareness of things; he is a stream of successive conscious states, or a stream of consciousness. The Real, according to Nagarjuna, is neither matter, Atman, nor a flux of consciousness, but *sunyata* (void); that is, the Absolute is unthinkable, unstatable, and verbally or intellectually indeterminate. It is a pure *That* which is beyond "form and speech." This is the doctrine of pure pantheistic, mystical idealism. From this point of view, which Nagarjuna defended with ruthless logic, all notions of substance, cause, identity, matter, soul, individuality, and the like are self-contradictory. The world of common sense and that of the talking philosophers are consequently mere illusion or "appearance." The Real or *sunyata* is, from the common standpoint of perceiving and thinking, nonsense or mere emptiness (*sunya*); it can only be grasped intuitively by speechless, spiritual insight. Salvation begins when we are spiritually reborn in a manner to discover the truth that all plurality, individuality, things, souls, time, space, and proud speculative thought with its futile logic are pure "appearance" or illusion.

Now this doctrine of a direct way to salvation, or the passage from personal illusion into impersonal Eternity, which we can anticipate here and now in spiritual consciousness, involves the recognition of two kinds of languages and two levels of truth. This is important, not only philosophically but for humanity as well. If philosophical truth alone provided salvation, most people would be doomed to hopelessness; for as intellectuals both in the East and West have repeatedly observed, in the words of Plato, "the public cannot possibly be a philosopher." Since this notion of salvation exclusively for the elect few is not to be contemplated, saving truth must somehow be accommodated to the public's capacity for truth. There must be, then, two levels of religious truth—literal theology for the philosopher and metaphorical or mythical theology for other people. This is the celebrated principle of "accommodation" adopted by theologians of all creeds and sects. Mahayana Buddhism has given extensive recognition to it. The philosophical idealist pursues the higher way to salvation: as the Diamond Cutter Sutra has it, the seeker who can abandon all beliefs in the reality of appearances will at once become a Buddha (enlightened one) and attain Nirvana or identification with the Eternal wherein is no plurality, no time, no change, and no self-consciousness. For those who are caught in the realm of illusion or appearance, Mahayana Buddhism has spun out a complex mythology of divine Buddhas, Bodhisattvas, heavens, and the use of prayers, which are pragmatically true and useful in the sense that they are imaginative helps to salvation for the unphilosophical mind.

A second school of pure pantheistic idealism, in modified form, was founded in the fourth century A.D. by the Buddhist brothers Asanga and Vasubandhu, who had been reared in orthodox Hinduism. Known as the Yogacara philosophy, perhaps because it sanctioned the spiritual use of Yoga or physical and mental discipline, it proposed to refine and slightly modify the *sunyata* doctrine. The Madhyamika theory had recognized only two kinds of truth, the absolute and the relative; the new philosophers held that this is inadequate, because "relative" hides an important distinction between two kinds of "appearances." If a man thinks he sees a snake and it turns out to be a rope, "that it is a rope" is less false than "that it is a snake." Similarly, the mind that knows truth, perceives appearances as such, or falls into the error of supposing they are more than appearances, cannot be "appearance" in the same sense that other things are: this mind is not mere *sunya* or nothing. Physical things, such as rocks, chairs, stars, ropes, and the like, are *sunya:* they belong to the imagination, like the world in the mirror, the dream world, the moon in the water, the hypnotic world made by the magician in the minds of his audience, or the world of fiery wheels produced by whirling torches. Such things are *maya* or illusion, mere thoughts in the mind. Of them, as Berkeley said later, "To be is to be perceived." The perceiver, however, who is a stream of consciousness and thought, is more real than they: he is a precipitate within the one Cosmic or Universal Mind (*alayavignana*), the storehouse of the past as memory. *Alayavignana* is also the home of eternal truth, in which finite minds can share by intuition, that is, by an extra-intellectual or spiritual kind of knowing. In some sense all finite minds are aspects of the Universal Mind; and human thought, it would seem, is a sort of "seeing all things in God." The Cosmic Mind, however, is itself, so to speak, only a distillation from the eternal Absolute that is beyond all thought. This Absolute the Buddhists variously refer to as *sunyata*, Thatness, Nirvana, Suchness, Buddha Essence, *dharmakaya*, *bodhi* (knowledge), Buddhahood, Mind-Essence, and the like.

As in other forms of Indian philosophy, the religious goal of the Yogacara philosophers was *mukti*, or in the Buddhist term, *nirvana*, the final release from personal existence and consciousness. The question repeatedly asked in India, why the That or Brahman has precipitated appearance, illusion, and evil out of itself and forced finite selves upon the long and wearisome trek back to the homeland, has received several answers. One is that it is God's sport (*lila*). The philosopher Asvaghosha is said to have explained it as due to ignorance (*avidya*), without stating why the That produced such a principle. Buddhists generally are content to mark off the question as an insoluble mystery which Buddhas alone understand. Christians can feel some sympathy with this confession of failure; for Christianity faces a similar impasse in seeking the reason why there is so much evil in a world that has been divinely ordered.

Vedantist Pantheism   If the Upanishads were the inspiration of the first systems of pure philosophic idealism, contributed by the Buddhists, these systems were in turn the source of systems of idealism which subsequently developed within the orthodox Brahman tradition. This development is known as Vedanta or Vedantism, to indicate that it claims to be the authoritative and definitive statement of the philosophy contained in the Upanishads or Vedanta. Since Mahayana Buddhism finally became practically extinct in India and survived only as exported to such other parts of Asia as Tibet, China, and Japan, its philosophical torch, so to speak, was passed on to later Vedantism; and this fact is important, because Vedantic idealism became the dominant religion of Indian intellectuals and on the whole probably remains the most popular view among them today. In Vedantism two wings or subtypes developed, the impersonalistic form represented predominantly by Sankara (c.800 A.D.), and the personalistic form of Ramanuja (c.1100 A.D.). The same sort of fission, interestingly enough, occurred in the West during the nineteenth century, among the idealistic philosophies stemming from Kant.

By far the more popular form of Vedantist idealism has been the impersonalistic type, known as Advaita Vedanta, that is, monistic or pantheistic idealism. Apart from terminological novelties, Sankara's philosophy differed from its Buddhist predecessors chiefly in two respects—in the richness and precision of its logical elaboration, and in its clearer distinction between the perceptual world, on the one hand, and the worlds of dreams and other illusory appearances, on the other. All such worlds are, of course, mere thought constructions or presentations: there is no real, ontological world of space and matter; but the one is shared by all finite minds as a common order of experience and it has to be taken into account as long as we exist; whereas the other realms are private and insignificant. Sankara accepted, like his Buddhist predecessors, a negative theology, with its doctrine that the Absolute is ineffable or beyond human conception. But he adopted the Upanishadic name of Brahman to indicate that, contrary to Buddhist doctrine, the Absolute is not a mere *sunyata* or Void, and that it is more truthful in a metaphorical sense to assert that it is consciousness than to maintain that it is without consciousness.

Sankara explained that error or the world of appearance is due to *maya*, an inscrutable power within the Absolute, the cosmic force of magic that makes for illusion; this is simply a renaming of the Yogacara doctrine of *avidya*.

Like other spiritual teachers in India, Sankara taught present salvation. Although the eventual religious goal is *mukti* or release from rebirth and consciousness, we can now possess a foretaste of eternity in high emotion, peace of soul, and spiritual bliss. Like the Buddhists, however, he recognized the need to accommodate religious truth to the lower capacities of the general public and offered them a mythical theology. Unphilosophical minds on the lower level of religion can pursue salvation by worshiping the Absolute under the "appearance" form of a personal God, Saguna Brahma or Isvara; and in this way of devotion they too can proceed, although at a slower pace, towards *mukti*. The high road to deliverance, however, is knowledge—specifically the knowledge that all things are "appearance" and that, in the formula of the Upanishads, "That art thou." Our identity with Brahman, or the proposition that we are God, does not mean that we as embodied persons or self-conscious beings are That: only our inner, unmanifested, and purely spiritual essence is the Absolute. Moreover, saving truth is not intellectual: the philosophic mind is released only when spiritually transformed, and this happens when the purely intellectual doctrine of the identity of ourselves and God becomes a vital, living experience in which, in some manner or degree, we intuit God. This living insight, of course, transforms life as well as the mind. Nonetheless, Sankara's idealism and his program of salvation are those of self-deification. With the loss of creature-consciousness and a sense of piety, his followers face Reality with Stoic imperturbability and an heroic quality of mind, but with a consciousness empty of love and lyricism.

The three methods of salvation most anciently practiced in India were those of cult sacrifice, ascetic discipline and mortification (*tapas*), and philosophical knowledge. As early as the fourth century B.C., however, another way had been adopted by sects of a semiphilosophical type, with a literature their own, theistic and devotional in character, and identified chiefly, as we have already noted, with the god Vishnu, who loves men and seeks their love in return. The most celebrated expression of this devotional and active way of *bhakti*, or selfless love of God, was the *Bhagavadgita* or Divine Song, which holds in India the place that the Gospel of John claims among Christians. In the Vedantist system of Ramanuja, among others, this theism and devotional religion attained to the status of philosophy, as a philosophical religion flanked by metaphysics and speculative logic. Although it did not win among the intellectuals the popularity gained by Sankara's system, it nonetheless holds a place of respect if not wide allegiance among them.

Ramanuja's idealism was ontologically semimonistic and personalistic in its account of both God and finite selves. Brahman or God is supreme personality, that is, eternal self-conscious Being, with attributes of grace and love as well as power and knowledge. Both the material world and the system of finite persons are real attributes of God, not mere transient appearances. Finite selves are uncreated, divine modes; yet they are intrinsically self-conscious and capable of creative activity. Salvation, for Ramanuja, continued to mean release from rebirth, but in his system it does not involve, as in most, the destruction of personal, conscious individuality; on the contrary, it enhances it. The perfected soul who has escaped from the wheel of rebirth lives intimately and forever in the presence of God; and within the fellowship of "the Kingdom of Heaven," he shares with others divine communion and the blessedness of the "beatific vision." God is in active communion even with human, earthbound persons who open themselves to him in devotion, prayer, and meditation; and he will assist them in their spiritual quest for perfection and deliverance. In this life the earnest and devout mind can enjoy a direct intuition of Divine Presence, gained not through philosophical knowledge, as Sankara proposed, but by the worshiping mind in prayer and meditation.

The fact that Ramanuja represents, on the strictly philosophical level, a minority viewpoint in India is significant. The great spiritual divide is that between love and community, on the one hand, and self-sufficiency and lovelessness, on the other. Christendom took the former way, India on the whole, in its philosophy, took the latter.

WESTERN IDEALISM: GREECE

If the idealistic theme were eliminated from Western philosophy there would be very little left to discuss. But as we have noted, "idealism" is a word of many meanings, and it is now necessary to introduce some new distinctions that must be kept in mind if idealism in the West is to be understood. Most of the idealisms we have thus far considered are what may be termed cases of *supernaturalism idealism;* that is, they have maintained that Nature, however understood, whether it be a kind of real being or mere "appearance" in the human mind, is subordinate to ideal or spiritual reality. In Zarathustra's philosophy, Nature is the neutral field that serves either good or evil. In Indian philosophical systems, the dominant view has been that Nature is the enemy of spirit and that salvation means an escape from it. In Chinese Confucianism and Taoism, Nature expresses or is a manifestation of spiritual being, whether this be conceived as Heaven or Tao; consequently it is good and the true home of mankind. This Chinese view—that Nature, as divine manifestation, operates for the general good according to universal rules of order, not arbitrarily or despotically or by special intervention on occasion, whether by miracle or in some other manner—is known as the theory of "general providence." Its alternative is known as "special providence." Philosophical religion has stood, on the whole, for the position of general providence; popular religion is almost invariably linked with the belief in special providence. Idealism linked with a doctrine of special providence we shall term *preternatural idealism.*

The original philosophy of the Greeks, with its anthropomorphic kind of personalistic theology derived from Homer and Hesiod, was a preternatural idealism. Popular religion (*eusebeia*), consequently, was motivated by a belief that the gods not only punish men for insolence (*hybris*), but will also, if properly petitioned, flattered, and fed (sacrifice), perform special services for those towards whom they are favorably disposed, vouchsafing assistance in war, protection during a journey, and aid in a business venture. Greek philosophy (from 600 B.C.) introduced a theological and religious revolution by rejecting outright the Olympian gods and by deifying Nature itself, now regarded, in the expression of Theognis, as the "Mother" of things. Nature in its unity as the *makrokosmos* is divine because it is eternal, and is the source of life and vitality, intelligence, order, harmony, and beauty. The new philosophical point of view was *naturalistic idealism,* with an impersonalistic theology which taught that Nature orders all things spontaneously rather than by purpose, and although ensouled, is not self-conscious. This standpoint eliminates the notion of special providence. The supreme ancient expression of this sort of idealism was Stoicism.

Popular thinking considers religion to be a means, and the Divine a utility serving man in his selfish pursuits. Religion is, so to speak, a life, health, and accident insurance policy, with special added benefits. According to the new philosophical way of thinking among the Greeks, philosophy is religion in the form of cosmic piety, and this religion is life rather than an extrinsic means supporting it. Among the fruits of philosophical religion three may be mentioned: first, it provides the supreme good man can possess, the sustained "beatific vision" of the world; second, it is the key to the blessed life by revealing the principles of cosmic order that we can apply to personal living; third, it saves us from the supreme indignity, the buffoonery, of being dupes of superstition and vain imaginings, for nothing is more comic or absurd than a man who seriously believes what is false and ridiculous.

The general complaint of all the philosophers, from beginning to end, against popular religion was that it is unspiritual, untruthful, and unworthy both of the Divine and man. First, it is simply esoteric materialism, motivated by fear and avarice, not by a concern for supreme and divine things. As Cicero let his Epicurean spokesman put it, "Mortals call Jupiter 'Best and Greatest,' not because they imagine that he makes them just or temperate or wise, but because they attribute to him their security, preservation, affluence, and comfort." [12] Second, the popular religious mind is thoughtless about the things that matter most and ought to be of most serious concern. This mind expresses *eupistis*—easy believing, thoughtless acquiescence, a taking things for granted; it accepts traditional theology and cult practice simply because accepting them is the thing to do according to conventional ways inherited from the forefathers. The true religious mind, on the contrary, follows the way of *skepsis*, the careful looking at things. Third, popular religious mentality is actually irreligious because it is afraid of truth, it is too cowardly to examine critically its own beliefs. "Men say," Plato observed, "that we ought not to enquire into the supreme God and the nature of the universe, nor busy ourselves in searching out the causes of things, and that such enquiries are impious, whereas the very opposite is the truth." [13] Fourth, popular theology is unworthy of the Divine and is an offense against spiritual intelligence. People piously believe the Homeric tales about the venality and lustfulness of the gods, or they think of God as a sort of superman. But this nonsense is really a desecration of sacred things: infantile theology and eupistic religion are alike pestiferous.

Socrates As depicted by Plato, Socrates introduced a fresh synthesis of the best in Greek thought by de-divinizing Nature, by divorcing religion from all connections with cosmological speculation, by freeing theology from all theosophical claims to any detailed knowledge of the divine order, and by considering pure religion as devotion exclusively to moral purpose and spiritual values. His theology amounted to the simple proposition that the divine world is a society of superhuman beings and divinities, probably with a supreme God at their head, perfectly good and righteous, in whom there is no shadow of evil, irrationality, or unrighteousness, whose common will is for general good, and to whom Nature is subordinate. Socrates accepted the notion of special providence, and thus the theory of preternatural idealism; but he freed religion from everything commercial, materialistic, and sordid. Spiritual beings are concerned for our welfare, and on occasion will reveal to us what it is wise to do, or at least not to do; but they assist us only in our pursuit of holiness or perfection and in the life devoted to wisdom. Apparently Socrates was not certain that he would survive death to share in a more felicitous fellowship with the divine community. He was convinced, however, of two things: that hope of immortality is reasonable only if there is something worth preserving from the ravages of time; and that individual destiny is determined by the best, that is, what is compatible with the total good.

Platonic Idealism The writings of Plato are the supreme expression of Greek idealism and Greek religion, and both directly as well as through their echoes in neo-Platonism and St. Augustine they have left a massive impression on the theology, spirituality, morality, and general culture of Christendom. Precisely what Plato's own detailed thoughts were is a matter of debate, but his general vision is unmistakable in outline. Accepting the principles of Socratic theology and religion, he returned to the traditional view of the philosophers that Reality can be known and that this knowledge is necessary for mature theology and spiritual life. On the one hand, religion or true piety is personal and social: it begins when a man is prepared "to honour his own soul," [14] which few do as they ought, and then spreads out laterally to enrich our relations with fellowman and organized society in a manner to give them a reverent and sacred quality. On the other hand, religion is cosmic or ontological: it involves participation in the Real so far as it is divine. Men, in fact, are only mirrors: they can embody the Good only by reflection and inspiration. But they cannot reflect or participate in it unless it has been found, and for this reason the spiritual life is dependent upon that regenerate vision which philosophical study alone provides, and upon devoted enquiry into metaphysics and theology.

The central thesis of Platonic idealism was that the Good (*agathon*) "must embrace and hold together all things." [15] This Absolute Good, however, was not the world soul of earlier philosophers; it was, rather, transcendent Being-in-itself, the eternal Good and the possibility of all existent good. It does not seem, however, that this Absolute Good was what Plato meant by "God," although this matter remains obscure. By "God" he apparently meant the supreme creative cosmic artist who, inspired by his union with the Good, wills beauty, order, and harmony in the spatial world. If so, Plato's theology was of two levels, that of the impersonal Good-in-itself and the personal God of creative and moral will. At any rate, his cosmic religion was aesthetic and ethical, but not one of reciprocal community between the Divine and the human person, just as there is none between a beautiful painting that we contemplate and ourselves, nor between man and the celestial sun that gives light, life, and warmth to the earth. We seek and live in the Divine; but the Divine does not seek as a conscious being to live in us.

True religion, then, is philosophy, which purposes, subjectively, to nourish the "divinest part" of the man, and objectively, to put him in contact with true Reality which is the ontological Divine. Through philosophy as high religion man "partakes of God," comes to have "a share of the divine attributes," and "imitates God." Religion, in sum, is "divine assimilation," which transforms our lives. The man who thus "holds converse with the divine order becomes orderly and divine, as far as the nature of man allows." [16] (Note this reservation: Plato was not a sentimentalist who claimed that human nature is thoroughly innocent and good.)

Plato characterized himself as a "partisan of the 'whole'." [17] No man, from his point of view, is genuinely religious or spiritual as long as he remains a self-centered egoist. In a passage later reflected in Stoicism and in the Christian doctrine of *resignatio ad infernum* (willingess to be damned for the glory of God) Plato writes:

> The ruler of the universe has ordered all things with a view to the excellence and preservation of the whole, and each part, as far as may be, has an action and passion appropriate to it. Over these, down to the least fraction of them, ministers have been appointed to preside, who have wrought out their perfection with infinitesimal exactness. And one of these portions of the universe is thine own, unhappy man, which, however little, contributes to the whole; and you do not seem to be aware that this and every other creation is for the sake of the whole, and in order that the life of the whole may be blessed; and that you are created for the sake of the whole, and not the whole for the sake of you. For every physician and every skilled artist does all things for the sake of the whole, directing his effort towards the common good, executing the part for the sake of the whole, and not the whole for the sake of the part. And you are annoyed because you are ignorant how what is best for you happens to you and to the universe, as far as the laws of the common creation admit.[18]

The theological axiom at the center of Plato's thinking, that "God is in no wise and in no manner unrighteous, but utterly and perfectly righteous," [19] then, does not mean that the so-called religionist, who is really a sentimental egoist, has the right to expect that the world is here merely to serve his wish for happiness.

On the question of human destiny, whether we have a right to hope for immortality, Plato in his writings supports the Indian doctrine of transmigration. In a discussion of the problem in the *Phaedo*, Simmias makes the following remarkable observation:

> I think, Socrates, as perhaps you do yourself, that it is either impossible or very difficult to acquire clear knowledge about these matters in this life. And yet he is a weakling who does not test in every way what is said about them and persevere until he is worn out by studying them on every side. For he must do one of two things; either he must learn or discover the truth about these matters, or if that is impossible, he must take whatever human doctrine is best and hardest to disprove and, embarking upon it as upon a raft, sail upon it through life in the midst of dangers, unless he can sail upon some stronger vessel, some divine revelation, and make his voyage more safely and securely.[20]

This suggestion is reflected, later on, in Kant's teaching.

In his final work, the *Laws,* Plato introduced the doctrine of special providence—that the gods keep their eyes on us. In this context he seems to have been concerned not only with the fact that men "are the most religious of all animals" [21] but also with the value of religion for social order among creatures that incline towards moral lawlessness and civil disobedience. Since the multitude, he held, cannot possess high religion, because they cannot be philosophers, religion has to be fitted to their capacity, on the principle of "accommodation." The mythical religion of the State, that is, not only supports public order but gives man religious value in pragmatic form. This justified Plato in protesting against some of his contemporaries who declared that "all religion is a cooking up of words and a make-believe." [22] Mythical religion, that is, is in a sense true.

WESTERN IDEALISM: CHRISTIAN PRETERNATURAL PERSONALISM

Since the conquest of Europe by Christianity, the West has been a Bible civilization; Bible idealism has been the nucleus of its general manner of thinking and valuing and at least the unseen background of its philosophy. With rare exceptions, all of its major philosophers have been serious Bible students and have been acquainted with the official theology of orthodox Christendom. Subsequent discussions of "religion" have understood the topic to be "Christianity"; and even in recent times this traditional religion has been the point of departure for a consideration of the subject.

Christianity We must here presuppose acquaintance with our own spiritual heritage which, in its supreme expression, has a lyrical quality unique among the great cultures. (It is significant that music is Christianity's paramount contribution to art.) Although the warp and woof of Semitic and Christian doctrine in the Bible compose a complex and controversial pattern, the thinking of modern philosophers about religion, and preeminently about Christianity, has focused on a certain fragment of the New Testament embedded in the Synoptic Gospels. In order to understand their philosophical interest in our traditional religion it is necessary to lift this fragment out of the whole and state what it was. The general philosophic frame of Christ's teaching was that of Semitic ethical and theological personalism: God is self-conscious, is concerned about man, who has high cosmic status, and is the will to righteousness. The essence of Christ's doctrine, and the only item of it that is systematized, as the quintessence of "the law and the prophets," is the Golden Rule and the Great Commandments (Matt. 7:12; 22:35 ff.). God is "Father" who, although "in the heavens," is also ubiquitous as both special and general Providence. He sends the rain for the benefit of all; he feeds the sparrows, not one of whom "shall fall on the ground without your Father." Even "the very hairs of your head are all numbered" (Matt. 10:29 ff.). Religion is an inner, spiritual life, ethical as well as filial, which extends outwards to fellowman as well as upwards to the Divine. The kernel of it is sincerity, earnest will to goodness, and helpful kindness. Most men substitute for this a hypocritical mask of pretense of public "face"; and they think of religion as a commercial transaction with the Almighty which is beneficial to the unregenerate, selfish, materialistic ego, unmindful of the fact that spirituality requires a second birth, an inner transformation of the soul. "Blessed are the pure in heart (*katharoi*), for they shall see God." Externals are at best secondary or peripheral: the Sabbath was made for man, not man for the Sabbath; it is not eating with unwashed hands or ceremonially uncleansed dishes that defiles a man, but rather the evils that proceed from the base motives and desires of the heart (Matt. 15:18 f.; Mark 7:4). The scum of the earth, so to speak—taxgatherers and notorious sinners—more easily enter into the kingdom of heaven than do holy hypocrites or self-complacent formalists; for the confessed sinners possess at least the virtue of wholeheartedness and forthrightness. Pure religion expresses itself in explicit duties, not first of all to God, but to our fellowmen. Zacchaeus and his family were not saved by a formula of theological repentance, nor by subscribing to a creed, nor by performance of required ritual, but by a regenerated heart that first expressed itself in his promise to repay with good measure those whom he had financially defrauded (Luke 19:8). If, for instance, a man is on the way to place a gift on the temple altar and recalls that someone has a grievance against him, he should leave his gift there, go and make peace with his brother man, and then return to the temple to offer it (Matt. 5:23 f.).

No matter how this fragment may fit into the total picture of the mind of the historical Jesus, at least it did not remain the simple content of the new world religion established by St. Paul, which as time went on expanded into a vast spiritual empire with a complex priesthood, ritual, and theology, composing an extraordinary synthesis of Mediterranean principles—Greek, Roman, Egyptian, and Semitic. The nucleus of a philosophical idealism, although not the whole, was the creed and doctrine of orthodox Christian theology, whose center was restated in the Council of Trent in 1546:

I believe in one God, the Father Almighty, Maker of Heaven and earth, of all things visible and invisible; and in one Lord Jesus Christ, the only-begotten Son of God, and born of the Father before all ages; God of God, light of light, true God of true God; begotten, not made, consubstantial with the Father, by whom all things were made, [who] now in heaven, "sitteth at the right hand of the Father" . . . and in the Holy Ghost, the Lord, and the giver of life, who proceedeth from the Father and the Son; who with the Father and the Son together is adored and glorified, who spoke by the prophets. . . . I confess one baptism for the remission of sins; and I look for the resurrection of the dead, and the life of the world to come.[23]

The trinitarian doctrine here reformulated, although by no means unique, expresses personalistic idealism on a new level. Ordinary personalism, represented in the Jewish theology of a divine Monarch, suggests on rationalistic grounds that a personal self must in some degree at least suffer from the loneliness of absolute privacy or estrangement from other persons. By resorting to a logic of paradox, Christian orthodoxy introduced the notion that the Godhead is a perfect society in absolute unity and thus suggested that in higher states of existence interpersonal relations may be altogether richer than they can be on the human level.

Modern Philosophy and the Religious Problem   With the maturing of the scientific revolution about 1600 a tensional relation began to develop between what may be called the philosophical and the antiphilosophical parties in religion. This became more virulent in the later years of the eighteenth century when the renaissance of the spirit of *skepsis* gained force through the spread of new ontological ideas and new scientific knowledge, and with the application of historical method to the study of the Scriptures and the evolution of theological tradition. Victor Cousin had this distinction in mind when in 1853, writing from France, he referred to "the deplorable strife between the clergy and the University." [24] Outside of Latin Christian circles, this strife has moderated more recently in favor of the University because there has been a steady shift of Protestant theological leadership over to the philosophical group; although in areas known by the rather pejorative label of the "Bible belt," the antiphilosophical position still remains dominant.

The controversy between the two religious parties, who share the same spiritual interests and on the whole the same name of "Christian," is on two levels, namely, that of principle and that of specific propositions of creed and doctrine. With respect to principle, the antiphilosophical party stands for external authoritarianism validated by miracles, and consequently for theological infallibilism and a closed system of dogma. Since religious truth has been supernaturally given, whether as the Mosaic Torah (divine law), or as a *kerygma* (proclamation from heaven), basic theology is not subject to critical review, modification, or revision by later generations. The philosophical party stands for the opposing point of view. It points out that Christianity, from its inception, has been committed to truth and the "spirit of truth"; it has always possessed profound metaphysical seriousness and has never been willing to compromise with what its leadership has taken to be mere mythology. It was from the outset, in other words, identified with *skepsis* and the philosophical principle. But it is argued that those who follow the letter of Christian tradition no more manifest its spirit, as embodied in its founder, than those who abjectly look to Aristotle as a speculative authority share genuinely in his spirit. The founder of Christianity stood for philosophical religion by demanding the free application of rational, moral, and spiritual intelligence to a rigidly authoritarian and ritualized faith of the fathers. Later orthodox Christianity has simply repeated the history of Judaism: in spirit and form it has abandoned its founder's principles and has become a neo-Judaism.

This criticism against antiphilosophical religion holds also, according to the philosophical party, on the level of specific doctrine. Christianity has been a neo-Judaism in its externalized and ritualized faith, its exclusivism, and its precisionist notion of what constitutes the conditions of salvation and acceptable piety. The starkness and pettiness of all this becomes loud and raucous in the ear of him who has come to share in the frame and spirit of mind evoked by the vastness and majesty of things that modern science reveals; much conventional theology now assumes the cast of childishness, unworthy to be linked with the Divine. Traditional religious authoritarianism, combined with preternatural idealism and theological teachings that are inextricably united with dated notions of the prescientific Biblical era, combined with the claim that belief in these is a necessary precondition of true faith, acceptable piety, spiritual life, and salvation, impose on the credulity of modern sophisticated consciousness an arbitrary burden it cannot bear. The philosophical party recognizes this and admits that religion must either keep step with knowledge and identify itself with *skepsis* or philosophical principle, or accept the demeaning status of a mythical cult. To choose the latter alternative is to be doomed, as far as the intellectual and practical leadership of mankind is concerned; and if this were to happen the priceless values that Western religion has contributed to the world might be lost. This is, from the standpoint of modern philosophy, the "religious problem."

Cambridge Platonism   Modern philosophical idealism has been the chief single factor in the active concern, since the scientific revolution, to illumine, enrich, refine, and support traditional Western religion, which, all parties have acknowledged, has given to the Western mind new truth, new values, new quality of life, and new hope. The first great constructive movement of this kind was that of the Cambridge Latitude Men during the middle of the seventeenth century in England. Founded by Benjamin Whichcote at Cambridge University, the group included More, Norris, Cudworth, Culverwell and John Smith, and the poets Vaughan and Traherne. The movement was "latitudinarian" as insisting that true religion is in essence a simple, ethical, and spiritual thing; that creed is subordinate to spiritual life; and that true and saving piety cannot be identified with subscribing to theological orthodoxy with its intellectualistic demand for conformity to a nice and complicated body of dogma. Later on the movement became known as Cambridge Platonism because its proponents were deeply influenced by Platonic thought in their interpretation of New Testament religion.

The century between Henry VIII and the Restoration had been one of violence, bloodletting, and stormy controversy, caused by religion mixed up with politics. During the Cromwellian Interregnum a many-sided struggle broke out among Presbyterians, Congregationalists, Non-Conformists, liberal Anglicans, and Anglican Sacerdotalists. There was clamor everywhere over theology and politics, and heated debate over bishops, presbyteries, local church control, apostolic succession, legitimate church symbols, appropriate vestments, the catechism, and the like, although none at all over the Golden Rule or the Great Commandments. In Holland, Spinoza at about this time was complaining that religion had become so deeply mixed up with complicated theories that "the Church seems like an academy, and religion like a science, or rather a dispute." [25] There was much ado about refined distinctions among such words as Regeneration, Conversion, Adoption, Vocation, Sanctification, Justification, Reconciliation, Redemption, Salvation, and Glorification, like a storm in Aristotle's classroom. This sort of business, Whichcote insisted, is useless, for they all mean the same thing. It fills us with "troublesome multiplicity" and possesses the minds of men "with thought that religion is a more voluminous and intricate thing than indeed it is: whereas truth lies in a little compass, and narrow room. Vitals in religion are few." [26]

Intellectual disputes, Whichcote declared, destroy spirituality in two ways: instead of bringing men of good will and earnestness into spiritual fellowship, they cause dissension and ill will; and they lead people to suppose that religion is scientific thinking, whereas it is a being and a doing. "The first thing in religion is to refine a man's temper and, second, to govern his practice." [27] One of his favorite passages from the Bible was Titus 2:11: "The Grace of God that bringeth salvation hath appeared to all men, teaching us that, denying ungodliness and worldly lusts, we should live soberly, righteously, and godly in this present world." This means that "If men contend for the effects of real goodness and deny wickedness, they do truly and properly preach Christ. . . . Whosoever doth deal with men to leave off sin, preaches Christ and carries on Christ's work." [28] Whatever name a man goes by, he is a Christian if he acts like one; and no man is such, who wears the label, unless he acts as he talks. "Universal charity is a thing final in religion." [29] John Smith restated this truth in precise Platonic terms: salvation "is nothing else but a true participation of the Divine Nature." Whichcote wrote in the same strain: "It is the proper employment of our intellectual faculties to be conversant about God, to conceive aright of Him; and then to resemble and imitate him." [30]

The main point of the Latitude Men, who claimed to be orthodox Christians and accepted preternatural religion, was the twofold proposition that religion is moral and spiritual and that it is philosophical. No man is truly religious until what he believes about religion has been gained by the most rigid and thorough examination of it and has earned the whole-souled acceptance of his total mind. Dishonesty, obscurantism, and self-deception have no place in it. Whichcote declared:

> Of all impotencies in the world, credulity in religion is the greatest. [A man's mature, settled, and confirmed religion] is the selfsame with the reason of his mind . . . they pass into one principle; they are no more two, but one: just as the light in the air makes one illuminated sphere; so reason and religion in the subject, are one principle.[31]

Traherne put it more bluntly when he proposed that "an ignorant Christian is a contradiction of terms."

> A Divine theologian includes a Philosopher and a Christian; a Christian includes a Divine and a Philosopher; a Philosopher includes a Christian and a Divine. [A Christian as a philosopher, of course,] may be defective, but so far as he is defective he is no Christian, for a Christian is not a Christian in his blemishes, but his excellencies. . . . Every man therefore according to his degree, so far forth as he is a Christian, is a philosopher.[32]

This thought rejoins that of the ancient patristics and Church fathers who were willing to call Christianity a "philosophy." It was St. Thomas, and Luther after him, who objected to this use of language.

Modern Speculative Idealism Before Kant The larger portion of religious thinking on a mature and sophisticated level, in modern times, has leaned directly or indirectly on the speculative writings of three modern idealists—Descartes, Leibniz, and Berkeley. The interests and purposes of the great philosophers have always been complex, but a concern for religion has invariably been a preeminent one. So it was with these men. Their attention was not directed, however, to the publicizing or restoring of original, philosophical Christianity, but rather to the significance of the new natural science. Descartes, who created the first novel cosmological theory since Aristotle, was inspired by a kind of practical religious interest to establish the scientific foundations of natural knowledge that could be put to use to improve man's needs on earth, particularly through scientific medicine. (This dream of a medical science was shared by all the philosophers.) In his philosophy, too, he reinforced the classical Christian view of the spiritual status of man and the divine axis of reality. He reinforced man's spiritual status, not only by an exalted notion of spiritual consciousness that suggested Platonism but also by putting man radically at the center of the cognitive enterprise. The celebrated maxim, "I think therefore I am," with which his philosophy began, meant to accent the fact that the thinking person knows himself more intimately and directly than anything else, that aside from God he is the one substantival being most certainly known to exist, and that he is the responsible judge of truth. Descartes further insisted that the existence of God is more certain than that of an external physical world, that theology is the presupposition of natural science, and that without the abiding presence and sustaining power of God the entire universe would collapse into mere nothingness (the doctrine of continuous creation). He was also responsible for the modern use of the Platonic term "idea," introducing it into the language to mean a human thought. In this new usage he employed it in connection with his cognitive theory known as "epistemological, subjectivistic idealism," that the human mind is directly or immediately aware only of its own private thoughts or "ideas"; whereas the external world is known only inferentially, that is, mediately, indirectly, or by re-presentation. This doctrine, later restated as the thesis that there is no object without a subject, was accepted in one form or another by thinkers generally, and thus provided the idealists with an argumentative advantage which permitted them to assert that there is better evidence to judge that the world is mental or spiritual in kind than that it is material.

Leibniz and Berkeley, however—the two original pure speculative idealists in the West—were concerned with the possibility that the new natural science of Descartes and Newton might lead to an ontological theory which would prove hostile to religion. Spinoza, although not interested in science as such, had nonetheless proceeded to construct a new metaphysical system in which, on the principles of Descartes, all religious values of the Bible were eliminated, and only its pure ethical doctrine remained standing. Leibniz and Berkeley essayed to defend Christian theism against all comers by offering to demonstrate that there is no real, self-existing space and no material substance. Reality, that is, is completely mental or spiritual. According to Leibniz, Nature is an infinite system of spaceless mental "atoms" or individuals, each self-contained and self-active. Berkeley proposed that it is the direct consequence of God's action on finite persons or minds which we know as perceptions. From either theory of Nature, religious theism remains justified.

Kant's Philosophy of Religion　During the past two centuries the principle of *skepsis*, that of the "University," has penetrated deeply into all areas of human interest. In this spread of "enlightenment" the key figure has been Immanuel Kant (1724-1804), whose main purpose was, in principle, to pick up the problem of philosophical religion where the Cambridge Platonists had left off. During the more than a century between them and Kant the intellectual climate had changed. In the scientific world of Descartes and Newton, man seemed to be an alien spectator stuck fast in the grinding process of a Nature mechanical in operation and empty of spiritual value. Natural science was discrediting traditional belief in the plenary, infallible truth of the Scriptures. The creation story and cosmological notions of these were mythical and prescientific, and in consequence the theological ideas associated with them had become dubious or meaningless. Historical science, moreover, was undermining the confidence of informed minds in the accuracy of Biblical narrative, and above all raised doubts about its miraculous stories and the reliability of alleged supernatural revelation. Such powerful thinkers as Spinoza and Hume had challenged man's cosmic status and the existence of a religious God. In the eyes of perceptive observers, then, the position of religion in general and conventional Christianity in particular had deteriorated.

The time had come for a reappraisal of the entire speculative situation, which Kant like other philosophers considered a single problem. The focus of all thought, it was commonly agreed, is the religious question. The driving force of ontological thought, Kant pointed out, has been religious and moral: the great questions have been of God, freedom, and immortality, on whose outcome hangs the existential issue between optimism and nihilism. The hope of happiness, he wrote, "first begins with religion." [33] The central business of modern man, therefore, was to reconsider what genuine religion is and on what grounds it is justified. But the path to wisdom, "if it is assured and not made impossible or misleading, must for us men unavoidably pass through science [*Wissenschaft*, the total field of established knowledge]"; [34] for inasmuch as religion belongs to the realm of "faith," it must wait upon our decision concerning what we know and what knowledge has to say in the matter.

This preliminary work Kant undertook in the *Critique of Pure Reason*, in which he essayed to demonstrate that Greek philosophical method could not provide the basis for religion—nor any objection to it. On the one hand speculative metaphysics yields no "theology whatsoever," because it produces no transcendent knowledge at all; as a pretended esoteric science it is fraudulent mythology. There is no theoretical information available about the unseen realm of things-in-themselves. On the other hand natural science cannot provide a theology because it deals with Nature, which is pure "appearance," not ontological reality.

Even if this were not so, as Hume had shown, a god of Nature has no religious value, because the natural world exhibits callousness and indifference to individual creatures, not kindness, love, grace, and concern.

Kant did not write on the question of Biblical criticism, as did philosophers like Hobbes and Spinoza, but was satisfied to point out that supernatural history can never provide the basis of universal religion and no longer is solid ground for religious conviction. Any faith based on history demands mental reservation which forbids wholehearted commitment; remote history, particularly when it relates to miracles, is always susceptible to discount or disproof by some factual discovery that might sometime turn up. Honest men, therefore, must remain open to possible evidence, accept preternatural history as tentative, and thus in religion are inevitably subject to wavering and instability of mind.

Religious faith based on intellectualistic grounds, in fact, is undesirable because it poisons at the root the genuine moral motive which is the kernel of true religion. Scientific proof of our destiny would destroy the spiritual principle and substitute for it considerations of egoistic self-interest; then religion would become even for good men what it popularly has always been—esoteric commercialism. This justifies Kant's paradoxical suggestion that "the unsearchable wisdom by which we exist is not less worthy of admiration [sustained wonder] in what it has denied than in what it has granted." These are the closing words of the *Critique of Practical Reason,* and accordingly the final message in his philosophical system: for creatures such as we, religion must be based on moral faith, not scientific knowledge.

The traditional derivation of religion from intellectualistic "truths" or "facts," according to Kant, is the source of its moral failure. Pure religion, all great teachers have agreed, involves spiritual rebirth in which egocentricity and self-deception give place to objective will and honesty. Long before the Freudians arrived, Kant taught us to consider carefully man's universal corrupt propensity, evil will, perversity of heart, hypocrisy, pretense, self-deception, coarseness, arrogance, vain self-love, and the will to cheat. "Self-interest," he observed, is "the god of this world," which is filled with "envy, the lust for power, greed, and the malignant inclinations." [35] (This is why Kant stressed so ruthlessly the moral law unadorned by diverting and compromising influences of feeling.)

Now positive religion plays right into the hands of man's unregenerate ego: it tends to sugar coat it, perfume it, soothe it, by offering substitutes for the one thing needful, that is, the earnest pursuit of holiness of motive and righteousness of action. Men try in every way to fulfill religious obligations, considered as externally imposed, in some circuitous manner by subscribing to a creed, by meticulous performance of ritual, by seeking to please God through "adoration and ingratiation," by heavenly feelings, by reverence without moral earnestness, by piety without worthiness, and by other forms of disguised hypocrisy and evasion. Man busies himself, Kant observed, with "every conceivable formality, designed to indicate how greatly he *respects* the divine [moral] commands, in order that it may not be necessary to *obey* them." [36] Contemplating this absurd and futile situation he indulged in an apostrophe to sincerity: "O sincerity! Thou Astraea, that hast fled from earth to heaven, how mayst thou (the basis of conscience, and hence of all inner religion) be drawn thence to us again?" [37]

The one alternative to an intellectualistic derivation of religion, that is, from objective necessity or empirical fact, is the *ought* to be. (Kant excluded the possibility of a mystical way.) Conscience, on which Christ's religion was founded, not dubious miraculous history, is the "great revelation" of "the divine man within us," [38] and the evidence of a spiritual world: from this one supernatural fact within human consciousness, that man belongs to the spiritual realm of "freedom" as well as psychological animality, flow pregnant implications for theology and religion; for "morality leads inevitably to religion." [39] These implications are moral, not speculative: they persuade only if a man accepts the full force of moral consciousness and the ideal self, which commands the will to seek holiness and righteousness by obedience to the Golden Rule and the Great Commandment, which Kant renamed the "categorical imperative." From this fact of conscience is morally deduced the right to faith in the existence of God as the ground of the possibility of fulfilling our moral vocation, the cosmic sanction of the pursuit of worthiness, and the hope that in the eternal "kingdom of God," the "intelligible world," worthiness and happiness will be reconciled perpetually as they are not here on earth.

Pure, moral, universal, or absolute religion, according to Kant, consists "not in dogmas and rites but in the heart's disposition to fulfill all human duties as divine commands." [40] This in no way dilutes the moral imperative nor does it lead to slavish mindedness as many religions do: "Religion is the recognition of all duties as divine commands, not as sanctions, i.e., as arbitrary and contingent ordinances of a foreign will, but as essential laws of any free will as such." [41] Moral religion ennobles morality by giving it cosmic meaning and rationality, by freeing it from plodding moralism with its tendency to tragicomic heroics. The logic of this religion is precisely what St. Paul said: "We live by faith (*pistis*), not scientific insight or demonstration (*eidos, gnosis*)." [42] This pure moral religion is the only one that can bind men into a universal fellowship of spirit, keep piety free of insidious commercialism, disentangle it from fetish faith and idolatry, and give man a solid religious foundation that no possible fact or speculative argument could ever destroy. An honest man does not need to keep an open mind about it: it can be for him a final, definitive decision. True, even a morally disposed person may waver; but he "can never be reduced to unbelief." [43]

Kant did not maintain, however, that this is the sum total of what a moral religion permits of belief nor the whole argument for it. We have the right to personal overbeliefs so long as these are reasonable, for instance in a specific philosophy of history, a Christology, or the persuasion that when we have done our level best to pursue holiness and righteousness God by divine grace will assist us in some mysterious way. Here there is room for decent difference of opinion. Such overbeliefs belong to the secondary level of personal judgment which William James named "the will to believe" or "the right to believe." The point is, these individual opinions must not be held dogmatically or fanatically in a manner to break communion with those who "will to believe" otherwise.

There are, moreover, personal sources of spiritual persuasion, which St. Paul referred to as *arrabona*, that is, pledge money or tokens of man's divine value and destiny (2 Cor. 5:5); to some of these Kant pointed in his *Critique of Judgment*. Moral action, for instance, inspires an idea of our spiritual destination, and sacrifice connected with the fulfillment of moral law "discloses in us an unfathomable depth of this supersensible [spiritual] faculty, with consequences extending beyond our ken." The feeling of the Sublime gives us a sense or hint (*Ahnung, Wink*) of "our supersensible destination," and sympathetic feeling for the beauty and vitality of Nature enlarges the mind "to surmise the existence of something" in our environment that is more than stark, meaningless process, and even hints of cosmic thought and purpose.[44] These and other sources of persuasion that reinforce our moral faith are legitimate, but they must never serve as substitutes for the moral argument itself, which is definitive. To fall into this temptation is to move away from the primary pursuit of holiness and to succumb to soft-headed, romantic sentimentality which invites back insidious egotism.

Kant, it might be said, offered a revision of Lutheranism, Hegel a revision of Calvinism. In sum, mature religion, according to the Hegelian philosophy, is paradoxically the union in a man of a totally satisfied yet tragic consciousness.[45]

Subsequent Idealism and Religion   The history of philosophy discloses that "idealism" is not a magic word which solves religious problems. This is indicated in the development of post-Kantian idealism in Germany, Britain, Italy, and America, much of which conflicts with basic teachings of Christianity. Hegel, for instance, whose theology is a pantheism somewht reminiscent of Vedantism, cut much of the heart out of Christianity by eliminating theological grace (*charis*) and love (*agape*) and apparently by rejecting the hope of personal immortality. He saw in history the logical, triumphant God (or Absolute) moving to his own fulfillment in man's philosophic consciousness; but whether his teaching is an optimism or a pessimism is perhaps a matter of words. Radical pessimism, at any rate, was vigorously asserted by Arthur Schopenhauer, whose theology, in a manner suggesting the *sunyata* doctrine of Nagarjuna, identifies the pantheistic Absolute with an ineffable abyss of "Will." The world is the self-objectification of this eternal, impersonal Will which precipitates out of itself embodied individuals who are inherently egoistic, engaged in a mutual "struggle for existence," and bent on pleasure consciousness. But happy existence is impossible; consequently consciousness is an evil, life is a gross mistake, and human history, which is enmeshed in "the *worst* possible world," is futility and madness. Salvation is gained, negatively, as in classical Buddhism, by destroying the ego-will with its self-assertion and its lusting for pleasure, and, positively, by achieving a mind of detached serenity or apathy. According to Schopenhauer the ethical-spiritual essence of the Christian religion, divorced from its superficial connection with Judaic notions of cosmic justice and reward, is similarly an ethical nihilism which teaches salvation by stifling the "will to live." Christianity, that is, is an inferior Western counterpart of Buddhism, with an occidental mythology of its own.

Another development in religion began with Friedrich Schleiermacher, a contemporary of Hegel's and a kind of realistic, Spinozistic pantheist, who insisted that religion is an autonomous, original area of experience or consciousness, not a deduction from something else, whether natural science, dialectic, or even morality. The essence of religion, contrary to Hegel, is the sense of dependence on the Infinite whose intrinsic nature cannot be known. Although Schleiermacher was profoundly religious, he did not believe in personal immortality and thus represented a point of view not remote from that of the Indian Upanishads. This move to give recognition to religion as a primary and unique sphere of fact, with its own criteria of truth, was further explored by Fries, Ritschl, Otto, and others, and is now a position well established.

Meanwhile in Germany Hermann Lotze pointed out that a post-Kantian type of pantheism can be modified rationally to permit, as Fichte had rather ambiguously suggested, the ontological reality of self-active persons within the one supreme Self or Person, in a manner compatible with the personalistic principles of Christian theism and reminiscent of Ramanuja. An attempt was later made in Scotland under the leadership of the Caird brothers to combine Hegelianism with Christianity, but this was found satisfactory only when reformulated in Lotzean terms. In England an impersonalistic monism based on Hegel was established by F. H. Bradley and B. Bosanquet, with a religion strictly Hegelian in character. Another Hegelian in England, J. M. E. McTaggart, produced a system of atheistic personalism, with a religion of love among uncreated, eternal persons. In the United States Josiah Royce combined a post-Kantian and Lotzean kind of pantheism with a remnant of Pauline doctrine by proposing that essential religion is loyalty to a group or community.

A more pluralistic personalism united with a liberal form of preternatural Christianity was defended in England by H. Rashdall and in the United States by B. P. Bowne and his followers. In right-wing pragmatism William James represented marginal idealism in the form of panpsychism, according to which the world is a sort of ocean of feeling which tends to congeal into conscious selves. He proposed a doctrine of special providence by teaching that divine influence can enter human consciousness through the subconscious. Both he and F. C. S. Schiller, representing pragmatism in its most personalistic form, defended a theology of a finite god. Henri Bergson, who came to a personalistic and Christian religious point of view from a musical environment and scientific studies, identified supreme value with mystical love.

More recently speculative thought has been inclined, under the influence of value-empty natural science and logic, to disregard value experience as philosophically important. Even Kant, who foreshadowed the new preoccupation with values, was inclined to lump them together under the psychological term "happiness." One of the latest and most significant developments in classical idealism is the exploration of values, by Max Scheler, Nicolai Hartmann, and others, as the content of significant spiritual experience and as basic to any spiritual view of personality, its life, the world, and religion. This restores a vital connection of modern idealism with Plato and St. Paul.

Speculative idealism has been of extraordinary service to Western religion by restoring its original status as a philosophical faith and by stimulating the elevation of religion to a major field of inquiry. Although its influence has been far-reaching, it is at present eclipsed by naturalism, language analysis, positivism, existence philosophy, neo-Calvinism, and other points of view.

Confessio Fidei My own confession of faith is briefly this: I judge that Plato and the pure religion of Christ, as Kant understood it, are the two most priceless gifts of the past to our Western spiritual inheritance, and that they offer in principle the lighted path out of nihilism. Philosophically put, the ultimate question turns, I think, on the importance of personality, however described metaphysically, as the sole principle of worth and dignity. The world view and life view of Socratism as well as Christianity is identified with it, and this seems to me the very heart-center of Westernism. The final issue is between a basic personalism and impersonalism. In a way, the ultimate choice among points of departure for an appraisal of man's situation is between Hegel and Kant, and I think that Kant, enlarged by Cambridge Platonism and a spiritual theory of values, is fundamentally right. The substance of it all, perhaps, has been expressed by Warner Fite in an observation that has always seemed to me impressive:

> Does "God" express an idea or is it only a word—a verbal expression which sophisticated reflection has shown to be without meaning? This I believe to be the form which the question tends finally to take. He to whom "God" conveys an intelligible meaning will, I suspect, ever hesitate before a final disbelief. The conclusive disbelief expresses itself by saying that, whatever the word may mean to others, it means nothing to me.[46]

NOTES FOR CHAPTER 2

1 *Chandogya Upanishad*, VIII, 23, 1.
2 *Mundaka Upanishad*, I, 7.
3 *Ibid.*, II, 1, 1.
4 *Katha Upanishad*, I, 2, 19.
5 *Ibid.*, II, 5, 12.
6 *Ibid.*, II, 6, 8.
7 *Chandogya Upanishad*, III, 1, 1.
8 *Ibid.*, III, 2, 8.
9 *Brihadaranyaka Upanishad*, I, 4, 5.
10 *Ibid.*, I, 3, 27.
11 *Chandogya Upanishad*, VI, 2, 11.
12 Cicero, *On the Nature of the Gods*, III, 36. Translated by Hubert M. Poteat, Chicago, University of Chicago Press, 1950, p. 329.
13 *Laws*, 821a (Jowett translation).
14 *Ibid.*, 727a.
15 *Phaedo*, 99c (Fowler translation).
16 *Republic*, VI, 500d (Jowett translation).
17 *Theaetetus*, 181a (Fowler translation).
18 *Laws*, X, 903b (Jowett translation).
19 *Theaetetus*, 176c (Fowler translation).
20 *Phaedo*, 85c (Fowler translation).
21 *Laws*, X, 902b (Jowett translation).
22 *Laws*, X, 886d (Jowett translation).
23 John H. Leith, *Creeds of the Churches*, New York, Doubleday and Co., 1963, pp. 401 f. Hegel's view of philosophy of religion has not been discussed in this chapter, since there is an extended treatment of his view below in Chapter 10, "Religion and Dialectical Philosophy," by Gustav E. Mueller.
24 Victor Cousin, *Lectures on the True, the Beautiful, and the Good*, New York, 1860, p. 345 n.
25 Spinoza, *A Theologico-Political Treatise*, ch. 13. *The Chief Works of Benedict De Spinoza*, translated by R. H. M. Elwes, New York, Dover Publications, 1951, pp. 175 f.
26 E. T. Campagnac, *The Cambridge Platonists*, Oxford, 1901, p. 72.

27 F. J. Powicke, *The Cambridge Platonists*, Cambridge, Mass., 1926, p. 63.
28 *Ibid.* Across the channel Spinoza was saying the same thing: "If a man is absolutely ignorant of the Scriptures, and none the less has right opinions and a true plan of life, he is absolutely blessed and truly possesses in himself the spirit of Christ" (Spinoza, *loc. cit.*, p. 79).
29 Campagnac, *op. cit.*, p. 196.
30 Powicke, *op. cit.*, p. 83.
31 Campagnac, *op. cit.*, pp. 54 f.
32 *Centuries of Meditations*, IV, 4, 5.
33 Kant, *Kritik der praktischen Vernunft*, II, 2, 5, par. 8.
34 Kant, *Critique of Practical Reason*, translated by Lewis White Beck, Chicago, University of Chicago Press, 1949, p. 243.
35 Kant, *Religion Within the Limits of Reason Alone*, translated by Theodore M. Greene and Hoyt H. Hudson, Chicago, Open Court Publishing Company, 1934, pp. 149, 85.
36 *Ibid.*, p. 189.
37 *Ibid.*, p. 178 n.
38 Kant, *Critique of Practical Reason*, p. 200; *Critique of Pure Reason*, translated by Norman Kemp Smith, New York, The Humanities Press, 1950, p. 486.
39 Kant, *Religion*, p. 7 n.
40 *Ibid.*, p. 79.
41 *Critique of Practical Reason*, p. 232.
42 2 Cor. 5:7.
43 Kant, *Critique of Practical Reason*, translated by Thomas Kingsmill Abbott, London, Longmans, Green, and Co., Ltd., 1927, p. 244.
44 Kant, *Critique of Judgement*, translated by J. H. Bernard, London, Macmillan and Co., Ltd., 1914, pp. 139, 168, 267.
45 Cf. Chapter 10 below, "Religion and Dialectical Philosophy" by Gustav E. Mueller.
46 Warner Fite, *Moral Philosophy*, New York, Lincoln MacVeagh, 1925, p. 278.

QUESTIONS

1 In your religious thinking what is the role or status of personality?
2 List what you consider the essential values that a satisfactory religion must provide for. From your religious viewpoint thus specified is a theology or doctrine of the Divine necessary? If so, is impersonalistic pantheism (Nagarjuna, Sankara) adequate? Explain.
3 The preceding question presupposes that vital spiritual or religious "needs" legitimately serve as criteria of objective or ontological truth. This is denied by intellectualistic theories of cognition. Which point of view do you accept? Why?
4 American personalists of the school of B. P. Bowne are inclined to maintain that although no religious doctrine can be immune from rational criticism, a theistic philosophy as such is not an adequate substitute for historical, positive religion and that an attempt to displace by abstract philosophy the spiritual community or Church based on history "would be absurd." According to A. C. Knudson (*The Philosophy of Personalism*, 254 f.) this school holds "the view that the highest revelation of divine truth is to be

found in the person of Christ rather than in his oral teaching"; and they "see in the Christian faith something which transcends their own personalism. They recognize in it a unique content that owes its origin to revelation or history or some other extralogical source." Kant took an opposing view, although he acknowledged that a Church with its unique symbolism and history was probably necessary as far as the public is concerned. Disregarding the question whether you consider yourself a "Christian," which position do you adopt? Why?

5 Sir Charles Eliot (*Hinduism and Buddhism*, I, xcvii) points out that "nearly all the propositions contained in a European creed involve matters of history or science which are obviously affected by research and discovery as much as are astronomy or medicine, and not only are the propositions out of date but they mostly refer to problems which have lost their interest." Do you consider this observation justified? What would be Kant's rejoinder? What solution would you suggest?

SUGGESTED READINGS

Immanuel Kant, *Religion Within the Limits of Reason Alone*, translated by Theodore M. Greene and Hoyt H. Hudson, Chicago, Open Court, 1934. Especially Book IV.

John Macquarrie, *Twentieth-Century Religious Thought*, New York, Harper and Row, 1963, pp. 23-94.

E. T. Campagnac, *The Cambridge Platonists*, Oxford, 1901. Selections.

Katha Upanishad, Mundaka Upanishad. Originally published in the Sacred Books of the East series; several good translations are now available.

3 *Patrick Romanell*

Religion from a Naturalistic Standpoint

NATURALISM AND RELIGION

Naturalism is the oldest tradition in Western philosophy, and its bearings on religion are evident from the very beginning. The first philosopher of ancient Greece on record is not only a prototype of the naturalist in metaphysics; significantly enough, he is also a prototype of the naturalist in religion. According to Aristotle, Thales declares that "all things are full of gods," as well as full of "water." About half a century later there appears on the Greek scene another pre-Socratic by the name of Xenophanes, who, though not officially called a naturalist in the standard textbooks, expresses picturesquely the naturalist's perennial attack on anthropomorphism in traditional religion, with his wry observation that men paint "their gods in their own likeness." Needless to add, the naturalistic tradition in Western thought develops this attack in sundry ways, from Lucretius in ancient times to Freud in ours.

As is plain to any competent student of the subject, religion is an important human activity in itself. But religion is important too in relation to naturalism because it serves as the acid test for this controversial philosophy. If naturalism as a philosophy cannot succeed somehow in making intelligible the supernatural of the historic religions in its own terms, then all its accomplishments elsewhere (in science, particularly) will be in vain. For were it not for the existence of religion in the first place, there would be no real justification for the emergence of supernaturalism as an alternative world view, and as a consequence everybody could then be a naturalist with alacrity. In short, if the philosophic naturalist makes a good case for religion, his battle is virtually won; if not, it is lost. *Aut Caesar, aut nihil.*

What philosophic naturalism has to say about religion will depend, for our purposes here, on two related matters: (1) the aspect of religion involved and (2) the kind of naturalism presupposed. To begin with, religion is a highly complex affair in human history, yet its essential components are fairly easy to analyze out. Every organized religion may be understood in terms of four distinct aspects: (1) its articles of faith, (2) its rules of conduct, (3) its rituals, (4) its forms of organization. These aspects constitute the four C's of religion—creed, code, cult, and church. Of these four, the aspect most relevant to the present subject is the first, the creedal aspect of religion. Historically, the great debate throughout the ages between the naturalists and the supernaturalists has always revolved around the question of the validity of religious beliefs, especially the belief in God. Logically, this is not at all surprising, since it is only the *theoretical* side of religion which has the possibility of being either methodologically suspect or significant. Concrete proof of the logic of the situation comes from the historic conflict between religious faith and natural science in the modern world.

The history of Western philosophy is studded with many varieties of naturalism, each of which would (in theory, at least) have its own implications for religion. Nevertheless, despite the great variety of naturalistic systems of philosophy since Thales, we may distinguish two primary types within the naturalistic tradition itself—a reductionist and an antireductionist. If we call the older reductionist type of naturalism (inspired in Democritus) by the classical name of "materialism," then we can reserve the term "naturalism" for the newer antireductionist type (inspired in Aristotle).[1] Although this distinction explicitly made by contemporary naturalists has not prevented critics from accusing the new naturalists of being old materialists in disguise, still it should help to clear the ground of an initial confusion and thereby make room for future criticism which may be fruitful and to the point in the end.

Even if the semantic difficulties were removed by some agreement at the outset, there would remain the major problem underlying the subject of naturalism and religion: *Which* of the forms of naturalism provides the most reliable interpretation of religion on the philosophical plane? Opinions on this crucial question vary greatly among the philosophic naturalists themselves. This is not really a bad sign: it keeps the road open for further inquiry. After all, as Plato the comic philosopher reveals so dramatically via a "laughing voice" at the close of the *Protagoras,* the real enemy of genuine thinking is not healthy disagreement but sterile dogmatism.

In order to see concretely and profitably how a naturalist in philosophy looks at religion, let us consider John Dewey, the last of the great naturalists, whose philosophy of religion provides perhaps the best test case for philosophic naturalism as a whole. We propose to examine Dewey's religious philosophy from a *fuller* naturalistic standpoint and show that his interpretation of religion on its creedal side, which professes to be thoroughly naturalistic in intent, is actually positivistic in execution, and hence, not naturalistic in fact. Thus my critique of Dewey, being in essence internal, rather than external, to naturalism itself, will lead me to reexamine religion from a more thorough naturalistic point of view. This I attempt to do in the final section of the essay, with a naturalistic defense of what Dewey and his followers deny categorically to religion—its cognitive significance.

DEWEY'S PHILOSOPHY OF RELIGION

Of the forty books left by John Dewey for posterity, the one which in my opinion typifies him best of all is *A Common Faith*. Though this slender volume of Terry Lectures is the only book of Dewey's on the subject of religion published during his long life, in it the sage of Columbia reveals himself most characteristically as a moral philosopher *par excellence*. The work itself stirred considerable controversy when it appeared in 1934. Now that it has virtually become a classic in the philosophy of religion, the time should be ripe to examine its contents in a more dispassionate perspective. My main concern here will be to show that Dewey's *confessio fidei* has the defects of its qualities. I am going to argue that while his interpretation of religion is very good as far as the *moral* side of life goes, it is, ironically enough, not so good when it comes to its *religious* side.

A Common Faith opens with a discussion of "religion versus the religious," and attempts to meet the problem involved by establishing painstakingly "the difference between religion, *a* religion, and the religious." [2] Submitting for consideration an "adjectival" as against a "substantival" analysis of religion, Dewey contends that all traditional religions in general and modern religious liberalism in particular "smother" the religious by shutting religious values up within a separate "compartment" of life. The reason he singles out this position (which was popular in certain religious circles a generation ago) is to make sure that his own experiential interpretation of religion is not mistaken for the view of those who hold that "the religious" denotes a special *kind* of experience, "something *sui generis*" which is marked off from other varieties of experience and is made "the ultimate basis of religion itself." In place of this substantival view of religion, whose assumption of a territorial division between scientific and religious experience leads inevitably to a dualistic conception of knowledge and its methods, he develops the alternative adjectival position that "the religious" is a special *phase* of experience, the function of which in our daily life is to introduce "genuine perspective" into "the piecemeal and shifting episodes of existence." [3]

According to Dewey, the adjective "religious" does not denote a specifiable entity that can exist all by itself, either under the traditional institutional name of *a* religion or under the subtler psychological name of "religious experience." Rather, it denotes a certain "quality of experience" which may belong to *all* our experiences, or a certain "quality of attitude" which may be displayed in *all* our activities. To be more specific, by "religious" Dewey refers to the "religious attitude," and by this he means "a *general* attitude" that may be taken "toward every object and every proposed end or ideal." Thus the adjective "religious" is an *attitudinal value* term with moral connotations of a nonrestrictive nature, that is, something not to be "confined to sect, class, or race." Given this adjectival definition of religion as the religious, signifying "a certain attitude and outlook," [4] it follows, strictly speaking, that there is no philosophy of *religion* as such for Dewey, there is only philosophy of *the religious*.

Dewey's whole point in starting his discussion with the difference between *the* religious and *a* religion is plain from the very first page of the book under study. He wants to make room for his own alternative to what we may call "the compartmental or the church conception of religion" inherent in the major religions of the world, to adapt to the field of religion the descriptive phrases Dewey coined in another book.[5]

As to his general appraisal of traditional religion itself, the author of *A Common Faith* boldly charges that the historic religions suffer from a multitude of "encumbrances," the net effect of which has been to prevent "whatever is basically religious in experience" from expressing itself freely. Therefore, he submits, what is urgently needed at present is a complete "emancipation" from the "outgrown traits of past religions." [6] How are we to achieve such religious emancipation? Dewey's answer uncovers the very heart of his entire book, and it comes in a paragraph which spells out in black and white the paramount lesson that the contemporary mind must be prepared to learn from the revolutionary impact of modern science upon the intellectual side of religion:

> The positive lesson is that religious qualities and values if they are real at all are not bound up with any single item of intellectual assent, not even that of the existence of the God of theism; and that, under existing conditions, the religious function in experience can be emancipated only through surrender of the whole notion of special truths that are religious by their own nature, together with the idea of peculiar avenues of access to such truths. For were we

to admit that there is but one method for ascertaining fact and truth—that conveyed by the word "scientific" in its most general and generous sense—no discovery in any branch of knowledge and inquiry could then disturb the faith that is religious. I should describe this faith as the unification of the self through allegiance to inclusive ideal ends, which imagination presents to us and to which the human will responds as worthy of controlling our desires and choices.[7]

This emancipation proclamation constituting Dewey's main thesis in *A Common Faith* is characteristically Deweyan and may be said to sum up beautifully his whole philosophy of religion, inasmuch as it includes within the same paragraph both his denial of the *cognitive* significance of religious faith and his assertion of its *conative* significance.

To take first an historical look at Dewey's theory of religion, it is worth noting that, even though religious thinkers differ widely among themselves as to the exact relation between morality and religion, men as far apart as Pascal and Spinoza in "the century of genius," and Bergson and Dewey in our own, all apparently agree on one thing—that the function of religion is essentially *moral*. In significant contrast to this agreement on the moral import of religious faith, there has been much debate since the Middle Ages with respect to its theoretical import—some, like Pascal and Bergson, taking the affirmative side; others, like Spinoza and Dewey, taking the negative. Long before we had in our midst an emotive theory of ethics to contend with, there was its more convincing counterpart in theory of religion, which Comte formulated in positivistic terms over a century ago. As a matter of fact, viewed historically, Dewey's philosophy of religion, whose aim is above all to effect an emotional as well as an intellectual union of religious faith with "the common faith of mankind" [8] in moral ideals, is an American version of Comte's "religion of humanity," shorn of its presumptuous quality and tinged with cosmic piety.

Turning next to an examination of Dewey's religious philosophy from a systematic angle, we may isolate at least two philosophical strains from his work—a naturalistic and a positivistic. On the one hand, our author is a naturalist as regards the human abode of religion; on the other hand he is a positivist as regards its intellectual content. While I sympathize fully with the naturalistic strain in his analysis, I have some doubts about its positivistic strain. As I see it, Dewey's interpretation of religion suffers from two serious defects which are bound up with each other—one having to do with subject matter, the other with method.

As to the first defect, Dewey gets himself into difficulty when he reduces the intellectual content of religion (as embodied in creeds) to its moral equivalent, and thereby transforms *religious* faith into "*moral* faith."

To be sure, the celebrated author of *A Common Faith* would be quick to deny that he has reduced religion to a glorified ethics, although he would be quite willing to admit that religious faith is moral faith under special conditions, and in fact says as much. For one thing, he not only denies that "all moral faith in ideal ends is by virtue of that fact religious in quality," but goes so far as to specify that a moral faith becomes religious in quality "only when the ends of moral conviction arouse emotions that are not only intense but are actuated and supported by ends so inclusive that they unify the self." [9] For another thing, he not only takes great pains to define the attitude that is religious in quality as a "comprehensive attitude" but in addition states emphatically that this attitude signifies something "much broader than anything indicated by 'moral' in its usual sense." [10]

Nevertheless, I submit, no matter how "inclusive" the ideal ends may be which prompt us to make the world of which we are an integral part a better place to live in, they as objects of our aspiration remain *moral* in nature, and not religious. For the "inclusiveness" of our ideals, which is regarded by Dewey as the "indispensable" condition that a moral faith must satisfy in order to qualify as religious in quality, is itself much too quantitative a criterion to be of real service in making intelligible the actual qualitative differences between the moral and the religious. If we go from the objective to the subjective side of the question, we arrive at the same conclusion. Thus, no matter how "comprehensive" may be our attitude displayed, say, in art, science, and politics, it too remains *moral* in quality, and not religious. For "comprehensiveness" as the differentiating mark of the attitude that is religious is no better than "inclusiveness" as the differentiating mark of the objects which fall within its purview. To claim with Dewey, for example, that man's faith in justice as a moral ideal takes on a religious quality on becoming "a *general* attitude" displayed in political life is to confuse the categories of the moral and the religious unnecessarily. Besides, if we go back to a much older work of which Dewey was co-author, the textbook entitled *Ethics* (1908), and compare it with *A Common Faith* (1934), we will find that his later distinction between the moral and the religious really amounts to one between two species of the "moral"—moral "in its usual sense" and moral in its higher sense—or in the language of the *Ethics*, "customary and reflective morality," respectively. In brief, to hold with Dewey that the religious is nothing but the moral *generalized* is to miss what is unique about the religious quality of experience itself, the unique thing about it being its irreducible accent on the sublime and the sacred. Man does not need religion to be *good*, he needs it to be *holy*.

If I may venture an opinion here in passing on the basic difference between the religious and the moral as aspects of human experience, I would say that the religious is the moral *idealized* (in the logical sense), that is, carried to its theoretical limits. Whereas it is characteristic of a moral outlook on life to regard man as *partially* bad and *partially* good, it is, on the other hand, characteristic of the religious outlook to view man as *totally* bad, that is, as sinner, and God (or its equivalent) as *totally* good, that is, as Savior (in one form or another).[11] Whence sin and salvation, as the *limiting* concepts of the religious as such, in contradistinction to the moral. This no more signifies that individual men *are* actually sinful, than the limiting concept (say) of the frictionless engine in classical physics signifies that individual engines are actually frictionless. All it really signifies is that man, *sub specie religionis*, is *viewed* as a sinner. Once sin is admitted as a limiting concept at one pole of the religious, then salvation follows necessarily as its counterpart at the other. Consequently, as the interdependent categories of freedom and responsibility are necessary to moral understanding, so the interdependent categories of sin and salvation are necessary to religious understanding.

We moderns may choose to dispose of sin and salvation as categories of an outmoded theology, but if we do we must realize that we may be doing so to our own disadvantage and at our own risk—the risk being not that of going to hell spiritually, as religionists in their angry moods would have us believe, but simply one of just going to seed intellectually. For aught we know, the logic of an old-fashioned theology like Calvinism, no matter how mythical in expression, may make more religious sense than the modern mind is aware of or even cares to recognize.

To return to Dewey, the adjectival analysis of religion in *A Common Faith* is in keeping with his whole functionalistic philosophy of experience, although, as I have already argued in print elsewhere,[12] the same type of analysis is not consistently carried out in his theory of art. Yet, quite apart from this instance of inconsistency, is Dewey's particular "conception of the nature of the religious phase of experience"[13] adequate to a philosophy of functionalism in general? As I understand it, a thoroughgoing functionalist in philosophy would be logically obliged to put each aspect or phase of human experience on the same metaphysical footing, so to speak. But, as I have been hinting all along, in Dewey the religious aspect of experience invariably suffers at the expense of its moral aspect. To see what happens when the primacy is accorded to one aspect of experience at the expense of another, let us consider how Dewey handles the distinction which is bound to come up sooner or later in any theory of religion, to wit, the axiological distinction between the sacred and the profane.

Starting with the premise that it "is of the nature of a religion based on the supernatural to draw a line between the religious and the secular," Dewey infers that a conception of the "religious" which is "independent of the supernatural, necessitates no such division."[14] Now, this conclusion of Dewey's certainly follows from his premise, but the premise itself is questionable, since it implies that only a *supernatural* religion requires the distinction stipulated. Suppose, however, it turns out that the polar distinction between the sacred and the profane is as empirically necessary for the *religious* aspect of experience as the polar distinction between the ideal and the real is for its *moral* aspect. Then what? Then, I say, we should accept it as graciously as we do any other empirical distinction, or at least, not reject it outright without the supporting evidence. In any case, why does Dewey reject the very distinction which is part and parcel of the religious itself—a distinction essential not to supernaturalism alone (which, after all, is only one species of religion—the dualistic) but to the whole of religion? Obviously, he rejects it because he is approaching religion from the *moral* side of experience, even though he thinks he is approaching it from the religious side. That his approach is not religious becomes plain when we notice that the sacred-profane distinction is irrelevant to the interpretation of religious experience only in its moral aspect. But—and this is a big "but"—the fact that religion viewed *morally* necessitates no distinction between the sacred and the profane does not signify that religion viewed *religiously* necessitates none.

To illustrate our point with a memorable example from the history of medicine, Hippocrates as a scientific physician is reputed to have said that a particular disease is neither "more divine nor more earthly than another" (on the ground that "nothing happens without a natural cause"), but Hippocrates as a pious man also said in the same breath that all diseases "are equally of divine origin." [15] Many of us today raise our eyebrows over the pious part of the Hippocratic passage from the famous essay on *Airs, Waters, Places,* but such a reaction on our part misses the point completely. Whether we personally approve of religion or not—be it as primitive or as sophisticated as you like—the fact remains that religion is what men actually do in response to what they regard as *sacred.* Any conception of religion constructed, as Dewey's is, without presupposing the distinction between the religious and the secular liquidates the religious itself *in theory.* This should not, however, be taken to imply that Dewey banishes the sacred *from practice.* Far from it: human ideals with a natural basis are just as sacred to him as God is to most people. On the other hand, there must be something wrong with a doctrine which rejects the sacred-profane distinction in theory, yet has to resort to it in practice, insofar as the idea of the divine, according to Dewey himself, "involves no miscellaneous worship of everything in general." [16]

Dewey is entitled to interpret religion as he sees fit, but I am afraid that his valiant and militant plea for a moral reconstruction of our historic faiths will appeal only to those relatively few secular and disillusioned souls who, like himself, "have abandoned supernaturalism," and in order to fill the ensuing spiritual void left and felt in their lives, "are devoted to making explicit the religious values implicit in the spirit of science as undogmatic reverence for truth in whatever form it presents itself, and the religious values implicit in our common life, especially in the moral significance of democracy as a way of living together." [17] With all due respect to John Dewey as a great reformer in philosophy, let it be said that he had to pay a high price for being so—the price in this instance being the irrelevancy of much of his religious theory to the ultimate concerns of religion, concerns which have hardly anything to do with the particular values he treasured.

I take it that religion at its best transcends as well as presupposes ethics—which signifies that it goes *beyond*, but not *against*, ethics. If this is so, do we really gain anything in the way of understanding by putting a religious halo around the moral values of our particular culture, such as those of science and democracy? Surely, Dewey as a philosophical naturalist is committed to the proposition that our moral faith in ideals must stand on its own feet, otherwise it is foredoomed to failure. In fact, as he wisely brings out in the course of his discussion, the authority of any object of faith "to determine our attitude and conduct" rests on its "intrinsic nature" [18] *as an ideal*, not on something extraneous to it. Yet, to take his own favorite example, isn't it most revealing that he is not content to describe the spirit of science with a moral term, that is, as *respect* for truth, but finds it necessary to resort to a religious term, *reverence* for truth, presumably on the ground that the latter term furnishes a more adequate explanation of the scientific spirit? Still, does a mere change of terminology here transform the nature of the spirit of science from something of *moral* value—which is what its value potentially and actually is—into something of *religious* value?

I strongly suspect that what Dewey is trying to convey through such transformation of values is that, if we define (say) the spirit of science in religious terms, then it might exert a greater claim on our allegiance and devotion than if we define it in moral terms. This may well be psychologically the case, I admit; but what difference does it make, logically? Besides, even though I share his faith in science as a method of inquiry and therefore have no desire whatsoever "to disparage the possibilities of intelligence as a force" in human life, I must confess that Dewey strikes me as romantic and optimistic when he maintains that there is "such a thing as faith in intelligence becoming religious in quality." [19] It is true that human intelligence may be used to split atoms, but it is equally true that it may be misused to split nations. *Abusus non tollit usum*, to be sure, but we must not slur over the abuses of intelligence in human history. These form part of the human tragedy, and we might as well acknowledge them as such. Finally, I fear that we do not alleviate the situation by raising intelligence to a religious status, as Dewey proposes (with the best of intentions, no doubt). On the contrary, we might make it worse, if a look at the dark side of religious history yields any indication at all.

To recapitulate, Dewey's adjectival analysis of religion deftly escapes one dilemma—"religion versus the religious"—but is caught in another: *the moral versus the religious.* The latter dilemma stems from the fact that once a theorist secularizes supernatural religion and brings it down to earth to dwell among men, he is immediately confronted with the disconcerting problem as to the crucial difference between the moral and the religious as axiological qualities of experience. Now, it seems to me that Dewey could have avoided his own predicament by declaring unequivocally that "the common faith of mankind" is simply *moral* faith. Had he been satisfied with declaring just that and no more, he would not have found it necessary to derive artificially a religious faith from an enlightened moral faith, because he would have seen with Thomas Jefferson that the only type of faith which could ever serve as the *common* faith of mankind is moral faith, the religious type of faith being too *uncommon* in nature to qualify in that unifying capacity.[20] But all this may be expecting too much of a late-nineteenth-century Vermonter who had reacted to a long Puritan tradition behind him. Anyhow, the dream of Dewey was the dream of each and every great religion: to have one common religious faith guide mankind. Even if the dream were realizable—which I seriously doubt—I am not sure that the outcome would be desirable in all respects. A common religious faith might well be of benefit to mankind from an ethical standpoint, but it could hardly be so from an aesthetic standpoint, since from the latter standpoint, the more articulate variety there is, the better.

Lest there be misunderstanding of my principal objection to Dewey's approach to religion as a whole, let me recall that our author was indignant with those critics of *A Common Faith* who accused him of an antireligious viewpoint, and to the extent that he deplores the "lack of natural piety"[21] in "aggressive atheism," as well as in supernaturalism, he was quite justified in his reaction of indignation. Despite his nonatheist protestations and intentions, I think that both Dewey and his religious critics were mistaken in their respective contentions, because his appeal to "a common faith" is neither proreligious nor antireligious. It is, to be exact, *nonreligious,* his newer concept of "a common faith" being his older concept of "reflective morality" adorned with reverence. In fact, Dewey's *normative* conception of religion (that is, his conception of religious values as he sees them) is essentially nothing but a contemporary restatement of a naturalistic and humanistic ethics.[22] So much for our examination of the first defect in the Deweyan interpretation of religion, bearing on its subject matter.

While the first flaw in Dewey's religious philosophy is its *moral* reductionism, the second is its *scientific* reductionism. These two flaws in Dewey's reasoning go together. For once "the primacy of the ideal" [23] is postulated and the value of religion is restricted to its moral or practical side, then the only consistent stand to take with respect to its methodological side is to deny the cognitive or theoretical significance of religious faith—which is precisely what Dewey does in his work. It should be perfectly clear from the context of the key paragraph we quoted already from *A Common Faith*, that the author rests his case against the truth value of religion on the twin positivistic assumptions that there is only *one* type of truth—the factual—and "that there is but one method for ascertaining" it—the "scientific." His argument could be put more or less as follows. Since all truths refer to statements of fact established scientifically and since religion cannot issue in such statements, there are no special religious truths and no peculiar ways of knowing them. What is wrong with the argument?

To begin with, there is something quite ironical about this whole argument of Dewey's. Dewey is as tender-minded in his approach to scientific method as he is tough-minded in his approach to religious truth. However, despite the difference in attitude on his part, no scientific method as such, even if conceived "in its most general and generous sense," could ever be broad enough to cover the entire realm of cognition without at the same time thinning out and losing its peculiar probative effectiveness. John Dewey, alas, can't have his scientific cake and eat it! Moreover, regardless of whether the Deweyan conception of scientific method is adequate for ascertaining matters of value as well as matters of fact—and this may turn out to be the greatest irony facing any position which claims that "the same experimental method" [24] of science is in theory as applicable to values as to facts—the fundamental trouble with Dewey's denial of the cognitive significance of religion originates in the dubious presupposition which he shares with the positivists, namely, that the term "cognitive" is coextensive with the term "scientific."

Now that we have but barely indicated the inherent weakness in our author's approach to the methodological side of religion, it is only fair to point out its strength before proceeding. As against the great number of supernaturalists (old and new) whose logical vice is that they are forever perverting ideals by converting them into facts already in existence, Dewey is on very firm ground when he accuses the historic religions of committing "the moral fallacy" [25] of reification and flatly refuses to accord *factual* significance to their creeds. Yet this in itself does not automatically imply that religion may not enjoy some other sort of theoretical significance. The fact that we should go to science for the findings about man is no reason for not going to religion for the teachings about his destiny.

THE COGNITIVE SIGNIFICANCE OF RELIGION

Turning now to my own approach to religion on its methodological side, I have no argument with Dewey and his school that religious faith at its best has a practical or moral function in human life, helping us to *live* better. But as this is only half of the story, I am going to maintain, on the contrary, that religious faith has also a theoretical or intellectual function, helping us to *know* better. I do not mean that faith is a source of knowledge in the ordinary sense—knowledge of facts (information) —or in the American sense—"know-how" (skill)—but in the more important Greek sense—knowledge of values (wisdom). In daily life we distinguish between being *informed* about matters of fact and being *wise* about matters of value. Being well-informed in this or that is no necessary guarantee for being wise concerning the meaning of life as a whole, as is painfully manifest in human history, and this Age of Science is certainly no exception. *Homo sapiens* is not just *homo sciens*, irrespective of Linnean taxonomy! These distinctions take us directly to the field of comparative logic.

What is the logic of religious faith, and how does it differ from the logic of natural science? To see the import of this question for the whole field of comparative logic, suppose we ask the further question: What is the logic of a formal discipline like mathematics, and how does it differ from the logic of a natural science like biology? Merely to pose these questions should be sufficient to counteract the modern mind's bias, that only statements of fact have cognitive significance. As if facts were the most important things we need to know in life!

Pure mathematics proceeds by deduction, while scientific biology proceeds by induction, to put it popularly. What does this difference in method of reasoning imply as to the nature of their respective subject matters? It implies that mathematics and biology represent two different types of cognition, reasoning (in the narrow sense) and knowledge (in the ordinary sense), respectively. To say that mathematics is a purely *formal* discipline is to say that its statements are not judged on *factual* grounds, that is, on grounds of being true or false in the material sense. In other words, factual truth or falsity is irrelevant to mathematical discourse. If mathematical propositions are not true or false in the factual sense, in what sense are they? They are true or false in the purely logical sense—which means that strictly speaking they are not true or false at all, but valid or fallacious. In mathematical reasoning the only thing you have to worry about is to think *straight*. This is doubtless not easy, as we have been rudely reminded of late on a national scale by Sputnik and Company. The miracle of pure mathematics is that such an apparently ethereal science is applicable to so many mundane things. To appreciate applied mathematics, witness all the feats of engineering and all the marvels of physics—not to mention the prospects of astronomy, which may shortly become an experimental science for the first time, in the opening age of rocketry.

The validity of a mathematical conclusion is not determined by its factual truth or falsity, but by its consistency or inconsistency with a given set of stipulated premises; yet no one seriously denies the cognitive significance of mathematics. If this is so, why should the fact that religious statements are not factually true or false either, imply necessarily that they have no cognitive significance at all? For the beliefs of religion, like the opinions of philosophy and the sayings of poetry, may represent a third and last type of cognition which is distinct from both formal truth (consistency) and factual truth (knowledge)—normative truth (wisdom). As a consequence, religious beliefs fall under a propositional status other than valid-or-fallacious and true-or-false, namely, *wise-or-foolish*. Conceding with the positivist that religious propositions *per se* are not materially true or false, yet to the extent that they are wise or foolish they may be said to enjoy a truth status—not the status of "special truths" in the *factual* sense, but the status of special truths in the *normative* sense. This is precisely my thesis.

It is fortunate that the English language distinguishes between the verbs "reason" and "know." But unfortunately there is no verb in common usage corresponding exactly to the noun "wisdom." (There is in the Romance languages.) Actually, one can find in a good English dictionary the verb "wit" (to be or become aware), which is derived from the same Anglo-Saxon root (*witan*, know) as the noun "wisdom." But again, unfortunately, the term is now archaic except in the specifying phrase "to wit." If we could reinstate the verb "wit" in the English language, then it might become just as easy for us to understand the difference between "to think wisely" and "to think factually" (to know), as we now presumably understand the difference between either of these and "to think straight" (to reason). Consider what semantic confusion could be averted in the future in our modes of thinking if we could employ the infinitive "to wit" for matters of wisdom and the infinitive "to know" for matters of fact! Meanwhile, perhaps the verb in usage closest to the meaning of wisdom is "comprehend," which is to know not simply through information but through appreciation.

There are many definitions of wisdom in Webster's dictionary, but the most relevant one to our discussion is this: wisdom is the "ability to judge soundly and deal sagaciously with facts, especially as they relate to life and conduct." According to this definition, wisdom presupposes scientific information, yet at the same time goes beyond the facts by introducing perspective into them. Science is usually defined as *organized knowledge;* a more exact definition would be *organized information.* The English poet William Cowper saw clearly that knowledge and wisdom are "far from being one," but he went too far when he added that they have "ofttimes no connection." The distinction being drawn here between knowledge and wisdom is between types of cognition, not types of men. Scientists as a group are like other men: some are wise, some are foolish, just as some know more, some know less. No one group has a monopoly on wisdom, not even, alas, philosophers, who are supposed to be lovers of wisdom, by etymology!

Aside from the difficulties in semantics we must overcome henceforth, we must call attention again to the paramount thing that must never be forgotten concerning the cognitive status of religious faith. Religious beliefs, in contrast to scientific beliefs, are not true or false; they are wise or foolish. Just as when we ask, for instance, whether the Pythagorean theorem of the hypotenuse is true or false, we really mean *formally* true or false, that is, valid or fallacious, and when we ask whether the Darwinian theory of evolution is true or false, we mean *factually* true or false, that is, true or false in the usual sense, so when we ask whether the Christian doctrine of original sin is true or false, we should mean *normatively* true or false, that is, wise or foolish. For if the Christian proposition, "All men are sinners," were actually an existential proposition reporting a matter of fact, rather than a normative proposition stating a judgment of value, its alleged truth could never be established on grounds of faith. As no claim to factual truth can be settled by formal logic alone, so none can be settled by religious faith alone. Therein lies the methodological dilemma of traditional religion, which makes factual claims for its beliefs, yet refuses to abide by the scientific rules required to establish their validity and resorts to faith on discovering that those rules are not applicable. Accordingly, since matters of faith are not open to empirical testing, that is, to the true-false test, the only accessible and legitimate way left to judge a religious belief is to determine whether it is wise or foolish. This is easier said than done.

It would be just as absurd to assert that a religious proposition is true or false in the factual sense as that a mathematical proposition is true or false in the same sense; and on the other hand, it would be equally absurd to assert that a biological proposition is wise or foolish. The Darwinian theory of evolution may be as true in fact as you like, but nobody except evolutionary fanatics would ever think of calling it wise. In this connection Julian Huxley may be perfectly justified in holding "that without some knowledge of evolution one cannot hope to arrive at a true picture of human destiny." [26] Nevertheless, the ensuing picture could never be "true" in the same sense as the theory of evolution foundational to it. Propositions about human destiny are by nature debatable, and like other matters of value, belong strictly to the realm of wisdom, not to the realm of knowledge.

It would certainly be less confusing all around if we could get ourselves to restrict the use of the terms truth and falsity to matters of fact alone, but I am afraid this would be psychologically and culturally difficult. So if we must insist on calling mathematical and religious propositions true or false, we should qualify them with their proper adverbs, *formally* true or false, and *normatively* true or false, respectively. In any case, "the truth" that religion is talking about is not the factual truth of science. To illustrate with the Gospel passage frequently quoted but usually taken out of context, "the truth shall make you free" (St. John 8:32), the truth that Jesus is referring to specifically is what shall make us free from *sin*, not what shall make us free from *ignorance*. Therefore, the classic passage has nothing to do with truth in the ordinary scientific sense, let alone with freedom in the political sense. Stated positively, it has to do with sin and salvation, beliefs about which, falling as they do under the domain of religious wisdom, may be either wise or foolish.

Having arrived at the crucial difference between scientific and religious beliefs in *propositional status*, we are now prepared to consider the specific logic of religion. As pure mathematics proceeds by deduction and natural science by induction, so religion proceeds by faith. Faith is a term of many meanings. What is its meaning in the methodological context? Faith (from the Latin *fides*, not *fiducia*, trust) is to religion what scientific method is to science. If we identify science with the *scientific* method, then we should by the same token identify faith with the *fideistic* method. Scientific method may be defined as the method of tested research. Now the lesson we have learned from the history of science is that the essence of science lies not in the particular conclusions it reaches with respect to this or that subject matter. It lies rather in its peculiar self-correcting *method* of reaching those conclusions, although it should be added that many recent interpreters of science tend to exaggerate here and talk as if the scientific method were everything and the conclusions reached by it nothing.

Be that as it may, we still have to learn from the history of religion the counterpart of the lesson from the history of science—that religion on its creedal side is not constituted so much by its subject matter, which is legion, as by its characteristic method, which is faith. In putting the accent on faith as the method of religion, I am not unmindful of the fact that most of us in the Western world at least, and especially Protestants, identify faith with special subject matter, that is to say, with specific articles of faith or *beliefs*. But this is no argument against our emphasis on faith as *method*: if we were counting noses, most of us would not equate science with its method either, but with specific subject matter. On the other hand, the majority are not altogether wrong here, because subject matter and method go together in any inquiry. Subject matter determines ultimately which methods are appropriate to it and which are not. This brings us to the heart of the matter: the nature of religious faith.

In my opinion, the most revealing idea on the subject of faith comes from the eleventh chapter of the Epistle of Paul to the Hebrews.[27] The first three verses deal with faith as a way of understanding, the remaining verses giving instances from the Old Testament of what can be accomplished through its power. It is of course the famous first verse of the chapter which is fundamental to our theme. We quote it from the Authorized Version of the New Testament: "Now faith is the substance of things hoped for, the evidence of things not seen" (Hebrews 11:1).

As might be expected, this Pauline passage has been interpreted and misinterpreted in various ways. The most serious misinterpretation is the one which accepts the definition of faith in the first part of the text as substantially sound, but rejects the second part on the ground that faith is not "evidence" for anything at all. This appraisal rests on the erroneous assumption that the two parts of the text express different ideas about faith. The assumption itself in turn rests on a misreading of the term "substance" (*hypostasis*, in Greek). According to Webster's dictionary, "substance" as used in the text means "basis" or "ground" or "*substantiation*" (in the methodological sense)—which is *evidence*. Hence the two parts of the text are only different languages for conveying the same idea about the nature of faith, its method and subject matter. As "substance" and "evidence" in the Pauline passage are equivalent terms germane to the method of faith, so "things hoped for" and "things not seen" are equivalent phrases for its subject matter. In other words, faith to St. Paul in Hebrews 11:1 at least is the substantiation of things hoped for *or* the evidence of things not seen. Consequently, we cannot accept one part of the text and reject the other: either all or none.

The Pauline text on faith just explicated is invaluable not only as a clue to the logic of religion but also in its implication as to the difference between the way of faith and the method of science. In fact, if we define faith with St. Paul as the substantiation of things *hoped for*, the evidence of things *not seen*, then we may say, correspondingly, that science is the substantiation of things *searched for*, the evidence of things *seen*. It is clear that science's method of research is applicable only to things searched for, that is, to objects of observation. Similarly, it should be clear that the experimental or research method of modern science is not applicable to things hoped for as such, that is, to objects of aspiration. As the Book of Job raises the problem in the form of a rhetorical question: "Canst thou by searching find out God?" (Job 11:7). Except in the purely scholarly sense, God is no object of research!

Two most profitable lessons may be derived from the Pauline definition of faith. The first confirms what we have said already about the nature of religious cognition. Since the subject matter of faith is the sphere of ultimate hopes, not of facts, religious beliefs are not true or false, but wise or foolish. For example, the religious belief in the brotherhood of man is either wise or foolish, not true or false, quite apart from the fact that modern physiology teaches that all men are brothers under the skin. For the religious belief, "All men are brothers," is based on the religious idea that all men are children of God, not on modern physiology. And even granting the convergence of thought here, there is still an important difference between the religious and scientific expression of it. Whereas the physiologist as such submits the evidence which has bearing on the brotherhood of man and lets it go at that, the religionist expresses a value conviction about human brotherhood which he urges all men to take to heart.

The second lesson we can learn from the Pauline text is just as important as the first, if not more so. Many religious believers sincerely maintain with all disbelievers, ironically enough, that faith rests on no evidence of any kind. On the contrary, it should be noted, St. Paul's view in Hebrews 11:1 puts the stress on faith as *evidence*. This should serve as a safeguard against irresponsible believing in religion. Without evidence we have no real basis for accepting religious beliefs as wise, or even for that matter, rejecting them as foolish. Why should we believe anything unless we have some evidence to support it? To be sure, no religious proposition can be verified by scientific means, but this does not necessarily signify that there is no sort of evidence whatever for its claim to wisdom. The Pauline definition of faith takes care of the verification problem here by implication, the evidence of things unseen being presumably different from the evidence of things seen. It is obvious that the religious proposition, "All men are brothers," is not verifiable in the same way as the biological proposition, "All men are animals." To confirm the probable truth of the latter all one has to do is to go to the relevant data of comparative anatomy and physiology.

The fact that the evidence for a religious proposition is not based on sensory perception is no more a reason for denying its possible *normative* validity than the fact that a mathematical proposition is not based on that particular kind of evidence either, leads us to deny in turn its possible *formal* validity. For what constitutes evidence in the realm of cognition varies with the nature of the subject matter. Now, just as we have learned that the propositions of pure mathematics rest solely on the evidence of formally necessary relations and that the statements of natural science rest in the final analysis on the evidence of the ordinary senses, so we must learn that the convictions of religion may rest on the evidence of the extraordinary senses, that is, on the *insights* of faith. I have suggested elsewhere[28] that insights are the mind's analogue of the body's senses. If I am not mistaken, then some religious convictions may be said to be wise on the ground that they rest on *religious evidence*. On hearing this, positivists will rise up in arms to contend with assurance that "religious evidence" is a contradiction in terms. But their contention only serves to provoke the embarrassing query as to what logical right they have for ruling out in advance its possibility. Moreover, if there are geniuses in the arts and sciences, there are also geniuses in religion—the prophets and the saints—to whom we owe much of our spiritual heritage. In fine, to say that the religious belief in the brotherhood of man is based on faith, does not mean that it is based on something out of the blue. It simply means that its claim to being a wise belief rests on sound religious vision—no more and no less.

To sum up my case for religion from a naturalistic standpoint, I have asserted against Dewey and the religious positivists that religion has cognitive significance, to the extent that religious truths are "special truths" of *value*. Negatively put, religious truths are *not* truths of fact, their propositional status being different from scientific truths. In other words, religious beliefs do not belong to the ordinary class of true-false statements, they belong to a certain class of wise-foolish ones. Whereas Dewey's thesis is that the religious represents a species of values alone, I hold that it represents both a species of values and a species of truths. Finally, lest our attempt at a *via media* between religious positivism and supernaturalism be misunderstood in its overall implications for the logic of religion, I close on a note of caution. The fact that, for the thoroughgoing naturalist in philosophy, religion with its peculiar method of faith has theoretical as well as moral significance in nowise implies that it enjoys for that reason the cognitive possibilities of natural science, let alone those of pure mathematics. As there is no royal road to ordinary truth, so, despite the vociferous claims of the supernaturalists, there is none either to religious truth.

NOTES FOR CHAPTER 3

1 For the differences between the two types, see my book, *Toward a Critical Naturalism*, New York, Macmillan, 1958.
2 John Dewey, *A Common Faith*, New Haven, Yale University Press, 1934, p. 3.
3 *Ibid.*, pp. 66, 13, 14, 10, 24.
4 *Ibid.*, pp. 10, 23, 87, 66.
5 For the analogy with what Dewey calls in protest "the museum conception of art" and "the compartmental conception of fine art," see his *Art as Experience*, New York, Minton, Balch, 1934, pp. 6, 8.
6 John Dewey, *A Common Faith*, p. 6.
7 *Ibid.*, pp. 32-33.
8 *Ibid.*, p. 87.
9 *Ibid.*, p. 22.

10 *Ibid.*, p. 23.
11 John Dewey is quite aware that life from a moral viewpoint involves "a *mixture* of good and evil," and the reason for his refusal to admit that life from a religious viewpoint presupposes their absolute *separation* in theory is that such a presupposition for him leads to "too easy a way out of difficulties" (*A Common Faith*, p. 47). As a result, he is so sensitive to the moral waste of a religion which is too otherworldly that he is not sensitive enough to the spiritual emptiness of one which is too this-worldly.
12 Patrick Romanell, "A Comment on Croce's and Dewey's Aesthetics," *Journal of Aesthetics and Art Criticism*, Vol. VII (1949), pp. 125-128. For Dewey's reply, see "Aesthetic Experience as a Primary Phase and as an Artistic Development," *ibid.*, Vol. IX (1950), pp. 56-58.
13 John Dewey, *A Common Faith*, p. 2.
14 *Ibid.*, p. 66.
15 *The Medical Works of Hippocrates*, translated by John Chadwick and W. N. Mann, Oxford, Blackwell, 1950, p. 107.
16 John Dewey, *A Common Faith*, p. 53.
17 John Dewey, "Experience, Knowledge and Value: A Rejoinder," in *The Philosophy of John Dewey*, ed. by Paul Arthur Schilpp, Evanston, Northwestern University Press, 1939, p. 597.
18 John Dewey, *A Common Faith*, p. 23.
19 *Ibid.*, p. 26.
20 Cf. T. Jefferson to J. Fishback, 1809, in Thomas Jefferson, *On Democracy*, ed. by Saul K. Padover, New York, New American Library, 1946, p. 116: "Reading, reflection and time have convinced me that the interests of society require the observation of those moral precepts only in which all religions agree (for all forbid us to murder, steal, plunder, or bear false witness) and that we should not intermeddle with the particular dogmas in which all religions differ, and which are totally unconnected with morality."
21 John Dewey, *A Common Faith*, p. 53. For Dewey's rejoinder to Edward L. Schaub, one of his religious critics, see the Schilpp volume listed above, pp. 594-597.
22 This conclusion is confirmed by the recent appearance of Dewey's hitherto unpublished correspondence with one of his pupils. See Corliss Lamont, "New Light on Dewey's *Common Faith*," *Journal of Philosophy*, Vol. LVIII (1961), pp. 21-28. It is clear from this correspondence that Dewey was willing to call himself a humanist in religion. But what is still left unclear is wherein lies the difference, if any at all, between *ethical* and *religious* humanism.
23 John Dewey, *A Common Faith*, p. 45.
24 *Ibid.*, p. 73.
25 John Dewey, *Experience and Nature*, Chicago, Open Court, 1926, p. 34; *A Common Faith*, pp. 21-24, 43-44.
26 Julian Huxley, *Evolution in Action*, New York, New American Library, 1957, pp. vii-viii.
27 There is disagreement among Biblical scholars as to the authorship of the Epistle to the Hebrews, and I am following here those who attribute it to St. Paul.
28 Patrick Romanell, "Are Religious Dogmas Cognitive and Meaningful?" *Journal of Philosophy*, Vol. LI (1954), pp. 153-155.

QUESTIONS

1 Why is religion the acid test for naturalism as a philosophy?
2 What are the four aspects of religion, and which of these aspects is relevant to the historic conflict between faith and science in the modern world?
3 Distinguish ethics and religion from a naturalistic standpoint.
4 Differentiate naturalism from positivism in religion.
5 In what sense is a religious belief true, according to a philosophic naturalist?

SUGGESTED READINGS

John Dewey, *A Common Faith*, New Haven, Yale University Press, 1934.
William P. Montague, *Belief Unbound*, New Haven, Yale University Press, 1930.
James B. Pratt, *Naturalism*, New Haven, Yale University Press, 1939.
George Santayana, *The Life of Reason*, Vol. 3: *Reason in Religion*, New York, Scribner's, 1930.
Frederick J. E. Woodbridge, *An Essay on Nature*, New York, Columbia University Press, 1940.

4 *Francis H. Parker*

The Realistic Position in Religion

What is here meant by realism in religion may initially and very roughly be denoted as the philosophy of religion characteristic of the tradition owing most to such Western thinkers as Aristotle, St. Augustine, and St. Thomas Aquinas. What I shall define as the essential core of realism in religion is given its starkest formulation by Aristotle. With the introduction into the West of Judaism, Christianity, and Islam, this essential core of realism in religion was accepted in appropriately modified forms by most of the great religious thinkers of the Middle Ages, and preeminently by St. Thomas. This essential core of realism in religion is far more characteristic of ancient and medieval than of modern thought, though many thinkers living in modern times (e.g. Etienne Gilson and Jacques Maritain) embrace it, and some characteristically modern thinkers (e.g., Descartes and Leibniz) espouse it explicitly even though it conflicts with the implications of their systems. What I mean by religious realism is, in short, similar to but not entirely the same as what Charles Hartshorne calls "classical theism." [1]

This is only a very rough indication of what I shall mean by realism in religion, however; and it is not primarily the history or tradition of religious realism that I shall here discuss but rather its essential core. What is the meaning and truth of this essential core of religious realism, and what are the main problems confronting it? I shall first try to define the nature of realism and to demonstrate its truth as a general theory of knowledge without reference to religion. I shall then try to demonstrate the truth of realism in religion, both as following from the truth of realism in general and also on specifically philosophical and religious grounds, and to solve certain fundamental problems confronting a realist philosophy of religion.

REALISM AS A THEORY OF KNOWLEDGE

The common core of realism is epistemological; realism is *essentially* an epistemological theory. This does not by any means prevent other areas of discourse, philosophical and nonphilosophical, from being realist too (indeed, the very point of this essay is that religion, specifically, is also realist in nature), but in this section we shall be concerned with realism only as an epistemological theory. Here a demonstration of realism as a theory of knowledge will (if valid) establish the *cognitively* realist status of the religious object, and in the next section a demonstration of realism from philosophical and religious considerations will (if valid) establish the *totally* realist status of the religious object. Yet the solution to the main problems confronting realism in religion will require again the application of realism as a theory of knowledge, so that in the last analysis the meaning and truth of realism as a theory of knowledge will turn out to be the most fundamental point in this essay.

The Essence of Realism   What is the essence or common core of realism in all its many and varied forms? It is *cognitive independence: the independence of an object of knowledge from the knowledge of it.*[2] But what exactly does this mean? To answer this question let us begin with some things that cognitive independence does not mean.

(1) It does not mean that the objects of knowledge are necessarily independent of any and every act of knowing or of thought or mind as such. Many of the things we apprehend are plainly themselves mental in nature and are therefore certainly not independent of mind or thought. For example, we are aware of purposes, ideas, and minds; and such things as these, being themselves mental in character, are of course dependent upon mind—even if mind should be shown, from a metaphysical point of view, to be itself material. Furthermore, while many of the other things which we apprehend—e.g., buildings, fields and trees—do not seem to be mental or mind-dependent, it is conceivable that a metaphysical understanding of them might show that they are really mental or spiritual or, if not, that they at least depend for their existence and nature upon something else which is mental or spiritual. Thus the thesis of cognitive independence which I shall try to demonstrate, and therefore the thesis of realism as a theory of knowledge, is not incompatible with—though neither does it entail—a metaphysical idealism or spiritualism, a metaphysical thesis that really everything is ultimately mental or spiritual in

nature. Cognitive independence and epistemological realism are incompatible, however, with idealism as a theory of *knowledge*, with idealism as a theory that things are mental *because* they are dependent, in nature or existence or both, upon the fact that they are known, with idealism of the Berkeleian type.

(2) Cognitive independence (and thus epistemological realism) does not mean that objects of knowledge are necessarily independent of the *physical conditions* of their being known. What we apprehend is at least sometimes dependent upon such things as the states of our bodies and their sensory organs, the nature of the media between our sense organs and their objects, and the various natural and artificial instruments (like spectacles) which we sometimes use to increase the accuracy or scope of our perceptions. Such dependence of the objects of knowledge upon the physical instruments used in knowing sometimes becomes very important. In microphysics, for example, the particles being observed are so small that either their positions or their velocities are significantly altered by the physical techniques necessarily used in their observation; this is the basis of the uncertainty principle. But the uncertainty principle should not be interpreted as asserting or implying that the very act of awareness itself alters the very small particles of which the physicist is aware, nor any large body composed of these small bodies; and if the demonstration below of the truth of cognitive independence is valid, then the uncertainty principle cannot consistently be so interpreted.

(3) Finally, cognitive independence or epistemological realism does not mean that the things we apprehend are necessarily independent, in either their nature or their existence, from cognitively mediated practical activities. Whenever we know an artifact, for example, we know something which is dependent upon some mind for its nature and existence since it has been constructed by some purposive activity which is infused and controlled by some idea and mind. In short, any or even every object of knowledge may in fact, or even by necessity, be dependent upon some purpose, some conscious act of will. Indeed, this possibility is asserted to be the actual state of affairs and even necessarily so by religion, or at least by religion in the realist tradition, so this consideration will assume great importance when we turn to religion in the next section. But independence of will or conscious purpose is not what is here meant by realism. What, then, is this cognitive independence which is the essence of realism?

This cognitive independence, this essence of realism, is the independence of a thing known *from the knowing of it*. A thing is cognitively independent, in the sense here defined, if and only if it in no way depends upon that act of knowing which uniquely corresponds to it as being the knowing of it, that single and exact act of apprehension whose unique and peculiar object that thing is and by virtue of which that thing may be said by an extrinsic denomination to be an *object*. To be an object is to be thrown before a mind for its attention, and a thing (or event, situation, etc.) is an object only by virtue of the precise, individual act of attending to it which logically and extrinsically bestows upon it the logical property of being the object of that act of attention. There are no objects in general; there is only *this* object *of this* awareness *of it*, *that* object *of that* awareness *of it*, and so on—though this does not exclude the religious claim that the world as a whole is one object of one divine act of awareness. Now it is only from the specific, exact, corresponding awareness of it that an object is independent, according to the definition of cognitive independence here presented—not necessarily from *other* acts of awareness nor from the *instruments* employed in such awareness nor from conscious *purposes* nor from *mind*.

This meaning of independence is so easily misunderstood that it should be repeated and clarified. A building depends upon the builder's antecedent idea of it, but after it is built *it* does not depend upon any *subsequent* idea of it which the builder or someone else may have—although a later, modified form of the building may indeed so depend. Your thought depends upon your mind, and it may (let us hope) even depend to some extent upon my mind; but your thought does not depend upon my thought *about* your thought—nor even upon your own thought *about that* thought. In like manner the thought that I am now thinking depends upon my thinking and upon my mind, but it does not depend upon any particular thought which I may or may not have *about* that thought. Each thought about another thought is at a different level than that thought which it's about. If T_1 is a thought and T_2 is a thought about T_1, then T_1 is independent of T_2—though of course dependent upon some mind. And if T_2 should then become an object of another thought —should become thought about by T_3—then T_2 will be directly dependent upon T_1 and indirectly dependent upon some mind; but it will be independent of T_3, the thought about T_2. And so on. Every object, whether or not it is dependent upon some *other* cognition, is independent of the cognition *of or about it*. The object's relation of being "known by," "apprehended by," "cognized by," the knower is not a real relation, not a real property of the object by which it would be dependent upon the knower, but rather only a logical or mental relation which arises only in reflection by reversing the real relation of "knower of." This point will be of great importance below in the solution of the most fundamental problem of all those that confront a realist philosophy of religion.

So much for the definition of that cognitive independence which is the essence or common core of realism in all its forms. Let us now turn to the demonstration of the truth of this cognitive independence, the truth of the essence of realism.

The Truth of Realism   What I want to try to demonstrate is the thesis
that an object of knowledge is independent,[3]
both in nature and in existence, from the knowing of it, where this independence is understood in the precise sense just defined. This demonstration consists in showing that any denial of this thesis of cognitive independence either concedes that very thesis or else involves a contradiction. Such a denial of the thesis of cognitive independence may take
either of two basic forms, one partial and restricted and the other total
and unrestricted. Let us examine each of these in turn.

A Refutation of Cognitive Constructionism   The form which is most
often given to the denial
of the central realist thesis of cognitive independence is the view that the
object of knowledge is dependent upon the mind and its operations by
virtue of being constructed by those operations out of independently
given sensory materials. On this view only the formal structure of the
object of knowledge is dependent upon the knowledge of it; the content
or matter of the object is independent of the mind and its activities and
derives from an independent, transcendent source. Thus this is only a
partial denial of the realist theory of cognitive independence; cognitive
dependence is here restricted to the formal structure of objects of knowledge. This view, most influentially asserted by Kant in his famous "Copernican" revolution in epistemology, I shall call the *constructionist
theory:* the theory that knowing consists in forming or ordering or constructing phenomenal objects out of independently given materials.

Let us now attempt to refute this constructionist theory. If the theory
maintains that the independent given is an object of knowledge, then the
contradiction results that knowledge of the independent given is not
knowledge of the independent given, because according to this theory
knowing consists in the transformation of that independent given into
something new and different, the phenomenal object. The knowledge of
x (the independent given) would then not be a knowledge of x itself at
all, but rather of x' (the phenomenal object, where the prime represents
the aspects of the object which are dependent upon, because imposed by,
the knowing mind). But this is plainly self-contradictory.

The constructionist will not of course grant that the independent given
is an object of knowledge, because to do so would be to concede the
realist thesis of cognitive independence from the very start. As Peter
Bertocci once put it, "it makes no sense to talk about being aware of x
itself,"[4] the antecedent, independent given; x is merely the material out
of which an object of knowledge is to be constructed. It is rather x', the
constructed object, which is the object of knowledge; and as soon as this
fact is recognized the alleged contradiction disappears. This is true. But
how, then, according to the constructionist, is the mentally constructed

object known? Since it is the constructed and thereby mentally dependent object which is, according to this theory, the object of knowledge, and since knowing is regarded as an activity of ordering, informing, or constructing, then this theory is obliged to declare that the transformed, constructed, dependent object (x') is also transformed and constructed— or rather *reconstructed*—by the act of knowing *it* into a new and different object, x''. If this is so, however, then x' cannot be an object of knowledge as it was asserted to be because *it* no longer even exists. It can only be x'' which is the object of knowledge. But this means that the constructionist's asserted knowing of x' is not the knowing of x' but rather of x''. And this is self-contradictory. If this contradiction is eluded by the claim that x', like x, is not itself an object of knowledge but only the material out of which such an object is constructed, then the process must be repeated all over again. The knowing of x'' must, if the constructionist's theory is consistent, be the transformation of x'' into x''' so that the knowing of x'' is not the knowing of x'' but rather of x'''; and this too is self-contradictory. And so on, *ad infinitum*. Thus the attempt to escape the contradiction only produces an infinite series of contradictions. Hence the constructionist theory that objects of knowledge are cognitively dependent for their formal structure can consistently have no object of knowledge at all, for every attempt to know an object succeeds only in thrusting it beyond the reach of knowledge.

Here the constructionist may object that for any particular object of knowledge the constructing process occurs only once, and that after it once occurs, the constructed, cognitively dependent object is just simply known. This stops the infinite regress of constructions and avoids the contradictions. This is exactly what Kant seems to do—though he remains significantly silent concerning that last act of just simply knowing the antecedently constructed phenomenon. This modified constructionism does, it is true, bar the regress and escape the contradiction in the earlier, unmodified theory. But it does so only by conceding the point, only by granting the realist thesis of cognitive independence as it has here been defined. Though the object which is thus known is constructed by and hence dependent upon *prior* mental acts, it is now, according to the modified theory, not constructed by or dependent upon that specific act whereby it is *known*. The realist has no objection to the constructionist's view that many complex mental (and physical) operations are often required so long as it is agreed that these operations are only preparations for a nonconstructionist knowing of something that is therefore not dependent upon that very act of knowing. Doubtless often, even usually, perhaps even always, various mental and physical operations must be performed in order to prepare the situation, both the potential knower and the thing to be known, so that the knower can actually know something: we must first put on our glasses or stain a cross section of tissue or fire a stream of electrons or organize something in our minds. But these operations cannot with consistency be identified with the actual act of knowing for which they prepare, since consistency demands, we have now seen, that the very act of knowing does not itself construct or alter its own proper object and that consequently that proper object is and remains quite independent of the corresponding act of knowing it. And this is just what the realist thesis of cognitive independence means as we have defined it.[5]

Thus one form of the denial of that cognitive independence which is the essence of realism—the restricted form of constructionism which claims that objects of knowledge are dependent upon the knowledge of them with respect to the formal structure which the knowing mind imposes upon them—either concedes the realist's cognitive independence which it claims to deny or else it contradicts itself by implying that the knowledge of something is not the knowledge of that something. Let us now turn to the other, unrestricted, total form of the denial of the realist thesis of cognitive independence.

A Refutation of Cognitive Creationism In contrast to cognitive constructionism, one might deny that there is any independently real material or thing in itself, in favor of the view that the content as well as the formal structure of objects of knowledge is constructed by and thus dependent upon the knowing mind. According to this form of the denial of the realist thesis of cognitive independence, knowing does not construct objects out of some independently given material but rather *creates* its objects out of itself. This total denial of cognitive independence I shall therefore call cognitive creationism. While cognitive creationism does as such avoid cognitive constructionism's initial partial concession of cognitive independence, it must join constructionism in either totally conceding realist cognitive independence or else lapsing into contradiction,[6] for it too must have a knowing without any object. This I shall now try to demonstrate.

According to this creationist theory, there exists no object to be known until after the cognitively creative act has occurred; this is the meaning of this theory. Hence that yet to be created object cannot be what is known, according to this theory, for it is not yet in existence. But may this object not be known *after* it has been cognitively created? No; the knowing of it after it has been created by the first act of knowing would have to be a second act of knowing—since the first act is over and done once it has finished creating its object—and the object of this second creative act of knowing would have to be a different object than that of the first creative act of knowing. Once more, it can now be seen, we are on the brink of an infinite abyss. For a *third* cognitively creative act aimed at knowing the *second* cognitively created object would succeed only in creating a *third* cognitively created object which would need to be known by a fourth act which would succeed only in creating a fourth object rather than in knowing the third one—and so on, *ad infinitum*. According to this creationist theory, therefore, when there is a (creative) act of knowing there is no corresponding object known, and when there is a (created) object to be known there is no corresponding (creative) act of knowing it. Once more, therefore, we find ourselves in an infinite regress, with knowing always thrusting its object out of reach. To put the situation in terms of the contradiction involved, cognitive creationism as well as cognitive constructionism implies the proposition that "knowing a thing is not knowing *that* thing."

The creationist may avoid this contradiction in the same way as the constructionist: by insisting that for any particular object of knowledge the creating process occurs only once and that once it has occurred its created object is just simply known. Again, however, this avoids the contradiction only by conceding the point, only by granting the realist thesis of the cognitive independence of the objects of knowledge; for now the specific act whereby the object is just simply known is one which does *not* create its object but which rather finds it and leaves it unchanged and independent.

The basic point in this whole argument that the denial of the cognitive independence of the object implies an infinite regress of contradictions is, it may have been surmised, that knowing *means* identifying an object which is *already there*. It is the logically implied denial of this basic point which forces both the constructionist and the creationist versions of the denial of cognitive independence into an infinite regress of contradictions. That the logic of the concept of knowing does in fact entail being presented with something already there has been manifested in the demonstration by the obvious oddity of having a knowing without any object being known. It has also been shown by the fact that the concept of knowing has actually been used by each of these variants of cognitive dependency to imply that there is already an object there to be known, in the fact, that is, that they lapse back into realist language and concede the thesis that the once constructed or created object is then known just as it independently is. As Etienne Gilson once wrote, "those who pretend to think otherwise, think in realistic terms as soon as they forget to act their part";[7] and it needs to be added only that they *must* forget to act their part because the very logic of the concept of knowing which they are trying to enact contradicts their enactment of it.

The proposition that objects of knowledge depend, partly or wholly, upon the knowing of them therefore either concedes the realist thesis of cognitive independence or else lapses into contradiction. Hence its contradictory, the thesis that objects of knowledge are independent of the knowing of them, is thereby demonstrated to be true.

The Inescapability of the Law of Noncontradiction   Does the fact that this denial of cognitive independence involves a contradiction imply that the denial is really false? Only if the law of noncontradiction is really true, clearly; but how do we know that it is? Can we prove the truth of the law of noncontradiction? We cannot do so indirectly, by a *reductio ad absurdum* argument, because, as we have just been seeing, such an argument presupposes the law of noncontradiction. Nor can it be proved by a direct argument, I believe—though this is a more debatable point— since the law of noncontradiction is definitive of and thereby presupposed by direct, deductive proof. The reason for this is that the very meaning of deduction is that the falsity of the conclusion, when taken together with the truth of the premises, involves a contradiction. And even if it could be demonstrated directly, deductively, we still would not be sure that it is true, for such a direct proof would, by its very meaning, presuppose *other* propositions as premises; and then *these* propositions—or the premises from which they are deduced or the premises from which *those* premises are deduced, etc.—would not be proved true. Hence every demonstration, and therefore our demonstration of realism, must presuppose the truth of at least one proposition which cannot be demonstrated either directly or indirectly. The mere postulation of such ultimate premises with no justification at all would at most permit the realism demonstrated from them to be valid; it would not establish it as really true. We are therefore faced with the fundamental problem of justifying unprovable propositions. How is this problem to be solved?

What is needed is a nondemonstrative verification, an ascertainment of the truth of these propositions without deriving them from other propositions, so that all the propositions validly derived from them will be known to be true. Is there any such thing? Yes, of course. There are logically necessary or "self-evident" propositions, such as "Bachelors are unmarried" or "Men are animals." Aristotle said that such nondemonstrative verification is effected by insight or intellectual intuition (*nous*), the act of that "thinking part of the soul" whose apprehension of the forms of things gives rise to "universal and necessary judgments" and "the first principles of scientific knowledge." [8] "We cannot know the truth of anything," he wrote elsewhere, "without also knowing its explanation. And . . . that is the most true which is the explanation of other truths. Consequently the ultimate principles of the permanent aspects of things must necessarily be true in the fullest sense; for such principles are not merely sometimes true, nor is there any ulterior explanation of their being, but on the contrary *they* are the explanation of other things. And so, as each thing stands in respect of being, it stands likewise in respect of truth." [9] With such an intellectual intuition of the principle of noncontradiction we can know that it is really true, therefore, without deriving it from any premise. Hence we can know that a proposition which violates that principle, as the denial of cognitive independence does, must really be false.

Or can we? Can we be sure that any thesis which involves a contradiction is thereby *really* false, false of *reality itself?* Knowing that a proposition is *really* false, false of *reality* itself, *because* it involves a contradiction implies that in knowing the truth of the law of noncontradiction we are knowing something of reality itself *independently of our knowledge of it.* But this is of course exactly what is at issue between the realist thesis of cognitive independence and the nonrealist thesis of cognitive dependence. So the argument for the realist thesis seems to be circular, for it seems to depend upon the claim that one thing, at least—the law of noncontradiction—is independent of the knowledge of it; and this is of course exactly what the opponent of cognitive independence does not admit. No necessary propositions "provide any information about matters of fact," as Ayer wrote.[10] "Analytic propositions are necessary and certain" because "they simply record our determination to use words in a certain fashion . . . As Wittgenstein puts it, our justification for holding that the world could not conceivably disobey the laws of logic is simply that we could not say of an unlogical world how it would look." [11] Since the necessity of even the laws of logic is dependent upon our linguistic or conceptual conventions, even the law of noncontradiction could be abandoned. True enough, as C. I. Lewis pointed out,

> The higher up a concept stands in our pyramid, the more reluctant we are to disturb it. . . . The decision that there are no such creatures as have been defined as "swans" would be unimportant. The conclusion that there are no such things as Euclidean triangles would be immensely disturbing. And if we should be forced to realize that nothing in our experience possesses any stability—that our principle, "Nothing can both be and not be," was merely a verbalism, applying to nothing more than momentarily—that denouement would rock our world to its foundations.[12]

And yet such a world-shaking event is still quite possible—in some ineffable use of the word "possible"—simply because, on this view, even the law of noncontradiction is dependent upon our cognition of it and is not necessarily independently true of the real world.

And so my effort to defend our demonstration of realist cognitive independence seems to have failed simply because it begs the question. The thesis that things known exist independently of their being known cannot be demonstrated to be really true by showing that its denial involves a contradiction, because this assumes that the principle of noncontradiction is a truth about the real world which exists independently of our knowledge of it.

Dark as the outlook for realism is, however, a ray of light may be seen shining through. While it does seem that the issue between realism and nonrealism is too fundamental to be resolved by logical demonstration, may there not be some other way of justifying realism's essential thesis of cognitive independence?[13] The light breaking through is a recollection of Aristotle's argument that the skeptic refutes himself by reducing himself to the vegetative state. Is it possible for us as humans, as thinking beings, to avoid believing that the principle of noncontradiction is necessarily true of the real world independently of our knowledge of it? To say "The law of noncontradiction is not true of objective reality independently of our knowledge of it" is to allow that the contradictory of this very proposition itself may really also be objectively true, that the law of noncontradiction *is* true of objective reality independently of our knowledge of it, because then independent reality may be other than and in contradiction to cognitively dependent reality. Hence the opponent of the realist thesis of cognitive independence is, at bottom, in the self-defeating position of denying his thesis in the same breath with which he affirms it, of implying that the principle of noncontradiction is true independently of our knowledge of it just in order consistently to deny it. But this is, on the one hand, exactly not to maintain any consistent position at all and also, on the other hand, to grant the independent truth of the principle of noncontradiction and hence also of the demonstration of the realist thesis of cognitive independence which is based upon the independent truth of that principle. This being the case, the realist in the final analysis need pay no more attention to the nonrealist than Aristotle did to his vegetable. Thus while the realist thesis of cognitive independence might possibly *be* false, by some unspeakable sense (or non-sense) of the word "might," it cannot be *asserted* or *believed* to be false. Put differently, while the *proposition* that things known are independent of the knowing of them can only, in the last analysis, be *seen* to be true, the *assertion* of or *belief* in that proposition can be demonstrated to be *inescapable* by any being who makes any assertion or holds any beliefs at all.

Summary of Realism as a Theory of Knowledge The essential core of realism as a theory of knowledge, of any and all knowledge in whatsoever area, is cognitive independence: the independence of things known, not necessarily from minds and their activities, but from those precise, corresponding acts of knowing those things. And the demonstration of the truth of realism thus defined consists in seeing that its denial involves a contradiction (or else concedes the point), and that the law of noncontradiction, upon which such a demonstration is therefore based, cannot be denied but must be asserted or believed in by any being who makes any assertions or holds any beliefs at all. Hence the nonrealist cannot assert his thesis; he is obliged to assert realism, for "those who pretend to think otherwise" must "think in realistic terms" [14] just in order to think at all.

Let us now apply this realist theory of knowledge in general to the question of realism in religion.

REALISM AS A THEORY OF RELIGION

Realism in religion means, roughly and as a first approximation, that the inward religious experience has, at least to some extent, an outward reference to an independently real deity who supports and justifies that inward experience. But what does this mean more precisely? And is it true? Our procedure will be first to try to show the precise meaning and the definite truth of realism as a theory of religion and second to try to solve certain fundamental problems necessarily faced by a realist philosophy of religion.

The Meaning and Truth of Realism in Religion Religion, like every distinctively human activity, has two fundamental dimensions: the cognitive and the conative, the theoretical and the practical. In trying to demonstrate the meaning and truth of realism in religion I shall try first to show that realism is true of the theoretical dimension of religion, of philosophical theology, and then to show that it is true of the practical dimension of religion, of religion itself in the narrower and commoner sense of the word.

Realism as Philosophically-Theologically Required Whether there truly is any such thing as theology—a *logos* about *theos*, a knowledge of God—we shall consider shortly. But if there is any genuine theology, any true knowledge of God, then that theology, that knowledge of God, must be realistic just because it is a knowledge. This is the first thing to see in seeing the truth of realism in theology. In preceding pages the truth of realism as a *general* theory of knowledge was demonstrated; it was demonstrated that the object of *any* and *every* act of knowing must be independent of the act of knowing it. From this it necessarily follows that a *divine* object of knowing must be independent of the acts of knowing it. The God who is known must be independent of the act whereby he is known; this is the essence of the truth of realism in theological knowledge. And this is true of a so-called negative theology as well as of a positive theology, for a negative theology, while denying that we can make true affirmative statements about God, affirms that we can make true negative statements about God; and if these negative statements are to be truly about God, then, by the preceding argument, the God whom they are about must be independent of these statements about him.

It is therefore not at all strange that denials that we can have knowledge of God as something objective and independently real should—at least usually—be accompanied by denials of realist epistemology, for a denial of realist cognitive independence, whether by a cognitive constructionism or a cognitive creationism, logically excludes the possibility of a knowledge of God as independently real. Thus in Kant's philosophy, for example, the putative refutations of the arguments for the existence of God which Kant gives in the Transcendental Dialectic are quite unnecessary and redundant, since beginning with his "Copernican" revolution (in the Preface to the second edition of the *Critique of Pure Reason*) it is a foregone conclusion that knowledge of God as an independent reality is impossible because *all* knowledge is restricted to cognitively constructed phenomena. The antirealist thesis of cognitive dependence is a sufficient condition for the rejection of realism in theology, and the realist thesis of cognitive independence is a necessary condition for the truth of realism in theology.

It is only a necessary condition and not a sufficient one, however, and for two reasons. First, an epistemological realism does not entail and does not suffice for a theological realism, because an epistemological realism says only that whatever objects of knowledge there may happen to be must be independent of the knowledge of them, and this statement does not entail that God is among these objects. It is compatible with epistemological realism to assert that God does not exist, or that if he does he cannot possibly be known. Hence a theological realism requires, in addition to a realist theory of knowledge in general, the propositions that God exists and that he can be known, at least to some extent. In the second place, granting the thesis that God exists and that he can be known, at least to some extent, a theological—and, as we shall see, also a religious—realism requires something more than that God exists independently of our *knowledge* of him; it requires also the thesis that God is independent of all other aspects of our nature, and, indeed, that he is independent of any and every aspect of nature as a whole. Hence epistemological realism, the theory that whatever we know is independent of our knowing it, is only one of the theses necessary for a theological and religious realism. Three other theses are also necessary: that God exists; that we can know at least something of him; and that he is independent, not merely of our acts of knowing him, but also of all aspects of nature.

These four theses, then, I take to be conjointly sufficient conditions of a theological and religious realism (though the knowing will also involve a response): (1) things known are independent of the knowing of them, (2) God exists, (3) we can know that God exists and something else about him, and (4) God is independent of any and every aspect of nature. Proposition (1) has already been established in the preceding pages, so it is the other three propositions which must now be established in order to obtain a realist philosophy of religion. Let us now try to demonstrate these last three propositions.

A demonstration of these three propositions would of course be some form of argument for the existence of God, of a God who can in some sense be known by us, and of a God who is independent of the world. Many such arguments have been proposed in the history of philosophy and theology, some of them invalid and some of them valid, I believe; and it is of course impossible to consider anywhere near all of these. Fortunately there is, I think, one argument which will suffice to establish all three of these propositions, at least so far as theology is concerned and so far as the theoretical dimension of religion is concerned, though this argument too will require some modification and explanation. This is the argument from contingency which has been most famously expressed by St. Thomas Aquinas in his "third way."

The starting point of this argument is that there are things about us which are actually existent and yet at the same time contingent. Here "contingent" means existentially contingent or dependent in being; existential contingency is the possibility of not existing. And the things about us certainly are existentially contingent, able not to exist; they come into existence and pass away. From this starting point Thomas concludes an existentially necessary being which is the first cause of the existence which the contingent things about us sometimes happen to have. His formulation of the argument in the *Summa Theologica* is as follows:

> We observe in our environment how things are born and die away; they may or may not exist; to be or not to be—they are open to either alternative. All things cannot be so contingent, for *what is able not to be may be reckoned as once a non-being,* and *were everything like that once there would have been nothing at all.* Now were this true, nothing would ever have begun, for what is does not begin to be except because of something which is, and so there would be nothing even now. This is clearly hollow. Therefore all things cannot be might-not-have-beens; among them must be being whose existence is necessary.[15]

This formulation of the argument contains two non-sequiturs, however. In the first place, from the fact that something *might* not exist it does not necessarily follow that it ever *does* not exist; on the contrary, it could conceivably exist forever as something which might not exist. Actuality does not necessarily follow from possibility. In the second place, even if we grant that *each* contingent thing fails to exist at some time *or other*, it does not follow that *all* contingent things fail to exist at the *same* time to produce a state of affairs of nothing at all. Like houseflies, contingent things could perfectly well be around forever even though no one of them lasts very long. Indeed, this is the position of Aristotle upon whose philosophy Thomas bases his own, so far as it is not based on divine revelation; and Thomas says that this position of Aristotle's of the everlastingness of the world is to be rejected on grounds of revelation only, not on grounds of reason. However, the formulation of the argument from contingency which Thomas gives in his *Summa Contra Gentiles* is free of these flaws:

> Everything that is a possible-to-be has a cause, since its essence as such is equally uncommitted to the alternatives of existing and not existing. If it be credited with existence, then this must be from some cause. Causality, however, is not an infinite process. Therefore a necessary being is the conclusion.[16]

The essence of this argument from contingency is very simple: "contingency" entails "necessity," "dependence" entails "independence," "relativity" entails "absoluteness." You can't have a thing which is just simply contingent. For a thing to be contingent is for it to be contingent *upon*, for a thing to be contingent upon is for it to be contingent upon *something*, and for a thing to be contingent upon something there must *be* that something upon which it is contingent. All this is involved simply in what it *means* to be contingent; it is the logic of the concept of contingency. Nor can it any longer be properly objected that this is true of contingency merely as it seems to us, merely of the way in which we use the word "contingency," because earlier pages have shown that what we know is independent of our knowing of it. And the logic of contingency is the same as that of dependence and relativity. If *everything* were dependent, nothing could be *dependent*, for there would be nothing for anything to be dependent *upon*.

The most frequent objection to this argument, and also to some other arguments, is that this series of contingent, dependent effects may regress to infinity, that it is false—or at least that it has not been shown to be true—that "causality is not an infinite process." But this objection is based upon a misunderstanding. While it may be argued that the series of *effects* may *progress* to infinity on the ground that the existence of the cause is not dependent upon a completed series of effects, the existence of the effect, by definition of "effect," is dependent upon the completion of the series of the actually existent causes of it. This is a logically necessary truth, as we have just seen. For anything to be dependent, there must be something else which is independent. And there is something which is dependent; this is an empirical matter of fact. Hence there must be something which is independent, necessary, or absolute.

This completed series is not, however, a *temporal* series—another common misunderstanding. As we have just seen, something could conceivably exist *forever* as contingent or dependent upon something else. This, again, was Aristotle's view which Thomas rejected only upon grounds of revelation. Furthermore, no temporally prior thing could be the cause of a temporally posterior thing because they are not co-existent. No past thing as past can be the cause of any present thing as present because the former, as past, is not even in existence—and the cause of anything must be existent. Hence the cause of a present thing, that upon which it actually depends for its existence, cannot be something "way, way back in ages dark when old man Noah built his sea-going ark"; it must rather be something *now* existing, something co-present with the contingent, dependent thing which depends upon it as the independent, necessary cause of its existence.

Hence follows the conclusion that there is and must be a necessary cause which is first in a completed series of real causes every member of which is co-present with the contingent existent which is their effect. And such a necessary first cause cannot be escaped by making the completed series a circle rather than a line, for this involves the contradiction that each simple item in the circle is both before and after itself since both cause and effect of itself. For Atlas to hold the world there must be the broad-bosomed sea to support the turtle upon which Atlas stands. Since there are contingent things, things which are but might not be, there must be something else which is necessary and independent, something which cannot help but be. "And this," as Thomas concludes his argument, "all men call God."

A more recent and sophisticated objection to this argument is that it entails, as Findlay has put it, "not only that there isn't a God, but that the Divine Existence is either senseless or impossible." [17] The reason advanced for this alleged absurdity is that " 'necessary' is a predicate of *propositions*, not of things," so "we shall have to interpret 'God is a necessary being' as 'The proposition "God exists" is logically necessary'." However, Smart goes on to say (and Findlay agrees), "No existential proposition can be logically necessary, for . . . the truth of a logically necessary proposition depends only on our symbolism. . . . 'Logically necessary being' is a self-contradictory expression like 'round square'." [18]

This objection makes two mistakes, however. One mistake, which is less relevant to our present problem, is the assertion that "no existential proposition can be logically necessary," that "the truth of a logically necessary proposition depends only on our symbolism." That this is a mistake follows from the fact that logically necessary propositions depend upon the law of noncontradiction (they are ones whose contradictories are self-contradictory) taken together with the fact (established earlier in these pages) that belief in the existential reference or objective truth of the law of noncontradiction is inescapable for beings who believe anything at all.[19] The other mistake, and the one which is most relevant to the present issue, is the assertion that " 'necessary' is a predicate of *propositions*, not of things." Logical necessity is indeed a property of propositions, not of things; and since God is plainly not a proposition, it is clear that God is not logically necessary. But from this it does not at all follow that God is not necessary in some other, *non*logical sense; and the argument we have been considering plainly shows that God must be necessary in some other such sense. The necessity of God is a *real* or *existential* or *ontological* necessity, not a logical necessity. This point is made against Smart and Findlay by another contributor to the same volume, Rainer (Windsor):

> The necessity of God's existence . . . means God's complete actuality, indestructibility, *aseitas* or independence of limiting conditions. It is a property ascribed to God, not a property of our assertions about God. To maintain that the ascription of such a property is logically absurd is to confuse the necessity of God's being with the necessity of our thinking about it. That is to commit the converse fallacy of Anselm's ontological argument, namely, to say that a Perfect Being cannot exist necessarily, because we cannot necessarily assert its existence. Our assertion of God's existence may be contingent, although God's existence is necessary in the sense of being indestructible or eternal.[20]

Hence the necessity of God does not mean that any proposition or knowledge about God is necessary; it means that while all other things would fail to exist without God upon whom they depend, there is nothing at all upon which the existence of God depends and in the absence of which God would fail to exist. Divine necessity is the real, not the logical, impossibility of God's not existing because he is independent of and nonrelative to all other things.

If the argument from contingency for the existence of God as a necessary, independent being is sound, then one of the conditions necessary for religious realism is established—namely, proposition (2), that God exists. But the argument also establishes the third condition necessary for theological realism, namely proposition (3), that we can know something about God, for it establishes at least that we know that God is independent of all other things as their necessary cause. Furthermore, knowing that God is independent of all other things implies, I believe, that we can also know some other things about God—for example that he is eternal or nontemporal, that he is immutable, etc. But I will not here press our knowledge of such other aspects of God, because knowing that God is necessary and independent of all other things is sufficient to establish proposition (3), that we know about God that he is independent of all other things. Finally, the argument also thereby establishes the fourth condition necessary for religious realism—namely, proposition (4), that God is independent of any and every aspect of nature. The first condition necessary for religious realism, proposition (1), that whatever is known is independent of the knowing of it, does not of course necessarily follow from the argument from contingency. And since this proposition, this epistemological realism, will be essential in solving the problems confronting religious realism, it is necessary to have the demonstration of it which has been presented in our first section.

If the argument from contingency for the existence of God as a necessary or independent cause of all other things is sound—at least in some form if not in the form which I have given—then it follows that realism, the objective and independent existence of God, is *philosophically-theologically* required, required by the theoretical component of religion. God must exist and must be independent of all other things simply because he is the cause upon whom all other things depend for their very existence and because for all other things to depend upon him for their very existence he must be really independent of them. A "God" which, *per contra*, depended upon other things could not possibly be *God* in the sense in which he is theoretically required, required by the necessity of seeing him as the cause of all other things. So the head tells us that God must be independent of all other things; the head is a theological realist. But what now about the heart? What about the practical or conative dimension of religion and its requirements?

Realism as Religiously Required The first thing to note is that God must be independent of the conative or practical dimension of religion, of religious responses, for the simple reason that God must be independent of everything other than himself whatsoever. Since this has been established in general in the preceding section, it follows that it must also be true of the special case of religious activities and practices. God must, theologically and ontologically, be independent of human religious attitudes and practices.

The second thing to note is that God must be independent of the element of awareness or cognition which is necessarily present in every genuinely religious activity, for the simple reason that *everything* known must be independent of the knowing of it. This has been established in our first section, and the apprehension of God which is necessarily present in every genuine religious activity is but a special case. Every religious activity necessarily contains, at the very least unconsciously, an awareness of God upon whom that religious activity centers; no *religious* practice can be blind, automatic, or mechanical. Some human behavior may seem outwardly to be religious—the saying of a prayer or the bending of a knee—but it surely cannot be allowed to be genuinely religious unless it is infused by an awareness of God as him to whom the response is directed. The most that can legitimately be said of such automatic behavior is that it is the kind of behavior which would be religious if it were consciously and voluntarily directed to God. Hence God as the object of religious awareness must, like any object of knowledge, be independent of the awareness of him.

Furthermore, this conclusion that God is independent of all other things is required by the religious attitude specifically and uniquely, just in so far as it is truly religious. Schleiermacher made this point when he noted that religion necessarily involves the feeling of absolute dependence on God; and so did Rudolf Otto in his description of the religious attitude as one's relation to the holy, the numinous, to that which is wholly other than the worshiper himself. A God who is regarded as in any way dependent upon the worshiper or upon man or the world may be an object of respect or even admiration, but he cannot be regarded with awe and reverence, the appropriately religious attitudes. This truth that the religious attitude necessarily regards God as absolute, necessary, and independent of the world has in recent years received increasing recognition; and it is most interesting and significant that this recognition has come from unbelievers as well as from believers.

The Flew and MacIntyre volume of *New Essays in Philosophical Theology* is an excellent illustration of this point. Of the four philosophers who discuss the question of the existence of God in Chapters III and IV of that volume, two maintain a theistic position and the other two a nontheistic position; but all four of them agree that God as "the 'adequate object of religious attitudes' " [21] must be absolute, necessary, or independent of the world. Smart writes, "if worship is to be what religion takes it to be, . . . then God must be a necessary being. . . . He must not be just one of the things in the world, however big. To concede that he was just one of the things in the world, even a big one, would reduce religion to something near idolatry. . . ." While "it is not a logical necessity that God exists," he continues, "it would clearly upset the structure of our religious attitudes in the most violent way if we denied it or even entertained the possibility of its falsehood." [22] Findlay agrees, and his account of the necessity, absoluteness, and independence of God as required by the religious attitude is worth quoting at some length:

. . . religious attitudes presume *superiority* in their objects, and such superiority, moreover, as reduces us, who feel the attitudes, to comparative nothingness. For having described a worshipful attitude as one in which we feel disposed to bend the knee before some object, to defer to it wholly, and the like, we find it natural to say that such an attitude can only be fitting where the object reverenced *exceeds* us very vastly. . . . To feel religiously is therefore to presume surpassing greatness in some object. . . . But now we advance further . . . and ask whether it isn't wholly anomalous to worship anything *limited* in any thinkable manner. For all limited superiorities are tainted with an obvious relativity, and can be dwarfed in thought by still mightier superiorities, in which process of being dwarfed they lose their claim upon our worshipful attitudes. And hence we are led on irresistibly to demand that our religious object should have an *unsurpassable* supremacy along all avenues, that it should tower *infinitely* above all other objects . . . there mustn't be anything capable of existing, or of displaying any virtue, without owing all of these absolutely to this single source. . . . But we are also led on irresistibly to a yet more stringent demand . . . we can't help feeling that the worthy object of our worship can never be a thing that merely *happens* to exist, nor one on which all other objects merely *happen* to depend. . . . And so we are led on insensibly to the barely intelligible notion of a Being in whom Essence and Existence lose their separateness. And all that the great medieval thinkers really did was to carry such a development to its logical limit.[23]

An object of any other sort, Findlay goes on to say, might "deserve respect and admiration, . . . but it would not deserve the utter self-abandonment peculiar to the religious frame of mind. It would deserve the *douleia* canonically accorded to the saints, but not the *latreia* that we properly owe to God. . . ."[24]

Of course after giving this correct description of the necessity and independence of God as a requirement of the religious attitude Findlay then argues that such a God "is either senseless or impossible" on the ground, as we saw earlier, that necessity is never existential and existence is never necessary.[25] But this nontheistic conclusion is based, we also saw there, upon a confusion of the real necessity and independence of God with the necessity and independence of a necessary proposition. Still, Findlay's account of the requirement of the religious attitude remains good phenomenology for all that. The religious man turns to God for strength to support him in his weakness, but he would never do so if he believed that God depended on him or upon some other natural thing. The religious man turns to God for help, but he would never do so if he thought that God himself depended on someone or something for help. The religious man turns to God for consolation, but, again, he would never do so if he thought that God himself needed someone to console him. The religious man stands before God in absolute awe and reverence, but he could never do so if he believed that God was relative and depended upon something outside himself for some property or for his very existence. And so on. The God of religion, the God of the heart, like the God of philosophy, the God of the head, must, in order to sustain these attitudes toward him, be necessary, absolute, and independent of the world.

------ ✷ ------

Three conditions, then, are severally necessary and conjointly sufficient for realism in religion: that God exists, that we know something about him and respond to him appropriately, and that he is independent of the world. That God, if he exists, is independent of our knowledge of him is established by the epistemological realism concluded in our first section. But that God does exist, that we know that he does and respond to him, and that we know that he is independent of the world are all established philosophically by the argument from contingency and religiously by the requirements which the religious attitude places upon the identification of its proper object. Therefore also are the meaning and the truth of religious realism established. The epistemological realism of our first section follows from the considerations of our second only as a specifically religious epistemology, not as a general theory of knowledge. In any case, since epistemological realism as a general theory will prove to be the key to the solution of the main problems confronting religious realism, the independent demonstration given earlier will turn out to be vital. These problems confronting religious *realism* arise, of course, from what is distinctively realistic in it; and this is the thesis of the absolute independence of God from all else. Let us turn now to these problems.

PROBLEMS CONFRONTING REALISM
IN RELIGION

Among the many problems associated with a realist philosophy of religion, i.e., connected with the thesis that God is absolutely independent of the world, I want to consider just three basic, interrelated problems arising from this realist thesis: the problems of God's love of the world, God's knowledge of the world, and God's causation of the world.[26] The problem of God's causation of the world in relation to his independence from the world underlies the other two problems, as we shall see.

God's Love of the World   Doesn't the fact that God loves or cares for the world mean that he is, contrary to the tenets of religious realism, dependent upon the world? God needs the world, it would seem, as the object of his loving care, just as the parent who loves his child needs and depends on his child. To love someone would seem to be to sympathize with him, to be concerned about him, to enter into his hopes and fears, to participate in his joys and sorrows. But surely this is to depend on him for those shared joys and sorrows, hopes and fears. So mustn't God too, in so far as he loves the world, depend upon the world for his love of it?

This argument, like any argument, may be met either by denying one of its premises or by denying that the conclusion follows. Aristotle's theological realism takes the former tack; and the religious realisms of Christianity, Judaism, and Islam take the latter.

Aristotle held that God—pure actuality, the unmoved mover, or self-thinking thought—does not love the world and is even oblivious of the world. On this view the problem of the compatibility of God's love of the world with his independence from the world does not even arise. Or perhaps it did arise in Aristotle's mind and perhaps his denial that God loves the world is his solution of the problem. While this move is clearly not open to the Christian, the Jew, or the Muslim, it can make a very strong case for itself, both logically and empirically.

Logically Aristotle's argument would seem to be unimpeachable. God is perfect (purely actual). Therefore he concerns himself only with what is perfect. But the world is imperfect. Hence God cannot concern himself with or love the world; he must rather be concerned only with himself, since he is the only being who is perfect. Epicurus also followed this line of argument except that he placed it in a polytheistic context: the gods live a life of blessedness, blessedness is imperturbability (*ataraxia*), the world is disturbed and disturbing. Therefore the gods are not concerned with the world; it would mar their peace of mind. However distasteful this argument may be to us who are the inheritors of the Judeo-Christian tradition, it is hard to find any logical loopholes in it (not in the polytheism but in the denial of divine concern with the world).

Experientially also the doctrine of divine unconcern can make a very strong case for itself. It is difficult to argue that experience shows us that God loves the world, for the person who claims that God does love the world will not allow any possible experience to count against that claim. The believer

tells us that God loves us as a father loves his children. We are reassured. But then we see a child dying of inoperable cancer of the throat. His earthly father is driven frantic, but his Heavenly Father reveals no obvious sign of concern. Some qualification is made—God's love is "not a merely human love" or it is "an inscrutable love," perhaps—and we realize that such sufferings are quite compatible with the truth of the assertion that "God loves us as a father (but, of course . . .)."[27]

So we begin to see that the person who believes that God loves us will reinterpret every experience which appears to be against that claim in such a way as to make it agree with that claim. We also begin to see that for the believer the claim that God loves us is not empirically falsifiable, and so we begin to wonder whether it is empirically verifiable. If every experience, no matter how opposed it may seem to be, is interpreted in favor of that claim, is any experience really a verification of that claim?

Here one might, however, take the line that the claim that God loves us is empirically falsifiable, and therefore also empirically verifiable, in principle though never in practice.

> Does anything count against the assertion that God is merciful? Yes, [Crombie writes],[28] suffering. Does anything count decisively against it? No, we reply, because it is true. Could anything count decisively against it? Yes, suffering which was utterly, eternally and irredeemably pointless. Can we then design a crucial experiment? No, because we can never see all the picture.

Thus the believer need not let any experience count as evidence against his belief that God loves us. Furthermore, as a believer, as a man of faith, he will not and cannot let any experience count as evidence against his belief that God loves us—or at least he cannot allow anything "to count decisively against it; for he is committed by his faith to trust in God."[29] For the Christian, at least, faith in a loving God is a *virtue*, so that one who does, or even would, let any possible experience lead him to abandon his belief that God loves us would lack the virtue of faith, would have a religious vice, and would therefore not be truly Christian.

Hence the assertion that God loves the world seems to be neither a matter of experience nor a matter of logic—or at least not until "love" is appropriately interpreted. The assertion that God loves the world would seem rather to be a matter of faith. And this brings us to the other way of dealing with the problem of the seeming incompatibility of God's love for the world with his independence from the world.

Aristotle's solution of the problem by means of denying that God does love the world is of course not open to the great revealed religions of the West—Judaism, Christianity, and Islam—for they accept on faith that God loves the world. "For God so loved the world that he gave his only begotten Son, that whosoever believeth on him should not perish but have everlasting life," the Fourth Gospel tells us; so within this context the problem of the seeming incompatibility of divine independence and divine love can be solved only by means of some appropriate understanding either of that love or of that independence or of both.

Of these possibilities it is the first which is the properly religious one, I believe—or at least the properly Christian one. According to Christianity—or at least the traditional understanding of Christianity—God's love of the world does not entail God's dependence upon the world because God's love of the world is charity, not desire. The distinctively divine love—at least so the New Testament tells us—is *agape* or *caritas*, not *eros* or *amor*; it is a love that flows from God's abundance and independence. not from any need to be completed or fulfilled. This is a point which has been made most famously by Anders Nygren in his *Agape and Eros*. God's love of the world is a *charity*—even in the present colloquial use of that term—it is a taking care of the world which arises because the world needs taking care of and is too weak and dependent to take care of itself and because God is able to take care of the world by virtue of his strength and independence. According at least to the traditional understanding of the Christian view, God "will never take . . . reward of any kind"; rather he "helps from the fullness of His love and spiritual strength, not because He needs anything . . . he gives much but receives nothing." [30] God's love is grace, gratis, free.

That God's love of the world does not entail his dependence upon the world—that, on the contrary, it entails his independence of the world— may also be established by an indirect argument. If God's love of the world did entail his dependence upon the world, then it would necessarily follow that God's love of the world would be only *eros*, desire, that it would arise from a deficiency and aim at a selfish gain. But this conflicts both with the philosophical requirement that God be necessary rather than contingent, the first cause of all rather than the effect, and also with the Judeo-Christian-Muslim religious requirement that God's love of the world be *selfless*. If God's love of the world meant that he depended upon the world, then he would be to that degree an effect rather than the first cause, contingent rather than necessary; and he would therefore not be the God required by philosophy. If God's love of the world meant that he depended upon the world, then he would be limited, imperfect, and weak and would thus not be an adequate object of the religious attitude; and he would therefore not be the God required by religion. Hence both the philosophical and the religious attitudes here concur that God's independence of the world is actually entailed by God's love of the world rather than inconsistent with it.

God's Knowledge of the World If God knows the world, either in part or in whole, does this not mean that God depends on the world as the object of his knowledge? This is the second of the fundamental problems confronting religious realism that we must consider and try to solve; and this problem, like the first one posed by God's love of the world, is one which Hartshorne has claimed to be insoluble by religious realism (or "classical theism"). A man depends on the objects of his knowledge for his knowledge of them; if they did not exist he could not know them—at least not truly. By the same token could God know the world if there were no world to know? And if he could not, mustn't he thereby be dependent upon the world and thus not be absolutely independent of it as the religious realist claims?

Like the argument from God's love of the world, this argument may be met either by denying the premise that God knows the world or by claiming that the conclusion of God's dependence upon the world does not follow from his knowledge of the world. Aristotle takes the former course, and the main line of the Judeo-Christian-Muslim tradition follows the latter.

From the point of view of Aristotle's theological realism the problem of the compatibility of God's knowledge of the world with his independence of the world does not even arise, any more than the problem of the compatibility of God's independence with his love did; for Aristotle held that God does *not* know the world. Or perhaps this problem did arise in Aristotle's mind after all, and his denial of God's knowledge of the world was his way of solving the problem. According to Aristotle, God must be oblivious of the world for exactly the same reasons that he cannot love the world: God is perfect, purely actual. The world is imperfect, partly potential. Therefore if God were to have knowledge of the world he would be involving himself in something imperfect. But this is self-contradictory and impossible. Therefore God cannot think about the world; he can think only about himself: he is self-thinking thought. This argument actually seems to concede the validity of the objection we are considering; it seems to concede that *if* God were aware of the world he could not be perfect and independent of the world. The Western religious tradition of realism will of course not concede this, as we shall shortly see. On the other hand, there is a sense in which God does know the world, according to Aristotle, for in knowing himself as pure actuality and as that at which all natural things aim and which they partially realize in becoming partially actual, God thereby knows the distilled essence or actuality *of* the world; by knowing himself God also knows the world just in so far as it is actual. As we shall shortly see, moreover, this view even approaches the view of the Western religious tradition of realism. But in knowing the world in so far as it is actual, God would seem not to be knowing the world in itself and properly speaking, according to Aristotle, because the world is also partly potential. Hence in the last analysis it seems correct to say that Aristotle solves—or dissolves—the problem of the compatibility of God's knowledge and independence of the world by asserting that God does not have any knowledge of the world.

While such a theory is unacceptable to the Jew, the Christian, and the Muslim, it should be noted that it can make a strong case for itself on both empirical and logical grounds—just like Aristotle's theory that God does not love the world. Aristotle can make a strong empirical case for his view that God has no knowledge of the world (*as* the *world*) in exactly the same way as that in which he could for his claim that God does not love the world.[31] If every possible thing in the world is known by God (if God is omniscient), then nothing in experience could possibly count against the claim that God is omniscient. On this basis it is hard to see how the claim that God knows the world could be an *empirical* claim—and, indeed, few or none who make this claim do hold it to be an empirical one.

Aristotle can *logically* sustain the view that God has no knowledge of the world, furthermore, because such a view is not at all incompatible with either of the two basic roles played by the concept of God in Aristotle's philosophy. One of these, the more general one, is that of being the first cause of the world. Without having to know the world, God can, in Aristotle's philosophy, be the first cause of the world in a certain sense—by his causing the world only as being its goal or final cause. God causes or moves the world as does the object of desire, according to Aristotle, without being himself caused or moved by what he moves. God is the unmoved mover, moving things while remaining wholly unmoved by and unaware of the things which he moves. Besides being consistent with the function of God as first cause, this conception of God as solely a telic cause avoids serious problems which arise from making God also an efficient cause—especially the problem whether God as an efficient cause can remain unmoved and uncaused as he must in order truly to remain God.

Yet this easier attainment of consistency manifests a serious limitation of God's causation in Aristotle's philosophy, for God can be solely a final or goal cause only because the *existence* of a world to *have* God for its goal is presupposed. In order for something to move toward a certain goal it must first exist, and this existence of the world seems not to have been considered by Aristotle in his recourse to God as the first cause. Aristotle's is "a god who is doubtless the cause of all being, including its intelligibility, efficiency, and finality—all, save existence itself," Gilson writes, while "on the Christian side" stands "a God Who causes the very existence of being." [32] This deeper question of the existence of the world and its corresponding answer of God as the cause of that existence is basically what requires the medieval addition of efficiency to the ancient finality of God's causation.

The other basic, but more restricted, role played by the concept of God in Aristotle's philosophy—the role of being the good at which all life aims—can also be sustained consistently with the view that God is unaware of the world: a natural ethic requires only that the moral agent be aware of his goal, not that the goal be aware of the moral agent. Once more, however, Aristotle's concept of God as unaware of the world can perform its function only by overlooking the fundamental question of the cause of the very existence of the world and of life. It is this question and the claim that God is the answer by being the cause of the very existence of the world which led medieval philosophy to regard God as efficient as well as final cause, and this in turn was perhaps the main natural (as distinguished from revealed) reason for the medieval claim that God knows the world.

Now isn't this claim of medieval religious realism that God knows the world incompatible with its assertion that God is independent of the world? Here clearly the realist can solve the problem only by showing that the conclusion does not follow from the premises. The view that God's knowledge of the world makes him dependent upon the world rests on a confusion of know*ing* with *that which* is known. Hartshorne makes this mistake, for example: ". . . knowledge is deficient unless it fully and literally contains its objects," he writes.[33] "In the clearest case of direct and certain knowing—thus . . . when we know a color, a sensory quality—it is . . . clear that this quality becomes a determination of our own actuality, our own experience." [34] But "knowing" and "experience" are here certainly ambiguous; from the fact that the knowing is part of the knower it does not follow that the known is.[35] Obviously and tautologically anything known or experienced is part of one's knowledge and experience, but it certainly does not follow from this that the thing known is part of the knower's "own actuality" or experienc*ing;* even one who sees red does not thereby become red. Hence things which are known need not be parts of the knowing or knower of them, and hence the knower need not depend on them; such does not follow from the fact that these things are known. Furthermore, when the knowing is a divine knowing and the knower is God and when the thing which is known is the world, then the thing which is known cannot be a part of the knowing or the knower on which the knower depends, for then the knower could not be God. This is true for a number of reasons.

In the first place God is simple; this follows from the conclusion of the argument from contingency that God is a necessary being. For if God were not simple but had parts, then it would be possible for those parts to be separated from each other and it would be necessary to have a cause of their being held together. But what could such a cause be? It could not be either of the parts, for the cause of the togetherness of the parts must be distinct from either of the parts being held together.

And the cause could not be God himself, for now God himself is merely the two parts taken together; and what needs explaining is exactly the togetherness of these two parts, that is to say, God himself. Hence the cause of the togetherness of these two parts, the cause of God himself, would have to be something other than God. But then God would be an *effect* rather than the cause of all, and as such he would be *contingent* rather than necessary. But then he would exactly not be God at all as he is required to be both by philosophy and by the religious attitude. Hence God cannot really have any parts at all, and *a fortiori* he cannot have the world or any of its parts as parts. Hence he cannot depend on the world as a part of himself.

In the second place God is unchanging, nontemporal, pure actuality. This also follows both from the argument from contingency and from the exigencies of the religious attitude, for if God were changing, or temporal, or partly potential he could not be either a necessary being and the first cause of all or the proper object of awe and reverence. But this world and all its parts are changing, temporal, and partly potential. Hence God cannot include the world or any parts of the world within himself. Therefore it follows again that God is not dependent upon any such things as parts of himself. If he were he would simply not be God; he would not satisfy either the philosophical or the religious requirements. Furthermore and finally, God is not dependent upon anything at all— parts of himself or not; this too follows from the philosophical requirement that God be necessary rather than contingent and the religious requirement that God be absolutely independent. Again, a dependent "God" would simply not be God.

The essence of this argument depends upon the simple logical fact, nicely described and illustrated by Smart,[36] that if an argument is valid one may argue from the falsity of its conclusion to the falsity of one or more of its premises just as well as from the truth of its premises to the truth of its conclusion. While the nonrealist, for example Hartshorne, argues from the truth of the premises that "God's knowledge of the world entails his dependence on the world" and "God has knowledge of the world" to the truth of the conclusion that "God depends on the world," the realist can just as validly argue from the falsity of the conclusion, "God does not depend on the world," to the falsity of either premise, that "God does not have knowledge of the world" (Aristotle) or that "God's knowledge of the world does not entail his dependence on the world" (e.g., St. Thomas). So the question really becomes: Is there more reason for believing in the falsity of the conclusion than in the truth of the premises? And to this question the realist, as we have seen, answers emphatically Yes. For he is convinced, by the arguments which have been presented, that the conclusion that God depends on the world must be false since it conflicts with both philosophical and religious requirements; so he concludes that one of the premises must be false—here that God's knowledge of the world entails his dependence upon it. All that the realist need do in addition is to show *how* that premise is false, and this we have just done by showing that while the knowledge is part of the knower, the thing which is known need not be.

At this point, however, the nonrealist may again object. "If I come into existence at a certain time, then doesn't God's knowing of me also come into existence at that time so that, once again, God depends upon something in the world for his knowledge of it?" No, the realist once more replies, for this objection too is based upon a misunderstanding of the nature of God; it forgets that it is *God* that we are talking about. God is eternal, nontemporal; we have seen that this is necessary both for philosophical and for religious reasons. Hence God's knowing must likewise be eternal or nontemporal. Hence God doesn't *come* to know me when I come to exist; he *timelessly* knows me in an eternal "now." It is this position which we earlier saw approximated by Aristotle's position concerning God's knowledge of the world.[37] The critic may rejoin that on this view God knows that I exist *before* I actually do—which is a contradiction. Not at all, the realist replies, because "before" is a time word and, once again, there can be no time in God. By the same token, it should here be noted, all talk about God's *fore*knowledge and its relation to his *fore*ordination is based upon the same mistake.

Knowing is thus a property of the knower; but that which is known need not be, and when it is the world which is known by God it cannot be. God is eternal and independent of all other things; this is required both by philosophical argument and by religious attitudes. From this it follows that God and his knowing are independent of the world. Here again the critic may object. Does not knowing the world entail and therefore logically depend upon an object, the world to be known? But in the first place, the realist replies, even supposing that God's knowing the *world* depends on the world. God's *knowing*, his knowing *something*, doesn't depend on the world, for God would still be omniscient even if there were no world. God's omniscience depends only on his knowing whatever there is, and there doesn't have to be a world—it is contingent. Hence God's omniscience doesn't depend on the world. In the second place, even if we were to grant the objection that God as knower of the *world* depends on the world as the object of his knowledge, God still remains, in the last analysis, independent of the world. For since the world itself depends for its very existence and nature upon God, the most that would follow is that God depends on that which depends upon himself—in short, that God depends only on himself. Hence again God is independent of the world. But this point about the world's depending on God takes us to the last of the three problems confronting religious realism: the problem of causation.

God's Causing of the World   If God is to some extent immanent in the
world, as all the great Western religions
claim, then isn't God thereby dependent upon the world? The first thing
to note here is that such divine immanence is a *causal* immanence: it
says that God wills and causes the world and the various things in it. The
next thing to note is that while the effect is by definition dependent upon
its cause, the cause is by definition independent of its effect. Hence it
follows that God's causal immanence in the world does not conflict with,
but on the contrary actually entails, his independence or transcendence
of the world.

But does not God *as* cause *of the world* logically and necessarily depend on the world? If there were no world that God caused, could God
be the cause of it? If there is no food in the icebox can you eat it? "God
causes the world but there isn't any world" makes no more sense, the
objection continues. Hence does not God's being the cause of the world
logically and ontologically require that he be *dependent* on the world?

Here we are at the essence of this third problem confronting religious
realism, and this essence of the third problem is also the root of the
other two problems—the problems of God's love and knowledge of the
world—for God's *caritas* of the world is a case of his causing the world
(or something in it), we have seen, and his knowing the world is also
a case of his causing the world and his knowing of it. Hence we are here
at the most basic general problem confronting a realist philosophy of
religion. This is the problem of the relation of a cause to its effect.

Now the realist maintains that cause-effect *means* independence-de-
pendence (necessity-contingency). The cause cannot with consistency be
said to depend on its effect. To say that E is the effect of C is to say that
E *depends* on C. Now if this means that C is also dependent on E by
virtue of being the cause of it, it necessarily follows that C is the *effect*
of E rather than its cause, and also that E is the *cause* of C rather that its
effect. But this is self-contradictory.

Here the critic may try to preserve his position that the cause is as
cause dependent upon its effect by dividing the cause, and also the effect,
into two parts. E_1 is then said to be the effect of and hence dependent
upon C_1, and C_1 the cause of and hence independent of E_1, while C_2 is
said to be the effect of and hence dependent upon E_2, and E_2 the cause
of and hence independent of C_2. Granted. But all this has done, the
realist points out, is to divide a complex situation into two different causal
connections; in each of these two it still remains true that the *cause* is
independent of *its* effect. E_2 is the cause of and hence independent of
C_2, and C_1 is the cause of and hence independent of E_1. Here, however,
the critic may rejoin that C_2 as well as C_1 is an aspect of God, and that
with respect to his C_2 aspect God is dependent upon E_2, dependent upon
the world as the cause of God. While God *as cause* is independent of the

world, the critic grants, God as cause *of the world* is the *effect* of the world and hence dependent upon it. This is the position of Whitehead and Hartshorne: God has both a primordial and a consequent nature; while his primordial nature is independent of the world, his consequent nature is dependent upon it.

This position seems to differ only verbally from the realist theory of the independence of God from the world, however; for isn't "God as dependent" (as effect) simply the *world?*[38] The critic's "consequent nature of God" is the realist's "world," and the realist's "world" is the critic's "consequent nature of God." Both positions maintain that reality contains both an independent, necessary, eternal factor and a dependent, contingent, temporal factor. Hence the issue is one to which the famous passage from the conclusion of Hume's *Dialogues Concerning Natural Religion* might well apply, *mutatis mutandis.* "I ask the [critic] if he does not allow that there is [in reality something independent, necessary, and eternal:] The more pious he is, the more readily will he assent. . . . I next turn to the [realist] and I ask him, whether [there is not also something dependent, contingent, and temporal:] He will readily acknowledge it. . . . Where then, cry I to both these antagonists, is the subject of your dispute?" And so far as the choice of words is concerned, granting that it is somewhat arbitrary, the realist must agree with Schopenhauer: "To call the world God is not to explain it, but only to enrich language with a superfluous synonym of the word 'world.' Whether . . . 'the world is God,' or 'the world is the world,' comes to the same thing." [39]

If the critic replies, however, that this is not a verbal disagreement at all, that the world is *really* an aspect of God, then he must contradict himself by having either two "Gods" or one God with two contradictory attributes—and both alternatives are, of course, unacceptable on both philosophical and religious grounds. The religions we are presumably talking about are all monotheistic; and besides, if there were two different "Gods" neither could be an adequate object of the religious attitude, for neither could possess the unsurpassable awesomeness which is the proper object of reverence. Nor could they satisfy the demands of the argument from contingency, for the secondness of each "God" would make it contingent upon the other "God" for its secondness, but then neither would be a noncontingent or necessary or independent being —neither would be *God*. Nor would one God with two contradictory attributes be any more acceptable—and they *would* be contradictory for, as we have seen, God must be simple, and a simple being cannot be both independent and dependent, both necessary and contingent. In reply to this, however, Hartshorne holds that these two attributes are not contradictory: they are both instances of absolute superiority or unsurpassability—and from God's possession of both types of superiority it follows that God cannot be simple. Divine superiority means, for Hartshorne, a superiority in dependence, contingency, and relativity just as much as a superiority in independence, necessity, and absoluteness: ". . . to depend . . . upon all other things, is . . . a unique maximum, since ordinary things depend only upon some other things. . . ." [40] But such a claim, the realist insists, rests on a misunderstanding of the nature of dependence, etc., for "superiority" in *dependence* is exactly *inferiority* and thus a contradiction in terms. The maximum of dependency is rather dependency *in every respect* than dependency on *everything*—to be helpless, to have next to no being. Furthermore, such utter dependency upon everything would violate the religious requirement by making God an inadequate object of reverence and worship. How can one worship something which is dependent upon everything, including oneself?

Although I do not think that *this* attempt to avoid verbalism can be sustained, I do believe that there is indeed a real, nonverbal difference between the realist and his critic; and this difference returns us to the most fundamental problem confronting realism: the problem of the relation of a cause to its effect. While I have argued that God cannot depend on the world since God is the cause rather than the effect of the world, the critic again objects: "(God-as-cause-of-the-world) depends on (the-world) because the latter is contained in the former as one of its essential parts." When the critic puts his point in this way the realist must agree. But—and this is the most basic question—what kind of dependence is this? It cannot be a *real, existential* dependence, for, as we have seen, there would then arise the contradiction that the cause of the world is not the cause of the world but its effect—or else the contradiction that there are two "Gods" or one "God" with two opposite natures.

Hence the critic's kind of dependence of the cause upon its effect, the dependence arising from the fact that "cause-of-the-world" entails "the-world," *can only be a logical or epistemic dependence.* Insofar as a thing is the real, existential cause of the *being* of something else, it cannot *really, existentially* depend on that something else for its *being.* But the cause can and often does depend on its effect for its being *known*, for our *knowledge* of it—both our knowledge of it in itself and also our knowledge of it as the cause of something else. The rain that makes the sidewalk wet isn't caused by, doesn't depend on, the wetness of the sidewalk; but our *knowledge* that it rained and that the rain caused the wetness of the sidewalk is caused by and does depend on the wetness of the sidewalk. Hence a real, existential cause can depend on its effect only epistemically or logically. The effect may be the cause of our *knowing* its existential cause; but the effect cannot, on pain of contradiction, be the cause of the *being* of its existential cause. The world is the cause of our knowing God, and God is the cause of the world. But the world cannot be said, without self-contradiction, to be the cause of *God* or of God's causing the world.

But what, it may be asked, is the justification for this distinction between a real or existential cause, on the one hand, and an epistemic or logical cause, on the other? The justification is simply the difference between *being* and *knowing*. Since being and knowing are different things, a property of knowing need not be a property of being. And in the present case it cannot be. That which is known is independent of the knowing of it. This was established in our first section and it is the essence of realism as a general theory of knowledge. Hence this independence of the real or existential order in a causal situation from the cognitive or epistemic order is simply a special case of realism, and it too is therefore true. Hence also the independence of the real causal order from the cognitive causal order in the case of our knowledge of God's causing the world is also simply a special case of the truth of the independence of *every* real causal order from the corresponding cognitive causal order, and therefore also a special case of realism, and it too is therefore true. Hence God's really causing the world does not entail his real dependence upon the world but on the contrary his real independence of the world. Hence God *is* and *remains* really independent of the world he causes, and of the world he loves, and of the world he knows.

So even though God as *known* to be the cause of the world ("God-as-cause-of-the-world")[41] is dependent upon the world as known to be the effect of God ("world-as-effect-of-God")—which is itself dependent on the real world—it does not follow and it cannot be the case that God *himself*, who *really is* the cause of the world and therefore of our knowledge of him, is *really*, existentially, dependent on the world.[42] Hence the epistemological realism established in our first section, while not directly necessary to the establishment of religious realism, turns out to be absolutely necessary for the maintenance and defense of religious realism against its opponents.

NOTES FOR CHAPTER 4

1   See, for example, Charles Hartshorne and William L. Reese, *Philosophers Speak of God*, Chicago, The University of Chicago Press, 1953.
2   In "A Demonstration of Epistemological Realism," *International Philosophical Quarterly*, Vol. II, No. 3 (September 1962), pp. 367-393, I tried to define and demonstrate realism as a theory of knowledge in terms of six propositions of which the thesis of cognitive independence was only one. But since this thesis is the most important of those six propositions (I believe) and since it states the very essence of realism, I shall here restrict myself to this one proposition. The following definition and demonstration of cognitive independence as the core of realism is a shortened form of the account given on pp. 378-384 of this "Demonstration."
3   At least in cases of genuine knowledge, in cases of veracious cognition. The question of the cognitive independence of the objects of erroneous cognitions I have discussed at length in "On the Being of Falsity," pp. 290-316 of

Philosophy of Knowledge, edited by Roland Houde and Joseph P. Mullally, Philadelphia, Lippincott, 1960.

4 Peter Bertocci, "The Nature of Cognition," *Review of Metaphysics*, Vol. VIII (1954), p. 59.

5 Although this revised constructionist position does escape, by conceding the point, the contradiction just discussed, there is another contradiction which it cannot escape even when it grants the realist thesis of cognitive independence. This is the contradiction of knowing something which it declares to be unknowable. On this see "A Demonstration of Epistemological Realism," *loc. cit.*, pp. 384-387.

6 Cognitive creationism also falls into another contradiction, that of knowing unknowables, namely other minds, human or divine, as independently real things in themselves not created by the acts of knowing them. To escape this contradiction cognitive creationism must maintain that there is only one knowing mind and that everything knowable is created by the knowing of this single mind. On this see "A Demonstration of Epistemological Realism," *loc. cit.*, pp. 387-388.

7 Etienne Gilson, "Le réalisme méthodique," translated by W. J. Quinn and printed in Houde and Mullally, *Philosophy of Knowledge*, p. 386.

8 Aristotle, *Nicomachean Ethics*, VI, 1139 b 31-1140 a 8.

9 Aristotle, *Metaphysics*, 993 b 24-31.

10 A. J. Ayer, *Language, Truth, and Logic*, London, 1946, p. 79.

11 *Ibid.*, p. 84.

12 C. L. Lewis, *Mind and the World Order*, New York, Scribner's, 1929, p. 306.

13 The argument in this passage was used in a different context in my "Traditional Reason and Modern Reason" in *Faith and Philosophy*, edited by Alvin Plantinga, Grand Rapids, Eerdmans, 1964, pp. 48-49.

14 Gilson, *loc. cit.*

15 Aquinas, *Summa Theologica*, Ia. ii. 3, from *St. Thomas Aquinas, Philosophical Texts*, translated and edited by Thomas Gilby, New York, Oxford University Press, 1951, p. 56. Italics mine.

16 Aquinas, *Summa Contra Gentiles*, I, 15, as translated in Gilby, *op. cit.*, p. 57.

17 A. Flew and A. MacIntyre, *New Essays in Philosophical Theology*, New York, Macmillan, 1955, p. 54.

18 *Ibid.*, pp. 38-39.

19 That some logically necessary propositions are also existential or factual I have tried to demonstrate in the essay referred to in Note 13 above. For other attempts to demonstrate it, see Henry Veatch, "On Trying to Say and to Know What's What," *Philosophy and Phenomenological Research*, Vol. XXIV, No. 1 (September 1963), pp. 83-96, and also his "The Truths of Metaphysics," *Review of Metaphysics*, Vol. XVII, No. 3 (March 1964), pp. 372-395.

20 Flew and MacIntyre, *op. cit.*, p. 68.

21 Flew and MacIntyre, *op. cit.*, p. 48 (Findlay).

22 *Ibid.*, p. 40.

23 *Ibid.*, pp. 51-52.

24 *Ibid.*, p. 53.

25 Pp. 93-94 above.

26 My appreciation of the importance of these problems and my struggles to solve them are due largely to the writings of Charles Hartshorne, who

maintains that God is independent of the world in only one aspect of his nature, that in another aspect of his nature he is dependent upon the world. While this section does try to deal very briefly with some of the problems Hartshorne has discussed at great length and with great subtlety and rigor, I am fully conscious that the following considerations will not be very adequate—and certainly not as extensive as the problems demand. One might therefore read in connection with this present section Hartshorne's essay in the present volume, and also some of his many other writings in the philosophy of religion.

27 Antony Flew, in Flew and MacIntyre, *op. cit.*, pp. 98-99.
28 *Ibid.*, p. 124.
29 *Ibid.*, p. 103 (Mitchell).
30 Alexander F. Skutch, *The Quest of the Divine*, Boston, Meador, 1956, p. 75. This book is nonrealist in certain respects, however.
31 See pp. 99-102 above.
32 Etienne Gilson, *The Spirit of Medieval Philosophy*, translated by A. H. C. Downes, New York, Scribner's, 1940, p. 81.
33 Hartshorne and Reese, *Philosophers Speak of God*, p. 18b.
34 *Ibid.*, p. 271a.
35 I tried to make this point in a discussion of *Philosophers Speak of God:* "Head, Heart, and God," *Review of Metaphysics*, Vol. XIV, No. 2 (December 1960), p. 345.
36 Flew and MacIntyre, *op. cit.*, pp. 30-31.
37 See p. 102 above.
38 This is a point I tried to make in "Head, Heart, and God," *loc. cit.*, pp. 348-349.
39 *Selected Essays of Schopenhauer*, translated by E. Belfort Bax, London, George Bell & Sons, 1914, Section 619 (pp. 192-193).
40 *Philosophers Speak of God*, p. 505a.
41 I suggest that it is very significant that Hartshorne frequently uses such argument by hyphenation. On this see "Head, Heart, and God," *loc. cit.*, pp. 338-339 and 344-345.
42 This independence of the real from our knowledge of it—of the existential from the cognitive—is exactly the reason that realists have historically rejected the ontological argument; for its validity presupposes a dependence of the real upon the cognitive. *If* the concept of existence is entailed in the concept of God, it is only the *concept* of existence, after all; and, without the antirealist presupposition that the real depends on the cognitive, it is a far cry from this concept of God's existence to its independent reality.

QUESTIONS

1 What is the core meaning of "realism," in all areas, according to this essay?
2 What is the basic structure of the proffered demonstration of realism as a general theory of knowledge?
3 How exactly does this essay argue that realism in religion is required philosophically or theoretically?
4 How exactly does this essay argue that realism in religion is required by religious attitudes?
5 What is the key to the solution of the final and most basic problem confronting realism as a philosophy of religion, according to this essay?

SUGGESTED READINGS

Charles Hartshorne and William L. Reese, *Philosophers Speak of God*, Chicago: The University of Chicago Press, 1953, especially the Introduction, Epilogue, and Chapters II, III, VII, and VIII.

Francis H. Parker, "Head, Heart, and God," *Review of Metaphysics, Vol.* XIV, No. 2 (December 1960), pp. 328-352.

————, "A Demonstration of Epistemological Realism," *International Philosophical Quarterly*, Vol. II, No. 3 (September 1962), pp. 367-393.

Thomas Gilby (translator and editor), *St. Thomas Aquinas Philosophical Texts*, New York, Oxford University Press, 1951, Chapters II-VI.

Antony Flew and Alasdair MacIntyre, *New Essays in Philosophical Theology*, New York, Macmillan, 1955, Chapters II-VI.

Charles Hartshorne and John Wild, debate in *Review of Metaphysics*, Vol. II (1948-49), pp. 65-77, and Vol. IV (1950-51), pp. 31-84.

5 *J. F. Ross*

Religion in the Neo-Scholastic Tradition

Religion has always been the object of *rational* investigation by the neo-scholastics, and this on the unconcealed hypothesis that such investigation will bring forth scientific support for religion which would not otherwise be available.

Scholastics and Neo-Scholastics   I. M. Bochenski has said: "Philosophy can construct a theory of natural religion in complete independence of revelation; Thomism has always done so, especially in recent times." [1]

Bochenski's statement reiterates the claim that neo-scholastic philosophy is intimately associated with *rational* (scientific) investigation of religion and has an object more specific than merely to discover the truth, whatever it may be; that object is to find *scientific evidence* for the truth or at least the reasonableness of what religion proposes for belief.

Some people, upon learning this, lose sympathy with the neo-scholastics, thinking that they have a preconception of the outcome of their investigation and cannot be objective. Such thinking involves two mistakes: (1) a forgetting that no useful and complex investigation can be conducted without a hypothesis or a series of hypotheses to be established or rejected; (2) a forgetting that there is no reason to believe that a man who thinks he knows what his investigation will disclose is thereby rendered incompetent to investigate; on the contrary should he happen to have conjectured well, he may be all the more competent to investigate.

Bochenski's statement also calls attention to three questions which must be settled at the outset of this essay: (1) What religion are we talking about? (There has been little or nothing of the Hindu religion considered in the tradition of neo-scholasticism, nor has there been anything of Muslemism). (2) What thinkers are neo-scholastic? Are they Thomists (disciples of St. Thomas Aquinas) as the quotation from Bochenski might suggest? (3) Are the neo-scholastics to be called philosophers, theologians, anthropologists, or what?

In this essay we shall speak of those neo-scholastic thinkers who are primarily philosophers, although very many of them are also theologians and although it is virtually impossible to ignore their theological environment; as philosophers they have espoused a special method of handling problems and of resolving disputes which does not entirely coincide with the method they employ as theologians. This must be remembered when the thoughts of these neo-scholastic philosophers on the subject of religion are compared with some works of other writers such as Tillich, Niebuhr, and Barth who are primarily theologians, employ different methods of theory construction and problem resolution, and do not make the distinction between theology and philosophy which has always been thought by neo-scholastics to be of paramount importance.

The term "neo-scholastic" is quite properly applicable to any thinker who attempts a systematic restatement and development of the doctrine of one of the medieval Aristotelian, Platonic, or Augustinian thinkers who have usually been called scholastics. Thus it is as proper to call a neo-Scotist (a philosopher who develops the position of the Franciscan Doctor John Duns Scotus) a neo-scholastic, as it is to so call a neo-Thomist (a follower of St. Thomas). In this broader sense there have been countless neo-scholastic philosophers in the last century, and their discussions of religion have been more varied than we shall be able to illustrate.

Yet the student interested in the philosophical investigation of religion ought to realize that there were several diverse tendencies among scholastic philosophers; for example, (1) the distaste for dialectical analysis expressed by Bernard of Clairvaux, with the resulting emphasis (by some recent philosophers) upon personal experience as the sole evidence for religious truth; (2) the emphasis upon vestigial or innate traces of God in the soul of man, characteristic of St. Bonaventure's thought and of many other Franciscan thinkers in the Middle Ages, an emphasis which has had its main modern expression in the claim that no one is *really* an atheist and that all moral experience is grounded in an inbred consciousness of the person of God;[2] and (3) the apriorism and logical formalism of Duns Scotus' approach to God. These tendencies are very much alive among neo-scholastic thinkers; and as historical scholarship on the teachings of the medieval originators of these tendencies becomes more refined, the modern expositors of their thought can be expected to make important contributions to the philosophy of religion by undertaking new theoretical expressions of these time-honored differences in attitude.

The scholastic and neo-scholastic philosophical tradition has been vitally and pre-eminently concerned with religion, but not with "religion" in the abstract (though there have been some penetrating discussions of the concept "religion"). Rather, neo-scholasticism has always been concerned with the *Christian faith as taught by the Catholic Church*. And while it is true that many of the arguments produced and many of the conclusions reached by the scholastic philosophers would be acceptable to any but the most "liberal" of Christian groups, the scholastic philosopher-theologians were not concerned with whether or not this broad acceptability of their conclusions would be a result of their work, but were primarily concerned with the presentation of justifications and explanations of the beliefs basic to the Christian faith (as taught by the Catholic Church) and with the systematic development of the revelation of God as they understood it.

This commitment to the Christian faith and to a particular exponent of what the Christian faith is is not due to some peculiarity of the philosophical method employed by these philosophers. Many conservative Protestant theologians might well be called neo-scholastic both with respect to their conclusions and with respect to their close adherence to the propositions which I shall indicate as especially characteristic of the neo-scholastic tradition. Yet it must be acknowledged that although there is a great similarity between the method and teaching of Aquinas and his non-Christian contemporary Moses Maimonides, it is a fact that thinkers are not usually called scholastic or neo-scholastic unless they work within the dogmatic framework of the Catholic Church; thus Maimonides was a non-scholastic medieval philosopher.

The enormous differences in philosophical doctrine which are found among the neo-scholastics are often concealed by our saying that they are strongly influenced by medieval Aristotelian philosophy; for this leads one to think that they agree in what they attribute to Aristotle's metaphysical system. Nothing could be further from the truth; there is *at most* among the thinkers a striking resemblance on the points that I shall emphasize and upon a few other basic philosophical conclusions. The mere fact that medieval scholastics were greatly influenced by Plato and Augustine, besides being influenced profoundly by Aristotle, should suggest the wide variety of doctrinal mixtures and emphases to be found in their work. The very great differences of basic outlook to which I referred above in mentioning Scotus, St. Bernard of Clairvaux, St. Bonaventure, and St. Thomas are important in this area of consideration because they show that the philosophical method employed by the scholastic writers is not dictated by the particular religion they primarily investigate; and the obvious divergency of method and emphasis in their work shows that their primary interest in the Christian faith as taught by the Catholic Church is not dictated by their methods either and apparently their religious commitments impose little restraint upon their philosophical speculations.

We consider the salient characteristics of this approach to religion in the following eight sections (of which the first is the longest and most fundamental).

Faith and Reason BOTH THE ACTIVITY OF FAITH AND THE ACTIVITY OF REASON ARE WAYS OF ARRIVING AT KNOWLEDGE. This has as a subsidiary the important claim: *Both faith and reason are ways of arriving at knowledge of God and of God's will for men.*

When one reads such writers as St. Thomas Aquinas, Francisco Suárez, and such modern writers as Maritain, Gilson, De Raeymaker and Garrigou-Lagrange,[3] one might (upon superficially considering them) be led to think that they do not consider faith to be a source of anything more than belief or opinion. But this is not so. The term "belief" functions in many ways in neo-scholastic thought, often designating the *state of adherence* to a proposition or to a way of life ("belief that" or "belief in"), often designating a *state of opinion* and often a *state of knowledge*. These are, of course, not the same thing, and the third is the most important. Something is known by someone only if he believes that it is the case, and if it *is* the case, and if he has a good reason for his holding it to be the case.

Aquinas and his successors (even the non-Thomists) have always tenaciously insisted that faith can fulfill just such conditions, that faith can be a source of knowledge.[4] Although faith is a state, it is also an activity. One is said to *exercise* faith, to come to God *by faith*, etc. So, there is at least one way other than reasoning for a man to acquire knowledge: and that is to exercise faith.

Faith is divided into human faith and divine faith, and is generally referred to as a way of arriving at belief (a *state* of adherence to the truth) through the acceptance of the testimony of someone else as being authoritative. The fact that the term "belief" occurs in this explication must not be contrasted with the fact that "knowledge" does not occur here. For it is assumed in the context that the religious propositions to be discussed are true and it is the origin of the *psychological* event of *acceptance* (which a man could have even if his belief were false), which must be explained, not the epistemic event of having a *true* belief.[5] Moreover the *quality* of the testimony is crucial to whether or not a state of *knowledge* or a state of *false* belief or a state of true but *unjustified* belief is produced. As a result the definition of "faith" is left neutral, and it is said that faith is *sometimes* a source of knowledge but need not always be. For example, if a fully authoritative professor of physics should tell me that something, *p*, is the case and should in fact be lying, I will have every reason to accept what he says as true (assuming that I have no corresponding expertise in the area and no reason to think that what he says is false), but while I will be brought to a state of *belief*, I shall not be brought to *know*, although, of course, I shall be brought to *think* I know something. Yet when such an authority tells me what *he knows* to be the truth, I shall by my acceptance of his authority and by my grasping his pronouncement be brought to know something which I might not have known otherwise. This activity of accepting the authoritative testimony of other people is the activity or exercise of "human faith."

The very fact that we know so many things which we have not discovered for ourselves shows that faith *can* give knowledge (assuming that we find out what we have not discovered only by *being told*). Would any American student deny that he knows who is the President of the United States? Yet in most cases he cannot truthfully say he has found it out for himself and he probably would not know in certain extreme circumstances how to go about discovering it for himself, should he begin to wonder about the reliability of the usual human witnesses.

Divine faith is also described as a state and as an activity. As an *activity* of some human being, the exercise of divine faith gives knowledge. As an activity, divine faith is the accepting of certain propositions upon the authority of God who is taken to reveal them. As a *state* of faith, a man has divine faith when he is in fact committed to the truth of some proposition because it has been revealed by God. This definition allows for the possibility that a man may be deceived into thinking that he accepts some proposition upon the teaching of God when he is in fact not doing so (because God has not revealed that proposition). In such a case, insofar as the activity of accepting what one takes to be revealed is virtuous, the act is virtuous or worthy; but insofar as the activity is supposed to result in knowledge, the activity fails. In such a case we have an activity *in accordance with* the virtue of divine faith, but an activity which is not an activity *of* divine faith.[6] Yet it must be noted (and this clarifies even more the essential distinction between true belief and knowledge) that a man may come to believe (e.g., that he is destined for salvation) by thinking that God has revealed it to him when in fact God has not done so. This has its parallel in human faith, when Jones takes it to be the case that a war has begun (when in fact it has) because he thinks a certain general who would know has said so (when he has in fact not said so). Jones would think he knows when he has only a true belief; for in our own case the distinction of true belief from knowledge tends to break down since *we* never have the equipment by which to make the distinction in our own present case even when such a distinction is applicable to us by someone else.

The distinction between true belief and knowledge need not be applied to the doctrines of the Christian faith as they are understood by the neo-scholastics. For they are considered to be revealed by God and are therefore true. Hence anyone who accepts these doctrines because God revealed them will have knowledge. This is the way the scholastics justify the claim that divine faith (when it is *act* of divine faith) always gives knowledge; they appear to assume that a person who mistakes a proposition for something revealed by God and accepts it, has acted *in accord with* the virtue of divine faith (perhaps by habit) but has not acted *from* it. This raises the nice question of whether to come to know something by faith (whether divine or human) a man must already know something on his own or by reason. Does a person have to know by reason that God revealed truths to man in order to accept a certain proposition *p* as having been revealed by God? The answer seems to be No, but the neo-scholastics have not made themselves unambiguous over whether a man must know by divine faith that God reveals himself or whether one can know this by human faith. This is a serious problem; for if one can know that God has revealed himself only by divine faith, then one must already know that God reveals himself in order to have the divine faith required to come to knowledge that God has revealed himself. If, on the other hand, one can come to know that God has actually revealed himself by human faith, then why is it that a man not aided by grace cannot acquire this knowledge? For the neo-scholastics have uniformly contended that a man may not come through his own powers to believe that God has revealed himself, but rather that all such cases of conversion require an intervention of divine grace.

With relatively few exceptions, the neo-scholastics have not developed extensive philosophical theories about the relationship between the public revelation of the gospel to the Christian Church and the process by which an individual comes to know these truths; in fact among orthodox theologians there is also great diversity of opinion. Generally the theologians have spoken of a special grace called the "grace of faith" which is given to men by which they become aware that God has revealed the things preached to them by the ministers of the gospel and by which they are moved to accept these preachings as guarantees of the fact that God asserted the doctrines preached. There are several interesting theories of how an individual comes to know that God did in fact reveal the "gospel" he hears. Most of those theories seem to postulate a special revelation to the new believer that the preaching heard is in fact the word of God. Such neo-scholastics as Bochenski have called this a supernatural perception. Aquinas himself is vague on what is involved, and with a very few exceptions so are the neo-scholastics. This is probably one of the areas which will receive development in our time.

No detailed explanation of the neo-scholastic doctrine that reason is a source of knowledge need be given. It is, on the one hand, a denial of philosophical skepticism and an espousal of what is loosely termed "common sense," and on the other, an adherence to the doctrine of moderate empiricism. Yet one might well wonder what is meant by "knowing by reason." It is a very broad concept closely akin to "finding out for oneself." Thus a man comes to know by reason that it is raining if he *looks at* the weather himself; he comes to know the same thing by faith, human faith, if he is *told* by someone who knows. Another way to make the distinction is this: a man knows '*p*' by reason, if he *sees* (either experientially or discursively) that it is so; a man knows '*p*' by faith if he accepts '*p*' because he has been *told* that it is so by one who knows. This is suggested by St. Thomas' saying: "Divine truth . . . descends on us in the manner of revelation, not however as something made clear to be seen, but as something spoken in words to be believed." [7]

Sometimes St. Thomas Aquinas and his followers employ the term "knowledge" to apply only to things arrived at by reason. This is the case in the discussion of whether something can be an object of faith and at the same time an object of knowledge. It would be quite mistaken to conclude from this context that something which is an object of faith cannot be an item of knowledge as we defined the term "knowledge" above. The definition given above includes both some objects of faith and some objects of reason, since in both cases we have true belief and a good reason for our believing. Rather, the Thomists often used "knowledge" in a more restricted sense by which the true belief has a special and direct relation to *what* is believed and has this relation apart from anyone's testimony or witness. What this relation is thought to be, this *cognitive relation*, cannot be explained apart from the complex Aristotelian theory of knowledge (if it can be explained at all) and need not detain us here. Rather, the point can be made by putting the question as follows: Can the same proposition be the object of faith and the object of reason for one and the same person at the same time? The Thomists uniformly replied that this cannot be. The reason for this answer can be simply illustrated. Suppose I ask you whether you have your wallet with you. If you pull it out to show me, I cannot properly (and nonhumorously) say, "I'll take your word for it." I cannot accept anyone's testimony for what I, independently of that testimony, know to be so. Hence, with regard to the creative activity of God, I cannot be staring at and apprehending the evidence for God's creative action (presuming that it is sufficient) and *at the same time* be taking God's word for it that he created the world. However, as the scholastics say, one can alternate one's attention in such a way as to hold different attitudes toward the same proposition at different times. Thus, if I do not recall that you showed me your wallet, I could a while later take your word for it that you had it with you earlier.

The expression "the divine faith" is also used to name the body of doctrine and rules which are revealed by God and proposed for belief to all men; this body is more usually called "the faith." The set of things which a particular man has taken to be revealed is called "his faith." Hence it is possible that the faith of Jones should not accord with the faith in one or another element. This would only show that Jones takes himself to have divine faith with regard to propositions where he lacks it, since God cannot guarantee a false or inconsistent set of propositions. There are many refinements of this point to be found among the scholastics, but they can be passed by for now.

With regard to the claim that *both faith and reason are ways of coming to knowledge of God*, all the neo-scholastics are in agreement; in fact, the doctrine has been incorporated by the Roman Catholic Church into its official teaching. If one admits the possibility of divine revelation to man, the first way is conceded. It is with regard to the second element that much dispute has arisen between the scholastics and their Christian colleagues: the claim that reason is a way of coming to knowledge of God; and it is on this and allied points that the neo-scholastic religious tradition is distinct from all the other traditions extending to our time.

Some distinctions are necessary with regard to what has been disputed. There is much less dispute over whether a man, without revelation or acquaintance with persons who have benefited from the revelations, can come by his own intellect to know something of God, than over whether such a person or any persons can, without receiving revealed truth, come to have *scientific* knowledge of God.

There are three main positions on this point. (1) Some thinkers have said that no one comes to know that God exists or comes to know anything additional to this without the revelatory grace of God. (2) Others have said that one can come to know some things of this sort but not *demonstratively* or scientifically. (3) Still others have said that one can come to know such things scientifically or demonstratively and also nonscientifically and nondemonstratively, for example, in a personal direct perception.

There have not been many who *both* make a distinction between the operations of reason and the production of knowledge through revelation or grace, *and* hold the first view; for it seems to run counter to many scriptural statements and to the tradition that good men not blessed with the knowledge of the Redeemer could yet discover some truths about God and stand in God's favor.

Many of those who have attacked the neo-scholastics did not, probably, notice that they themselves held view (2) and that whether the scholastic view (3) was true or false could have no practical significance, since scientific or theoretical knowledge on the matter would very probably never come to a man who did not have the personal and experiential knowledge of God that both groups agree is possible apart from revelation.

The neo-scholastics and most of the medieval philosopher-theologians hold the third position. They hold, first, that a man untutored in the standards of argument or reasoning might be led from his wonder of the operations of nature, his observing the orderly behavior of things, and his experience of the contingency of existence to an *apprehension* of the being of the Creator and of his perfection. Such a man in a very personal experience would come to *see* (it is an experience best compared to visual seeing) that there is a perfect and almighty Creator of the world. He would not be able to *cite* (with scientific formality) the factors of his experience which supply adequate *evidence* for his position; but it need not follow from *that* that he must have erred in his reasoning. Rather, he need not have done any deductive reasoning at all, he may merely have had *insight* (just as we do not *reason* from his visual and auditory appearances or effects to the existence of a person who addresses us). This experiential knowledge is not scientific or demonstrative, yet it is possible, at least in principle, without revelatory grace from God. What disputes there have been between scholastic and non-scholastic thinkers have been primarily concerned with the logical supposition of some non-scholastics that all knowledge of God comes via revelation. As a result it has been a technical scriptural and theological dispute. Two of its aspects are, however, philosophical. First, the scholastics contend that it is necessary that a man should be able to *have* evidence and to proceed *in accordance with* and on the *basis of* evidence which he cannot detail, in order for him to know God in an experience which he cannot formulate in terms of an inferential relationship; otherwise there would be no cognitive relation but only a true belief. The scholastic theories of knowledge all insist that such processes of knowledge are normal, a view supported by our experiences of other minds and our recognition of other persons from their visual appearances. This claim has been quite widely recognized.

However, the other element of the neo-scholastic position on natural knowledge of God is very widely disputed by other Christian theologians and by most philosophers. The scholastics have almost universally maintained that there are certain propositions concerning the existence and nature of God which can be proved or demonstrated to be true, even by a person not possessed of the truths of revelation. Despite the virtual unanimity and near identity of terms on this point among these writers, there is considerable vagueness as to just what is maintained. Even the neo-scholastic theologians, guided by their understanding of the statements of the First Vatican Council [8] (which seem to admit interpretation as an assertion of the second position explained above, rather than as an explicit commitment to the third position which the neo-scholastics hold) have not been clear on what they claim to be able to do when they are "demonstrating." At the time Aquinas was writing, the issue was not so complex. He claimed to have found some true premises, confirmed in experience, from which the existence of God would follow deductively. But of course this is not the definition of a demonstration, nor did he think it was. If the proposition "God exists" is true, it follows truth-functionally[9] from any true premises whatever in the form:

If p, then God exists
p
Therefore God exists.

So if the proposition "God exists" is true, then it is evident that there is a sound argument for its truth (an argument with true premises in a valid form). Clearly this is not sufficient for proof or for a demonstration, since in this sense every true proposition is in principle demonstrable. This cannot be the scholastic position. One way to show this is for us to notice that all the doctrines said to be revealed are (*ex hypothesi*) true, and *some* are said to be indemonstrable or unprovable. Given that these doctrines are revealed and therefore true, they should follow truth-functionally from any other true proposition. For consider. There are some other propositions which we know to be true. Let us call those propositions p and make them premises for any truths of revelation that the scholastics say is indemonstrable. By the rule *modus ponens*, the conclusion (whatever truth of faith you choose) will follow. Since the scholastics have explicitly and unanimously maintained that not every truth of faith can be demonstrated, they must, therefore, universally deny that the mere presentation of a sound argument constitutes a demonstration of a truth of faith. This leads us to ask what is meant by "a demonstration." What are we to be offered? In some cases the scholastics are clear; but in those cases the term is clearly not used in the sense required to conform to the Thomist arguments and other well-known arguments for the existence of God. For, a demonstration is often considered to be a valid argument with *necessarily* true premises, as Duns Scotus explicitly said. (He constructed his arguments in conformity with this definition, but none of the classical arguments fit it.) Almost none of the neo-scholastics are willing to say that the two statements "every change has a cause" and "every contingent being depends upon some other being which is not contingent" are *logically* necessary (in the sense that denying them involves a contradiction). Rather, the notion of demonstration appropriate to the neo-scholastic claim that God's existence can be demonstrated seems to be this:

> Valid arguments with true premises can be found such that they entail the conclusion 'God exists' *and* such that these premises either belong to the body of generally acknowledged philosophical truths or can be shown to deserve the status of acknowledged truth in an adequate systematic philosophy.

Putting the scholastic claim this way does not eliminate any of the opposition to the position by non-scholastics; both the liberal theologians who think demonstrations to be inappropriate to matters of religious faith and the cautious philosophers who think the task of providing such premises will be hopeless will say and have promptly said, "Show us the arguments in question and we will show you either (*a*) that they are invalid, (*b*) that the premises are false, or (*c*) that the premises do not have the scientific or established status you attribute to them." Usually the charge of invalidity has been of no avail, since all parties know that no matter what the conclusion and what the premises, a *valid* argument can be constructed by the addition of appropriate assumptions. The reason why non-scholastics have attacked the validity of the scholastic argument is that they hope to show that other premises than the ones stated have been assumed, and by implication, these attacks suggest that those previously unnoted premises certainly do not have the "evident" status needed for theoretical proof. Attempts at this procedure have been relatively unsuccessful, since the scholastics have usually rejected alleged proofs of the falsity of their premises or of the doubtfulness of their implied assumptions; for example, Garrigou-Lagrange devotes considerable effort to the refutation of Kant on the subject of causality and on the possibility of transcendental knowledge, since it was on these points that Kant criticized and rejected traditional arguments for the existence of God. The third course (*c*) has also reached no decisive outcome; for when opponents have said they did not acknowledge "every change has a cause" or "an infinity of causes is impossible" as generally accepted truths, the scholastics have made intricate appeals to the metaphysical system they employ. The opponents have seldom been convinced that such appeals have sufficed to establish the scientific status of the premises of the argument, since they do not find the philosophical system in which they are integral to be an adequate philosophy.

However, the outcome of the debates is of less importance to us than its *structure*. The scholastic thinkers have clearly espoused the cause of supplying demonstrations in the sense of that term which we explained above. They certainly have not undertaken to convince everyone of the truth of the conclusion, however obdurate or stupid he may be. They must, then, have promised to provide arguments with true premises where the premises conform to some standard such that the whole argument will qualify as a demonstration, a standard given above. The fact that many philosophers and theologians have disputed whether or not the neo-scholastics have succeeded is not relevant to what has been undertaken and is compatible even with success in their undertaking.

We cannot delve further into the question of how one provides true premises of "scientific status" or "acknowledged truth" for such arguments or what standards must be met. The purpose of exposition is achieved when it is clear that the neo-scholastics are devoted to providing arguments with such premises and not to providing arguments which will convince everyone or which will have such obvious premises that everyone will know them to be true.

The neo-scholastics and their medieval predecessors have always conceived philosophy as a science, as an organized body of general knowledge for which we possess adequate evidence. If they are in fact in possession of such a body of science, then it is quite appropriate for them to take general truths from the science as premises for their arguments. Thus when Aquinas takes "an infinite regress in ordered causes is impossible" as a premise, he is implicitly appealing to the systematic metaphysics of Aristotle in which this claim is an integral part and which he has adapted for his philosophical purpose. Aquinas and many of his followers considered this as obvious a truth as we now consider the principle of entropy to be.

The very nature of the claim to provide demonstrations makes it clear that the providing of such arguments for the existence of God is not a simple matter of selecting some few propositions in isolation from the rest of the metaphysical system. Rather, the *status* of those premises as *suitable* for a demonstration rests upon their status as part of an acknowledged body of established truth. It is therefore a substantial error for anyone to take the Five Ways of Aquinas or the later scholastic presentations of these Five Ways in isolation from the whole system and examine them independently of the system as arguments for the existence of God. Taken in independence, the arguments lack one of the necessary conditions of their status as demonstrations, i.e., that the premises should have an acknowledged place among truths established in a science.

Some neo-scholastics, like Garrigou-Lagrange, faced with the refusal of many thinkers to accept the Aristotelian metaphysics and physics supposed by Aquinas' arguments, have—perhaps without realizing the effects of such a decision—tried to reduce all the arguments for the existence of God to one simple, superpremise: The principle of sufficient reason or sufficient explanation; a principle they feel is acceptable apart from a particular metaphysical system. These writers feel that principles like "every change has a cause" and "an infinite regress of causes is impossible" are deducible from the general claim that whatever is or is the case has an explanation either in itself or in something else. They have uniformly maintained that this principle is self-evident and therefore holds the best possible status as an acknowledged truth. They have, in effect, held that their demonstrations begin with premises whose "scientifically established status" is guaranteed by their self-evidence. Of course, we are not told what self-evidence consists in, and we are not provided with an explanation of how what is self-evident (to whom?) can seem doubtful to reasonable men of intellectual honesty.

So far we have seen that the scholastics held (1) that faith is a source of knowledge and in particular a source of knowledge about God, and (2) that reason, unaided by revelation, is a source of knowledge about God in two ways—(a) in an experiential, personal, and direct way and (b) in a scientific, impersonal, and publicly accessible way through philosophical demonstrations, that is, arguments based upon well-established or self-evident premises.

Divine and Mundane Wisdom　THE NEO-SCHOLASTICS ARE COMMITTED TO TWO KINDS OF PURSUIT OF WISDOM. The one, taking a term from Aquinas we call *sapientia divina*, divine wisdom or science; the other, coining a correlate term, we call *scientia mundana* —mundane wisdom or science. This distinction does not quite parallel that between philosophy and theology, a distinction also important to the neo-scholastics. Instead, divine wisdom includes all of philosophy, all mundane wisdom; it is not restricted in subject matter but embraces the whole universe as seen not only in the light of unaided human knowledge but as seen also in the light of divine revelation; this is the science of Christian wisdom, an integrated world-view In the construction of this body of knowledge, *everything* man know: (however he may have acquired the knowledge) serves as a premise to the discovery or deductive ordering of other truths. This is the broadest of all endeavors; it produces the most profound wisdom possible to *homo viator;* furthermore it is a model of the manner in which man in the presence of God extends his knowledge throughout his immortal life. On the other hand, the *mundane science* is philosophy as the pagans understood it, philosophy carried on in terms of what we know by our intellect unaided by revelation. *Theology,* on the other hand, has become the scientific elaboration and integration of things known by revelation or deduced from what is revealed by means of the knowledge we have through philosophy or *scientia mundana.* Here the doctrines revealed are taken as first principles. The difference between theology and divine science is primarily that the latter includes theology as a part, but also contributes revealed premises to the development of answers to questions which would have in the days of the pagans been called philosophical and not religious at all. For instance, the question whether man is immortal can be decided by such divine science simply by an appeal to the revealed doctrine of the resurrection of all men. Explanations of how this resurrection could come about might be recognizably philosophical in form; but the basic fact can be established merely by an appeal to revealed truths. The unitary body of knowledge that results from the conjunction of what we know by faith and reason is divine science or wisdom. The scientific or philosophical elaboration of revelation is dogmatic theology (which is only a part of divine science).

Nevertheless, the neo-scholastics and their medieval predecessors quite rigorously distinguished their rational or philosophical arguments from the arguments in which revealed truths appear as *premises*. Thus Aquinas attempts to establish the existence, omnipotence, infinity, perfection, and goodness of God without appeal to revealed truths, as evidence for his conclusions in virtue of their status as revealed. The reason for this is that these writers consider themselves engaged in a scientific dialectic with thinkers who do not possess their revealed premises and in the process of developing and expanding the Christian faith they wish to establish its philosophic respectability by supporting its basic commitments with arguments acceptable even to nonbelievers. There has no doubt always been a mixture, if not a confusion, of purposes on the part of these writers. They have always considered the possibility of conversion to the faith through these arguments to be real and yet have not made converting others the primary objective; rather the *philosophia perennis* common to both Christian and pagans has always seemed worthy of preservation and of dialectical development even though the Christian thinkers needed no such argument to support their own beliefs. In the discussion of such matters as the fact of evil in the world, these writers have seldom argued from their revealed premises that there cannot be a conflict with God's goodness; instead they have proposed what might be called rational reconciliations of the goodness of God and of the evil in the world. But there has not been among the neo-scholastic writers a sufficient concern over why these various strategies are employed, or concern to make clear just what borderline is invoked between divine faith and human reason. This borderline may have been sufficiently clear for Aquinas' purposes but has remained without further precision from his followers, although the disputes after the Reformation have required a more precise statement of it than was necessary in Thomas's time. This is perhaps the greatest failure of neo-scholasticism to make an enduring contribution to contemporary thought on religion, i.e., the failure to make what non-scholastics will consider a precise distinction between divine faith and reason as distinct ways of coming to knowledge. The key to this distinction lies in an elaboration of the concept of 'revelation' on the one hand and of 'finding out for one's self' on the other.

Compatibility of Faith and Reason SOME THINGS CAN BE KNOWN THROUGH DIVINE FAITH WHICH CANNOT BE DISCOVERED IN ANY OTHER WAY, AND SOME THINGS CAN BE KNOWN BY REASON WHICH ARE NOT REVEALED, AND SOME THINGS CAN BE KNOWN IN BOTH WAYS. This is the third principle held in common by the neo-scholastic writers and has often been taken to be the essence of the Thomist reconciliation of faith and reason. However, it is not a position peculiar to the Thomists, since most neo-scholastics have accepted it. There is another feature which is also taken to be basic. *No one can come to know something by divine faith which is incompatible with something one can come to know by employment of reason.* This is taken to be evident from the fact that the proposition and its negation cannot be true at the same time and from the fact that whatever is known by divine faith is known by divine revelation and whatever is known by divine revelation must be true, since otherwise it could not be said to have been *revealed.* This does not deny that a man might *believe* he has discovered something incompatible with what is revealed, that a man might *believe* that God has revealed something incompatible with what he *knows* by reason to be so. A man might do either thing but he would in each case believe something incorrectly.

The things which can be known only by revelation are called strict mysteries, *mysteria stricte dicta;* they are truths for which no adequate evidence would ever be available to a man deprived of revelation and which one would have no reason to believe (even if they were proposed by a preacher of the faith) unless God's revealing grace acted in the soul. Such things are that God is three persons in one substance, that the Logos has been incarnated, that Christ is present in body, blood, soul, and divinity in the Eucharist. These operations of the Persons of God could not be apprehended either to be facts or to be the work of distinct Persons without a revelation, since all the Persons have the same nature and are therefore not distinguishable in their effects to a mind unaided by grace.

The things which are objects both of reason and of faith are those truths which, though possible of discovery to men, are difficult for men to discover and which are necessary for a man's faith. Thus, the existence of God, while in principle demonstrable, is not an object of natural knowledge to most men, either because of their weakness of intellect, their lack of information, their preoccupation with other matters, or their emotive unsuitability to such investigation. For these men, the majority of mankind, the revelation of these matters is a practical necessity, since they would otherwise be unable to come to the Christian faith even if it were preached to them. This body of propositions common to both faith and reason is what is called the *Preambula Fidei,* the prerequisites or preambles of faith, the truths logically presupposed to the truth of the things revealed. It is here too that faith is supported by reason, since such doctrines of faith are demonstrated to have rational grounds, and by extension, the whole of the faith is made more credible to one who does not possess it. However, as was suggested earlier, this apologetic function of reason in behalf of the faith is not clearly distinguished from the merely theoretical and scientific functions of reason in pursuing the establishment of these propositions.

Yet it is important that the neo-scholastic tradition has unanimously held that there are *some* religious claims, those that state the strict mysteries, which cannot in principle be discovered to be true by means of any purely rational investigation. Such propositions are unverifiable and unfalsifiable by any purely rational means. This doctrine plunges the neo-scholastic tradition into the midst of the dispute over the meaningfulness and meaninglessness of religious claims, since the doctrine commits the philosopher to holding that some meaningful propositions cannot in principle be verified or falsified. There seems to be relatively little awareness among the scholastic writers, at least in our century, of how fundamental this issue is. As a result, there has been almost no development of the problem of meaning in the scholastic position, although the scholastic position, as we shall say in the latter part of this chapter, has in the theory of analogy the basis of an extensive answer to the problem of meaning of religious statements.

The Existence of God   Neo-scholastic thought is uniformly committed to the doctrine that the *existence of God* (where the name "God" has associated those attributes considered essential among Christians: creator, omnipotent, omniscient, perfect, morally excellent, etc.) *can be rigorously established from premises based upon the structure of the observable universe.* Not all the neo-scholastics have faithfully adhered to the Five Ways of St. Thomas in the form in which he presented them. Rather, many non-Thomists have employed Scotist arguments; others have been original (at least in attempts); the Thomists have very often interpreted Aquinas' arguments as schemata or forms of argument. Thus instead of arguing in terms of a cause of local motion among natural bodies, many writers have developed sophisticated cosmological arguments which employ the principles of evolution and entropy as premises, and which radically redefine the notion of unmoved mover which is implied in the claim that a cause of all physical change, an unmoved mover, exists. For example, Vincent Smith and Maritain have done this, as has Van-Steenberghen. The same thing has occurred with regard to St. Thomas's argument from the order in the universe; in this argument he wished to allege that since things in nature move toward goals which are not determined by the things themselves but which are achieved in an orderly and nonrandom manner, the whole end-directed activity of natural objects must have been preordained by a divine designer. But many of his followers present the argument as Hume interpreted it: as an argument that the structural complexity and lawlike behavior of nature must have a designer.

These derivations or developments, as some would call them, in no way constitute an abandonment of the main claim, stated in italics above, which is characteristic of neo-scholasticism and has very probably been made part of the doctrine of the Catholic Faith (through the decrees of the First Vatican Council).

Many influential neo-scholastics also hold that all these various arguments from the structure of the world fit a general schema of argument, although there is some divergence over what that superargument is. Garrigou-Lagrange says:

> All these arguments can be summed up in a more general one, based on the principle of causality, which may be stated as follows: that which does not exist by itself, can exist only by another which is self-existent. Now experience shows that there are beings endowed with activity, life, and intelligence, which do not exist by and of themselves, since they are born to die. Therefore, they received their existence from another who must be existence, life and intelligence itself. If such were not the case, we should have to say that the greater comes from the less, the higher form of life from the lower and that the plurality of being comes from a primary being less perfect than all of the others taken together.[10]

While there is something in what Father Garrigou-Lagrange, the noted Thomist and original neo-scholastic philosopher, says, his statements are not satisfactory. For the conclusion of *his* argument does not follow from its premises, which say nothing about "existence, life and intelligence itself." When we introduce an auxiliary premise to the effect that an infinite series of causes "born to die" cannot be postulated to account for the presently existing beings, we find that this general form of argument is based on at least one premise additional to the principle of causality.

Moreover, there is no reason given why we should have to say any one of the things the writer says we would have to say if it were not the case that the existing beings received their being from a self-existing being; and there is no reason at all why we should have to say all these diverse things all together rather than disjunctively. Lastly, if we take the first statement of the argument literally, as the claim "it is impossible for anything which is not self-existent to exist unless it does so by another which is self-existent," we see that this is the same as saying that nothing exists unless a self-existent being exists. This hardly seems to be an appropriate premise for a general statement of the a posteriori arguments since if this premise is true, none of the other arguments is in any way relevant and the whole distinction between a priori and a posteriori arguments will have collapsed; for the truth value of premises about what is *necessary* is not discovered by observation, but by analysis a priori (as the author would himself be quick to point out). This argument is a perfect example of an a priori argument (since its main premise is a verbal or necessary statement) and cannot serve as the general form of a set of arguments which are *really* a posteriori (based upon experience). Perhaps the one untoward but really profound effect of this failure in consistency by the writer in question is to suggest that although St. Thomas's arguments *appear* to be a posteriori, they are *in fact* a priori or analytic arguments. Despite these disadvantages, many neo-scholastics have thought that this or something quite similar is the general form of argument employed (as is evident in almost every neo-scholastic textbook since the eighteenth century).[11]

Sometimes it has been said—and it has been said by Garrigou-Lagrange —that the principle upon which all the proofs for the existence of God rest is the principle of sufficient reason: that whatever is the case must have an explanation either in itself or in something else. Thus, the existence of contingent beings cannot be explained by their production from other contingent beings, since those in turn need explanation. If an infinite set of such producers is postulated, it may be treated as one conjunctive contingent event in need of an explanation. If the whole set of contingent but actual events be taken as a conjunctive set, it can be treated as an event (or being) in need of explanation. The only *possible* explanation (if any at all would be possible) under such circumstances is a noncontingent or self-explanatory being. Hence if the principle of sufficient reason is true, it follows not only that a sufficient reason or explanation is possible but also that it is actual and is found in a noncontingent or self-explanatory being.

There is very good reason to think that this sort of reasoning (for it is better to consider the above as a process of reasoning than a particular argument) is fairly close to what is supposed by most of the neo-scholastic arguments (perhaps even the arguments given by St. Thomas Aquinas) even though these writers have not *said* exactly this. So let us consider what results when such an argument is *granted* to be correct.

Two very important problems arise for the neo-scholastics: (1) Is this a *proof of the existence of God* either in some general form or in one of the five particular applications of this reasoning which have been part of this tradition? (2) Does this noncontingent being exist necessarily, and if so, why does not a contradiction arise from the denial that such a being exists?

The scholastic reply to the first question is that even if one grants that the premises of the general or specific arguments belong to the body of acknowledged scientific truth or can be shown to have such scientific status, or if one knows the premise to be true and the arguments to be valid, *still* the existence of God is not, properly speaking, proved; rather the existence of the being *who is God* has been proved; but it remains to be shown *that* the being whose existence has been proved is *God*. The better neo-scholastic philosophers like Garrigou-Lagrange, DesCoques, Maritain, and Gilson have always recognized that the proof of the existence of God is not completed until this Necessary Being, First Mover, First Cause, Designer, or Perfect Being has been shown to have the properties associated inextricably with the concept "God." Hence, St. Thomas spends far more time in the development of the attributes of the self-existent being than he does in showing that there is such a being. For if the self-existent being does not turn out to have the attributes Christians ascribe to God, then either something is wrong with the argument for the existence of such a being or there is a self-existent being not identical with God. Of course, while this disjunction is admitted as a guide to investigation, these philosophers know from their faith that God has produced *everything else* and that there cannot be two self-explanatory beings. They will thus have to ascribe failure to arrive at a recognition that the self-existent being has the properties of God to the stupidity of men, the poverty of their philosophical system, or the inherent frailty of the intellect.

Rarely since the time of Aquinas has the investigation been pushed far enough to demand the election of one of these paths. Most of the neo-scholastics have concentrated upon showing the existence of a being *who is God*, rarely taking the next step to a developed claim that they have shown that the being is God. This is to a large degree a matter of accident and an effect of the vastly increasing detail involved in the very first steps of showing the existence of a being which could have the properties ascribed to God. Yet some confusion of terms has arisen among neo-scholastics so that a man is said to be offering a proof of the existence of God when he is offering an argument that there is a first cause, a necessary being, a perfect being, or a world designer. Nevertheless, these writers are all aware of the two distinct stages I have mentioned above, the existential stage and the identification stage; and in view of the fact that it is the existential arguments which have been primary targets of writers who think the existence of God cannot be proved, it is to be expected that the stage which has been most hotly contested should gradually inherit the name more properly applied to the whole enterprise.

With regard to question (2), whether the self-explanatory or self-existent being *necessarily* exists and whether a contradiction follows from a denial of the proposition "a self-explanatory or self-existent being exists," the neo-scholastics seem to be divided, both in opinion and in emphasis.

Such a distinguished author as Garrigou-Lagrange does not even discuss this point. He does say that Anselm's method of a priori reasoning to the existence of God is incorrect, and yet (as we have shown above) employs an a priori argument himself, *calling* it a posteriori. Actually the neo-scholastics tend to urge *separately* rather than conjointly two of St. Thomas's claims: (*a*) that the existence of God is a *necessitas de re* (a real necessity) although as *we* understand the proposition "God exists," its negation is not contradictory; (*b*) that there is a proposition closely corresponding to "God exists" which God knows and which is self-evident in itself. Sometimes the neo-scholastic interprets (*a*) as a hypothetical necessity: that "God exists" must be true because "something contingent exists" is true. But this is the less authoritative group of neo-Thomists. For Aquinas' Dominican followers have always said that God's existence is an unconditional necessity: it could not have been otherwise than that God exists. Then in answer to the charge that a proposition which is unconditionally necessary ought to have a contradictory denial, appeal is made to St. Thomas's distinction between what is self-evident to us and what is self-evident in itself; we are said not to have a rich enough concept of God, and we are unable to acquire such a concept in this life, to see the absurdity of the denial of this proposition: hence, it is not self-evident to us. Much remains to be done by the neo-scholastics to develop this approach into a set of satisfactory replies to Hume's arguments and to the arguments of such contemporary writers as Terrence Penelhum (*Mind* 1960). For if the self-explanatory being exists with unconditional necessity, then either the denial of the claim that the being exists entails a contradiction or some new sense of necessity is being employed which must be explained and related to the well-entrenched notions of necessity we now possess.

The neo-scholastic tradition has not materially advanced St. Thomas's claim that the existence of God can be rigorously established upon the basis of premises taken from among the things we know about the structure of the observable universe, although this tradition has never failed to adhere to that claim and to urge it in terms of the Five Ways of Saint Thomas and in terms of certain so-called developments of his arguments, the most notable of which is the general form of argument that was stated above.

The Meaningfulness of Theology   We now turn to the most significant contribution made by the neo-scholastic tradition to the philosophical investigation of religion. The whole body of neo-scholastic writers has accepted the doctrine that *there is built into the structure of our language and of our thought a series of procedures for the meaningful extension of concepts from one context to another; and since the terms in metaphysical and theological discourse have been extended in use in accord with those natural procedures, such discourse is meaningful.* The description of these procedures or their formulation into rules which are justified by the actual behavior of thinkers and by the properties of our natural language is called the *theory of analogy.* While there has been a great disagreement over what the theory of analogy that Thomas Aquinas proposed (and that many other medievals considered) actually maintained, apart from the general purpose stated above, and while there has been a great confusion over whether the theory is primarily a logical theory or a metaphysical doctrine, the neo-scholastics have been invariant and unyielding in reiterating the claim that religious discourse is essentially analogical and that it is meaningful not metaphorically, but literally. The fact that some of the more trivial efforts in the direction of exposition and justification of the theory of analogy have become the works best known to non-scholastics has tended to produce widespread misunderstanding, but luckily has not destroyed the expectation of most philosophers that there is something worthwhile in this complex semantical doctrine, something we would see if only its proponents would elaborate it carefully and systematically.

The object of the theory is to explain how it can be that terms like *good, just* and *cause* do not have exactly the same sense when applied to God that they have when applied to creatures, while (1) arguments from the properties of creatures to the properties of God do not equivocate; (2) we can understand what assertions attributing such predicates to God mean; (3) God has nothing *precisely* in common with any creature. The theory of analogy is designed to steer a middle course between a doctrine which would say that God is so different from his creatures that nothing intelligible can be said of him in our creature-oriented language, and a doctrine which would say that God is so similar to creatures that no alteration in the meaning of our ordinary predicates is necessary to express truths about his nature and operation. The one view is a complete agnosticism, popular among Neoplatonists and some modern theologians who hold that all religious language is symbolic and must be taken nonliterally. The other view is anthropomorphism, which pictures God as merely quantitatively different from objects of experience. The neo-scholastics insist upon the fundamental qualitative and transcendent difference between God and creature, but at the same time insist that our religious language literally expresses truths about God; that it takes terms from ordinary human experience and alters them in meaning according to two basic procedures for such alteration which are part of the structure of our natural language and which guarantee the meaningfulness of the religious assertions despite the alteration in the meaning vis-à-vis the other ordinary uses of such terms.

I shall explain somewhat further the language theory, since it is the matter most relevant to present-day discussion of religion, leaving the associated metaphysical theory unexplained but unmitigated in importance as an integral element of the neo-scholastic conception of God's relation to the world.

The first thing to be noted, although it is more obvious in the writings of St. Thomas than in the scholastic followers of the Angelic Doctor (who often failed to mention the matter at all) is that the religious utterances which are characteristic of the Christian's expression of faith are not in a technical language and do not employ a scientific vocabulary. Rather, such utterances as "God is almighty," "God loves the world," "God created the heavens and the earth," "God is good," are as much part of ordinary language as are utterances concerning the weather, domestic or business affairs, and community relationships. Theological statements of truths about God in a scientifically refined systematic discourse are *derived* in meaningfulness from ordinary discourse. Hence the extended or restricted meaning of those predicates of religious claims which occur in ordinary discourse must first be justified; then the theoretically developed language of theology and philosophy can be justified.

We cannot hope to describe the full theory of analogy which is thought to serve both these functions. Rather, we can only indicate how the ordinary religious predicates are related to other ordinary employments of terms and hope that this gives some moderately effective idea of the analogy theory.

Let us call statements which attribute some predicates P to God, G-statements, and statements which attribute some predicate P to creatures, E-statements (that is, statements about objects of natural experience). Wherever a predicate P occurs in a G-statement, it is not univocal with (does not have exactly the same meaning as) P when it occurs in an E-statement. Thus, sentence (1) "Socrates is good" employs *good* in a sense different from its sense in (2) "God is good." But the uses are not totally equivocal. *What is signified* by P in (1) is the same as what is signified by P in (2). But the *mode* of signification is different, since the *mode of signification* depends upon the *mode of being* by which the subject possesses or could possess the predicate. For instance, God is by nature or essentially good; the creature is contingently good, dependently good. Secondly, God's existence is independent and necessary, the creature's existence is dependent and contingent. Hence, the mode of being appropriate to each is different. This affects the sense of the predicate in a way that cannot be spelled out.

Let us see why this difference cannot be spelled out. The divergence of sense cannot be eliminated by the construction of any new predicate Q, since the only way we can understand what saying "God is Q" means would be by first understanding what it would mean to say of some creature, "X is Q"; but since Q by supposition is a predicate not applicable to creatures (since it was designed to express the mode of being proper to

God), it follows that we could not understand the assertion "X is Q." Hence, the analogical predicate cannot be eliminated in favor of a univocal predicate. This is why the neo-scholastics have invariably insisted that analogy is the *form* of human language about God, and that the analogous predicate cannot be eliminated without the abandonment of all sense for our God-statements.

Now consider what it means to say that a predicate is analogous. A predicate cannot be analogous by itself; rather, it is analogous in one use with respect to another use or class of uses (in statements). Thus the term *good* is analogous in its G-statement uses with respect to its E-statement uses. Neo-scholastics have generally, but not exclusively, adopted two different sets of conditions which are sufficient for its being the case that a predicate has been used analogously with respect to several uses. The sets of conditions are found to relate different usages of the same term in ordinary language and are thus said to preserve the meaningfulness of the term when religious discourse conforms to those rules, simply because it is obvious that the ordinary-language changes in the sense of predicates according to these rules do not debar meaningfulness for the derived assertion.

The first rule is called the *analogy of attribution*. It states that the same term *t* can occur as predicate in two different statements, e.g., (A) "Fido is healthy" and (B) "Fido's complexion is healthy," where the subject of the one statement (A) actually possesses the property of health, while the subject of the other (B) is merely a cause, a sign, or a condition of the subject-of-(A)'s having that property. In (B) the predicate *t* is attributed to a subject which does not possess it (i.e., the complexion has health attributed to it), on account of that subject's relationship to what does possess it, the dog. The predicate *healthy* in the two cases is equivocal, but not entirely so; rather the entire definition of *t* in (A) is part of the definition of *t* in (B). There are other conditions for this kind of analogy too, notably conditions of *priority* of predication; but this will do as a sketch.

Thus it will be seen that some things will be predicated of God—for example, being-our-life—which God does not possess formally, but only possesses by attribution, possesses on account of his causal or conserving relationship to our experiencing certain effects. Some neo-scholastics have thought that this is the most fundamental sense in which predicates are attributed to God; but these thinkers are very much in the minority and are surely in error. The analogy of attribution has many important functions but it is not fundamental to the neo-scholastic theory of religious language in the sense that all predicates in assertion about God are used by analogy of attribution with respect to other basic ordinary-language uses. Many things are attributed to God which God possesses both formally and essentially—for example, intelligence, existence, power, love.

The second analogy rule, called the *analogy of proper proportionality*, is generally considered to be the basis of the meaningfulness of religious language. It is assumed by the conditions for this sort of analogy that there are similarities between God's relationships to his actual and possible operations and man's (or some other creature's) relationship to his actual or possible operations. Thus if "Socrates is good" is true, Socrates stands in a relationship to some activity or act of his in a way similar to that in which God stands to his being or act when it is true that God is good. The term *good* is employed in speaking of God just because we recognize that similarity of relationship to the relationship we call "being good" with respect to a creature. So also with all other terms applied to God. The reason why the term is not *univocal* (of exactly the same meaning) in these divergent uses is that there is an essential difference between the beings, a difference in *mode* of being. Thus it is correct to say "Fido knows his master" and "Socrates knows his teacher." But the term *knows*, while expressing a similar relationship, does not express the same relationship since the *mode* of knowledge possessed by Socrates is different from that possessed by Fido. This example is given to suggest, without the elaboration necessary for a full explanation, how the same sort of shift in sense which is held by the neo-scholastics to characterize religious discourse also occurs in other areas of ordinary language and follows the same rule. Perhaps the most striking example of such a shift in sense is in the statements "Hamlet exists," "Socrates exists," and "the number 1 exists." In these three statements the term *exists* differs slightly in meaning depending upon the mode of being properly attributable to each one of the subjects; after all, Hamlet does not exist as numbers do and numbers do not inhabit space and time.

(1) The neo-scholastics hold that between the world described in E-statements—the world of sensible experience—and some entity not part of that world there obtain several relations e.g., (1) "being moved by"; (2) "being efficiently caused by"; (3) "being conserved in existence by"; (4) "being excelled by"; (5) "being designed by." (Each relation is established by one of the five existential arguments of St. Thomas.)

(2) A term which signifies these relations—let us take only one for consideration, say "being caused by"—cannot be used in exactly the same way as it is used in a sentence like this: "My black eye was caused by John." For this is an E-statement, and the fundamental *assumption* is that God will not have any properties or relations in the same way as any of his creatures, since God's being is self-explanatory and the creature's is not.

So, the argument is: God is at most *proportionally* similar to John (that is, is not *directly* similar) because the relation "being caused by" is similar (but not identical) in the statements of the form (A) WCg (The world is caused by God) and (B) BCj (The black eye is caused by John). And the term "being caused by" is *analogous by proportionality:* in its two occurrences the term is used equivocally but not totally equivocally. The reason why we cannot replace this term ("being caused by") with a univocal term is that in (A) the *mode of signification* which is proper to C in (B) has been canceled out. Because we do not know the distinguishing characteristics of the *mode of possession* by which God has his properties, we cannot fill in the part of the signification which is canceled out.

So, the term "being caused by," while having all elements of its meaning present which are necessary to distinguish "being caused by" from any other relation, still does not have present the elements by which to distinguish the divine mode of being from the finite mode. And yet, even if these latter modal elements were present, the term would still be equivocal because the modal elements of C in (A) and C in (B) would be different.

(3) All natural knowledge of God consists basically in discovering that certain relationships with possible worlds actually obtain between things that exist and God.

(4) These relation terms, which are analogous by proper proportionality with instances of the same terms in statements about the world, are then transferred into *names* of the other relatum, "God." This transference of relation terms into names follows the rule of analogy of attribution: you can call a person by the names of his actions because he is the cause of his actions. Thus we call a man who smokes a smoker and a man who judges Judge, and a man who designs a designer. And transforming the name of an effect to become a name of the cause is an instance of analogy of attribution. So, the entity X which has the relation "being remote or immediate cause" of all other entities and events is called "First Cause."

(5) Next, utilizing the fact that secondary employments of terms analogous by attribution still tell us something about the subject, St. Thomas and the neo-scholastic writers generally proceed to decide what properties God would have to have if he is the cause, the judge, the conserver, etc. And thus, they arrive at the properties of intelligence, free will, simplicity, etc. But *these* terms can all be turned into relation predicates and shown to be analogous by proportionality with respect to ordinary-language occurrences of the same terms—occurrences which are psychologically prior.

(6) Hence, all statements about God employ terms which are analogous by proper proportionality with respect to psychologically prior instances of the same terms in ordinary experience-describing statements. And analogy of proper proportionality is the general form of language about God.

Thus, the neo-scholastics, following Aquinas, suppose that there are two basic sets of statements made in discussing the existence and nature of God: (A) the statements which assert that some relation R obtains between entities of a certain kind (the things of the world) and some entity not a member of that kind, God; and (B) the statements which employ cognate forms of the relation term R as common nouns or adjectives to either name or describe the entity. An example of (A) is "Everything which has really distinct properties is causally dependent upon some entity which does not have distinct properties; and there are some entities which have distinct properties." An example of (B) is "There exists a First Cause." It is immediately obvious that statements of set (B) logically presuppose both the truth and meaningfulness of statements of set (A). How set (B) is derived from (A) is described in the next paragraph (7). The relation terms that occur in sentences of set (A) are said to be analogous by proper proportionality with ordinary-language occurrences of the same terms.

(7) Some statements about God employ terms which, besides being used analogously by proportionality with respect to E-statements, are also used analogously by attribution with respect to other and logically prior G-statements. That is, the statement "The world is caused by God" is logically prior to "God is the First Cause." The statements which attribute common names to God employ predicates analogous by attribution with respect to instances of the same predicates occurring in statements asserting that certain relations obtain between the world and God. Thus, to say "God is the artificer, the designer, the judge," etc., is to employ as a common name a term which by both logical and psychological priority is employed in a statement which says "The world is made, planned, and judged by God."

This in briefest outline is the theory of analogy, but it must be remembered that it is an outline, that the neo-scholastic philosophers vehemently disagree on what is the authentic doctrine of Aquinas on the matter and vary greatly in their statements of this theory of meaning.

A theory of this sort is undoubtedly the only theory which can make plausible the case of the more conservative Christians that their religious utterances are meant to be taken literally but with appropriate alterations in the sense of the predicates from their use in utterances about finite things and that these alterations will both preserve the transcendence and perfection of God and the meaningfulness of the utterance itself. This theory, together with the doctrine of our first section that faith and reason are *both* sources of knowledge and of knowledge of God, constitute the most enduring and important elements of the neo-scholastic position on religion.

Verification Since the neo-scholastics think basic orthodox religious utterances (such as those in the Creeds) are to be taken literally, it is natural to ask whether they think that they can be confirmed or falsified by experience. This is not a question a neo-scholastic is likely to ask himself, and hence is not a point which has figured in the overall tradition; but it is a question likely to be put to the neo-scholastics by a positivist, an empiricist, or a pragmatist. For example, A. J. Ayer confronted Father F. J. Copleston, S.J., in their BBC discussion[12] with various forms of this question, and it is to be found in all the discussions of religious utterances by philosophers influenced by the analytic and pragmatist movements. The neo-scholastics, as we have said, have not addressed themselves to the question systematically; yet there are in the neo-scholastic position indications of at least one approach. That is to interpret the question of whether experience can verify or falsify such claims as a request for an explanation of how we *find out* that religious claims are true (or false), since no one pretends that they are all analytic. On this point the neo-scholastics (who are often theologians as well as philosophers) possess two answers, neither of which has yet been extensively developed. The first is to say that the truth of some religious claims is discovered by one's finding out that God has revealed them. The second method, related to the first, is possessed by the Catholic theologians who say that *the truth or falsity of religious claims can be determined by an inquiry into whether or not the Church actually teaches them or their negations* or something which entails them or their negations. *Whether or not the Christian Church teaches 'that p' has almost always been thought to be an empirically decidable matter.* Hence, the ultimate appeal for the guarantee or falsity of religious claims is the *experience* of the Christian Church, and it is admitted by almost all the neo-scholastics that sometimes the Church has to *grow* in awareness of some truth and defer decision to a later date (this is the development-of-dogma hypothesis). Hence, while the method of verification or falsification of nonanalytic religious claims may not appeal to the non-scholastic philosopher as a reliable method for discovery of truth, it must be conceded that neo-scholastic tradition possesses a method (a method employed in practice) and has at least one way to answer the question of what experiences would falsify or verify a religious claim. And there is no reason to think a priori that this sort of appeal cannot be developed into a satisfactory reply (at least logically) to the conundrums of verification and falsification which have been so widely circulated in recent years. The fact that the method of verification would be reliable only if the major part of what is found to be true by this method actually is true is not a peculiarity of the procedures for confirming religious claims; it is a general characteristic of all empiricist criteria for verification.

Reason's Service to Faith   It follows from all these points that the neo-scholastic tradition is firmly committed to the project of developing, supporting, and making precise religious beliefs (specifically, the Christian faith as expounded by the Catholic Church) by the development of a systematic scientific thought or wisdom which has as a recognizable part a system of philosophy. After all, if what experience confirms were not, on the whole, the case, what sense would there be in our appealing to confirmability by *that* method as a guarantee of sense rather than to some quite disparate rule? It has always been alien to this position to avoid problems by appealing either to the transcendence of God or to the feebleness of man's intellect. The greatest service an intellect can offer to divine faith, this tradition has always held, is that of systematic analysis of religious belief and defense against error. This does not mean that these writers think that the truth of the Christian faith *depends* upon such philosophical arguments, or even any particular man's *knowledge* of the truth of the faith depends upon such arguments and analyses; nor does it mean that these writers think that one will come to apprehend the truth of the faith through such analyses or arguments (for such a position would be inconsistent with the claim that Christianity is a faith, an acceptance on verbal guarantee in the absence of one's own seeing that what is proposed is true). Despite certain ambiguities as to just what this service of reason is said to consist in, the best justified view is that *the service of reason to faith is in the construction of a scientific philosophy and through that, the development of a universal science called Christian Wisdom.*

Trends in Neo-Scholasticism   The neo-scholastic tradition is becoming fragmented at the present time into what appear to be five distinct directions. First, some European neo-scholastics, particularly some of those associated with Louvain University (one of the great strongholds of the Thomist revival early in this century) are showing marked influences from the phenomenologist and existentialist movements and are attempting to express the neo-scholastic commitments in new ways. Secondly, there is a group both in America and in Europe which is concentrating upon rigorous exegetical expurgation of textbook presentations of the Thomist doctrine and are attempting to make precise historical statements on what St. Thomas and other medieval scholastics really thought. Thirdly, there is a small number of philosophers, primarily in Europe, who are markedly influenced by American pragmatism and by scientific operationalism and are seeking this mode of expression. Fourthly, there is a significant group of neo-scholastics who are diverting most of their efforts to accommodating the Thomist system to contemporary science, with the result that in their work the discussion of religion is only tangential. Lastly, there is a group of neo-scholastic philosophers, for example, D. J. B. Hawkins and Frederick Copleston (the historian) who are attracted by the analytic and linguistic philosophies of England and America and are pursuing this method of development. Which of these tendencies will become dominant among the neo-scholastics is difficult to predict. However, I shall conclude this essay by saying which one ought to become dominant and why.

The scholastic tradition ought to be revitalized by a plenteous infusion of analytical methods and of sophisticated formal logical techniques, for this alone will both preserve the method of the medieval scholastics (who were formidable logicians) and allow for a successful updating of those systems. Analytical scholasticism is the only hope of those conservative Christians who wish to approach religion with rational support and develop a viable philosophy for this century. One must accept this general orientation and a commitment to the points italicized in this chapter and then proceed to give new analyses and arguments—not necessarily opposed to the traditional ones, but entirely in conformity with the standards of excellence in philosophical reasoning which are current in our day.

An outstanding example of the application of formalized techniques was given by I. M. Bochenski, O.P., in the *Thomist* (1948), where he presented the essence of the analogy theory in a formal semantic system.

Anyone who reads Aquinas, Duns Scotus, or Occam will find that there is no opposition in method between their work and the more worthwhile analytical products of our time; rather, there is a surprising similarity. (Of course, this same thing has been said by others about the methods of existentialism and phenomenology.) The more complicated theories of Aquinas and the neo-scholastics—for example, the theory of analogy, the theory of participation in being, the theory of powers of the soul, the theory of essentially ordered causes, the doctrine of universals—would benefit immeasurably from formalized techniques; not only would they derive increased precision but also such treatment would direct philosophers to points which demand original development.

Conclusion In this brief survey I have indicated that each of the basic commitments of the neo-scholastic tradition requires a systematic development on a cardinal point.

(1) The distinction between faith as acceptance of something proposed upon testimony and reason as a kind of discovering for one's self must be subjected to a further elaboration in order to justify (*a*) the distinction between philosophy and theology; (*b*) the practice of the Christian philosophers of not using everything they know (particularly, the things they know by faith) as premises in philosophical arguments; (*c*) the claim that there are some propositions which, though not analytic, cannot be known to be true by any effort of human reason (although these propositions are meaningful); and (*d*) the claim by many neo-scholastics (e.g., Gilson) that there is no such thing as a Christian Philosophy although there are many Christian philosophers.

(2) It is necessary to redefine the distinction between philosophy and

theology so that it will more adequately justify the neo-scholastic in debating with one hand behind his back (his knowledge derived from divine revelation); for the neo-scholastics let anyone else use any premise he knows to be true, and yet do not follow suit. This distinction is needed to make clear the various strategies the Christians are using in their philosophical discussions of religion and to make evident just what will count as having resolved a problem. For if the object is to convert those who disagree into those who agree, the task is hopeless. If it is something else, that should be explained, for it will have a bearing upon what premises can be employed.

(3) The neo-scholastic philosophers must decide what they are going to do about specific arguments for the existence of God or for the existence of some being which they intend to show is the same as the one believers put their hope in and call by the name "God." Neither the logical subtlety of the formulations of these arguments nor the selection of premises has been in tune with the philosophical criticism of non-scholastics for many decades. The result is that arguments which were at one time of the greatest philosophical weight are now dismissed by non-scholastics as unworthy of detailed examination.

(4) Neo-scholastics must decide the question whether the proposition "God exists" is a necessary one or a contingent one, and if necessary, in what sense it is so. Moreover, it would be a fatal *ignoratio elenchi* to take Copleston's answer that it is necessary because it is certain (BBC discussion with A. J. Ayer); for anything we *know* is certain, even a contingent proposition.

(5) The nature of demonstration must be more fully explained. (*a*) If all it consists in is valid argument with premises that the author knows to be true, any Christian can demonstrate the existence of God. In particular it must be stated what standards are to be employed to determine whether a given argument with true premises and a valid form is or is not a demonstration. Why was it not a demonstration for Moses to have said, if a fool had raised the question, "Of course God exists; I spoke to him."? (*b*) If being a demonstration consists in having premises *everyone* knows to be true, there probably never will be any such arguments since there is no reason to think that there is any set of premises which everyone knows to be true (in any straightforward sense of the expression *knows*). (*c*) If demonstration consists of something else, as I have suggested, this must be made clear (for the explanation I have offered is only hypothetical), since the most commonly cited distinguishing feature of neo-scholasticism on the subject of religion—i.e., the claims that the existence of God can be demonstrated—otherwise appears ambiguous if not confused.

(6) The theory of analogy must be (and gradually can be) developed into a full-scale theory of meaning for religious discourse and this must

be done by an exhaustive study of the actual statements whose meaning-fulness is to be explained. This means that a subsidiary investigation into the methods by which the truth or falsity of religious claims is determined is required to make the theory accord with recent discussion on the subject of falsification and verification. It is with respect to the question of meaning that the neo-scholastics have the most to offer and have done the least to aid the contemporary investigation of religion.

In this chapter I have tried to show that the neo-scholastic position is inextricably bound to the *rational*, the philosophical investigation of religious faith, and that this position holds (*a*) that man can come to know God partly by reason and more fully by divine faith; (*b*) that a natural science of God is possible to man; (*c*) that the existence and nature of God are properly to be established by philosophical investigation while at the same time they have been revealed; (*d*) that there is a Christian wisdom or divine science which embraces all that man knows into one organized system of knowledge; (*e*) that there are some truths, the strict mysteries, which are undecidable in principle by any intellectual effort of man apart from revelation; (*f*) that there is a theory called the theory of analogy which explains and justifies the claim that orthodox religious doctrines are literally meaningful and which parallels the metaphysical structure of the universe in which God both transcends all creation and is partially visible in it; (*g*) that the Christian possesses an empirical means of determining whether God has revealed a certain proposition for his belief by an appeal to whether or not the Christian Church teaches that proposition as part of its faith.

I have suggested that neo-scholasticism is a complex and integrated system in which the elements relative to religion are not really separable from the epistemological, metaphysical, and psychological doctrines. Finally, after indicating various incompletenesses in the neo-scholastic theories, I have said that those can best be supplied by an increasing application of analytical and formalistic philosophical techniques, both because of the nature of the problems to be solved and because of the great resemblance between this method and the careful logical and analytical method employed by Aquinas and the greatest of his scholastic contemporaries and successors.

NOTES FOR CHAPTER 5

1 I. M. Bochenski, *Contemporary European Philosophy*, Berkeley and Los Angeles, University of California Press, 1956, p. 246.
2 See the works of the British theologian Austin Farrer; e.g., *The Freedom of the Will*, London, Adam and Charles Black, Ltd., 1958.
3 *God, His Existence and Nature* by Pierre Garrigou-Lagrange (full reference under Selected Readings) is one of the most comprehensive neo-

scholastic works in systematic natural theology available in the English language.

4 While the neo-scholastics, following medieval practice, consider faith to be an adequate source of knowledge and hence capable of providing principles or premises of scientific knowledge, things known by faith are not said to be arrived at scientifically, since the *activity* of science is essentially that of ratiocination, of discursive investigation.

5 Neo-scholastic interests diverge from those of many non-Christians in this matter. The latter wish to concentrate their analyses upon the question of whether faith is a reliable guide to true belief, a question which the former answer summarily and affirmatively, concentrating upon the explanation of what such mental states consist in and upon how they are distinguished from states of direct knowledge or discovery. The difference in interest is, of course, complementary; but it must be remarked in order to place the neo-scholastic position in proper perspective.

6 It would be possible to define *divine faith* in such a way that anyone who accepts a certain belief because he takes God to have revealed it has exercised divine faith. But then one could not say that *every* exercise of divine faith gives knowledge or even true belief, as the neo-scholastics most often claim. There are many varying terminologies to be found among different writers, but on the whole the differences seem merely verbal and I am confident that the way the matter is explained here is a correct and sympathetic explanation of the prevailing elements of the traditional position.

7 Aquinas, *Summa Contra Gentiles*, Book 4, Chapter 1, No. 5.

8 Denzinger, *Enchiridion Symbolorum*, No. 1785: Vatican Council I: "Eadem sancta mater Ecclesia tenet et docet Deum, rerum omnium principium et finem, naturali humanae rationis lumine e rebus creatis certe congnosci posse." Translated: "The same Holy Mother the Church holds and teaches that God, the beginning and end of all things, can certainly be known by the light of natural reason on the basis of things made."

It will be obvious that this statement is ambiguous with respect to the latter two of the three positions described on page 121 above. Garrigou-Lagrange interprets the Council (see his Vol. I, pp. 8-32) as espousing position (3) by citing less authoritative statements which are more explicit. This seems hardly decisive. One statement of considerable authority is the Oath Against Modernism which was required of scholastic professors for a while, and which clearly states the neo-scholastic position:

Denzinger, *op. cit.* No. 2145: "Ego firmiter amplecto ac recipio omnia et singula quae ab inerranti Ecclesiae magisterio definita, adserta ac declarata sunt. . . . Ac primum quidem: Deum, rerum omnium principium et finem naturali rationis lumine per quae facta sunt, hoc est, per visibilia creationis opera, tamquam causam per effectus, certo cognosci, adeque demonstrari etiam posse, profiteor." Translated: "I firmly embrace and receive each and every thing which is defined asserted and declared by the inerrant teaching authority of the Church. . . . And first: I profess that God, the beginning and end of all things, can be known with certainty through the light of natural reason on the basis of what has been made, just as a cause through its effect, and moreover, can be demonstrated."

9 "Truth-functionally" is a term associated with the propositional calculus in modern symbolic logic and is closely associated with the concept of material implication. The latter notion was well understood by the medieval scholastic logicians. One cannot, however, say that the neo-scholastics of

recent times have been acute logicians. As a result there is great confusion about the more recent concepts of demonstration.

10 Garrigou-Lagrange, *God, His Existence and Nature*, Vol. 1, Appendix, p. 381.

11 Cf. John Edwin Gurr, S.J., *The Principle of Sufficient Reason in Some Scholastic Systems, 1750-1900*, Milwaukee, Marquette University Press, 1959.

12 A transcript of this discussion is reprinted in Geddes MacGregor and J. Wesley Robb, eds., *Readings in Religious Philosophy*, Boston, Houghton Mifflin Company, 1962, p. 328.

QUESTIONS

1 What are three or four of the doctrines which clearly distinguish the neo-scholastic tradition from other approaches to religion?

2 What do the neo-scholastics think will be achieved by theistic proofs, and what conditions must such proofs satisfy?

3 Why do the neo-scholastics hold that the terms applied to God cannot be either univocal or totally equivocal with respect to their other ordinary-language uses?

4 Just what is the analogy theory, and what is it supposed to explain?

5 What are the main problems confronting the neo-scholastic philosophical perspective on religion today?

SUGGESTED READINGS

Jules Baisnée, S.S., *Readings in Natural Theology*, Westminster, Maryland, Newman Press. Paperback.

James Collins, *God in Modern Philosophy*, Chicago, Henry Regnery Co., 1959.

Etienne Gilson, *God and Philosophy*, Oxford, Oxford University Press, 1941; also Yale University Press. Paperback.

Gabriel Marcel, *The Philosophy of Existence*, translated by Manya Harari, London, Harvill Press, 1948.

Reginald Garrigou-Lagrange, O.P., *God, His Existence and Nature*, translated by Dom Bede Rose, O.S.B., 2 vols., St. Louis and London, B. Herder Book Co., 1949.

6 *Paul L. Holmer*

Religion from an Existential Standpoint

The question "What is philosophy?" is posed at two extremes of sophistication—by beginners and by acknowledged experts. Novices want to know about it in the same way they want to know "What is philology?" or "What is geography?" The experts ask their question the way mathematicians do when long preoccupation has made their subject very complex and the easy definitions somewhat bizarre.

Among the philosophical the simple question compounds anxieties. On the one hand, it might well appear that no one knows if the experts cannot agree; and this is what amateurs often conclude. On the other hand, some professionals, unwilling to identify philosophy by a distinctive subject matter, resolve that it is only an activity. So, too, this book might well confuse some readers with its several positions, its many points of view, perspectives, even philosophies. And this is the way a reader might well feel about the current theologies that compete for the readers' attention. Where there are so many alternatives; and where every attempt at mediating between the alternatives seems to be one more position, the matter does become confusing. It is one thing to be confused by one's ignorance and some partial views, but it is quite another to be embarrassed by the plethora of positions.

There are, of course, differences in many fields of learning. But in the humanities, and not least in philosophy and theology, the differences confuse the reader because they are fundamental and often mutually negating. Seldom can the differences be attributed solely to preoccupation with different areas of concern. Furthermore, differences in many disciplines are successive in time, and the later hypothesis supplants the earlier. But no such easy understanding works very well in the difficult and abstract matters at hand. Hence the pertinence of the questions "What is philosophy?" and "What is theology?"

The author confesses to a bewilderment, a bewilderment born of long preoccupation. But out of a concern with an almost maddening array of views and out of a rediscovery and renewed interest in some very elementary matters of the religious life, at least a few modest proposals have come forth. These are much too unostentatious to represent anything so grand as a whole new philosophy and probably too familiar, if spelled out, to be anything like a new theology. These things are said in the confidence that each reader has an immediate access to the point of departure for important reflective matters—that philosophy does not depend upon occult essences, unexpressible things, or an unfamiliar realm of substances. There is, in other words, no quaint nor esoteric subject matter yet to be discovered by the reader whereby reflective issues can be resolved. The dogged and continuing effort that reflection requires might still make philosophizing as difficult as anything one can do. About religious matters, something analogous can be said, with the qualification here that most of us begin with a kind of social exposure to doctrines and rituals, churches and synagogues. Theology issues in the master proposal that we know God, and here its way swings off, as we shall subsequently note.

In what follows, the reader will not be offered so much a position as a new way to think about the array of problems now dominating the literature. It will be disappointing if all of this is taken to be one more position rather than an encouragement to some new habits and even a new way of looking at things. Sören Kierkegaard told the story of the raw recruit who was told by the army sergeant to be quiet, whereupon the recruit said, "Yes sir!" The sergeant yelled, "I said, be quiet!" The recruit, seeking to assure the anxious sergeant that he had really heard and understood, said "Yes sir; I heard you and I understand."

First some words about how we get started in these matters. It must be apparent to most readers how we get started in things religious. We are taught to say prayers at meals, at bedtime, and on special occasions; we are brought to special places to hear sermons, songs, and Scripture; we are taught to answer certain difficult catechetical questions and to do such odd things as to kneel, to sing responses, and to repeat creeds; we are admonished to believe certain abstract teachings and to do a number of strenuous things, such as loving the neighbors, giving to the poor, and remembering the sick and the dying. We learn to pray, to worship, to listen, to care, to preach, to be hopeful, loving, and faithful, among other things by way of becoming religious. It is not easy to say whether all of these suffice to make one religious or not; neither am I suggesting that this will make one a Christian or a Jew, liberal or conservative. The aim is rather to remind us that becoming religious often happens in quite ordinary ways, ways that are undertaken by mothers and fathers, monks and sisters, laymen and ministers, and yet are surprisingly effective in sons and daughters.

No highly technical devices seem ever to have been invented for teaching these things. While one must admit only partial success, the failures are not clearly a matter of poor methods and amateur instruction any more than the successes are due to professional means and superior teaching. People who dare to instruct in these matters do very much like parents who must constantly improvise a tremendous range of admonitions and precepts—"Wash your hands!" "Be nice to Suzy," "Don't bite the baby!"—and they do so without ever supposing a vast understanding in the children or without possessing a technical mastery of professional skills themselves. Most parsons, priests, and rabbis are effective when they can continually improvise the sense of things religious within the range that is already common. So, too, parents teach ways of behaving, something we call manners and maybe later, morals, by advising, commanding, threatening, yelling, commending, and all sorts of other ways. If the parent says, "I want you to be good today—don't blow bubbles in your milk," even this, in that context, is very plain talk. Certainly the parent is not preparing the child for a new and master concept, the concept of the good, however much the language might seem to lend itself to such a reading in the eyes of a later reader.

Neither is this to say that all kinds of specialties might not be developed; but most of the specialties are for experts who teach the teachers. There seem to be big differences between teaching physics, for example, and teaching religion and morals. In the first instance, physics is so specialized that everything one does teaching it has to be special and technical too. But if religion is taught at all, it is taught with means that may be queer to outsiders but are not, for all of that, inappropriate or ineffective. Most religion is taught in nontechnical language and ways. There are no experiments, no mathematical symbols, few artifices of a technical variety at all.

Much religion is taught almost inadvertently. Using a contemporary word we can describe the processes of teaching and learning as a matter of enculturation. A host of stimuli, a variety of stories, admonitions, and parables, certain rituals and formulae—these dominate the pedagogy of religion. Even the pages of the Old Testament and the New—besides offering a strange variety of chronicles, poems, prophecies, anecdotes, laws—depict several teachers in some detail. One of them, Jesus of Nazareth, was known even to his contemporaries as a teacher, but his teaching was strangely unsystematic, almost casual, intertwining apparently fortuitous adjustments to circumstances with pointed diatribes and commands. Besides that, he asked for a kind of emulation and following that was at least nonacademic, whatever else it might be. But there were and are people who "learned" to be religious from him, just as there were and are Jews, Hindus, Moslems, and others who learn in somewhat analogous ways.

There is almost no end to the pedagogical lore available on these matters. Much of it is a lore, not a science. It is probably clear to every reader that chemistry and physics, for example, demand pedagogical devices that are intimately appropriate. Almost without reflection on the specifics of the matter, most teachers of the special sciences also become scientific in their teaching. But religion, like moral behavior, suggests no single and no precise method; and one must resist very strongly the temptation to shape the pedagogy of faith by analogy with science or art or any number of other teachable subjects, even if rationality and order seem to be thereby served. Perhaps it is also rational and just to acknowledge the oddness of our several human activities without always seeking supposed common methods of teaching them and loose analogies between them.

It is at this very juncture that philosophizing about religious matters begins. For religion is often taught, as we have noted, in parables, in pictorial and imaginative ways; also it is taught by injunctions and rules. Thus, God is likened to a father or a king; the world is his creation and kingdom; men are pilgrims and wanderers without their proper home; and salvation is likened to being redeemed in the refiner's fire, or to being saved as a lost sheep, or to being put on the right path. Much of the language of religion is like that. A certain kind of reflection grows up very easily and is one root of the philosophic concern. For we easily learn to ask: What is salvation? And, we are often not happy with the various answers already noted. What we want is something the philosophers call a concept. The concept *salvation* is not clear to us, we say, even though we have probably not had particular difficulty understanding the expressions "refiner's fire," "lost sheep," or "right path."

Comparable difficulties are discovered with *sin, guilt, atonement, God's will, creation, providence, God, Virgin Birth, law, Trinity*, and a host of others. These terms are surely familiar to people schooled in the Holy

Bible, but somewhat similar issues arise for readers of other scriptures too. Most of the perplexities we will note could be shown to arise in a variety of religions and societies.

However, a proposal is now in order. Philosophy seems to arise because some people are intent upon conceptualizing, upon articulating, upon systematizing and cohering a host of commonsensical matters. Thus a distinction is hereby introduced: on the one side, there are our many common-sense concerns and convictions, widely shared, taught, and practiced; on the other side, there is the somewhat rare and aristocratic task of worrying about these commonsensical matters.

For example, human beings draw pictures, write poems and novels, sculpture, and compose. Most of this we now call aesthetic behavior, on the assumption that such activities have something in common. All kinds of ways have been found to teach these things; and many kinds of interests and many ways to appreciate their consequents are constantly being fomented among us. Scarcely anyone escapes exposure to these matters, though, indeed, very few prosper in them to any marked degree. It is a truism that everyone has to do with beauty, with goodness, truth, and God. Most people certainly discriminate somewhere and at some time between what is beautiful and what is ugly, even if it is only to make invidious comparisons of the opposite sex or disingenuous remarks about another's taste.

It seems almost generically human to be concerned with making one's home attractive, to choose a pretty wife if one has a choice, and to have beautiful things rather than ugly. For the moment, it is not my point to note the ambiguities here, but only to remark upon the widespread and well-nigh universal interest. Likewise and in a thousand ways, men distinguish right from wrong, good from bad, and stupid and bungling behavior from that which is appropriate and just. Of course these things are also taught, but in an almost formless number of ways, by policemen, mothers, and army sergeants, as well as lawyers and judges. No matter whether the distinctions are well drawn, the fact is that the ordering and judging of behavior, planning for tomorrows, discussing what one ought to do—these and more are as common as men themselves. To do these things is part of our lot, and we need only the slightest participation in our common life to learn the rudiments of doing them.

There are common languages too that grow up with and sometimes foster these concerns. The languages "of" aesthetics and "of" morals are truly ubiquitous. They are not initially scholarly and technical, and certainly they are not learned via aesthetic and moral theories. The theories are an account of what is already there rather than the cause of what is there. More often than not, these languages "of" are one with other aspects of truly aesthetic and moral behavior. Much the same can be said of religious language and its relation to other religious activities. There are, nonetheless, conditions for understanding all of these ways of talking; but most of the time we teach our young people through their early life, and properly so, the very forms of living that go with such ways of speaking. And the conditions for understanding usually lie in reduplicating those ways and forms of life, not in another explanation or a kind of third-person shorthand account.

Already then we have noted that behavior called aesthetic and behavior commonly called moral grows up among us because of a variety of dispositions and needs. We can name other major activities too. For example, Aristotle noted centuries ago how everyone was curious and wanted to know. Accordingly, we have all kinds of knowing and all kinds of knowledge, and the most abstract and concentrated kinds we include under the generous rubrics of the humane disciplines and the sciences. However, our interest here is in the origin and scope of philosophizing. The points of departure for the aesthetic, the ethical, and the knowing enterprise seem to be rather ordinary and even commonsensical, whereas the philosophical interest is extraordinary and out-of-the-way. For philosophy is the conceptualized, coherent, and articulated common sense of mankind. Philosophy usually is fed by a *meta* interest. It comes "after" something else has been asserted, believed, and studied.

This proposal is meant to differentiate two uses of the word "philosophy." For some people use the word "philosophy" to describe simply having views on or about anything, and perhaps collecting and rather ostentatiously parading them. There are, then, "philosophies," and they can be philosophies of antique collecting, of educating, of playing chess; but these are instances of a vulgar conception of philosophy, one which likens philosophy to simply having and collecting views. Our proposal, in contrast, proposes a technical and sophisticated view, one which denotes the highly demanding business of rendering, let us hope without loss and even with gain, a subject matter in concepts rather than in the vernacular language of everyday life. Thus philosophies in the manner of Plato, Aristotle, Socrates, and Descartes and also the academic traditions which we know as idealism, materialism, scholasticism, and logical positivism are technical philosophies rather than vulgar and vernacular philosophies.

There is a loose sense, then, in which all men are philosophers, but this is only to say that all men are occasionally concerned with one or more of the issues previously noted and have corresponding views. Very few people lack a sense for discriminating, however badly and infrequently, wrong from right, the better from the worse, the lie from the truth. And to do this on purpose and with one's heart in it is not altogether rare either. However, this is not quite enough to make one a technical philosopher. For only the rarest of talents, men with altogether exceptional concerns and gifts, are able to philosophize in the logical and abstract manner to which we have alluded. This is not to say that such philosophers are therefore correct in all that they say or do, or even that all men stand to profit by reading them and becoming preoccupied with the same issues. On the contrary, it might well be that the persistent effort to convert commonsensical matters into more refined and subtle conceptual, coherent, and systematic forms is often mistaken. This will be argued later in some detail.

But it is time to return to the specific issues of religion. As we have insisted, men in the name of religion, not least in virtue of Christian and Jewish training, do all kinds of things. They worship, pray, attend services, change their habits, and come to believe all kinds of things. But the highly talented and reflective interest is usually directed to the beliefs. For better or for worse, there seems to have been an almost continuous tradition of philosophical inquiry upon the very subject matter of theology itself. Whatever else theology includes, it appears to be, certainly, a kind of knowledge about God. Even the etymology of the word "theology" suggests that, and much of the professional literature gives the historical usage some substance. It is a little less clear whether every religious man claims to know God the way theologians often suggest, but a religious man certainly believes all kinds of things. In any case, at least three big issues are perennially germane. First there is the very meaning of "God," what we will herewith call the God concept; second, there is the philosophic concern with the question of God's existence; and, third, there is the broad issue of the meaning of religious language.

Our point is a simple one. Out of religious exposure and training there has developed a kind of philosophizing about religion. This happens because reflective people believe very easily that they can conceptualize where formerly there were perhaps only pictorial and imaginative ways of speaking. And the topics noted loom large as engaging issues. Some of what is here said will seem a little too negative and will be construed as an attack upon all intellectual inquiry, but this must be considered again. For the author freely acknowledges a debt to Sören A. Kierkegaard and Ludwig Wittgenstein, both of whom taught hearty respect for the ordinary ways in which we learn and talk our morals and many other things, including our faiths. It may be that many elaborated expressions are, for all of their precision and abstractness, also less appropriate, less meaningful, and even pointless. Contrariwise it might be well to be reminded even in a context like this, that none of us can afford to neglect our daily life, our hour by hour existence. If this be existentialism, make of it what you will. Also, none of us can neglect the originating languages of faith, for they are the norms of our elaborated speech. If this be linguistic analysis, make of it what you will. But in either case or both, there is not less thoughtfulness, but more.

------- ✳ -------

Concepts are meaning-complexes by which we refer but do not assert. The word "concept" belongs in the noble lexicon of logic, where it keeps company with other lofty expressions—"terms," "judgments," "propositions," "theories," "hypotheses," and their like. For a long while it has been said that a proposition (or a judgment) is a meaning-complex by which one asserts or makes a claim, whereas a concept only refers and does not assert. Therefore propositions such as "God is a Trinity" contain at least two concepts, "God" and "Trinity," whereas the concepts contain no propositions.

The word "concept" has been nearly synonymous with "general notion," "idea," and "thought"; all of them bespeak the same kind of object or stuff (above we called it "meaning") which we think. Part of the task of philosophizing has been simply to declare that "meaning"—to make explicit the concept as though it were that which was already addressed in other ways. Thus, in our example, the word "God" might initially be learned in stories about how the world was made. There God is the name of a somebody who makes everything, including Adam and his wife. This God also watches over Israel and he neither slumbers nor does he sleep. As the story gets longer, we learn more things about him, for he sends a Son to earth who says in turn that God, the father, and he, the son, are one.

In these many uses of the expression "God" a certain kind of meaning-complex is surely being drawn up for us. If one exposes himself to this long story, a kind of familiarity with the term "God" is gradually acquired. But if we ask, "Is there only familiarity with the term?" the answer seems clearly to be "No." For most of us would be strongly moved to say that we understand the meaning of the term, not just the term. We find ourselves saying that we "see" and "hear" the term, but we "think" the meaning. There are any number of things to be said about this, but for the present, we can at least note how plausible it is to believe that meanings are different than words, that the former are conceived and the latter perhaps perceived.

But another step is usually proposed. If the many uses of the term "God" are for purposes of getting a general meaning clear to oneself, then these first uses are like means to an end, not expressions to be understood in their own right. So it is often asserted that the many times the word "God" is used is to effect our own awareness of the meaning of that term. Without being very clear about the details, most of us, and certainly very often the brightest among us, are inclined to think that the many uses are incomplete uses, that many meanings are by themselves incomplete meanings, and that the many particulars need a general and commanding notion.

Getting the concept clear for oneself appears, then, to be a most laudable goal. To revert to our earlier example, we will remember how religion is in fact taught, seldom if ever by the bare concept or even a net of such concepts. Instead parables, anecdotes, and stories are told and perhaps creeds which summarize them. However, once one has acquired a taste for concepts and conceptual meanings, the whole shape of popular religion seems quite different and inadequate. For then, the concepts seem to have been involved all along; they seem to have been there in some sense, maybe implicitly, prior to their discovery. It is as if they were meant all along, as if the concepts (i.e., the meaning-complexes) were present in some immaterial and mysterious way long before the philosophically minded reader came along. We then say, confidently, that the God concept is of an "immaterial substance," "omnipotent being" "necessarily existing" and all sorts of other things and, furthermore, that the earlier uses of the word "God" in the stories and parables are the warrant for our saying these more startling and abstract things.

The God-concept is an excellent instance of how philosophical issues arise. One can also readily see how the issue becomes apparently crucial, for one can scarcely resist the thought that this is a veritable foundation of the religious life. Few of us can afford to appear so churlish as to deny the importance of being clear on the concept of God! For that is how the matter comes to mind. Ordinary religion, including Scripture and the rest of our nontechnical talk, seems nonconceptual and humdrum, if not downright mixed up and incoherent. When the dialectical and sophisticated reader gets at it, the promise is very great indeed, for he seeks the general notion that includes all the rest, the idea that makes the others but the examples, the meaning of which the others are but fragmentary expressions.

Most of us, in fact, live our days not only with ordinary interests but also with a common-sense view of the world. Furthermore, we are convinced, and rightly, that this view is in most respects completely true. Every sane man who also has the use of his eyes and ears believes and knows in a commonsensical way. And this sense is common to people of all societies and places. G. E. Moore, the British philosopher, speaking of this matter, says: "Does one need to add: And of which, for many centuries, it would have been true to say this?" [1] Moore and others have noted that this view includes "numbers of things which everybody knows or believes," such as "that he was born," "the existence of other minds," that we have a hand with five fingers, that there are tables and chairs, that there is a world, and so on.[2] But it is also true that this common view is not organized and articulated by those who share it. Nor is the view itself usually a philosophy, even in the vulgar sense of that term. No one who is plainly commonsensical bothers to collect such propositions or even bothers much to see whether every item or every proposition is believed by everybody.

Religious teachings of the West, including the large doctrinal claims, certainly are by and large congruous only with a common-sense view of the world. Doctrines about God, church, and the rest are added to such common components as noted. Teachings of a metaphysical sort which say that there is no world or that the common-sense view is illusory (and such views we find linked with Hindu and other religions) are quite alien to, among others, Christianity, Judaism, and Islam. Indeed, some religions seem to be taught via some large and inclusive views of the world. Being taught in this way is like getting your religion through and with a metaphysical scheme—some kind of view as to what the generic features of the world really are. Such religion is immediately dependent upon a very uncommon and perhaps adulterated view.

I have been arguing that religion is usually taught us in a variety of ways and not by understanding first a view of the world which repudiates these common-sense convictions. But a variety does not imply a completely shapeless and haphazard teaching; such teaching also includes a number of things which *everybody* knows and believes, plus a number of things which religious people in other ways come to know and believe.

We noted earlier that most philosophy arises in the attempt to conceptualize much of what we have learned and believed. Religion is learned not via a philosophy but in quite ordinary ways. Most people do not even come by it through doctrinal teachings though these when coupled with other activities are often effective teaching devices. An analogy might be useful here. Sometimes it is said that scientists are materialists. And there are people who even say that one must be a materialist in order to be a proper scientist. But this is a confusion and not because the insistence is simply upon materialism. All men who study the sciences also share the common-sense view. It may well be that some scientists will conclude after reflection upon their work that they are also materialists and that other views are wrong; but it is a downright mistake to insist that believing in materialism—and this view of the world is often believed to be typically philosophical—is the condition for scientific work. Today we have a host of new and modest emphases in the philosophy of science which make these large claims suspicious. Most philosophers of science are trying to define the concepts and clarify their relations as these arise in scientific work, rather than repudiate them or propose new ones. The point to remember is that scientists are not taught their science via a general philosophical view except in very rare and thoroughly bizarre instances, instances which make the whole process most unscientific. This is not to deny that all kinds of issues arise in the matrix of the common-sense adaptations of the sciences, which become the germinating point for philosophical inquiry. For example, persons of scientific temper and training often wonder about the concept of matter, for this concept seems suggested by a variety of scientific usages by which people refer to what is.

Yet there is a fault produced by philosophizing and it is a very great one; and philosophy frequently produces a whole nest of problems, problems which are often used to dignify a person as being very subtle and profound. With the pursuit of the meaning-complex that supposedly goes with, for example, the word "God," comes the theme that the meaning is really missing. If not missing it is only intimated and suggested in shadowy fashion by the discussion already at hand. Thus philosophizing becomes a time-consuming and endless search for the full meaning which goes with the concept "God." All kinds of interests become relevant. Some people look to expressions like "the unknown," others to "the unknowable," others to a first cause of all the causes, to being-in-itself, to the ground-of-being, to the *Ding an sich*, to un-caused causes, to substance, to the *nisus* in events, to "the power which makes for good in the universe" and a bevy of other possibilities too. Today there are philosophers who do ontology in the interest of getting the God concept cleared up and still others with maximal logical talents pursue idealizations that can only be articulated in abstract and artificial languages.

My concern is to insist that these are unsatisfactory ways of pursuing the meaning of "God." Surely we are tricked by the language into thinking that there is one master meaning which goes with "God." And philosophical interests which feed and sustain this quest ought to be most thoroughly examined. It is questionable whether there is any meaning lying in wait for our discovery and analysis, be it of God or otherwise. Certainly God is being referred to when religious men speak; but the philosophical interest is not simply in the referent but in the supposed meaning-complex, which like a mysterious correlate corresponds to it and supposedly relates to other meanings too that are correlative to most of the other significant words in our everyday language.

Philosophers then purport to have a major problem. Some of them know the vocabulary of faith and they know his name, but the relevant meanings are missing. It is altogether easy to go as Plato did to the con-viction that there exists for reflection a world of numberless, colorless, insensible Ideas (though we would say meanings) which impart character and quality to everyday objects. But meanings and Ideas, so the tempting account goes, like many other supersensible things, can only be thought, not otherwise perceived. The difficulty is only that such meanings are not completely known. It is as if philosophers knew in some strange way that they must be there in principle—or in possibility—though they are not known in fact. So the problem of knowing them becomes the unrequited task of understanding.

All of this must clearly be a misunderstanding. For one and surely a most pertinent reminder is that the meaning of a word consists in its use in the language.[3] Therefore, it is salutary for every reader and learner of religious practices and doctrines to understand that the languages of faith, the ordinary ways of talking of prophets, psalmists, Apostles, probably even some later preachers, are usually quite enough for us to come to full understanding. But it is also well to remember that the uses of the word "God" within a literature as many-sided and as many-purposed as the Bible are as various as the uses of many familiar things, for example, our car, our tools, or the numbers from 1 to 10. The variety is probably too wide to be brought under any single formula. We are again tricked into believing that the word "God," because it is discrete, recognizable, unvarying, and a peculiar kind of thing, must also have an equally discrete, recognizable, and unvarying kind of meaning. What we cannot then find, we sooner or later pursue and eventually invent. This is the stuff from which much philosophizing in religion is made. In contrast, we suggest that the better part of wisdom is to remember that the word "God" has indeed these many uses, but these uses are not unlimited in number and not random in scope either.

We must then be reminded that a certain kind of philosophizing is a trap for the unwary. And it takes great efforts to get out of such traps as these. Kierkegaard likened such difficulties to the habit of getting drunk on the most expensive liquors, a habit which is all the more difficult to cure because of the expense involved.

This is not to say there is no sense to philosophical inquiry, but it is to admit that many philosophical difficulties seem to arise from misunderstandings which have the character of depth. For these forms of language, like that noted with God and present also with a host of related religious expressions, are all-pervasive and ostensibly basic. Therefore they are not unimportant, even though they are induced by properties that are justly spoken of as being verbal. The near-tragic but also humorous side of this is that the best educated and most talented people are the only ones subject to such problems. It is ironic to note that most ordinary men and most Biblical writers, too, speak meaningfully; but later readers, infinitely more gifted, and heirs to countless increments of knowledge, though heirs also to their words, conclude that the meanings are missing. They have puzzles which get more deeply set the longer they think in this way.

Therefore the proposal is both negative and positive, negative because we must learn to curb all the tendencies, philosophical or otherwise which make us think more highly of indiscernible and unspeakable meanings than we ought to think, positive because we must learn to take with utter seriousness the actual religious use of language and not allow our philosophizing to interfere with or to slight those uses. But this brings us to the other aspect of philosophizing respecting religious matters which surely is legitimate—namely, to keep the sense of religious words straight and clear. We began by saying that philosophy was the conceptualized common sense of mankind, but we also noted that attempts to supply meanings for these concepts, as if their uses were already insufficient, was a gratuitous creative and constructive function. But there are concepts—and we mean by concepts those complexes by which we refer but do not assert: "God" is such a concept—for an understanding of which we need to recover everything, to do everything whereby the use of a word becomes lively and relevant, efficacious and appropriate. In short, religious words need contrite hearts, guilty consciences, a sense of wonder and awe, before they can be well used and hence understood. Short of this there is yet another task that is philosophical. For religious needs and especially the most significant ones, do become all too easily confused. What is their apparent enrichment, when alien usages like the idea of God in scientific explanation or God as the name for "the aesthetic unity of the manifold" are fed into the corpus of religious teachings, may actually breed confusions. It is at this point that conceptual study is needed simply to break up the easily wrought syntheses and amalgams of meanings.

Surely there are great differences between the uses of the word God in religious contexts and those we find in metaphysical treatises like Spinoza's or Whitehead's or in scientific-speculative accounts like Teilhard de Chardin's or Carl Jung's. Searching out the differences is much more difficult than asserting the analogy, for the analogy, again, is suggested by the very word "God" and related words (divine, theistic, transcendent, etc.). Neither is this task trifling. It is clear that we can make mistakes even in ordinary unlettered discourse; and if we can mistake Baal and the God of Abraham and Isaac, if we can judge as Pascal did that the God of Abraham is not the God of the philosophers, then there is order even in our common and most ordinary discourse. The fact that everyday speech is effective, and markedly so, suggests that such words are often in order as they are and need no translation before becoming clear and powerful. But that very order means that philosophers have something to describe and something by which to correct the confusions that continually arise. This order does not have to be invented nor contrived. In the case of religion, the order is discernible in the language of worship, of creeds, of stories, and of parables. The task is to recover their proper use, not their esoteric meaning. More of the task is to discern the patterns and perhaps formulate some rules of usage in addition to simply noting them.

It is of no small consequence, then, to be able to discern with confidence the differences between the God concept when it is used in contexts of scientific explanation and when it is used in church. It might well be that this concept is inappropriate in all scientific work, and its inappropriateness might also be the reason for the progressive disuse of the expression in the history of scientific research. Rather than this being a retreat and a sign of growing irreligiousness, this disuse by scientists also might be real progress, a progress which, with more and more things asserted about the world, made very clear that the concepts necessary to explain, to predict, and to know in certain refined and precise ways did not demand the long familiar God idea. It is a different matter whether the scientist, rather than the science, can do without the concept. It is the claim of religion that every man needs God, though this is not to say that every conceptual scheme needs the God concept.

Such a confusion is not a small thing. On the contrary, to be able to say as much in a responsible and considerate manner is a large part of wisdom. And philosophy is wisdom. Our point is that the pursuit of the meaning to go with the big word "God" is a vanity if it entails the invention of a new vocabulary, a new language of the pure meaning, by which the old ways of speaking are then refurbished and redefined. No, the concepts are indeed to be taken with seriousness, but this happens only when one returns to the primitive expressions and learns to use them. Meaning is not a thing about which one can write or at which one can peer. We cannot tell anyone the meaning, as if it were something to be added to the words. The point is that by learning to use the original expressions, one comes to use the language meaningfully. And here is the issue—not the noun, "meaning," to go with the word "God," but rather the variety of uses. A concept is a meaning-complex but a meaning-complex is largely a complex of uses.

------ ✳ ------

Over and over again, philosophically oriented writers have professed difficulty with religion. One of the principal issues is whether or not God exists, and this issue is now dignified as a problem, one to suffer and, we may hope, resolve. In tracing the lineaments of this problem we hope here to do, over again, our own philosophizing.

It is quite clear that the question of God's existence does not arise as we learn our religion. In fact, the bulk of religious literature is only tangentially concerned with it, and it does not arise as a philosophical issue with St. Paul, Jeremiah, St. Francis, Luther, or the Psalmist. Instead, the question is associated with Anselm, Thomas Aquinas, Kant, students of all kinds, and what one might call the academic tradition. This is not to denigrate the issue nor to resolve it. Such a consideration only places it in its usual context. Typically the issue of God's existence marks a philosopher (but one who also might be religious) rather than a religious writer or thinker.

Again we might refer to the common-sense view of the world which all of us imbibe so freely. All of us know that there is a world around us, that the sun, moon, and stars are a long ways away, and that we have hands, feet, and internal organs. But if the issue is raised—how do you know there is an external world? Does the world exist?—we are hard pressed to give an answer. Our learning that there are all these things is entirely inadvertent, and when someone presses us to declare how we came to know we simply are unable to say. The proposal of philosophers to make advertent the belief that there is a world seems bizarre at first, for in one sense we all know that already. But when the demand becomes insistent and we are unable to oblige, there again appears to be a major lack. Once again a major philosophic problem emerges. Philosophers who have thought long about this and who conclude from some kind of reflection that there is a real world are called realists; but it is quite apparent that most persons have no problem and that they are certain without evidence even being sought.

The issue of God's existence has always seemed terribly difficult. For one thing, it is true that many persons distinguish the idea of God from God's existence. Just as we say that gnomes exist only in the story and nowhere else, so there are persons who say God is only an idea, a meaning-complex, a concept, but that he does not otherwise exist. With such a prospect the religious life begins to fade, for how can there be faith if there is no God? The issue again seems paramount, and everything else in the array of doctrines ostensibly depends upon this issue. Philosophy appears to be basic. Where others have taken for granted God's existence, the philosopher now inquires.

So we have irresolution and uncertainty. Is there a God? Much effort has been spent to show that we can infer God's existence if we only mean by God certain things. For example, if God is what we also can call a first cause, then it has been asserted that a first cause must exist; if God is a first mover, then it has been contended that a prime mover must necessarily exist. Some men have philosophized even to the end of showing that the concept of God is so strange and unlike other concepts that existence is a characteristic included within the very meaning itself. Therefore to deny God's existence is absurd. Analogous arguments have been proposed about God as designer, as purpose, as perfection, and many other but perhaps less persuasive convictions. There is something deep about all of these matters too, and one cannot dismiss them easily. But all of the arguments noted surely depend for their validity upon agreeing that the God concept can be enlarged in one or more of the directions noted. Thus if the meaning of God does not cover "designer," or "first cause," or "perfection," then the argument falls flat. And it is not clear from religious literature that God does mean any of these things. Usually the meanings have been already declared by a kind of philosophizing and reflective inquiry before such arguments really can move at all. The claim of most philosophers is that the meanings are implicit all along and that they are being educed not added; but we have already noted reasons for denying this kind of claim. We have antecedent ways of talking about God and they invite only rules which govern further usage; they do not evoke meanings in other senses.

The arguments for God's existence, furthermore, are pertinent only if reflection has broken the natural and ineradicable bond between words and objects, consciousness and things. For it is an inalienable feature of consciousness always to think and to speak "of," "about," "to," "for," etc. Prepositions in ordinary speech have no peculiar corresponding mental acts or ideas to go with them. But a feature of a kind of intellectual analysis to which all of us are heirs is to distinguish between an idea and a thing. We speak of "an idea of the tree," "an idea of God," and we find it easy to separate "the idea-God" from "the existing God" and "the idea-tree" from "the tree." We then must reconstitute the "of" and the "about." With the idea or concept of God, an inordinately rich and flexible concept at this juncture in history, the issue is even more confounding; for we have a singularly rich content—God the Father, Son, and Holy Ghost inextricably tangled up with causes, motion, perfection, Being-in-itself and a galaxy of other meanings—but also a pervasive disquiet about whether such a God exists.

Once the distinction is drawn between concepts and things, words and objects, there seems to be a most singular rift. Only very bright and self-conscious people are able to make such a distinction; and this must be why philosophizing is so exciting, for the problem of God's existence is not for the obtuse and the crude, only for very good minds. We are sure that the idea exists: to think an idea is to give it existence. But God's existence is another matter altogether. And what began as an idea or concept "of" God is now a God concept, and whether it is "of" anything is the reflective issue. Again this matter is analogous to a host of convictions which we have in our common-sense view of the world. Most of us know that there are sticks and stones, other people, and an impressive array of heavenly bodies. Once the distinction is drawn between those words, "sticks," "stones," "other people," "bodies," and objects, then their relations become a moot point. The question of the truth and falsity of our descriptions of these things is altogether separable from the question whether there is anything to which such words (and concepts) stand related. The common-sense view of the world includes simply our knowing that there are such things; and all of us will admit that more detailed descriptions, some of them of a most magnificent and scientific sort, can be proposed, sometimes as corrections and most often as supplementations to everyday knowledge. But the point is that both elaborate descriptions and plain ones, both science and, for example, newspaper talk, are subject to philosophical scrutiny. Neither kind has really resolved the above-noted existential question: Are there such objects?

Whether one speaks of the ordinary talk of the pious layman or of the sophisticated descriptions of the virtuoso theologian and Biblical scholar, the same distinction can be drawn and the same question forced upon that language. This is how philosophy gets rooted. But now another matter must be engaged if only in order to reflect our way out of this set of difficulties. For there certainly is no profit in engaging the issue of God's existence, except as a salutary intellectual exercise. If the prosperity of faith is really dependent upon being sure of God's existence, as it certainly appears to be, then there is very little prospect of return for the would-be believer in attention to these arguments. At best, the arguments are inconclusive and even sophistical. Again the issues must be thought about more deeply, rather than less so.

The so-called existential question cannot be solved as though it were a problem for which thinking men were seeking an answer. It has never had an answer save a peculiar and temporary one that might thrive until the thinker became aware of the legerdemain and juggling of conceptual meanings that was going on. Once that was clear, then the search went right on. The point to be remembered here is that we are victims again of a captious way of proposing the issue. We have for too long been treating ideas and concepts, meanings and notions, by analogy with physical things. This practice goes back to ancient times, but it has been reinforced by all kinds of British empiricists and recent thinkers as well. For treating ideas as things has had obvious advantages, but they all are short-lived. Once ideas and other so-called mental contents (perception, sensation, notion, etc.) were thus defined, they seemed only to need description in order to be known. A kind of armchair description has not been wanting in the past one hundred years. But important features were then forgotten, namely, that ideas and mental contents are not things at all, and they are not like things in any important respect. For example, we add all kinds of relations to a thing—we use it "for" this and that, we contrive one thing to do for another, etc. but with ideas it is altogether different. Ideas have no "for" or "of" added to them, for they do not exist in that independent and detached way at all. They are already "of" and "about"—these are not added, they are already constitutive.

Therefore, there is no general problem of existence, of which God's existence is but one instance. For such a problem depends upon our saying that concepts are meaning-complexes laid up somewhere (in heads or "out there") and that their relation to existence is an optional matter to be done by the thinker if he deems it wise. Ideas and concepts are not stored up anywhere. To think conceptually requires that one practice the uses that are appropriate. Therefore, most existential issues (of the logical and epistemological variety) can be resolved only if we remind ourselves of what the original usage was. For example, the problem of the existence of the external world cannot be solved on its own terms. The way one solves it is to recover slowly and in piecemeal fashion the ability once again to talk about sticks and stones, hands and feet, and all kinds of other things. Once the habit of distinguishing between the concept of a stick and the stick is vanquished by thinking the stick, the issue will gradually disappear. Of course, there are pink elephants, green giants, elves, and gnomes; but the existential problem does not really arise here anyway, for we all learn to talk about these creatures too in a responsible way without much confusion.

With God the matter is not quite so easy. For religious persons come to believe in God in such a way that they do not know that they are also believing in his existence. Therefore, it is always something of a surprise to have a philosopher delineate that believing in God and church and other doctrines logically entails that one also believes in God's existence. The difficulty inheres in the fact that the use of the word "God" in religious discourse is such that the word or the idea is already "of." There are not two acts—first, entertaining the idea or concept, and then, believing that God exists. The idea of God, like other ideas ingredient in the common-sense view of the world and our ordinary language, is already a referring notion. We don't think the idea, we think about God. That is the way with all ideas, until we are erroneously caused to think about ideas and to construe them as objects. Furthermore, we do not ordinarily first think an idea and then refer it to a something; we simply think the thing.

What philosophizing has wrought, more philosophizing must undo. We need to remind ourselves of the fact that coming to believe in God is coming to believe in a religious manner. And the proper way to believe in God is to worship him, to love him increasingly, to do his commandments, and many other things. In so doing, people believe in God. It is a mistake, therefore, to tackle the issue of God's existence frontally, as if it were a plain problem demanding a plain answer. The issue of God's existence can be dealt with only indirectly. "And by this we may be sure that we know him, if we keep his commandments." [4] The use of God's name must be learned in the religious context, and when it is learned there, it brings its own assurances. Indeed there are a host of other questions which can be raised about the existence issues too (for example, whether "existence" is a predicate), but these are subsidiary to the question just noted.

Apparently it is the case that the religious life, with all of its strenuousness and demands, does also have its compensations, not least of which is the certainty that God exists. But this certainty is a common-sense assurance, not made plausible by evidence and not in any sense a proof. Furthermore, it is not as if a proposition or claim were being vindicated. Rather, the religious life teaches the use of the religious language so firmly and unequivocally that the assurance is also immediate. This is why religious people do not have a need for arguments for God's existence, and if they conceive them, they usually do it for the unbelievers. But for the latter, as Pascal noted, they are usually not convincing and for the former they are unnecessary. This assurance is as native as the fact that the religious man uses the word "God" always to refer to God, not to the idea of God. This assurance is very much like the conviction so widespread among people of common sense, that, of course, there is a world, and who would dare to think otherwise? Religious living does as much for the question of God's existence.

It may be that assurances about God are more hedged about than the other characteristically existential commitments of our common-sense view. The religious literature is replete with such suggestions. "If with all your hearts, ye truly seek me, ye shall ever surely find me." It also might be a matter of wisdom to remember such sayings in order to keep the similarities and differences between the supposed philosophic problem, now often called the ontological problem, or the existential reference, or the problem of existence, very clear. In religious contexts, the issue of God's existence turns out to be similar only in trivial respects to other existential issues, and the differences involved between believing in God and believing in the world are all the differences already marked out in the differences between the activities of daily life and those enjoined by a distinctive religious way of life.

In another context we might admit that the numerous ways to live a religious life will not invariably lead to ineluctable clarity respecting the God concept and what is involved. Just as we are easily led to assume that concepts ought to have clear definitions and meanings, so we can be led to think that the Scripture's many ways of talking are examples of a common meaning that we are presently unable to state. But the religious life and religious ways of talking are not an indirect way of getting to the issue in default of proofs and clear concepts. The how of the religious life is also the how of the language; and there is sufficient material to tell anyone what the religious way is. Kierkegaard helped make it clear that though many of the words might be the same in different views of life, still putting those words to aesthetic uses, to ethical uses, and even to religious uses, certainly made them quite different. So it is with religious words. Even the confidence to use the word "God" comes with the religious way of life; and the fact that it can be used lightly to swear and strongly to found a new life is but testimony that the particular way and how of taking it is the secret.

------ ✳ ------

We come, finally, to a third problematic issue, one again which comes to birth with the application of philosophical talents and concentrated intellectual attention. This is the problem called so casually "the meaning of religious language." Already I have noted religious concepts as the locus of one kind of meaning issue. The question of God's existence seems so crucial to many thinkers because a conviction about it strikes one as being the difference between faith and faithlessness. Here the theme pretends to being the supposition of all the rest, a necessary condition though not sufficient, for the meaningfulness of all the rest. For if there is no God, we say, how can it be meaningful to talk about him? This is like saying, "If there is no world, how can we describe it?"

At this juncture it is well to be reminded of something that otherwise we forget, and some of the thinkers we call existentialists serve here to do that. Oftentimes we do not need novelties to bring ourselves to understanding as much as we need reminders of what we already have encompassed. Repeatedly the issue of the meaning of religious language has been couched as though either (a) religious persons did not know the criterion of what made their language meaningful or (b) that their language was "now" in fact meaningless and had to be made meaningful by new concepts and relevant ploys and inventions. Usually the first way has been used to club theologians and religious thinkers into silence, purportedly because they simply were ignorant and/or irresponsible, maybe both. The second way has been practiced by both theologians and philosophers as a kind of subtle apology, warranted to make the everlasting quest for meanings part of the religious life itself. But neither way of handling the matter is quite adequate.

Philosophy has often been very obliging in both of these respects. Many contemporary philosophers have even tried to provide criteria of meaning—indeed, to discover them. There have been inclusive and exclusive views, revivals of older philosophies which ostensibly are rich in kinds of criteria and the newer positivisms which have proposed very tight and circumscribed criteria, so circumscribed that they make religion and morals suspect because they mean, it is said, only emotively and not cognitively. Recently, the revival of ontologies along with existentialisms of certain kinds have given the theologians a new lease on life by offering an array of dodges by which to escape the strictures of positivism and other restrained views. Again, certain avant-garde theologians are gleaning all they can from these advanced philosophies in order to show that theology is after all really meaningful if refurbished and redefined. New theologies today are hopefully proposed in order to be more "meaningful," and often their license is granted by some supposedly new philosophical perspective. Sometimes an objectless thought is proposed for which, it is asserted, the entire subject matter is the meaning and no interest whatsoever is given to historical personages and an existing God.

However, we return to the matter at hand by saying that religious language is neither simply description nor simply evocation, neither just expression nor artful trickery. The bald fact is that one must learn to fit one's life to religious language and theology as well as to fit religious language to one's life. This is not to say that its significances are therefore only autobiographical or that it serves only as a kind of public litmus for the internal chemistry of the human spirit. On the contrary, religious language is very much like ordinary speech—it refers to and is about all kinds of things, including God. This still does not mean that one can address its claims directly by comparing the language and the religious object and according it *ipso facto* veridical values. In fact, it is impossible for anybody to declare the meaning or even the truth of any language, including religious language, by reference to any special experience or a special performance or a single occasion. The pursuit of a criterion for meaning—a kind of insightfulness about how language means or refers or counts up—is a real will-o'-the-wisp. Most of us are captured by the possibility of a kind of outside view, a kind of peep-sight perspective, by which we can know the meaning once and for all and then fit all the religious expressions to it. But there are, to date, no rules or patterns to be seen independently of our practices of speech, and there is no way to know the meaning of any speech in advance of the speaking and writing, except through long practice with so speaking and writing. Only a long series of performances and occasions will ever be enough, and certainly no single and unique kind of philosophical experience, call it insight or the criterion of meaning or what one will, will ever declare it.

We like to believe that the pursuit of the criterion of meaning is a fundamentally serious matter, but this is certainly one of the oddest of illusions. For philosophy here seems to promise that we are going to know a criterion which we can grasp in a moment and then use to construe all kinds of writings, including religious, as if they were but applications and interpretations. Most of our language describing human consciousness is also replete with such considerations, almost as though consciousness were the organism in which the ideas, the understanding, the meanings, are located as an ethereal stuff waiting to be expended upon mundane matters of reading, writing, and speaking. Consciousness then becomes an incorporeal arena of thought in which activities go on that make and inspire our words and deeds.

But our point is here to address the question of meaning. Religious language must, of course, be learned; it does not, as Luther said, arise in the kitchen. But how does it come to mean anything except by being put to its appropriate employment? For the religious life is a continuing practice, a way of responding to the world and to God, and religious language reveals itself only in the long series of words, doings, occasions, and beliefs that make up that life. We are only deluded if we think that there is another mental process encapsulating the whole array as it were in a nutshell and for which the long series is but applications and expressions. No; it is to the continuing practice and way of responding that we must turn, even for the meaning!

Here a peculiar belief has to be put to rest. Often we are prone to conclude that there is a religious meaning to be grasped in virtue of which words are then religiously employed. Theology is sometimes construed to be that profound yet elementary understanding in virtue of which other things, ritualistic and dogmatic, could be properly construed. Some kind of profound mental act, ostensibly philosophical and maybe theological, is understood to be prior, at least in a logical sense, to the more mundane religious expressions. But this view is false. The analogy to employ instead is that provided by how children learn their native language. They do not first understand the meanings and then say the word; rather, they are taught the word and words and then after a while they know the meanings. To know the meanings is really a shorthand expression for knowing the range of phenomena, the time and place, the way to say or to write. When the child shows such knowledge not once and by chance but regularly, then and then only can we say he knows the meaning. In this common-sense way, language also becomes religious; but the practice and the how is absolutely ingredient to the what, just as it is with the learning of the child.

Apart from the abstract considerations just noted, there is also the very existence of the man to consider (though here another kind of existence concern is being alluded to). For the teaching of religious faiths is also a teaching of how to handle the world and oneself in it. The point of the religious teachings is not adequately marked until there is a transformation also of the human subject. That is the chief aim of the teachings—namely, to give cause and reasons for a new mode of life and behavior, a new hope, a victory over despair and evil. Our proposal is not something new; it is only a reminder of what people already know well enough. When we said above that religious people are taught to handle the world, we were also proposing that this expression be used to make meaningful the expression "consciousness." For every human being is a synthesis of abilities, dispositions and wishes, hopes and fears, by which he handles and "intends" his world. We intend and handle the world by our expectations, our wishing, our believing, our imagining, our hating and loving. Among other things, the religious teachings are designed to transform and to reconstitute our way of comporting ourselves with respect to the world and all things therein. Therefore we can say with justice that these teachings aim to produce a distinctive religious consciousness.

Religious teachings, doctrines, admonitions, and worship produce the religious consciousness in a variety of ways. And religious language is both an expression of so doing and the cause of it. Sometimes the language is the occasion for the discovery that it has been done or that it can be done; at other times, as with the Psalmist and the Apostle Paul, it is an expression, even a confession, of the doing. This is not to say that "intending" goes on within all of these activities, but rather that to do any or all of these is what we mean by intending the world, or better, by being conscious and handling the world. Being religious, then, is only one way to be conscious; but nothing esoteric or mysterious, atmospheric or incorporeal, is meant. Instead, the many ways to behave— to love one's neighbors, to hate evil, to love God with all one's heart, to care for one another, to honor mother and father—these are the ways by which we are conscious in a religious manner.

Language is ingredient to most of these, sometimes in one way, sometimes in another. It is clear that religious people also come to believe in God and in his love. They also come to believe in their own guilt and sin. But the design of all this is to remind us of the salient fact that this wide array of behavior in which the fittingness of the speech is to be discovered is also the preoccupations in which the language comes to mean. Once again we are back at *how* the language is employed, for here is the crucial matter.

Nothing we have said denies that religious language refers to God and not just the idea of God. But the aspect to be marked is that even the "referent" is achieved in the religious activities and usages, not by an independent philosophical or ontological insight. For the religious way of intending the world and God makes language very important. That language is not simply a sign of an internal religiosity, deep within subjectivity, nor is it an artifact, arbitrary to the age and to be discarded with the passage of time. To confess with the mouth, a New Testament writer reminds us, that Jesus is Lord is one way to be a Christian. Confessing with your mouth is no trivial matter to be done either by rote or second hand; and that in part is what we learn by reflecting upon the stream of particular occasions in which the religious life is defined and enjoined.

Thus the existence of the man again comes to the fore. And here we are not concerned with "existence" as a concept, if such there be. For religious teachings neither give nor presuppose such a concept; instead, they primarily teach us how to live. We learn to hope, to love, to believe in distinctive ways if we submit to them. But all too easily, learned men assume that the teachings must make for and even disguise an array of concepts. Then we are led by this reflection to assume that the concepts and their hidden meanings actually clarify and abbreviate the teachings as well as instruct more firmly and precisely the would-be learner. But there are no such "abstract" mediating concepts. There are, of course, the many uses and gradually a complex of these is brought together such that we can distinguish *agape* from *eros*, *nomos* from "grace," God from a vital force, and so on. Nonetheless, there is no way to the complex of meanings except by the miscellany and complex of teachings, in which practice becomes all-important. The gradual association that goes on as we read the religious literature, the appropriateness of themes and motifs, the fittingness of grace and God, sin and guilt—these and more are what the concepts turn out to be. The complexes of meaning are learned by the juxtaposition of stories and parables, commands and beliefs, that religious training recites from the lives and teachings of others and renews and refounds in the life of the learner. After a while, through constant conjunction and repeated practice, the language and beliefs become meaningful. There is seldom or never, then, any one experience that is the key to the meaning of religious language; rather, there are a large number of experiences and occasions, sometimes alternatives among them, which are characteristic and cause the language to spring to life.

The ways in which religious language becomes meaningful are rich and various. Let us take an example familiar to all. The Egyptians, we learn, have slaves. One day many of them are gone, wandering ostensibly in search of another land. The big words in their story seem to be that God had called them out of Egypt to be his people, that God had covenanted with them so that even under the odd circumstances of their present life they were still chosen by him. Gradually God's will was declared in some commandments and his purposes were identified in a number of other ways. All of this is, in a certain sense, familiar enough to all of us. But how does this story become meaningful?

Without any particular technicalities involved, we can undoubtedly make it meaningful simply as a good story. We can treat it as we would the stories of Faust, of Don Giovanni, or of *The Magic Mountain*. It can arouse thoughts, stir feeling, recreate another society for us, move us to tears, enlarge our appreciations, and relieve our boredom. Even the literature of the Old Testament can be read simply and solely for aesthetic sustenance and gratification. This is one way to make it meaningful. Perhaps as a story thus read, the issue of whether or not it is true or whether God exists is not paramount. However, there are many people who are so constituted, whether by nature or disposition, that they cannot respond to it even aesthetically. If one were a teacher anxious to effect a response, there are many things to be done at such a time. For example, one might dramatize the story, tell it more slowly, acquaint the student with other and nearer examples of slavery and freedom, and so on.

Others might say, "But there is another point to be learned from all this. Look at the story again. Is there not a moral lesson too?" Suffice it to say that morality is ubiquitous and almost everything human, old and new, is imbued with moral factors. Making promises and breaking them, perseverance and patience, lightmindedness and sobriety—all of these are also part of the story. To exploit these in the story and in the reader will probably also make that account meaningful. But thus far, though the story, in one sense, is the same, the kinds of meanings it gets are in consequence both of the story and all that it is plus the uses to which the reader puts it.

Significantly such readings as those proposed have not broken down on the big words like "God," "covenant," and "chosen." For they can be either disregarded in the kinds of readings proposed or they can be ingredient simply as a way of talking, much as we use religious words really in vain, almost pointlessly, in everyday speech. Nor is it enough to say that only the perspective has changed; for words also do so many things that they work for us and mean for us in a wide variety of ways and often really create what we call perspectives.

But how do they come to mean religiously? There is no access to the meaning of the words of the Old Testament via some special theory, philosophical theme, or entertainment of an abstract noun. The meaning is not another thing, apart from the text or even hidden within that text. Neither is the meaning apart from the text the way justice is said to be apart from and different from the compromising actions of the court and slow-moving arrangements of societies. No; the meanings are only the names we use to describe putting the literature to certain aims, purposes, achievements, accomplishments, satisfactions, interests, and the like. We know a great deal about the religion of Israel and we know enough to be able to talk a little about what went before and what came after most of those utterances.

Jews and Christians, though with differences, have used these stories not simply for amusement and not simply for moral strengthening but also to declare who God was, what he did, what the world was, how men ought to live in relation to him and others, and a host of other things. They have used the story of the exodus of the Israelites to identify themselves and to give reasons for saying something about themselves centuries later.

There is nothing obvious about God, about being chosen or being a child of God. To say these things is part of the strangeness of religious language. But that very strangeness demands the strangeness of the religious life before it becomes meaningful and apt. The capacity to use this language, language about a living God whose ways are like the refiner's fire, comes only with discipline and patience—it is small wonder it cannot all be understood at once or immediately bestowed like other trivialities. Though it can be said that the words are easy enough to learn simply as sounds and signs, their meaning is not easy to grasp; but the difficulty does not lie in the abstruseness of the corresponding concept nor the intellectual difficulties to be met in the formulation. Most of the difficulties demand acquaintance but even more, they demand the willingness to make one's life their subject matter too. There are conditions of the subject to be met before the objective references can even be approached and simulated.

The facts of Israel's history are open to all. The historian can "know" in a certain way so as to leave God out. Perhaps this is the way most Egyptians reflected about the escaping slaves centuries ago; and some of the slaves themselves were quick to lapse into such a conviction too. Maybe the drama of it all was exciting to others, both actors and spectators, sufficient to make it a story worth remembering. Maybe some saw moral causes and moral consequences and therefore vowed to change their slovenly ways. Some said God had his hand in the enterprise. Perhaps to most of us, at this distance as among the contemporaries, springs forth the question—"Is this true?"

Oddly enough there is no answer that is really in kind. For the facts available to historians now can never be greater than what the Egyptians had, and there was uncertainty among them. Is it, therefore, only a matter of interpretation? Is there something so odd about what they meant about God that if we knew what they meant we would then agree with their sayings?

Some concerns like these have generated philosophical issues through the centuries. By searching out the conceptual meanings, all kinds of temporary alleviations have been granted to awesome questions. But what I have been suggesting is both easier in one sense and more difficult in another. It seems clear that what the Israelites meant can only be learned in the many stories that the Old Testament literature and its uses in worship provide. One grows into that, and it comes only with patience and honesty, preoccupation and fidelity. Once one sees and knows the how, one no longer asks for proofs for God's existence; for God's existence is an assurance given only the way the conviction that there is a world is given. Indeed one knows God; and one knows enough to recognize mistakes in judgment and conceptual errors; and one knows enough also to identify the meaning-complexes and keep them straight.

Such sober and straightening reflection is more difficult because it requires restraint and attention, not least in respect to oneself, so that one will not be bewitched. Perhaps this chapter is an admonition with two thrusts: "Watch your language!" and "Don't forget yourself!" Together they might be said to blend the merits of linguistic analysis and existentialism. But it is hoped, instead, that everyone will agree that these are matters of common sense, which if taken with seriousness, are the high roads to God and eternal life.

NOTES FOR CHAPTER 6

1 G. E. Moore, *Commonplace Book, 1919-1953*, edited by C. Lewy, London, Allen & Unwin, 1962, p. 280.
2 Note here "A Defense of Common Sense" by G. E. Moore in *Philosophical Papers*, London, 1959, and several papers in the Moore volume in The Library of Living Philosophers.
3 Ludwig Wittgenstein, *Philosophical Investigations*, No. 43.
4 First Letter of John, 2:3.

QUESTIONS

1 What is a concept? Illustrate. Can all language be made conceptual?
2 Do we learn religion by learning concepts? How do we learn religion?
3 What is the task for philosophy in respect to religion? to science? Does the author agree or disagree with others in this volume?
4 Distinguish two uses of the words "existence" and "existential."
5 In what sense or senses were these pages "linguistic analysis"? In what, "existentialism"?

SUGGESTED READINGS

Sören Kierkegaard, *Philosophical Fragments*. New York, 1945. Note that the author-pseudonym, Johannes Climacus, was trying to translate Christianity "into concepts."
Norman Malcolm, *Ludwig Wittgenstein: A Memoir*, Oxford, 1958.
Ludwig Wittgenstein, *The Blue and the Brown Books*, Oxford, 1958.
Erich Frank, *Philosophical Understanding and Religious Truth*, Oxford, 1944.
John Henry Newman, *The Grammar of Assent*. Available in paperback and many editions.

7 *Peter Koestenbaum*

Religion in the Tradition of Phenomenology

The present chapter examines the impact of phenomenology on religion from a philosophical rather than a historical point of view. Our interest focuses on what phenomenology has to offer to the reformulation and consequent justification of traditional religious insights. Religion has been a major historical, cultural, and philosophical force for millenniums; it has manifested itself on numerous levels, from introspection to ethics, from asceticism to sexuality, from love to hate, from protection to persecution, and from peace to war. We must therefore be clear about the referent of the word "religion" intended in this chapter. Religion has had something significant to say about the nature of man, the good life, the human condition, has expressed views about some pervasive characteristics of the universe, and has commented on the structure of being itself. As a consequence, the study of religion can be taken as the examination of man's deepest problems and highest aspirations. It is with this general conception of religion that the present chapter is concerned. Historical and anthropological roots, comparative analyses of rituals and creeds, these are not our present concern. Questions of the truth of specific religious beliefs—e.g., the existence of God and the immortality of the soul —are left neutral in the definition. Our delimitation of the subject matter must not be construed to imply either a humanistic or a supernatural interpretation of religion. In fact, the phenomenological approach seeks to avoid both extremes. Our first task, then, in assessing the impact of phenomenology on religion, is to show to what extent the phenomenological approach to philosophical and theological problems differs from others.

Phenomenology   Phenomenology has become a force in philosophy since Hegel wrote his *Phenomenology of Mind* in 1807. Its most notable formulation as a philosophic method was given by Edmund Husserl (1859-1938), who provided the methodological background and theoretical justification of much of the existentialist philosophy today.

(*a*) In brief, phenomenology holds that all knowledge about ourselves and about the world must begin, in the last analysis, with our own highly personal experience. That principle had been voiced earlier by the American philosopher William James (1842-1910) under the expression *radical empiricism*, and in general it is today a widely accepted philosophical principle. The real, in James's words, is the experienced. The radical empiricism of phenomenology is to be contrasted to the rationalistic tradition in the theory of knowledge. Rationalistic epistemology—ably represented in modern philosophy by Descartes, Spinoza, and Leibniz—held that a priori or innate knowledge of the world is possible. Certain truths, among which we find mathematical and geometric theorems, certain laws of physics, and often also the existence of God, were thought to embody important knowledge about the world but to be nonetheless based on pure reason alone, that is, reason unaided by experience. The empiricist approach, characteristic of the British philosophers in modern history, is traditionally represented by Locke, Berkeley, and especially David Hume (1711-1776). It holds—in sharp contrast to rationalism—that all knowledge about existence (and there can be no exception) must be traced ultimately to experience or observations of sense (internal or external). This view harmonizes with the contemporary scientific outlook, an approach to knowledge that was still inchoate in the eighteenth century but which certainly has reached fruition in our day. Phenomenology is merely an extension (perhaps even the ultimate extension) of the empiricist spirit. It is an extension, however, that incorporates into its total vision some of the insights of rationalists and some of the intuitions of poets. Thus the first defining principle of phenomenology is that all understanding, which includes of course knowledge about religion, is to be based on first-person data and experiences.

(*b*) True to the spirit of radical empiricism, phenomenology concentrates on descriptions of experience. Phenomenological descriptions differ from descriptions of other types in that they deal with the ambiguous fringes of experience—say, the feelings of guilt and euphoria—rather than with simple shapes and colors. These descriptions have been useful in recasting psychological categories and are equally helpful in understanding the nature of religion and its place in the life of man. It follows that the phenomenological approach to religion consists in carefully describing the experiences which give rise to typically religious statements and beliefs. Phenomenological descriptions of religious states of consciousness have a dual advantage: they disclose the structure of the experiences in uncommon detail and they justify the disclosures of these experiences on philosophical foundations that are far sounder than the traditional arguments of rational or natural theology.

(c) Phenomenology contends that ordinary categories of description are philosophically unwarranted and consequently misleading in the effort to understand religion, since they involve a plethora of assumptions about the nature of man, the nature of the world, the nature of emotions, and the like. Most nonphenomenological descriptions of human or nonhuman events presuppose, without any attempt at justification, that some occurrences are external to our minds or persons (e.g., a tree in front of a house), while others are internal (e.g., the feelings of hunger and of joy). Poets and artists have made it amply clear that such facile ego-world distinction does not agree with the facts of immediate human experience. The key to understanding art lies in the realization that emotions and moods are projected onto the world and thereby change the appearance of the world. But the experience of the world thus transfigured does not automatically separate itself into mood and fact. That separation is a subsequent and partially arbitrary superimposition on and interpretation of experience as it gives itself to man in actual fact. A gloomy landscape is mood and fact intertwined. Our ordinary analysis of such an experience is that the landscape is a composite experience: part of it can be classified as mood, and part of it as objective fact. If we are asked to point out which lines, colors, or regions of the painting are mood and which are objective fact, we of course cannot provide an answer. The fact is that the separation is artificial, in the sense that it is our particular interpretation which is imposed on the immediate data of experience. Another way to state the same point is that fact and value are not clearly separable on the grounds of the actually present structure of experience.

Our common-sense categories go even further than has already been suggested in distorting the actual data of experience. The emotional aspect of a painting is presumed to be localized in the perceiving subject, notwithstanding the fact that it is experienced as external, whereas the factual part of it is interpreted to be external to the individual observer. If the sky is charged with mood, the mood and the sky are experienced on the same level, a level which need not be characterized as either external or internal. Finally, in common sense as well as in traditional philosophic views, more credibility and trust are placed in the so-called objective features of the experience than in the putative subjective projections. Emotions are not "real" in the sense in which perceptions are thought to be "real." Phenomenology avoids unwarranted assumptions entailed by these inarticulate world views by describing experience—experience with which knowledge about anything must begin—as it truly manifests itself. Phenomenology thus develops its own categories of description.

The common-sense or naively philosophical analysis of the affective experience of a landscape may be, for all we know, quite accurate. The phenomenological position does not reject, willy-nilly, common sense as false, but points out that ordinary categories are in fact unexamined assumptions and that experience does not uniformly correspond to these assumptions. If we wish to get to the truth about ourselves and the world, we must rely on the pure, uninterpreted, given facts of experience. And that is what phenomenology hopes to do.[1]

The Phenomenological Approach to Religion   How do these considerations affect the study of religion? In approaching the study of religion, phenomenology disregards the common and sharp distinctions made between soul, body, world, creator, emotion, reason, and the like. It endeavors, instead, to discover what in human experience the notions of God, faith, prayer, immortality, perfection, salvation, and the rest correspond to.

The phenomenological tradition must be clearly separated from logical, psychological, anthropological, historical, and comparative studies. The study of comparative religion gives us a list of objective facts about the religions of the world and is only tangentially relevant to the philosophic problem of the meaning and truth of religious assertions. The same can be said of historical studies. From the philosophical point of view, the most that can be expected from these aerial photographs of the outward manifestation of religious consciousness is a perspective of toleration and an escape from narrow provincialism and pedestrian orthodoxy in religious beliefs. Anthropological and psychological studies of religion display certain significant similarities with phenomenological approaches, but also show important differences. Anthropology and psychology study religion as a manifestation of man's existence on earth; the study of religion is for them based on a theory of man of a special kind. From the phenomenological perspective, however, psychological and anthropological theories of man are grossly defective for any ultimate understanding of what it means to exist as a human being in the world. Both anthropology and psychology see man as an object in the world, as something external to the human subjectivity that thinks of him. In actual fact, man is the center of all experience, not an extremity or a distant object which he himself sees. He is the subject that sees. To study man objectively is to study him the way an entomologist studies a butterfly. Phenomenology contends that genuine understanding of man must proceed by the introspective analysis of his own subjective states. While psychology may study religion by drawing correlations between father-child relations in infancy and religious affiliations at maturity, and anthropology may study it by describing the genesis of religious rituals in primitive society, phenomenology studies religion by describing how it feels to be in a state of religious concern and devotion. The latter, according to phenomenological procedures, is philosophically more basic than the scientific approaches, since it fulfills the demands of presuppositionless investigations: it examines the most direct and private data about the world and human existence to which we have access. Phenomenological researches are introspective, and with respect to the question of the truth and value of religion, are more likely to reach significant conclusions with their radical empiricism than are detached scientific observations.

Finally, the phenomenological approach to religion is distinct from the traditional philosophical, theological, and logical attitude. It differs from the traditional rational approach, that is, the approach through the arguments for the existence of God and the immortality of the soul, in holding that the arguments are logically invalid, epistemologically defective, and axiologically misplaced. Religion is a manifestation of man's deepest anxieties and highest concerns; it is not a pursuit of inferring the existence of certain entities in the world. In this connection, the distinction between the metaphysical and the religious God is in order. Aquinas presumably proves the existence of a *primum mobile*. The Unmoved Mover is a metaphysical principle. As such, it is no more worthy of reverence and worship than the law or force of gravitation. The transition from the First Mover to the God of religion—that is, the object of devotion— is carried out by Aquinas with the facile words "and this everyone calls God." He overlooks the fact that the difference between the two is immense. The arguments for the existence of God may be relevant to the metaphysical principle needed to account for the existence of motion in the world, but they are quite beside the point in relation to the problem of the ultimate meaning and fulfillment of human existence, the problem of death, and the like. Here, the religious God becomes relevant, and that God is to be understood in terms of the experiences that evoke him. Yet an important aspect of the phenomenological approach to religion has been the reinterpretation and reformulation of the traditional arguments for the existence of God, a matter that will be touched on later in this chapter.

It is not always easy to dissociate phenomenology from existentialism. The simplest way to differentiate the two is to adopt the view that phenomenology is a philosophical methodology while existentialism is a theory of man that emerges upon the application of that method. It follows that existentialist views about man and the human condition will provide the background into which religious concerns can be fitted.

The Death of God The death of God (Nietzsche's expression) is a fact of modern life. The phenomenological reassessment of religion must be seen against this macabre background. The statement "God is dead" is taken in a context in which it becomes a profound religious concern, in full recognition of the difficulties that such concern faces. Only a man deeply impressed with the need for and potential of religion can see the tragedy and meaninglessness of life as did the atheists Camus and Sartre.

The death of God has been brought about primarily by three historical and philosophical trends: skepticism, science, and totalitarianism.

The development of philosophy from the apex of religiosity in the thirteenth century synthesis of Aquinas, Dante, and Maimonides to the present day is one of increasing skepticism with respect to God. In the eighteenth century Hume and Kant undermined irrevocably the arguments for the existence of God. The philosophy of the twentieth century —in its extreme of logical positivism—has gone as far as to call all religious propositions meaningless. Such increasing skepticism about all knowledge whatever and religious knowledge in particular has signalized the end of religious respectability for the sophisticated intellectual. Philosophical skepticism has caused the death of God.

The growth of science over the last three hundred years has had the similar effect of displacing God as a principle of explanation. If God is needed at all in theoretical construction, it is solely in connection with the problem of the beginning of the universe. God has been pushed into the farthest distance, a transition usually designated as one from theism to deism, as a useless and ailing grandfather may be placed in an old-people's home by a more vigorous younger generation. Natural law has effectively displaced divine intervention and purpose in explaining events. God as a theoretical necessity or scientific hypothesis is also dead.

The existence of evil is a powerful argument against the existence of God. Hume stated it succinctly in his *Dialogues Concerning Natural Religion* when he pointed out that an all-good and all-powerful God could not, would not, and need not tolerate the presence of evil in the world. World wars, totalitarianism, secret police, genocide, and nuclear threats have signalized the twentieth century as one of the vilest in history. The spectacle, to quote Nietzsche, must be "the noise of the gravediggers who are burying God." The absence, on a mammoth scale, of even a pretense to ethics has been another factor in displacing God from the firmament of man's consciousness.

Thus, philosophical skepticism, scientific progress, and political disasters have conspired to give our age an aura of godlessness. Into this vacuum steps the phenomenological approach. It is an approach that recognizes the importance of religion for a meaningful human existence in the face of the theoretical and practical impossibility of traditional religious views. Religion is like woman in the old Hindu story—one cannot live with her nor without her. To man in the twentieth century religion is both necessary and impossible. Phenomenology therefore hopes to reevaluate the meaning of religion and develop a new foundation for its reconstruction. We now turn to illustrations of these efforts.

Salvation Salvation and God—these two central theological themes represent apparent extremes of emotion and reason (although in essence they are very much alike). Exploration of them will be fruitful for our effort to uncover the full range of religion in the tradition of phenomenology.

THE PHENOMENOLOGY OF SALVATION. Salvation is the religious answer to the problem of the meaning of life. "Salvation" is a term with analogical meaning, in this point resembling mystical terms generally. Salvation, like the idea of the Holy for Rudolf Otto,[1a] does not designate a condition in the world; it means a state of being or state of consciousness that is, strictly speaking, conceived to be "otherworldly." The phenomenological analysis of human experience in general allows for a reasonably lucid and convincing interpretation of the meaning of salvation. The phenomenological understanding of salvation is not reductionistic: the experience of the anticipation of salvation is not reduced to feelings or to psychological, sociological, or anthropological frames of reference. Neither is that experience accounted for blindly in the terms and categories of traditional theology. Phenomenology examines life "from within" and locates the experience of salvation within the human situation. Similarly, salvation is examined from within as an *experience*, not as an inference and not as a hypothesis of a future life.

As an actually encountered experience, salvation has two salient features. First, it is not an immediately present experience, like the pain of a pin prick, but it is an experience of *anticipation*. The phenomenological analysis of salvation must therefore focus on what that experience anticipates, what promises it claims to fulfill. Second, careful phenomenological disclosure of the actually present experience of the anticipation of salvation clearly indicates that it points to something outside and *beyond* ordinary human consciousness. This is an important point, since it implies that phenomenological analyses of salvation must not be interpreted in humanistic terms. Faith in salvation is not experienced as a subjective psychological state. It is experienced as pointing to a fulfilling objective and transcending condition. The external reference of the experience of salvation is a manifestation of that experience as it appears to consciousness. The careful analysis of the experience of salvation—which is the radically empirical approach of phenomenology—is neither psychological (that is, subjective) nor theological (that is, objective), but shows how the two elements are subtly combined.

To understand the structure of salvation, let us examine how the need for it arises out of the human condition. It would be presumptuous indeed to attempt to characterize the salient and pervasive features of the human condition. It would be even more presumptuous to make general statements about the corresponding phenomenological characterizations of this condition, a typology usually referred to as philosophical anthropology or existentialism. Nonetheless, since the phenomenological study of religion emanates from such general studies, a brief sketch is needed.

PHILOSOPHICAL ANTHROPOLOGY. Four great names in the phenomenological-existential tradition shall serve as guides in our delimitation of that aspect of human experience which gives rise to the religious need for salvation. Franz Kafka's (1883-1924) novels, short stories, and parables deal with a lonely man trying unsuccessfully to communicate with or in some manner reach an important otherness—from K's search for Count Westwest in *The Castle* to that of the immediate members of Gregor Samsa's family in *Metamorphosis*. Man's condition is to reach for some perfection, some otherness, some solution to his yearnings, something that leads him to a region beyond his personal ego. Man in search of his *summum bonum* is in effect seeking self-transcendence.

We find a parallel insight, in altogether different contexts, in Husserl's notion of intentionality. All conscious activity—in this case mostly cognition—is a reaching out from the center of personality to an external reality. In the knowledge situation, Husserl refers to the objects towards which man's thoughts (*cogitationes*) are directed as the *cogitata*. The knowing process is a one-directional quest for meanings, aptly represented by the extension of the famous Cartesian formula (*ego cogito*) into Husserl's paradigm *ego-cogito-cogitatum*.

On the basis of these two brief allusions we conclude that man's affective (Kafka) and cognitive (Husserl) nature is to transcend himself. Jean-Paul Sartre (1905-   ) has encapsuled this expansive character of human existence in the expression "Man's project is God." ("Project" is a term borrowed from Heidegger.) The nature of man is defined as pure consciousness—which Sartre calls the *pour soi* or nothingness, since pure objectless awareness is nothing to our eyes—seeking to become concrete being—which he calls *en soi* or being. The ultimate symbol for this ubiquitous human tendency of self-transcendence is God. Hence, the human condition is phenomenologically described in the above-mentioned paradigm, "Man's project is God." "God" thus becomes a significant symbol for theists, atheists, and agnostics alike. For the theist it is the highest reality and the repository of absolute values to which man must conform and towards which human life is to be directed. To atheists and agnostics, "God" is a symbol, in Tillich's phrase, for man's *ultimate concern*, his highest aspirations. The phenomenological structure—that is, the directly present context of the experience—of God as the repository of highest values is the same, irrespective of whether God is thought to be an objective reality or a subjective projection.

Martin Heidegger (1889-   ) was one of the first phenomenologically oriented thinkers to define man's existence as something determined by the anticipation of death. In his words, "Life is a being-unto-death." The inevitable anticipation of death is perhaps the most forceful and certainly the most dramatic reminder of our finitude. Finitude contradicts the very essence of man's infinite quest for self-transcendence; it denies his unassailable project to be God. Meaning in life is thus unequivocally tethered to the possibility of an indefinitely prolonged self-transcendence, while actual human life forever and with supreme tragedy contradicts that possibility. The contradiction between man's projection towards infinity (i.e., God) and his finitude as symbolized by death gives rise to the paradox of human existence, a paradox which leads, in the terminology of Albert Camus (1913-1960) to the utter absurdity of life. This absurdity—or the essentially meaningless character of life—is not brought about by a particular age or by disease or by pain, poverty, and wars, but stems from the ineluctable nature of man himself.

Theological concern with eschatology makes plain the intimate connection between the purpose of religion and the paradox of human finitude. The doctrine of the resurrection in Christianity and its corresponding centrality in Christian theology makes evident the extent to which that religion preoccupies itself with the paradox. In this context, religion is to be interpreted phenomenologically as man's effort to do something about the desperate conditions (to him) of his finitude. To remedy the destruction to his being that finitude, especially death, represents, man must seek solutions outside the ordinary world of experience that he knows. These considerations suggest strongly that finitude, death in particular, must be overcome before life can have meaning. Salvation is the religious name given to the search for a way to overcome this paradox, as much as it is the name for the promised fulfillment of its resolution.

SOLUTIONS TO THE PARADOX. Religious answers to this universal and primal paradox can be roughly classified into three categories: resignation, immortality, and identity with God. The first solution is to learn to accept one's finitude as ultimately good and inherently desirable in spite of its totally incomprehensible and seemingly unjust nature. The cheerful acceptance of the human condition—after that condition has been recognized as meaningless and desperate—is embodied in the universal prayer "Thy will be done." It is also seen in expressions of gratitude for all that befalls one, expressions typical of the prayers of most religions. Humility, self-immolation, and even some forms of asceticism are concomitants of this religious solution to the paradox of human existence.

The second solution is perhaps the one most widely adopted in practice. It is the traditional doctrine of the immortality of the soul, a doctrine whose philosophical roots can be traced to Plato's *Phaedo*. That doctrine denies the reality of death and, with it, rejects the powerful symbol of finitude that death represents. To understand the phenomenology of immortality we must first realize that belief in immortality is belief in a sense different in kind from belief in scientific propositions. Above all, belief in immortality is a belief to be distinguished structurally from a belief in the certainty of death and finitude. In fact, only because he believes in death does an individual's belief in immortality become significant.

Let us amplify this point. To say that belief in immortality refers only to the soul while belief in death refers only to the body is a superficial distinction. The two types of belief are to be distinguished not by their objects (i.e., death of the body and continuation of the soul) but by their inner, phenomenologically disclosed, nature. Here we find a perfect example of total ambiguity. The single word "belief" refers to two uncompromisingly different types of experiences. The act of believing in death is to be distinguished fundamentally from the act of believing in immortality. The structures of the acts themselves show the difference. Belief in death is a certainty that no logic or evidence can dispel. In fact, psychological studies have indicated that people who believe in immortality possess deeper anxieties about death than people who hold no such convictions. Epicurus' feeble effort to eradicate the fear of death through the logical consideration—that while we are alive death is not, and when we are dead, the fear of death has died with us—is unconvincing. The act of believing in immortality, on the other hand, is of the order of a commitment rather than of an unremitting logical certainty. He who believes in immortality has dedicated his life (a dedication possible only in the light of inexorable death) to the following difficult but important commitment: he will spend his life determined to doubt the reality of death by seeking out experiences, attitudes, proofs, and evidences that suggest immortality. His life is deliberately and forcefully surrendered to the exploration of religious meanings. Such dedication, surrender, and devotion is an attitude and a direction suffusing the life of man. It is not a belief in the sense in which he believes the expansion of gases with heat to be true or in the sense in which he is convinced of the certainty of his own death. Belief in immortality is never a firm conviction; it is man's lifelong effort to persuade himself of the unreality of death.

The final solution to the dismal paradox of human existence is associated with mysticism and can take many forms. Although different verbalizations give rise to the view that there are various forms of mysticism, they may be the same in the end. Mysticism hopes to solve the problem of man's meaningless finitude in one of two ways: the individual ego is either absorbed completely in the Godhead, or it discovers that in essence it already is God himself. The phenomenological structure of these two goals of human experience may be identical, since in either case the consciousness of the normal individual disappears and in its stead all that remains is an awareness of and unity with God. Through ascetic practices—from the ethics of humility and self-sacrificial love to monasticism, asceticism, and yoga—the individual endeavors to minimize and eventually to destroy his common self. The phenomenologically disclosed content of bona fide experiences of religious self-immolation is the deeply felt practical (rather than the purely logical, intellectual, and theoretical) extinction of human existence in the world. The assumption in the background of ascetic practices is that the world of ordinary experience, together with the body and the self that make it possible, must be eliminated in order to make room for the superior religious experience of salvation. After such "acosmism" has been experienced, what remains is inner peace, a state of desirelessness and possibly also one of euphoria, a state that can be described well in traditional theological terms—words like "God," "holy," "redemption," "revelation," and "salvation."

Phenomenological descriptions of the inner sense of time, descriptions that have been consummated with exquisite skill by Henri Bergson, Edmund Husserl, Martin Heidegger, and Eugen Minkowski, disclose that the future and not the present or the past is the basic dimension in man's temporal quest for meaning in life. Although mysticism emphasizes the virtues of the spontaneous present, it does so with a view to the future. From the practical point of view of the religious life, the Beatific Vision, that is, the experience of oneness with God, is not a *fait accompli*. It is a hope; it is the direction given to life. Similarly, man does not actually experience his death, but he does experience the anticipation of his death. Mysticism is that religious solution to the existential paradox which substitutes the *anticipation* of the Beatific Vision for the *anticipation* of death. The mystical solution differs from the more common quest for immortality in that mysticism does not wait for death to bring about, almost mechanically, the Beatific Vision, but expects to achieve it in the immediate and lived future. The life of a mystic is thus dedicated to the pursuit of that experience. That dimension of time which defines man is the future. It follows that death is experienced as in the future, and so is salvation.

The Transcendental Ego   We now turn to an elaboration of the nature of the mystical experience, which is described as a feeling of identity with God. The phenomenological description of the insights of mysticism are *ipso facto* phenomenological descriptions of God. We begin this analysis with an exposition of Husserl's notion of the Transcendental Ego, through which he has provided the basis for an understanding of the mystical solution to the existential paradox. Husserl developed it in epistemological contexts only—to account for the ultimate source of our constitution of the world—and not much attention has been paid to it in recent philosophy. His doctrine of the Transcendental Ego is also reminiscent of the absolute idealism of Georg Wilhelm Friedrich Hegel (1770-1831) and, especially, of Josiah Royce (1855-1916), as well as of some forms of Oriental nondual idealism. The winds of doctrine are currently blowing the other way. As a consequence, Husserl's idealistic leanings late in life have been frequently dismissed as aberrations from his more productive thoughts. The paradigm of the intentionality of consciousness mentioned earlier (i.e., the *ego-cogito-cogitatum* triad) can serve as basis for a brief explication of the Transcendental Ego and its religious implications. Though Husserl did not give religious significance to his doctrine of Transcendental Ego, the doctrine lends itself to such implications. To them we now turn.

When I focus my attention on any object of apprehension—a physical object, an abstraction, a feeling—no problem regarding the nature of the ego appears. But when the intentionality of consciousness directs itself on the ego proper, when I explore my own ego, then the above analysis of consciousness demands that we postulate two different egos in experience: the ego that is perceived (called the *empirical* or the *psychological* ego) and the ego that does the perceiving or apprehending (called the *Transcendental Ego*). The Transcendental Ego is the ultimate core of consciousness. It cannot be apprehended in the manner of an object—since it is the perennial subject—but it is nonetheless present in experience.

Phenomenological analysis makes it plain that the Transcendental Ego manifests itself in consciousness in a manner altogether distinct from ordinary objects of experience. A description of the appearance of the phenomenon of the Transcendental Ego discloses it to be closely related to the mystical experience of the inner self, the "Deeper Self," as Royce called it, or the Atman or Purusha, as the Vedanta and Sankhya forms of Hindu philosophy respectively have called it.

(1) The Transcendental Ego is experienced as the source of consciousness whenever experiencing takes place, that is, whenever man is conscious. Anyone can disclose to himself the introspectively verifiable characteristics of the Transcendental Ego. First of all, the Tran-

scendental Ego is experienced as distinct from the body and the psychological states of the individual. I experience my anxiety, my joy, and my body. The I that does the experiencing is structurally different from that which it experiences; the I is the Transcendental Ego, and the anxiety, joy, and body represent the empirical or psychological ego. The two egos are at opposite extremes of the intentional stream of consciousness. Our new triad therefore is *Transcendental Ego-cogito-empirical ego.* The properties of the empirical ego (the *cogitatum*) are not the same as those of the Transcendental Ego. Both egos, however, are clearly present in consciousness. Philosophy has not concerned itself much with the phenomenological description of the appearance of the Transcendental Ego. Sartre, in fact, denies its existence altogether. But in denying it he merely uses the term "nothing" to describe this unique and ever-present locus and source of experience. Since the Transcendental Ego is no object in the ordinary sense, that is, no *cogitatum*, "nothing" is a not altogether inept term to evoke a suggestion of that peculiar locus in experience. As a consequence of this philosophical neglect, our language is deficient in vocabulary dealing with the Transcendental Ego.

The persistence of negative theology in the religions of the world can be understood in the light of the independence of the Transcendental Ego here mentioned. The Transcendental Ego is an experienced locus in consciousness, but a locus which does not disclose itself in the manner of an object. That locus is and remains the ultimate subjectivity and inwardness of experience; consequently, the language of objectivity cannot legitimately make reference to the Transcendental Ego. If we now assume that an exposition of the Transcendental Ego is one clue to the phenomenological understanding of God, then we can make sense of many of the manifestations of religion, including negative theology. The view that awareness of God can be evoked only by designating what He is *not*, corresponds to the fact that the Transcendental Ego is inaccessible to ordinary forms of experiencing and their linguistic equivalents. Negative statements are needed, not only for God, but for an apprehension, suggestion, and appreciation of the Transcendental Ego.

(2) The Transcendental Ego is experienced as always the same. It is the continuous background of changes in the empirical ego. These changes in the empirical ego are shifts in mood, focus, growth, outlook, attitudes, and so on. In the midst of such chaos, the individual experiences himself to be the same throughout. That sense of personal continuity and identity has its source in the experience of the Transcendental Ego. The Transcendental Ego is experienced as permanent. It is the peculiar mode in which we experience the Transcendental Ego that assures us that we are the same individual who was born twenty, forty, sixty, or eighty years ago.

(3) The conception of both the death and the birth (i.e., the non-existence) of the Transcendental Ego is impossible. It requires the Transcendental Ego to think, imagine, or conceive the death and birth of an ego. It also takes the Transcendental Ego to think of sleep or unconsciousness of the empirical ego. The ego whose death is anticipated and the ego whose birth is thought is the empirical ego. Birth and death are properties of objects and apply only to the empirical ego. The Transcendental Ego is given as the subject that is capable of thinking in terms of birth and death. This leads us to our next point.

(4) The Transcendental Ego is *experienced as existing by virtue of its own necessity*. Its nonexistence is inconceivable. The connection of the theory of the Transcendental Ego with mysticism, in fact, with the conception of God, is obvious. Let us explore it further.

If we subject the rationalistic doctrine of logical necessity to careful phenomenological scrutiny, we discover that the thin analysis that modern logic has given to it is not the whole story. Logical necessity, for Anselm and Aquinas, as well as for Descartes, meant an *experienced* connection. We see in Kant's analysis of the necessity that joins 5 and 7 to make 12 an *experiential* basis. It is a phenomenologically discovered fact of our experience that certain ideas are connected by a certain unavoidable and hard-to-describe "force." That force is called necessary connection or self-evidence. It is not correct to call it, as some modern logicians would, either a matter of arbitrary definition or a psychological habit (each refers to a different aspect of logical necessity). Necessity in nature is experienced neither as a psychological projection—one which we can through proper habituation remove—nor as the rule of a game of language. Modern analyses of necessity have not been true to the facts of experience intended by the rationalists' use of that concept.

Since the modern view of the a priori sharply contrasts with that of the tradition of rationalism, a few comments on the phenomenological revival and reinterpretation of that notion are in order. We are not concerned at this time with the conception of the a priori as an imposition or projection on experience, that is, with the a priori as an antecedent decision on how experience is to be seen, organized, and understood. That notion of the a priori will be invoked later, in the section on purity of heart.

Philosophical analysis usually distinguishes at least two different meanings of a priori. On the one hand, the history of philosophy has talked about a priori *connections* (such as Kant's famous proposition "5 + 7 = 12" and his "All bodies are extended") and on the other it has concerned itself with a priori proofs for *existence* (such as St. Anselm's ontological argument and Descartes' *cogito, ergo sum*). Modern philosophical analysis tends to view the first as a legitimate and the second as an illegitimate use of the a priori, provided, of course, that the connections stated are purely formal or symbolic and make no a priori reference to empirical reality. In fact, it was Kant who first criticized the a priori proof of existence. Phenomenological analysis of the experience and of the intentional constitution of the a priori discloses that the distinction between the assertion of a connection and the affirmation of existence is spurious. If we mean by a priori *absolute certainty, intellectual indubitability*, and if we mean by a priori the conscious fact that the most careful examination of a region of experience discloses it either to be there or to have a certain structure (which has been the rationalistic view), then it is of very little consequence whether we are certain of a linguistic connection, a correspondence of two types of experience (idea and fact, proposition and states of affairs), a certain manifest structure of a region within experience, or of the presence—that is, existence—of a certain area or aspect of experience. It is the certainty of the phenomenon that matters. Such certainty exists, and it is an important aspect of the theoretical and practical aspects of human existence.

It is not enough to dismiss certainty as a psychological phenomenon, problem, or category as Ayer and others have attempted. Certainty is a fundamental mode of being, part of our transcendental constitution of the world, and as such it precedes, logically and ontologically, any psychological considerations. The complex that is psychology, or any proposition within it, is given to us in experience as either certain or probable. Certainty may or may not be a manner in which psychological contentions manifest themselves to us. The phenomenon of certainty may be used to account for views held in psychology, but we may not put the cart before the horse and use psychological categories to account for elements in our ontological constitution of the world. The category of the a priori is constituted on a level far more basic than categories of any science, including psychology.

The possibility of discovering existence a priori is more important philosophically than the matter of merely disclosing connections. In fact, many a priori disclosed connections entail implicitly an a priori assertion of existence. For example, the a priori statement S_1 "Space is infinite" is to be translated into the phenomenological statement S_2 "Space is a presence experienced as having no clear limits in the ordinary, two-sided, conception of limits." This statement gives expression to the gray fringes of space that the concept of space carries with it. Furthermore, and this is what is important, that statement expresses not only the necessary *connection* between space and no-limit, but it also entails the implicit assertion that space *exists*. The intent of the statement is clearly existential. Statement S_1 is thus analyzed phenomenologically into two. One of these (S_2) describes the event or entity and asserts requisite and necessary subject-predicate connections. The other (S_3: "Space exists") is implied and existential. Statement S_1, therefore, has existential import.

And that import is given directly and with certainty. That is the existential dimension of the phenomenological concept of the a priori.

The phenomenological analysis of necessary connection and self-evidence becomes of the first importance when we examine the medieval and rationalistic notion of *aseity* or *necessary being*. Some things, such as space and time, are experienced in an unusual mode, a mode properly described as *necessary existence*. We now return to the Transcendental Ego.

The Transcendental Ego is experienced as existing necessarily. The reason for such a statement is that the presence of the Transcendental Ego is required in order to conceive of its nonexistence. To conceive of even the possibility of the nonexistence of the Transcendental Ego presupposes the presence, in experience, of the Transcendental Ego. This paradoxical situation makes it impossible to attach any genuine meaning to the expression "The Transcendental Ego does not exist." The name for such an experienced situation has been, traditionally, "necessary existence." This approach to the exploration of the Transcendental Ego is reminiscent of the ontological argument. In fact, the ontological *proof* for the existence of God is the same as the phenomenological disclosure of the element of necessary existence in the Transcendental Ego.

Aquinas criticized the ontological argument on the grounds that a connection in the mind does not guarantee a connection in reality. Phenomenological analysis tends to reject the distinction between "in the mind" and "in reality" as being unclear, imprecise, and in many respects arbitrary and without philosophical foundations. A similar rejection of dualism is found in analytic philosophy. With the denial of dualism, the problems it engenders either disappear or are reformulated. Aquinas' criticism can therefore no longer be taken at face value.

(5) The Transcendental Ego is experienced as external to both space and time. Space and time are, strictly speaking, *cogitata*, that is, intentions and constitutions of the Transcendental Ego. That this is the case can be seen from a number of relevant observations. First of all, space and time are not uniform notions; they refer to at least three clearly distinguishable and mutually exclusive contents or cogitata within experience. Space, for instance (and the same considerations apply to time), may be perceptual, conceptual, or theoretical. Perceptual space is that aspect of our immediate sensory experience which we call extension, perspective, the matrix for motion, etc. Conceptual space is the generalized and abstractive image that we have of all space. This is the most common conception of space, and it is a concept that may have its roots in perceptual space, but extends far beyond the actual and possible experience of perceptual space. It is to conceptual space that we ascribe the predicates infinite, one, three-dimensional, and the rest. Finally, theoretical space is found in modern physics, where space is a set of mathematical dimensions, but

no longer either a sensory, a conceptually imaginable, or a representational construct. Speaking phenomenologically, each of these notions of space excludes the other, from which we must infer that no one of them can be ubiquitous, that is, coextensive with all of being.

The second consideration in support of the thesis that space and time are experienced as external to the Transcendental Ego is that since space and time are cogitata to the Transcendental Ego, they are not coeval with all of being. The totality of being, the vast sea of consciousness that being appears to be, includes the observing Transcendental Ego, an observer *of* space and time, but is not included in them. Third and finally, several elements within our experience clearly exclude the representation of space—numbers, ideals, propositions of logic, and in general, universal concepts—although the exclusion of time is not equally and immediately obvious. However, time itself is an atemporal notion, since it cannot be said to exist in the same time that it designates. In other words, the thought or idea of time is always structurally different, ontologically distinct from and intentionally unlike the referent of that idea.

In sum, the phenomenological analysis of the Transcendental Ego—which is an empirical and quasi-scientific examination of the structure of everyday experience—discloses the Transcendental Ego to be atemporal and nonspatial, since both space and time are observed and meant by it and do not apply to it. Space and time are intended to apply to the physical universe, but no such intention is apparent in the attempt to examine the Transcendental Ego reflexively. Infinity and eternity are therefore permissible metaphors with which to designate the manner in which the Transcendental Ego gives itself to introspection. And these have been traditional attributes of God.

(6) Experience discloses only one Transcendental Ego. Such a view may be akin to the unity and singularity of a universal Spirit found in Absolute Idealism, but it certainly is not a form of solipsism. In terms of the Husserlian categories here developed, solipsism becomes the mistaken identification of the empirical ego (to be precise, of one particular empirical ego) with the totality of being. Analysis of the empirically given structure of being clearly and immediately shows that this identification contradicts the facts of experience. In fact, this identification is absurd. Any empirical ego, including one's own, is seen to be but an infinitesimal speck in the totality of spatiotemporal being.

Furthermore, in connection with the singularity of the Transcendental Ego, it does not make sense to talk of *another* Transcendental Ego, since that Ego would be merely an object or cogitatum to the original Transcendental Ego. What is important to remember in this connection is that the Transcendental Ego is clearly to be differentiated from that entity in the realm of being referred to as "my body." A powerful antidote to the venom of solipsism is found in the fact that the Transcendental Ego, for all its singularity, is given in Husserl's own terminology, as *intersubjective*. The Transcendental Ego is given as a *social reality;* it is made real by an *encounter,* by an I-Thou confrontation. Josiah Royce combined a monistic type of idealism with the notion of community. In a related sense, the full exploration of the Transcendental Ego discloses not only its detachment from any particular empirical ego, but also its intersubjective structure. We have here a quasi-Spinozistic God.

The singularity of the Transcendental Ego has its counterpart in the religious insistence on monotheistic theologies and monistic metaphysics typical of the great religions of the world. If the fact that experience discloses but one Transcendental Ego seems to conflict with the data of being as experienced, then the following further considerations might help to solidify the position here developed: the *continuity* of the Transcendental Ego and the Transcendental Realm. To this consideration we now turn.

(7) The Transcendental Ego has close affinity and may be considered as even identical with the Transcendental Realm or the totality of Being. It has been an insight of the idealistic philosophies throughout history that by the very nature of experience, all being is given as being related to a single core, the Transcendental Ego. The intentional stream of consciousness, symbolized by the ego-cogito-cogitatum triad, and one that emanates from a singular Transcendental Ego and is directed, in myriads of rays, to all of being, makes up the totality of consciousness. It follows both from definition and from intuition that all of Being is experienced as suffused with consciousness, that is, as related to the Transcendental Ego (which I am); futhermore, consciousness—like space and time—is given to us as *one,* that is, as being a single because continuous totality. On the basis of these empirical and descriptive considerations we can view absolute idealism as a natural, albeit metaphoric, expression of these two insights: the ubiquitous experienced relation of all of Being to the Transcendental Ego (which I am), and the continuity of the intentional stream of consciousness. Some religious expressions that have served traditionally as terminological metaphors or symbols for these two insights about the Transcendental Ego and its intimate relation to Being as such are the Beatific Vision, the union of God and man, the identity of Atman and Brahman, and the absorption of man in God (as in Schleiermacher's feeling of infinite dependence or creature-feeling).

The basic continuity and, in a sense, identity of the Transcendental Ego with the totality of being is an insight not limited to idealism, although it does form a central tenet of that philosophical position. When a philosophy uses the word "consciousness" to designate the totality of being, it is in effect asserting the truth of the equation "being = consciousness." That assertion is to be interpreted as an attempt at phenomenological description, and what singles out this particular description from others is that it describes being with special emphasis on its relation to the subjective center of experience, that is, the Transcendental Ego. If the emphasis in description is on the objective pole of experience rather than on its subjective pole, then we come face to face with naturalistic positions in metaphysics. Naturalistic metaphysics tend to postulate or discover a similar unity of nature. In this case the root metaphor is not "mind" or "consciousness" but "matter" or "nature." The emphasis is shifted from the *ego* to the *cogitatum*, without sacrificing the underlying insight of unity. The unity is the same in either case; what differ are the metaphors invoked to decribe them. Both naturalism and idealism speak of a *unity* of all of being that is given in experience. This oneness is a feature of being as being presents itself, irrespective of the categorial a priori with which we organize reality.

It is obvious that anyone familiar with the rigorous development of philosophy in the twentieth century cannot glibly accept a revival of absolute idealism. The core difficulty for absolute idealism lies perhaps in the ambiguous concept of consciousness. Although consciousness is certainly not a "thing" (Sartre has aptly designated it as "nothing," and so have logical positivists, but with an altogether different intent), nonetheless the term is philosophically significant. It makes reference to an experienced unity of being, a unity which has the Transcendental Ego at its source, and calls attention to the subjective commitment apparent in all experience.

(8) It may be possible to comment on the manner of appearance of the pure Transcendental Ego. And this point should be made for the sake of completeness. The height of religious illumination, be it the vision of God in Western mysticism or *nirvana* or *samadhi* in Oriental mysticism, can be described metaphysically as the experience of *empty consciousness*. Consciousness is there (or, what is the same thing, being is there), but the contents are gone, the particular determinations and differentiations have been eliminated. Such would be the experience of the pure Transcendental Ego. Husserl has designated it as the "pure look," the outward gaze without objects. Such a vacuous "look," such an empty universe, is always present in consciousness—at least as one of its constituents—and it is a mere gaze; it is the experience of pure subjectivity.

(9) The ninth characteristic of the Transcendental Ego, its complete freedom, is one of its most important aspects, in part because, although self-evident in one sense, it is contradicted by experience in another. Let us examine this characteristic in some detail.

The Transcendental Ego is experienced as both active and passive. In other words, the Transcendental Ego has its passive and active modes or aspects. In the passive sense it is the observer of being; in that sense, it "opens itself up to being," it makes being possible through its apprehension of it. Heidegger encased this insight in the metaphor that man is the shepherd of being. Since the Transcendental Ego is, by definition, the observer of all of being, the metaphor of omniscience is not misapplied. To know all means to be the observer of all. Omniscience is one kind of freedom; it is the freedom of knowledge. From the point of view of activity, the Transcendental Ego is experienced as free in another sense. Here "freedom" is used in the pervasive sense characteristic of Sartre. Freedom, although limited, is experienced as absolute. For one thing, man's freedom to commitment, to embrace any way of looking at reality or any *Lebenswelt* he chooses is well-nigh total. Again, man's attitude and response to life and being in general are fully and freely in his power—an insight as old as the Stoic's *apatheia* and as new as Frankl's logotherapy. Descartes thought of man's experience of free will as a replica of the divine because, in his words, "Free will . . . I experience to be so great in myself that I cannot conceive the idea of any other more ample and extended, so that this is what principally indicates to me that I am made in the image and likeness of God." [2] Finally, Husserl's notion that the Transcendental Ego *constitutes* the *Lebenswelt*, including the empirical ego, fits into this pattern of explanation. The idea of constitution is not new with Husserl. Philosophers have always known that the world as it appears to us is an admixture of refractory data or qualia, upon which the mind of man, eventually the Transcendental Ego, imposes a certain meaning by virtue of its particular organization, classification, and interpretation of the world of the impressions. For Kant, these interpretative subjective projections are the pure forms of intuition (space and time) and the categories (quantity, quality, relation, and modality). For Husserl, constitution is far more radical and complex than it was for Kant, although the principle is the same. It follows from these various considerations about the freedom of the active aspect of the Transcendental Ego that omnipotence is a good metaphor in terms of which to describe the experience of boundlessness that accompanies the understanding of that freedom.

What was said above about the difficulty and danger of defending some of the insights of absolute idealism in the twentieth century applies with even more force to the ascription of omnipotence, that is, total freedom, both passive and active, to the Transcendental Ego. The following considerations, therefore, cannot be construed to meet the demands for rigor consistent with philosophical analysis, but are rather general outlines indicating, for the sake of completeness, the direction for subsequent phenomenological research.

The Transcendental Ego, as the passive observer and active "constituter" of the world possesses the omniscience and omnipotence ascribed to God. Specifically, the sense of active and passive freedom here invoked can be described phenomenologically as follows. When we focus attention on the Transcendental Ego, to the extent that non-objective apprehension is possible, the experience is one of *pervasiveness* (i.e., omniscience) and *nonresistance* (i.e., omnipotence). But these attributes apply only when the Transcendental Ego is seen in isolation, as the vacuous and pure look, and not when it is experienced as intermeshed with the cogitata of the world. Although these facts may follow from introspective intuition of the general *ego-cogito-cogitatum* stream of consciousness and from the overall outlines of the relation between the Transcendental Ego and being, certain obvious factors—e.g., loss of memory, ignorance, the refractory nature of experience, the anticipation of death, and frustration—contradict these initial insights. In this connection religion has developed some perhaps dubious *ad hoc* hypotheses. The value and truth of religion may well be said to stand or fall with the success with which it can reconcile the apparent contradiction between the intuitions of the omniscience and omnipotence of the Transcendental Ego and the obvious finitude of human experience. If there is an answer within the context of phenomenology, it must be found in immediate experience, not in metaphysical inference; it must be disclosed through careful description of the structure of experience and not through deductive arguments. It may not be possible to achieve such a synthesis, but let the following paragraphs represent attempted phenomenological reformulations of traditional suggestions.

The answer must be worked out by making some order in the confused array of areas of experience. Freedom of observation, commitment, and constitution may not be actual, but it does seem possible. The qualia of experience, however, the pure shapes, colors, and feelings, are refractory indeed. One solution to this aspect of the contradiction is to assume that the Transcendental Ego constituted these pure refractory qualia (called "matter" or "material substance" in older forms of theology) so as to be in the presence of genuine otherness. One of the oldest theological problems is that of the creation of matter. If God, as the Transcendental Ego, is coeternal with matter, then the pure otherness represented by the refractory qualia in experience has always existed, and although the Transcendental Ego is experienced as one, including the apprehension of the refractory qualia, and the structure of experience is in some measure determined, the spirit's otherness (nature, for Hegel, "matter" for Aristotle) has always been in existence. On the other hand, if God is conceived as the Creator in an absolute sense, then he brought about matter in order that it might appear as genuine and independent otherness to him. Free will was retained as a reminder of his true nature. We shall return later to an elaboration of this particular solution.

Another proffered solution is that the experience of finitude applies solely to our experience of an empirical ego: since we tend to confuse (through unanalyzed identification) one particular empirical ego with the Transcendental Ego, we transfer to the Transcendental Ego the sense of finitude associated with the empirical ego. It follows, conversely, that the sense of finitude emerges only when man tries to impose the capabilities of the Transcendental Ego onto an empirical ego. As long as the focus of consciousness is on the Transcendental Ego, the sense of limitation does not arise. These considerations suggest one rather common answer to the problem of the meaning of life, an answer found in many forms of religious mysticism. To experience the infinite bliss which is the Transcendental Ego—that is, omnipotence and peace—the individual must dissociate the Transcendental Ego from its entanglements with the world, and specifically, with an empirical ego. The view is defensible that ascetic practices and meditation exercises reinforce the conscious distinction between the empirical ego and the Transcendental Ego. The meaning of life, i.e., ultimate satisfaction, is to be attained merely through the clear understanding of the Transcendental Ego itself.

In the brief space here available, the above view can be presented only as a tentative suggestion. It must be viewed as the general direction in which phenomenological researches concerning religion, that is, the phenomenological analysis of typically religious experiences, are to proceed. Later, we will endeavor to resolve these paradoxes further. At the moment, let us concentrate on some illustrations.

How can the frustration of desire—the great impediment to finding fulfillment and meaning in life—be thought of as consistent with the omniscience and omnipotence of the Transcendental Ego, which, presumably, resides at the very heart of my being? These are the problems of evil and of man's finitude, problems to which religion has addressed itself since the dawn of civilization. Desire is frustrated when a student fails an examination; desire is frustrated when an erstwhile athlete is permanently crippled by arthritis; desire is frustrated when a politician loses an election, when a salesman loses a sale, or when a great composer becomes deaf. How can we say that the Transcendental Ego is omnipotent in the face of such extensive contrary evidence? How can we reconcile man's sense of absolute freedom with the obvious encroachments on that freedom? Religion has faced this problem and replied that there is a hidden purpose in the light of which all misery is for the best—and that it is the only possible path to the best. That view can be reassessed, and perhaps even be reestablished, through the phenomenological tradition in religion.

In the first place, all the limitations invoked in the examples apply to an empirical ego and are thus properties of cogitata and not of the Transcendental Ego. But such an explanation leaves "the single one," the individual in Kierkegaard's emphatic sense, untouched whenever he truly suffers. Let us therefore turn to a phenomenological disclosure of the experience of frustration itself.

The phenomenological analysis of the experience of frustration involves three dimensions. It includes the experience of desire—the apparently uncontrollable presence of a want—the experience of the frustration of that desire—that is, the experience of obstacles apparently negating the possibility of such fulfillment—and the consequent experience of tension between the two. Our question now is, How can the presence of such a state of affairs be accounted for in terms of the theory of the Transcendental Ego and of the theory of satisfaction, in the sense of self-transcendence developed here (see the section in Love, below)? The phenomenological answer to the problem of evil must be explored according to the following six guidelines.

(1) The desire (or *project*, in Heidegger's and Sartre's terminology) may be inauthentic. Careful examination of the desire in question—in relation to man's basic nature, interests, potential for satisfaction, and the general context of his life—may disclose it to be a surrogate, an error due to ignorance, in short, a misguided project, a project contrary to his own interests, a project that is fraudulent in that it does not yield the satisfaction, fulfillment, and meaning that it promises. He who does not heed the warning of this analysis, when applicable, may be bitterly—and perhaps irrevocably—disappointed.

The quest for fulfillment that follows the path suggested and demanded by desires as they are ordinarily given to us in consciousness leads to ennui and bitterness. The demand for fulfillment, even in apparently minor, unrelated, and atypical instances, carries with it the demand for eternity and the cessation or dissolution of opposing otherness. Neither of these demands, made by the Transcendental Ego within us, can be met by following the path that seeks the satisfaction of desires in the quest for a meaningful life. In other words, the solution to the problem of finding ultimate meaning and total fulfillment in life is not to be given in terms of the alternatives that the demands of desire suggest. The direct satisfaction of desire may not be the most efficient path to fulfillment.

(2) The analysis of the experience of frustration leads to significant insights about the nature of ultimate satisfaction itself. The impact of frustration on the reflective man is that it brings into focus his real and authentic values. The attempted fulfillment of desire often merely leads to further frustration—a theme common to current cynicism in both literature and the theater. A life dedicated to the satisfaction of desires frequently leads to an overpowering sense of emptiness and meaninglessness. The reasons are easy to find. He whose desires have not yet been satisfied lives in the hope that in the future, when his desires will be met and fulfilled, he will achieve the euphoria of Elysium and the eternity of the

Beatific Vision. On the other hand, he whose desires have been met no longer cherishes this ultimate hope, since he has tasted the bitter fraud entailed by such an existence. He has discovered for himself that it is not of the nature of desire to be capable of fulfillment. His cynicism is thus total. It follows that frustration is an important key—a beginning— to the recognition of mankind's true values. Religion has traditionally emphasized that there are such things as "true" or absolute values (i.e., not values to any individual man, but to the one Transcendental Ego within us all) and that they are, in some sense, eternal. This emphasis is a direct consequence of the insights winnowed from the experience of the frustration of desire.

(3) In equating happiness with the satisfaction of desires, we in effect demand the elimination of otherness. Man thinks of himself as frustrated as long as any refractoriness whatever remains in this experience. If one of the many hard cores within his *Lebenswelt* gives in and succumbs to the conquering phalanx of his desires, he demands more; in fact, in the presence of his desires, he demands the same dissolution of the remaining concrete otherness in his life, a demand that has become habitual. But further investigation discloses that what man actually demands in the elimination of otherness is the destruction of all possibility for satisfaction whatever. As we saw already, some frustration—even to the Transcendental Ego and in the sense of an opposing otherness—is an essential ingredient to the acquisition of fulfillment. Frustration, therefore, is not altogether evil. Its presence has something to do—both cognitively and affectively—with the very nature and the possibility of ultimate satisfaction.

(4) Frustrating situations are not as refractory and unchangeable as we often think. Man has the free will and the power to circumvent many obstacles and make good his gratifications. As a last resort, that is, if he cannot change the circumstances in his life that account for frustration, man is nevertheless able to modify and adjust his attitudes and responses to these obstacles. In other words, man must not think of his frustrations as final and irrevocable. Nor must he think of himself as the victim of fate. If his *Weltanschauung* is fatalistic, it is so because he has freely chosen to view life fatalistically. He may choose, with equal freedom, to make every effort to change his environment or to adjust himself to it. In other words, he has the freedom to choose to see the world as partially pliable and as responsive to his demands.

(5) The desire that seeks satisfaction may be neurotic. Being neurotic does not make a desire *ipso facto* undesirable. But neuroticism is an indication of a deeper problem, a problem that resides at the core of the desire that is neurotic. Neurotic desires must be interpreted in the present context to be free *commitments to fantasy rather than to reality*. The neurotic individual has thrust himself into a fantasy world, a world that

has no genuine otherness, while the healthy individual has involved and intermeshed himself with a world that is real, a world in which otherness is concrete and independent.

Existentialist theories of man have suggested that the distinction between reality and fantasy is, at best, unclear. That is true up to a point. If we take as the criterion of differentiation between these two worlds the attitude towards otherness, then the distinction between reality and fantasy is unambiguous. There are still many possible *real* worlds to which man's commitment may be directed. What these different worlds have in common, however, is the seriousness with which the individual takes his confronting otherness.

Fantasy commitments—which in exaggerated form become outright insanity—are unsatisfactory and inauthentic, and that is why they are neurotic. Their inauthentic character stems from their mistaken conception of otherness and of its function in the experience of fulfillment. The neurotic man wishes otherness to disappear, thereby inadvertently flouting his very own demands for satisfaction. It may be argued that the fantasy world is as solid to the neurotic or psychotic as the reality world is to the so-called normal individual. That is not true, since the fantasy world of the neurotic *consists* either of the belief and insistence that his impossible demands be satisfied or of the free, clear, and deliberate distortions of the facts to serve his own inner purposes. In other words, the neurotic knows that his world is unreal, but he chooses to repress that knowledge. In fantasy, the other responds as told. In reality, an encounter with another is unpredictable. In either case, man depends for the quality of his being on the manner in which others respond to him. The neurotic demands that the other respond with the slavishness of fantasies. The reality-committed individual realizes the self-destructive and contradictory nature of such demands. The neurotic is unrealistic because he does not recognize or accept the "facts." But what are the facts? Facts can be changed. The neurotic is characterized by his rejection of—or at least his insistence on rejecting—all otherness or *factuality* (Heidegger's "facticity") altogether. His unrealism consists of the refusal to accept the need for and virtues of otherness.

On the other hand, a reality commitment has the potential for satisfaction because it is a life "in-the-world," and because it is free and full dedication to the acceptance of otherness as essential to the good life. The neurotic, having misled himself into fantasy commitments, always wishes the world to be other than it is. He is an eternal pessimist, hating the world. The realist, however, the *homme engagé*, the man who is reality-committed, is an optimist, one whose life is suffused with *joie de vivre*, since he accepts the world in its manifest form as necessary otherness, not forgetting of course that this otherness is at the same time pliable.

(6) The structure of ultimate satisfaction that emanates from the pres-

ent and from previous considerations is that ultimate fulfillment means the experienced oneness of the Transcendental Ego with the totality of being, as that being is given to consciousness. Since life is the perennial quest for self-transcendence (see the section below on Love), the terminal point of such expansion is union with the totality of being. Since the Transcendental Ego is experienced as continuous with being, the goal of union is a hope and appears to be even a possibility. In this sense, then, the metaphors of omnipotence and omniscience may indeed refer to the ultimate possibilities of human existence. That has been a traditional goal of religious doctrine, from which it follows that life as man finds it must be interpreted as offering him the optimum number of possibilities for the acquisition of such a noble state.

The above nine characteristics of the Transcendental Ego, emanating from the empirical analysis of everyday experience, parallel religious conceptions in general and mystical ones in particular. The mystic insists in detaching himself from bodily, psychological, and worldly concerns. That is in effect the "practical" process of isolating the Transcendental Ego, so that the latter is all that remains in consciousness. The eternity and singularity of the Transcendental Ego, as well as its seven other characteristics, are in keeping with the almost universal religious doctrines of immortality and the nature of God. Phenomenology promises to give these religious views a new interpretation and a rejuvenated justification.

God In our discussion of salvation and the Transcendental Ego we inescapably transferred our examination from the area of religious experiences to considerations concerning the existence of God. This pedagogically unprudential overlap can be accounted for by the fact that in the phenomenology of mysticism, God and salvation are indistinguishable religious concepts. Nonetheless, we must separate at this time for purposes of discussion certain phenomenological considerations applicable primarily to the metaphysical concept of God. The phenomenological interpretation of the existence of God was based on the analysis of the phenomenon of necessary existence. While the analysis of the problem of salvation had affective overtones, the phenomenological reevaluation of the concept of God emphasizes the intellectual aspects of religion. Let us now elaborate on these considerations.

Trenchant analyses throughout the history of modern philosophy have rejected the traditional arguments for the existence of God. The rejection is based on considerations of at least three kinds. First, the logic of the arguments is faulty. Some steps are omitted and others are invalid. Second, the rationalistic premises of the arguments—for example, that logic suffices to prove the existence of a being—are seen as altogether unwarranted by our empirically oriented age. Finally, the conclusion of these putative arguments, the existence of God, is meaningless. The concept of a being transcending nature, and one that possesses the nebulous characteristics of omnipotence, goodness, omniscience, incorporeality, and the rest, is an entity whose existence cannot be verified even in principle through observations of any kind.

The phenomenological tradition in religion accepts these criticisms; consequently, the phenomenological approach is important precisely because it does not deny the results of modern and contemporary philosophical researches, but because it endeavors to reevaluate, reconstruct, and reinterpret the meaning of God in human experience.

The positivistic criticism—that "God" is a nonempirical concept and that propositions about God are nonverifiable and hence meaningless—is disallowed by phenomenology as being excessively narrow. It is unwarranted to restrict observational verifiability to simple sensations, irrespective of the additional problem of whether the pragmatic or positivistic view of verifiability is legitimately the sole criterion for meaningfulness. The Transcendental Ego is as much an experience as a reading on an ammeter, and the sense of necessity in logic is as much a matter of experience as a pain in the appendix. The merit of phenomenology, as we saw earlier, is to have extended the meaning of facts and data to a region which allows for the reconception of religious ideas.

The arguments for the existence of God can be reinterpreted phenomenologically in two directions: the concept of the miracle or mystery of being and that of aseity mentioned earlier. Let us discuss these.

Perhaps the most important traditional arguments for the existence of God are the cosmological and the ontological ones. In Aquinas' presentation of the cosmological argument, the third way—the argument from possibility and necessity or from the contingency of the world—is usually considered to be the most difficult but also the most significant of them all. Both conclude that God exists by virtue of his own necessity. Anselm's ontological argument (as well as later versions of it, including a famous one by Descartes) finds that an examination of the idea of God leads to the discovery of necessary existence as part of that idea. Modern logic has rejected the validity of that logical derivation: existence is absurd—it is discovered and irrational. However, if we interpret God to mean the Transcendental Ego or the Ground of Being (to be discussed shortly), then, what C. I. Lewis has called the "presentation," that is, the actual immediate given experience, of the referent of those concepts contains within it an unavoidable element of certainty, conviction, and assurance which can only be properly described with the expressions "necessary being" or "necessary existence." Lately these descriptive expressions have been formalized and abstracted so as to lose their experiential content altogether. As suggested earlier, we must reintroduce the experiential aspect of these notions to see how phenomenology can relate them once more to religious concerns.

It matters little whether the phenomenological experience of God is interpreted to mean the Transcendental Ego or Being. Both notions are part of our experience: the perennial subjective, "nonobjectifiable," core of all experience is there as the Transcendental Ego; and existence *per se*, pure Being (*Sein*, in Heidegger's terminology) is always present as the background and matrix of all experience. Careful phenomenological examination and description of these ever-present but not commonly articulated aspects of experience disclose their necessary character. The concept of nothingness—even of the most vacuous conceivable nothingness—is always a presentation *to* the Transcendental Ego *against* a background of Being. Even nothingness has a mode of manifestation, a type of presentness; it is a kind of Being in turn. Irrespective of final merit, phenomenological considerations such as the above have revitalized the ontological argument for the existence of God.

The argument from the contingency of the world is related to the ontological argument and presupposes the Leibnizian rationalistic principle that there is a sufficient reason—a logical cause and explanation—for all events. That principle is to be interpreted phenomenologically to mean nothing else than that everything can be *thought*. Every individual item or event within the universe is to be explained in terms of something other than that individual item or event. In the last analysis, such external causation or explanation is no explanation at all unless the whole claim could be traced to some first principle which is not subject to these causal and explanatory limitations. So runs the argument from the contingency of the world.

Interpreted phenomenologically, the argument from contingency is merely the assertion that the universe must have a reason. To say that God exists is equivalent to the expression "I experience the universe in such a way as to demand a reason for its being." That phenomenological insight is called the *Ground of Being*. To say there is a Ground of Being (Tillich's expression) is to ask Heidegger's famous question "Why are there beings rather than nothing?" On the premise of the principle of sufficient reason, there is no answer to Heidegger's question. But there is a typical response to it: it is the recognition that there is a Ground of Being, a Ground that exists necessarily, but also a Ground that is even in principle beyond comprehension. The recognition of these paradoxical features of the Ground of Being leads to the phenomenologically descriptive phrase "the miracle or mystery of Being." As stated before, Being is a surd: it is inexplicable, yet it needs to be understood. This paradox is essentially and forever without resolution. The mind's response to it is awe, reverence, the transvaluation of values, humility, purposiveness, and hope—all of which are typically religious emotions.

In the end, all these disparate considerations coalesce. Both the ontological and the cosmological arguments explicate the notion of aseity or necessary being, a notion that can be reintroduced into the spirit of modern empirical methods through the expanded conception of what constitutes a legitimate datum of experience and observation found in the tradition of phenomenology. The notion of necessary existence is to be associated preeminently with two pervasive but commonly unnamed aspects of our experience—the ultimate source and the ultimate intention of experience. These two loci are the Transcendental Ego and the Ground of Being, the ego and the universe. The above-mentioned properties of the experience of the Transcendental Ego apply as well to the experience of Being as such. That is particularly the case in connection with existence. The nonexistence of Being is as inconceivable as the nonexistence of the Transcendental Ego. Non-Being is always conceived of against a background of empty Being. Space and time, as Kant has suggested, can be emptied of all content, but cannot be thought away. The same is true of Being as such.

If this view can be accused of pantheism (an accurate observation) it must be noted that pantheism, objective idealism, and views of God as a transcendent rather than an immanent being can be interpreted to be articulations and descriptions of what is fundamentally one and the same insight: the fundamental identity of the Transcendental Ego and the Ground of Being.

Love   In the religions of the world, love (and its ethical concomitants) is a pervasive command and goal. It is therefore apparent that a phenomenological analysis of the experience of love in its various forms will throw further light on the nature of religion.

An earlier section, on Salvation, pointed out that what has here been called "transcendence" or "self-transcendence" is a ubiquitous aspect of human existence and a pervasive trait of all experience. Let us now both review and amplify this point. All of man's conscious states (both active and passive) may be analyzed as being efforts of or events for his ego to project itself onto the world. As was pointed out in that section, Sartre's paradigm "Man's project is God" describes well the limiting condition, the asymptote, of that pervasively dynamic aspect of the human situation. The desire of the ego to go beyond itself, "to conquer the universe," in Nietzsche's phrase—to reach out literally or symbolically to the most distant corners of a reality that appears to be external to it, to appropriate and make its own that which appears to be at an insurmountable psychic distance from the inner subjective core—that search for adventure is at the heart of human competition, ambition, quest for values, search for status, roles, peace of mind, and happiness and the demand for fulfillment, meaning, and salvation in life.

But it is not enough to describe the human situation in terms of the universal quest for self-transcendence. For an exhaustive statement, two additional features of man's *conatus* must be mentioned. One of them is that the *goal* of self-transcendence is a *consciousness* or some sort of surrogate for subjectivity. The poet who meditates on nature seeks not only to transcend himself, that is to say, to "expand his ego to the size of Mother Nature," to become "one" with the larger entity that is Nature, but he looks for a consciousness or subjectivity that resides in nature, that confronts his own inwardness, and that will respond to it. Nature poetry is animistic and hylozoic. The astrophysicist who explores the impersonal universe already envisions, beyond the immediate yield of his scholarly inquiries, the response that the social reality will give to his discoveries and acumen. He shares the conclusions of his research with the consciousness that social reality presents to him. The orchestral conductor dedicated to the creation of magnificent and touching sound is not concerned solely with the music but reaches out to his conscious audience, while the composer may have reached out to all mankind. The ultimate goal towards which the artist's aesthetic efforts are directed is an encounter with both his own authentic and conscious values and the conscious social reality that is the permanent backdrop for all his striving. Even the hermit reaches out to consciousness, appearances to the contrary notwithstanding. Through his prayers, poetry, and meditations, he seeks God or Nature, or clarity about his own authentic values, or simply peace for expression and creation. In all these endeavors, his consciousness is always goal-directed towards a consciousness without. Whether such a consciousness exists, either in a personal God, in animistic nature, or in social reality, is not the question here. The point is the empirically introspectively discovered fact that consciousness is a goal towards which all human activity *intends* to go; it is a fact that to make contact with consciousness is the hope of all human activity, even of that which prima facie seems turned away from consciousness. These are empirically discerned facts of human experience, and not metaphysical or scientific inferences and hypotheses.

The man who builds up his business may not look upon a thriving practice or a large factory as a consciousness in the literal sense, but he has increased the phenomenological "size" of his own ego substantially through the magnitude of his success in business, and he is now ready to show himself to society with that larger, more important, more respectable, secure, and concrete ego. While before the consummation of his business ambition he was "nothing," a weak and insecure, i.e., "small" ego, now he is solid, secure, and large. That is the phenomenologically described nature of his happiness and his drive. By using the phenomenological size of his business to show himself to the world, his ultimate goal in that activity is to reach out towards and be accepted by what the phenomenologically oriented sociologists call "social reality." His business is the mask or *persona* he shows to the world. It is his self-chosen incarnation; it is the "body" that he shows the world. And of course the social reality towards which his being is directed is given in experience as made up of consciousness. In the presence of consciousness we see our own being in a manner altogether distinct from our self-image when we are truly alone. The presence of a consciousness forces us to see ourselves through different eyes, eyes external to us. The confrontation with consciousness, well described phenomenologically in Martin Buber's timeless *I and Thou*, is a *reflexive* act; it enables (indeed, it coerces) the ego to look upon itself; in fact, this reflexivity *creates* the ego. It is clear that men comport themselves differently (because they experience themselves differently) in the presence of people than when they are alone.

Finally, self-transcendence is not only directed towards consciousness, but it also demands *otherness*. The phenomenological analysis of otherness is a major theme in philosophical anthropology, and its significance can only be suggested here, although an earlier reference was made to it in connection with the theory of the Transcendental Ego. Otherness is the antidote to loneliness. The airplane needs the opposition of air in order to fly, the ship needs the upward force of the water to float. In a similar way, man needs the presence of otherness—i.e., some sort of opposition—in order to realize himself as a concrete and distinct human entity. No one wishes to see the world crumble or dissolve before his eyes. Man depends for his existence on the reliability, predictability, and consequent security represented by the refractory otherness of the world around him. The unremitting need as well as the pervasive presence of otherness contradicts the demand for expansion and appropriation that is inherent in the primary urge for self-transcendence. That contradiction is experienced as a tension, a paradox, a dialectic, or a dialogue, and it is a central fact in human experience for the explanation of fulfillment. To that we now turn.

We are concerned with a phenomenological disclosure of the experience of love and its significance for the understanding of religion. In order to achieve the necessary insights, we must recognize the manner in which the experience of love fits into the ubiquitous pattern of human existence described in terms of self-transcendence, goal-consciousness, and otherness. In the last analysis, love may be seen as a component of the experience of salvation.

What then are happiness, hope, and fulfillment and how are they related to love? When the process of self-transcendence proceeds smoothly and with promise, then its expansive tendencies are fulfilled, its conquests achieved. At the same time the presence of happiness, hope, and fulfillment is an indication that the goal of consciousness is being approached. Above all, however, these states of joy and satisfaction exist only to the extent that they are made possible by the confrontation with otherness. Otherness is to man's self-transcendence towards a goal of consciousness as is the wind to a child's kite, the kite it lifts into the skies. But if otherness becomes overwhelming, then the kite, destroyed by the gale, falls to the ground; hope evanesces, and depression ensues. Conversely, insufficient otherness leads to a flabby sense of selfhood, a weak and insignificant ego. Excessive otherness is evil and destructive suffering—it shatters the ego; while inadequate otherness, like insufficient buoyancy, sinks the ship that is the ego. There is an optimum amount of otherness, sought, for instance, both in sports and in love, which elevates and inspires the ego to the security of a strong and solid sense of inwardness. It follows that the supremely positive experiences of man, designated by "joy," "happiness," "bliss," "inspiration," and "love," possess the soaring character of quick, smooth, hopeful, and successful self-transcendence towards a conscious goal experienced as worthwhile, and are made possible by an optimum amount of otherness. Love, therefore, depends for its being on the presence of an optimum amount of otherness.

Love also entails the experience of "psychical distance" between the ego and the other. Although love is the endeavor of an ego to appropriate or identify itself with the object of its love, complete identity is not the ultimate stage or goal in the fulfillment of love. The optimum amount of otherness requisite for the encounter that is love means also an optimum psychical distance between the ego and the object loved. Too much distance estranges the two, transforming Buber's I-Thou relationship into a mere I-It relation. Similarly, insufficient psychical distance erodes the fulfilling experience of love or encounter until it becomes the jejune loneliness of what might be called by extension an I-I relationship.

Religious literature often distinguishes at least three types of love— *eros, philia,* and *agape*—which we might adapt to our own purposes of exposition. The experience of love, as man's highest fulfillment, depends for its existence on the presence of the optimum quantity of otherness and the optimum amount of psychical distance. This phenomenological generalization applies to all three types of love. Let us investigate each in turn.

Eros. The sexual act itself is no guarantee of love, although it is doubtful that the act has any meaning without love. Consequently, we must allow eros to stand for *love* between the sexes, a love that includes sexual interests and experiences, but is not exhausted by these. From the male perspective, eros (which we might call sexual or romantic love) fulfills the conditions of satisfaction enunciated earlier in connection with man's ubiquitous demands for self-transcendence. The lover embraces (figuratively even more than literally) and conquers his momentary *Lebenswelt* (his partner), thereby achieving self-transcendence. He seeks to coalesce with the object of his love. However, the fulfillment of heterosexual love degenerates into the fraud of prostitution and autoeroticism if both goal-consciousness and otherness are not carefully preserved. The preservation of goal-consciousness means that the woman loved is clearly experienced as a consciousness, a confronting inwardness, a Thou, while the preservation of otherness means that the woman must be experienced as retaining her independence, individuality, dignity, and selfhood—that is, her psychical distance and concrete separate being. If the otherness is excessive, then sexual love vanishes altogether; whereas if otherness is insufficient, sexual love degrades itself into a parody. The spiritual and physical characteristics desired in women for the possibility of fulfilled romantic love (a "feminine" disposition and a "youthful" body, for example) and celebrated by Anacreontic poetry throughout the ages—from Ovid to E. E. Cummings—are precisely those which make possible the tripartite complex of self-transcendence, goal-consciousness, and optimum-independent-otherness. We find an insightful and detailed analysis of this situation in Sartre's *L'Être et le Néant*.

From the woman's point of view, to fit her experience of sexual love into the general human pattern of self-transcendence is considerably more difficult than for the male. The difficulty is due in part to both the social and physiological roles of women. As a consequence of that difficulty, woman's sexual adjustment is considerably more painful than that of man and is also more rarely achieved. Differences between man and woman can often be traced to the disparate roles they play in sexual love. Certainly the social and physiological conditions are only part of the total picture. In fact, woman cannot fulfill her drive for self-transcendence through sexual love as readily as can man. Satisfaction means to a woman, as it does to all human beings, successful self-transcendence. But a woman cannot achieve fulfillment in love by approaching the relation with her lover with the directness of the male. She is first of all forced to choose freely to identify herself with her lover, to give herself to him entirely (something that can be done only if she thinks of him as a god—impossible or at best rare), and then she is able to seek self-transcendence through the love relationship, through the projection of her own ego onto his, a relationship that she has effected. That projection is the decision of total love. Woman, in the sexual relationship, assumes the role of *otherness*. That role must be freely chosen; the only way in which such a choice can be made is by total identification with her lover. The parallel with man's mystical surrender to God is obvious. Equally obvious is the difficulty that such a situation presents to woman. For sexual love to be fulfilling to woman, she must be able to look upon her lover as a redeemer, that is, as an individual who, in the role of God, transforms her in order to make ultimate fulfillment possible for her. Simone de Beauvoir has described this aspect of woman's lot perceptively in her book *Le Deuxième Sexe*. Because of the extraordinary difficulties and the great dangers facing woman in sexual love, frigidity can be readily accounted for.

Romantic love promises fulfillment to the paradox of human existence notwithstanding the fact that much has been and can be said to point out the nefarious consequences of a romantic outlook on life. Romanticism, as Denis de Rougemont has pointed out in his *Love in the Western World*, contradicts the marriage relationship, in that the two are founded on opposing principles and needs; and it also fosters the severe internal conflicts, especially in women, just mentioned. The decadence of romanticism is therefore seen by many as a healthful and stabilizing sign of Western civilization. Be that as it may, the experience of eros or romantic love illustrates quite plainly that otherness (complete and independent otherness) is a *sine qua non* for the existence of the experiences of joy, happiness, bliss, fulfillment, and love. In short, otherness is required to find meaning in life. The loved object must be seen as having the spiritual and physical characteristics which make it pliable enough for absorption, conquest, and union and yet independent and firm enough to ensure the proper psychical distance and quantity of otherness.

Eros is Kierkegaard's aesthetic stage. It symbolizes man's relation to being as a whole. Its fascination suggests that it contains in germinal form the answer to the problem of the meaning of life offered by religion through its command "Love thy neighbor." We must therefore show that other forms of love are but expansions of this primordial manifestation of self-transcendence, and that all forms of love can thus be recognized as profound means of achieving fulfillment and consequently as worthy of the highest religious eulogies. We now turn to other forms of love.

PHILIA. The general principles that have been discussed under the eros aspect of love apply equally well to a kind of love, called here *philia*, a love that may manifest itself either as universal compassion for and empathy with all sentient beings, especially human beings, or with restricted segments of humanity. Philia is the love of friendship, companionship, concern, and social conscience. From the point of view of the phenomenological structure of the experience of *philia*, the cluster of phenomena so designated is a less intense but more expanded version of eros. It possesses the same paradigmatic characteristics as eros, since philia is merely another—but a more expansive—relation of man to being. We may compare the situation to a beam of light, which may be focused sharply on a point, as in eros, or may diffuse itself over a large area, as in philia. This is not to say, as some Freudians have suggested, that philia is to be reduced to eros, that philia is a manifestation or sublimation of eros. Philia and eros stand on an equal ontological footing. Both are instantiations of man's generalized quest for self-transcendence.

Both exemplify the same general tendency and embody the same defining characteristics. From the point of view of immediate introspection or description of experience, no priority can be ascribed to any illustrative instantiation.

Philia as here described is certainly a social phenomenon. Its existence, its very possibility, presuppose a social setting. Philia is always directed to the consciousness that is represented in a social reality. Man's self-transcendence is here directed not at a single conscious object (really, a conscious subject) as in eros, but at a subgroup of society. Loving concern for other people demands both the existence of goal-consciousness—represented as individual egos or as a kind of amorphous consciousness associated with the group—and of otherness. A hermit is capable of the experience of philia only to the extent that he at least *imagines* a mankind towards which his love is extended.

As was also true of eros, in philia excessive psychical distance from that otherness leads to the detached, abstractive, and nonaffective relation to being that is characteristic of the scientific posture. Insufficient distance degenerates philia into dependency, possessiveness, sadism, and other aberrations in which the individual does not *serve* the object of his love, but *uses* it. In philia, self-transcendence is directed to social reality. Identification with or appropriation of social reality represents the goal of the expansive ego. That goal is a consciousness towards which the emerging ego strives. Finally, social reality is given as independent and refractory, as responsive but free; and these are the requirements of otherness needed for the experience of fulfillment. Love of mankind, therefore, has the phenomenological structure of all of man's successful projects.

AGAPE. We may reserve the word *agape* (and here we veer away from its ritualistic meaning for early Christianity) for something like Spinoza's *amor intellectualis Dei*. Agape is the next and last step in the amplification, in the ever-widening horizon, of the object of one's love. Whereas in eros self-transcendence is restricted to a single member of the opposite sex, and in philia self-transcendence expands itself upon a much larger region of consciousness, in agape the object of love is all of being. The love of God, which is related to (but not identical with) the experience of salvation, is self-transcendence directed towards Being itself. In this manner the ego strives for union with Nature or with God, retaining at all times its independence, at least as an observer. When St. John of the Cross writes, in the *Dark Night of the Soul*,[3] "The soul seems to be God rather than itself, and indeed is God by participation, though in reality preserving its own natural substance as distinct from God," he may have indeed "disappeared" as an effective ego. Nonetheless, and here we return to the Cartesian *cogito*, he must exist as an independent entity to be invaded by God in the first place, and he must retain his independence as an observer of divine reality, even while he feels himself to be totally absorbed in God. Even in agape—perhaps especially here—the tripartite nature of human awareness, that is, of the intentionality of consciousness, is manifest. The mystic who seeks union with God is expanding the projection of his ego towards the totality of being. Furthermore, that totality is his goal and it is a consciousness, since God is referred to as Spirit or Person. The totality of Being with which the mystic wishes to achieve union in his ecstasy is a responsive consciousness and meets thereby one of the paradigmatic requirements of otherness. Finally, a psychical distance, a dialectic pendulum, and dialogic interaction remain as part of the tension that is both inevitable and desirable, thereby fulfilling a second paradigmatic demand of otherness.

The above considerations show that the word "love" represents and designates at least three successive stages in the pinnacle of man's fulfillment. The analysis of the nature of ultimate satisfaction, of the meaning of life, of happiness and other such matters, and how love meets these requirements, must be undertaken within the context of the pervasive characteristics of the human situation here outlined. In that context, love fulfills the three postulated requirements of self-transcendence. To the extent that religion is concerned with the problem of man's ultimate meaning, satisfaction, or concern, it must engage the faithful in pursuit of love. Love, therefore—above all, of course, in the sense of agape—is the religious equivalent or explanation of man's ultimate fulfillment. Love means happiness; to love is to have found meaning in life. There is, however, in addition to the emotional aspect of love, a cognitive one. To it we now turn.

Purity of Heart Love demands purity of heart. What does this mean?
A pure heart is one that has overcome the problem of evil. A pure heart sees only good, divine good, in all creation. No evil is present to the pure heart. Confessing, atonement, self-sacrifice, good will, and abhorrence of sin are all expressions of man's demand for a pure heart; they are efforts to achieve it. Purity of heart is another important religious notion which can be explained and clarified in terms of the phenomenological analysis here presented.

Stated simply and directly, purity of heart is given to us in experience (and can therefore be described phenomenologically) as *love that is cognitive*. The insight that love is not only a feeling but also a form of knowing (in the ancient Hebrew the words "love" and "knowing" are synonymous) is not new. The cognitive character of love is a fundamental principle to romanticism in philosophy and the arts as well as in religious mysticism. The phenomenological analysis of the religious demand for purity of heart discloses mysticism as the effort to see the world through love. The religious man puts on the glasses of love before he looks out at the world. Thus, love is an a priori category in the

Kantian sense. Love, for the religious man, is not "discovered," but is imposed by him upon all his experience, and it becomes thereby a transcendental property of being. Since, as Husserl saw (and Kant before him), all experience is intentional—which means, among other things, that the ego brings about or *constitutes* the world as it appears to us, that the ego injects meaning into the world—the ego can constitute the world with the a priori intention of love as well. For the religious consciousness the world contains no evil because that consciousness has made the prior decision (intention) to see everything as the manifestation of infinite love. No contrary evidence has any relevance to the religious recognition of pervasive love in the universe, since love is an a priori intention, not an a posteriori discovery. Love is imposed on existence from without, not discovered from within. There is nothing unreal or illegitimate in this procedure, since man is free to decide how he is to interpret being. Being does not interpret itself to us, but we interpret it. The principles of that interpretation are absolutely free and self-determined. The religious ego has chosen universal love as the unifying interpretative principle. To that extent love is cognitive.

The cognitive character of love, seen in the demand for purity of heart, is importantly connected to our earlier considerations of the Transcendental Ego. We now turn to these observations.

It was noted earlier that several of the characteristics of the Transcendental Ego have traditionally been ascribed to God. We inferred from that coincidence the fact that the Transcendental Ego represents one phenomenological description of the meaning of God in human experience. The analysis, however, did disclose two substantial lacunae. These were discussed in the theory of the Transcendental Ego, and are now brought to bear on the exposition of the cognitive character of love. God, traditionally, is not only one, eternal, coextensive with Being, and so on, but he is also *creator, omnipotent*, and *omniscient*. These three characteristics are clearly not manifest in our experience of the Transcendental Ego when it is committed to the world. In fact, the Transcendental Ego seems to confront many clear strictures: the refractory character of the world, sleep, forgetting, the presence of evil as injustice and as suffering, to list but a few. How does the religious ego neutralize the contradiction between its implicit assertion that God is the Transcendental Ego and that the Transcendental Ego, although in many respects like the conception of God, is nonetheless unlike him in that it does not possess the traits of omnipotent and omniscient creativity? Earlier we discussed possible answers to this problem (which is the phenomenological reformulation of the theological problems of theodicy and eschatology); now we can see how love is the religious answer to the problems of evil and man's finitude.

The religious answer has been that if *man makes the decision to train himself to view all existence with the a priori categorial intention of universal love, then he will see the reason for and basic unreality of the strictures imposed upon the Transcendental Ego as he experiences it.* Let us examine that answer in some detail.

We must here make reference to a view first enunciated by the man who also used the word "phenomenology" for the first time—Hegel. Hegel, through his dialectic, endeavored to give reasons for "Spirit's" creation of Nature. Briefly stated, Spirit created Nature, then identified itself with it, and is now slowly emerging from that identification. The rationale behind Hegel's convoluted but inspired theory is that Spirit must create an otherness in order to achieve complete fulfillment which, in this case, is self-conscious self-possession. We may take our clue from that once influential and now derided view.

The religious ego has decided to see this world as suffused with love. Availing ourselves of Leibniz's terminology, made infamous by Voltaire's *Candide*, we must say that the religious ego has decided to see this as the best of all possible worlds. In fact, of course, the world does not appear to be such. Consequently, the a priori decision of the religious ego demands certain ad hoc hypotheses to bring consistency into his view. These hypotheses must account for the presence of evil, for the strictures and limitations militating against the creative omnipotence and omniscience of the Transcendental Ego. But love (especially in the sense of agape) is needed in order to see the "truth" of these hypotheses.

Analysis of the Transcendental Ego disclosed that it is *experienced* as totally free in the initiation of action. Yet this freedom is not borne out in experience. The religious consciousness must therefore conclude that (*a*) the limitations upon the Transcendental Ego are self-imposed and self-willed, (*b*) the reasons for those self-limitations are deliberately hidden from it, and (*c*) the knowledge of the potential for infinite creativity is deliberately, freely, and consciously repressed. These are indeed weighty assumptions, but the religious consciousness is willing to make them, and it is capable of making them through the cognitive a priori of love.

Why would the Transcendental Ego freely limit itself? And why would it limit itself in the particular manner that defines an individual man, that is, the generic limitations as well as the particular ones that constitute a unique human situation? The answer that religion has given to that question, reinterpreted phenomenologically, is that fulfillment requires otherness. Ultimate meaning in existence can be achieved only through the presence of otherness that exists against a background of consciousness. The important aspect of the possibility for fulfillment lies in the presence of otherness. Otherness, to be true otherness, must be totally independent of its creator. We have, in this connection, the religious image of God creating man free to deny his Creator. The Transcendental

Ego, to achieve bliss, fulfillment, meaning, and satisfaction, must bring about refractory and independent otherness. The limitations that the Transcendental Ego experiences when it wishes to exercise its intuitively present omnipotent and omnipresent freedom must be interpreted as self-willed. Of course, the ego's ignorance of that self-willing must also be self-willed.

Only through the a priori intention of love can the religious man see the world in this light. In that sense, love is cognitive. Purity of heart demands that the ego replace all strictures and all evil with the ad hoc hypothesis that they are all self-willed because that kind of otherness is, in the last analysis, for the best. This is not to say that the world as we find it is, as Leibniz would have it, the best of all possible worlds. To account for man's freedom, the religious man must say that *the world as he finds it offers him the maximum possible opportunities* (in the sense of the presence of otherness) *for ultimate satisfaction.* This outlook is manifested in the religious stance that looks upon all events—good or evil—as expressions of God's love and intones the prayers "Thy will be done" and "We thank You. . . ." Each man must then reflect on his own life, his own particular situation in the world, his inner demands and his outer realities, and *discover in precisely what way the strictures to his life represent the optimum otherness for his free utilization of them to achieve ultimate meaning in life.* The cognitive character of love illustrated in the demand for purity of heart has been traditionally formulated by St. Augustine and St. Anselm in the expression *credo ut intelligam,* I believe so that I may understand.

The lowest level of the bliss that comes with love is pleasure. If a man seeks pleasure, he may resent the obstacles to it that emerge at every turn. Brief reflection, however, will show him that certain obstacles are necessary for the very existence of pleasure. If he were God and found no resistance to his desires in the world, that is, no resistance whatever, he would also find no world that could offer him pleasure. As God, he must first create some form of independent and opposing otherness in order to render the experience of pleasure possible at all. We may then generalize and say that the complex form of otherness that we find contains within it the *potential* (not the actuality) for the exercise of our freedom, a freedom that can fashion infinite bliss out of the materials that the world has to offer. The details each man must work out for himself, and therein lies his life's task.

Is the above view open to empirical verification? Yes and no. To the extent that the above position interprets religion as an a priori categorial imposition on experience, it is as impervious to empirical test as are all a priori propositions. On the other hand, the view is consistent and possible, and is therefore a permissible a priori, as also are non-Euclidean geometries. However, from the pragmatic perspective the view here presented is susceptible to empirical test. It stands in agreement with the data of immediate experience as disclosed by the repeated applications of the phenomenological *epoche* (reduction, bracketing), and its experienced value is of course also a matter of empirical verification.

------ ✳ ------

It goes without saying that the view of love as cognitive sketched here, although quite common in the history of philosophy and of religion, must be explored, defined, and defended in detail before it can be considered acceptable. Modern criticism of traditional metaphysics, insightful and necessary though it may be, nonetheless overlooks some of the profound visions to which these systems tried to give expression. Phenomenology hopes to preserve these insights and reformulate them within the context of twentieth-century logical rigor and scientific empiricism. The positions here developed are therefore but a guiding outline of necessary research and cannot be construed to be final statements.

The above illustrations should indicate the potential of phenomenology for religious investigations. Through phenomenology it is possible to preserve what have been the greatest insights of religion, cast these in the categorial mold of twentieth-century philosophy, and discover how these insights happen to have found the particular rational and mythological forms that the religions and theologies of the world have given them. Phenomenology is not humanism nor is it transcendentalism. Both of these world views make fundamental assumptions about man and his relation to the world which are not confirmed in a close examination of the data of human experience. But symbols developed by these world views, properly understood, help to reveal us to ourselves. Phenomenology thus stands on its own in relation to the world's philosophies.

Phenomenology studies religion through the unprejudiced and accurate analysis of the manner in which the religious consciousness manifests itself subjectively in each individual. Religion is, in the last analysis, man's experience of religion, recorded at its deepest and most sensitive levels. The phenomenological tradition concedes that man is how and what he feels authentically about himself, and that self-knowledge includes religion. St. Augustine expressed the philosophical importance of introspection for religion very well when he said "My love is my weight."

NOTES FOR CHAPTER 7

1   *Cf.* Peter Koestenbaum, "Phenomenological Foundations for the Behavioral Sciences," *Journal of Existentialism*, Spring 1966 (No. 23), pp. 305-341.
1ª Cf. Rudolf Otto, *The Idea of the Holy*.
2   R. Descartes, *Meditations*, translated by L. J. Lafleur, New York, The Liberal Arts Press, 1951, p. 51.

3   St. John of the Cross, *Collected Works*, translated by David Lewis. Quoted in J. A. Mourant, *Readings in the Philosophy of Religion*, New York, Thomas Y. Crowell Company, 1956, p. 183.

QUESTIONS

1   What is phenomenology? What are three of its defining characteristics? In what ways does the phenomenological approach to religion differ from other methods of examining religion? Do you find the phenomenological approach sensible and useful? Explain.

2   What is the meaning of Sartre's expression "Man's project is God"? How can an atheist subscribe to that formula? Can you explain how Heidegger's and Camus' views fit into this same pattern? In connection with these considerations, explain the "paradox of human existence," and discuss three possible solutions to it. Can you think of others?

3   What is the Transcendental Ego? How is it to be distinguished from the empirical or psychological ego? What are some of the characteristics of the Transcendental Ego and how are these related to the traditional religious conceptions of God? Examine critically these characteristics; in particular, discuss the phenomenological conception of the rationalistic doctrine of necessary existence.

4   What is the phenomenological interpretation of the solutions to the problem of evil? What is the significance of matter? of frustration? What considerations can be adduced to reconcile the omnipotence and frustrations of the Transcendental Ego? What do you think of these ad hoc hypotheses?

5   What are the three elements of self-transcendence? In what way is love a paradigm for self-transcendence? What are the similarities between *eros*, *philia*, and *agape?* What is meant by the position that purity of heart is a cognitive a priori? Do you think that the phenomenological analysis of love presented in the essay is correct? Discuss.

SUGGESTED READINGS

Martin Buber, *I and Thou*, 2nd ed., translated by R. G. Smith, New York, Scribner's, 1958.

Edmund Husserl, *The Paris Lectures*, translated and introduced by Peter Koestenbaum, The Hague, Martinus Nijhoff, 1964.

Max Scheler, *Vom Ewigen im Menschen*, 1921.

Pierre Thévenaz, *What Is Phenomenology?* edited by J. M. Edie, Chicago, Quadrangle Books, 1962.

Paul Tillich, *Dynamics of Faith*, New York, Harper, 1957.

———, *Systematic Theology*, Vol. I, Chicago, University of Chicago Press, 1951.

G. van der Leeuw, *Religion in Essence and Manifestation*, translated by J. E. Turner, London, Allen & Unwin, 1938. Reprinted in Harper Torchbooks, 2 vols.

Alan W. Watts, *The Supreme Identity*, New York, Noonday Press, 1957.

8 *Ben Kimpel*

Religion in the Tradition of Linguistic Philosophy

Linguistic Analysis Is One Type of Philosophy An analysis of language is one type of philosophy, or one type of philosophical procedure. A stronger estimate of the philosophical significance of such a procedure is that philosophy itself is linguistic analysis. This estimate is a position which is stated by Wittgenstein when he says that all philosophy is critique of language.[1] Whether linguistic analysis is regarded as a philosophical procedure or as the nature of all philosophy is, of course, a matter of opinion. A much less controversial matter of opinion, however, is that such analysis, as Randall points out, is one of "the most important present-day philosophical concerns." [2]

Linguistic philosophy may be defined as "the philosophical analysis of language." [3] As analysis, or as analytical procedure, it may therefore be regarded as "a specialized part of analytical philosophy." [4] Thus again, it is a matter of opinion whether a "philosophical analysis of language" is itself "analytical philosophy" or is one of the procedures in a philosophy which is regarded as more inclusive than linguistic analysis. What is not equally optional, however, is taking account of the fact that an analysis of "scientific words or concepts" is today regarded as a "philosophy of science." That is, a present-day interpretation of the scope of philosophy of science is that it is an analysis of the language which is used in the sciences. Such an analysis constitutes the type of "philosophy of science" which is associated with the names of Heisenberg, Bohr, and Einstein: it is a clarification of the meaning of the language used in physics. So characterized, one type of philosophy of science is a linguistic analysis "of basic concepts in physics." [5] A comparable type of linguistic procedures applied to the language used in mathematics constitutes a philosophy of mathematics, which is a type of "philosophy of mathematics" associated with the names of Brouwer, Hilbert, and Russell.[6] The so-called subject matter of this type of mathematical analysis and of this type of analytical physics is the language used in mathematics and in physics. Such an analysis may be applied to any type of statement, provided it affirms a concept or has a meaning which can be understood and so can be restated.

If linguistic analysis is a procedure for the clarification of the meaning of "any class of statements," then there may also be a linguistic analysis of meaningful affirmations in religion.[7] Yet the proposal to extend the procedures of linguistic philosophy beyond the scope of mathematics and the sciences is a controversial issue in present-day analytical philosophy. Every philosophical analyst would agree that the scope of philosophical analysis includes any language which is meaningful, but many philosophical analysts maintain that the language used in religion or for religious purposes is not meaningful. On the principle that the language used in religion is not meaningful or does not convey "concepts" or conceptual meaning, the preceding proposal would indeed be rejected by many contemporary philosophical analysts. The issue, of course, whether the discourse in religion is meaningful or meaningless is controversial; and a consideration of this issue itself constitutes a major part of any philosophy of religion which is influenced by contemporary linguistic philosophy. A fundamental problem, both in linguistic philosophy and in a philosophy of religion, concerns the criteria of "meaningful discourse": What constitute the conditions for meaningful language or for language which conveys conceptual meaning?

Philosophical analysis, it must be acknowledged, considers only one aspect of language—the meaningful character of language. The nature of such "meaning," however, as has been pointed out, constitutes one of the fundamental problems in contemporary philosophy. Insofar as philosophical analysis identifies the meaning of language with concepts, the only type of language used in religion which would come within the scope of philosophical analysis would be language used to affirm concepts or "ideas" or "interpretations." If it is granted that at least some of the language used in religion performs the function of affirming concepts, then at least that much language might well come within the scope of linguistic analysis.

This essay assumes that *some* of the discourse identified with "religion" performs this function of affirming concepts or conveying ideas or articulating interpretations which are "religious." Just what constitute "religious" interpretations or concepts or ideas is one of the problems which must be clarified before the procedures of philosophical analysis can be applied to a language used for specifically "religious" purposes.

If it is admitted that at least *some* language which is used for "religious" purposes has meaning or is meaningful, and so is capable of being clarified in concepts, then it will also be granted that the procedures of linguistic philosophy may apply to one aspect of religion, just as it applies to one aspect of the sciences. Insofar, however, as a philosophy of religion comes within the scope of linguistic philosophy or philosophical analysis it will be very restricted in its scope: it will be confined to an analysis of only the meaningful language used in religion or of language used for a religious purpose of affirming a religious interpretation. Such language must *by definition* be meaningful; otherwise it would not come within the scope of "linguistic analysis" or "philosophical analysis." Such meaning must accordingly be conceptual or consist of concepts; otherwise the language which conveys the meaning would not come within the scope of a linguistic philosophy which is defined as "conceptual analysis." If, therefore, at least some language which is identified as "religious," is "meaningful discourse," then at least that much language may be regarded as coming within the range of "analytical philosophy," whose objective is a clarification of meaningful language; or it may be characterized as "seek(ing) to clarify what we mean." [8] Philosophy of religion of this type would then be comparable to philosophy of science of the type which also comes within the scope of philosophical analysis or linguistic philosophy: it would consist of an analysis of "words or concepts." [9] This parallelism, of course, is rejected by logical positivists on the principle that there are no meaningful affirmations in the entire discourse of religion—in creeds, in theologies, and in scriptures.[10]

Since logical positivists regard themselves as philosophical analysts or as linguistic philosophers, it is obvious that the scope itself of philosophical analysis, as a type of philosophy, is controversial in the sense that there is a difference of opinion about what specific types of analytical procedure constitute the unique procedures of philosophical analysis, as a type of philosophy distinguishable from other types of philosophy. According to logical positivists, philosophical analysis would not be differentiated from other types of philosophies if it were to include the discourse of theology, metaphysics, and religion in its subject matter. If the objection of logical positivists can be met by a defense of the meaningful character of at least some religious affirmations, then one type of philosophy of religion may be defined as a philosophical analysis of discourse which conveys uniquely religious meaning. The concern of such a philosophy of religion would be "with meaning rather than with truth." It would thus not presume "to discover truths about God and the universe." It would rather be modest enough to undertake an analysis of affirmations of religious life only for the purpose of understanding the meaning they convey.[11] The scope of such a philosophy of religion would indeed be very restricted, but in its restriction, it would parallel philosophy of science and the philosophy of mathematics of the types which are also instances of linguistic philosophy. Rather than defending religious interpretations with an apologetic, it would instead undertake to clarify the linguistic structure of discourse used in the service of religious life. For example, it would scrutinize the meaning of the question: "Does God exist?" and it would point out that, as stated, this question is not a proper question because it cannot be answered until the meaning of the critical term "God" is clarified, or is defined. Neither an affirmative nor a negative answer to this question will be an intelligent response unless the question itself is intelligible. And it will not be intelligible or capable of being understood until its critical term is clarified.

Whereas many theologies include assertions about the necessity of God —e.g., "God is a necessary being"—a philosophical analyst maintains that no existence is necessary, that there is no reality whose existence is a necessity. "Necessity" is a term used by philosophical analysts in a very restricted way—i.e., to speak about the logical relation of one proposition to another. They regard the use of this term with any sense other than this as a misuse, and consequently they regard any statement in which such a misuse is included as a meaningless expression. A principle which is fundamental to philosophical analysis is that "no existential proposition can be logically necessary." [12] A proposition about existence or about a reality which exists may be mistaken; and therefore it may not be regarded as logically necessary. An existing reality likewise cannot possibly be regarded as necessary, or as a necessity. Hence the only admissible use of the terms "necessity" or "necessary" is in speaking about the relation of implication between one proposition and other propositions, but not between a proposition or a linguistic expression and a reality which is other than language. Necessity, in other words, is a type of relation internal to a language system and the term is not appropriately used to speak of the relation of such a language structure to a reality other than language itself. A failure to understand the strictures of the term "necessity" accounts, for example, for many blunders in Descartes' arguments about the nature of what reality *must* be because of the character of logical argument. Necessity is a character internal to a logical structure; and a logical structure, in turn, is one type of linguistic system.

Much of the confusion in the so-called "ex nihilo doctrine" might also be eliminated by considering the meaning of the term "nothing." [13] This doctrine, for instance, does not affirm that God created the world out of nothing, in the sense of creating something from a total absence of anything. It means rather that the world, as a determinate thing, was not created out of another determinate thing. Plato makes this distinction in the *Timaeus*, where he points out that the determinate character of the world was preceded by an indeterminate reality, called the "Recipient," or the "Receptacle." As purely indeterminate, it cannot be called "spatial" or "temporal" or "material"; the same point is made in the ex nihilo doctrine, when that doctrine affirms that there was no one *thing* out of which the world, as another *thing*, was created. Insofar, therefore, as God is defined as *the* ultimate reality, it would be logically inconsistent to speak of any *thing* else which is also ultimate, or as not contingent upon God for its reality.

Much confusion likewise could be eliminated from the controversies of long standing about the "freedom of man" being qualified by the "grace" of God. Feigl points out that the meaning of the term "freedom" is confused when it is construed as an opposite of "determination," rather than as an opposite of "compulsion." [14] According to this distinction (and with apologies to Professor Feigl), man may well choose to have his life "determined" by the law or will of God; and when so interpreted, there is no contradiction between man's freedom and man's dependence upon the determination of his life by a reality which he himself chooses to revere.

This same type of analysis may be offered for many controversies in the history of theology about the qualification of man's freedom insofar as man's life is "determined" by its relation to God. So treated, the controversies themselves could be resolved, because in many instances they are verbal, arising out of disputes about equivocal statements whose equivocal character is derived from the ambiguity of one or more of its terms.

The Principles of Linguistic Analysis Are Logical Linguistic or philosophical analysis is logical analysis. These terms are synonymous; interchangeability of expressions follows from a common character of the principles of this type of philosophy. The principles of philosophical analysis are logical, and these principles are applied in the analysis of any meaningful linguistic expression. Thus the same set of principles is used for an analysis of the language which constitutes the discourse of the sciences as for the language which constitutes discourse of religion or of religions.

Even classifying the discourse of religion confronts an analyst of language with a problem: What term is suitable for speaking about the discourse that constitutes scriptures, creeds, theologies, and religious affirmations of all types? The elliptical expression, "religious language," is certainly not satisfactory, since there is no language which is peculiar to religion.[15] There are languages peculiar to the various sciences and to mathematics; but there is no comparable uniqueness of language in the discourse of religions. Thus the expression "religious discourse" is equally unsatisfactory.[16] The same may be said about the expression "religious talk." [17] What is peculiar to religious life is religious interpretations; and it is these which constitute the meaning of the discourse of religious life. But the language used to affirm such meaning is not peculiar to religious life or to religion. As Bultmann points out, "There may well be Christian cobblers: but there is no Christian shoe-making." [18] The same applies to language. The language used by religious people for a specifically religious purpose—reciting a liturgy, affirming a creed of faith—is not unique to religion, since it is appropriated from nonreligious uses to perform some uniquely religious function. As Locke points out, the language used in Scripture is also employed by "those whose hand is used to the plough," or as Bacon says, it is appropriated from the "market place."

The *meaning* of a term in a discourse which constitutes a creed of faith is derived from religious life or from religious experience, and as such, is unique to religious life. But the same analysis does not apply to the grammatical rules for forming the affirmations of creeds of faith; and it is this point which Martin makes in pointing out that "there are no terms which apply to [religion] and it alone." In other words, religious life "has no vocabulary of its own." [19] Instead, it uses a language which admits of uses which are other than affirming *religious* interpretations, or religious beliefs. Hence, Hepburn proposes the expression, "the religious use of language" for language which is used to affirm a religious interpretation or religious faith.[20] Another equally satisfactory expression is proposed by Flew and MacKinnon, i.e., "the language of religion." [21] Stead also proposes, in addition to the expression "the language of religion," the expressions "religious pronouncements" and "theological statements." [22] This discussion of the terminology itself for speaking about one use of language helps to illustrate how the misplacing of an adjective constitutes inaccurate language and so confuses, rather than clarifies the discourse of the very analysis which presumes to clarify other discourse.

All discourse is intelligible or understandable only when it is formed according to the rules of a grammar of a particular language and according to the principles of logic, which are the rules of consistency for the use of any language. The rules by which a statement is affirmed as an inference from another statement are the fundamental principles of formal logic. These were formulated by Aristotle and in some measure by Plato.

Such principles of formal logic are conditions for an intelligent use of any language, insofar as language is used to affirm an idea or a concept, which may be called "conceptual meaning."

A language used to affirm interpretations of the nature of God may be referred to as "theological discourse" when what is unique to it is an interpretation of the nature of God. The meaning of the term "God" in such discourse is, however, a religious interpretation, and apart from such a uniquely religious interpretation, there is nothing uniquely religious either about the grammar of theological discourse or about the logic with which such discourse is formulated into an internally coherent set of statements.

The present emphasis upon the logical analysis of language may be traced to three principal sources: "movements," or "schools," or "circles" of analytical philosophy linked with the names of Cambridge, Vienna, and Berlin. With the single exception of G. E. Moore in the Cambridge movement, the interest of the philosophers identified with these three sources has principally been in science and mathematics. Hence the dominant influence of philosophical analysis until recent years has been in the sciences and in mathematics. The most influential members of the Cambridge movement are Moore and Russell; and although both have written in moral philosophy, neither has directly contributed to a philosophy of religion in any writings that may be regarded as instances of linguistic analysis.

There are many notable members of the Vienna Circle, among them Feigl, Neurath, Carnap, Waismann, and Schlick. This philosophical movement or circle has in fact been referred to as "formed . . . around Schlick," who, like the other members of this school, was primarily a physicist.[23] He became aware of linguistic problems in his studies with Max Planck, who was influential in the formulation of the theory of relativity and so in the logical critique of such concepts in Newtonian physics as "absolute space," "absolute time," and "simultaneity." Although Wittgenstein was "never personally present" in this circle, he was nevertheless influential in its thought by virtue of his contact with Schlick and Waismann.[24]

Even though the circle formally dissolved in 1938, at the outbreak of World War II, it subsequently became an international philosophical movement, and at present there is no critical discipline which is not in one way or another affected by its emphasis upon the linguistic, and so upon the logical, aspect of language.[25] This type of analytical philosophy is called by various names—e.g., neo-positivism, neo-empiricism, logical empiricism. Carnap prefers "logical empiricism" since he believes that any derivative of the term "positivism" applied to a discipline that lays emphasis upon logic and syntax might be misleading, because it might be confused with positivism of the type represented either by Comte or by Mach.

The third principal source in the development of philosophical analysis as a type of philosophy is the Berlin school, commonly referred to as logical empiricism, since its principal interest is in the logical analysis of the language used in the various empirical sciences. This emphasis upon language, in distinction from nonlinguistic sensory or perceptual experience, sets off logical empiricism from empiricism of other types—for instance, the type represented by Hume.

Linguistic Analysis Is Discourse About Discourse Linguistic analysis as logical analysis consists of philosophical statements about statements which may be affirmed in philosophical or scientific or moral or religious uses. As such, it is a type of discourse about various types of discourse. The discourse which constitutes a logical analysis is, therefore, a different order of statement from the statements about which such analysis is given. Logical analysis may be called second-order discourse, in distinction from first-order discourse, which constitutes the data for a logical analysis. A logical analysis of science, for example, is "a way of talking about science and is not a part of science itself." [26] A logical analysis of the language used in religion would likewise be language about language, or discourse about discourse. The orders of such discourse thus are different: one order consists of language affirmed by scientists or religious people about whatever reality they presume to interpret; whereas the order of discourse of logical analysis consists of affirmations about such affirmations. The affirmations or statements of a scientist about whatever reality it is that he proposes to investigate constitute a science; and an analysis of the statements which constitute such a science is logical discourse about science. One set of statements constitutes a science or a "knowledge within science," whereas statements about such statements constitute a linguistic analysis, which is one type of "knowledge about science." [27] The former consists of "object-sentences," and the latter consists of "syntactic sentences." Sentences of both types are meaningful or "genuine," but they are affirmations about different "realities." [28] The first are about whatever a scientist investigates by his methods of research; and the latter are about the statements which such a scientist makes in speaking about what he presumes to know by means of such research.

A distinction of the same type may be made between so-called moral judgments or moral evaluations and clarifications of the meaning of such judgments or evaluations. Whatever a person approves may be said to be good. An analysis of the meaning of "good" as a predicate or in an estimate is not a moral judgment, but is rather a philosophical analysis of such a moral judgment. Ogden and Richards make this distinction when they speak of "good things" as "those which we approve of approving." [29]

Approving of an act or a decision is one order of approval, whereas approving of the approval is another order.

A distinction of this type may also be made between affirmations of religious faith and comments about the meaning of such affirmations. Whereas a religious person affirms a religious interpretation or states a religious belief, a philosophical analyst may attempt to restate the meaning of such an affirmation. In so doing, he does not affirm a religious belief, but rather affirms what he understands to be the meaning of such an affirmed belief. Farrer makes this distinction between "a belief" which is peculiar to a religious life, and "a belief about that belief," which may be the comment by a linguistic analyst and which may exhibit an understanding of the principles of language and logic, but exhibit no understanding whatever of the basis or the justification for affirming such a religious belief.[30] Such a distinction is also made by contemporary philosophers of existence (existentialists) when they distinguish between "the existential understanding" and "the existentialist understanding." As Bultmann points out, a "philosophical analysis" of a certain type is an instance of "the existentialist understanding," whereas the type of experience which constitutes a mode of living or a way of life is an "existential understanding" and as such is a unique sense of significance.[31] When this sense of significance becomes the meaning of an affirmation such as an affirmation of religious belief, it may then be commented upon by another who knows the procedures of logical analysis, even though he has no acquaintance whatever with the quality of life which constitutes such a "religious" sense of significance. The distinction here made, between having a faith which is affirmed in a statement and commenting on the meaning of such an affirmed statement, parallels the distinction which Heidegger makes between "looking-toward being from within being" and reflecting about the affirmations of such a person.[32]

A logical analysis of a religiously significant affirmation may well yield an enrichment to a philosophical analyst's life, provided such a person is in search of something more than a logical analysis. But if he is not seeking something more than such an analysis, his understanding of the significance of an affirmation of religious faith will be restricted to the principles of logic and language, and he will be acquainted only with the tools of analysis of affirmations, not with the significance of religious living which is the source for the religious meaning of such affirmations.

One type of religious affirmation is a declaration of belief about the nature of God or about the dependence of a person's life upon God. Such belief, as Bultmann says, "speaks of God, and indeed *to* God." [33] In contrast, a philosophical analyst may speak about such religious affirmations without any conviction which is peculiar to religious life. His qualifications may be exclusively linguistic, insofar as he has a knowledge of the rules of language. A knowledge of every aspect of language, however, is not equivalent to the religious faith which underlies the use of some language to state a religious interpretation of reality. Heidegger makes this distinction when he differentiates "an essential clarification of the essence of being," and "linguistic and grammatical investigations" directed toward a clarification of the meaning of affirmations made about such "being." [34]

The same kind of distinction was made centuries ago by philosophers who commented upon Parmenides' philosophical discourse "Concerning Truth" or "Concerning Being." Proclus, for instance, in the fifth century A.D., was aware of the two orders of discourse when he pointed out that the poem by Parmenides may be regarded as discourse about philosophical discourse, such as terms "being," and "reality." There are indeed two radically different ways of regarding Parmenides' "Concerning Being." One is a logical analyst's interpretation of it as discourse about the philosophical vocabulary of "being." The other is a metaphysician's interpretation of it as discourse about ultimate reality or "being." It is the latter interpretation which would be respected as serious philosophy by Plato and by those who look upon one function of language as Plato does. Aristotle also takes this interpretation when he speaks about "first principles of being." A linguistic analyst, on the other hand, respects as serious philosophy a logical analysis of the structure of language; and from his point of view, philosophy is analysis of language, and not of a reality about which such language is presumed by some to be affirmed. A consistent linguistic analyst, for instance, presumes to know the various meanings of the term "being," but not the nature of being or reality about which traditional ontologists have presumed to be informed. Whereas linguistic analysts speak about the term "being" as it is used by metaphysicians, metaphysicians not only speak about the term and about *its* meaning but also presume to know something of the nature of reality or of being by means of such meaningful discourse. A presumption that such knowledge is possible differentiates traditional metaphysicians from contemporary philosophical analysts. Hence Heidegger speaks from the point of view of traditional metaphysicians when he maintains that "the question of being is not a matter of grammar." He insists that "as long as we dwell on the word form and its meaning, we have not yet come to the 'thing,' to . . . being." He, therefore, proposes a sound philosophical directive when he declares that "If we expect to apprehend the essence of the thing, here of being, by mere discussions of the word and its meaning, we shall obviously be making a mistake . . . it would be like trying to investigate . . . atomic processes, by grammatical studies of the word 'atom' . . . rather than by the necessary physical experiments." [35]

If the term "God" were to be spoken about rather than the term "being," a theologian would insist that what is of utmost importance is what is known about the reality referred to by this term. The primary theological concern, from the point of view of a theologian, is the reality to which discourse refers that is other than discourse, whereas the primary concern of a philosophical analyst of theology is the discourse which constitutes the linguistic structure of theology. The primary concern of such an analyst is not with the ultimate reality, designated, for example, by a religious person with the word "God," but it is rather with the word itself or with the meaning with which this word is used in theological discourse. A theologian's discourse about God is first-order discourse, whereas the discourse of philosophical analysts about a theologian's discourse is second-order discourse.

All Contemporary Critical Studies   It is safe to say that there are no im-
of Religion Consider Language   portant studies of the phenomenon
of religion today which do not in
one way or another take account of the nature of language. Malinowski, for example, as a representative of modern anthropological studies, maintains that "an intimate connection exists between the word, the mythos, the sacred tales of a tribe, on the one hand, and their ritual acts, their moral deeds, their social organization, and even their practical activities, on the other." [36] Malinowski considers this linguistic consideration to be basic to the anthropological studies of Sir James Frazer, who, according to Malinowski, "has established the intimate relation between the word and the deed in primitive faith," and has shown that "the words of the story and of the spell, and the acts of ritual and ceremony are the two aspects of primitive belief." [37] What Malinowski refers to as "the perspective of linguistic approach" is thus of fundamental significance in anthropological studies.[38] Conversely, no study of the phenomenon of language can be considered either scientific or empirical without a consideration of ethnography—a study of the influence of geographical or environmental factors upon the character of a people's language. Insofar as language is an essential aspect of human culture, which includes religion, whatever can be known about the phenomenon of language is also an essential condition for understanding religion as a cultural phenomenon. Malinowski says that "the Ethnographer can make himself useful to the Philosopher of Language," and in turn, to a philosopher of religion, insofar as language is a means for the affirmation of religious interpretations, which in one way or another condition the aspect of human behavior that is classified by anthropologists as "religious" or as "religion." [39]

Rudolf Otto's *The Idea of the Holy*, one of the most influential books in the study of religion published within the last forty or fifty years, puts a primary emphasis upon language, since the thesis of the book is that what is essentially religious is "the numinous consciousness" which cannot be reduced to language and cannot be "handed down in concepts and passed on in school instruction." [40] McPherson points out that what is unique to "Otto's view" is that "the distinctive thing in religion" is "the numinous experience [which] cannot be put into words." [41] Anything approaching an adequate commentary on Otto's point of view about the nonrational aspect of religion would, of course, be nothing less than an extended study, impossible within the limits of this chapter. The only point which is made here is that Otto's study of religion comes within the scope of linguistic philosophy insofar as its basic thesis is that the nature of religious experience cannot be articulated or formulated in language. To gain some idea of the linguistic consideration which is basic to Otto's study, consider the single affirmation that "more of the experience [of the numinous] lives in reverent attitude and gesture, in tone and voice and demeanour, expressing its momentousness, and in the solemn devotional assembly of a congregation at prayer, than in all the phrases and negative nomenclature which we have found to designate it." [42]

Otto also diagnoses some of the confusions which have arisen in the history of theology in the same way that a philosophical analyst diagnoses them when he declares that the reason for the "blasphemous and horrible . . . caricatures" of some theological doctrines arise from "a mistaken choice of expressions." [43]

Notwithstanding the very great differences between philosophical analysis and existentialist analyses, there are some emphases in common in these two approaches to religion. Common emphasis may be illustrated by a comment made by Marcel: "The answer to a . . . question, 'Do you believe in God?' ought to be in the great majority of cases, 'I don't know whether I believe in God or not—and I am not even quite sure that I know what "believing in God" is.'" He points out that the impossibility of understanding the exact meaning of such a question makes it impossible to give an intelligent answer; and in maintaining this, he analyzes one problem of modern bewildered life as a linguistic philosopher would analyze it. In stressing the failure to understand the meaning of an assertion or a question in which the term "God" is included, he points out a difference between the doubt with which a contemporary philosopher of existence is concerned and the type of doubt with which an agnostic philosopher of the last century was concerned. A representative of "the agnosticism of the last century" would say: "I don't know whether there is a God or not." Speaking as a linguistic analyst would, Marcel says that one cannot be "quite sure" about the meaning itself of any statement about God, unless the critical terms in such a statement are clarified.[44] Attempting to understand the meaning of assertions about God is at least one interest which modern existentialists share in common with contemporary philosophical analysts. A. N. Prior, for example, as a representative of contemporary philosophical analysis, says that "the real intellectual difficulty for the believer or would-be believer is not the problem of proof but the problem of meaning." [45] Whereas the philosophical agnostic of the last century was primarily concerned with the adequacy of proof in support of the religious belief that there is a divine reality or God, contemporary philosophers of existence, as well as contemporary philosophical analysts, are concerned with the meaning of affirmations of such belief.

Since reference has already been made to the influential writings of Heidegger, it may be sufficient at this point merely to recall the similarity of *one aspect* of Heidegger's approach to the procedures of philosophical analysts' approach: his assertion that "essence and being express themselves in language." [46] Any adequate commentary on this statement would go far beyond the scope of this chapter.

Our commentary upon the tendency in representative modern studies of religion to take account of the phenomenon of language would show a notable gap if it did not refer to Martin Buber's writings, e.g., the *Eclipse of God*, a work in which Buber too is concerned with the use of language that has lost its religious meaning. He points out, for instance, that the term "God" does not as such express religious significance, since it is so often used in discourse without a shred of religious meaning.[47] He also remarks that a religious person, in addressing himself to God, characteristically uses the second-person pronoun "Thou," instead of a third-person pronoun. On the other hand, Otto maintains, in criticism of this analysis by Buber, that " 'third person' hymns . . . under certain conditions may even be more genuine and first-hand utterances than those which address God as 'Thou.' " Otto maintains that a religious person's use of the second-person pronoun in addressing himself to God tends "to lose sight of just the mysterious transcendent aspect of deity." [48] Otto thereby directs a very disturbing question to those who uncritically adopt Buber's prescription of one type of language as alone appropriate to express religious faith: "Does this Power that impresses us with such awe admit of . . . question and answer in the second person?" [49] Another equally disturbing principle about the type of language appropriate for affirming religious faith is proposed by Otto when he says that "utterance should not be so continually in the form of an address *to* God as to exclude prayerful and thoughtful discourse *about* Him." [50] This principle is a basis also for a critique of many hymns used in religious services; and it is also basic to a rethinking of much language used in prayer.

There is, it may be pointed out, no expression in popular philosophies of religion which is more used, and also more misused, than "demythologizing of scripture." This expression, which has been popularized by the writings of Rudolf Bultmann, is now a part of current discourse about scripture and about religion, and as Lohmeyer says, refers to "a methodological or logical" principle.[51] So interpreted, the emphasis of Bultmann, and his followers, comes within the scope of at least one type of linguistic analysis. Bultmann's interest in scripture is in "the language of myth," in distinction from "the language of faith." [52] According to him, the language of myth may or may not be a handicap to affirming a religious interpretation, since its adequacy depends upon the meaning with which such metaphorical language is used. Insofar as myth is metaphorical or a figure of speech, and insofar as metaphors are characteristic of much language in religion, the problem of scrutinizing myth in religion is almost coterminous with reflecting on religion itself.[53] A basic thesis of Bultmann is that "mythological sayings as a whole contain a . . . deeper meaning which is concealed under the cover of mythology," and on the basis of this assumption, he argues: "If that is so, let us abandon the mythological conceptions precisely because we want to retain their deeper meaning." He therefore defines "de-mythologizing" as the "method of interpretation of the New Testament which tries to recover the deeper meaning behind the mythological conceptions." [54] This definition is obviously not very satisfactory, since it is circular: it amounts to asserting that "de-mythologizing" is removing "mythological conceptions," and as is evident, such a procedure cannot be understood until the nature itself of mythology is clarified. Yet it is this very clarification by Bultmann which leaves much to be desired, since he uses the term "mythology" with various meanings. Because it is ambiguous, any affirmation about "de-mythologizing" is, in some sense, equivocal.

Our purpose in this chapter is not to present a commentary on Bultmann's procedure, but merely to point out that this procedure comes within the scope of linguistic analysis, in the sense that since myth is a figure of speech, demythologizing is an operation upon language. Insofar as myth is treated by the procedures of linguistic analysis, Hepburn reminds us, myth "as a form of language" must not be confused with "the *content* of any particular myths." [55] A commentary on the meaning of any particular myth is a hermeneutical analysis, and what alone is important in this chapter is pointing out that the method itself of distinguishing meaning from a particular form of language, in which such meaning is affirmed, comes within the general range of linguistic analysis. "The project of demythologizing," therefore, Hepburn points out, "raises in an acute form the general problem of the religious use of language," and in particular, it raises the problem of "the logical nature of statements about God." [56]

Insofar, however, as Bultmann defines "de-mythologizing" as "freeing the Word of God from a by-gone world-view," he raises questions which are outside the scope of linguistic analysis, since what is believed to constitute such a presumably inadmissible "world-view" is contingent upon what is regarded as an admissible "world-view"; and such a world view is a metaphysic.[57] But a metaphysic is just what many philosophical analysts regard as inadmissible in any defensible philosophy. On the other hand, insofar as Bultmann defines mythology as a version of anthropomorphism, he does not raise a problem about which world view is admissible. In defining mythology as a version of anthropomorphism, he identifies it with a type of discourse about "gods as if they were men and [about] their actions as human actions." [58] When mythology is so defined, it is very simple to decide which affirmations in religion ought to be "de-mythologized." But when mythology is defined in terms of a "by-gone" or indefensible world view, the very disturbing problem arises about which world view, even though historically "by-gone," is, nevertheless, not conceptually indefensible. Deciding which of such interpretations of reality are historically antiquated is very simple; but it is not equally simple to decide which historically ancient views of reality are also cognitively indefensible. Aristotle, for example, interprets reality in terms of purpose or a *telos,* and although such a point of view is obviously outside the scope of scientific explanations, it is not necessarily outside the scope of possibly sound religious and metaphysical interpretations of reality. Notwithstanding the antipathy of many philosophical analysts for metaphysics, this particular teleological metaphysic may be cognitively significant even though many philosophers and many scientists think otherwise. What is thought by any person or group of people to be a defensible world view is, fortunately, not the criterion of its soundness. What is thought about a world view only indicates what *is thought* at the time about such a view. If anyone agrees with the view here stated, he will then also be aware of a very weak principle underlying Bultmann's methodology; Bultmann declares that "the world-view of the Scripture is mythological and is therefore unacceptable to modern man whose thinking has been shaped by science and is therefore no longer mythological." [59]

The unacknowledged presuppositions in this criterion of what is unacceptable to "modern man" are only too obvious. If what is now regarded as sound and is therefore classified as science is not as sound as it is at present thought to be, then the very criterion on the basis of which Bultmann proposes a reformulation of meaning affirmed in the Scriptures would itself be discredited. Speaking about science as if it were a fixed criterion of defensible views about reality is almost too naïve to be admitted into philosophically critical discourse; and yet Bultmann does speak in this way about science when he says that the "conception of the world we call mythological . . . is different from the conception of the world which has been formed and developed by science . . . and which has been accepted by all modern men." [60] If anyone should be naïve enough to assume that what is "accepted by all modern men" is a fixed criterion for ascertaining which world views are sound, he would simply disqualify himself from critical philosophical analysis, since the very principle by which philosophical analysts themselves define "empirical discourse," such as is used in the empirical sciences, is that it is "falsifiable" or is *in princi-*

ple capable of being false. Thus to propose a criterion which *in principle* is capable of being rejected in the light of subsequent learning, with the assumption that it should supersede all other criteria such as are respected in religious interpretations, is to express what is little more than a matter of preference.

What has been said about Bultmann's methodology, as coming within the scope of linguistic analysis, may also be said about all hermeneutical methods. Hermeneutics is a procedure for understanding the meaning of various types of human expressions, principally of language. This definition, proposed by Dilthey and accepted by Bultmann, indicates the relation of linguistic analysis to the principles of hermeneutics.[61] When hermeneutics is regarded as a methodology of interpretation, it is evident that all scriptural exegesis also comes within its scope and within the range of the principles of linguistic analysis. Even if scripture is interpreted as the Word of God, the language of such scripture is a human phenomenon; and insofar as the language of scripture is interpreted by a religious person, his interpretation, whether called an instance of hermeneutics or of exegesis, is also an instance of linguistic analysis.

Attempts to understand the meaning of a scripture or a creed or any other type of linguistic expression of religious interpretation come within the range of the general principles of linguistic philosophy. This may also be said of the type of studies of the New Testament which endeavor to formulate the *kerygma*, the "proclamation" of the Christian Gospel. Although there are many ways to regard the *kerygma*, the procedures for formulating it are fundamentally those of linguistic philosophy, since the *language* of the New Testament is the source from which such a *formulation* of the *kerygma* must come.

Considerations of Language Are of the Utmost Practical Importance in Religious Institutions Malinowski points out that "language . . . is an instrument [for] . . . the communication of thought," and since this is the case, it is an indispensable factor in a religious institution, because it is a means for the communication of beliefs which constitute interpretations of reality that are basic to behavior included in religious institutions.[63] The continuity, in fact, of a religious institution is contingent upon the effectiveness of a means such as language for affirming beliefs which underlie the practices of such an institution. As Marcel says, "if illumination is to be communicated, it must inevitably become language." This fact thus confronts a person who is concerned with perpetuating religious life through the meanings of religious institutions with a problem of which Marcel speaks: "From the moment [any illumination] has passed into a sentence, it runs, in some degree, . . . the sad destiny of the sentence itself, which in the end will be repeated mechanically without the person who repeats it any longer recognizing its meaning." [64] An understanding of the critical relation between the "spiritual" function of a religious institution and the adequacy of language for communicating its convictions or creed of faith is expressed, for instance, in the Dean of St. Paul's "Plea for a New Statement of the Christian Faith as Understood by The Church of England." According to Dean Matthews, "one of the most urgent needs of the Church of England is a reconsideration . . . of the Thirty-Nine Articles," and this amounts to "a new *statement* of the Christian faith as understood by [the] Church." [65] Professor Thielicke of Germany expresses the same awareness of the urgency for a reconsideration of the language with which the basic belief or faith of the Church may be affirmed today, when he declares that: "the Church is challenged . . . to take a confessional stand." [66] Such a "confessional stand" is, of course, an affirmation of an interpretation of life and reality in relation to God, which constitutes the creed of the Protestant Church for which Professor Thielicke is so able a spokesman.

The problem likewise of selecting a suitable language to convey religious interpretations which are affirmed in the New Testament is, as Hans W. Bartsch, the editor of *Kerygma and Myth*, says, "the fundamental problem of all New Testament exposition." That this problem is not merely an incidental consideration, but is rather of the utmost importance for the Church, is pointed out when he also says that "it faces both the theologian in the lecture room and the parish priest in the preparation of his sermons." [67]

The adequacy or effectiveness of a language which is selected by the representatives of the Church or any other religious institution to convey its basic creed of belief is of such importance that it "affects the very foundation" of such institutions.[68] A consideration, therefore, of the type of language capable of conveying whatever religious interpretation is essential to the "foundation" of a religious institution is, as Bultmann says, "a burning issue." [69] Selecting "an intelligible language" is the only means, Bultmann declares, by which "the Church can re-establish communication with modern man and speak with an authentic voice." [70] The principle which underlies this plea made by Professor Bultmann, as well as by Professor Thielicke and by Dean Matthews, is that one "cannot truly believe . . . without understanding." [71] Implied in this principle is the conviction that any significant development in the life of a religious institution must depend upon making the *affirmations* or the *statements* of its faith intelligible. This procedure is at least one way to revitalize the influence of the Church in the modern world.

This operation upon the language of the Church, however, would not be of such urgent importance as it is, were it not that the world itself, which is served by the Church, is in the throes of what Heidegger calls a "darkening." By this "darkening of the world," he means a spiritual or moral "disintegration," or "wasting away." [72] This tragic phenomenon of the loss of the Church's influence upon modern men, including many of its own nominal members, is traced by Heidegger in part to the poverty of meaning of the language still used by the representatives of the Church; as he points out, many of the critical terms in the discourse of the Church have "become no more . . . than . . . empty word[s]." [73] Insofar as the language with which the Church addresses itself to people has lost its spiritual or its genuinely religious meaning, it "no longer applies to anything" that is of *utmost* significance in the lives of people. Heidegger points out that "we have fallen away from what" the words of religious life affirm of religious faith, "and for the moment cannot find our way back." [74] Although finding our way back will surely not be merely a matter of improving language, a serious consideration of language can at least remove some of the obstacles to reaffirming genuine religious conviction by means of the language used in religious institutions.

Even though it is a fact that the religious significance of much language still preserved by religious institutions has evaporated from such language, yet a diagnosis of the critical problems of the modern church would indeed be pathetically superficial if an emphasis were placed primarily on language. What is of primary importance is the *meaning* of the language used in religious institutions; and such meaning is not communicated to language by rules of language. Hence no operation upon language by the procedures of philosophical analysis would make any appreciable difference whatever in the *religious* significance of any language. The religious significance of a language is derived from religious living, and not from the logical or syntactical rules with which language is formed. A basic tragedy of modern life is an impoverishment of the reverence itself which is the minimum condition for all religious interpretations of life and reality. What Heidegger refers to as "the flight of the gods," or what Nietzsche speaks of as the "death of God," is actually not a comment about God, but about the impoverishment of the spiritual significance of this word in the vocabulary of modern men. What Heidegger refers to as an "evaporation" of the spiritual meaning from the vocabulary of religious institutions is what Ogden and Richards refer to as "symbolically starved." [75] A basic factor in such impoverishment of language in religious institutions is not a deficiency of language, but rather a deficiency in religious life. Without a reverence for an ultimate reality, without an awesome sense of the majesty of a Creator of the world, the terminology "the world," as well as "God" or "Creator," will be devoid of religious significance. "The general exhaustion of language" is not the only modern tragedy; such also is the more general exhaustion of the spiritual character of modern life.[76] The language in religious institutions is certainly not the primary cause of a decline in the vitality of religious institutions; such a cause is rather to be sought in a basically irreligious life which uses the language of religious traditions without the meaning of such traditions. Thus "the evaporation of [the] being" of religious life itself is the primary factor in the impoverishment of the religious significance of language used in religious institutions.

Heidegger, therefore, declares a major principle about the nature of the meaning of language when he says that "the destiny of language is grounded in a . . . relation to *being*." [77] The importance of this principle might be more fully appreciated if it were stated in a slightly different way: the meaning of words for a person who uses them is determined by the significance of the reality to which he refers by such words. If there is no reality with utmost significance to a man, no amount of language he may use will evoke a sense of utmost significance, unless, for example, a person has a sense for the awesome character of the heavens, no recitation of the expression "the heavens declare Thy glory" will mean much *to him*.

There is indeed an integral relation between the religious significance of the discourse of religious institutions and the religious life of members of such institutions, but the vitality of religious life is not brought about by the language of a religious institution. Rather, language is effective for affirming religious faith only when there is such faith to affirm. Language, for instance, can declare a reverence for God only when there is such reverence; and the source for such reverence is not language, but the relation of human life to the reality about which religious life affirms its faith. Heidegger, therefore, is right: "As we prepare to set forth . . . the fact of the evaporation of being, we find ourselves compelled to take linguistic considerations as our starting point." [78] But, it must be added, the religious significance with which any language is used in religious institutions, is derived from religious life, and not from language, as a structure which is determined by rules of grammar and rules of logic. The religious meaning of the discourse of religious institutions is determined only by the religious life within such institutions; and so there must first be a religious interpretation of life and reality before any language used in religious institutions can affirm religious meaning. The religious meaning of a language is a religious interpretation or a religious belief or religious faith; and in the absence of such faith or belief, no discourse has religious meaning.

It is not only the language of traditional religious institutions which is undergoing a radical change today, but also the entire linguistic aspect of modern life. Basic to this phenomenon are a few fundamental moral principles about the relation between what a man is and most wants in life and the significance with which he uses his entire vocabulary. The tenth Psalm, for instance, helps us at this point to understand at least one aspect of the tragic plight of great numbers of people today: "the man greedy for gain . . . renounces the Lord." Whatever is of *utmost* importance to a person is the key to the meaning of words with which he refers to whatever it is that has utmost meaning for him. The significance of words or their signifying role is an index to a man's character, to his life.

Heidegger points out that "the crux of the matter is the reinterpretation of the spirit as . . . mere cleverness in . . . calculating . . . [when] this cleverness is a matter of mere talent and practice." [79] Hence, it is not the techniques of modern sciences which are responsible for a fundamental alteration in the *significance* of modern man's vocabulary, including the vocabulary of the Church: it is rather what modern man most wants by means of such techniques. Basic, therefore, to an analysis of what must be done by the Church to introduce new spiritual significance into its discourse is a consideration of values: what men most value or most want in life determines the significance or the meaning of whatever terms they use to refer to what they regard as "reality." Whatever is regarded as having supreme importance in a man's life will determine the range of application of his entire vocabulary. What a scientist, for instance, or a person trained in the techniques of scientific investigation considers to be the justification for such training will also determine what he thinks of the nature of science itself. It will, therefore, constitute the very meaning of the term "science" for him. Insofar as "science today is," as Heidegger says, "a technical, practical business of gaining and transmitting information," it is incapable of contributing a shred of spiritual or moral significance either to man's life or to his vocabulary. One of the profoundest insights into the tragic impoverishment of modern life, in spite of all of its education, is Heidegger's insistence that "an awakening of the spirit cannot take its departure from such science," since "it is itself in need of an awakening." [80]

The meaning with which language is used in any aspect of human life is an index of the spiritual level or character of such life. Hence an analysis of the meaning with which language is used is one way to understand much of the character of the life which employs it. Analysis of language is in a profound sense a philosophy of culture, when "culture" has the widest possible sense, embracing whatever makes a difference in the quality of a people or a society and thereby makes a difference in the quality of the life of individuals in such a social context. Thus, "the critique of language and of the linguistic form of thinking becomes," as Cassirer declares, "an integral part" of all aspects of culture—science, philosophy, morality, and religion. [81]

Awareness of the Problem of Language Is Not of Recent Origin The present emphasis upon language as a philosophical problem is not new: it may be traced to the beginning of Western philosophy itself. Cassirer points this out when he says that "philosophical inquiry into the origin and nature of language is as old as that into the essence and origin of being." [82] Randall likewise points out that the Greek philosophers' consideration of the nature of reality includes a consideration also of the discourse about such reality: " 'Discourse' and 'reason' are one and the same thing—in Greek they are designated by one and the same word, *Logos*." [83]

Even a superficial glance at the major philosophers of ancient Greece will confirm what both Cassirer and Randall point out. Heraclitus, for instance, is impressed with the fact that although there is one ultimate source of order in the world, that one source is called by as many names as men choose to refer to it. Heraclitus says that "everyone gives [it] the name he pleases." [84] This comment indicates a problem which troubled Heraclitus: the relation between what reality is and what men say of it. This problem includes, of course, a consideration of the conventional character of language, in distinction from the conditions for the truth character of language. The conventional character of language is an expression of what men think and say, whereas the nature of reality is the criterion for the truth of what they both think and say. Heraclitus is convinced that "the sun will not overstep his bounds" because there is an ultimate factor of cosmic order, notwithstanding men's ignorance of it, and so not withstanding what they think or *say* about it.[85]

Another explanation for the poverty of men's knowledge, and so for the vacuity of the truth character of their discourse, is pointed out by Cratylus, a disciple of Heraclitus: the nature of the world in which men live is in constant flux, or is process; accordingly, there is no possibility for knowing such reality, since this so-called "object" of knowledge has no persistent status. It is this implication of the view of Heraclitus which Socrates states in Plato's *Cratylus:* "We cannot even say that there is any knowledge, if all things are changing and nothing remains fixed." [86] Plato's *Cratylus* is, as Fowler says, "the earliest extant attempt to discuss the origin of language." [87] Though a minor dialogue, it is one in which the primary problem of Plato is very clearly stated. This problem is accounting for the possibility of knowledge, if it is the case that the world in which men live is one of "becoming." And Plato indeed shows the influence of Heraclitus and Cratylus in maintaining that the physical world is an order of change or flux or process and as such is not an object of *knowledge.* By Plato's definition, knowledge is of a persistent or enduring or changeless reality.

Plato indicates his awareness of the philosophical problem of the relation between language and reality when he speaks both about signs (*sema*) and also reality (*ousia*).[88] Since the term *ousia* is one of the ambiguous words in a philosophical vocabulary, this statement may well be in need of clarifying. But what alone is important at this point is taking account of the fact that Plato is not satisfied with the then current interpretation of language as a purely conventional phenomenon. Although language has a conventional aspect, according to Plato it also has another aspect; and he struggles with this latter aspect through his entire writings. He believes that over and above the conventional features of language, there is also some aspect of language which is determined by the nature of realities designated by language. This belief underlies whatever he says about the so-called "correctness of names." The notion that "there is a kind of inherent correctness in names, which is the same for all men, both Greeks and barbarians," entails, to be sure, some bizarre consequences; and Plato is perfectly aware of this undesirable aspect of his analysis of language.[89] But he is so totally dissatisfied with the conventionalist point of view that he is willing to entertain any notion which will offer a way to defend the possibility of knowledge, as he interprets knowledge. One philosophy of language which Plato regards as intolerable is that "convention and agreement" are sufficient to account for the entire nature of language.[90] He is convinced that knowledge, as he defines knowledge, is possible; and he therefore believes that a philosophy in defense of such possibility is achievable. This conviction may be referred to as Plato's premise that some language has cognitive character or fulfills a cognitive function.

What is unfortunate in this early study of language by Plato is the very restricted notion of what constitutes knowledge. According to Plato, it is "the quality of showing the nature of the thing named." [91] Whereas this general definition is clear, what is not equally clear is what aspect of language is presumed by Plato to accomplish this. He considers language as an "imitation" of reality. But this terminology itself creates an impasse in this dialogue because it appears that Plato is not aware of the ambiguous character of the term "imitate." When this term is used with the sense of "being like" *in some respect,* the impasse is averted; but when it is used with the sense of *identical with* or the same as, the impasse is simply insurmountable. That it was regarded as insurmountable by Plato is indicated by the fact that this dialogue ends as all of the tentative dialogues end: it has no clarification of the problem which satisfies Plato. The very way that Plato defines "imitate" accounts for his inability to proceed to a satisfactory philosophy of languages. He thinks of language being *like* reality; and he thinks of "being like" in the sense of agreeing in all respects with reality. He declares: "Names which are rightly given are *like* the things named and are images of them." [92] The analysis of the cognitive aspect of language in terms of an "image" of reality only confuses Plato, because he cannot see how there is in any feature of *physical* language a parallel to the physical features of nonlinguistic realities. Something of his despair in struggling with this problem is indicated by his suggestion that "the name is the representation of a thing." Unfortunately, the term "representation" is one of the most ambiguous of all terms in the vocabulary of philosophy. It is therefore not surprising that the use of this term did not clarify the problem, but only added to its bewildering character. Plato expresses his bewilderment most acutely when he uses both ambiguous terms, "representing" and "likeness," in one statement. This combination yields the thoroughly equivocal assertion about the cognitive function of language as "representing by likeness the thing represented." To clarify this notion by making it concrete, he suggests the absurd notion that "the letters of which the primary names are to be formed must be by their very nature *like* the things." [93] Of course, this suggestion is a last-ditch stand in support of his critique of conventionalism, and it confronts Plato himself with the necessity of considering a function of language which is not exhausted by its physical character. Another unfortunate oversight of Plato in this particular analysis is his unawareness of the limitations of his use of analogy. He argues that an instrument is a "good one" if it is physically suited for its presumed function; and he carries over this analogy to language, arguing that "if a name . . . is to be a good one, it must have the proper letters." [94] Even suggesting this is a *reductio ad absurdum*. Still insufficiently critical of his use of analogy for pointing out features of language which parallel nonlinguistic realities, he proposes the parallel of a painting and the imitative function of language. This most unfortunate analogy is stated by Plato in the question: "Can I not step up to a man and say to him, 'This is your portrait,' and show him perhaps his own likeness . . . can I not step up to the same man again and say, 'This is your name'?" On the basis of this specious similarity, he generalizes that "a name is an imitation, just as a picture is." [95] The uncritical use of analogy in this particular dialogue may be traced to Plato's insufficient attention to the ambiguity of the critical terms whose meanings he sought to clarify by use of analogies. It need not be pointed out that no analogy can be helpful for clarifying a term when the term itself is used with so many meanings that one doesn't even know which meaning is being illustrated.

What Plato himself calls the "ridiculous" features of his attempt to formulate a defense of the cognitive character of language might so easily have been averted, if instead of considering the thesis that "names belong to things," he had considered the proposal made by Ogden and Richards that "words . . . *symbolize* thoughts." [96] This point of view, which appears so obvious today, makes the cognitive function of language much less bewildering, since it removes the bewilderment from the physical features of language to the *interpretation*, to the meaning assigned to language, a meaning which is nonphysical; and this aspect of language, which constitutes its cognitive character, is entirely independent of its physical features. Plato was justifiably convinced that "that speech which says things as they are is true, and that which says them as they are not is false." [97] But he was unable to account for the truth character of affirmations within the scope of his analysis of language, as that analysis is presented in this dialogue.

In this very superficial sketch of the ancient origins of philosophical considerations of language it is impossible to do justice either to Plato's philosophy or to others', such as Parmenides'. It may, however, be sufficient to repeat what Heidegger has said about Parmenides' "Concerning Truth": it "might perfectly well replace whole libraries of supposedly indispensable philosophical literature. Anyone living today who knows the measure of such thinking discourse must lose all desire to write books." [98] The profound importance of Parmenides' discourse about the language of "being" was acknowledged by Plato in his dialogue *Parmenides,* and for an appreciation of its significance in the history of a philosophy of language, one should read Cornford's, *Plato and Parmenides.*[99]

Only an acquaintance with the major writings of Aristotle would be sufficient to impress one with Aristotle's awareness of the philosophical importance of language. For an appreciation of this aspect of Aristotle's philosophy, one might, however, read Professor Randall's important study, entitled *Aristotle,* in which he points out "Aristotle's careful analysis of language," basic to which is the presupposition that "the world lends itself to the grasp of language." [100] In other words, Aristotle, following Plato, is convinced of the cognitive function of some language: "Knowledge can find that structure (of the world), and express it in words and discourse." Professor Randall points out how naïve this assumption of Aristotle is in taking for granted that "the Greek language is a natural instrument for knowing and expressing the world's structure"; and then he confronts us with the sobering question: "But is it really more naïve than our modern conviction that the structure of mathematics and the structure of the world are the same?" [101]

The serious consideration of language in antiquity is not confined to philosophical discourse: it is also evident in the serious attempts of the early Christian church to affirm its faith, and to communicate its basic beliefs. Such a concern for a suitable language with which to affirm a sense of the importance of the Gospel for human life is already expressed, as Bultmann points out, "in the New Testament itself." [102] An adequate support of this statement is, of course, impossible here. One might receive considerable help in understanding this, however, by taking account of what I. T. Ramsey calls "logical analysis" in New Testament studies, which is a "search for appropriate logical structures in the Gospel narratives." [103] Much of the effort of the Church in the first centuries of its formation may likewise be considered to fall within the scope of a concern to select language which is capable of affirming Christian faith. Such affirming of faith is communicating by means of language; and in this respect, the early Church was concerned with "rules for . . . talking" about what is essential to Christian faith and Christian life.[104] The attempts of the early Church to formulate a creed capable of stating what is essential to Christian faith come within the general range of a consideration of the use of language in the service of religious life. Such formulation of faith likewise includes an articulation of what is believed about the nature of ultimate reality or God. Such a formulation is a theology. As Seeberg points out, the efforts of the Apostolic Fathers constitute "the beginnings of theology in the church," and are "the earliest attempts of ecclesiastical theology." [105] Insofar as the efforts of the Apologists were directed to "setting forth Christianity in forms intelligible to the cultured classes of their age," they were necessarily confronted with selecting a language capable of conveying the creed and theology of the Christian Church.[106] A term, for example, with which educated but non-Christian people were familiar was *logos*, one part of whose meaning is eternal wisdom; and on the basis of this meaning, the Apostolic Fathers selected the term "logos" to interpret the eternal and divine character of Christ, in whom Christian faith centers its hope.[107] The term "logos" was already in the vocabulary of Stoic philosophy; bringing it into the terminology of the Christian Church presented the challenging task of redefining this term to divest it of some aspects of Stoic thought and to assign to it other aspects unique to Christian faith. The very fact that the philosophical term "logos" had already acquired a vast range of meanings in the tradition of Greek philosophy helps to account for some of the problems with which the Church struggled in formulating its faith after it adopted this particular term. It may well have been Irenaeus' awareness of the ambiguity of "logos" that explains why he interprets Christ as "Son of God," rather than as logos. But in stressing the sonship of Christ, Irenaeus introduces many more problems, such as are inevitable when anthropomorphic language is used to speak about realities other than human. He speaks, for instance, of the "Son of God, who was actually born, lived and suffered as a man, and died." [108] To give some idea of the doctrinal problems created by this single statement one need only consider the view of Praxeas of Asia Minor, who argued that the interpretation of Christ as Son, implies that he came after the Father, and therefore is not eternal in the same sense as is God. There was, in other words, "a time when he was not." Praxeas also points out that insofar as Christ is identified with God, God becomes identified with Christ, and therefore the birth and death of Jesus the Christ are occurrences in God. The Church obviously was not long in realizing that this type of analysis discredits the very basis for Christian faith, which is in an immutable, changeless, reality to which men may turn for a help they cannot receive in the changing order in which they live. The *logical* implication, however, of interpreting Christ as Son was so evident to some Christian philosophers that their considerations of logic superseded their attention to the affirmation of faith in the eternal and so changeless character of both God and Christ. Noëtus of Smyrna, for instance, and Epigonus of Rome, argued that after identifying the Father and the Son and after acknowledging the birth and death of God in Christ, faith in the eternal status of God could be retained by considering his nature before such birth: "when the Father had not yet been born, he was rightly *called* Father."[109] This way of reconciling two contradictory affirmations about one reality is, of course, purely verbal: the affirmations alone are commented upon, and, in this respect, attention focuses upon what is *said* about God, rather than upon the nature of God.

The centuries of the Christian Church preceding St. Augustine are a chapter in the formation of creeds and theologies, and, therefore, much of this epoch in the history of the Church also comes within the scope of a use of language in the service of religious life. Augustine points out, for instance, that the basis for the long and tragic Arian controversy is stressing "that if Christ is a Son, then He was born; if He was born, there was a time when the Son was not," etc.[110] The intolerable logical consequences of affirming this concept accounted for the efforts of Alexander of Alexandria to interpret the birth as "without beginning," and by this verbal means he assumed he had preserved the eternal and immutable character of Christ. Thus he affirms that Christ is "immutable and unvariable, and is rightly worshiped as is the Father." [111] Athanasius endeavored to defend the same view about the eternal character of Christ by supporting the use of the philosophical term *homoousia*, which stresses that the essence or nature of God and Christ are the same. This insistence upon *homoousia* aims at repudiating the Arian doctrine that Christ is like God, the so-called *homoiousian* doctrine.

Even the most superficial survey of the history of Christian doctrine cannot be compressed within the scope of a single chapter. All that can possibly be done in this fragment of a chapter is to point out the linguistic aspect of the history of formulating the creed of Christian faith. This history includes taking account of the impact upon the Church of Neo-Platonic philosophy, of gnosticism, and of many other philosophies. In every encounter with such non-Christian philosophies, a new problem of language confronted the Church. The doctrine of the Trinity, for instance, challenged it to *state* in what respect one godhead may be *spoken* of as three. Hippolytus proposes that "three are one God because there belongs to them one power." [112] Origen introduces another philosophical term to clarify this relation: it is *hypostasis*, by which he stresses a "personal mode of existence" which differentiates the Son from the Father, while he maintains there is one God. He argues that the Son and the Father are "two things in hypostasis, but one in sameness of thought and . . . in sameness of will." [113] Many other churchmen took the same approach, such as Paul of Samosata, bishop of Antioch. Yet, when any distinction whatever is made between God as Father and God as Son, there is already the beginning of a view such as is associated with Origen, that "the Son is the 'second God' "; and when this is stressed, some version of Subordinationism logically develops.

Something of the tragic aspect of language in the history of the Church is wonderfully well stated by St. Augustine when he points out that "the Greeks speak of three hypostases, the Latins of three persons [whereas] Scripture nowhere speaks of three persons in one God." He points out that "our Greek friends have spoken of one essence, three substancs; . . . the Latins of one essence, or substance, three persons [whereas] we do not find that Scripture anywhere mentions three persons." [114] Augustine's acquaintance with the problems created by language in the formulation of theologies and creeds accounts for his wise comment that "God is more truly thought than He is uttered, and exists more truly than He is thought." [115]

This single comment constitutes a basis for an entire philosophy of religion and also for an entire reappraisal of a linguistic analysis of religion which presumes that what is essential to religion can be reduced to language and that the meaning of such language is exhausted within the scope of principles of language—grammar and logic.

NOTES FOR CHAPTER 8

1 Ludwig Wittgenstein, *Tractatus Logico-Philosophicus*, London, Kegan Paul, 1947, § 4.0031, p. 63.
2 John Herman Randall, *Aristotle*, New York, Columbia University Press, 1960, p. viii.
3 M. B. Foster, " 'We' in Modern Philosophy," in Basil Mitchell (ed.), *Faith and Logic*, London, Allen & Unwin, 1957, p. 195.
4 May Brodbeck, "The Nature and Function of the Philosophy of Science," in Herbert Feigl and May Brodbeck (eds.), *Readings in the Philosophy of Science*, New York, Appleton-Century-Crofts, 1953.
5 Herbert Feigl, "Logical Empiricism," in Herbert Feigl and Wilfrid Sellars (eds.), *Readings in Philosophical Analysis*, New York, Appleton-Century-Crofts, 1949, p. 3.
6 *Ibid.*, p. 6.
7 Mitchell, *Faith and Logic*, "Introduction," p. 5.
8 Brodbeck, *Readings*, p. 5.
9 Brodbeck, *Readings*, p. 4.
10 Antony Flew and Alasdair MacIntyre (eds.), *New Essays in Philosophical Theology*, London, SCM Press, 1955, "Preface," p. ix.
11 Mitchell, *Faith and Logic*, p. 2.
12 J. J. C. Smart, "The Existence of God," in Flew and MacIntyre, *New Essays*, pp. 38, 41.
13 R. M. Hare, "Religion and Morals," in Mitchell, *Faith and Logic*, p. 192.
14 Feigl and Sellars, *Readings*, p. 21.
15 Antony Flew and D. M. MacKinnon, "Creation," in Flew and MacIntyre, *New Essays*, p. 185; and R. M. Hare, in Mitchell, *Faith and Logic*, p. 179.

16 R. M. Hare, in Mitchell, *Faith and Logic*, p. 188.
17 Mitchell, *Faith and Logic*, p. 4.
18 Rudolf Bultmann, *Essays Philosophical and Theological*, translated by James C. G. Greig from *Glauben und Verstehen*, London, SCM Press, 1955, "Humanism and Christianity," p. 156.
19 Martin, "A Religious Way of Knowing," in Flew and MacIntyre, *New Essays*, p. 80.
20 Hepburn, "Demythologizing and the Problem of Validity," in Flew and MacIntyre, *New Essays*, p. 236.
21 Flew and MacKinnon, "Creation," in Flew and MacIntyre, *New Essays*, p. 183.
22 Stead, "How Theologians Reason," in Mitchell, *Faith and Logic*, p. 108.
23 Victor Kraft, *The Vienna Circle*, translated by Arthur Pap, New York, Philosophical Library, 1953, p. 3.
24 *Ibid.*, p. 4.
25 *Ibid.*, p. 5.
26 Brodbeck, *Readings*, p. 3.
27 *Ibid.*, p. 5.
28 Kraft, *The Vienna Circle*, p. 76.
29 Ogden and Richards, *Meaning of Meaning*, London, Routledge and Kegan Paul, 1948, p. 119.
30 Austin Farrer, "Revelation," in Mitchell, *Faith and Logic*, p. 88.
31 Bultmann, *Jesus Christ and Mythology*, New York, Scribner's, 1958, p. 74.
32 Martin Heidegger, *An Introduction to Metaphysics*, translated by Ralph Manheim, New Haven, Yale University Press, 1959, p. 96.
33 Bultmann, *Essays*, "The Crisis in Belief," p. 11.
34 Heidegger, *Introduction to Metaphysics*, p. 54.
35 *Ibid.*, p. 87.
36 Bronislaw K. Malinowski, *Magic, Science and Religion*, Garden City, N.Y., Doubleday, 1954, p. 96.
37 *Ibid.*, p. 147.
38 Ogden and Richards, *Meaning of Meaning*, "Supplement I," p. 333.
39 *Ibid.*, p. 322.
40 Rudolf Otto, *The Idea of the Holy*, translated by John W. Harvey, New York, Oxford University Press, 1943.
41 McPherson, "Religion as the Inexpressible," in Flew and MacIntyre, *New Essays*, p. 137.
42 Otto, *Idea of the Holy*, p. 62.
43 *Ibid.*, p. 105.
44 Gabriel Marcel, *The Mystery of Being*, Vol. I, translated by G. S. Fraser, Chicago, Regnery, 1950, "Reflection and Mystery," p. 12.
45 A. N. Prior, "Can Religion be Discussed?," in Flew and MacIntyre, *New Essays*, p. 3.
46 Heidegger, *Introduction to Metaphysics*, p. 53.
47 Martin Buber, *The Eclipse of God*, New York, Harper, 1952, p. 24.
48 Otto, *Idea of the Holy*, p. 208.
49 *Ibid.*, p. 203.
50 *Ibid.*, p. 208.
51 Lohmeyer, "The Right Interpretation of the Mythological," in H. W. Bartsch (ed.), *Kerygma and Myth*, translated by R. H. Fuller, London, S.P.C.K., 1954, p. 133.

52 Bultmann, *Jesus Christ and Mythology*, p. 67.
53 *Ibid.*, p. 21.
54 *Ibid.*, p. 18.
55 Hepburn, in Flew and MacIntyre, *New Essays*, p. 229.
56 *Ibid.*, p. 236.
57 Bultmann, *Jesus Christ and Mythology*, p. 43.
58 *Ibid.*, p. 19.
59 *Ibid.*, p. 36.
60 *Ibid.*, p. 15.
61 Bultmann, *Essays*, "The Problem of Hermeneutics," p. 235; cf. H. A. Hodges, *The Philosophy of Wilhelm Dilthey*, London, Routledge and Kegan Paul, 1952, p. 137.
62 Bultmann, *Jesus Christ and Mythology*, pp. 45, 46.
63 Malinowski, "The Problem of Meaning in Primitive Languages," Supplement I of Ogden and Richards, *Meaning of Meaning*, p. 297.
64 Marcel, *Mystery of Being*, p. 53.
65 Matthews, *The Thirty-Nine Articles*, London, Hodder and Stoughton, 1961, p. 5.
66 H. Thielicke, "The Restatement of New Testament Mythology," in Bartsch, *Kerygma and Myth*, p. 139.
67 Bartsch (ed.), *Kerygma and Myth*, "Foreword," p. viii.
68 H. Thielicke, in Bartsch, *Kerygma and Myth*, p. 139.
69 Bultmann, "A Reply to the Theses of J. Schniewind," in Bartsch, *Kerygma and Myth*, p. 123.
70 *Ibid.*, p. 122.
71 Bultmann, *Jesus Christ and Mythology*, p. 44.
72 Heidegger, *Introduction to Metaphysics*, p. 45.
73 *Ibid.*, p. 52.
74 *Ibid.*, p. 40.
75 Ogden and Richards, *Meaning of Meaning*, p. 131.
76 Heidegger, *Introduction to Metaphysics*, p. 51.
77 *Ibid.*, p. 51.
78 *Ibid.*, p. 51.
79 *Ibid.*, p. 46.
80 *Ibid.*, p. 49.
81 Ernst Cassirer, *The Philosophy of Symbolic Forms*, translated by Ralph Manheim, New Haven, Yale University Press, 1953, p. 82.
82 *Ibid.*, p. 117.
83 J. H. Randall, *Aristotle*, p. 6.
84 Heraclitus, Fragment 36, in Milton C. Nahm (ed.), *Selections from Early Greek Philosophy*, 2d ed. New York, Crofts, 1940, p. 91.
85 Heraclitus, Fragment 29.
86 Plato, *Cratylus* 440A. Translated by H. N. Fowler, in *Plato with an English Translation*, Vol. VI, London, William Heinemann, 1926.
87 *Ibid.*, "Introduction to the Cratylus," p. 4.
88 *Cratylus*, 401C-D.
89 *Cratylus*, 383A.
90 *Cratylus*, 384C.
91 *Cratylus*, 428E.
92 *Cratylus*, 439A.
93 *Cratylus*, 434A.

94 *Cratylus*, 430B.
95 *Cratylus*, 431B.
96 *Cratylus*, 390D; Ogden and Richards, *Meaning of Meaning*, p. 100.
97 *Cratylus*, 385B.
98 Heidegger, *Introduction to Metaphysics*, p. 96.
99 F. M. Cornford, *Plato and Parmenides*, New York, The Liberal Arts Press, 1957.
100 H. Randall, *Aristotle*, p. viii.
101 *Ibid.*, p. 7.
102 Bultmann, *Jesus Christ and Mythology*, p. 34.
103 I. T. Ramsey, *Religious Language*, New York, Macmillan, 1957, p. 141.
104 *Ibid.*, p. 202.
105 Reinhold Seeberg, *History of Doctrines*, Philadelphia, Lutheran Publication Society, 1905, pp. 118, 111.
106 *Ibid.*, p. 110.
107 *Ibid.*, p. 113.
108 *Ibid.*, p. 124.
109 *Ibid.*, p. 167.
110 Marcus Dods (ed.), *The Works of Aurelius Augustine*, Vol. VII, translated by A. W. Haddan, Edinburgh, 1873, "On the Trinity," p. 165.
111 Seeberg, *History of Doctrines*, p. 205.
112 *Ibid.*, p. 121.
113 *Ibid.*, p. 150.
114 Dods (ed.), *Works of Augustine*, VII, iv, sec. 7, p. 189; sec. 8, p. 192.
115 *Ibid.*, VII, iv, sec. 7, p. 190.

QUESTIONS

1 In what sense is linguistic analysis a type of empiricism? In what sense is its subject matter different from traditional empiricisms, such as Locke's and Hume's?

2 For what logical reason is the problem of truth distinguished from the problem of meaning? In light of this distinction, why is a "logic of science," as one type of philosophical analysis, not itself a so-called empirical science?

3 Why is a linguistic analyst's clarification of statements made by empirical scientists an order of discourse which differs from such scientists' statements? What parallelism may be pointed out in an analyst's clarification of the statements, for example, in a scripture?

4 In what way are the anthropological studies of primitive societies of utmost importance to philosophers of language? In what sense are studies of this type indispensable for an understanding of the function of languages?

5 In what way may a philosophy about the function of language condition the estimate of scientists about their empirical studies with language? Analyze how Malinowski has been influenced by Ogden and Richards' definition of the noncognitive character of language used in religion.

SUGGESTED READINGS

A. J. Ayer, *Language, Truth and Logic*, London, Gollancz, 1946.
Gustav Bergmann, *The Metaphysics of Logical Positivism*, New York, Longmans, Green and Co., 1954.

Basil Mitchell (ed.), *Faith and Logic*, London, George Allen and Unwin, 1957.

A. Pap, *Elements of Analytic Philosophy*, New York, Macmillan, 1949.

Ian I. Ramsey, *Religious Language: An Empirical Placing of Theological Phrases*, New York, Macmillan, 1957.

W. M. Urban, *Language and Reality*, New York, Macmillan, 1939.

9 Charles Hartshorne

Religion in Process Philosophy

In all the higher religions, philosophical speculations have played an important part, at least in the theoretical accounts which these religions have given of themselves.[1] Christian theology, in particular, inherited certain concepts of Greek metaphysics—as witness the creedal expression, "of one 'substance' with the Father." In the past four centuries, and especially since about 1850, a new type of metaphysics has been emerging, the importance of which has been obscured by the simultaneous development of certain skeptical or antimetaphysical doctrines which themselves had Greek forerunners. It is time that students of religion, and educated persons generally, became aware of what has been happening.

The old metaphysics was based on a logic of things and properties, or subjects and predicates; the new employs a logic of terms and relations. It may perhaps be objected that relations are also properties, "relational properties," so that the thing-property concept is still all-inclusive. But this obscures, more than it exhibits, the truth. If A experiences B, for example, one may, if one wishes, say that A has the relational property "experiencing B." But then note that we have, not a single subject and its predicate, as when we say "A is happy" or "has the property 'being happy'," but rather two subjects, one of which is a constituent of the relational property of the other. In "A experiences B," what characterizes A is not simply "experiences" or "experiences something," but "experiences B." Relation-to-B has to be taken as a unit; otherwise we shall have a relation between the relation and B, and a truly vicious regress will be set up. Relation-to-B includes B and cannot exist without it. Thus, for A's relational property, B is as necessary (in the logical sense of necessary) as A. A must then be taken as partly constituted, made what it is, by B. Reality thus is shown to be irreducibly relative. Subjects are what they are, not through mere private predicates or properties, but through the references which it is their natures to make to certain other subjects.

This is really common sense. What is a man apart from the world which he experiences, loves, fears, contends and cooperates with, grows out of? Actuality is relative through and through. To know is to be related (or to relate oneself); to love is to be related; to be an effect is to be related. And what, pray, is life and actual existence except as knowing, loving, acting, and being acted upon?

But there is another objection to the thing-property language. Many important relations are not between what is normally meant by "things," but rather between events, states, or phases of process. Consider spatio-temporal relations. Is it really the stone, *simpliciter*, which is here and the cloud which is yonder? At another moment, the stone may be yonder, hurled by an explosion, and the cloud may be here, grazing the hilltop on which, let us suppose, we have been standing. True, we are still speaking of the stone or cloud as being somewhere; but really it is the state of the one or the other at a given moment, the stony or cloudy event or process then going on, which has a certain spatial locus.

Is the stone, considered as identical through time, "before" or "after" itself? Its self-relation is that of identity, which does not seem to be the relation of temporal succession. Hence, as furnishing a term of temporal relations, the stone is not what we require, but rather the event or state, the something-going-on-now. And this term of temporal relations also gives us all we need as term for spatial relations. For the event is not simply now, it is here-now. What then is added if we say, "But really, the event is a property of the stone"? Are we thus reporting a relation of event to thing? The open secret of this matter is that "stone" merely designates a certain stability and intimacy of relatedness in a sequence of events, and this stability is a property, a predicate, of the events, rather than a final subject of predicates. From Aristotle to Kant (and, we may add, to Strawson) the confusion about this can be traced.[2] Science at least has finally escaped from the muddle. Science is concerned with the spatio-temporal-causal relations of events, or phases of process, and with nothing else. By "thing" a scientist simply means a certain sequential order in events, a "world line" of unusual persistence of character, and this persistence or stability of character is for him simply a special strand of the orderly causal relatedness of events.[3] "Person" for psychology differs only in the type of relatedness and of events involved. Some psychologists still choose to talk about an identical soul or self; but as scientists what they actually do is to trace the relationships among experiences or behavioral occurrences. They relate these, not to a soul, but to one another. To say that the relationships are "explained" by the identity of the soul is, I submit, to betray verbal-mindedness. For the word "soul" has in turn to be explained exhaustively by the observed characters and relationships of events, since nothing else could be observed. Any observation is an event or event-sequence whose concrete data are also events or characters of events. The Buddhists discovered this long ago and insofar anticipated what clear-headed analysis is gradually forcing upon us. Self-identity as found by observation—even introspective observation—in the form of abiding personality traits, fixed purposes, continuity of memories, is describable as a common character or relationship of the experiences and occurrences in the individual world line. The persistence of the character is itself a relation, and whether it be of similarity or of "partial identity" makes no difference for our present concern. The logical point is that the identity is at most only "partial": that is, what has persisted throughout my life—say, from the beginning until now—is only a part or aspect of what "I" am now, not the whole. Recall that if a whole is not a new whole, nothing in it is new, for the least new item produces a new total reality, by the mere meanings of "new" and "total." At each moment, therefore, the total personal reality is numerically new, just as the Buddhist writings of long ago said it was. This was a fine anticipation of modern logic and science—and metaphysics. (Hume's account was inferior to the Buddhistic, for he denied relationships, in a manner in which they did not. But their account of the relatedness was not adequate either.) Whitehead is the first Western philosopher to get close to the bottom of this matter. Of course the view is still not widespread. To think with logical sharpness is not the line of least resistance in any age. It is toilsome and often painful for the best of us.

As an example of how easy it is to fall into confusion in this matter, consider the argument (which James Ward presented as well as anyone) that if there are perceptions there is a perceiver, if thoughts, a thinker. Suppose we grant this as in some sense correct. Does it follow that the perceiver or thinker is identical from birth to death? Not in the least. This is a quite distinct question. Each momentary experience may have its own unique "subject-pole" (Husserl's term), numerically distinct from that of its predecessors. And if this is denied, then one must suppose that the same believer believes contradictory beliefs, insofar as a man repudiates his childish or youthful errors. But—you may say—he does not hold contradictory beliefs at the same time. Does this really help? The subject of the childish beliefs was entirely innocent of the adult beliefs; the later beliefs with their later date then must be insinuated into the same total reality without altering its identity. But this is contradiction, no matter what is said about dates. Any novelty at all means a novel totality.

And please note that the subject which really has beliefs and other forms of experience must be the whole of which they are aspects. The subject having a certain total experience can only be the total reality constituted by that experience; it cannot be less. The "subject," as Whitehead explains, is the experience in its total self-active or creative functioning. But this can never acquire additional content. Only a new subject can have new content, as a new self-active totality integrates additional terms.

Let us consider still another common confusion. It is said that a momentary self could not know succession, that only a self "above time" can know time. Or it is said that the identity of the soul explains memory. But as we have already pointed out, the relation of present to past, which is the temporal structure of memory, is not the relation of identity. "Well," you may say, "but still identity is required." Yes indeed, it is, and here is where Hume—and perhaps even the Buddhists—went astray, as compared to Whitehead. The remembered past event must be the identical event which in itself was not past but, for itself, the latest verge of time. However, this identity is that of the event, not of the soul. (We shall return to this identity of the event presently.) But, runs a possible objection, do we not say, "I remember how *I* did thus and thus"; we do not say, "I, number n, remember how I, number $n - m$, did thus and thus." No, we do not pedantically speak like this. But is this the only elliptical element in language, the only simplification required for practical everyday purposes? All language is more or less elliptical. You say, "I remember," your neighbor says, "I remember," but only a Hindu mystic denies that "I" here means two entities. If difference in space—you here, your neighbor there—alters the referent, it is a fair question if temporal differences do not also alter it. Pronouns are "token-reflexives," context-dependent labels, changing their referents from occasion to occasion. That common sense is more aware of this with respect to spatial than to temporal distance between various utterances of "I" is no great puzzle to Buddhists or Whiteheadians, since the relations of similarity and of memory are in general most intimate in the merely temporal case. The latest referent of "I" coming from a given person is much closer, in many ways, to an earlier referent in the same "personally ordered" sequence. This, too, the Buddhists saw clearly enough, and they saw that it was compatible with their main doctrine.

The old metaphysical question was, "What is it for a thing or substance to be or exist?" The new question runs, "What is it for events or total states or units of becoming to occur, for acts to be enacted, or experiences to be realized?" "What is it to happen, occur, become, or experience?"—not, "What is it to *be?*" I think that most philosophers do not, even yet, suspect the radical transformation involved in this new form of the philosophical question. (Preoccupation with "ordinary language" has on the whole impeded the full realization of the transformation, without—in my opinion—invalidating it.)

There are many who will triumphantly ask at this point (or sooner), "Granted something becomes, does this not mean that it comes to *be?* And thus is not 'being' the final upshot of the matter?" But the very same people are also likely to say, "No sooner has an event 'become' than it drops into the past and thus 'ceases to be,'" from which it appears to follow that 'non-being,' rather than being, is the final upshot of becoming! To escape this weird double unreality of what at first lacks being and then presently and forever after loses being, we must, it is urged, turn away from becoming to a form of being which simply and absolutely is.

However, when an event becomes, the "being" which it thereby achieves is not something additional to its becoming as such, but a mere analytic aspect of it. The "being" of an event, once it has become, is its status as relatum for subsequent events in their relational natures. Relations can be no more real than their terms. If B becomes, as relative to A, if it has, as its relational property, "succeeding A," then the determinate nature of B includes that of A. The relativity of events to predecessors means the indestructibility of events! It is the undying merit of Bergson to have been the first to see this clearly. But Whitehead is the first to work out with systematic thoroughness what is implied in the discovery. Events do not cease to have status by "becoming past"; on the contrary, they can become past only by becoming constituents of the events whose past they constitute.

Perhaps the philosopher of being will object: the being of an event cannot be preserved in later events unless there is this being. But what is being or reality? I submit that it is the same as definiteness, determinateness. It is fictions that fail to correspond to the law of excluded middle. How many hairs on Mr. Micawber's head? There is no definite number, and this indefiniteness, multiplied to something like infinity, is the unreality of Mr. Micawber. This cannot be denied without paradox.

If, even for God, the possible can be as definite as the actual, then when the possible is actualized, only an absolutely indefinite something has been added. I hold that this is nonsense. If reality *is* definiteness, what is the definiteness of an event? Simply its becoming, as completed. Take an experience, a total act of experiencing. Of course it has its unique overall quality. This quality does not "die" as the event is taken over by later events as their relatum. On the contrary it is just the quality of the act as a whole that is taken over as "predecessor."

Pastness is not unreality, which would mean indefiniteness; pastness is constituent reality, definiteness as relatum of new relational wholes. We need no philosophy of pure being to protect us against the destruction of reality: the concrete realities which are events logically cannot be destroyed, if they are to have successors—and without successors how could it be true that they have been destroyed? This would have meaning only with reference to a succeeding state of affairs, and therefore would imply successors after all. The destruction of actuality against which the philosophers of being offer us protection is a fiction or absurdity which they themselves have invented.

But men and trees and cities can be destroyed! Yes, things, "substances," are subject to "destruction" in the common-sense meaning. But this simply connotes that an event-sequence with a certain persistence of character, and with peculiarly intimate relationships among the member events, may have a final member, like the last chapter of a book. The book is not destroyed by virtue of the limited number of its chapters, and neither is a life, properly seen as an event-sequence, turned into naught by virtue of the limited number of its experiences and behavioral occurrences. It may be that the book of an individual's life is painfully incomplete, truncated; but it may also be rather well-rounded, with a good and suitable last chapter.

Those who make the concept of thing or substance final must resort to all sorts of pseudo-permanences (as I must regard them) to achieve the indestructible reality which events, as the concrete units of the real or definite, cannot fail to achieve as they become ingredients in their successors. But having invented the pseudo-concept of the destruction of events, one cannot stop there—like the liar who must always go on lying. How much of man's history is summed up in this: think of the heavens and hells, the inquisitions and wars justified as means of keeping people from inheriting the hells, the theories of transmigration (found even in Buddhism), and the rest of it! These doctrines give too little heed to the question, "Is not all experience, as occurrent, and about to become past for every future event, immortal?"

We have discussed the reality of past events. What about that of events "in the future?" This, according to the modern philosophers of process (Buddhists seem to have seen the matter otherwise) is a different question. The future is the as-yet-uncreated, the partly unsettled or indefinite, that concerning which choices and decisions still have to be made, and even now in part are being made. Of course, therefore, the future lacks the full reality or definiteness of the past; for that is altogether settled, by the very meaning of "past." On the basis of what has happened we decide what to do next; but how could we do this if subsequent happenings were already in all details decided? This would mean either that the pending choice or decision was to have no future effects, or that it was itself already decided—before it was decided. Decision must be step by step, each step presupposing its predecessors but not its successors.

We should also note this: if B is successor to A and C to B, then the temporal order, C following B following A, is fully defined. It is at best redundant to add the reverse or prospective order, *A* preceding *B* preceding *C*. It is worse than redundant, for succession does not have such a prospective structure; an event is not related to its successors as definite or real events. There are various ways of showing this. If *A* had the relational property, "preceding *B*," then since this property includes *B*, *B* must have been there before it happened. And since it must also be true that *B* has the relational property, "succeeding *A*," *A* and *B* would become mutual constituents of one another, and the entire succession of becomings would thus be viewed as a single whole of mutually implicative elements. This would amount to saying that nothing could become in any intelligible sense, but rather, all events simply and timelessly are. But then they are not events!

Of course, dates on a calendar can be related prospectively, and so can planned or predicted events associated with these dates. But these are "events" only in a somewhat abstract sense: they are not fully defined actualities, but are kinds of event—e.g., "political convention of the Republican Party for 1980." Only afterwards will this denote a definite set of fully defined, i.e., real, events.

We can now shed new light upon the old dichotomy relative-absolute. The very same event can and must be relative with respect to some terms, and absolute with respect to others. Effects are relative to causes, but causes are absolute, so far as their effects are concerned. Regardless of what comes of a situation, it is what it is. One cannot similarly say that regardless of what a situation resulted from, it is what it is. For had it resulted from other causes, this must have made a difference. The most striking aspect of this is seen in memory. So far as memory goes, experiences intrinsically refer to their origins. Some would claim a similar role for anticipation or intuitive foreknowledge, as intrinsic references to later events. I cannot argue this here, but I believe that the evidence for clairvoyance of the future does not go beyond tendencies and probabilities, even though a plausible case can be made against me at this point.

To be "absolute," we see, is not a special property belonging only to some one thing or class, but a universal status in which anything whatever stands, at least in some respect. Ordinary realities, i.e., events, are universally absolute, so far as later events are concerned. Absoluteness, insofar, is not a strange, remote, awesome business, but one side, and the negative side, of the basic asymmetry inherent in becoming as such. The past is settled, hence absolute, wholly independent of anything that anybody may do.

Nevertheless, there is an aspect of mystery about absoluteness. Past events are indeed inviolate to subsequent influence, and insofar absolute; they are absolute ingredient relata in later events which, with reference to them, are relative. But *how* are past events ingredients in subsequent events? There are two forms of such ingredience. One is memory—not imagination of the past plus belief, but memory in the primary Bergsonian-Whiteheadian sense of direct possession of the past in and by the present. The other is perception, in which also—I hold—past events are given. Perception taken in this way may be called impersonal memory, since its data belong not to one's own sequence of experiences but to sequences constituting one's body and, less directly, environment. I shall use "memory" henceforth to cover both personal and impersonal forms. Yet how far, in our human case, does this true or immediate memory go, and where does inference from memory begin? At best we seem to lack really adequate memories even of the most recent events. Only an ideally perfect memory, possessing total recall, could fulfill the requirements of the logic of relativity, which calls for inviolate or absolute constituent relata for relative terms. If temporal order is real, then later events must intrinsically and definitely refer to their predecessors. But this requirement is not entirely fulfilled in human experience, so far as introspection reveals it to us. The conclusion can only be that the events called human experiences contain more than our introspection is able to detect. And what this introspection misses must include the equivalent of perfect memory. How shall this be?

There is but one way, so far as I can see, to render this intelligible: human experiences must have a side, largely hidden from us, which renders these experiences more than merely human, which in fact renders them divine experiences as well. "Divine," however, must not mean what it does in a philosophy of pure being, a timeless act of cognition whose object is the totality of events. For, according to the process doctrine, the notion of such a totality is self-contradictory or meaningless. Even divine knowing must have a settled past and an open future. This does not imply that it must or can be "ignorant," for it is a misuse of terms to speak of ignorance where there is nothing to know; and "future events" are an empty class: there are no such events. All definite or actual events are present or past. God can know them all perfectly, and when a new present becomes, and the totality of elapsed happenings has thus been enriched, there will be more for him to know. But only then. For him to know definite events "eternally," although no event can be eternally real or definite, would be divine error or illusion, not knowledge. Thus the paradoxes of divine "foreknowledge" (or eternal knowledge) of our future actions and experiences arise from taking seriously an empty concept or pseudo-concept. There is no problem of reconciling human freedom with omniscience; for, until we have decided, there are no human decisions for God either to know or fail to know. Such decisions are real neither beforehand nor eternally. The elimination of this famous problem is one of the many merits of the new doctrine.

We have seen that the absoluteness of past events, as ingredients in present events, is not clearly and directly discernible in experience and is to be conceived only by thinking of a divine equivalent of what in us is called memory, taken (as many philosophers refuse to take it) as actual possession of the past itself. What we need God for is thus not to furnish a merely nonrelative or "absolute" actuality, but rather, to furnish that adequate form of relativity without which events as successive, and hence relative to predecessors which are not relative to them, cannot be positively understood. All memory is relative to what it remembers, and the more perfect or exact this relativity, the more completely it exhibits the absoluteness of the past. This absoluteness of the past, or relativity of the present to the past which was not relative to it, is the asymmetry of process. Absoluteness and relativity are thus correlative. Neither can have exemplification unless the other does. An event qua absolute is the event qua potentially or actually past, and this means the event qua potentially or actually inviolate ingredient in subsequent events, i.e., events as relative. To be successive is to be relative, and relative to that which is not, in turn, relative—in this relationship. Absoluteness and relativity are the same fact, viewed in reverse order. But the exact or definitive absoluteness-relativity can only be furnished by a divine mode of relativity which has the structure of perfect memory. I term this divine mode of relativity, *Transcendental Relativity*, a mode of transparent relatedness which completely, or if you will "absolutely," sums up that to which it is relative. The "transparency" of the divine relativity is the meaning of "omniscient." Each new act of divine relativity is of course absolute, so far as subsequent acts are concerned; but it is also relative, both to its own previous acts and to acts of nondivine relating, such as human experiencings.

There is, however, one further sense of "absolute," which was exhibited in the above employed adverbial term "absolutely." We need to consider the question: Is there anything which is nonrelative, not merely in a certain respect, as events are nonrelative with respect to later events, but in any and every respect? The answer is Yes; there is something which in no relationship is relative, but is in every contingent relationship independent or inviolate. This is the generic adverbial property of the divine acts of self-relating. In all possible instances, the divine relates itself adequately, completely, perfectly, "absolutely," to its relata. It expresses the entire truth about them, takes account of them in every detail and subtle nuance. "*The* absolute"—meaning the unconditionally independent or in every respect nonrelative—is adverbial, not adjectival. There is and can be no individual thing, act, or person in all respects absolute; but there is a *mode of action* which in all respects is absolute, and the thing or person with this mode of action is God. Each particular divine act is itself, in some respects, relative; for it is an act of self-relating, experiencing, knowing; but if we ask, "How in general does the divine relate itself to things?" the answer is, "Absolutely," i.e., without the slightest lack of transparency. The generic adverb applying to God is thus the long-sought referent of the old term "the absolute." But the adjective applying to God is, "absolutely self-relating or Transcendentally Relative," TR.

I contend that not only is there no contradiction in this but there is no other way to avoid contradictions in speaking of the relative and the non-relative. The contradictions in traditional views are well-known, and have increasingly tended to discredit metaphysics. But the avoidance of metaphysics is not achieved by declaring that "everything is relative." In the first place, this dictum merely makes "relative" unmeaning, since it expresses no contrast. Since without contrast meaning collapses, the dictum fails to express anything. In the second place, if everything thinkable is relative, then relativity is itself absolute, since it must be realized no matter what. The solution of the paradox is to see: (1) that each event has a relative side and an absolute side, the asymmetry expressing "time's arrow"; (2) that the relative side is the event as embracing the absoluteness of previous events, so that it is relativity, not absoluteness, which is the inclusive principle; (3) that only an adequate or Transcendental Relativity can fully define events as absolute; (4) that this Transcendental Relativity, as a generic adverbial aspect of the Transcendental acts of self-relating, is itself relative to nothing, for it is bound to be exemplified. Otherwise there would be nothing definite at all, whether relative or absolute, inasmuch as this mode of self-relating is essential to the relational structure apart from which no conceptions can have meaning.

Is TR the same as deity, as God the Creator? Let us consider again what our categorial basis is. Reality is process as creative and cumulative. Events sum up their predecessors (as terms of their relativities) but not their successors. Hence the latter will be additions, creations, not deducible from, nor in any sense whatever contained in, the present events. Becoming is thus, as Bergson put it, "invention [creation] or nothing." It is of little use to say that the cause "makes" the effect if this means a relation whereby an event contains or necessitates a later event as relative; for this entails the double, or symmetrical, relativity which we have rejected. Such symmetry (a) makes "time's arrow" an enigma, (b) treats as elementary what we know from general relational logic ought to be derivative (asymmetrical relations are primary), (c) implies that the future is real before it happens, since it is a real constituent of present relative events, and (d) doubles every temporal relation of succession with a redundant inversion. It also (e) fails to shed light on the statistical nature of law which science seems more and more unambiguously to affirm as the only useful one. So let us persist in rejecting the symmetrical view, and in affirming the absoluteness or nonrelativity of present events with respect to later events, and, therefore, the creative character of becoming.

In what sense, then, if any, is there causal necessity? If we can predict with certainty or if one with ideal knowledge of the past could do so, *in so far* the future is indeed entailed by the present, and the present is therefore relative to it. For nothing is independent of what it entails, since for X to be independent of Y means that the denial of Y does not contradict X, and this in turn means that X does not entail Y. But only insofar as the future is certainly predictable must it be entailed. According to the statistical or indeterministic view of causality, what is predictable is never particular events but classes of events—not the later happening itself, but the sort of happening, the class of more or less probable happenings, of which there must be some instance or other. The particular happening is never implicated or entailed, but must be created. This creation is free in the too often despised sense of causally indeterminate or arbitrary, subject only to the probabilities mentioned. Certain more or less definite trends are given which the creative process must exhibit, but that is all.

What this means is that ordinary events are as truly self-creative as—in some aspects—they are causally determined or necessitated. (If you object to "self-creative," substitute "spontaneous and neither determinable nor predictable in advance.") Our doctrine then brings down the exalted theological idea of "creating" and makes it a universal feature of reality as such. There can be no reality which is simply "made" to be what it is by some power other than itself. Every reality, in some degree, escapes full determination by any other reality whatever.

TR is not in contradiction with this. Even the perfect relativity, whereby each ordinary relative event is enabled to have also a face of absoluteness turned toward the future, must not itself be supposed fully to determine subsequent events; for this would defeat the very purpose for which the concept was introduced, namely, to preserve the independence or absoluteness without which subsequent relative events would lack suitable terms. The absolute cannot entail the relative, for to entail is to depend upon. Only the neutral is independent, and the neutral is just what does not entail. To attribute to deity the power to determine events completely is to make deity in this respect of power, qua exercised, relative. Deity as transparently referring to events in the past is indeed relative, but not because it determines, decides, their natures; rather, because it accepts their natures as already self-decided and "immortalizes" them by accepting them into itself, its own life and value.

How can I put this plainly and strongly enough to do justice to what I think I see? The absolute is not the greatest of all things, but is merely the foundation for ever new relativities, and in this function all its value consists! Moreover, this value will be included as ingredient in the new relativities, as relative terms include their relata. The class of new acts of Transcendental Relativity is the greatest, most exalted, of classes; but no such act is the greatest possible in its class, for it would then exhaust inexhaustible possibilities.

What then is left of the idea of divine creation? A great deal—all that ever made genuine sense, so far as I can see. The basic creative activity is becoming as such. Events are free, not predetermined or determined from above. This is included in the meaning of events as successive, uni-directional, asymmetrical, ordered, and relative. Thus to "create" another cannot in this philosophy mean to make or force a reality (an event) to be what it is. Yet this deprives us of no conception that we ever really possessed. For with all the talk in our tradition about "creation," no genuine category was provided for this term. X creates Y, "God creates or causes the world," was verbally asserted. But what did the words connote? When Hume challenged philosophers to show the basis in direct and concrete experience or in clear analysis for the idea of cause, they were at a loss, and even though Kant did his best to meet the challenge, this best was not good enough. How can the prior (or the eternal) reality of X imply the subsequent (or temporal) reality of Y? In God is a de-cision of will, "Let the world exist." What is the link of necessity between this fiat in God and the existence of the world? For this our theologians had only words like "power," which is the problem over again. To get beyond mere verbalism we must find causation or creation as a character exhibited in some experience. Can we do this?

There is one point in experience where we can find a cause issuing in an effect, and where the natures of the cause and the effect are both given. This is in immediate memory. I feel a pain, and then immediately I try to escape the pain I have just begun to feel. I hear kind words, and immediately afterward feel encouraged, as I sense what I have just heard. I make a decision for immediate execution, and then, aware of what I have just decided, I make appropriate subdecisions as to details. Here the remembered element causes a present response. To remember *is* to be in-fluenced by what one remembers. Memory is an effect or it is nothing. How then does God influence us? If we can have direct awareness of the divine fiat, as we have direct awareness in immediate memory of our own past experience, then this fiat will influence us. The awareness need not be conscious in the sense of being introspectively evident. Immediate memory is mostly not conscious in this sense. I begin a sentence, and without saying to myself that I have begun it, I yet feel this beginning, so that I am able to go on appropriately. In such fashion we must be supposed to feel the divine fiat, without usually telling ourselves, or even being able to tell ourselves, that and what we feel.

But, you may argue, is it not possible to be aware of a fiat without obeying it? Certainly the idea of disobedience to divine fiats is not without its standing in religion! On the other hand, there must be some mode of divine power which cannot simply be disregarded. Can the lower animals disobey God? His fiat concerns them too.

Let us recall that to disobey is not the same as to disregard. The disobedient is not uninfluenced by the command he refuses to accept; for it puts him in a state of rebellion or resistance to suggestion which is not the same as the state of simple unawareness of the suggestion. As for the lower animals, they are no great problem here. Since they lack the power of thought, save on some minimal level, there is very little they can do with a suggestion, if they feel it at all, except to act in accordance with it.

The basic point here is the unique preeminence of the divine influence over all others. Any individual can furnish suggestions to others, give them an impetus in some direction; but with most individuals such power is sharply restricted, first in scope, in that only near neighbors are appreciably affected at any one moment, and second in degree, in that even some near neighbors may not be appreciably affected. I am not appreciably affected by any one of my brain cells, though it is certainly close enough to me. The preeminence of the divine influence is that (1) all things are neighbors of God, nothing is remote from him; (2) all things are appreciably, and indeed incomparably, influenced by him.

We now ask ourselves, why is the divine fiat universally and incomparably influential? I answer with an old doctrine (perhaps first stated by Aristotle), somewhat transformed: God is uniquely influential because he is uniquely good or beautiful. As Whitehead puts it, "the power of God is the worship he inspires." Not, the power inspires the worship, but the worshipfulness is the power. The creatures do not behold the divine power in its effects and therefore admire or worship God, they directly feel his worshipful excellence and beauty, and this inspires and influences them, which inspiring beauty is the power. The principle here is: no creature can respond to anything except value, goodness, or beauty in some form. All power is of the nature of appeal, attractiveness, or "charm," acting either directly or indirectly. A tyrant need not charm all his subjects, it is true, but he "charms" at least the members of his own physical body, or they would not act in accordance with his thoughts and purposes, and the movements of his body "charm" the surrounding molecules, or they would not vibrate to constitute the sounds of his voice, and so on. The tyrant may also—to some extent must—charm his personal followers. Each link in this chain is either inexplicable, a mere mystery, or a case of the appeal of value to some creature. There is, I suggest, no second positive clue to "power," whose nature so puzzled Locke and Hume. The rest is words.

It is easy to be skeptical concerning the view just sketched. But the question in metaphysics is not what is probable, or most easily believed or understood. Metaphysical truth is never very easy or perfectly clear, for neither is human thinking. And metaphysically ill-judged statements are never simply improbable; they are meaningless or contradictory. They do not say something wrong, they fail to say anything positive at all. For instance, one can in words say that a divine fiat "causes" mere bits of matter, but of the "dependence" of the latter upon the former we have not the faintest glimmering of a conception. Of the dependence of an experiencing subject for its values upon values experienced in another, however, we do have some idea; at least if we have any idea of what it is to know another mind than our own. To grasp the different feelings or thoughts of another is to receive increments to our own thought or feeling; to feel the intense or happy feelings of another is to participate to some extent in this intensity or happiness; to grasp the complexity and harmony of another's ideas is, insofar, to possess this complex harmony oneself. Whatever another finds valuable we can also value if we can share his perspective. The more value the other achieves the more it is worth being aware of the other, so that by participation we may appropriate as much as we can of his blessed state.

We must have some idea of how mind can influence mind. This concept is indispensable. But the possibility of an influence of mind upon mere matter is a gratuitous problem wholly created by the absolute denial of feeling or experience to large parts of nature, a denial which outruns not only any actual but any conceivable evidence. No one will ever inspect atoms and find there as manifest fact "no feeling or experience of any kind (not even in very primitive or strange forms, compared to the human)." No such absolutely negative observation could take place. We cannot form a conception even of God making such an observation, for he would be experiencing the sheer absence of experience in something, and we have no notion of what such an absence would look like. That a chair does not feel we can indeed observe, for the chair does nothing which could be appropriate to feeling; but the real action in chairs, we know today, is on the micro level. To forget this is to relapse into Aristotle's attitude toward physics (and many there are who do not seem to mind doing this). Of the things which are really "done" in a chair, on the level where definite actions take place in it, all one can say is that any feelings expressed in these actions must be very different from human feelings. But why not? What anthropomorphism it is to suppose that the human way of feeling is anything like the only way. How does a bee feel? One thing seems sure: in no way closely similar to any human mode of feeling.

One can, if one wishes, define feeling as something which accompanies vertebrate animal responses, but all that one has really defined in this way is "vertebrate feeling," and "vertebrate feeling" implies the possibility of nonvertebrate feeling. Moreover, all argument from the necessity of nerves for feeling is a mere vicious circle. Our feelings require human

nerves, a dog's feelings require doggish nerves, all vertebrate feelings require vertebrate nerves; but a "protozoan feeling," by definition, could
not require separate nerve cells, since there can be no separate cells in
the case. Unless, then, one can look into the amoeba and simply see its
lack of feeling (and one cannot), one has to judge from behavior, internal
and external. The behavior shows definite analogies between what the
metazoa do by means of nerves and what the protozoa do without nerves.
So the only evidence there could be favors the view that the protozoa
have feelings, but more or less different feelings from the metazoa. Go
farther down. Does not an atom behave, respond, organize its parts, and
under stimulation reorganize them, act also without external stimulus
(when radioactive at least)? Moreover, it is no mere odd fact of science
that the parts of "inert" matter are not themselves inert. Until we do
get to something not inert we have no reason to think we have reached
the essential structures of nature. Process is not a detail, but the essence.
The appearance of mere stuff in which nothing goes on could be no more
than appearance. Aristotle was wrong to trust it. The "deadness" of
matter is the same as its elusiveness because of the grossness, the coarse
scale of our senses, a coarseness highly useful, nay indispensable, biologically, but deceptive theoretically.

The model of "influence" which we all know in ourselves is the following: our past thoughts and feelings readily influence us simply because
we are aware of them and because they are our sort of thoughts and
feelings. Further, we influence what goes on in our bodies, and the
bodily processes influence our thought and feeling. Why? How? Many
great men have thought this a riddle we could never penetrate. But they
have taken this despairing view because of assumptions which are not
obligatory. Thus they have uncritically accepted the notion of mere
matter, and they have equally uncritically thought of the mind-body
relation as a one-one, not a one-many, relation. There is no possibility
of really comprehending how "*the* mind" influences "*the* body" and vice
versa. Aristotle pretended to explain it, but he merely provided the problem with some neat labels. Mind "informs" and "actualizes" "matter,"
whose nature is potentiality for form, and what forms can be actualized
depends upon the particular matter, this particularity, so far as it is
qualitative, being explained as a lower level of form. This is all verbal;
no positive insight is had. But what is called *the* body is in truth a multi-
billionfold society of cells. The true question is, How does each of my
successive experiences influence billions of cells, and how do they collec-
tively (for the single cell has but slight effect) influence my experiences?
I am a sort of king in my "animal republic." It is, in bare essentials, the
situation of one ruling over many. For I (or my thought) at a given
moment sway a billion cells; no cell at a given moment sways a billion
cells or (very strongly) even one human experience. On the other hand,

each cell, at least in the activated cortex, does slightly influence my thought of the moment. What does this amount to? I submit, to this: I rule over my cells as none of them rules over its fellows; but also I am responsive to them as they are not to each other, for I respond on what for them is a vast spatial scale, whereas they respond directly and effectively only to a few neighbors. I am incomparably the most influential, but also incomparably the most open to being influenced, of the entities in my psychophysical system. Almost by magic thinkers failed to put these two truths together. They are really, I suggest, one and the same truth. The most sensitively and widely responsive individual is the very one who will be most readily and widely responded to. By response one appropriates the values of others, makes them in a measure one's own; accordingly, he who responds to all shares the values of all. But then they will have the best possible motive for responding to him, since he tends to sum up all the values anywhere around. The influential is what is in some relevant aspect good, and goodness is socially achieved, i.e., it arises through sensitivity to others, whereby their values are integrated into a unity which belongs to none of them individually. We love those who love us, and who love others besides us, for through this love they tend to equal or surpass those they love. The Greeks thought of love as essentially lack, defect, and thereby missed almost wholly the secret of divine power. The power of God is his beauty—this Aristotle did see; but this eminent beauty is the same as eminent love, and this no Greek, it seems, was quite capable of seeing.

So, to the question, "Why is the divine fiat so efficacious?" the reply is, "Because it offers to each creature what the creature most wants or appreciates in the way of intrinsic value." In short, the fiat is uniquely eloquent and appealing. Any other view of divine power is slavish groveling before brute force (which only means, indirect power whose direct links are left unexplained). We love God neither because of his power nor in spite of his power; rather, his lovableness (which includes his wisdom) is the sole and entire reality of this power. God can "speak" to creatures so eloquently, beautifully, wisely, and hence relevantly to their natures that they cannot, except within narrow limits, even wish not to respond. (In somewhat this fashion, but not on the same eminent level, I can "speak" to my brain cells and thus indirectly my muscle cells, so that they do as I wish. I do not compel them, I charm them; they "cannot choose but hear.")

It does not follow and it cannot follow that the precise response of the creatures is determined by the divine eloquence. No stimulus can absolutely determine a response; which rather, as we have seen, must determine itself. But the stimulus determines the range of possible or probable responses. God determines what creatures can do, but only they determine what they do do. Even the least creatures must be so conceived, according to this philosophy. The divinely furnished relatum cannot wholly determine the relation; in general, data cannot logically contain the response to themselves. This would be nonsense or self-contradiction. Thus God cannot simply "coerce" anything; he can only inspire it to act in a certain sort of way. But an act is no mere sort of act, just as a particular is never the universal of which it is an instance. Thus freedom is metaphysically universal. Enslavement, even to the divine, cannot be absolute —not only because the divine is generous, but because power means influence of one free act upon another free act. (Or else we do not know wherein power consists.)

It might seem to some readers that I have been hasty in deciding that the relativity of events—that is, influence, power—must be conceived in such psychological terms as "memory" or as stimulus and response. Can there not perhaps be a merely physical relativity, whereby events are effects referring back to causes? I reply that I think Hume furnished unanswerable arguments against this. The only way to observe relatedness, as temporal or causal property of events, is precisely in "psychological" terms. This is one of various arguments against materialism or dualism (it comes to the same, for the point is that the only intelligible monism is a psychical, not a merely physical one). I shall not further discuss the issue here; but for me it is as clear as anything philosophical is likely to be that the notion of matter, as irreducible to the concept of experience, is a pseudo-conception. The question is not, "Are there bits of such matter?" but "What could be meant by matter as a mere surd to 'mind' (in every sense of this word)?" I find no meaning; and if I am right, the question of fact does not arise.

Although in rejecting the notion of mere matter we are agreeing with Bishop Berkeley, it does not follow that we must also agree with him in reducing the physical world to a set of ideas in the mind of God as well as in human minds. I think that here he was fantastically wrong (not simply factually, but conceptually or as a matter of meanings), and that we must suppose that the totality of experiences includes, not only the divine superexperiences and our human experiences, or vertebrate animal experiences, but also an enormous variety of subvertebrate experiences, the lowest of which constitute the reality of such things as crystals and atoms. In addition, there are presumably the experiences of creatures on the billions of inhabitable planets of which astronomers now speak.

We now have before us something of an outline of the new metaphysics; and we have seen how some at least of the old problems are transformed by it. I should like to consider some other examples of this transformation. First, the venerable "problem of evil." Is God too weak to prevent evil or too indifferent to try? Neither. He is ideally strong and ideally interested in his creatures. Why then is there evil? Because it is inherent in the very meaning of "strong" and of "interested in" that the power and the interest are relations whose relata have their own independence. Otherwise, the power would be power over nothing, the interest, interest in nothing. Moreover, if reality consists, and can only consist, in events (since "beings" are but ordered sequences of events) and if events or becomings can only be creative-cumulative, the notion of power over events so great that it deprived the events of their creativity or self-determination must be a pseudo-conception, not a genuine ideal or definition of the divine. There is no need and no possible role for divine power in this sense. Accordingly, we need not "limit" the power of God; we need only understand what is meant by "power," whether divine or not divine. Thus we get rid of the problem of evil, without admitting any weakness or indifference in God. He "cannot" save us entirely from evils which may result from our free acts, and those of other creatures, because this saving would be nonsense: it would mean overdetermining the creatures to the point at which they would not be creatures and would be nothing definite whatever. The "cannot" is logical, a lack of sense in the rejected assumption.

What is the importance of the foregoing? Go through biographies and note how common it is to find a sensitive and gifted person who has given up the idea of God essentially because of the problem of evil. But this is a pseudo-problem, produced by philosophies of being, with their imaginary, or rather, implicitly self-contradictory, notions of "omnipotence," contrasted to the equally illegitimate alternative of a God less than ideal in power.

By the same token, the hoary problem of reconciling divine power and human freedom is a pseudo-problem. In a philosophy of creative-cumulative becoming, ideal power cannot mean the suppression of creaturely self-determination. There is nothing ideal about the longing to monopolize power, to reduce others to powerlessness. On the contrary, this longing is a sign of weakness. Power cannot be maximized by trying to suppose a being who decides beforehand or eternally what happens; for this would amount to deciding that nothing was to happen. Ideal power does two things: it decides upon the cosmic limits of law (traditionally called "general providence") within which lie the possibilities for happenings, and it decides upon its own final evaluation ("special providence") of what, by decisions of the creatures, within these limits, does happen. Otherwise put, ideal power decides upon its own way of utilizing the self-determined creatures as items in its deathless memory of them. This evaluation is necessarily transparent, i.e., it must express every detail and nuance of quality in the creatures, but this necessity is not enough to determine the evaluation. It is somewhat as though one had to invent a perfect language to describe something; what is to be described is given, but more than one perfect language is possible for its description.

Let us now consider the interrelated religious questions of motivation and immortality. It is an important reason for the rejection of conventional religious ideas that they seem to enshrine self-interest as ultimate. Whereas the unbeliever may die for humanity, the conventional believer knows (?) that he cannot properly relate himself to the whole of things without bringing back upon himself an everlasting reward, in comparison with which no personal advantage he might renounce would count as significant. Thus Archdeacon Paley could even say that Christianity was transcendental hedonism: Christians seek pleasure for themselves, he said, but in heaven, not primarily on earth. Meanwhile, there is no telling how many of our fellows may receive, not an eternal reward, but an everlasting punishment. Berdyaev called this "the most disgusting morality ever conceived."

The philosophy of process does away with it. For—as the subtlest Buddhists, for deep spiritual reasons, insisted—there is no simply identical self reaping rewards and punishments. Each momentary agent and sufferer is numerically new; from which it follows that the I which now acts never can receive either reward or punishment, beyond the intrinsic reward or punishment of acting and experiencing as it now does. The account is immediately closed. Anything one demands for the future is demanded for another, even though this other is termed "one's self." (This means, it will belong to the same ordered sequence of agents, the same world line.) There is no metaphysical reason for limiting one's concern regarding the future to this sequence. A man seeing a child about to be run over by a car, and acting to prevent this, is not contemplating primarily his own future, but the child's. It is a pity that the philosophies of being should have frequently led religions to adopt a theory of motivation more self-centered than the experiences of everyday life illustrate or require! And it is philosophies of being and the tendencies in this direction found in "common sense" or "everyday discourse" (a heterogeneous mixture of elements—some indeed essential to wisdom, and some mere bits of pre-scientific guessing and crude philosophizing) which have brought religion to this unfortunate outcome. For the whole theory of heaven and hell seems largely the result of the concept of personal "substance." Let us see why.

First, this concept seemed to present us with the alternative: either death is sheer destruction of each personal life or else this life "goes on" after death; one awakens, as it were, and begins to act as a glorified human being, doing the sort of things one only longed to do on earth (or if less fortunate, the sort of things one had deluded oneself with thinking one had forever escaped doing). But this is a pseudo-alternative, a false dilemma. As remarked earlier, the affixing of a final chapter to life no more destroys the life than FINIS at the close of a book destroys the book. The essential meaning of immortality is the everlasting transparency of our lives to the divine. God alone is the "authorized" and permanent reader of the book. To object that this immortality is God's possession, not ours, is to bring out into the open unashamedly the secret egotism inherent in most substance metaphysics. It is to betray the fact that what we have really wanted is to be the Immortal Person ourselves, to enjoy divine privileges, not just our own human ones; or that we have regarded God, not as the end of ends, but as means to our own end, the achievement of permanence!

Second, the notion that the logic of motivation is, "I love myself because I am myself, and if I love you that must be because you are useful to me," is full of errors. For one thing, love is not explained by identity. Self-hatred is a real phenomenon, and if it has limits so has hatred of others. For another thing, the enduring self is not the source of self-love or other relationships occurring in experience, but rather, this self *consists* in the intimate mode of relational unification between successive experiences whereby they form a single personal sequence, one aspect of which unification is called self-love and another self-hatred. But relational unifications of love and hate also bind members of one sequence to members of other sequences. Human personality is merely one important kind of order in experient events, merely one sort of world line. There are others, and the unities they involve are just as genuine, though they may be less intimate or complete in most cases.

When the confusions arising from the attempt to make beings rather than becomings (or acts) final are cleared away, the theoretical religious sources of egotism and (in the bad sense) otherworldliness are also laid bare. What harm this egotism and otherworldiness have done! To what other source (apart from mere wickedness) are to be attributed the persecutions, the acts of hate in the name of divine love, and the neglect of genuine human problems in favor of supposed problems concerning proper seating arrangements in the hereafter? The excuse for this sort of thing vanishes once we become clear that the personal reality of the moment, the now acting and experiencing self, in its concrete actuality, cannot be rewarded or punished beyond the present. It may indeed have ideal ends which can be fulfilled in the future, but only if these ends transcend that self and its experience. Such a self can live only by "losing" itself, by contributing its decisions and qualities of enjoyment as absolute relata for future selves to enjoy and profit by. Even God, in each actual phase of himself, in this sense lives altruistically, for the sake of future phases of both his own life and other lives.

The immeasurable exaltation of God's altruism over that of any other being is seen, from one point of view, in this, that in any future, however remote, the divine sequence will be represented by new members, in which all nondivine events will be transparently expressed, whereas the other sequences will (so far as we know) not always be represented by new members, but only by their one-time members, everlastingly transparent to members of the divine sequence. The notion of losing one's life to save it thus acquires a deeper and more metaphysical meaning than most Christians (but perhaps not than some Buddhists) have given it.[4] And therewith also the quarrel between humanism and theistic religion ceases to be the hopeless impasse that it otherwise is likely to seem. For what the humanist has to say about "social immortality," living for posterity, is included in theistic immortality as conceived in the philosophy of process. Each momentary self indeed aspires to be remembered, cherished, and turned to profit in the society of future members of its own personal sequence, also of other sequences, and above all (this alone being absolutely essential) in the society of members of the divine sequence, for which alone it can be fully transparent, or by which alone it can be adequately evaluated and appreciated or given its full quota of significance. Thus all the nobler conceptions of human motivation are here fused together. If there really is any point in the idea of endlessly prolonged (nondivine) personal sequences—which I find hard to believe —there is no more obstacle to this belief in the philosophy of process than in any other. All that is here given up is the alleged necessity for the belief as sole alternative to the admission that death is the destruction of personal reality. If the philosophy of process is sound, such destruction is impossible, and therefore there is no need to search for an alternative to this merely verbal possibility.

I shall mention but one more religious value in the doctrine of creative-cumulative process. By making it clear that no one agent can decide a situation, since every agent involved contributes to the decision, our new metaphysics protects us against yet another curse due to a confused metaphysical tradition. If one asks the philosopher of process why there is "injustice" in life, he can answer, "Because process involves multiple freedom, the partial self-determination of each and every actuality, every becoming, and this multiple freedom means genuine chance at the points of intersection between diverse free acts." I decide my act, you decide yours, but how my act and yours flow together to constitute a new total situation of potential absolute relata for subsequent acts of self-relating neither I nor you nor anyone, and not God, decides. Nor does any necessity bring it about. It simply happens. In other words, if "by chance" is equivalent to, "neither by necessity nor by intention," then literally all things, in their concrete details, happen by chance. How much bitterness has been due to the notion that, whatever happens, someone must have been "responsible"! Situations being multiply decided, they are not in their entirety decided by anyone. Resentment against the details of life is unwittingly resentment against chance; but one cannot consciously hate chance. And yet it is the cause of all our woes—aided here and there, no doubt, by wickedness and carelessness, but never attributable to these alone. So far as the divine contribution to situations is concerned, there can be neither wickedness nor carelessness; in this sense, not providence but chance alone is the cause of evil. God ideally intends, and ideally operates to produce, the good of the creatures; but this good must in part be furnished freely by the creatures for themselves and for one another; and this, once more, because any other supposition involves pseudo-conceptions. "Creatures not in any degree determining their own and one another's welfare" is a meaningless or self-contradictory notion.

The mature acceptance of life seems not fully intelligible except as we admit the reality of chance, on the one hand, and the everlasting transparency by which our acts have their inviolate reality, on the other. In this way we are released from the old sterile search for the one to blame in misfortune; and at the same time, we are saved from despair lest our lives fall into a meaningless abyss of nonentity as we begin to grow old, to forget, and to be forgotten. The ideal of disinterested love acquires a metaphysical, as it has always had a psychological, meaning. We understand the deeper import of the psychoanalytic truth that sanity is love, and that love in each new life is kindled only by love in some life already there. This deeper meaning is the enfolding of all achieved values, from everlasting to everlasting, in the divine love, which is the same as the divine transparency, evermore cherishing every least detail and nuance of definite created actuality, to whose increase there can be no end.

It is curious that a poem by Longfellow seems almost to embody our doctrine: "All are architects of fate . . ." [Not artisans, mere executors of the world-design; no, designers!]

> "For the structure that we raise
>   Time is with materials filled;
> Our todays and yesterdays
>   Are the blocks with which we build."

Events themselves, actions, experiences, are the "substance" of which the great Achievement is composed. But the reality of the Achievement, while it must bear the marks of our free decisions, can hardly consist merely in the structure of our lives as enjoyed by us. It must rather consist in the Ideal Interpretation of that structure, and of all actualized structures, in the truly immortal consciousness, absolutely (or in an immutably perfect manner) self-related to all that happens, and thereby constituting itself the Process inclusive of all actualized process, and the Relativity definitive of all relative things.

NOTES FOR CHAPTER 9

1 I wish to express thanks to Professors Howard Parsons and Nolan Jacobson for having, in a way known to them, inspired this essay.

2 See P. Strawson, *Individuals,* London, 1959 and 1961, for an attempt to prove the inadequacy of the event-language, presented, however, in a weak, imperfect form. Note pages 46-57.
3 See E. Schrödinger, *Science and Humanism,* London, Cambridge University Press, 1951, pp. 16-21, 27. For a startling comparison, see Strawson, *op. cit.,* p. 44.
4 J. H. M. Whiteman, "The Early Buddhist Teaching Concerning 'Birth,'" *Journal of Religion,* 37: 189-200 (1957).

QUESTIONS

1 In what principal respects may a philosophy which focuses upon relations arrive at a different view of reality from one focusing upon nonrelative predicates?
2 How may becoming be so conceived that it illustrates "absoluteness" and "relativity" as aspects of the very same entities?
3 How does process philosophy interpret the idea of individual or substance?
4 Is becoming a deficient form of being, or being a mere aspect of becoming? What arguments can be used, one way or the other?
5 What happens to the idea of God in Process Philosophy?

SUGGESTED READINGS

Charles Hartshorne, *The Divine Relativity,* New Haven, Yale University Press, 1964. Paperback.
——— and W. L. Reese, *Philosophers Speak of God,* Chicago, University of Chicago Press, 1963. Paperback.
A. N. Whitehead, *Adventures of Ideas,* New York, Macmillan, 1933, esp. Parts III and IV.
Donald W. Sherburne, *A Key to Whitehead's Process and Reality,* New York, Macmillan, 1966.
W. P. Montague, *The Ways of Things,* New York, Prentice Hall, 1940.
H. Bergson, *Creative Mind,* New York, Philosophical Library, 1946.

10 *Gustav E. Mueller*

Religion and Dialectical Philosophy

Definition of Dialectic   Everybody knows what marriage is. Except for a few unfortunate exceptions, everybody has been born in one, grown up in one. Almost everybody, after enjoying a brief spree of independence, again joyfully accepts a marriage situation as a lifelong enterprise and moral task.[1]

Marriage is composed of sexual partners who are attracted to one another, but this sexual difference alone would never be a sufficient basis for marriage. It could only be a sufficient basis for promiscuity. The natural difference alone by itself is not only the source of attraction, but also the source of all troubles and difficulties. The partners as natural biological organisms complement each other in such a way that man becomes man through woman, and woman becomes woman through man; but they are not merely natural, they are also moral persons, who respect and treat each other as such. As Kant formulates his moral law: Treat the other not *merely* as a means to your pleasure or profit, but *also* as an end in himself. This dignity of being an end in itself is rooted in Being. The Greek word for it is *On*. Philosophy, therefore, speaks of the ontological dignity or status of each individual human being. Each person represents this Being in all beings to the "other," besides appearing also naturally different, as male or female, old or young, child or parent. Being is present in truth, which says that all things are what they are and not otherwise. Truth is openness to whatever *is*. Truthfulness is also the spiritual bond of marriage. The partners are open to one another, not hiding their weaknesses and troubles, because they can trust in the mutual sacred unity, which is not at all identical with erotic satisfactions or attractions. The wedding ceremony which speaks of this unity "for better or worse, in sickness and in health" truly expresses the spiritual, insoluble principle of marriage. The sexual polarity is intersected by the polarity of selfish, vital orientation versus universal, spiritual orientation.

Everybody also knows himself. He is that being which says "I am." I relate myself to myself. This "I am" expresses an ontological, objective being which knows itself as responsible subject of all its functions. I know that all my various interests, functions, and experiences are mine and no one else's. I know myself to be involved in them, but I also know them as different from myself. When I look at a diary which I wrote twenty years ago, I cannot disclaim my past interests and outlooks as my own, and yet I know myself, *now*, to be different from them, *then*. I distinguish my many functions from myself, but at the same time retain my unity and identity in all of them.

What marriage and self-experience have in common is this: in both there is *a concrete or living unity of two or more opposite functions or participating "partners"; each is what it is for itself (identity); but at the same time also is what it is, by not being its own other partner (difference). Dialectic is the unity of identity and difference, as well as the distinction of identity and difference.* The dialectic of "existence" is not the same as the dialectic of family life. There are many dialectics, according to the many different opposites which unite and differentiate themselves.

Dialectic from Plato to Hegel   My book *Plato: The Founder of Philosophy as Dialectic* shows both in detail and at length, why dialectic must be the logic of philosophy, the way of philosophizing ("method," which is the Greek word *methodos,* means a way that gets you from your starting point to your goal while remaining the same for both directions). Let us here quite informally recall some of the essentials of that book.

First, Plato (427-348 B.C.) used the *dialogue* as form of philosophizing together. The Greek *dialegein* means to clarify your thought in meeting a partner with a different point of view. If "the one," A, is willing to listen to the "other," B, then both will profit from this meeting. A will become A,b, while B will become B,a. The community of good will, of honest openness, of mutual respect is more than the different standpoints, which discover their mutual imitations in a common life of "discourse," the Latin equivalent (*discursus*) of the Greek "dialogue."

Dialogue is a *structural* dialectic of give and take, the kind of thing we have in mind when we refer to a "democratic" procedure, by means of which we arrive at a common agreement.

There is also a temporal or *historical* dialectic. I start out by imbibing a world view, an evaluation of life, from my parents, my educators, my environment and historical situation. Later on I may come to see that my former position was rather limited, narrow, unsatisfactory. It will be included, preserved in its limitations, in a wider, more comprehensive horizon. In such a case *dialectic is a maturing process.*

Plato formulates this maturing process as a *law of value.* If you get stuck on a lower, more primitive level, if you refuse to "ascend," to move, you then not only lose or fail to attain a more mature insight, but even your lower values will sour on you and become perversions.

For example, if your love of money, which has its value and its place, is the only value you can understand, then the evils of a miserly plutocracy will corrupt the "state of your soul." Or if you isolate your love of honor and rest satisfied with an honorable achievement, then your good achievement turns into an enemy of further expansion. The achieved good becomes the block to something better.

This relationship of lower versus higher values is formulated by Plato as *dialectic of contradictions.* Evil consists in frustrating a higher good, and good consists in combating a frustrating evil. They are inseparable, yet different. If I do not insist that my natural, vital desires ought to be satisfied, then I cannot experience their lack of satisfaction as evil. If I do not expect *spiritual demands* to be lived up to, then lies and treason cannot be experienced as evil.

According to the Socratic principle of ethics no man desires to be evil or to have a miserable life. All men desire a good or happy life, because none is in sure possession of it; and if you believe that you are in possession of some good, then you will fight or strive to preserve it.

The dialectic of contradiction, consequently, appears as hostility of lower values against higher ones, because they "do not know what they do." The philosophical critic is stoned to death in Plato's myth of the cave, just as Socrates was poisoned in historical reality. The search for good is tragically divided against itself, owing to different levels or degrees of practical insight; Kant calls it "practical comprehension" (*Vernunft*).

Plato distinguishes repeatedly four such levels in all *realms* of experiences: The first and lowest is the level of immediate experience, where all impressions and desires are subjective, momentary, relative to the organism experiencing them, and relative among themselves; what appears large or important in one changing situation appears small and unimportant in an opposite situation; as gray appears white against a black background, and black against a white one.

The second level Plato calls "right opinion," which is the level of technical manipulations of practical obstacles and scientific formulations of behavior patterns of objects selected for study in special sciences.

The third level is the level of reflection or self-knowledge, where we know what we are doing when we are doing it. What I say reality is, at the same time characterizes myself. I begin to know myself in my limitation.

The fourth and highest level is reached when I know my limited perspectives or assumptions (Plato says "hypotheses") as regional or provincial segments of the whole of reality, called the Unconditional or all-embracing Absolute, which is both the ground as well as the annihilation of everything that is conditional or finite within this whole. In this dialectic of the Absolute, Plato shows the reality of all that is nonabsolute, relative, and negative. Evils, lies, deceptions, errors are as real as their ideal opposites. The absolute Being is also present in that which it is not, in its own negations.

Against this dialectic of contradictory levels of consciousness, to which correspond realities evident to those various levels of the mind, Plato contrasts the dialectic of *complementaries*. These are the above-mentioned realms or dimensions of experience.

To the various levels of *theoretical* consciousness correspond levels of reality conceived as objects of knowledge; the Absolute appears here as the unconditional value of truth.

To the various levels of practical consciousness correspond various political, economic, legal and moral constitutions of states as well as of individual characters. The Absolute appears here as the unconditional value of the Good.

To the various levels of aesthetic enjoyments correspond various levels of beauty; Beauty is the Absolute, appearing in sensuous symbols. It also is an unconditional value, which is imitated or actualized in the various arts and in the festive art of living.

Here we come to religion and its place in dialectic. *If reality is responded to in faith and worship, then the Absolute appears in the sign of the Holy.*

Plato has written no major dialogue on this religious way of life, but there are hints in every major dialogue from which his philosophy of religion can be reconstructed. In the chapter of my Plato book dedicated to this reconstruction, I have found the same four levels of religious maturity as in the other correlations between consciousness and its intentional objectives or goals.

On the lowest level the Holy is bound up with superstition, magic, and idolatry. Gods are bribed for specific selfish purposes. There are demonology and literal-minded mythological stories.

On the second level the Holy is conceived in a dualism of good versus evil. God or the gods are helping man in his moral struggle for the good.

On the third level the symbolic-mythical language of religion is seen through as an inadequate "hypothesis"; "God" is now the mythical, personifying name for the all-encompassing Absolute which cannot be moralized. "God" cannot be courageous for example, because he has no obstacle outside of Him. He is present in all parties alike and cannot be appealed to as blessing our arms, our cause, our victory.

In his negative dialectic, God cannot be a party. This negative dialectic is completed when God is known on the fourth and final level as "the father and maker of this All," in whom Being and Value are One, which is the definition of the Holy.

God is the religious name for the Absolute. In general, this dialectic of contraries, of realm or type of consciousness and of discourse, is known both by that which it is in and for itself (a Platonic formula!) and by that which it is not.

If I know that religious worship is not a political-moral or legal matter, or that it is not to be confused with statues or mythical stories of the gods, or that it is not a logical-scientific theory, then what religion is in and for itself is defined and clarified by the dialectical opposites that are dialectically excluded from it and at the same time related to it. But all such essential distinctions of *realms* of experience, together with their levels of maturity, are self-distinctions of and within the whole. Nothing can drop out of Being. And we are allowed to participate (in our limited way) in its eternal life. The Absolute maintains its concrete identity: in creating, in canceling, and in preserving its own finite otherness in its eternal activity.

Hegel (1770-1831) began to appropriate dialectic from Plato when he was a theology student in Tübingen. He repeatedly praises the most dialectical of all the Platonic dialogues, the *Parmenides*, as the greatest masterpiece of Greek philosophy. As a student of Christian theology he began to apply dialectic to the Christian religion and to all religions.

The way was prepared for him by the Christian theology. Abelard (1079-1142) introduced the dialectical method into scholastic philosophy in his famous book *Sic et Non*. He shows that it is as important to investigate what follows from an affirmative premise as what follows from a negative premise. It is as important to truly affirm the one or the other as it is to truly deny the one or the other. And if authorities differ, Abelard says, then it is unprobable that a genuine conviction does not rest on a true vision of something that is real and important in and for life. Each authority, therefore, must be listened to and treated with respect. *Dialectic is the end of all authoritarianism.*

The most important scholastic philosopher, Thomas Aquinas (1225-1274) develops his whole immense *Summa Theologica* in dialectical form. Every assertion is considered in the light of one or several objections, and the result is usually a dialectical modification of the original assertion brought about by having considered its possible limitation. Not only is his *logic* or method dialectical, but also the *religious content* of his theology.

I illustrate what I mean with Aquinas' famous argument entitled *analogia entis*, which was reformulated by Leibniz (1646-1716). To put it first negatively: Thomas rejects one-sided, abstract, undialectical positions. God cannot be not-related to the world; if he were, we would know nothing about him. God cannot be identical with the world, if he were, he would be the sum total of all imperfection, incompetence, and evil. The first position, *dualism*, which separates God and world absolutely, would make the world satanic; the absolute denial of dualism would falsely absolutize our finite mortality, which is evidently neither necessary or final, but accidental and contingent.

Positively stated, the "analogy of Being" says that God as Creator of the world would not be what he is (Creator) without or apart from the creature; just as a father is not what he is without the son: the son makes the father just as much as the father makes the son.

God, in other words, is one with that which he is not, the limited and suffering creature.

Man as "created in the image of God," then, reflects the same proportion: as God is a Being in and for itself (*ens a se*), present in that which he is not, the "other-than-himself" (*ens ab alio*); so man as soul or subject of all his activities, which he knows himself to be or which he is for himself (*ens per se*), is at the same time meeting himself in his physical alienation or organic embodiment (*ens in alio*). The dialectical proportion of God and man, then, is like a mathematical proportion, where the ratio of 6 : 4 is analogous to the ratio of 3 : 2. Similarly:

$$\frac{\text{God} : ens\ a\ se}{\text{Creation} : ens\ ab\ alio} \simeq \frac{\text{man as subject} : ens\ per\ se}{\text{man as object} : ens\ in\ alio}$$

We now turn to five different and opposite approaches which constitute Hegel's dialectical philosophy of religion in general, and of Christianity in particular.

RELIGION IN HEGEL'S DIALECTIC

On Terminology   Since Hegel uses his terms as no one else does, every approach to him necessitates a preliminary explanation of certain key words.

One such key word is *Begriff*, which I have translated "Concept"; other English translations use the word "notion." If it is not clear that Hegel's Concept has nothing to do with the ordinary concept, it is impossible to understand Hegel.

Hegel's Concept is always a living organic unity of two or more opposite *moments* or phases of a process. Thus, the Concept tree is not an abstract class retaining what is common to all different trees; but the tree is a concrete process of life being nourished by its roots as the roots in turn are nourished by the leaves. The Concept water is not the abstract class H_2O but it is the ocean from which arise the clouds, which turn into rain or snow, which sinks underground, which springs forth as wells, swelling to brooks and rivers, and ending in the ocean again. Each of those moments of the Concept "water" is different from the others, and yet each is necessary for the being of the others.

Likewise, the religious Concept is engendered out of five roots or origins which in turn are all manifestations of its concrete dialectical unity.

Hegel stubbornly refuses to use words in the way that everybody else uses them and blames the dictionary for what he calls false definition; for example: "by concept one usually understands an abstract and one-sided termination of rational thought." [2] To illustrate: the ordinary, rational concept animal is a general class of those characteristics which fleas and elephants, fish and butterflies have in common. Such abstract concepts disregard or abstract from what distinguishes these animals. The more abstract and the more general the concepts of formal logic become, the less content can be contained and the more content must be dropped. The dialectical or speculative Concept, on the other hand, is a living whole of tensional opposites and is called "the soul of life, the self of an existence . . . the existence of the pure Concept is an individual which he chooses as a vessel of his sorrow." [3] What we call soul and more precisely ego, is the Concept itself in his free existence.[4] From those definitions it will be already evident that such a logic will be capable of coping with such religious expressions as the beginning of the gospel of John where the Concept or *logos* becomes flesh.

Two other terms which have caused infinite confusion in English translations are *Verstand* and *Vernunft*. *Verstand* is never "understanding," but is always reason (*ratio*) as defined in formal logic. Reason always thinks in abstract concepts. They are abstracted from an organic whole which they disregard. There are general classes which are never identical with their nonlogical or irrational individual contents. This dualism of form and material characterizes reason. Reason tries in vain to classify rationally what remains to it nonrational. This demand or postulate to see the object as a system of coordinated and subordinated classes discovers that immediate experience will always appear as unclear and irrational. The irrationality of immediate experience could not be discovered without or apart from this rational will to see it as a logical system. In other words, reason, without knowing it, is an aspect of the concrete Concept in that it is an effort, a struggle, a process, a never ending and never successful battle with its own other which is irrational.

As such a living historical enterprise, reason is a part of a *Vernunft* which I have always translated as comprehension and comprehensiveness. *Vernunft is never reason.* If *Vernunft* is translated by reason, then any understanding of Hegel becomes impossible. *Vernunft* is an all-encompassing, comprehensive totality, whose living members are the Concepts. When *Vernunft*, or comprehensiveness becomes aware of itself, then it knows itself as "absolute spirit." In it all these necessary and essential opposites are both distinguished as well as united:

"There are three aspects in every thought which is logically real or true: the abstract or rational form, which says what something is; the dialectical negation, which says what something is not; the speculative-concrete comprehension: A is also that which it is not, A is non-A. These three aspects do not constitute three parts of logic, but are moments of everything that is logically real or true. They belong to every philosophical Concept. Every Concept is rational, is abstractly opposed to another, and is united in comprehension together with its opposites. *This is the definition of dialectic.* Thinking as *reason* (Verstand) requires fixed or identical determinations in clear distinction from other identities. To reason, such limited abstractions are evident as valid and as real. The dialectical movement, in contrast to reason, cancels such one-sided determinations. Dialectically they are related to that which they are not. It is this negative relation which defines them. They themselves require their opposites and are determined by them. When dialectic is exclusively rational, it leads to skepticism. Reason, as an isolated aspect of dialectic, points to the untruth of every thought.

Historically, dialectic is considered a sophistic trick which arbitrarily and deliberately produces confusion in conception. This confusion, it is supposed, is destroyed by reason; and this formal destruction of illusions is proudly proclaimed as truth. Reason, as the correction of all one-sided determinations and of historical misconceptions, remains tied to their irrationality. In comprehending reason as such a struggle, dialectical reflection passes beyond or transcends reason.

While rational terms are preserved in their limited validity, they belong to complex relationships in which they constantly change their functions. Dialectic is not an external reflection, but belongs immanently to the transitoriness of all finite, one-sided, and merely rational positions. It is their own negation which they are, without knowing it. It is the moving soul of the world-as-process. It guarantees to philosophy the immanent connection or necessary consistency between its contrary and essential disciplines. Speculative comprehension grasps and is the unity of all essential opposites. It is the principle of systematic philosophizing. In realizing the limitation of every finite standpoint, it realizes the infinity of Being through the nonfinality in all finite beings. The Absolute maintains itself in the transition of all its own nonabsolute or partial manifestations.

The positive result of dialectic is not an abstract void, an abyss into which everything is thrown. Dialectic denies absolutely one thing alone: the claim that any particular thing of the finite world exists absolutely. The Absolute appears as *nothing* to those finite positions which want to cling to their pseudo-absolute claims. This does not mean that "nothing is." To suppose this is to confuse thoughtlessly the dialectical-ontological negation with a formal-logical self-contradiction, wherein reason isolates the negative function of comprehensiveness as if it were a simple identity beyond all definite contents. Rather, the identity of speculative comprehension is the concrete unity of all essential opposites in the world itself. This alone is the ultimate concern of philosophy. The abstractions of reason are pierced, so that reason may reach its own concrete thought (or be reintegrated as a "moment" of *Vernunft*). The logic of philosophy retains and includes the formal logic of reason. Leave out dialectical comprehension and formal logic remains! Formal logic may unravel the tale of finite object-thinking in the sciences; but if the story of the sciences is absolutized, science degenerates into scientism. Concepts of philosophy are concrete realities and values of Being, thought together with their opposites. Philosophy contemplates them as they are in themselves as well as what they are for those to whom they are evident. Contents are thereby realized as manifestation of Being, which is both in and for itself; or which relates itself to itself in an eternal movement. The ontological categories are thus also the foundation for the self-comprehension of mind and spirit. Form and content of Concepts are not abstractly separated. As self-manifestations and self-determinations of the living whole, they are at once its forms and its value contents.

The formal logic of reason, on the other hand, handles forms in abstraction from contents. Neither form nor content expresses self-knowledge. Since they are not true for themselves, they are not forms of living truth. It is even essential that material data of formal logic remain alien to their forms. The logic of speculative philosophy, in contrast, thinks that which is real in and for itself. The Absolute is present in the subject thinking it. The Concept is absolute in thinking subjects together with their intersubjective unity, as well as in their difference. Concept (*noesis noeseos*) is what Aristotle called the principle of his First Philosophy or metaphysics.

As Concept [*Begriff*], reality becomes conscious of itself in the thinking mind. Herein philosophy seems to be occupied exclusively with the thinking mind and sundered from the richness of the sensuous world, and from the more concrete and intelligible historical world. But the dialectic of philosophy is not confined to the actual subject. It pertains equally to the structures of Being, to essential universals. Philosophy, in this enlarged sense, is cognition of reality as such.

The dialectic of philosophy is also present in the oppositeness of essential universal structures of Being (ontology); also the realistic treasures of the world presuppose onto-logic. These treasures also belong to the all-pervasive ultimacy of Truth. The concrete universals abstractly presented in logic prefigure all essential values of the spirit. The highest among them is religion. On its highest plane philosophy contemplates the Concept of all Concepts, the eternal Absolute—the God who is worshiped in religion. Philosophy then culminates in speculative theology." [5]

It is evident from this quotation that this religious Concept is a comprehensive one (*Vernunftbegriff*). It expresses itself in such terms as God and world, creator and creation, holiness and sin, moral law and grace.

Religion is thus a particular form of the absolute spirit. It maintains its concrete unity of a life in that which is the finite and temporal. And conversely, the religious man discovers the religious Concept in himself by negating his particular natural self in order to unite it with the eternal.

The Logical Origin of Religion   Hegel understands the Greek term "logical" in the comprehensive sense of truthful. This truth is close to the Greek meaning of *aletheia* in which being shows itself or becomes manifest when prejudices are removed. The philological root of the German term *wahr* is connected with trust in that which is reliable. Negatively, Hegel's concept of truth is not confined to dualistic concept of truth as a correspondence between a subjective concept and a given object. The essential nature of truth comprises this object-subject cleavage. The struggle of a knowing subject with an alien other is a concrete process or Concept. But scientific struggle with objective, given materials is only one way in which truth is cultivated. Truth is thus an original presence of Being-as-Process in man, which Being is a living and spiritual power and not a dead thing. Man becomes truly human when he matures beyond a mere organic natural process of being born and aging and dying. The criterion of truth is the realization of what one essentially is. The dynamic nature of truth shows itself in its contradictory which is the stagnation in prejudice and untruth.

The logical origin of religion, then, has to do with the relation of religion to truth. Because dialectic, the logic of philosophy, is not confined to the formal logical rules by which object-science proceeds, there is nothing in heaven and earth that could escape the question as to its truth.

I have quoted Hegel's definition of dialectic in his *Encyclopedia*. I think this passage is so crucial that it will not be superfluous to paraphrase it once more:

- Every comprehensive Concept is identical with that which essentially and truly is; for example, the good consists in fighting the evil which it defines as evil.
- The good is the negation of its own nonbeing—the evil—just as, on the other hand, evil cannot be, unless it fights its own opposite. In breaking down that which says it ought not to be, it becomes evil. In formal logic this dialectical negation or contradiction is abstractly expressed in the formula: A is not non-A.
- Each comprehensive Concept gains its concrete equality by its limitation. In finding its limitation by other equally concrete Concepts, it gains its place in a whole of such dialectical relations. Only if you know yourself in your limitation do you know yourself truly. For example: a moral action is not a work of art, and vice versa. Not to be a work of art is just as essential to being a moral action as not to be morally relevant is essential to a work of art. These are not contradictory opposites, but contrary or complementary opposites.

By virtue of such dialectical movements the various comprehensive Concepts take part in the life of the whole. On the one hand, they would be nothing in abstract isolation; and on the other hand, the whole would be nothing without each of them. All are living modifications of the whole. Any one standpoint or Concept is thereby prevented from falsely absolutizing itself. Whoever tries to isolate himself and to hold on to this splendid isolation experiences the absolute whole as his negation or annihilation, as his Nothing. Each living Concept is posited in the whole, dialectically negated by the whole, and is by virtue of this limitation preserved in the whole. The whole of this eternal movement Hegel calls *Idea*. The formula is: A is non-A—the Absolute preserves its concrete unity in that which it is not in the nonabsolute, finite relative and temporal, by both positing and canceling it in its own process.

Hegel's *Logic* develops on four (not three) levels.

- *Being* in the first part is discovered as an essential struggle between finite and infinite, eternal and temporal, measure and measureless, quality and quantity—to mention only these.
- In reflecting on this result, Being is discovered to be *essentially dialectical*. Its essence (*Wesen*) is to be a dialectic unity of opposites. This it is in itself but not yet for itself.
- As the essence of being becomes for itself what it is in itself, then it becomes conscious of itself and grasps itself as its own *Concept*.

- If now the conscious subject or Concept participates in the eternal life of the whole, in which it has become for itself what it is in itself, then it rises to be the absolute spirit. The Absolute then is mirrored in the highest forms of spiritual culture, art, religion, and philosophy. They together unconditionally cultivate the beautiful, the good, and the true.

Let us now see what happens to religion when this dialectical logic is applied to it.

- As one particular form of the absolute spirit, the religious Concept is for itself that which it knows itself to be.
- At the same time, the religious Concept is also and essentially determined by that which it is not: it is not that which is merely profane, worldly, or temporal.
- The religious worship of the Absolute is never the Absolute itself, but only one actuality of the absolute spirit which is necessarily distinguished from other equally actual forms of it. Through such mutual limitation within the whole, each of these forms becomes consciously aware of its value within its limitation.

If this dialectical comprehensiveness is not understood, then immature or one-sided conceptions of truth are applied to religion. The first level of reason is governed by its abstract identity and by its equally abstract "either-or." Religion claims to be all the truth. If we assume this, then all the other truths must be disregarded or damned. The Christian obscurantists who burned the Alexandrian library argued in this fashion: either the whole Greek literature from Homer to Plotinos contains that which is also contained in the word of God, in which case it would be superfluous; or it contains things that are not in the word of God and then it must be the Devil's. This is a very old story, but the idea lurking behind it has been advocated time and again.

Hegel, of course, could have learned nothing from this pious irrationalism and has always branded it as leading to totalitarian despotism. The rationalistic assumption that faith must not be mediated by anything else, or that it is sufficient in its abstract identity or its immediacy, is nothing else but the rationalistic principle of reason: A is A. The religious irrationalism is, without knowing it, based on the rationalistic principle of identity. "Either," Kierkegaard says, "you believe or you only think what others believe," as if one could not believe in order to understand, or as if to comprehend faith would distort its truth.

Such abstract decisions of either/or are according to Hegel valid only in finite situations. But the infinite truth of religion stands in a whole of truth in which it is mediated with all other members of that truth.

Hegel understands this Christian anti-intellectualism as a dialectical perversion of an abstract reasoning which can see no truth except in itself. Religious anti-intellectualism is thus governed by the very thing it condemns: the abstract identity of a falsely isolated reason!

A second logical possibility to determine the relation of religion to truth consists in the device to divide truth as if it were a cake. Such is the famous Thomistic harmony of faith and reason in which the truth of the one is thought to be compatible with the entirely different truth of the other. For Hegel such a double truth is impossible and can only lead to compromises, a "rotten peace" as he calls it, or to indifference.

The idea of harmony of a double truth is based on the logical principle of the excluded middle: A is not non-A: the wisdom of God is not the wisdom of the world, and vice versa. Denying that such contradictory opposites are contradictory, this standpoint contradicts itself. Thomas practices contradiction when he denies there is contradiction, because this denial is a contradiction; but it isn't truthful or honest to deny an opposition, if this opposition exists in truth; nor does it make sense, to deny the whole within which the opposites are mediated.

This opposition of knowledge and faith belongs to the whole of human existence. The faith in knowledge is just as essential as is the knowledge of faith. The truth has the primacy over its different modifications. Truth is one as Being is one. It unfolds itself as that unity of essential opposites which in men become conscious of themselves. This is the "concrete Concept": "The truth is the whole." [6]

Philosophical comprehension, according to Hegel, comprehends the very same truth which in religion is mythically imagined. Religion is the Absolute in the form of mythical *Vorstellung*. This is a crucial and technical term. *Vorstellung* means a personal introduction, a dramatic or cultic performance, a symbolic representation (like the Christian cross) in which man can participate with his life. I have rendered it by the term myth. Thus, the term "God" is that mythical personifying *Vorstellung* by means of which the Absolute becomes available to faith and prayer.

Religion is thus shown to be a Concept of comprehension which is equally present in the other two major forms of the absolute spirit, in art and in philosophy. The primacy of truth shows itself in this: faith can become articulate for itself if there is faith in truth; but truth of religion does not comprehend the other Concepts of comprehension.

Before religion had reached its philosophical self-comprehension, religion had to develop in many less adequate world-shapes. This long way of religious development must be understood, transcended, and preserved. This leads us to the second—the phenomenological—origin of religion.

The Phenomenological Origin of Religion This topic deals with the gradual fragmentary self-manifestation of the Absolute in the historical religions of the world.

Religion like every other Concept of comprehension is an essential living or spiritual being which develops itself from its potentiality to its actuality; or as Hegel likes to say, it must become for itself what it is in itself. Each Concept must *become* what it *is*. It must work out its own essence. The first sketch of this bold conception is found in the *Phenomenology of Mind* (1806). Twenty years later the lectures in Berlin carried out in great detail and with boundless patient work the sketch of the *Phenomenology*. The phenomenologist observes the religious consciousness as it is in itself and as it appears for itself; he sees the correlation between different acts of apprehension to that which is apprehended. Every religious consciousness is an act of worship which relates itself to its intentional goal of worship.

For the thinking observer or phenomenologist, religions are logically ordered in a sequence of steps, phases, or levels—somewhat like the circles of hell, purgatory, and heaven in Dante's *Divine Comedy*. But this logical sequence, as Hegel emphasizes several times, need not coincide with a temporal historical succession. Regression into earlier or more primitive forms of religious Concept are always possible. For example, as I shall show in detail later, Marxism is a regression from the religion of the absolute spirit into a rather primitive religion of Essence (*Wesen*).

In each historical religion the Absolute is partly revealed. This revelation may break through in mystics or prophets apparently without prior mediation; or it may come about through a disappointment in a previous form of religion. This latter case will become particularly important in Hegel's phenomenological critique of the New Testament. For that religious consciousness which remains tied to a particular set of revealed mythical symbols, there would be no such sequence and order of revelations.

A few samples may illustrate what is meant by a phenomenological understanding of religions.

Magic, the wishful but illusory religious control of material powers; *idolatry*, the religious worship of holy images; *superstition*, the religious assumptions of meanings that are not there; these primitive levels of the religious consciousness correspond to an immediate experience of nature. This nature is alienated from its own life; it is not for itself what it is in itself. Thus in *nature religion*, man also becomes estranged or alienated: he loses himself to images which take possession of the soul, or he tries to bribe or bring under control the uncanny powers which lurk in the background of the appearance of nature. In idolatry the images do not mean a god but are immediately one with him; the sun, for example, does not mean a sun god but is divine in itself. "This is the immediate and substantial unity of the absolute in its religious significances with its existence as natural shape inseparable from it." [7] Hegel points out that such primitive religious phenomena are still with us, but do not occupy the core of the religious consciousness as they once did.

The experience that all immediate appearances come and go, appear and disappear, leads to a higher level of religion. The disappointment with that which immediate experience tries to hold on to, as if it were real and for itself, leads to the thought of a unity of being which maintains its unbroken and eternal presence in all these ups and downs and changing images of immediate experience. Hegel calls this eternal unity and presence in nature *substance*. The religions of substance worship nature as a living whole.

Hegel illustrates the nature religion of substance in Chinese Confucianism and Taoism, but also in the religious attitude of Spinoza. He even discovered the *I Ging* [I Ching], *The Book of Transformations* as the original source of the Chinese pantheistic nature-religion. Leibniz already had brought it to Germany around 1700 from the Jesuit missionaries in Rome and was fascinated by it. Natural images and states of mind, external and internal experiences are woven together as in a dream. In the external and visible changes of the world, together with their mood values for feeling, the eternal unity of nature maintains itself. Ethically this corresponds to an attitude of patience and of a flexible adaption to the assumed harmony of the whole in the infinite mutations of worldly constellations.

The situation is quite different in Hinduism and Buddhism. Here Being appears as the Nothing, as the annihilation of all beings, each of which falsely imagines that it is unconditional or final. This is the great metaphysical deception, Maya, which must be seen through and must be overcome. Thus, religious life is like a pilgrimage towards Nirvana in which Being as cessation of all particular desires and experiences is reached; life is a continuing sacrifice. This negative conception of Being produces its own paradoxes. Either this way: if the finite appearances ultimately are nothing but deception and illusions, then to overcome them is not a merit; or that way: the will to resign or to sacrifice remains conditioned by that which it wants to sacrifice. Therefore, the will to sacrifice must be sacrificed too. Only then is the perfect unity of the annihilating Being with the annihilated self reached.

In the Hindu trinity, the Trimurti, Hegel discovered an early mythical expression of his dialectical concept of Being. Vishnu, the absolute One is both creation and preservation, Brahma, as well as annihilation and destruction, Shiva.

As in Hegel's logic, the phenomenology of religion develops Being as a unity of opposites in the consciousness of religion; it is parallel or analogous to the ontological dialectic in Hegel's logic. Consequently, we reach the level of the *religion of Essence* (*Wesen*): in analogy to the second level of the logic dealing with the logic of Essence. As we have seen, Essence is the transition from Being to Concept. Being is essentially the concrete unity of its own opposites. But this it is only in itself, not yet for itself. Only when the subject takes upon itself this living and concrete unity of all opposites has the substantial Being become the concrete subject or Concept. Then Being is revealed both in and for itself. In analogy to this logical development, the religions of Essence oscillate between the religions of nature on the one hand and the religion of the absolute spirit on the other hand.

Historically speaking we enter the Orient, the morning-land (*Morgen-land*): a geographical continent defined by sand deserts, oases, date palms, and camels. Politically speaking this continent was united twice, first by the Persian Empire and later by Islam.

In the Persian religion of Essence the myth represents the world as a battle of good and evil, Ormuzd and Ahriman. Light and dark, opposites of nature, become the significant mythical symbols of this struggle. This great dualism, as Hegel calls it, remains preserved as a moment in the religion of the absolute spirit. It has been several times renewed in the Western world, for instance, in Manichaeanism in the early Christian centuries. But it seems to me that in Marxism also we have regression to a moral dualism presented in naturalistic terminology. Good and evil with a prophecy of a final victory at the end are mixed up with natural-istic classes such as "bourgeoisie" and "proletariat." I shall return to the Marxistic religion after we have acquainted ourselves with Hegel.

In the Syrian Adonis (the Lord), an incarnate, suffering, dying, and resurrected lord of salvation is mythically presented. Passionate feeling of sorrow and jubilating gratitude belong to his cult; the evil, the nega-tive, suffering, and death belong here to the eternal life of the deity; in union with the cult of the dying nature in winter and its coming back to life in spring.

For reason, nature appears as a *riddle* which ought to be figured out. Practically speaking this reason is embodied in what Hegel calls the "work-master" (*Werkmeister*) who tries to compress nature into abstract and geometrical forms. Nature as riddle of reason and as something to be controlled remains an obstacle, refusing success to both the effort to understand and the effort to control. But failures do not discourage reason and its techniques from continuing in their enterprise. Hegel sees in the Egyptian religion the archetype of this rationalistic religion. The human head growing out of the animal body of the Sphinx symbolizes the attempt as well as the failure of a half-rational and half-naturalistic religion; and the geometrical tombs of the pyramids confuse immortality with the preservation of dead bodies.

"I will, thou shalt." This is the way the god of the Jewish religion speaks to his chosen people. The struggle to keep the commandments is also a struggle for the preservation of this particular national existence.

This naturalistic or nationalistic ingredient of a particular people is done away with in Islam, where God is no longer the god of a particular people but the god of all men who believe. But in its getting rid of a onesided concreteness, the abstract character of this religion of sublimity, as Hegel calls it, is all the more evident. The god of the religions of sublimity is only a being-for-itself, beyond all reality, which is left to its worldly "prose." Creator and creature are connected only by a mutual negation or exclusion.

All this changes in the Greek religion of beauty: "All divine, human all!" Many divine powers, essentially different and opposed to one another, pervade both nature and human history. The most central myth of Greek religion is the battle of the Olympian gods with the Titans. The latter represent vital natural interests and powers who are vanquished in the interest of a higher spiritual life, making political culture possible. They are vanquished but they are also reconciled and preserved. Man carries divine ideals in his soul. He dedicates himself to them and tries to give them shape in the works and institutions of this cultural life; and the gods on the other hand confer immortal values to mortal men.

The cult of this religion is art—essentially the tragedy which projects the battle of the gods and the Titans into the human soul. The mortal and natural side of man is sacrificed and suffers for the sake of being loyal to unconditional values; and by his loyalty to them the sacrifice is also man's redemption.

Hegel points out that the identification of religion and aesthetics was also its limitation. The imagined gods or the gods of aesthetic imagination are not sufficient to establish a religion of the absolute spirit. The images of the gods are broken. Man now finds himself in a godless world. The empirical individual becomes the last remnant of reality. Philosophy shrinks to a desperate existentialism. In religion, this corresponds to the cult of the abstract individual as we see it in emperor worship in Rome; or the deification of the individual in the Asian Dalai Lama.

What motivated Hegel to undertake this phenomenological journey through the major religions of the world? Since the Renaissance, European nations—particularly the Spanish, Portuguese, French, and English— had spread over the world and had established their colonial empires. The religions encountered in those raids were construed only as occasions for missions and conversions. Hegel's phenomenology of religion is a loving countermove; here these religions are no longer merely "pagan," but valid expressions of the divine and human mind. Only a religion of the absolute spirit can appreciate each level of religious consciousness and do justice to it; conversely, only those who can appreciate the genuine values in each level of religious consciousness may claim to stand in a religion which is unconditional and all-embracing. This meeting of Christianity with other religions constitutes one aspect of its Crisis.

The Encyclopedic Origin of Religion   This third origin of Hegel's philosophy of religion is found in
his *Encyclopedia;* it deals with the ontological place of religion within
the whole of Being. The ugly and rather meaningless foreign word
"encyclopedia" is derived from the pretty and meaningful Greek *en-
kyklo-paideia,* all-around culture or education.

The infinite cycle (*kyklos*) is a mathematical symbol for the universe
of philosophy. "All Being is *Comprehensiveness conscious of itself.* Philosophy is the *Encyclopedia of Philosophical Sciences.* Its self-engendered
movement is free, but each of its steps is necessary; it distinguishes its
disciplines or "parts" and links them all together. Each of its "parts" is
itself a philosophical whole. Each encompasses in itself a self-completing
sphere in which the whole is present. The oneness of this whole is nevertheless determined differently in its many particularized elements or media.
The presence of the whole in each of its singular spheres renders each a
whole; each contains this insufficiency and this longing to break its own
restricting barrier and to en-whole itself. Each sphere is established in
itself as well as grounded in and by a negative relation to further spheres.
The whole becomes systematically articulate, therefore, as a *circle of
circles of which each is a necessary moment of the whole movement.*
Philosophy is essentially encyclopedic, that is, encompassing or encircling.
In distinguishing as well as connecting its own self-distinctions, the whole
is both the necessity of its parts as well as its own freedom. The Truth
can exist only as such a totality systematically developed; only the whole
is the truth." [8]

In this infinite cycle each already may be at once an immediate beginning; but when we have gone through the circle and come back to that
beginning, it then will have become the result mediated by the whole
movement; I begin to draw the cycle and return at the end to the beginning.

A Latin equivalent to this Hegelian symbol of the cycle is the term
universum. It, too, is a whole of many essential differences which all grow
together and contribute to the concrete unity of the whole. Among the
many essential realms of Being, religion too may be such an immediate
beginning, prompting man to philosophize about it; and religion, too,
may appear at the end as having been mediated by all other philosophical
disciplines.

This does not mean, however, as is often assumed, that religion may
be replaced by philosophy. This perversion or misconception of Hegel's
encyclopedic understanding of religion follows from quoting certain passages where Hegel uses his language in an ambiguous way, a sloppiness
which nourished the prejudice against him. Two passages where this linguistic ambiguity is quite apparent may suffice to illustrate this point.

Very well known, and always quoted to make Hegel ridiculous, is the famous passage from the introduction to his large logic. He says there that his Logic "represents God as He is in His eternal essence prior to the creation of nature and to the finite spirit." [9] The mythical-religious term "God" simply does not fit at all into the perfectly clear reflection on the nature of logical truth. Equally misleading is the title of his last lecture on philosophy of religion entitled "Proofs of the Existence of God." [10] If one studies these magnificent notes serving as a basis for his oral lectures, one discovers that Hegel completely agrees with Kant, that there are no proofs about the existence of "God," because "God" is a mythical term which does not exist apart from the religious consciousness or community in which He functions; it is like proving the existence of Goethe's Faust outside of the tragedy, Part One and Part Two. What Hegel does prove, however, is the absoluteness of Being; and to this *corresponds*, in terms of religious worship, the mythical term "God." This *analogy* or correspondence between ontology and religious language is not a reduction of the one to the other. I consider it a most important discovery of Hegel's philosophy of religion. All that is needed to make Hegel's meaning clear is to use his own terms more consistently than he does.

I return then to the *Encyclopedia*, to the comprehension of religion within the eternal movement of the whole of Being. This comprehension is essential to systematic philosophy. Philosophy is that form of the absolute spirit which not only understands itself but also understands all other forms of the same spirit. To compare religion with other equally real forms of the spirit is a matter of systematic thinking and not a matter of religious worship. Philosophy, in comprehending religion as another form of the absolute spirit within itself, is a first and most essential limitation of religion.

"The dialectical negation of single individuals in their living immediacy mediates their participation in the life of an objective whole; this necessary participation is identical with a free dedication. The ethical community rests on such sacrificial life of all its members. This life of sacrifice, further, is the ethical root of philosophy. All worldly existence is posited by and in the Absolute; it is also sacrificed for the sake of the Absolute in its eternal life. Philosophical contemplation, in thinking this through, participates in the sacrificial life of the Absolute; like the Absolute, it transcends the dialectical essence of nature as well as of finite mind.

Absolute spirit is the living and actual identity of the eternal being which *is what it is in itself*, but which also is its own eternal self-differentiation, eternally reabsorbed by itself. As this absolute knowledge, absolute spirit is this process *for itself*.

Religion represents this same process and this absolute knowledge in the medium of faith; on the one hand, faith begins in the feeling of the finite subject and is not found outside of it; on the other hand, God absolutely establishes himself in the community of faith as their absolute ground; the absolute spirit is evident to the spirit of the faithful." [11]

A second limitation of religion is art. It also is a legitimate form of the absolute spirit.

"The aesthetic *Ideal,* called Beauty, is the absolute spirit immediately presented to the senses and to imagination. All arts imitate the Ideal.

Natural materials are rendered unessential in the art of the Ideal; they are transparent expressions of the absolute idea. The artistic spirit works out [*einbildend*] its imagination in symbolic media. In this transfiguration of the material into a symbol, all foreignness is overcome. The shape of beauty in a work of art shows nothing but its own perfection. It does not point beyond itself (as scientific and practical languages always do).

The finite aspect of art remains tied to its natural media or carriers. Thus, separate works of art are scattered in space and time. This external existence of art brings about a distance between the work—in itself a shaped living whole [*Gestalt*] born from and expressive of spirit—and the creative artists, and congenial admirers and appreciators." [12]

The relationship between religion and art is violently oscillating. On the one extreme lies the identification of religion and art as Hegel sees it in the Greek religion of beauty; at the other extreme lies a religion which wants to purge itself of all art because art is felt to be a seduction glorifying this life and this world. This ambiguity is inseparable from the religious myth or *Vorstellung* which uses word-images, but only for the purpose of breaking them and pointing to a Beyond or transcendence. Art on the other hand rests blessed in itself. In the artistic symbols the concrete unity of all essential opposites of life is beheld or contemplated in the form of sensuous appearance.

A third limitation of religion is its opposition to godless, profane, worldly activity in the sciences, practical techniques, and political power maneuvers. This opposition appears historically in the relationship between church and state in European history.

Since those opposites truly exist, it would be unphilosophical or dishonest either to deny the opposition or to blur it: if I seek my rights I go to the lawyer and not to the minister; and if I have to solve a scientific question, I shall not make use of a hypothetical "god."

Hegel calls this realm of scientific and practical culture the realm of the objective mind. It unfurls itself in labor and within the society in political power contentions, in natural and historical sciences, in morality and law, all of which are independent of religions.

But this objective mind, which is the driving force in human history, is severely limited. On the one hand, it is limited by the natural needs and wants against which it pits its energies in a never ending struggle; and on the other hand it is limited by the forms of the absolute spirit in art, religion, and philosophy. If the secular culture does not limit itself in order to make room for them, it would terminate in a fanatical totalitarianism of limited and temporal interests. Man would imprison himself in the three-dimensional space-time world as one object among other objects. Neither religious freedom of worship nor philosophical freedom of thought would be possible if finite ends were treated as if they were ultimate. This finitism of the objective mind is the great metaphysical lie.

This objective spirit faces nature as a being that is completely other or foreign to it, and is never overcome, and is always limiting it. The spirit remains thus in its existence both as knowing and as willing tied to this other side and thus constitutes merely another aspect of nature. In this fear lies the finitude of the theoretical as well as the practical spirit, limited in its scientific knowledge and confined to a mere ought in realizing the good. Here as well as in nature the appearance of the spirit is not adequate to its true essence. Thus, we receive a confusing view of skills, purposes, opinions, and talents which seek and flee each other, which work for and against each other, and which cross each other out; the most manifold shapes of contingency mix themselves in, sometimes disturbing, sometimes favorable, with the life of knowing and willing. This is the standpoint of that spirit which insists on being scientific, temporal, self-contradictory, and therefore mortal, unsatisfied, and deluded. The satisfactions available in this sphere of finitude, are limited, relative and isolated. The willing thinking consciousness therefore lifts itself high above this sphere and seeks and finds its own true universality, its concrete unity and blessedness somewhere else: in the infinite truth. This unity and blessedness, towards which the comprehensiveness of the spirit is driven to transfigure the stuff of its finitude, becomes then the true revelation of that Concept which the world of appearance potentially contains. This spirit comprehends its own finitude as the negative aspect of itself and thereby enters and achieves its infinity. The truth of the finite mind is the absolute spirit. . . .[13]

This standpoint [of the absolute spirit] which endows art with its highest and truest dignity at the same time makes clear that which finds itself on the same absolute level with religion and philosophy. In all spheres of the absolute spirit the spirit evaluates itself out of the contracting barriers of its real existence [*Da-sein*]. . . .[14]

The Critical Origin of Religion The fourth source of Hegel's philosophy of religion deals with critical reason as the negative critique of every standpoint, which would deny its limitation. Critical reason is for Hegel no final standpoint, no end in itself. If it turns itself into an isolated standpoint, it becomes a *merely negative* or skeptical criticalism.[15] Critical reason (*Verstand*) remains healthy only if it is no more than a necessary aspect or "moment" *within* a concrete or "speculative" philosophical comprehension. "When dialectic is exclusively rational, it leads to *skepticism*. Reason, as an isolated aspect of dialectic, points to the untruth of every thought." [16]

Rational critique, then, is the fourth origin of Hegel's philosophy of religion. The English meaning of "critique," a word Greek in origin, would be something like the decision of a judge or a judgment of conscience. Cognate with "critique" is another Greek word, "crisis," in which something stands or does not stand a trial of its strength. In critique and in crisis each form of consciousness is reminded of its limitation.

Both were present in all movements of the phenomenology of religion. But we concentrate here on the critique and on the crisis by which Hegel dissects and dissolves the source book of the Christian religion.

There is an immensely meritorious book by Albert Schweitzer—*The Quest of the Historical Jesus: A Critical Study of Its Progress from Reimarus to Wrede*—which tells the story of this gradual critical demolition of the trustworthiness or historical veracity of the so-called New Testament. The original German title—*Geschichte der Leben Jesu Forschung* (1906)—gives the idea more accurately than the English title.

The greatest weakness of Schweitzer's book is the absence of a chapter on Hegel; it is in Hegel's critique of the New Testament that all the rational and historical criticisms of the Enlightenment are condensed. At the same time the application of his own phenomenological method to his problem anticipates the new critical approach in the nineteenth and twentieth centuries which would be unthinkable without him.

The two major directions of the critique in the Enlightenment converge in Hegel. One direction is the logical or rational one, which refuses belief in the miracles that fill half of the New Testament. What was begun in Nikolaus von Kues (Cusanus) and Spinoza, in Leibniz and Lessing, in Kant, Fichte, and Schelling, is completed in Hegel: the author of the "holy scripture" is not "God." The second *historical* critique undoes another major part of the New Testament as being incompatible with historical fact. It was particularly Gibbon's *Decline and Fall of the Roman Empire*—Hegel read it and partly translated it for himself when he was a tutor in Bern—that confirmed his own view, a view which he had arrived at before he read Gibbon. He saw that there was a close affinity between the earliest spirit of Christianity and the decadence and despotism of the late Roman and Byzantine Empire. According to Hegel, early Christianity is the complete contempt of man. The early Christians sneak around with petitions for mercy in their pockets. They do not dare to approach the heavenly despot or emperor and therefore try to approach him through mediating "saints" or through the Virgin Mary. All human values of which humanity was deprived were projected into the *image* of the Savior.

Hegel sees this logical and historical destruction of the Jesus literature as the inevitable and ironical outcome of the so-called scriptural principle, proclaimed by the Reformation. It assumed that the Church was founded on the Scripture. This assumption led to hundreds of different sects. This was due, not to faulty interpretations, but to the fact that the Jesus literature was the product of a changing Christian religious consciousness which projected its contradictory and dogmatic standpoints back into the Jesus of their imagination. This phenomenological approach is the new, decisive insight of Hegel's. His quite irreverent and contemptuous study of the Jesus literature leads him to view the Christian consciousness as it changed, prompted by one disappointment after another. By this method the New Testament—a term which Hegel sees through as a construction by Paul and which he refutes—is overcome in criticizing itself. This phenomenological or immanent criticism of the "Scripture" has been taken up and has led to the modern eschatological understanding of a historical Jesus who identifies himself with bringing about the end of the world:

> Hereby the flag is unfurled around which all people may assemble, the flag of the *free spirit* who is both for itself and in the truth and is only free by being in this truth. . . . Luther has rejected the authority of the church in order to place in its stead the Bible and the testimony of the human spirit . . . this is an immense revolution; the whole tradition and edifice of the church became problematic.[17]

This result was not intended by the Reformation because it believed that in the Christian source book it had the word of God as an absolute and given truth:

> The content, however, which was to proceed from the book, and the truth which should become alive in us, have been assumed by Luther to be something given, something revealed by this re-

ligion. Now, however, the new principle is this, that this content must be a present one, of which our minds must be convinced, and that everything must be based upon this inner ground in ourselves.[18]

That this given revelation had no inner unity was feared by the enforced conformity of the old church; the "scriptural principle" brought to light against its own will the correlation between various deposits in the scripture and the many churches and sects: "Nothing has so many different meanings as the modern concept of what Christianity is. . . . Incompatible dogmas were historically derived from scripture texts." [19]

This is the historical reason, according to Hegel, why a philosophy of the Christian religion, which asks, What does Christianity mean or what is its truth? cannot be answered by presupposed authoritative texts. If religion is to correspond to its philosophical comprehension "then we must demand that we start from religion itself and not from any texts, and we may claim the right to develop religion openly and truly out of comprehension and thus to contemplate the meaning of 'God' without taking our starting point from any given words. . . . The Christian religion must *not at all* be based on mere sayings of Christ." By "Christ" here Hegel means the historical Jesus. "Only in the apostles is it presented as a developed and posited [*gesetzt*] truth. This content was *evolving* in the Christian community." [20]

Hegel sees his philosophy of religion as the ironical outcome of the "scriptural principle" of the Reformation, which in its consequences brought about the exact opposite of what it intended: the "scriptural principle" dissolved the authority of the "Scripture." The Roman Church, on the other hand, at the council of Trent, countered the dogma of the scriptural principle with the counterdogma of the infallible authority of itself. Not the Scripture is the origin of the church; the infallible church has not only produced the Scripture, but also is the authoritative interpreter thereof, and the Pope is the sole legitimate successor of the Savior. "After the decisions of this council, reunion became impossible." [21]

What are some of the major aspects of Hegel's critique of the New Testament?

In the first place, he rejects this title as a false and unwarranted construction by Paul, who has torn the Jewish Bible out of the hands of the Jewish people and transformed it into the Old Testament as a mere preface to a theological dogma of Christ. But the national god of the Jews, Jahveh, is radically different from the Christian Trinity.

From this decisive rejection follows another phenomenological insight. Hegel sees much of the Christian text as dramatizations of sayings found in the Jewish Bible, the major example being the suffering servant of God of the second Isaiah more than the Christ story; or the Twenty-Second Psalm furnishing the text attributed to Christ on the cross.

Since Hegel discredits the historical value of the whole Jesus literature, the question is, Why did the authors of the later first and early second centuries project into Jesus what they did? The answer is that post-Pauline dogmatic requirements led to their illustrations in pseudo-historical gospels. Both Luke and Matthew, having accepted Paul's theology, transfer the birth of Jesus from Nazareth to Bethlehem "in order that the scripture be fulfilled," according to which the Messiah must be born in Bethlehem; for Paul, the Messiah had to be a descendent of King David and had to be born in Bethlehem. Another example: the pro-Semitic Matthew gives to Jesus twelve apostles because each of the twelve Jewish tribes had to be one; whereas the anti-Semitic Luke gives to Jesus seventy apostles because there are, according to a sociological conception at the time, seventy pagan nations which needed them.

The most remarkable achievement of Hegel's critique of the Jesus book is his clear vision of a historical Jesus being the occasion for his theological transformation into the myth and later into the dogma of a Christ. Arthur Drews, therefore, has no right to quote Hegel as being in agreement with his book *The Christ Myth*, in which he tries to show that there is no evidence whatsoever for any historical Jesus.

Hegel, however, does see a historical Jesus: as one who oscillates between a persecution complex and megalomania; as one who curses and damns all values of and in this world and on the other hand hides his "Messianic consciousness" behind secrecy; as one who not only *entertains* gnostic apocalyptic visions about the end of the world, but has identified himself with this illusion. This historical gnostic Jesus prophesies that his appearance means the disappearance of this world. But this "truly I say unto you" remained unfulfilled. Disappointed and furious, he throws himself against the Jewish god in order to force the Jewish priests to condemn him as blasphemous and in order to bring about the end of the world by this—his own sacrifice.

There is no ethics and no "teaching" in this historical Jesus, but merely a cursing and damning of those who do not "believe" and equally primitive promises of rewards in the "kingdom come" for those who do believe. A collection of sayings, edited by the pro-Jewish Matthew as the Sermon on the Mount and in the anti-Semitic Luke as scattered sayings to the non-Jewish Samarians, are all based upon the expectation that this world will not last any longer, and all are accompanied with savage threats of hellfire and damnation and with promises of rewards in the "kingdom come."

The first Christians overcame their disappointment that the Messianic promise had not been fulfilled in the formation of the first dogma, that of an expected second coming on clouds at the head of an army of angels, Jesus being of angelic nature himself. They sell all they have and arrange a communism of consumption. They sit on their housetops expecting the end. Those who do not "believe" are those who do not want to contribute everything they have to the common fund as the entrance ticket to the "kingdom come," as Hegel says, are prayed to death; "and fear possessed them all," as Acts has it.

This fanaticism and narrow conception of love, Hegel comments, could only be the mentality of a small sect, whose only business was to spread the name of Jesus. "The loss of freedom," Hegel comments further, "and of all human values have prepared the masses for a heaven." This revolution was to be brought about without their cooperation by a divine being. The first ones who spread this Christian religion hoped for the end, but when this hope evaporated, it was transferred to an indefinite future.[22]

But this so-called *parousia* could not be indefinitely postponed. Here Paul steps in with his very radical transformation of the Christ dogma. According to him a second coming has already taken place in a resurrection of the Christ from the dead. In the second place, Paul fuses the Jewish Messiah with the appearing, suffering, and resurrected god of the Syrian mystery religion. Christ, therefore, and the religion of Christianity, does not begin with the historical Jesus, but with the double Pauline dogma of the resurrected Christ, falsifying the Jewish Bible into an Old Testament as a preface to the New Testament.

It seems, indeed, that Peter and Paul are actually the two pillars of the Christian Church, Peter furnishing the story of the historical Jesus as preserved in the gospel of Mark (which was written in Rome about the year 70) and in some of the oldest layers in Matthew; and Paul transforming this historical Jesus into the Christ myth in which one participated through a magic sacramentalism of "the blood of Christ."

Hegel's application of his phenomenological method has proved its immense fruitfulness. Hegel has actually anticipated the whole reconstruction of a historical Jesus as a gnostic and paranoiac visionary, as he appears in the research of the twentieth century. Hegel has shown how the Christian consciousness has changed itself together with its intended Savior.

The Pauline theology, which promised immortality through the participation in a magic baptism, proved insufficient to stem a new wave of disappointment; people kept on dying as before, and this disappointment in the efficacy of Paul's magical sacramentalism led to a final transformation of the Christ myth, which found its expression in the trinitarian dogma of the Gospel of John in the second century.

It is this final myth (*Vorstellung*), which found its authoritative and dogmatic formulation in the Nicene Creed, that interested Hegel the most. In it he sees the religious analogy to his own conception of truth, according to which the Absolute maintains its unbroken unity in revealing itself in its individuation and in taking back the mortal and individual suffering into its own eternal life. It is this dogma which carried Christianity to victory, and not an obscure, unknown historical Jesus.

This explains Hegel's unconditional opposition to the theology of Schleiermacher and the whole liberal theology that followed him in the nineteenth century. Liberal theology, having become aware of the development of the dogma, tried to cast it aside in order to discover a superhuman historical Jesus. This demythologizing, as continued in this century by Bultmann, was for Hegel utterly perverse, because he was convinced of the inferiority of the character of the historical Jesus. To him this search ended with an insane man; whereas the later development of the Christ myth and the dogmatic formulation of that myth contained a profound religious truth. "Through this impoverishment of the life of the spirit, through this removal of the myth [*Vorstellung*] from the community . . . a mere single externality, a historical and immediate appearance and a meaningless remembering of a particular individual and its past, has replaced the religious Concept." [23]

"Since the dogmas in the Christian religion have been developed by Greek philosophy, one must not contend, therefore, that they are alien to Christ and of no account. It is perfectly indifferent, where they have come from; the only question is, Do they contain a truth which is true in and for itself?" [24] This distinction which Hegel made between a worthless historical Jesus and a religiously significant myth has been fully confirmed in the discussion of the twentieth century since Albert Schweitzer's *Quest of the Historical Jesus* appeared in 1906.

Failing to make this distinction leads, according to Hegel, to a despotic fanaticism. One is not allowed to look critically into the obscure mixture of *religious faith* on the one hand with a *pseudo-historical belief in or assent to doubtful so-called facts*. This mixture of a falsified history with a religious myth had to be protected. This need for protection against truth has transformed Christianity into a book-burning religion, beginning with the burning of the Alexandrian Library, the details of which are described in Gibbon's *Decline and Fall of the Roman Empire*. Book burning has been a periodic episode in the history of the Church.

From the burning of books to the burning of heretics is only a short step. The New Testament basis for the Inquisition, which literally murdered hundreds of thousands of people, quite apart from the religious wars between Christian churches, is found in the second-century Gospel of John. His Jesus, who has developed into the second person of the Trinity, states that those who are not incorporated in him are like dry and thrown-away branches which must be gathered and burned.[25] The anti-intellectual fear not only of critical reason but even of philosophical comprehension is a dominant trend in the Christian theology of most churches. Tertullian demands the sacrifice of the intellect in order to be a Christian; the Platonic and philosophic primacy of truth is flouted.

Thomas Aquinas—the official philosopher of the Roman Catholic Church, declared to be infallible by an infallible Pope of an infallible Church—gives reason this choice: either to be a handmaiden of the Church or to be silenced as a subversive element and a heretic danger.

The Reformation, of course, is famous for its extreme antiphilosophical and anti-intellectual fervor—Luther speaking of philosophy as the "Grecian whore" whose eyes ought to be gouged out; and Calvin burning the scientist Servetus for heretical doubts. No other religion has such a bloody record as the Christian Church.

It is through the work of critical reason in the enlightenment, beginning with Spinoza, that the whole dogmatic background of this weakness is exposed and overcome. In Hegel the primacy of truth is fully restored, as I have shown above in the section The Logical Origin of Religion.

Religion as the Analogy of Being Hegel is surely justified when he insists that the expansion and victory of the Christian religion in the Roman Empire was not due to an obscure and unknown historical individual Jesus, but was due entirely to the religious myth which in 325 in the council of Nicaea hardened into the infallible dogma. The Christians believed that God himself, the creator of heaven and earth, had appeared in the midst of his own creation and revealed himself in the uniqueness of the one Savior; had taken upon himself the pain and suffering, the hatred and injustice of this world; had died on the cross as a criminal; and had returned in his resurrection and ascension to his eternal glory in heaven.

As we have seen, Hegel's word for myth is *Vorstellung*. It is the religious analogy of the truth, of the Concept. He interprets the Christian Trinity, as just described, as the mythical religious expression of the eternal truth: Being itself or the Absolute discloses itself as finite and personal life and again cancels this "othering" or self-alienation in an eternally present process. We are living this truth whether we want to or not, whether we know it or not. But if we do know and affirm it, then we can discover in ourselves the truth of religion; we are emancipated from any Biblicism, be it orthodox or be it liberal, fundamentalistic or dogmatic. The living religion of the absolute spirit in us is the analogy to the dialectical Being in us, which pervades all essential realms of reality. Religion, as one of these essential realms or Concepts of comprehension, therefore does not make an exception. The trinitarian God of Christianity is the mythical-religious symbol for the dialectical constitution of reality as such, the unconditional Being, the Absolute.

The eternal unconditional Being retains or maintains its own concrete identity in that which is the very opposite of itself, in the finite, conditional, and temporal life of man. But in canceling again this its own self-alienation or estrangement, it also preserves this finite existence as an eternal moment within its life. *A is non-A: The Absolute mediates itself to itself through being both eternal and temporal at the same time.*

To put the same dialectic negatively: the eternal or absolute Being would be nothing apart from its manifestation in the temporal world; and the temporal world, if taken by itself, would be nothing; it must confess its insufficiency and futility when isolated and falsely absolutized.

In religious language this corresponds to saying that God as the creator is both distinguished from and identical with his creation. Thus neither is the world in and for itself divine, nor is God anything apart from his creation.

The first document in which Hegel formulates Christ as a symbol of this comprehensive dialectic is a long manuscript which he never published; it was written in Bern, when he was about twenty-four years old and is entitled "The Life of Jesus." But as is very frequently the case with Hegel, the title is misleading. He is not trying to write the life of Jesus at all, but rather selects a very few sayings in order to show that "Jesus" is a symbol of a dialectical comprehension which is autonomous and true in and for itself. His "Jesus" points to that autonomy and freedom in every soul—almost the exact opposite of the meaning in those texts.

If we go from this beginning to Hegel's very last lecture in Berlin, the so-called Proof of the Existence of God, we find a steady continuity. This title also is misleading. If one looks more closely into the lectures, one finds that Hegel is in perfect agreement with Kant that the existence of God cannot be proved, because "God" is a mythical religious term serving to personify the Absolute and make it available to prayers and cultic performance. Apart or aside of this religious performance in a community of faith, the term "God" has as little existence as Goethe's Faust would have outside the tragedy, Parts I and II. Hegel agrees with Kant's refutation of a pseudo-ontological argument, which defines God as a perfect being and infers that the perfection of a being entails the existence of the being that is perfect. This is invalid because the conclusion merely repeats the premises and is really tautological. The abstract reason applied here thinks of the abstraction "God," as if it were a given physical thing; it is obvious that in all such abstract reasoning, classes or concepts are never identical with the individual appearance or unique life, which they vainly try to think according to the rules of formal logic.

But what can be proved is the absoluteness or unconditionality of Being for which "God" is the religious analogy or equivalent. These proofs are formulated mainly in three movements.

(1) The *ontological proof* thinks the whole of reality, but then a rational concept, such as "the whole is reality," is *not* the whole of reality. Hegel is the first philosopher after Anselm who understood the latter's ontological argument. That "Being greater than which nothing can be conceived" cannot be an absolute conception in my head, because such a conception is not a being greater than which nothing can be conceived. In this dialectical negation, in this "not," the Absolute shows its absoluteness in breaking down any attempt to identify a rational formulation with it. It is through this dialectical negation of reason that the Absolute mediates itself as itself: A is through its non-A.

(2) The second movement is known as the *cosmological argument*. Every finite appearance or experience in the world is relative and dependent on others which are also relative. None of them can say of itself, "I am eternal, necessary." No one can say of himself, "it is impossible that I might not be." But if we admit this to be true then we have already measured the finite, temporal and relative world of existence by the idea of an absolute, necessary Being, which appears in the breakdown of all finite positions that would claim to be absolute or final. The truth of Being becomes manifest in the breakdown of all finite certainties of reason which is, as scientific, oriented towards objects over against itself. The infinite and encompassing Being, however, is not such an object. But neither is it beyond, behind, or separate from the relative beings; it appears in them as that which posits them and as that which limits and cancels them. Man experiences the Absolute in the experience of his limitation. The insufficiency of finitude becomes aware of itself in itself.

(3) This leads to the third movement, labeled the *teleological proof* of the Absolute. It starts from the moral incompetence of man. There is, as Hegel says, "no absolute but only relative wisdom in the world." [26] There are no finite purposes which do not engender their own opposites, with which they struggle; and there are no purposes in which the agent will not be disappointed if he lives long enough. Purposes are crossing each other out. It is therefore impossible to moralize the Absolute or to think of it as a Being with a plan or design. The absolute Good is evident in our sufferings, in the infinite sorrow, as Hegel calls it, concerning our incompetence.

The much misunderstood Hegelian insight into the insufficient nature of the moral ought has a profound religious meaning and truth. What ought to be belongs essentially to every finite will. The fact that I always ought to be what I am not, reveals the finality of our moral incompetence, which we cannot escape. This situation of struggle is absolutely accepted in faith. The Absolute thus appears as the ground of the whole practical realm of life. It is one with its finite negations. In this sense alone the ought coincides with the factually given, the holy with the profane, comprehensiveness with actuality. This is never the case in finite wills. It is not possible for us to experience ourselves other than as ambiguous; if we absolutize this our ambiguous and finite will, where "ought" and "is" always fall apart, then we cannot but experience the absolute perfection of Being as our annihilation.

These purely dialectical and philosophical formulations have a precise analogy in the language of the Christian religion; this correspondence with ontology makes Christianity the religion of the absolute spirit. "That the absolute essence appears in human existence is the simple content of the absolute religion." [27]

God himself takes upon himself the futility of immediate existence and gives himself to suffering and death in order to negate this negativity and thereby affirm himself as the eternal and holy spirit.

This Christ is, according to Hegel, the mythical image (*Vorstellung*) of the Holy as it lives in the Christian community or church. Thousands of years have enriched it, as it has enriched the religious life of generations. For Hegel this Christian image of the Holy is the perfect and absolute symbol of it; and he describes the various aspects of religious satisfaction in the interaction between the Lord as revealed in this unique individual, and the community of the Christian faith.

In his chapters on the Christian cult he describes the Holy in the same categories that Rudolf Otto has worked out in abstractions from history. [28]

Christ assembles all of them in his holiness.

He is the *mysterium tremendum*. He shakes man to his root in the absolute anxiety that his natural existence and this world is *doomed*. The Crucifixion—"God is dead"—is the absolute sacrifice, the annihilation, the Nothing made manifest.

He is the *mysterium mirum*. His resurrection and ascension is the miraculous itself. He is not bound by our categories of space and time. He is absolutely beyond the filters of our finite minds.

But the mysterium mirum does not strike with awe and terror, but with wonder and admiration.

He is the *mysterium fascinosum*. Let those who suffer, who are burdened, come to him. He has taken our death and sin upon himself; they are forgiven in his boundless goodness and kindness.

He is the *mysterium martyrium*. He is confirmed by the blood of all the martyrs, who have taken persecution upon themselves, thereby binding themselves in imitation to him in suffering the hate and injustice of the world.

He is the *mysterium sanctum*. He guarantees safety and rewards in heaven for those who give themselves to his "body," the Holy Church. The mighty and weighty tradition of centuries is added to his absolute authority.

Hegel has described all those categories of the Holy as they are assembled in a full accord. This concrete unity of opposite "moments" renders the Holy analogous to the comprehensive or "speculative concept," which finds itself in this religious analogy of itself. Only to reason it will forever remain an incomprehensible mystery! "This content of religion is called *mysterium*, because to reason its meaning is concealed, for reason does not reach the process which is the unity of all its moments: this speculative unity, therefore, remains a mystery to reason." [29]

Hegel's Relation to Schleiermacher and Hamann Hegel discusses two undialectical theologies of his time: one is the liberal or unitarian theology of Friedrich Ernest Daniel Schleiermacher (1768-1834); the other is the Christian existentialism of Johann Georg Hamann (1730-1788). For Hamann one might substitute the later Sören Kierkegaard (1813-1855); Hegel would have seen nothing new in him.

Hegel had greeted Schleiermacher's *Discourses on Religion* (1789) with great joy and reviewed it favorably. What attracted him was Schleiermacher's understanding of religious dogmas as symbols of the religious consciousness. What Hegel missed, however, was that Schleiermacher did not see this as a two-way traffic. The symbols, in other words, were not only products of a religious community, but in turn, reacting back, formed the community in their image, uniting it in their "names." But when Hegel and Schleiermacher became colleagues at the University of Berlin, a fight between the two became inevitable. Schleiermacher had started his theological reflections by denying Christ, the second person of the Trinity; but wanted to find, instead, a historical Jesus as an exemplary religious individual, in whom "the feeling of absolute dependence" on God was exemplary. The poet Heinrich Heine, who was a student of Hegel, says Schleiermacher preached in the Berlin Cathedral a Christianity without a Christ—which was like a turtle soup without a turtle. For Hegel, as we saw, this *historical Jesus* was a pathological individual and a false prophet, and the second-century dogma formulating the *mythical Christ* as the second person of the Trinity, was the unifying core of the Christian churches.

The theological research since then has been in favor of Hegel's dialectical understanding of the whole situation; whereas Schleiermacher's liberal unitarianism is historically untenable. Almost every tale in the New Testament about the life of Jesus is fiction.

Georg Hamann's Christian existentialism is much appreciated by Hegel, who reviewed Hamann's complete works in a review of 72 pages.

The individual has ultimate, ontological dignity and value. Individuation, for Hegel, is an absolute ontological category. "No individual is indifferent." Every individual is unique and irreplaceable. This is central to Christianity, in that Christ is this "one, this only son of God"! And insofar as Hamann expresses this religious value of the individual, in contrast to generalities and memberships in societies, parties, trends, or churches, Hegel is with him. What he criticizes is the abstract or isolated intensity, the infinite subjective passion without any interest in or orientation of other dimensions of the Absolute which are also important and real.

NOTES FOR CHAPTER 10

1 For a background of this essay compare my English version of *Hegel: Encyclopedia of Philosophy*, translated and annotated by Gustav E. Mueller, New York, Philosophical Library, 1959; *Plato: The Founder of Philosophy as Dialectic*, New York, Philosophical Library, 1964; *Hegel: The Man, His Vision and His Work*, Chicago, Open Court Publishing Co., 1964.
2 Hegel, *Sämtliche Werke*, Stuttgart, Frommann, Vol. XII, p. 136.
3 *Ibid.*, II, 538.
4 *Ibid.*, XII, 157.
5 Hegel, *Encyclopedia of Philosophy*, New York, Philosophical Library, 1959, pp. 82-84.
6 Hegel, *Sämtliche Werke*, II, 24.
7 *Ibid.*, XII, p. 428.
8 Hegel, *Encyclopedia of Philosophy*, pp. 71-72.
9 Hegel, *Sämtliche Werke*, IV, 46.
10 *Ibid.*, XVI, 359, 553.
11 Hegel, *Encyclopedia*, pp. 269-270.
12 *Ibid.*, pp. 270-271.
13 Hegel, *Sämtliche Werke*, XII, pp. 137-138.
14 *Ibid.*, p. 139.
15 Hegel, *Encyclopedia*, p. 93.
16 *Ibid.*, p. 82.
17 Hegel, *Sämtliche Werke*, XI, 524-525.
18 *Ibid.*, XI, 552.
19 *Ibid.*, XII, 39.
20 *Ibid.*, XI, 421.
21 *Ibid.*, XI, 526.
22 NOHL, p. 224.
23 Hegel, *Sämtliche Werke*, II, 582-583.
24 *Ibid.*, XII, 424.
25 John 14, 6.
26 Hegel, *Sämtliche Werke*, XVI, 523.
27 *Ibid.*, II, 577.
28 R. Otto, *Das Heilige*, Breslau, 1922.
29 Hegel, *Sämtliche Werke*, XVI, 553.

QUESTIONS

1 What is dialectic (*a*) as negative dialectic; (*b*) as dialectic of contrary opposites; (*c*) as dialectic of contradictory opposites?

2 What would be an undialectical position in philosophy?
3 Why is dialectic incompatible with authoritarianism?
4 Why is dialectic the logic of systematic philosophy?
5 Why is philosophy of religion a necessary discipline of systematic philosophy?

SUGGESTED READINGS

Georg Wilhelm Friedrich Hegel, *Early Theological Writings,* translated by T. M. Knox, Chicago, University of Chicago Press, 1948.

———, *Encyclopedia of Philosophy,* translated by Gustav E. Mueller, New York, Philosophical Library, 1959.

Gustav E. Mueller, *Dialectic: A Way Into and Within Philosophy,* New York, Bookman Associates, 1953.

———, *Discourses on Religion,* New York, Bookman Associates, 1951.

———*Origins and Dimensions of Philosophy,* New York, Pageant Press, 1966.

PART II

Religion in Cultural

Perspective

In dealing with experience, one must include its relevant aspects. In the physical and organic areas of existence, among nonhuman phenomena, culture is irrelevant although it may play some role in the perspectives of particular scientific men. When, however, we cross the line to human experience, culture is never irrelevant.

M. K. Opler ⋮ *CULTURE AND MENTAL HEALTH*

Our problem is not how to get outside experience but how to discriminate within it. . . .

H. D. Lewis ⋮ *OUR EXPERIENCE OF GOD*

Culture . . . has some of the attractive elusive qualities of the rainbow. So has religion in its deepest essence as distinct from its routine, ritual, conventional practices. Religion may perhaps be said to stand in much the same sort of relation to culture as one half of a double rainbow stands to the other. On a religious interpretation the cultural half would be the weakest, a pale reflection, of the real thing, the last to appear and the first to vanish. A purely humanistic cultural interpretation might try to reverse the roles, but on a mystical metaphysical plane the religious interpretation would not lack a final comment. Like the sun from which both halves of the double rainbow derive their being, both religion and culture could be said to be manifestations of that reality which lies beyond the appearances with which mankind seems currently content to deal.

F. R. Cowell ⋮ *CULTURE*

II *William Horosz*

Religion and Culture in Modern Perspective

To view the problem of the relationship of religion and culture "in modern perspective" is to regard it from the standpoint of the functional approach. The fact is that the modern mind is readily more concerned with the processes, activities, and functions of experience than it is with entities which reflect static forms and fixed structures. The happenings in experience are more amenable to reflective scrutiny because they radiate their energy, potency, or dynamism in the context of human experience more than entities of a more substantival nature. Having to grasp the topics of religion and culture functionally, by relating them to the individual, to the group, and to the social techniques and circumstances that give rise to these functionings, the modern man can more properly evaluate the social and cultural roots of religion as well as the spiritual and ideational aspects of the cultural order. In brief, the truth seems more accessible from the functional standpoint than from a more substantival point of view.

The modern mind is equally fascinated with another facet of inquiry, to wit, the attitude of critical assessment. The poet-philosopher George Santayana gives the best literary expression to this attitude in his work *Obiter Scripta:* "Just as the spirit has the right to soliloquize, and to regard existence as a strange dream, so any society or nation or living interest has a right to treat the world as its field of action, and to recast the human mind, as far as possible, so as to adapt it exclusively to that public function." That, in fact, is precisely what each of the great religions and cultures has tried to do in attempting to remake the human mind more in conformity to its image. The culture is free to recast its religion; and the religion is free to transform the culture in which it operates. The history of thought is replete with examples of the claims of each and the counterclaims of both. Consequently, their relationship, as well as their respective attitudes toward it, has been subject to sharp fluctuations of intensity and even inconsistency, in the rise and fall of both religions and cultures.

In elaborating on the nature and function of religion and culture, and their respective claims, my intent is to utilize the functional approach in an attitude of critical assessment. To begin this task I propose to use Zen Buddhism as a positive molding factor of Japanese culture, and Christianity as a negative influence on modern science. The Zen impact on Japanese culture is direct and all-embracing, habituating its people to the religion of immediacy and mysticism for a period of eight hundred years, according to Daisetz T. Suzuki, the foremost expositor of Zen to the West. Zen has influenced the culture of Japan in numerous ways: (a) by its focus on the importance of personal experience in the realization of selfhood, (b) by cultivating a mystic sensitivity toward life, which neglects the structured forms of existence and art, and underlines originality and spontaneity in the life of pure spirit, (c) by emphasizing the innerliness of experience as the best expression of existence, (d) by an emphasis on directness and simplicity of living and communicating, (e) by discovering the self-sufficiency of existence even under the cover of poverty, (f) by an emphasis on the immediate facts of existence as over against the mediate realm of symbolization, (g) by the quality of "eternal loneliness" which registers the loneliness, silence, and mystery of existence, (h) by the quality of aesthetic awareness of self, nature, and the arts, (i) and by a certain quality of love and mystical rapport with nature.

Zen's influence on the culture of the East, particularly on Japan, is still felt as an attitude which conveys to the Japanese mind the importance of the immediate form of experience in the atmospheric current of mystic overtones. It suggests to the Oriental man the need for purity and transparency of the immediate form of experience which is discoverable in all walks of life under the inspiration of Zen religion. A statement from Suzuki conveys a sense of this strange universe without the medium of the conceptual: "To state the matter in a practical manner, religion requires us to put away everything that we have for some reason or other put upon ourselves and that does not really belong to us. . . . When there is nothing to screen oneself from outside views one comes to oneself." [1] Zen has been a great power in the whole existence of the Japanese people, teaching them to unload the wares of life and to be close to existence. It has affected the artistic, political, intellectual, social, and religious life of Orientals and stands as an expression of the Japanese character even when it indulges in the art of tea or the art of swordsmanship. In short, Zen has been in vital collaboration with the culture of Japan and remains the spiritual and ideational foundation of Japanese culture.

Although equally powerful influences can be discovered in Christianity's impact on the culture of the West, a negative example will be more in accord with the writer's purpose. Even in the historic periods of its most benevolent intent the Christian faith has had a negative attitude toward Western science; it has never assigned any greater role to science than an instrumental function. From the standpoint of the Christian ideology, science was never permitted to shape the destiny of man, because its alleged task was merely the instrumental function of seeking facts and the dissemination of information regarding those facts. There the influence of science ended. Whenever science misbehaved, as by increasingly preoccupying men's minds and dominating their interests and lives, it was quickly informed of a new-coined term "scientism," to remind the scientists that science could not function as an end by legislating for men's needs and suggesting goals for their destiny.

It was the liberal movement within Christianity which established some measure of commerce with science in the late nineteenth and early twentieth centuries. Edward Scribner Ames voiced the ideology of most American liberals when he said, in effect, that Christianity had but one alternative to choose from, either that of becoming a religion of this world or of having no appeal to this age. Liberalism was obligated to make Christianity "credible in a scientific age." The detractors of liberalism, those of more orthodox or neo-orthodox persuasion, have claimed that liberal theology has accepted the position of "servitude to modern culture" in showing a "deference to science," both in its methodology and in its substantive theory. Liberal attitudes toward science ranged anywhere from a complacent regard for its methods and conclusions to an actual alliance with science in the more modernistic circles. Henry P. Van Dusen of Union Theological Seminary in New York City, has restated his qualified endorsement of science and liberal Christianity in the following manner:

> Again, Christian Theology must make the fateful decision: will it venture forth into the mysteries of the newest Science and seek to establish contact between it and Christian Faith? Or will it take refuge in a world-view—if you will, the "Biblical world-view"—

formed before men knew the truth about the world in which men of today are fated to dwell and thunder largely unintelligible and irrational "myths" which compel a dual, a schizophrenic existence? The issue is that with which we began: fidelity to truth.[2]

Except for this neo-liberal wing of Christianity, however, there is little fidelity to truth in its general understanding. The truth of the matter is that the perpetuation of certain beliefs comes first and fidelity to truth second.

Although liberalism has done much to communicate Christianity to a scientific age, it was supplanted by the neo-orthodox movement, which was more critical of science—of its methods and conclusions as well as of its presuppositions. Henry P. Van Dusen speaks for the neo-liberal movement, which has accepted some of the doctrines of neo-orthodoxy, particularly its reinterpretation of the doctrine of man, along with more radical criticisms of modern science and its underlying metaphysical assumptions. The point is that even the most liberal movement within the Christian fold has not accepted the discipline of science with whole-hearted concern. The bulk of the Christian movement either denied its value or tolerated its work or showed a complacent regard. The most hospitable attitude on the part of Christian faith toward science has been the schizophrenic attitude that science is all right as something instrumental, but that it should not dictate the goals, ends, and purposes of men.

This hesitant attitude stems from the Christian metaphysics that says, in effect, that the object of Christian veneration is far superior to the objects of science, that the latter are specifically concerned with immediate, provisional, and phenomenal aspects of man's existence, but not with man's ultimate concern. The attitude has its source in the transcendent character of the Christian faith which asserts that this earth is not its final form of self-realization. A theologically created tension becomes the source of a cultural imbalance in that an irrational faith is set in competition with an enlightened discipline that has been the source of real values in modern culture. This tendency in modern theology has pushed Christian values further into the background of transcendent acquiescence, with less regard and less relevance for contemporary living.

Meanwhile, the work of science continues and its prestige rises. Since the difference between Christian theology and science is deeply imbedded in the question of standards, and there is no common value to mediate this difference, the impact of the Christian faith on Western science has been negligible, even negative. It lacks the creative interchange expressed earlier in Zen's impact on Japanese culture. Modern culture has registered its complaint against this kind of negative collective behavior against one of its respected disciplines by placing in exile all the claims of religion to transcendent truth and continues its explorations of the universe with its multifunctional approaches.

Having learned to distrust religion in various specific cultural situations, the modern mind has gone one step forward in instituting a universal critique of religion in general, to the effect that religion is not an adequate molder of modern culture. Religion is either obsolete in its solutions to the problems of a rapidly developing culture (John Dewey) or it is infantile in its attitudes of wish-thinking and wish-believing in solving the problems of real existence (Sigmund Freud); or (Karl Marx) it lacks the revolutionary zeal and the power necessary to bring about required cultural transformations. What is questioned by these three systems is the omnicompetence of religion to effect a vital culture in which modern man can find a meaningful life. Religion is denied its traditional role of being a culture-building agency. Dewey's naturalistic moralism denies it in favor of the specific sources of knowledge in the sciences. Freud's naturalistic psychology denies it in favor of more adult responses to the realities of existence under the enlightenment of psychoanalytic knowledge. Marx's naturalistic sociology denies it in favor of humanistic and communistic solutions to man's problems of alienation from existence. Their charge against religion is that even under the best possible conditions the relation between religion and culture must be terminated if mankind would achieve the stage of mature humanity, that unless the relationship is terminated, man's tendency of myth making, wish believing, and life denying and his susceptibility to superstition, credulity, and social inadequacy will assert themselves afresh and man will be hopelessly lost in secondary solutions to the problems of existence.

Sigmund Freud's Debate with Religion: A common mistake in the study
Projection and Responsibility of religion is to identify the constructs of religion with religious experience itself. Martin Buber points to this common fallacy, in discussing the individual's relationship to God in the tradition of Judaism, when he states: "Whenever we both, Christian and Jew, care more for God himself than for our images of God, we are united in the feeling that our Father's house is differently constructed than our human models take it to be." [3] It is Buber's view that God as reality is far greater than our projections of his nature. Thomas Aquinas claimed a similar truth when he insisted that God, as the object of man's faith, is infinitely more than the propositional understanding of his nature. Martin Luther gives credence to the same belief in a hidden God, *Deus absconditus*, who is, "something more" than our images of him. Traditional religion in general respects the belief that God, man, and religion are far more than our

constructed human models take them to be. They maintain a sharp distinction between man's symbolic understanding of religion and the religious experience *per se*. My empirical concern with religious experience agrees with this line of thought, to wit, that religious experience as projection and religious experience as reality or empirical fact are two clearly distinguishable aspects of religious affirmations.

To say that religion is the product of man's fears, hopes, anxieties, and wishes, as Feuerbach and Freud contend, is to give intellectual assent to the misconception of religious phenomena mentioned above. Ludwig Feuerbach claims that man "projects his being into objectivity," [4] that religion is merely the projection of one's wish-world and the gods men worship are wish-beings. Thereby Feuerbach denies the distinction between religion as projection and religion as an empirical fact. Freud's projective theory of religion similarly identifies the religious experience with projection itself, by relating projection *of* with projection *upon*.

By reducing religion to projection, Freud denies the factual, empirical nature of the religious experience. Religion proper no longer has its own authentic being in the residual core of inner experience, because projection *of* is viewed by Freud as the main mechanism in the formation of religious beliefs. The empirical nature of religious experience is denied because it is totally absorbed by the ego's defensive mechanism of projection. Faith is denied its conscious relation to the Other and is viewed as a psychological condition in the defensive behavior of the ego. Freud's basic choice is that between religion as projection and religion as reality. In choosing the former he denies the residual, inner, empirical experience of religion as reality. From his projective point of view one can no longer reminisce in the belief that religious experience is the immediate certainty of the uncertain: that religion is the immediate assurance of power, of love, of healing, of salvation. It is this primary form of immediate experience, and its inner core of residual meaning, that Freud rejects by equating it with the mechanism of projection. Since he regards religion as projection, it is not possible to hold a distinctive religious stand in reality, for religion is nothing more than the psychological outcome of defensive behavior. The empirical component in religious experience, its distinctive and qualitative sentiment, is given the status of an illusion.

Projection is a theory about the ego; it is a theory about how the wishes and desires of the ego operate. It is twice removed from religious experience in that it is a theory about the ego and its mechanisms of defense, a theory about its wishes and desires as they relate to religious experience. To miss this mediate characteristic about projection is the error of most theorists on the topic of the projective theory of religion. Projection can more appropriately be said to be one of the main mechanisms of the ego that reveal the formation of the ego in some stages of its operation than the formation of religious belief.

It is the thesis of this chapter that projective religion is the name of a theory about religion, that it is merely a way of talking about religion, from the psychoanalytic point of view. Since it is merely a secularized construct of religious experience (which is a primary form of immediate reality), it belongs specifically to the realm of discourse. It is basically only a theory of communication about religion. The projective activity is a form of transcendent meaning or mediate knowledge, not actually inhabiting the inner core of religious experience. Freud's psychoanalytic approach substitutes the projections of the ego for the religious experience itself; it thus equates projection *of* with projection *upon*.

Projection is expressive of religious affirmations, but not formative of religious beliefs. It has no power to produce religious experience, since it is a matter of discourse only. In his essay *The Psychopathology of Everyday Life* Freud views religion as "nothing other than psychological processes projected into the outer world." [5] In his defensive behavior the individual, in projecting his fears, hopes, wishes, and anxieties onto the outer world, is going through the process of doing something with the religious experience, but the process itself is secondary, and not the primary creative moment of religious experience. Freud is stating here what one does with religious experience and how one does it, not what it is in its immediate creativity. His words have to do with the expression of religious experience, not with what it is.

To claim that Freud's view is functional and dynamic, that he is not interested in the static structures of religious affirmations, but only in the formations of these beliefs, is to miss the point. No pure functionalism can survive inspection. For any activity is an activity of "something." Religious projection is a mediate form of activity about another activity rooted in the creative moment of the immediate form of religious experience. The basic psychological processes or wishes do not meet the requirements of the inner core of religious experience; they are secondary constructs and not primary data. Projection is what one does with empirical facts; it is the psychoanalytic way of communicating religious affirmations. The projective world is a subjectivized world of personal interpretations. Projection might be regarded as a synonym for interpretation. It is interpretation, and not the empirical fact of religion.

The projective view of religion lifts out for emphasis the symbolic or mythological nature of all religious beliefs, but neglects to treat as important the truth and reality which these symbols point to. That would be relating illusion with reality, which Freud's method prevents him from doing. Although the truth of religious experience can no longer be viewed as literal or scientific, meanings are attributed to the referents of these symbols which are entirely different from the meanings which Freud attributes to religious experience through his symbolism. Religious symbols are symbols of something; they are symbols of something other than literal facts and scientific facts. One might call them symbols referring to the fact-world of man, or the human *Lebenswelt*. If religious beliefs contain this something else, they cannot be reduced to pure forms of "wish projections." If religious statements are not literally true of the nature of things, it does not follow that they are not expressive of the nature of religious reality. The method devours the subject matter it is supposed to point to.

There are two basic meanings of projection in Freud's writings, according to Leopold Bellak, to wit, projection as a defense mechanism of the ego and projection as an epistemological issue having to do with perception.[6] Projection is a name for one of the defensive mechanisms of the ego; it means the "process of ascribing one's own drives, feelings, and sentiments to other people or to the outside world as a defensive process that permits one to be unaware of these 'undesirable' phenomena in oneself." [7] The term "projection" originated in the study of psychoses and neuroses as early as 1894.

The second meaning of projection assumes that "memories of percepts influence perception of contemporary stimuli." [8] Bellak has renamed this process "apperceptive distortion."

> It is suggested that the term 'projection' be reserved for the greatest degree of apperceptive distortion. Its opposite pole would be, hypothetically, a completely objective perception. . . . We may say that in the case of true projection we are dealing not only with an ascription of feelings and sentiments which remain unconscious, in the service of defense, but which are unacceptable to the ego and are therefore ascribed to objects of the outside world.[9]

The second meaning of projection has been a fruitful concept for projective psychology. But the topic of religion is primarily tied to the first meaning of projection as a defensive maneuver of the ego. What is at issue is Freud's definition of religion as a defensive process against anxiety.

In *The Future of an Illusion* (1927) Freud points out that religion is the product of human needs and desires.[10] The religious affirmations, as culture transmits them to the individual, consist of certain dogmas, ideas, assertions. Religious ideas are primarily "illusions, fulfillments of the oldest, strongest and most insistent wishes of mankind; the secret of their strength is the strength of these wishes." [11] Religious experience is the resultant of human wishes and desires. Having asserted that religious beliefs are mere 'illusions' Freud does not feel the need to relate illusion to reality; he disregards its relationship to reality, for it is capable neither of proof nor disproof. An illusion is void of truth and reality, as it is on the side of wishes and desires alone, with no objective reference in religious experience itself.

It is my intention to show that these wishes and desires, which Freud thinks are primary psychological data, are secondary constructs and belong to the side of *discourse* and communication about religion. The world of wish fulfillment is already a highly subjectivized construct, an interpretation of man's biosocial structure. Freud reifies these constructs to make them elemental wishes determinative of religious experience. They involve to a high degree psychoanalytic distortion.

Just how elemental are these Freudian wishes which, if projected on the outside world, are formative of religious beliefs? From a behaviorist perspective, Edwin Holt views the Freudian wish as a dynamic process, a "course of action which some mechanism of the body is set to carry out." [12] The wish, which dictates the religious beliefs, is located exclusively in the ego's mechanism of projection. The motive power of these wishes comes from behind; they are not of a forward intention. The wish, in short, is the ego's plan of action with reference to outer reality. In the case of projective religion, it is a defensive action. The ego itself in Freud's writings is a construct with many projective functions. Thus projection is neither the form nor the content of religious experience, but a course of reactive behavior of what to do with religious experience. Religion is man's way of protecting himself against reality. When he succeeds in this defensive action, he lives not in the world of reality, but in the world of his own making—his own wish-world. The Freudian wishes are secondary constructs; they are reactive experiences of the ego to religious experience, or away from it. They involve a high degree of distortion in reacting to these religious experiences.

David Trueblood's view of adult religion is an interesting rebuttal to this Freudian wish. He points out that religious convictions are "frequently at variance with wishes." [13] Religious affirmations are seldom or never flattering to the ego. What defenses does the ego have against the use of religion as a defensive pattern of behavior? It might be argued that the Freudian wishes are quite flexible and that these "unwanted encounters" in life, these varying wishes express another wish still, one associated with masochistic character traits. This is what Erich Fromm has in mind, with his humanistic perspective of religion. Arguing against the authoritarian view of religion, Fromm writes:

We find people who have a tendency to incur sickness, accidents, humiliating situations, who belittle and weaken themselves . . . they are driven by one of the most irrational tendencies to be found in man, namely, by an unconscious desire to be weak and powerless; they tend to shift the center of their life to powers over which they feel no control, thus escaping from freedom and from personal responsibility.[14]

Although this character trait is a prominent one in psychoanalytic literature, it is not enough to offset the fact of religious experience that more often than not, religious affirmations are at variance with human wishes and desires. The wish for unwanted wishes is not the normal pattern of religious behavior: it is the trait of a sick personality, a deviant from the norm. The fact that religious assertions are often at variance with human wishes and desires would indicate that projections are not a formative power in the manufacture of religious beliefs, but merely the psychoanalytic way of giving projective meanings and patterns to the given core of inner religious experience. Freud's positivistic attack on religion was part of the atmospheric current of his age.

Freud's problem in viewing the religious world as the realm of wish fulfillment is "methogenic" in nature rather than "empiriogenic." By reducing religious experience to projective experience, which is a repetition of early childhood experience ("familism, dependence, authority, wishful thinking, and magical practice," says Gordon Allport[15]), one cannot have a responsible attitude toward religion as a whole, because, as Allport points out, "To feel oneself meaningfully linked to the whole of Being is not possible before puberty. This fact helps explain the one-sided emphasis we encounter in many psychological discussions of religion." The psychoanalytic method cannot rightly understand the religious stand in experience, of a wholly committed self, and all that goes with it. By denying the autonomy and distinctive quality of empirical religious experience the psychoanalytic approach leaves itself no substance to work on.

If the view of projective religion conceives the world not as it is, but as a wish-world, in what sense does the concept of responsibility relate to projection? What is the relationship between wish projections and responsibility? With reference to God as reality there is no responsibility in Freud's theory because all our human notions of God are projections, and there is no Other as the culmination of these projections. Man cannot live by projections alone. The world of projection is the pure world of symbolism with no objective reference to reality. When religionists talk about symbols, symbols point to a reality beyond themselves; the case is not so in Freud. One is thus absolved from responsibility to the divine in the projective view of religion.

In the projective view of the deity, which is merely the objectification of one's wishes and desires, one is absolved from responsibility to God in the sense that it is an expression of a need. A deterministic framework prevents the person from revealing an attitude to responsibility. Unless one posits the assumption of freedom, it is meaningless to speak of genuine responsibility, for behavior becomes merely a habitual way of handling conflicts of anxiety by the institutionalized ego. One cannot help oneself; it is the expressions of one's need.

The projective view of religion creates an attitude of irresponsibility toward the self as well. The defensive behavior of the ego prevents it from functioning as a mature, free, and responsible self. This thesis is made explicit by Maurice Temerlin.[16] He puts all the defensive mechanisms of the ego under the category of projection, in that the ego uses these defensive maneuvers as techniques for avoiding the anxieties and choices of personal responsibility. It is easy to shrug off one's responsibility with the belief that in one's own eyes, at least, one is not responsible for repressed wishes. The defenses of the ego are means of avoiding responsibility. Although Freud's term "defense" is not primarily a moral category but a dynamic concept, the defensive behavior of the ego certainly has implications for morality. If one assumes that man's environment or history is primarily responsible for his fate, one is tacitly absolved from responsibility for his acts:

> Any defense, regardless of its explicit verbal content, seems based upon an implicit reference to personal responsibility which rarely is made explicit in a deterministic system. Even in the case of repression, the most basic and least verbal ego defense, there is presupposed an implicit experience of personal responsibility as the motive for repression. There is no need to repress, or to avoid in any way, experiences which do not define, reflect, or effect the self. Repression is not an abstract force, but a decision: "I refuse to think about it."

To view all the defense mechanisms of the ego as projections, as "responsibility-avoiding functions," has tremendous implications for selfhood. The self is thereby deprived of the character-building agency of decision making and responsibility. The affirmations of selfhood, of its identity, are lost in the process of reducing its responsibility and anxiety to the ego's defensive behavior. The defenses of the ego save the self from certain undesirable troubles and anxieties, but leave it weakened and unable to cope with the given realities of existence since man lacks the capacity for self-direction.

Ruth Munroe's attitude is typical of deterministic reactions to this problem. She states:

> Naturally, one might wish that the individual would appreciate realistically the total situation confronting him: his inner wishes and their possibilities for fulfillment in the external world. Unfortunately, this kind of insight is impossible for the infant and the young child.

What inevitably happens is that the child's ego forms its own concept of the dangers confronting it from without and from within and its own methods of handling them. These methods of handling conflict tend to become more or less firmly institutionalized as "mechanisms of defense." [17]

While this position is realistic (deterministic), it is morally inadequate from the standpoint of human behavior.

Gordon Allport speaks of a similar deficiency in the projective theory of religion, to wit, that in locating religion "exclusively in the defensive functions of the ego," rather than in the spiritual core of selfhood, the psychoanalytic view deprives man of the "forward intention" needed to relate himself to reality.[18] The self's functioning is absolved of responsibility and decision-making considerations in the process of fictionizing and wishful thinking. "Hence the developed personality will not fabricate his religion out of some emotional fragment but will seek a theory of Being in which all fragments are meaningfully ordered." [19]

Through projective religion modern man absolves himself from responsibility to the eternal, from responsibility to himself, and also from responsibility to the given nature of all primary religious assertions. This has been amply demonstrated in the paragraphs above—namely, that in reducing religious affirmations to projection and in identifying the two, one overlooks the empirical nature of given religious experiences. Empirically Freud's projective theory emanates an irresponsible attitude. If projection is primarily the realm of symbolism, devoid of objective reality and truth, then it is no longer possible to make empirical claims for religious experience. Religious experience, from this point of view, is an "illusion" rooted solely in one's personal desires and wishes.

Karl Marx performs a similar reduction of the religious phenomenon by the psychosociological approach. One is more apt to see the implications and consequences of the projective technique when it is fused with the highly charged symbolic notion of alienation.

Karl Marx's Debate with Religion   The theme of this section is alienation and responsibility in Marx's view of religion. To the extent that Marx is receptive to the projective theory of religion, via Ludwig Feuerbach's *Wesen des Christenthums*, our criticism of Freud is equally applicable to Marx. But to the extent that he was critical of Feuerbach's psychology of religion, special attention must be given to the sociophilosophic concept of alienation (*alienatio*) which is Marx's chief instrument for effecting a sociological reduction of the religious phenomenon.

Marx qualifies Feuerbach's psychological reduction of religious beliefs as having terrifying implications of degradation for man and society which Feuerbach did not suspect. However, both reductions, the psychological and the sociological, mark religion as an ineffectual instrument for the betterment of man and society. There is loss of individuality, community, and reality when religion is viewed as projection and alienation. Religion is replaced by a mechanistic collectivism, derived from a materialistic interpretation of history, which overcomes man's estrangement from existence. These needs come before a concern for God and religion. Since religion nurtures the life of illusion and fiction and creates societal disharmony and degradation, it is not a satisfactory concern of man; consequently its relation to culture must be terminated.

It is precisely at this point that traditional religion departs from Feuerbach, Freud, and Marx. Religion regards man's transcendence beyond nature, self, and community as an elevation of humanity in that humanity finds its final resting place in the eternal. In the eyes of Feuerbach and Marx this attitude of projection is a fictitious effort on the part of man to improve upon his earthly lot. As Nathan Rotenstreich views it: "In Marx man goes outside himself not to find himself at home in the divine realm, but to find himself as an object." [20] Consequently, the act of self-transcendence is the ground for alienation in that it brings about a loss of individuality and humanity. In Marx man is primarily responsible to himself and to the community, but not to God. To act out of a concern for religion is to act with utter irresponsibility, since it is tantamount to acting against one's humanity.

Friedrich Engels reflects this attitude of Marx in his work *Herrn Eugen Dührings Umwälzung der Wissenschaft* [Anti-Dühring], which views all religious affirmations as projections of sociological conditions. "All religion, however, is nothing but the phantastic reflection in men's minds of those external forces which control their daily life, a reflection in which the terrestrial forces assume the form of supernatural forces." [21] These projections are the product of man's theoretical intellect and reflect his imagination more than reality. "Religion is the table of contents [Marx declares] of the theoretical struggles of man." [22]

Religion is both a projected reflection of civil society and a compensation for its miseries. Since religion reflects the immediate and sentimental relation of man to nature and history, it is expected to maintain itself so long as men share these attitudes. It will continue to manifest itself in the form of "Die Phantasiegestalten" [fantasy figures] so long as men view their transcendent fictions as extraneous forces, as intruders from without, once they are mistakenly objictified by man. When they refrain from objectifying secondary causes (their own mental productions) as primary causes having a transcendental source, then religion will die a natural death, since there will be nothing more to reflect and project. This will take place when man knows the primary economic and material causes of his existence as being the true source of his humanity and society. Men will have to actively intercede to bring the relation of religion and culture to a halt. The necessity for this intercession becomes apparent when it is realized there is no transcendent realm which overcomes man's alienation.

Marx's sociological critique of religion rejects various solutions to the problem of man's alienation. The religious solution is rejected because it evaporates into a realm of transcendent fictions. The classical philosophical solution is rejected because it also evaporates into a realm of speculative fictions. The psychological solution, which in Feuerbach also includes the theoretical solution, is rejected, not because religion in its attempts to overcome alienation reaches a fictional end, but because projection does not take man beyond the realm of his humanity but rather injures the potentiality of his humanity "by way of a total perversion of the human position, turning the subject into its own object." [23] Marx gave quite an expanse to the process of alienation [*Entäusserung, Entfremdung*]. In capitalist society the product of man's work, and man's total environment, are alienated from man and his true culture. Man's labor exemplifies alienation in that it dominates man. Man is similarly alienated from his true essence or social being, from his generic human quality, from nature, from other men, and so on. Religion is thus in the class, with private property, of things which must be dispensed with if society is to reclaim a genuine culture. Marx contends that the various aspects of historical existence have turned man into a piece of property, and man has been objectivated to the point where the subject self has been lost. Religion has contributed to this lostness of human nature because there is no transcendent context in which man's alienation is overcome. Man's projections remain all too human, and they take on the character of "fetishistic fiction" and bespeak a historical reality. Consequently, only social action will convert the problem of man's alienation into a solution of man's well-being. When man has learned to command the economic and social forces of history, and culturally mold them to meet his deepest needs, only then will religion become dispensable to modern society.

Man has a responsibility to work his way out of religion to a true material existence. To the extent that religion remains a function of culture, as in "bourgeois culture," to that extent it is to be dubbed an irresponsible aspect of that culture. In fact, Marx declares, organized religion is at present an ineffectual instrument for molding culture, since its conservative nature merely protects the *status quo* of the existing class structure and leaves it impotent as an instrument of revolutionary change.

There are three plausible explanations of why Marx was preoccupied with the problem of man's alienation, and why he rejected other solutions to it, such as those of Feuerbach and Hegel. One is the gloomy view that sees alienation as degradation—a belief consequent upon the projective theory of religion. Marx was preoccupied with this theme very early in his career. He gave expression to it as early as 1844 in his *Kritik des Hegelschen Rechtsphilosophie*, where he states in the introduction that as far as he was concerned the critique of religion was final and complete.[24] He asserts that religion is "das Opium des Volks" which preoccupies men's minds with timeless abstractions and leads them to a realm of illusion. In that religion provides man with a distorted world view it is both an expression of the misery of the world and a protest against this misery. At any rate religion does not provide the real answer for man, but deepens the rift within his nature and adds to his progressive self-alienation. This dark picture of man's alienation, evoked specifically by the religious experience and its fictionlike function, is in part the motive for the radical action-centered solution which Marx offers to the problem of man's estrangement. This view of alienation is also endorsed by his work *Die heilige Familie*, in which he views religion as an inverted compensatory expression of man's values.

Another plausible explanation involves the youthful Marx's moral dedication to the wholeness of man and the dignity of human nature. Erich Fromm develops this humanistic naturalism of Marx in his book, *Marx's Concept of Man*. It is Fromm's contention that Marx fought religion because it fragmented man's nature and did not satisfy his true needs. Man's life is to be fulfilled in a true humanity and within the context of human nature, not in some transcendent realm. A revolutionary change had to be instituted in history to reverse the tide of man's transcendent perspective.[25] This position can be adhered to only if it is taken for granted that Marx was primarily interested in the individual, not in collective society; and that his socialism was not primarily scientific but was motivated by messianic or religious fervor.

The third plausible explanation for dispensing with religion and overcoming the process of self-alienation has its source in Marx's overall theory of man and history. This dialectical materialism denies to man the significance of all transcendent values. Here is basically an outside reason which motivates Marx in rejecting the religious experience. He endeavors to substitute a secular religion in its place. From the perspective of this presumed ideology Marx asserts that religious ideas have no real content and meaning in themselves, but rather have their source of meaning in the modes of economic production and within the material aspect of culture. The intrinsic content and meaning of religious affirmations are ruled out at the beginning of the inquiry on the grounds that dialectical materialism provides all the true values of man and society. Thus communism is the only available radical solution to man's estrangement from nature and history. It alone provides the proper stimulus for the rational society.

This third alternative, even more than the two explanations that precede it, requires taking the strongest possible measures against religion.

The solution is strongly encouraged by history. Since alienation is a historical event, it requires a historical solution. Since religion is the product of man's projective behavior, the manufacture of it must be curtailed by man's action.

If the above analysis is correct, there is no single solution to man's estrangement from existence in the writings of Karl Marx. Marx's opinion of alienation was not always the same, and his proposed solutions for overcoming it also varied. He viewed the problem of alienation from many perspectives, and the problem of its reconciliation varied from the early to the mature Marx. There is a shift away from a manifest interest in the human qualities of the individual in the mature Marx, who is intent on the realization of the collective rational society.

It matters very little whether alienation is viewed as an attitude by which man alienates something from himself or by which he alienates himself from something. Religion is in a similar fix with either alternative. In either case, what is involved is man's alienation from himself.[26] With respect to religion, alienation means that man is not at home when he is practicing religion, for he is outside the structure of his essential nature in taking part in such a fictional enterprise. What is basically at issue is man's separation, in existence, from his essence or original nature. Man's true essence is to be a creative, practical, and historical being. By trafficking with transcendent values man disrupts the unity idealized in his essential structure. To put it simply, man's capacity for self-transcendence is not part of the anatomy of human selfhood, as religionists claim it is.

Man's true essence turns out to be a bigger problem than the term "alienation." The Marxian attack on religion depends in part on the analysis of the essential structure of the human being. Man's essence is not the common denominator of what men represent universally; it is not something they all have in common. It is neither something fixed and eternal, nor the actually existing historical person. Man's true essence is his real "historically created possibility."[27] "That man alienates himself from his nature would mean, then, that man alienates himself from the realization of his historically created human possibilities."[28]

But the difficulties multiply at this point for the simple reason that possibilities are possibilities and not actualities. There is little difference in perspective whether one views the essence of selfhood from the standpoint of eternity as a timeless abstraction or as a historical abstraction in terms of the redundant phrase "real possibilities." Both views involve a preconceived notion of what man ought to be in his true humanity. Future possibilities are just as much mysteries as transcendent possibilities. Both views may claim what man will be (or ought to be) on the grounds of history, in terms of what he in fact is. Both sides can point to the essence of selfhood and each view may see its source in factuality. Marx does not have a monopoly on this issue, as the history of thought makes plain. Religion, too, has claimed that it promises "real possibilities" for living on the grounds of what one is. The techniques may differ slightly—how one derives its theme from actuality, and how the other interprets its claims. One view may go a little farther with its promises than the other. But essentially both views face the same irreducible issue, to wit, a transcendent impasse in not knowing what the essence of man is without some preconceived notion of what it ought to be. Religion usually faces this transcendental impasse in vertical perspective, and Marxism in the horizontal plane of historicity. To label religion an "inhuman possibility," as Marx says, bespeaks in effect an arbitrary and selective point of view. The fact remains that man's essence is construed by Marx from the perspective of his own preoccupations and historical studies. The negation of alienation rests on this preconceived notion of the essence of man.

I believe the choice Marx faces is limited. Either one's essence is given, in history (or outside it, which Marx denies) or else it is experimentally discovered. If it is scientifically and/or historically achieved (as Marx seems to think), then one does not know in advance where the inquiry and process will terminate. Such, at any rate, are the rules of experimentalism. Marx did not knowingly anticipate how Russian communism would fulfill the intentions of his thought. (He might even have changed his mind about the essence of man, had he seen this "real possibility" coming to fruition.) The case is more unpredictable with historical experimentalism than with scientific kinds because in the former existential man acts as an agent in the causal chain, creating patterns of unpredictableness.

The fact remains that Marx does not disclose the essence of man either historically or scientifically. Essence is a futuristic concept. With regard to the future, Marx is as much a prophet as is all mankind. If the essence of man is a creative achievement of history, Marx cannot have a predetermined pattern of the achievement; otherwise it is not a creative venture. He can be expectant about it, and vague about it, and even hopeful about its realization. But man's essence is not in the purview of man's cognitive faculty. Because Marx does not know what the essence of man is, and because the essence of selfhood is not given, he has no right to legislate religious experience out of human existence in such a cavalier fashion.

Although Marx uses history as a prop to support a definition of man in essential terms, the term "essence" remains a problem of Marxian scholarship, since it is a term with multiple meanings. The early Marx views the "essence of man" as a synonym for universal humanistic values; the mature Marx views authentic human nature as the sum of all the productive forces of history. From the latter perspective the process of socialization actually creates the essence of man. Aside from the problem of scholarship there is the practical problem of implementation of the historically normative image of man and culture.

From a more transcendent perspective the realization of vision by human techniques is a serious mistake. Reinhold Niebuhr, who used Marxian criticism in his attacks on American secular and religious liberalism, would charge the Marxian image of man with naturalistic naiveté:

> To say all this is really to confess that history of mankind is a personal tragedy; for the highest ideals which the individual may project are ideals which he can never realize in social and collective terms. If there is a law in our members which wars against the law that is in our minds as individuals, this is even more true when we think of society. Individuals set the goal for society but society itself must achieve the goal, and society is, and always will remain sub-human. The goal which a sensitive individual sets for society must therefore always be something which is a little outside and beyond history. Love may qualify the social struggle of history but it will never abolish it, and those who make the attempt to bring society under the dominion of perfect love will die on the cross. And those who behold the cross are quite right in seeing it as a revelation of the divine, of what man ought to be and cannot be, at least not so long as he is enmeshed in the processes of history.[29]

It is not necessary to agree with Niebuhr's metaphysical orientation, that society is necessarily subhuman and will remain so, nor does one have to agree with him that important human problems cannot be solved within the context of history or deny there is a measure of progress in history, in order to catch the significance of the above statement for Marx's normative vision of man.

Are the social techniques which Marx has devised adequate to the implementation of his image of man? Is the dialectical materialism sufficient philosophic ground to unite man's existence to its essence? Even if it is supposed that his vision is adequate, is the collective society Marx envisions equal to the task of implementing it? Does Marx have the answer that will take man beyond tragedy while man is enmeshed in its processes? History may provide the opportunity of viewing the faults both of the Marxian vision of man and its cultural implementation. That man's personal and social life should be shorn of its ethical and religious controls in order to make a contribution to humanity and history is yet to be tested by the facts of history. Both from the perspective of scholarship, and from that of the practical problems besetting the concept of man's essence, it seems clear that "essence" is as much a "historically transient phenomenon" as the concept of alienation. What Marx claims for man, that history promises to reunite man's existence with his essence, Christianity claims God alone can do, since He alone has unity of essence and existence, and man can be reconstituted in His image alone.

The fact remains that moralizing about man and culture, whether Christian or Marxian, is an inadequate approach to the problems of human existence. What is required is a better knowledge of the inner constitution of man and the structures of society, of their creative interchange, and of the relative potency both of the motives of man and of modern culture. Arthur O. Lovejoy put it well when he said: "The presentation of excellent ideals . . . has not been lacking; the question is, why they have so little efficacy in shaping the actual life of man." [30]

The Marxian critique of religion undercuts both the nature and function of religious assertions. On the other hand, Marx undercuts the value of religion for civilization, in that religion provides communal fiction, not communal solidarity, and also in the sense that it has the disvalue of being a disintegrating function in culture, rather than providing man with cultural integration. On the other hand, Marx attacks religious experience *per se.* Our second criticism of Marx has to do with the latter charge against religion.

Religious experience, like every other empirically identifiable phenomenon, has the double quality of being both independent as experience and of having a relation to other enterprises of human experience. As a distinguishable type of human experience, religious experience has an identifiable quality of its own, and fulfills a human need to be perfected. One might even call it the need for belongingness. Marx illegitimately denies this claim of religious experience to be itself, on the grounds of a presumed ideology that religious experience is derivative in nature and secondary in function, that it has no meaning and content of its own, but is merely the reflection of the productive forces of history.

On the other hand, religious experience intersects human experience of many other kinds because of its relation to other cultural enterprises. Marx does not do justice to this outside aspect of religious experience either. In secularizing religion and regarding it as a subdivision of politics and economics, as being derivable from their productive forces, he places it in the realm of fiction. Even the secularized version of religion is degraded in that the intersecting relations which it has with other human experience are dismissed as being fictitious in character. Like Freud, Marx knows religion from the outside and misconstrues even its secular content and meaning, as well as its inside meaning. One does not have to view his metaphysics from some transcendent vantage point to conclude that his reductionist naturalism is too narrow in method and theory to cope with the religious phenomenon.

Religion has the right to claim a distinctive experience, but not a distinctive knowledge. In my claim for understanding the distinctive claim of religious experience on empirical grounds, it is not my intent to make this claim unique. Since religious experience is both experience of autonomy and experience of relation, its claims to unique knowledge have to be related to the general approach to truth and justified by what it contributes to knowledge in general. If religion is related to human self-direction and purposiveness, it cannot be viewed simply as suprarational truth which is a focal point of illumination for truth in general. To the extent it is experience of relation, religious truth must relate to knowledge in general. To the extent it is autonomous, it cannot be replaced by politics, economics, or some other secular discipline: for religion alone can provide the goods which it yields to its adherents. Marx, we have concluded, ignores the experience of religion in both aspects of its claims in that he views the religious phenomenon reductively as purely psychosociological experience.

The human phenomena of projection and alienation, in their psychological and sociological forms, can be given more positive religious meanings. But this would entail a new effort to relate religion as a phenomenon to human self-direction and purposes in general. Alienation, for example, can be viewed as a doctrine of health, when viewed as an offense-mechanism of human self-direction. The self, in being drawn out of itself, by science or religion, comes to see itself in this projected posture, both in its subjective and objective creations, as the enlarged self. The self grows in self-direction by techniques of alienation and projects of self-direction. It is presumptuous to believe that Freud's view of projection and Marx's view of alienation are the only legitimate interpretations of the religious phenomenon. These same terms can be utilized for more positive perspectives of the *homo religiosus*, if we regard them as deliberate participants in the reconstruction of religious life. This endeavor to show how self-direction is the key both to the interpretation of science and religion must await further research and will be the concern of the author in the near future. The alleged inadequacies of religion may simply be the inadequate way in which projection and alienation have been interpreted by Marx and Freud, and how the two terms have been related to the religious phenomenon. But the modern debate between religion and culture continues, and we turn now to the writings of Niebuhr.

Reinhold Niebuhr's Debate with Modern Culture   In 1926 as he was debunking "Our Secular Civilization," Reinhold Niebuhr referred to society as being "sub-human"; in 1932, he changed the word into the phrase "immoral society." In his mature period (1960), Niebuhr had somewhat softened his polemic against culture:

> I never regarded secularism as the source of all modern evil, in the way some Christian apologists do. Christian humanism must make

common ground with the different kinds of secular humanism to protect the dignity of the person against the perils of dehumanization in an increasingly technical age. But it must also do so in contrite awareness that the secular humanist may be more honest and courageous in meeting large ethical problems than religious people. . . . Christians must be prompted to a more modest estimate of the role of piety in the ethical encounters of our society.[31]

Although Niebuhr's polemic against modern culture has become more humanistically oriented, the pattern of the debate remains largely the same. Modern culture is still breeding generations of men "who in their youth subsist on physical thrills, in their maturity glory in physical power and in their old age desire nothing more than physical comfort." [32]

The structure of the debate remains the same because the dichotomy between selfhood and culture remains on the same dialectical plane. Culture is still inferior to the individual because the self has a radical freedom and a transcendent capacity which culture does not possess. Man is next to God, and culture is next to man. The depth of man's total behavioral environment is neglected in Niebuhr's frantic attempts to relate modern man to an ancient God.

When one compares Niebuhr to someone like Karl Barth, Niebuhr looks good when he establishes some commerce between his transcendent perspective and the disciplines of modern culture. But such a comparison is deceiving; it is a comparison with someone in the same religious camp. When one compares Niebuhr to the behavioral sciences and their cumulative knowledge of man, there is an impasse which Niebuhr's transcendent perspective cannot overcome. Neibuhr's commerce with modern culture is "from without." The crucial issue for Christianity is being determined between man and his God, not between Christianity and its confrontation with the secular world.

In spite of the many volumes which Niebuhr writes on the theme of Christianity's need for commerce with culture, it is a secondary theme from the point of view of his transcendent outlook. Niebuhr attacked religious liberals on the grounds that with them the Christian faith was functioning in servitude to modern culture in deference to both the methods and theories of science. The position of Niebuhr's neo-orthodoxy is rather that modern culture, in its naturalized, humanized, and secularized forms, cannot function without an adequate transcendent perspective. Consequently, religion is superior to modern culture, since the latter cannot have meaningfulness apart from the transcendent values of the Hebrew-Christian Faith. In Niebuhr's view there is a uniqueness to this tradition that cannot be equaled by the totality of the cultural disciplines. The implications of this position for culture are ominous.

Niebuhr's position is restrictive of human culture in holding that culture does not possess the capacity for self-transcendence which the individual has. Transcendent ethical and religious values reside in the individual alone, since he is endowed with a higher level of self-consciousness than is manifest in culture. Man must tolerate the cultural order, but his true values come from his dialogue with God. It is precisely this superiority of the religious self-consciousness which Freud and Marx set out to destroy. From their psychological and sociological perspectives, any attempt to make the individual superior to his total behavioral environment to the point of spiritual exclusiveness (spirit is usually defined as otherness) would be a complete misrepresentation of the human predicament.

It was precisely this transcendent position that F. R. Cowell was attacking when he said that culture, too, can be a true source for transcendent values of another variety. It has the power to induce in man the attitude of "self-forgetfulness of the ordinary claims of self-interest, personal pleasure and private advantage" and enables a man to seek for new cultural meanings in truth, goodness, and beauty.[33] Cowell is not recommending the transcendental quality of culture as a substitute for the transcendental position of theology. He merely means devotedness to cultural pursuits in which the individual transcends the private claims of personal desires:

> Culture can be a powerful influence in men's lives without being developed into a substitute theology in that way. It can exercise its power anonymously, not in the name of culture, nor in the cause of truth, beauty or goodness, but by provoking patient devoted efforts to learn and think aright, make aright and to act aright in the many spheres of worthy human endeavors.[34]

For Cowell, culture is neither subhuman nor immoral nor something to be tolerated, but is permeated with a transcendental quality which it alone can contribute to human well-being. It is tributary to man's total behavioral environment. The transcendental quality within culture, in contrast to the Marxian materialistic quality in culture, is a collective human endeavor along lines not so much materialistic as symbolic. What primarily interests Cowell is not the category of individuality, but that of universality—the general quality generated by the universal experience of man in his search for happiness. Cowell wants what Kierkegaard and Marx both rejected in Hegel (for different reasons) and what Niebuhr rejects in Hegel—the importance of the general and the universal over the category of the individual. The individual's infinite outreach is absorbed in cultural pursuits, for Cowell. The dichotomy appears to be the following: the individual and God, culture and the universal. F. R. Cowell, along with Hegel, subscribes to the latter view.

In Niebuhr's position, it is required that man's relationship to nature, culture, and history, be as tenuous as possible, for what is essential to authentic Christian behavior is that the self establish strong ties with the eternal. This dialogue with the eternal is carried on in the medium of spirit, not in the medium of natural processes. Spirit in man is given a special motive power of its own, a directedness that is separate from the empirical self-directives of man. This extreme individualism, familiar in the writings of Kierkegaard, becomes the sole support of man's dignity and of his relationship to the eternal. Man is saved from the world of nature and of history by his unique ties to the infinite; he is saved by the special faculty of spirit, defined as otherness, and by the operations of self-transcendence, which is the primal characteristic of spirit. Consequently, man is disfranchised in his capacity for self-direction, and his total human situation—his ties to nature, culture, and history—is discounted for the religious dimension of existence.

Religion, it appears, is no longer functioning as a process related to total human self-direction; it is functioning with a directedness of its own, to whose steering man must submit and give up a portion of human self-direction in ultimate commitment to the singular relationship between man and God. The religious consciousness has a superintendency over the human consciousness in directive powers. Man capitulates his powers of self-direction to the directive agency of spirit, which has more in common with divinity than with man. This is extreme religious individualism that supplants human self-direction and thus berates the individual with natural self-direction in his total behavioral environment. Cowell speaks to this condition, making reference to another work, Christopher Dawson's, *Religion and Culture*: "It is difficult to accept such a generalization. The rude forefathers of the hamlet, the crusaders who fought for the Holy Land, the Swiss mobs who followed Calvin, the Scottish mobs who were swayed by John Knox, were all religious, but it is difficult to believe that their level of consciousness was higher, more developed or superior to that, say, of merely cultivated characters such as Cicero, Voltaire, David Hume or Bernard Shaw." [35]

The question might well be raised, as it was in fact raised by D. W. Ferm, whether Christianity can continue its main emphasis on uniqueness and particularity without losing its universal appeal and without endangering its power to be of service in the coming one-world community.[36] Can Christianity maintain its tenuous relationship to nature and culture in its doctrine of extreme individualism and remain a significant factor in that culture? I have touched on this problem in my second criticism of Marx, to the effect that the independence of the individual's religious experience cannot possibly entail his uniqueness apart from his total behavioral environment. This attitude cuts off all possible communication with modern culture. If the Christian faith has contributed creatively to society in the past with its tense unity of the eternal and the temporal, which enabled it to hold an extreme individualism by attributing the eternal dimension to the individual, it happened only because previous centuries were not aware of the structuring of society and the individual as the modern mind has come to see it. I am doubtful whether the same emphasis of the Christian faith will produce as creative an interchange with the world orientation of the present. The modern mind wants a comprehensive, intelligible, and convincing presentation of religion, not one which is embarrassing to his intellect and degrading to his cultural disciplines.

Niebuhr has difficulty pressing his individualism even within the tradition of his own faith. He has been criticized by Daniel D. Williams, a neo-liberal theologian, for not advocating a message of redemption in the Church and within the context of history, and for neglecting the community. If religious experience is a matter of relations as well as an autonomous experience, the claims of uniqueness cannot be made on its behalf. The claim of a unique religious experience does not necessitate making a similar claim for unique knowledge. The uniqueness of the experience comes to be generally known as part of human knowledge.

Niebuhr's substitute—the integrity of the human spirit for the integrity of the total behavioral environment and for an integral view of culture—is a poor substitute indeed. It betrays the total personality of man, in its total behavioral environment, to a facet of the human personality, to the spiritual side of selfhood. This kind of abstractionism is dangerous in the atmospheric current of modern culture: it encourages a schizophrenic attitude on the part of the believers in that particular tradition and makes them ineffectual workers in the modern setting. Spiritual inwardness does not show the noiseless life Niebuhr attributes to it. Spirit is something which traffics with the world, not in some discarnate I-Thou relationship, but through concrete individuals who are absorbed in a total behavioral complex in which they are constrained to operate. The point is that culture is internalized within the self even at the highest levels of self-consciousness, and the individual's spiritual life is, to that extent at least, a certain level of cultural development, too, and not a unique or distinctive kind of self-consciousness operating in a vacuum through acts of self-transcendence.

The basic question in Niebuhr's debate with modern culture is the question of standards. His dialectical evaluation of the individual and culture puts the weight on the side of the individual in terms of quality, on the side of culture in terms of quantity. Culture merely outweighs the individual as an "omnipotent variable." It is precisely this dialectical nimbleness that the modern cultural disciplines will not subscribe to. They reject the distinction in standards between the qualitied transcendent standard and the quantitive one. To be more specific, Niebuhr's position sets up an extranatural standard for judging human behavior, and consequently, human behavior is found wanting in a peculiar way. But much is also wanting in the transcendent standard, in the perspective of the cultural disciplines; it, too, has limitations and some definite perils. The

real issue is between the extranatural standard for judging human behavior and naturalistic and humanistic modes of evaluating man's behavior.
Even if the transcendent standard were properly employed to measure the
condition of human nature, even then it would demand more of man than
his human condition alone could supply. Niebuhr's method disrupts the
organic and cultural unity of man for the sake of transcendent unity. The
dialectical relationship existing between man and God, on the one hand,
and man, nature, and culture (or simply between culture and personality),
favors more the insulation of the individual from his total behavioral environment than his connections with it. Man and culture are not equi-
pollent terms, as I indicated above. Man has a vertical dimension which
makes him superior to culture. Although man finds both fulfillment and
frustration in community, the fulfillments are limited and provisional compared with the frustrations. The dialectics has cut man off from culture to
such an extent that man's attitude to it can, even at best, be only hesitant
and schizophrenic, never wholehearted. The individual's hopes are pinned
to naked aspiration rather than to promised fulfillments in community.

The Challenge of Rapid Cultural Change What are the problems of
rapid social change for the
current debate between science and religion? The basic issue between
religion and culture is the individual and his freedom. Freud and Marx,
although they appear as antagonists of religion, have made some contributions to its study. Freud narrates the story of religion as having roots
in the psychological constitution of man and says, in effect, that religion
cannot be understood apart from human psychological needs. Marx narrates the story of religion as having roots in the cultural conditions of
existence and says, in effect, that religion cannot be understood apart from
the cultural order in which it arises. Niebuhr, who appears as an antago-
nist of modern culture, narrates the story of religion in its more traditional
garb and states, in effect, that modern man cannot understand his cultural
order apart from its spiritual and ideational roots. Freud and Marx emphasized the biosocial and psychosocial structures of selfhood almost to the
exclusion of freedom. Niebuhr has emphasized the freedom of man, almost to the exclusion of his biological, psychological, and social inheritance. The behavioral sciences have improved upon Freud and Marx, but
they are still operating in the naturalistic tradition. They claim that man
has freedom, but that he has this freedom only within the structures of
his inheritance. Niebuhr continues as the spokesman for the religious traditions and claims that man has a freedom beyond the structures of his
total behavioral environment. The issue of the relation between religion
and culture depends on the resolution of this conflict: freedom within
structure and freedom beyond structure. Religion, it would seem, depends
on the amount and kind of freedom man possesses. The cultural disciplines

are not so readily inclined to give man the kind of freedom that will enable him to go beyond experience in transcendent acts and thoughts, for they do not have the methods and techniques for tracing and observing man at that transcendent distance. The religious disciplines, on the other hand, do not have a sufficient interest in man in temporal depth, and do not care to study man in his relatedness to nature and culture. Now that the behavioral sciences admit some measure of freedom within the structure of man and culture, and religious traditions admit having some commerce with the human disciplines, it is safe to assume the beginnings of a new debate between religion and modern culture. The meeting ground for the debate is between religion and the behavioral sciences.

By including Freud and Marx in this chapter, I am not advocating a conflict between religion and culture. By including Niebuhr in my discussion I am not advocating tension between culture and religion. Nor am I advocating harmony between religion and culture in general. It is premature to talk effectively of harmony between religion, science, and culture. Nor am I attempting to say that culture and religion are interrelated terms, as T. S. Eliot states in his work, *Notes Toward a Definition of Culture*. My intention is merely to indicate that there have been enough changes in the cultural disciplines and in the realm of theology to warrant another attempt at negotiations. History is replete with examples where little communication has taken place between religion and culture on an equal footing. The beginnings of a new dialogue are possible now between religion and culture if the matter is approached on the intellectual level of communication. The existential movement in theology will hold up this process of communication to some extent because it advertises personal encounter at the expense of knowledge of the experience, and its ordering in the general process of human experience. This attitude will create an attitude rather of arrogance and intolerance than of understanding. Positivism in the behavioral sciences will have a similar negative impact on the communication. This attitude creates an arrogance and an intolerance toward effective communication. Anything that will create an imbalance in the modern world, anything that perpetuates the schizophrenic attitude in cultural and religious pursuits ought to be doubly scrutinized in the perspective of the health problem of modern culture.

In presenting the tradition of Freud, Marx, and the recent behavioral sciences it is necessary to elaborate on the theme how they have come to accept the value of human freedom within the structures of human existence. The most conspicuous example of this theme is discoverable in cultural anthropology. Since the 1930's the anthropologists have been concerned with the topic of individual variation in man's behavioral environment. They assign a certain measure of freedom and uniqueness to the personality which was not adequately presented by older forms of cultural determinism. The individual is regarded as more than a passive recipient of cultural impressions, since he is viewed as playing a more creative role as agent in the cultural matrix. While typological studies of behavior are still emphasized, such as the patterned, the modal, and the normal types in behavior, individual variations are coming more and more to the attention of the theorists. Personal variations are significant in the areas of perception, selectivity, and subjective choices of value. One expects the present-day anthropologist to pay more attention to the interplay of personal and interpersonal relationships, their creative interchange in the sociocultural dimensions of the personality-culture complex. The individual is still seen primarily through the primary complex of culture, but the emphasis on individual variation within that complex has achieved a certain amount of new emphasis. The individual is viewed as a more responsible agent of evolving processes within culture; his participation makes a difference in that complex.

Social anthropologists now also emphasize individual variations in their analysis of status and role dimensions of experience, in the realm of symbolic communication, and within interpersonal relationships. Although it is recognized that training in culture places significant limitations on individual uniqueness (understood as autonomy), it is equally recognized that the individual emerges from these studies somewhat "idiosyncratic." Whether social anthropology begins its study with the varying individual and then moves toward the analysis of the typological aspects of behavior, as Felix M. Keesing holds, or whether culture is posited as the primary independent variable, and the culture-personality complex is studied from this perspective, as Marvin K. Opler holds, does not so much matter. What matters is that from both points of view, the stress is on individual variation. This gives a measure of acceptability to the idea that the individual has some limited autonomy and freedom within the cultural matrix; that man is free within a certain structure in his total behavioral environment.

There is, then, a new focus on the individual, but not at the expense of the sociocultural dimensions of experience. Although man's unique endowments are increasingly coming to be recognized, man's distinctive traits are not permitted to stand off by themselves. The individual as a participant in culture is more than interacting, and the shaping influences of this interaction are as significant as the idiosyncratic actions of the person involved in the cultural matrix.

This emphasis on individual variation and limited freedom within the cultural matrix is also emphasized in other behavioral sciences, in psychology and social psychology, psychiatry and social psychiatry, and to a certain extent in sociology. The upshot is that individual variation does contribute to the individual a certain measure of freedom and uniqueness, but that his autonomy is to an extent governed by the structure in which he operates. What is unique about man is not his distinctive spirit, but the total human behavioral environment. Nature and culture are included as part of the unique human situation which makes man discontinuous as well as continuous with the lower kingdom of animals. There are glimpses of self-determinate activity on the part of the individual in his relations with nature and culture. Culture as a pan-deterministic framework is no longer the dominant emphasis in the behavioral and social sciences. Man has a measure of dignity within the structures in which he operates. The method most instrumental in bringing about these changes in the various disciplines we call behavioral sciences has been antireductionist in nature and intent. Gordon Allport in the field of psychology, for example, has been in vital collaboration with existentialist and personalistic philosophies as a practicing psychologist, in helping to effect some of the shifts toward personality in his discipline.

Although emphasis on individual variation and the limited uniqueness of the total human situation does not indicate a rapprochement with religion, it provides a talking point which should encourage effective communication between religion and modern culture. No intelligible communication is possible between the two disciplines on the grounds of Freud or Marx or Niebuhr. Their systems merely pave the way for the possibility of effective communication. When either religion or culture is mutilated by a method of analysis there is little hope for effective communication. Freud and Marx have claimed that religion obscures man's image in existence. Niebuhr has claimed that Freud, Marx, and the modern behavioral sciences have obscured the image of man in existence. Niebuhr's claim is that there has been a loss of individuality and man's title to freedom in the evaluations of man in the behavioral sciences. This, we have seen, is not an accurate evaluation of the situation, since there has been ample evidence of stress in these disciplines on individual variation and on a measure of individual freedom within the structures of man's existence. It is unfortunate that Niebuhr has used the "badge of individuality" as a threat to the sciences, particularly so, since the sciences do not make individuality the final criterion either of their methods or their conclusions.

When Niebuhr charges the modern sciences with threatening to destroy man's individuality he is using man and religion as a badge of distinction and privilege. He is saying, in effect, that the only important thing about man is his spiritual nature, of which religion alone can be the true custodian. It is alleged by him that the true equivalent of the individual is the transcendent ego, which is free above and beyond the limitations of biosocial structures. The individual's privileged status (as spirit, as otherness) is supported by religious institutions, and its claim to distinction is its relationship to the eternal. When so much is claimed for this somewhat discarnate individual, whose selfhood transcends, fulfills, and negates all the other cultural enterprises, communication comes to an impasse between religion and culture. To the extent that Niebuhr's theory of the individual is a claim to distinction and privilege, to that extent it is irrelevant to the conclusions of science, and it lessens the possibilities of rapprochement with science.

What is to be said of Niebuhr's theme that the individual has a freedom above and beyond reason, nature, culture, and his own biosocial structure? No one has exploited the quality of individual freedom as much as Niebuhr. His role as a protagonist for man's free will makes him the spokesman for numerous religious traditions. The individual has a radical freedom with a locus in his subjectivity and a source and destiny in the divine. The self, in its capacity for self-transcendence, is above its functions and has a unity which transcends the organic unity of its functions. What concerns Niebuhr is the totality, independence, and the spirituality of the self. Even if the sciences progress in their study of man, by expanding in wider contexts, by instituting greater conceptual schemes, and even by surmounting the present categories, methods, and techniques, there is little hope they can meet the stringent requirements of Niebuhr's construct of the self. The spiritual individual, as Niebuhr defines him, is qualitatively inaccessible to any kind of orderly inquiry into human nature. The final characterization of man as radically free and as self-transcendent removes the self completely beyond the competence of any human mode of knowing. Man, in his transcendent detachedness, has a poetic, dramatic, and spiritual license to defy any systematic evaluation of the nature and function of the self. The self is free beyond the norms of rationality and has interests, loyalties, and commitments beyond the rules and principles of logic. In fact, man is like God, transcendent to "any conceivable order." The final majesty of man is the self's ability and freedom to be over the structures of its existence.

The value of Niebuhr's writings in the current debate between religion and modern culture, on the obscure image of man in existence, lies precisely in focusing on the place of the individual in religion, science, and society. But the focus, as we have indicated, is out of perspective, and man's place remains insecure in the modern debate. Although the concept of man's radical freedom has long been banished from the disciplines of science, man refuses to be legislated out of existence by his own objective creations. His subjective creations rebel at the thought of it. His personal preoccupations and self-directives are at stake in this game. To be sure, Niebuhr has reactivated man's concern for himself, for the self's interior life and its acts of self-will and self-transcendence. But he has achieved this at the cost of human self-direction. His concern for the place of the individual in modern life is legitimate, but his focus on man is out of perspective. By relating man to the special directive agency of the spirit, Niebuhr can no longer have a whole view of man in terms of self-direction. Man's spiritual direction conflicts with his empirical self-directives; he has separated the religious directives from human self-direction and left us with the traditional problem of man's relation to the infinite.

Whether there is effective communication between religion and modern society on the theory of man depends on the solution we give to the problem of relating the directives of the spirit to human self-direction. How can we relate religion more honestly to human self-direction? If it is possible to harmonize freedom within structure to freedom beyond structure, or the directive agency of spirit with human self-direction, then, perhaps, history will have gained a new perspective on the works of Freud, Marx, and Niebuhr. Freud and Marx have rebelled against religion because it deprives man of self-direction, through projection and alienation, even though their naturalistic reductionism prevented them from seeing the proper significance of human self-direction. Niebuhr has shortsightedly misplaced human self-direction in the special domain of the spirit which has a directive agency of its own. If men as divergent as Socrates, Isaiah, and St. Paul can say, in effect, "Come, let us reason together," the poet's hope can be shared by the present generation of men, "till hope creates from its own wreck the thing it contemplates." [37]

Recall the pointed dialogue between Odysseus, the self-willed solitary, and the old man in the epigraph at the beginning of Part One. The unusual display of dialectical skill stimulates the reader precisely because it speaks the language of every man who has studied the anatomy of selfhood. But man does not think or live by dialects alone. The dialogue sets up a false dichotomy between man as a determined creature and man as the defiant one, who in his freedom dares even to defy his biosocial structures and functions. The polarity is too distant to be comforting to us and too embarrassing to the intellect. We have attempted in this chapter to narrow the gap between man and himself, and between man and God. We have done this by suggesting that the key to effective communication between science and culture, on the one hand, and religion on the other, depends on finding a solution to man's freedom beyond structure and man's freedom within structure, or between the special directives of the spirit and man's total empirical self-directives. It appears that the humanistically oriented sciences have recently made some concessions and revealed some modifications of man's freedom in structure; they have shown concern for the dimension of personal being, as man relates to nature and history. Religion, however, remains more imperial in its design by adhering to the orthodox stand of man's freedom beyond structure, of saying that spirit has a right to its own directive agency, contrary to man's empirical self-directives. The difference between man's biosocial freedom and religious freedom must be modified and adjusted before effective communication can exist between the disciplines of culture and religion. What we regard as the normative vision of man can in our day no longer exclude man's biosocial and psychosocial inheritance.

The achievement of an authentic communication between religion and science on the theory of man in an advanced technological age requires a redefinition of directive agency in human reality. This would require redefining freedom beyond structure and freedom within structure in such a way that man's potentiality for self-direction is seen in a radically new light. How does science relate to human self-direction? How is self-direction viewed in terms of these objective creations of science? How do we regard religious assertions in the light of the language of self-direction? How does self-direction assert itself in these subjective creations of man? What is needed is a more comprehensive view of human purpose, if we are to create effective communication between science and religion, and this means readjustment between the claims of man in his freedom beyond structure and his claims regarding freedom within structure.

The act of proud defiance, exemplified in the Odyssean fantasy, which had the effect of transporting Odysseus from the plane of materiality to that of pure spirit, is a problem that belongs to the past. We must look forward to more meaningful solutions of human self-direction as man seeks to enlarge his life by scientific study, by religious worship, and by philosophical perspectives. The "turn from flesh and bone into pure spirit, lightning, joy, and deeds," [38] is too sharp a turn, and an unsteady one at that, since man has had little of his own energy to contribute to the turn in his capacity of self-direction. For this reason, and others which the reader may himself surmise, it is imperative to reduce the polarity between spirit and matter to more manageable proportions in order to expedite the current debate between religion, science and society. We have stated the need to make other turns on the road to a resolution of the problem of the two freedoms, and the two directives, those of the spirit and those of man. In stating the problem we have gained much. The next task is to facilitate effective communication between these opposing disciplines, between the objective and the subjective creations of man, in his endeavors to enlarge the meaning of his existence through self-direction and purposive living. The more we steer a course of action away from a religion that is unacceptable to cultural disciplines and away from a culture that is unacceptable to religion, the more the need to solve the issue of the two freedoms and the two directives will become apparent, and the more will the distance of the artificial polarity be reduced to manageable size and to more realistic proximity. The new turns in the road may eventually force us to work out a new harmony between projection, alienation, and the autonomy of man, more related to the reality of human self-direction.[39]

1 Bernard Phillips (ed.), *The Essentials of Zen Buddhism*, New York, Dutton, 1962, pp. 392, 415-91. An anthology of the writings of Daisets T. Suzuki.

2 Henry P. Van Dusen, *The Vindication of Liberal Theology*, New York, Scribner's, 1963, "Liberal Theology Reassessed."

3 G. L. Abernathy and T. A. Langford (eds.), *Philosophy of Religion*, New York, Macmillan, 1962, p. 91.

4 *Ibid.*, p. 33.

5 Ernest Jones, *The Life and Works of Sigmund Freud*, Vol. III, New York, Basic Books, 1957, pp. 352-3.

6 L. E. Abt and L. Bellak (eds.), *Projective Psychology*, New York, Knopf, 1950, pp. 7-33.

7 *Ibid.*, p. 8.

8 *Ibid.*, p. 10.

9 *Ibid.*, p. 13.

10 S. Freud, *The Future of an Illusion*, New York, Doubleday, p. 34.

11 *Ibid.*, p. 51.

12 Edwin B. Holt, *The Freudian Wish*, New York, Holt, 1915, pp. 3-4. The ego, as the projected construct of the larger construct of the personality, has additional projections within its sphere of influence. The ego's entire set of mechanisms of defense may be viewed as one such projection.

13 David E. Trueblood, *Philosophy of Religion*, New York, Harper, 1957, pp. 186 ff.

14 Abernathy and Langford, *op. cit.*, p. 67.

15 Gordon W. Allport, *Becoming*, New Haven, Yale University Press, 1955, pp. 94-95.

16 Maurice Kahn Temerlin, "On Choice and Responsibility in a Humanistic Psychotherapy," *Journal of Humanistic Psychology*, Spring, 1963.

17 Ruth L. Munroe, *Schools of Psychoanalytic Thought*, New York, Holt, 1955, p. 91.

18 Allport, *op. cit.*, p. 96.

19 *Ibid.*, p. 94.

20 Nathan Rotenstreich, "On the Ecstatic Sources of the Concept of 'Alienation'," *Review of Metaphysics*, March 1963, pp. 550-55.

21 Institut für Marxismus-Leninismus, *Marx-Engels Werke*, Vol. 20, Berlin, Dietz Verlag, 1962, p. 294. "Nun ist alle Religion nichts andres als die phantastische Widerspiegelung, in den Köpten der Menschen, derjenigen äussern Mächte, die ihr alltägliches Dasein beherrschen, eine Widerspiegelung, in der die irdischen Mächte die Form von überirdischen annehmen."

22 Eugene Kamenka, *The Ethical Foundations of Marxism*, London, Routledge and Kegan Paul, 1962, p. 62.

23 Rotenstreich, *op. cit.*, p. 555.

24 *Marx-Engels Werke*, Vol. I, pp. 378, 378-91.

25 Erich Fromm, *Marx's Concept of Man*, New York, Frederick Ungar Publishing Co., 1961. It is Fromm's contention that the early humanistic naturalism of Marx is consistent with the later Marxian emphasis on mechanistic collectivism.

26 Gajo Petrovic, "Marx's Theory of Alienation," *Philosophy and Phenomenological Research*, Vol. XXIII, No. 3, March 1963, pp. 421, 419-426.

27 *Ibid.*, p. 422.
28 *Ibid.*, p. 422.
29 H. E. Fey and M. Frakes (eds.), *The Christian Century Reader*, New York, Association Press, 1962, p. 227.
30 Arthur O. Lovejoy, *Reflections on Human Nature*, Baltimore, The Johns Hopkins Press, 1961, pp. 9 ff.
31 Reinhold Niebuhr, "The Quality of Our Lives," *The Christian Century*, May 11, 1960, pp. 568-72. In 1926 he blamed the increasing secularization and naturalization of society on the modern advance of science and the impotence of Protestantism. This article is in Fey and Frakes, *The Christian Century Reader*, pp. 22-28.
32 Fey and Frakes, *op. cit.*, p. 24.
33 F. R. Cowell, *Culture in Private and Public Life*, New York, Frederick A. Praeger, 1959, p. 89.
34 *Ibid.*, p. 89.
35 *Ibid.*, p. 93.
36 D. W. Ferm, "The Road Ahead in Religion," *The Christian Century*, May 25, 1960, pp. 636-39.
37 Shelley, *Prometheus Unbound*, end of Act IV.
38 Nikos Kazantzakis, *The Odyssey: A Modern Sequel*, New York, Simon & Schuster, 1958, p. 714.
39 Cf. my book, *Escape from Destiny: Self-Directive Theory of Man and Culture*, Springfield, Ill., Charles C Thomas, 1966. This volume is an attempt to view self-direction as the proto-attitude of human purposive behavior, redefined as a term of interaction. The perspective of the author is to view philosophy as a third force, a new movement of thought making its way between naturalistic and transcendental schools of thought.

QUESTIONS

1 What is the key to new negotiations between religion and science? Specify the course along which a "creative interchange" can take place between the two disciplines.
2 Summarize the Freudian position on projective religion and offer your own defense or critique of this view.
3 Summarize the Marxian view of "alienation" and offer your own defense and/or critique of this view.
4 Summarize Niebuhr's theory of man and offer a secular, cultural, naturalistic critique of the concept of self-transcendence.
5 List some objectionable solutions to the problem of relating religion to culture, and state the reasons why they are objectionable to you.

SUGGESTED READINGS

F. R. Cowell, *Culture in Private and Public Life*, New York, Praeger, 1959.
Merle Curti, *The Social Ideas of American Educators*, Paterson, N. J., Pageant Books, 1959.
William Horosz, *Escape from Destiny: Self-Directive Theory of Man and Culture*, Springfield Ill., Charles C Thomas, 1966.
H. D. Lewis, *Our Experience of God*, George Allen, Ltd., 1959.
M. K. Opler, *Culture, Psychiatry and Human Values*, Springfield, Ill., Charles C Thomas, 1956.

12 *Oliver L. Reiser*

Religion from the Standpoint of a Scientific Humanism

The Bewitchments of Language While the word "religion" is a single term, the various phenomena it supposedly describes are numerous and complex. Depending on what one chooses to isolate for study, "religion" can refer to rituals, belief systems, kinships, magical cults, shaman and priestly activities, ceremonial calendars, or states of mind called the "religious experience" (to keep the list short). All of these overlap, though they differ too; but what aspect is considered most important depends on whether one approaches the field from the viewpoint of anthropology or of psychology; whether one is chiefly interested in the cognitive (intellectual) or in the emotive aspects, and so on.

The problem of the nature of religion and its relations to science and philosophy can be discussed profitably only in the light of one's definition of these key terms. Since in the present essay I shall discuss the nature, functions, and future of religion from the standpoint of a "naturalistic humanism," it will be necessary to give definitions of these terms as we proceed. (I use the terms "naturalistic humanism" and "scientific humanism" interchangeably. This is not the "literary humanism" of Paul Elmer More. Still less is it the "true humanism" of Jacques Maritain. Historically it resembles more "renaissance humanism"—with scientific methodology and social reform as added components. Because my own variety of humanism is pantheistic in its cosmology—something not congenial to the agnostic or atheistic inclinations of some contemporary humanists— I have in recent years adopted the term "cosmic humanism" to designate this variant of the theme.)

Most of us are constantly using terms like "religion," "democracy," "communism," tossing them around like coin of the realm, and therefore tend to assume that we are all using these words in pretty much the same sense. But a little study of the bewitchments of language (as the "ordinary language analysis" school terms them) teaches the alert student that this "linguistic naiveté" must be replaced by a more "sophisticated" approach, if we are to have clarity of thought.

The importance of definition in this instance is illustrated by the following episode. Not long ago there was a discussion via the radio in which the panelists talked about the "future of religion." Toward the end of this half-hour program it became obvious that the discussants were not going to be able to agree on the "future of religion"—whether indeed it had a future. Quite properly one panelist suggested that since apparently the word did not mean the same thing to the various participants, perhaps each member of the panel should state how he was using the term. But at this stage all their time had been used up, and the thing they should have done at the outset was never even begun. Another illustration of the complexity of the manifestations of "religions" and resulting vagueness of meaning for the term is provided by the story of the graduate student in one of our great universities. He "earned" a master's degree by cataloging in his thesis the various definitions of religion that appear in the literature, stopping when he had culled fifty definitions. A cynic might point out that if this had been a doctoral dissertation, the student could have gone on with his "research" and collected one hundred definitions.

One might surmise that a major conclusion to result from an adequate discussion of the future of religion would be this: if one employs a narrow and rigid definition, then religion in its organized and institutionalized forms may have little future; but if one recognizes that religion is a dynamic thing capable of flexibility, it may have a future as bright as that of the human race—indeed, it might even help light the way to this uncertain world of tomorrow.

The "Essence" of Religion   As an example of the use of the broader definition, we think of the effort of Professor H. R. Mussey to show that Russian Communism, especially in its first decade, fulfilled the requirements of a religion. Similarly, Harry Emerson Fosdick once declared that Nazism is (was) a religion, though a bad one. Using a broad definition, it is possible to show that as long as men earnestly believe anything, religion will remain a fact of society. By carrying this procedure further, one can also prove—as indeed Albert Einstein once proposed—that science itself could serve as the religion of the devoted scientist.[1] If this is admitted, even atheism can become a religion—the religion of those who passionately deny the existence of the accepted gods of others. The historical fact that the term "atheist" was first applied by the Romans to the Christians (Lucian slurringly puts Epicureans, atheists, and Christians into one class), only in turn to be applied later on by the Christians to the atheistic unbelievers in the God of Christianity, confirms this broad use of the term, i.e., its possible dissociation from theism.

It is true that this inclusive meaning of the term "religion" violates those popular definitions which associate religion with a necessary belief in a god (monotheism) or in many gods (polytheism). However, the *New Century Dictionary* defines religion as the "recognition on the part of man of a controlling, superhuman power entitled to reverence and worship." If this "superhuman power" is not limited to a personalized (anthropomorphic) entity, but is broad enough to include the more abstractly conceived realities such as the universal lawfulness of nature of the pantheists and the "infinite eternal energy" of Herbert Spencer, there is no difficulty in accepting the *New Century Dictionary* definition. This dictionary meaning fits in with the broad interpretation and does no violence to semantic principles.

The importance of the problem of definition in determining the character of one's conclusions was brought out in an interesting manner when *Life* magazine in an article on the Huxley brothers[2] described Julian Huxley as "an atheist" and "a materialist, denying the need for religion or God." Commenting on the article,[3] Dr. Charles Francis Potter, founder of the First Humanist Society of New York, accused the writer of a *non sequitur*. Dr. Potter agreed that Julian Huxley does deny the need for God, but stated that the assertion that Dr. Huxley therefore denies the need for religion is evidently based on the false assumption that one must believe in God to have a religion. This, Dr. Potter pointed out, is false, for any student of comparative religion knows that there have been and are many nontheistic religions.

To prove that Julian Huxley is not opposed to religion, Dr. Potter quoted from Huxley's *Man Stands Alone* a passage in which Sir Julian affirms that "religion to continue as an element of first-rate importance in the life of the community, must drop the idea of God." This is a significant statement from a scientist who formerly served as Director General of the United Nations Educational, Scientific and Cultural Organization (UNESCO). The attitude thus exemplified is entirely in accord with what John Dewey in his book on *The Common Faith* calls the "religious spirit." Doubtless Dr. Potter is correct in regarding Huxley and Dewey as "religious humanists"; both are also well described as "scientific humanists." In passing, it is worth noting that Sir Julian reaffirms the need for a nontheistic (atheistic) religion in his chapter (by the same title) in the symposium, *The Humanist Frame* (1961).

From all this it appears that we face a dilemma: if our definition is too narrow, we exclude the possibilities for those novel developments which give new life to old forms; and if our definition is so broad that it includes everything (so that, for example, one can say that "golf is his religion"), it means nothing specific and therefore is practically useless.

If in a mood of optimism one hopes to resolve this problem of fixing the "essence" of religion through a "semantic" approach, it should be remembered that there are *two* kinds of semantics, namely, *descriptive semantics*, such as ordinary language analysis, and *creative semantics*, which is the reinterpretation or redefinition of terms in the light of new circumstances. One must preserve some measure of historical continuity in the use of words; but room must also be provided to allow for new conceptions, when this seems called for. For the present, however, it seems appropriate to stick to the broad *New Century Dictionary* definition, as given above.

The Motivations of Religion Religions have persisted for so long because they meet human needs. Man is a rational animal, more or less, and a social creature too, and as such has certain fundamental needs. As a member of the animal kingdom man has needs that characterize all living creatures: needs for food, shelter, defense against enemies, reproduction of the species, and the like. But as a member of the genus *Homo*, man has additional intellectual and emotional needs which distinguish him from other, subhuman animals. It is this second class of needs which is responsible for man's religions, his philosophies, his arts, and his sciences.

As a creature with intelligence—with curiosity and the ability to understand—man has need of a theory of the world in which he lives, a theory of nature and the forces that control the universe, and how he may adjust to these forces and use them for his benefit. This may be called a world view, a cosmology. As a member of a human social group, man has an additional need—the need for a moral code, a way of life, a theory of ethics.

Note that religion and philosophy serve the same psychological functions or purposes in human nature—they satisfy these two common needs of mankind. A religion gives a world view and a way of life, and a philosophy does the same. The difference is in the way you come by them. The individual thinks out his philosophy, but he is born into his religion and accepts it largely on faith.

Anthropologists inform us that only human individuals build cultures;

subhuman beings do not create cultures. Many social scientists also state that all (or at any rate most) human societies exhibit practices, beliefs, forms of cultural behavior that are "religious." Starting with these facts, the psychologists will then point out the obvious conclusion: behind the ever-present fact of religion lies human nature—the universal needs of man. If we are to understand why religions exist, we must examine the psychological motivations and the sociological factors that are present wherever religions are found. We have already noted that the function of religion is to satisfy the intellectual and emotional needs of human beings. The proportions of these two ingredients in human behavior will vary in different religions. Let us briefly consider the role of each of these components in the religious consciousness.

The emotional elements vary in different religions. In the more primitive religions *fear* and *awe* in the presence of the mysterious forces of nature are predominant. The advanced religions provide more significant roles for love, reverence, mercy, and the like. Students of human nature are not entirely agreed on the psychological mechanisms of religion. As everyone knows, the Freudian theorists believe that the gods of the religions are what they term "father substitutes," and that such religions are examples of wishful thinking and delusional systems. Some Freudians also argue that religion and art are sublimations of sexual desires, i.e., disguised manifestations of impulses that have not been satisfied in their most elemental ways because social conventions prohibit this.

In touching upon these controversial matters, one must, of course, point out that other students of the human mind take a more sympathetic attitude toward religion. For example, Freud's wayward disciple Carl Jung was more congenial in his views toward the purposes and claims of religion. This is an exceedingly complex field, and one must expect differences of points of view. But I see no reason why Freud and Jung should not both be correct in some degree.

Primitive religions are indeed related to the emotions of fear and the anxieties that result when fears are not relieved. Man, when he is afflicted with emotions that are unpleasant, seeks ways of removing the causes that produce them. Men are therefore always seeking constructive forms of behavior that will abolish the sources of insecurity and anxiety. This brings us to the function of magic in primitive society. *Magic* consists of the positive things to be done in order to control the forces of nature, while *taboos* are the prohibitions—things not to be done. Magic is a set of rituals—compulsive forms of behavior—which give people a feeling of confidence, thus relieving the feeling of insecurity. Today we know that many of the practices of primitive peoples were not efficacious, and so we label them as superstitions; but we know also that primitive man had no science and for him his magic had value. That was its psychological function—it restored his confidence in himself. When man does not have this release from anxiety, he becomes neurotic, as modern men do when they lose their religion and have nothing to take its place. When this feeling of anxiety is associated with feelings of guilt, the individual has a sense of having sinned and he languishes in a state of depression until he has expiated his sins.

The widespread uses of water in all forms and stages of religion illustrate how the foregoing psychological mechanisms operate in relation to the external phenomena of nature. For the early Greek philosophers, water was one of the four elements. For the modern chemist it is H_2O. But for primitive man water was a living thing; it moved, it made sounds —from the patter of rain, the murmuring of brooks, and the roar of the storm to the crash of ocean waves—so primitive peoples believed that water contained a spirit that was to be worshiped and placated. Not only did water quench thirst, but it cleansed the body; and its beneficent powers warded off evil spirits. Hence water was used for religious purposes in exorcism, purification, baptism, and many other functions. The Hindu cleanses himself from sin by immersion in the sacred Ganges, the Jew cleansed himself in the river Jordan, and the Roman in the Tiber— while Pontius Pilate "washed his hands"!

There is a theory that "religion is the invention of the priests"—that the medicine man or shaman created magic and taboo to strengthen his power over the group. This theory—never taken seriously by scholars— fails because it does not explain how the priestcraft came into existence in the first place. Once established, priests frequently did use religion as a supernatural sanction for customs that otherwise would have been intolerable to the group, and to this extent the shamans have used the services of religion to defend what became their "vested interests."

So much by way of a brief survey of some of the emotional factors in religion. Let us next consider religion as the result of an effort at understanding the world in which men live.

Primitive Religions as World Views The most primitive religions are associated with what is known as animism, the doctrine that the forces of nature are alive, are animated by spirits with feelings and purposes which control the phenomena of nature. This personification or "humanization" of the forces of the outer world is a result of the spilling over of man's subjective attitudes and purposes. Thus primitive man anthropomorphizes the processes of nature, treating inanimate things as though they were persons—and that is the "mystical participation" that Lévy-Bruhl has described.

We need to remember that animism is entirely natural and inevitable in certain stages of man's cultural development. Doubtless in its earliest form, personification is not even an intellectual response—it is largely a result of habit. Since primitive people are social in nature ("group minded"), it is the normal thing to respond to other people, who by *em-pathy* (the pathetic fallacy) are judged to have feelings akin to our own. If we transfer this "humanizing" response to what a later society calls the inanimate world, we have put "spirits" into nature. Insofar as animism results in a theory of the powers that rule the universe, it rests on what the science of logic later came to designate as "reasoning by analogy." External phenomena are like living things; they exhibit activity just as a man does; therefore they are alive. The pattern is simply the familiar ratio: A:B::C:D, or concretely:

$$\frac{\text{Spirits}}{\text{Natural phenomena}} = \frac{\text{human purposes}}{\text{human behavior}}$$

Thus primitive people put spirits into nature, powers like human beings in that they can be flattered by gifts and placated by sacrifices and rituals. Ceremonials, sacrifices (human and animal), totemism, fetishes, magical practices, taboos, and folkways—all these represent man's efforts at retaining the good will of the spirits and gaining their assistance in fighting wars, reproducing the species (fertility rites), and carrying on the other enterprises of the group.

In the course of time animism of the crudest sort gave way to polytheism, the worship of the personalized spirits elevated to the position of deities. Fire, wind, trees, clouds, mountains, rivers—all these were deified and entered the pantheon of primitive religion. Here, on a higher level of polytheism, the worship of the forces of nature is subordinated to a supernatural world. Among the powers of nature that were worshiped as deities was the sun. Sun worship is invariably a part of nature worship. The ancient peoples of England built a temple at Stonehenge, where the stones still point to the place of sunrise of the summer solstice; the early Egyptians well before 3000 B.C. had established a solar religion, with Heliopolis as its center of worship; the early Greeks thought that Zeus the sky god had placed the stars in the sky to guide mariners. In these, and many other cases that come to mind, we find the evidence of worship of the sun and the stars.[4]

Solar religion frequently had associated with it a belief in divine kingship—the worship of an earthly ruler who reigned by divine right or heavenly authority. This authority could take the form of a supposed descent from the solar deity, as according to Shintoism in Japan, or it may only be that the earthly ruler receives his power from a higher source through an intermediary, as did King Hammurabi of Chaldea (about 1700 B.C.), who claimed that he had received his codification of the law from the sun god. According to J. G. Frazer, this belief in the solar origin of kingship was shared by Aryans from India to Ireland.

So much for the inner compulsions, emotional and rational, that lie behind the manifestations of religions. Let us now turn to the factors which condition the structure of religion as a conserver of social values.

Religion as a Conserver of Social Values In primitive societies, i.e., those preliterate ethnic groups which preceded the early civilizations, religions frequently function in a conservative manner in seeking to maintain the integrity and continuity of the culture as it is passed on through social heredity from one generation to the next. To illustrate this, consider the processes of integration and organization as general characteristics of all natural systems.

All natural systems are integrated, i.e., they are complex configurations of component parts maintaining themselves through the interactions between the parts. Thus atoms, molecules, cells, organisms, and human social groups (families, tribes, nations) are integrated organizations. So long as a human social organization has integrity, there is an equilibrium between the component parts of the system. A system is in *dynamic equilibrium* when the various forces are in balance and hold each other in check.

The group must have some way of personalizing the processes which maintain cultural integrity. As Emile Durkheim observes in his classic, *The Elementary Forms of Religious Life,* the function of ceremony in primitive societies is to set up group symbols. Social rituals and ceremonials provide a way of dramatizing the themes with selected individuals of the group playing the roles which symbolize and make manifest the traditional patterns ("compulsions") which give meaning to life. The function of the pantomimes and rituals of those who play the "roles" (chiefs, priests, warriors, *et al.*) is to reiterate to the group the accepted patterns or stereotypes and thus stabilize the social bonds.

Associated with these integrated social systems are types of *values,* and these help to reinforce the social structure. All this is summed up in Durkheim's concept of sacredness, that is, social relationships which have final and absolute value to the group.

Even though social systems are integrated, there is usually a tendency toward disintegration, the breakup of organization. These are manifestations of departures from the socially transmitted cultural patterns. There are two ways in which disintegration may occur, both sometimes going on at the same time. To develop this idea, let us glance at Diagram I, The Three Levels of Human Conduct. Primitive societies for the most part function on Level II, the level of customary morality as exhibited by "mass man." In opposition to the dictates of folkways, traditions, and conventions, the heretics, the reformers, the ethical geniuses may rebel and try to lift their society to a new and higher plane of existence, to Level III. Their vision is frequently that of a more inclusive group, looking toward a higher level of social integration. We have termed such creative individuals the AVATARS of social evolution.

Diagram 1 · THE THREE LEVELS OF HUMAN CONDUCT

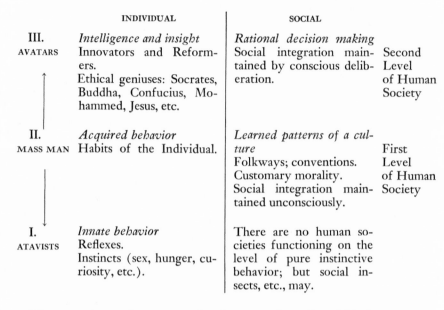

	INDIVIDUAL	SOCIAL	
III. AVATARS	*Intelligence and insight* Innovators and Reformers. Ethical geniuses: Socrates, Buddha, Confucius, Mohammed, Jesus, etc.	*Rational decision making* Social integration maintained by conscious deliberation.	Second Level of Human Society
II. MASS MAN	*Acquired behavior* Habits of the Individual.	*Learned patterns of a culture* Folkways; conventions. Customary morality. Social integration maintained unconsciously.	First Level of Human Society
I. ATAVISTS	*Innate behavior* Reflexes. Instincts (sex, hunger, curiosity, etc.).	There are no human societies functioning on the level of pure instinctive behavior; but social insects, etc., may.	

The opposite tendency, namely, departure from Level II of customary morality to Level I by regression toward the selfish (egoistic) satisfactions of the instinctual desires of the Id (sex, property, powers, etc.), is designated by the ATAVISTS, as opposed to AVATARS. This recidivism from cultural patterns through personal atavism negates the restraints of social conventions and leads to "delinquency," "criminality," and the like. When this is widespread, we have a "decadent" society. Either this society will then have to recreate itself through invention or adoption of new patterns, or it will disappear or stagnate. Arnold Toynbee has built a reputation on the simple formula of *challenge and response.*

In recent times the gradual disappearance of the "sacred" from society has been encouraged by the growth of scientific knowledge (which undermines religious myths), by the recognition of the cultural relativity of values, and by the increasing tempo of social changes which weaken the integrative power of social institutions such as the family, the church, and even the school. In our modern Western societies hardly anything is sacred; even life itself has little sanctity.

Along with this evidence of social disintegration of old value-systems, we have the parallel growth of what is termed "alienation." This term refers to the separation of persons from their environment, so that a sense of poverty and forlornness emerges in the individuals of such societies. The spread of industrialization (now termed automation) has increased this feeling of alienation in the worker from the world he lives in. Technologically our societies are becoming more highly integrated, but in terms of accepted moral values the individuals in it feel more alienated, more disorganized morally. Anguish, frustration, and despair are prevailing moods. This suggests that a new culture with new values is called for, if men are to survive in a satisfying existence.

The Evolution of Religion Some people think that "evolution" and "religion" are opposed to each other. But religion, far from being antithetical to the theory of evolution, offers one of the best proofs of evolution. This is why it is so difficult to analyze out the "essence" of religion. To support this claim, while at the same time enriching our ideas of what religions may be and do, let us glance at some of the stages in the development of religion.

We have elsewhere outlined the stages of religious evolution.[5] The religious patterns parallel the social stages in somewhat the following manner:

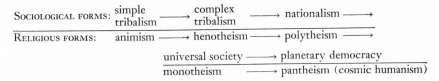

Since they represent more advanced stages of social development, the monotheistic religions made a relatively late appearance in the history of mankind. Monotheism is both a cause and an effect of the processes of social integration, an integration that is related to the economic, political, and ideological forces at work. But monotheisms usually do not come into existence suddenly and out of a clear sky. The bridge of continuity from a more loosely formed polytheistic tribalism to a more inclusive nationalism is usually provided by the intermediate form of religious-social development known as henotheism. Here the group recognizes that there is a variety of deities, all of whom are worshiped—this god by this tribe and that god by that tribe—but there is one god supreme over all who should be worshiped by all tribes. Later on, the supreme deity is declared to be the only god to be worshiped—and we then have a monotheism.

There has been much discussion as to which of the world's religions was the first monotheism to appear. According to some, Judaism—the worship of One God, Jehovah—represents the earliest monotheism. But this has been disputed. According to other scholars—for example, James H. Breasted, in his book, *The Dawn of Conscience*—the first clear monotheism was the religion taught by the ancient Egyptian ruler Akhenaton, a great religious reformer who for a while succeeded in replacing the polytheism of the earlier Egyptian religion with a monotheism—the acceptance of Aton as the supreme deity with the sun as his symbolic image in the Universe. This view, in a modified form, was also adopted by Freud in his last book, *Moses and Monotheism*.

It is further argued by some investigators that Moses, brought up and educated in Egypt in the court of Pharaoh at the time Akhenaton's reforms were in effect, borrowed the essential of this monotheistic pattern and then superimposed it on the henotheistic (or even polytheistic) Hebrew tribes. This "diffusion" is a possibility, if (as some claim) Moses and Akhenaton were contemporaries. But whether Moses was in fact influenced by Akhenaton's religious reforms before Atonism was submerged by a recrudescent Egyptian polytheism is a controversial point. Orthodox Jews claim that their monotheism dates back to Abraham, a thousand years earlier. Fortunately, we do not need to arbitrate these rival claims. In any event, it is certainly true that several other religions with a long cultural history did succeed in making the transition from polytheism to monotheism. One interesting and important feature of this phenomenon of religious evolution is which henotheism provides the bridge.

In looking back over the long course of religious evolution, we discern how, especially in the later stages, religious geniuses with ideological innovations guide the course of social development. Because this is so, it is necessary to examine the role of the religious genius (hero) in serving as the spearhead of religious development.

The Role of the Religious Genius Students of mankind have frequently observed that man's unique position in nature is based on the dominance of symbols in his life. Except for the satisfaction of universal biological needs, man lives, not in a world of things, but in a world of symbols. Picture writing, cuneiform inscriptions, hieroglyphics, money, wedding rings, handshakes, words like "time," "distance," "mass," flags, traffic signals, maps—all these are conventional symbols. The knowledge possessed by any social system consists of the sum total of its symbols, the record of their meanings, and the sense of their interrelationships.

Investigations by anthropologists lead to the conclusion that religious rituals play a symbolic role in human life. Throughout man's history the gods, the magic, and the litanies of religion have fitted a general pattern. In her book, *The Myth of the Magus*, Eliza Butler has isolated the components of the pattern into the following themes:

1 Supernatural or mysterious origin of the hero.
2 Portents at birth.

3 Perils menacing his infancy.
4 Some kind of initiation.
5 Far distant wanderings.
6 A magical contest.
7 A trial or persecution.
8 A last scene.
9 A violent or mysterious death.
10 A resurrection and/or ascension.

Specific examples of the mythological motifs which function as transfiguration symbols are Dante's *Divine Comedy* and the King Arthur legend of the Grail Knights. Some of these imaginative-creative symbols function as Jungian archetypes in setting the ideal patterns of life through the "roles" enacted by humans on their way to becoming divine personalities.

These movements of the pattern are illustrated to a greater or lesser degree in the lives of Zoroaster, Moses, Pythagoras, Krishna, Christ, Merlin, and others. This theme was handled by Kersey Graves in his once-popular book, *The World's Sixteen Crucified Saviors.* For the followers of the religions which were thus founded by their "saviors," the messiah, once accepted as fulfilling the role, attains the status of a superhuman divinity. But from a psychoanalytic viewpoint, the pattern of the myth is repeated in history because the group recognizes the embodiment of the role. As others have pointed out, if Christ did not exist, it would be necessary to invent him.

This theory may not prove congenial to religious devotees on the level of conscious acceptance, even though it has the sanction of unconscious motivations. Many religionists will distrust this intrusion of science into their kingdom of godliness. But the study of motivations and mechanisms is a part of scientific psychology. The religious devotee will take Dr. Anatol Rapoport[6] at his own word when he states that "the Humanist sees the scientific enterprise as the continuous and persistent effort to divest events of their mystery," and conclude that this is just another reason for suspicion of the scientific enterprise. "Science would clip the wings of the angels"—so it was said in an earlier day.

My own attitude toward the function of science—or rather, the interpretation of the results of scientific methodology—is somewhat different. From the viewpoint of a cosmic humanism, the enterprise of science need not be detrimental to the cause of the religious spirit. In such a world view, God, the Supreme Imagination, is the *guiding field;* but this impersonal reality finds its vehicles of manifestation in the lives of Jesus, Buddha, Confucius, Lao-tzu, and other prophets and seers. In India Christ is accepted as an avatar who was incarnated in Krishna. If we could take the Christian mystery and lift it out of the Hebraic-Palestinian background and generalize it, we would have something in the tradition of an ancient wisdom religion (the *pistis sophia*), reborn for today's needs in the religion of a cosmic humanism.

This conception of the future of religion is close to the view of Scott Buchanan,[7] who states well the case for a tradition of religious symbolism. Admitting the coercions of the past in the present as this reappears in the cultural survival of compulsive religious rituals, there still shines through all the trappings and mimesis man's personal need for symbolization and society's collective need for a spiritual alchemy of regeneration.

The sacramental use of analogies, which Professor Buchanan mentions, may still serve as a therapeutic agent in bringing grace and insight, the vital spark of illumination which can jump between the artificial forms and the realities they supposedly point to and symbolize. This "transubstantiation"—if I may call it that—is an implicit light which comes forth to explain, and Gratry and the Booles have described it.[8] A basic sacramental language, deliberately constructed by psychiatry and anthropology for a new wisdom religion, might well spearhead a renaissance of spiritual growth and rescue mankind from decadence and alienation in a world still replete with mysterious depths beyond the visible or manifest world. Salvation through scientific mysticism is perhaps man's last hope for a creative evolution through self-transcendence.

Mysticism, Religion, and Cosmic Consciousness We have made the point that religion has evolved; it has changed greatly in the long course of human history. Its future survival may well depend on whether it is capable of further changes in the world that is coming toward us. Today it no longer matters so much whether primitive religions were a "sublimation of sex," or a "father substitute," or whatnot; but it does matter *what religion can become in the age of the conquest of space, automation, and overpopulation among teeming billions of humans who have had their roots torn from the soil of ancestral traditions and loyalties.*

Perhaps a higher manifestation of religion can be seen in the phenomena of the religious experience, so called, as this is now being studied in mysticism. These various phenomena have been closely examined by William James and reported in his *Varieties of Religious Experience*. It has also been studied by Evelyn Underhill in her book on *Mysticism*, and by Walter T. Stace in his volume on *Mysticism and Philosophy*. According to James, if we disregard the "overbeliefs" which seek to "understand" mysticism, the generic trait of the consciousness which personal religion exemplifies is *the fact that the conscious person is continuous with a wider self through which saving experience comes*. For James, this plunges one into another dimension of existence than the sensible world. It may well be that the mystical experience as described by

James and others has a common core and that this unitary and timeless experience if it is to be described (perhaps a mistake?) will perforce be described in the language of the culture which the mystic employs.

It may also be the case that this experience has pretty much the characteristics which Maurice Bucke found and reported in his book on *Cosmic Consciousness* and which Professor F. S. C. Northrop, in his provocative volume *The Meeting of East and West*, designates as the *aesthetic continuum.* Beyond that, it may even be the case that this experience makes contact at some point with the fantasies of the psychopharmacological drugs as reported on by Aldous Huxley in his book *The Doors of Perception* and more recently expounded in Jane Dunlap's *Exploring Inner Space* and in Alan W. Watts's *The Joyous Cosmology.* In all these cases one allegedly feels that the finite human self has merged with a larger consciousness and that a union with the higher reality is man's true end. If this be so—and a scientific psychology should make it its business to find out the truth of such matters—then prayer as an inner communion with that unmanifest universe from which guiding fields of energy may flow is a legitimate and perhaps even necessary part of a complete existence for man. This is not stated as a fact; it is posed as a hypothesis—something to be investigated by proper research tools and a well-designed program of investigation.

Religion and Morality Religion and morality have been intimately associated throughout the long history of man's social development—"religion is morality touched by emotion," as one student put it. As examples from Western man's religiously conditioned morals, consider the impact of the Puritan tradition (as we now term it) on his views concerning the nature of the sex instinct and its role in life; or the former religious opposition to the use of anesthesia in child birth; or the present opposition on religious grounds to birth control, voluntary euthanasia, and so on. In these instances we see how the moral ideals of the Western nations have derived from ancient sources as these were stabilized in Christendom in the theology of St. Paul, later to be steamed and pressed into the orthodoxies of St. Augustine, Thomas Aquinas, Martin Luther, John Calvin, and other "authorities" of the organized churches. If we trace this ethical dualism of a "higher" or "spiritual" nature and a "lower" or "animalistic" nature to its primary sources, we discover, as historical studies reveal, that the theory which undergirds the above attitude is an outgrowth of the metaphysical dualism of the earlier Persian religion of Zoroaster as this was absorbed and transmitted by the Jewish refugees from Palestine during the years of their Babylonian captivity, approximately six centuries B.C. That this Iranian dualism (Mazdaism) should survive and reappear centuries later in the Mithraism of the Roman world, and be reborn in the Qumran monastic sect living along the shores of the Dead Sea—this indeed is one of the epics of human history. All the world knows about the Dead Sea scrolls, inscribed almost two millennia ago (as carbon-14 dating proves) by the ascetics of the Essene community, which were secreted in caves, to be rediscovered in 1947 by an Arab shepherd boy who wandered into a cave on the hillside by the Dead Sea. These precious scrolls were preserved in jars through twenty centuries of Palestinian ebb and flow of history. The discoveries of the scrolls in the many caves along the hills of Judaea is one of the highlights of archaeology.

Among these scrolls is a *Manual of Discipline* which prophesies a final struggle between the "Children of Light" and the "Children of Darkness," and this theme of a "day of judgment" seems to echo the earlier Zoroastrianism and to adumbrate both the evanescent Manichaeism and the more enduring Christian dualism which were on the horizon of time. The precise manner and extent to which the teachings of the Essene order at Qumran foreshadowed coming Christianity, and even helped to mold its basic teachings, is a matter about which scholars will dispute for decades to come.[9]

The main conclusion of all this is that at whatever level we take our Judeo-Christian tradition—ancient, medieval, or modern—we see clearly how religious notions helped to shape the moral outlook. To be sure, we also discern how these religious views in turn reflect the sociological forces at work in molding and modifying the evolving moral conceptions. This is the familiar feedback principle we recognize in many types of integrations.

This, of course, is the historical relation. But how about the contemporary relation? Certainly any survey of the role of religion in society must come to terms with the important issues which confront the troubled world in which we live. Such an analysis involves a consideration of touchy questions concerning the sources of friction between church and state in our modern democracies.

The Church and the State   Time and again we have heard pronouncements by our politicians and other leaders that "this country was founded on religious principles." When we and our Western Allies fought the Nazis, we were warned that "Christian values are at stake." Today we are informed that our enemy is "atheistic communism"—which we must defeat if our religion and our political democracy are to survive.

There are several inaccuracies in the above conception of the task we face. For one thing, there are not merely two alternatives, namely, atheistic communism versus Christian democracy; but there is in fact a third block of neutral peoples who are neither Christian nor communist. Secondly, the dogma that our own nation was founded on religious principles and is committed to the Christian (or even Judeo-Christian) ideology and way of life is historically false and ethically dangerous.

The United States was not founded on religious principles, though to be sure the religious tradition of the Western world did add one component. A more complete picture of the sources of Western democracy is given in Diagram II. Here it is evident that philosophy also added some constituents, and these, indeed, have pagan (non-Christian) origins. For that matter, much of what came to be accepted as a part of organized Christianity was Greek metaphysics (Plato and Aristotle primarily) and Roman philosophy (Stoicism). When one reminds himself of these considerations, does it not seem naïve to regard Chritsianity as a single entity? Christianity is a symphony which includes many notes, some of them discordant, in fact, and that is why it can be "all things to all men."

Diagram II · ORIGINS OF AMERICAN DEMOCRACY

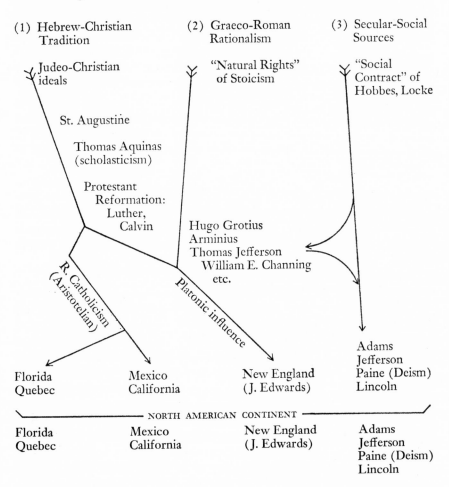

(1) Hebrew-Christian Tradition

(2) Graeco-Roman Rationalism

(3) Secular-Social Sources

Judeo-Christian ideals

"Natural Rights" of Stoicism

"Social Contract" of Hobbes, Locke

St. Augustine

Thomas Aquinas (scholasticism)

Protestant Reformation: Luther, Calvin

Hugo Grotius
Arminius
Thomas Jefferson
William E. Channing etc.

R. Catholicism (Aristotelian)

Platonic influence

Florida
Quebec

Mexico
California

New England (J. Edwards)

Adams
Jefferson
Paine (Deism)
Lincoln

——— NORTH AMERICAN CONTINENT ———

Florida
Quebec

Mexico
California

New England (J. Edwards)

Adams
Jefferson
Paine (Deism)
Lincoln

We have regarded religion as a serious, emotional attitude toward some reality or being(s) superior to man. Theology is the study of this postulated Being or Reality. But surely a measure of humility suggests that no man can "know" God, even though men may have partial and momentary experiences of a higher reality to which that term may be applied. In pantheism God is not a person. The pantheist holds that it is only arrogance which leads some persons to talk about "God" as if they had a private telephone connection with Him. This delusion becomes dangerous when such persons constitute a priestly class and presume to tell the remainder of the human family what it is that God requires of men in the way of obedience to "His Will."

This is not the place to rehearse the story of the harmful effects of the incomplete separation of Church and State, theology and politics. Other builders of the "wall of separation" have done this in full detail. Fortunately, the role of organized religions in politics is diminishing, and there is less to worry about than formerly.

Does the foregoing statement mean that we wish religion to disappear from the human scene? Not at all! There is a place for the religions of the world, provided they satisfy certain conditions. The conditions for the existence of religions in a democratic world are several in number, and briefly stated are as follows:

1. *The mutual toleration by each religion of other religions.* "Tolerance" is a word that seems to imply smugness—"I will tolerate you, even though your religion is not as good as mine." But we have stated a minimal condition; if beyond that it is possible to respect other religions, that is even better—provided the religion is worthy of respect. The point here is that the right to the observance of the beliefs and rituals of your religion (e.g., Protestantism, Roman Catholicism, Judaism, Mohammedanism) implies the right of peoples of other persuasions to their (different) religion. Freedom of religion is one of the Four Freedoms only when it is coupled with the extension of this same right to others.

2. *Complete separation of Church and State.* If one's own religion (or its spokesman in the churches) is permitted to dictate to the members of the congregation (or congregations of other churches) what the attitudes on socialized medicine, birth control, labor unions, child labor, or other controversial issues, shall be, this would revive ancient religious wars and stir up new conflicts born of modern circumstances.

3. *The right of each person to choose his religion, to change his religion, or to have no religion at all.* On becoming a mature individual, the citizen should be permitted to "shop around" and see what is available— visit synagogues, mosques, temples, cathedrals, spiritualist camps, Christian Science churches—and then choose what seems best suited to meet his own needs. Relatives should not ostracize their deviate offspring who "go astray." Religious convictions are of no value unless chosen freely.

This freedom of religion has another implication which is frequently overlooked. The precious right to conscience means that each individual should be free to have no religion at all, if that is his preference. The atheists and agnostics are not "un-American" (or un-whatnot) for that reason alone. Those who protest our so-called secular education because it is "godless" are not thinking philosophically. They are guilty of pride and arrogance.

All this is in the interest of making religion significant in human life. It is not an effort to denigrate the religious life of man in contemporary society. It represents the view of one student (myself) who has struggled with this problem; in the process he has passed through orthodoxy in youth, to agnosticism in the university, to a Cosmic Humanism as a world view in more mature years. But when I present this viewpoint to my students in university classes in philosophy, the occasional reaction from some is that if we take morality out of the field of religion, we have no firm supports for morality, no objective (absolute) standards, and so there really is no reason why a person should behave himself. "Anything goes"—and why not?

Just because this is such an important question, it is desirable to glance at the foundations for a humanistic ethics. In seeking to sketch the basis for a morality based on reason, it will be necessary at the same time to deal with the view of many of the logical positivists that a science of ethics cannot be made reasonable, since value judgments—they argue—are emotive in origin and justification, and therefore are not scientifically verifiable.

Linguistic Analysis and Values It goes without saying that we are dealing with complex and difficult problems. Not only are the conflicts of science and religion involved, but the incompatible claims of rival religions obtrude themselves. Beyond that, the champions of ethics as a secular social science also enter the arena of conflict to defend their interests. The field of ethics is itself a battleground on which ethical theories of many different types compete for victory. As yet there are no clear-cut decisions.

Recently some scholars have persuaded themselves that they could make progress toward elucidation of the issues if they were to focus attention on the observation that ethical theories and religious viewpoints tend to split on whether they are using the language of moral judgments in ethics and religion as primarily "cognitive" or "noncognitive" in function—that is, whether the terms employed are mainly intellectual (rational) or emotional in reference. Thus the noncognitive theories of ethics —such as that of Professor Charles L. Stevenson as set forth in his book on *Ethics and Language*—lead to the conclusion that there can be no rational science of ethics. The viewpoint of logical positivism also decrees that there can be no "truth values" to poetry, metaphysics, and ethics.

In my considered opinion this dichotomy in the uses of language is a heritage of the disappearing positivism which afflicted the world of philosophy for several decades following the termination of the Second World War. In pursuing this matter, I shall state briefly the idea behind this analysis of the several functions of language, then indicate why it seems unsound, and next suggest how our own formulation may escape the dilemma that was created. In this manner we hope to rise to a higher level in which the dualism is overcome.

We begin by referring to the well-known work of Ogden and Richards, *The Meaning of Meaning*, where several functions of language as they see them are presented. The elementalistic theory of psychic atoms, which provides the theoretical underpinning of much of our cultural fragmentation, is illustrated in the Ogden-Richards analysis of the functions of language in terms of the types of purposes that language serves, namely, the emotive function and the cognitive function. The supposition that there is a dualism of an emotive use of language and an intellectualistic use of language is certainly Aristotelian in spirit and reflects a faculty psychology from which, as one might suppose, such enlightened individuals as Ogden and Richards should be free. That this addiction to dualism is not an isolated phenomenon, but is shared by other theorists, is indicated by the fact that the Logical Positivists also succumbed to this traditional elementalistic type of analysis. Here is the dichotomy that is set up:

WAYS IN WHICH LANGUAGE IS EMPLOYED

I. COGNITIVE USE OF LANGUAGE (REASON)	1. Formal mode of speech (purely symbolic, e.g., mathematics) 2. Material mode of speech (factual statements, e.g., physics)
II. EMOTIVE USE OF LANGUAGE (VALUES)	1. Poetry and religion 2. Metaphysics and politics

This analysis of the two types of judgment—judgments of the cognitive function and judgments of value—is the consequence of a theory of human nature in which emotions can be isolated from the intellectual life. This mutual exclusiveness reflects the two-valued logic of the either-or antithesis: if a response (judgment) illustrates one of the alternatives, it excludes the other. As the logical positivists would put it, "there is no logic in ethics, and there is no ethics in logic." In our own analysis of the situation, we hold that these two types of response are not necessarily exclusive of each other; indeed, we go further and assert that there never is a response which is purely intellectual or purely emotional. All responses in man are organismic, a fusion in which one side, perhaps the emotional, may prevail over the other, the rational; but a sound psychology will recognize that ideas are always emotionally conditioned and emotions in man are ideationally guided in some degree.

If we adopt the following symbolism, the several classes of response and types of judgment that are logically possible are four in number, as follows (F = judgments of fact, intellectual; V = judgments of value, emotional):

$$(1) \quad (2) \quad (3) \quad (4)$$
$$FV \quad FV' \quad F'V \quad F'V'$$

The interpretation of the four classes is this: (1) judgments that are both fact and value responses; (2) judgments of fact, but not of value; (3) judgments of value, but not of fact; (4) judgments neither of fact nor of value. While (4) seems to be a logically possible class, it is really a null class, in the sense that it has no members (i.e., there are no human responses that lack both intellectual and emotional content); and (2) and (3) differ only in degree in which emotion and reason are present. Cases of the complete absence of emotion (pure judgments of fact) and the complete absence of ideation (pure judgments of value) represent limiting cases in which one or the other is reduced in amount to the vanishing point, i.e., they approach zero as a limit, without actually reaching it.

If our rejection of the above elementalistic psychology is sound, religion cannot be dismissed in favor of science because the former is emotive in nature and the latter rational and objective. This faculty psychology of "thinking," "feeling," and "willing," ill accords with the gestalt and holistic views of human nature which, in my opinion, come closer to a true psychology. Moreover, our integrative viewpoint now puts us in a position to sketch the ethical theory which, as indicated, will combine features of the cognitive-rational and noncognitive-emotive analyses in a higher synthesis. The most that we can do here is suggest the outlines of a more complete theory.

It is the presupposition of the present essay that a science of ethics is concerned not only with *what men do*, and why they behave as they do, but it is also concerned with *what men ought to do*, human nature and our social institutions being what they are. In the past this had to be stated as functions of time, place, and even altitude. Today, in a rapidly integrating world, our pressing problem is to formulate a set of moral principles which is independent of latitude, longitude, altitude, and time. This means that the function of philosophy is to provide vision and guidance—cultural planning—for the future.

There is a superabundance of textbooks devoted to the exposition of ethical systems, the language of ethics, and the like. These careful studies operate on a high level of linguistic sophistication. But they have no effects on the political and economic decisions of our statesmen, industrialists, and other "practical" people. What is needed is a bridge between the high-level ethical analyses and the lower-level "use-enjoyment" phases of social life. This bridge would be a *philosophical technology*.[10] Just as medicine and industry are technologies—practical applications of physics, chemistry, biology, and pharmacology—so a scientific humanism, as a technology, would aim at social applications of the moral principles of ethics to personal behavior and social conduct and evolution. Let us develop this idea somewhat.

Scientific Humanism as a Technology Much of what has preceded and is here further developed presupposes the idea of planning—*individual planning and social planning*. But what operational procedures do we possess for securing unity and coordination in such planning? This brings us to the crucial issue of the problem-solving techniques which are adequate and available for handling ethical-social questions in a scientific (reasonable) manner. Such a philosophical technology must recognize the two poles of the ethical situation, the *individual person* and the *field* or *social context*.

We have recognized that a critical test for a scientific humanism is its ability to formulate a naturalistic ethics, a code of moral conduct, for contemporary man. Before one can get a statement of objectives for the good society, one must find a methodology, a problem-solving procedure, which those who accept the humanist viewpoint can utilize. Given that methodology, one may then decide in specific cases what are the best courses of action. For the naturalistic humanists, the answer of the organized religions, "Do the will of God," is not good enough. Even if we knew what *is* the "will of God," and if his injunctions were the same in all authoritarian religions, this would not be sufficient.

A bit of reflection will indicate that a modern system of ethics—for the East *and* the West—must consider a number of fundamental problems, among which are the following:

(1) What is moral conduct? What is the good life for man?

(2) Is any act in itself (e.g., lying, cheating, stealing, killing) inherently and of its own nature always and everywhere evil? Or if one thinks of the opposites, is the act always good?

(3) Might two people solve the same problems (e.g., breaking a contract or permitting voluntary euthanasia) in different ways and yet both persons be considered moral, i.e., good citizens in the community?

(4) In general, would intelligent and educated people solve the same moral problems in much the same way, i.e., come up with the same answers?

(5) Are there general rules which ought to guide us? Under what conditions may they be set aside?

(6) What is the relation of moral principles to the laws of the state? Is political revolution ever justified? Is it ethical to break statutory laws on occasion?

(7) Has there been any general trend in the moral evolution of mankind?

It is not possible to deal with all these questions now (I shall consider the first problem in a moment), but in order to outline a *method* for handling these problems, it is necessary to state some fundamental concepts which seem essential to a system of ethics. These are as follows:

THE CONCEPT OF MORAL RESPONSIBILITY. This is a psychological notion which has to do with the degree to which a person is to be held responsible for his actions. A person is responsible to the extent to which he can be aware of the probable consequences of present actions and can choose his course of action in the light of these consequences. To have moral properties, an act must be voluntarily chosen. The acceptance of a behavioristic psychology does not wipe out the distinction between voluntary and involuntary acts, since these are describable in terms of cortical-striped-muscle responses and lower-level responses.

This means that any person who cannot be aware of what he is doing, who cannot consciously control his behavior in the light of anticipated consequences, is nonmoral. Thus the behavior of imbeciles, idiots, morons, insane persons, very young children, somnambulists, and those suffering from senility is amoral, to a degree which varies with intelligence and an education which develops one's innate abilities; that is:

$$\text{Moral responsibility} = \text{intelligence} \times \text{education}$$

Note that the place of rewards and punishments is not determined solely in terms of "responsibility" for acts; there is also the question of whether praise or blame modifies the conduct of such amoral organisms.

THE CONCEPT OF MORAL OBLIGATION. This deals with a fundamental ethical problem: *Why should I be good?* Why behave myself? Why should I consider the interests and values of other people?

The answer which authoritarian religions give to this question—"Because God commands it"—is not sufficient. Philosophy, like science, is secular—neither *for* nor *against* articles of religious faith, at least so long as these refer to a supernatural spiritual world about which there is no verified knowledge.

The answer of philosophy to the question, Why should I accept moral obligations? is this, I believe: Because this is a rule of the game of social existence. It is a rule of fair play or good sportsmanship. We cannot play the game of social life if one takes from society without giving something in return for values received. This is the familiar principle, "every right implies a duty," e.g., the right to freedom of speech, religious worship, and right to vote, implies the obligation to respect this same right in others.

We see, therefore, that any human act, to have moral significance, must (*a*) be voluntarily chosen and have a motive and (*b*) affect others for better or for worse—it must have social consequences. The first (motive, purpose) is the *subjective* aspect of conduct, and the second (social consequences) is the *objective* aspect. We may distinguish these as the *why* (motive) and the *what* (content) of moral conduct. This, then, brings us to a third concept of ethics.

THE CONCEPT OF A MORAL PROBLEM. A problem arises whenever one faces a situation to which one must respond, for which one does not have a ready-made response (reflex, instinct, habit), so that one must think out the solution. Thinking is problem-solving. This felt difficulty becomes a moral problem when the consequences of what one chooses affect others for better or for worse. Until the man Friday appeared, Robinson Crusoe did not have any moral decisions. If he chose to abuse himself, this was neither right nor wrong; but as soon as another person appeared (it takes only two people to make a society), moral obligations and responsibilities appeared. If, as a hermit, Robinson chose to judge his conduct as "bad" (let us say he salvaged some whiskey and drank himself into a stupor), because it was "sinful" in the eyes of God, this is his privilege—but it is not ethics. Man-in-society is a precondition for ethical judgments. Of course, if Robinson expects to rejoin society (as he did), then he is potentially a member of society and must judge his conduct in the light of its probable consequences in a future society.

Now we come to the question: suppose I am morally responsible, and accept my ethical obligations: (1) *How shall I know what to do?* (2) What *is* right conduct? (3) How do I find out?

Universal Ethics and Its Methodology To answer these questions, it is necessary to return to the distinction between motives (the subjective *why*) and the consequences (the objective *what*). It must next be noted that each of these may be described as "good" or "bad" (or "indifferent," in which case we lose interest as ethicists).

A good act, we observe, is one that is inspired by a good motive or attitude; it issues from a feeling of love or good will, the desire to help another. A bad act is one that springs from a desire to injure some person or group. It issues from a feeling of hatred or jealousy or fear or conceit. It is a simple fact of introspective psychology that some of our acts originate in feelings of kindness, sympathy, or love (the "love thy neighbor" of the ethics of Jesus), while other acts are manifestations of the desire to harm, get revenge, and so on.

Of course there are difficulties here. It is not easy to know one's own motives or to discover the motives of others. Psychoanalysis reveals the depths of hidden motives and the extent to which we rationalize. But in spite of difficulties, and a behavioristic psychology to the contrary notwithstanding, a knowledge of motives is important for ethics, as witness the difference in law between first and second degree murder.

Moreover, we know that good motives are not enough. We say that the road to hell is paved with good intentions, and many a well-meaning but ill-resulting action has been excused on the ground that "I meant well." Accordingly, the other aspect of conduct, without which no act is fully moral, is that the act must lead to the right objective results. What "good" results or consequences are is sometimes not easy to say in a specific case, but in general good acts lead toward socially desirable consequences—contribute to the general welfare and social progress. *So a general ideology or social ethics implies a vision of a better society.* For a humanist-scientific ideology this includes two things: (*a*) the creation of conditions in which each person is provided with the minimal material requirements of food, shelter, clothing, housing, and sanitation for physical well-being and (*b*) the development of social institutions and a cultural environment which make it possible for every person to receive an education adequate to his maximum growth as a creative agent with various talents and abilities. In general, the ideal society would be one in which each person had enough to do of the sort of thing he likes to do and can do successfully to make life fruitful and zestful. Such a world does not exist today, but is not beyond realization.

We have stated that every moral act has two aspects, subjective-motivational and objective-social, and we have seen that each in turn can be either good or bad. Now let us work out the possible combinations of acts in terms of this analysis. If M stands for motives and C for consequences, and g stands for good and b for bad, we can construct the following four classes of acts.

(1) *Mg Cg*–Man rescues child in danger; wise social legislation; intelligent philanthropy; doctor tells a sick patient a falsehood concerning his condition.

(2) *Mg Cb*–Prohibitory laws of misguided reformers; anti-evolution legislation.

(3) *Mb Cg*–Desire to harm but unwittingly do good. Philanthropy for the sake of publicity.

(4) *Mb Cb*–Criminal assassinates a good citizen.

In the first and the fourth cases the motives and the consequences are congruent; one accomplishes what he sets out to do. When the motives and consequences do not coincide (as in the second and third cases), this indicates a lack of sufficient foresight to accomplish one's purposes. No man, of course, is omniscient, and in a complex and changing world even the most far-seeing individual will make mistakes (as judged by wisdom after the fact).

We see now that we have the answer to our first question: the good act (or right conduct) is that motivated by a good intention or attitude and leading to the best social consequences. Since good consequences—those which promote social progress—can be achieved only through the use of human intelligence, our definition agrees with that proposed by Bertrand Russell: *the good life is the life inspired by love and guided by knowledge* (intelligence). From this scheme it is possible to work out the answers to the other questions in our list. For example, in answering Question 2, we may conclude that no specific act, inherently and of itself, is always good or always bad—it depends on the motives, circumstances, and probable consequences. There are occasions when lying, killing, stealing, or other acts which set aside the Mosaic law, are proper.

It is clear from this that the ethics of a scientific humanism places a premium on intelligence; in this respect it is opposed to an unintelligent morality which demands blind obedience to absolute commands "from above." Man's highest duty includes the obligation to be as intelligent and well-informed as his biological heredity and social environment permit. The virtue of intelligence is that with it one can learn from his mistakes, so that ordinarily the damage done by miscalculations is not irreparable.

In my opinion, the foregoing analysis has several merits. It provides a meeting ground for the cognitive and emotive theories of ethics and overcomes the harmful elementalism which vitiates so much writing in the field. Secondly, *it provides a proper place for religion in our modern world*. The virtue of religion is that it can teach the "brotherhood of man." Love guided by knowledge is the integrative force in society. The teachings of Jesus and other prophets as emphasizing the emotional basis —love thy neighbor—recognize the deeper affective basis of the good life. Our educational systems are falling short in their task of cultivating this nonrational aspect of life.

We now seem to have the main components of a methodology for the ethics that is required as we move into the new world that is opening up, a world of unprecedented needs and challenges. Our separation of philosophical technology (ethics as an ideological field) from the field of religion may seem a bit dogmatic; but it really is not so. The Pennsylvania Dutch, Jehovah's Witnesses, the Christian Scientists, and other religious groups, must abide by the statutory regulations concerning public health (e.g., vaccination) because preventive medicine is based on *publicly verified knowledge* concerning germs, viruses, etc., as causative agents in the spread of contagious diseases. When such knowledge can be shown to be false, through the further use of scientific methods, such regulations should be repealed. But clearly it is not verified knowledge which dictates that God forbids games of chance (gambling), or forbids extramarital sex relations, and the like. Obviously, at this point no particular practice is being defended or attacked; we are only noting that sin as a religious concept (i.e., a violation of the law of God) can have no place in ethics as a normative social science.

But it should be kept in mind that a scientific humanism is scientific primarily in the sense that at present it is committed to the use of a method. Let us hope that as a result of the prolonged use of scientific method, we will come up with a body of propositions for general acceptance—not only for public sanitation and hygiene, but also for eliminating the hazards of thermonuclear war, the social evils of automation, overpopulation, starvation, ignorance, and so on.

Outlines of a Cosmic Humanism In the preceding pages we have sketched the outlines of a possible religion for the future—a revival of the pantheistic tradition, but adapted to the concepts of modern knowledge. This viewpoint we have designated as a *Cosmic Humanism*. Here these suggestions are brought into sharper focus.[11] The major components are as follows:

(1) Behind our perceived universe of material things in space and time there is a *Cosmic Field of Energy*—infinite, eternal, uncreated, and indestructible. Within this universal and undifferentiated ocean of energy there is a Supreme Imagination which, by way of the *Cosmic Lens*, acts as a focusing and guiding field of influence in controlling the creation and evolution of matter. Thus, high above the local gods of our earth's regional religions, there is a Divinity, an immanent guiding field, maintaining the balance between the visible or *manifest* world and the invisible or *unmanifest* world (as required by Einstein's equation for the equivalence of matter and energy, $E = mc^2$). This guiding influence organizes matter into the forms of evolution, from the inorganic to the organic world, from atoms to human beings.

(2) Since God is not a personality distinct from nature, "miracles" and "special providences" as violations of nature's laws cannot occur. Therefore, there are no revealed religions and the doctrine of the verbal inspiration of scripture has no foundation in fact. The Supreme Imagination appears as an invisible field of influence permeating the visible physical universe, but since this impersonal and divine influence can never in man's thoughts be any greater than man's capacity to envision, man will become more like Divinity as he reverences and increasingly understands the infinite and everlasting cosmos in which all things live and move and have their being (to use a Stoic phrase which Christianity borrowed).

(3) There is no "sacred" literature; there is no special religious experience; there are no chosen peoples; and sin as a violation of the laws of

God as revealed to some prophet is sheer superstition. The clergy have no private contacts with supernatural powers, and they have no unique status as the interpreters of God's will.

(4) Human consciousness in its awareness, and in its time-spanning properties, is man's most immediate experience of the cosmic guiding field in its organic expression. The invisible Supreme Imagination which guides the course of evolution in the visible physical world is a nonmoral force, is neither good nor bad, *until it reaches up into human consciousness to appear as integrated personality, at which point the Cosmic Energy acquires moral attributes.* If there are other universes—planetary systems with living and conscious creatures inhabiting them—there, too, problems of moral choice will arise. But here on this earth man alone is the bearer of that godlike quality of creative imagination which is the precondition for moral behavior.

(5) Since a Pantheist does not pray to a personal god for special favors, he must seek for human "salvation" through the "therapy of knowledge"! The Pantheist cannot go to war because some god commands it, and if some day man brings peace to the world, it will come as a result of the fact that man is endowed with the divine quality of creative imagination and has forged a social lens for constructive social synthesis. But if a Pantheist cannot be lured into virtue by promises of everlasting life in paradise, neither can he be tormented by fears of eternal punishment in hell. In a word, the sources and sanctions of the good life are natural from beginning to end. Man must fashion for himself a social lens for collective vision; but the potentialities of human nature are much richer than the materialists, ancient or modern, are willing to admit.

These affirmations are stated in prosaic terms. In more poetic form, the attitude toward nature appropriate to a Cosmic Humanism was well stated by Walt Whitman—friend of Maurice Bucke—in the following lines:

MIRACLES

Why, who makes much of a miracle?
As to me I know of nothing but miracles
Whether I walk the streets of Cape Town,
Or dart my sight over the roofs of houses toward the sky,
Or wade with naked feet along the beach just in the edge of the water,
Or sit at dinner table with the rest,
Or look at strangers opposite me riding in the tram,
These . . . one and all, are to me miracles.
To me every hour of the light and dark is a miracle,
Every cubic inch of space is a miracle,
Every square yard of the surface of the earth is spread with the same,
To me the sea is a continual miracle,
The fishes that swim, the rocks, the motion of the waves, the ships with
    men in them,
What stranger miracles are there?

This eloquently presents the attitude of Pantheism toward the universe. But how about the attitude toward man himself?

Archetypal Man in a Cosmic Religion   From the present viewpoint, the universe is a powerhouse for the transformation of cosmic energy, and mankind is an evolutionary outlet for this power. Man—originally the planetary species and now the cosmic species—cannot separate himself from the powerhouse which is the environing universe, though he may limit or extend the manifestations of its capacities. In doing this the effects of each man's actions impinge upon others. What every individual does is part of the cosmic whole. Democracy grows out of that fact. On the human level, individualism takes on a new dimension; it implies not selfish rights but consciousness of universal relations. It is through the fulfillment of his individuality that man has evolved from the subperson, enmeshed in mass patterns of behavior, into the individual capable of choice and direction, at last to emerge as archetypal man—the being who is consciously creative, moral, and self-transcendent!

Man, the product of emergent evolution, is in turn the creator of new products. Thus man gains his existence from a cosmic field of energy he did not create, and he pays his debt to the cosmos by contributing to a reservoir of human achievement, the funded knowledge of men's minds and the material products of men's hands. If each man serves as an outlet for the formative energies of the universe, then mankind constitutes a collective outlet, a high-tension transmission system for the utilization of cosmic energies, omnipresent and inexhaustible. But to create the better world, human wishes are not enough. The human volition must be mobilized into a unified instrument that will energize the world society that must come into being as the vehicle for the imaginative creation of archetypal man. So many people seem to have built their own little powerhouses along the river banks of the stream of life and have failed to realize the cosmic background of this power availability. But the socialization of the benefits of power and knowledge is implicit in the spirit of cooperativeness whereby men share their results as they probe the depths and shoals of a universe that is endless in space and time. Man's earthly and outer-space enterprises depend on the directed guidance, the social imagination, he pours into his creations in industry, education, religion, and law.

The present moment sees us living in a world ready for the greatest forward movement in all human history. In this age of atomic energy, automation, electronic computers, communications satellites, there is no standing still. Either we move upward into the life more abundant, or we move downward and deathward into chaos and annihilation. But science must lead the way, and the religions of the world must supply the love, sympathy, and good will that can humanize the awesome undertaking.

NOTES FOR CHAPTER 12

1 See Albert Einstein's article "Cosmic Religion," first published in the *New York Times* and reprinted in the book, *Planetary Democracy*, by Oliver L. Reiser and Blodwen Davies.
2 *LIFE*, March 24, 1947.
3 *LIFE*, letter column, April 14, 1947.
4 See the article "Astronomy in Primitive Religions," by N. W. Makenson, *Journal of Bible and Religion*, Vol. 22 (1954), pp. 163-171.
5 See Oliver L. Reiser, *Man's New Image of Man*, 1961, p. 130.
6 See Anatol Rapoport, "Signal Reactions to Religious Symbols," *Humanist*, Vol. 18 (1958), pp. 195-206.
7 See Scott Buchanan, "Some Unnoted Aspects of Therapy," *Illinois Conference on Public Welfare*, Chicago, 1933.
8 This matter is discussed in more detail in my volume *World Philosophy: A Search for Synthesis*, University of Pittsburgh Press, 1948, pp. 113-120.
9 The literature in this field is considerable. Among the many books the student may consult are the following: *The Message of the Scrolls*, by Yigael Yadin; *The Essene Writings from Qumran*, by A. Dupont-Sommer; *The Dead Sea Scrolls*, by J. M. Allegro; *The Scrolls from the Dead Sea*, by Edmund Wilson; *From the Stone Age to Christianity*, by William F. Albright (1957 edition); *The Meaning of the Dead Sea Scrolls*, by A. Powell Davies; and *The Scrolls and the New Testament*, a symposium edited by Kristen Stendhall. Most of these volumes are available in paperback editions.
10 This term was suggested to me by Sir Julian Huxley. I made use of the concept and the word in the symposium, *The Humanist Frame*, edited by Sir Julian Huxley, published in England by George Allen and Unwin, and in the United States by Harper and Brothers, 1961. The title of my essay is, "The Integration of Knowledge."
11 These theses are taken from my volume, *The Integration of Human Knowledge*, Boston, Porter Sargent, 1958, pp. 34-36.

QUESTIONS

1 Explain why the belief in miracles and the notion of sin (in a religious sense) can have no place in a naturalistic humanism.
2 Why do some psychiatrists reject the sense of guilt as a valid and useful component of human nature? Do you agree?
3 Trace the history of pantheism in human thought. How does it resemble atheism? How does it differ from traditional materialism?
4 In what ways may a scientific humanism serve as a mediating position between Judeo-Christian supernaturalism and atheistic communism (*Diamat*)?
5 State the cosmological argument for the existence of God. What stand would a pantheistic humanism take with respect to this "proof"?

SUGGESTED READINGS

Erich Fromm, *Man for Himself*, New York, Rinehart, 1947.

Julian Huxley, *Religion Without Revelation*, New York, Harper, 1957.

Walter A. Kaufmann, *Critique of Religion and Philosophy*, New York, Harper, 1958.

Corliss Lamont, *Humanism as a Philosophy*, New York, Philosophical Library, 1949.

Charles Francis Potter, *Humanism: A New Religion*, New York, Simon and Schuster, 1957.

Oliver L. Reiser, *The Integration of Human Knowledge*, Boston, Porter Sargent Publishing Co., 1958; see also *Cosmic Humanism*, Schenkman, 1966.

13 O. Hobart Mowrer

Christianity and Psychoanalysis:
Is a New Synthesis Needed?

For nearly twenty years I have been persuaded, on the basis of both personal and professional experience, that in psychopathology we are confronted by profound moral and spiritual ("existential") issues which the secular healing professions have not at all adequately recognized.[1] I had come to see that so-called neurosis arises, not from an excess of virtue, i.e., unrealistic fear of "natural" sources of pleasure (as the psychoanalysts have held), but from *improper conduct* which has been protected and compounded by concealment and duplicity. And gradually it dawned on me that the only radically and specifically effective remedy for such a state of affairs is a *reversal* of the practices which have brought all this about—namely, confession to significant others in one's life of a hidden past *and* amendment of life, which includes not only discontinuation of sin and hypocrisy, but also a sustained effort at restitution.

I knew, of course, that such a conception of mental (or more accurately, *moral*) "disease" and its correction was by no means original. I knew that in at least certain great periods of the Church's history a similar position had been taken; and since there was at this time so little in professional thought and practice to support my views, I decided, some ten years ago, to reunite (after thirty years of estrangement) with a Protestant church and see what sources of encouragement and further enlightenment

I might thus discover. A great surprise was in store for me. Almost immediately I found that in Protestant Christendom in general "nobody was at home." Figuratively or literally, they were all over where I had just come from, getting themselves psychoanalyzed. There were, to be sure, exceptions. Some individuals in all denominations had refused to go along with this trend, and some denominations as such had resisted it. But the trend was and is unmistakable and pervasive.

One of the reasons I had left the church of my youth was its obstinacy with regard to Darwin's conception of organic evolution; but here, in a matter which challenges the Church much more fundamentally and for which there is much less empirical justification, there had been relatively rapid and widespread capitulation. This was to me such an astonishing phenomenon that I have spent no small part of the past decade trying to understand it. The present chapter will present the highlights of my findings.

------ ✳ ------

As a psychologist I had for some time been vaguely aware of the pastoral counseling movement in this country but had taken no special interest in it. Now I began to read avidly in this field and soon discovered that it was dominated by Freudianism even more systematically than the Church at large. In fact, it was from the seminary training which ministers were receiving in this area that much of the emphasis on psychoanalytic concepts seemed to be coming. So I began to delve into the origins and history of this enterprise. Here all signs pointed back to the life and work of a man by the name of Anton T. Boisen. In 1919-1920, while in middle life, he (himself an ordained minister) had experienced a period of psychotic disturbance; and from this had come a conviction that the churches have a great undeveloped potentiality and unmet responsibility. In an article entitled "The Challenge to Our Seminaries" which appeared in 1926, Dr. Boisen had expressed his views as follows:

> But of any such possibilities the Church is utterly oblivious. She takes no interest in cases of pronounced mental disorder. . . . We have therefore this truly remarkable situation—a Church which has always been interested in the care of the sick, confining her efforts to the types of cases [physical illness] in which religion has least concern and least to contribute, while in those types in which it is impossible to tell where the domain of the medical worker leaves off and that of the religious worker begins, there the Church is doing nothing.[2]

Since Fundamentalism preached only a hell to come and liberal theology preached no hell at all, both, argued Boisen, were "blind to the hell which is right before our eyes."

When we remember that what we know today about the human body has come very largely through the study of disease conditions, is it any wonder that a Church which has so completely ignored the problem of the soul that is sick, is able to speak with so little authority concerning the laws of the spiritual world? [3]

During the preceding year (1925) Boisen had already started a chaplaincy-training program at Worcester State Hospital in Massachusetts; and with the appearance of this article and others of like nature, the program grew in scope and influence. Then in 1936 Boisen published a book which he hoped would provide guidelines for the future of this movement. Entitled *The Exploration of the Inner World,* this volume set forth a conception of psychopathology and its treatment which is epitomized in the following excerpts.

The form of psychotherapy now most in the public eye is psychoanalysis. This in its aims is the exact opposite of faith healing. It has often been compared by its proponents to surgery, and major surgery at that. It is an attempt to lay bare and bring into clear consciousness the disowned sexual desires and cravings which it assumes have become detached from the conscious self and are responsible for the neurotic symptoms. Its aim is to make over the harsh conscience and the rigid ethical standards which have led to the disowning of these sex cravings so as to permit of their incorporation in the personality. To this end the psychoanalyst tries to get his patient to live through again his early experiences. The entire procedure is designed to detach the patient from his early loyalties in order to enable him to build up a new philosophy of life in which the dissociated craving may be properly assimilated. . . .[4]

In all my efforts [as a hospital chaplain and therapist] I rely upon a simple principle derived from my theological training which seems to me far too little understood. I refer to the view that *the real evil in mental disorder is not to be found in the conflict but in the sense of isolation or estrangement.* It is the fear and guilt which result from the presence in one's life of that which one is afraid to tell. For this reason I do not consider it necessary to lower the conscience threshold in order to get rid of the conflict. What is needed is forgiveness and restoration to the fellowship of that social something we call God.[5]

I would furthermore [suggest] that our findings indicate that the sense of guilt, the self-blame and the emotional disturbance which accompany it are not themselves evils but attempts at a cure. The real evil is the failure to attain the level of adjustment called for in some new period of development and the short-circuiting of the vital energies through easy satisfaction.[6]

Here is a conception of personality disturbance which, in its full elaboration, is very far from the conjectures of Freud (and very *close* to the position at which I have independently arrived); yet by mid-century the movement which Boisen had inspired had become predominantly Freudian. In the autumn of 1956, at a professional meeting in New York City, I had the privilege of meeting Dr. Boisen; and during the course of several extended conversations with him, I asked if it were not true that since 1936 the pastoral counseling movement has developed along lines very different from those he had originally conceived for it. Boisen's reply was: "Yes, that is so, but there were extenuating circumstances." And shortly afterwards he sent me a typescript copy of his autobiography, which has since appeared under the title, *Out of the Depths.* In this book Boisen reports that soon after he completed reading the proof and doing the indexes for *The Exploration of the Inner World,* he had a recurrence of his emotional difficulties and had to be hospitalized again for a brief time. This development was so traumatic for a number of the younger men and women who had been attracted to his program that he never regained leadership of the movement, either personally or conceptually. As a result of this temporary collapse, Boisen lost the confidence of some of the most gifted and dedicated persons in the field, who now began to look elsewhere for inspiration and guidance. This they found in Sigmund Freud and in some measure also in Carl Rogers. The result is the pastoral counseling movement and the general religious ethos which we know today.[7]

What the situation in our seminaries and in our churches would now have been if Anton Boisen had not suffered a recurrence of his emotional problems in 1936 no one can, with confidence, say. But it is by no means certain that things would not still have moved in much the same direction. In taking the position which he did, Boisen stood very much alone. His call to the Church to recover its historic interest and role in the cure of souls was timely and on the whole well received. But his further specification of the *way* in which this was to be done pleased neither of the major institutions with which he had to deal. Although he was usually restrained and respectful when he spoke of psychoanalysis, psychiatry, and medicine, it was clear that Boisen was not prepared to stress the role of permissiveness which has become the stock in trade of these professions. And thus he insured an attitude of supreme indifference on the part of many medical psychotherapists, and some he inspired to active recrimination and denunciation.

More subtly though hardly less definitely, Boisen's position was such as to make him suspect also in religious circles. In one of the passages already quoted, he speaks of the emotionally disturbed person's needing "forgiveness and restoration"; but he did not stress sufficiently, for the tastes of many, the *vertical* aspects of this transaction. In the passage alluded to, he goes on to add "forgiveness and restoration to the fellowship of that *social* something we call God"; and at various other points in *The Exploration of the Inner World* it is sufficiently evident that this particular phrasing was by no means accidental. Consider, for example, the following statements:

We may have *progressive unification on a basis conceived as universal* with attitudes of aspiration, reverence, and faith. Such an end result involves the sense of fellowship with that which is best in one's social experience and may be attained through confession and forgiveness for one's shortcomings and the reinforcement of the will to do right. The religious man at his best and the socially minded and disciplined man who may not call himself religious but who is none the less consistently loyal to the best he knows are exemplifications. It is the goal of all education to produce men of these types through normal development and without eruptive experiences.[8]

And again, somewhat more specifically, Boisen says:

Concealment devices are of greatest interest from the standpoint of our inquiry because of the light which they throw upon the social nature of man. In the accusing voices and other manifestations of the morbid conscience we have striking confirmation of the view that the sense of guilt is essentially a social judgment which operates within the personality itself. We may be impressed by the marvelous devices and the strange lengths to which men will go to escape the sense of condemnation and by the relationship between mental health and the systematization or structuralization of ideas. The paranoiac who succeeds in achieving some sort of systematization in his misinterpretation may be socially isolated but he does manage to keep his head above water.[9]

It is thus in no way surprising that many theologians came to regard Boisen as "scarcely more than a humanist." And he gave religionists further cause for distrust by his *rejection of revelation and advocacy of empirical inquiry*.

I take it [that] one of our great needs today [is] to provide through empirical observation and tested experience a basis for our generalizations regarding those types of conduct which make for the richer and more abundant personal and social life. . . . I hold that the shift from faith in a revealed religion, which is responsible for so much of the present confusion, to an empirical basis, must be not merely accepted but eagerly furthered. It is furthermore my conviction that the remaking of the outer world and the cure of the desperate sickness which now threatens to destroy our civilization is inseparably associated with the problems of the inner world and that out of the efforts to understand and help the mentally distressed should come a new vision of the great Reality to whom we give the name of God, in whom alone we are to find the end and meaning of personal and social life and the sources of power and of renewal.[10]

Boisen and his program thus faced danger on the right and danger on the left. Even without his personal collapse in 1936, it is doubtful if the vision he had for the new profession of pastoral counseling could have long withstood the crossfire from both psychiatry and religion. Nor was Boisen himself unaware of this predicament, for near the end of his book he says:

> In these particulars we find a striking contrast between the training of the medical man and that of the clergyman. . . .
> Now I have no brief for either profession. I have had almost as much difficulty with the one as with the other. I can only say that from the standpoint of the mentally ill, in whose behalf I speak, I scarcely know which is worse, to have to depend upon a clergyman who has never come to close grips with the realities of human nature, or to be at the mercy of a physician who has no understanding of the spiritual needs and aspirations and of the nobler potentialities of mankind. I am merely convinced that *our present system of training experts in the maladies of the personality is in need of improvement.*[11]

Yet the spectacle which confronts us today is that of psychiatry and religion appearing to have miraculously made peace with each other, without ever acknowledging the cogency of the analysis and argument which Boisen adduced. If at this point the reader is still baffled by what has transpired in this field, he has every right to be; for here we are surely dealing with mystery within mystery, ambiguity compounded by ambiguity.[12]

It would be tedious and in no way illuminating if at this point I attempted to indicate the exact nature and course of my reading after I arrived at the perception of the situation which has just been set forth. I was even more perplexed than I had been in the beginning; and the only option now open to me, it seemed, was to dip much more deeply into the historical background and determinants of prevailing attitudes and practices. The Reformation quickly became a period of lively interest for me; but I also read about the medieval church, the early church, the life and times of Jesus, and the immediately preceding developments which were represented by the Essenes and their remarkable community at Qumran. I read about classical Judaism; and I followed, in at least a cursory way, developments down to such contemporary works as Freud's *Moses and Monotheism* and David Bakan's *Sigmund Freud and the Jewish Mystical Tradition*. Naturally, I read extensively in both the Old and the New Testament, and I also resorted to standard biblical dictionaries, commentaries, and textbooks. But my interest throughout lay primarily in *Christian* history and ideology. And here my concern was further specialized and focused in that, as a psychologist, I had constantly before me the question as to what religion, throughout the ages, has said and done about the phenomenon which today we call *mental illness*.

Among the several books I have read on the Dead Sea scrolls and the life and thought of the Essenes which they portray, none has been more illuminating than Dr. Charles Francis Potter's trenchant but too sensationally titled book, *The Lost Years of Jesus Revealed*.[13] Here the thesis is persuasively advanced that the Essenes were a transitional link between classical Judaism and early Christianity which, later, both Christians and Jews systematically and deliberately repudiated and ignored (a strategy facilitated by the sacking of Qumran and the destruction of its communal life by the Roman army in 70 A.D.). Christians were interested in suppressing the fact of continuity and cultural evolution in favor of the more dramatic thesis of a divine revelation; and Jews, as the rift with Christians widened, tried equally hard to disavow any trace of kinship with this heresy. But the historical reality of the Essenes and the salient nature of their teachings and practices (thanks to the recent discovery of the contents of their library, which before taking flight from Qumran they had hidden in nearby caves) can no longer be questioned; and the evidence that they had a direct affinity both with Judaism and with Christianity is specific and compelling. The Apostle John was almost certainly a converted Essene; and the fact that John the Baptist "cried in the wilderness" and baptized in the Jordan River only two or three miles from Qumran and stressed (as did the Essenes) the purifying power of immersion suggests close association on his part as well. With perhaps less documentary proof, but not implausibly, Potter suggests that Jesus himself studied protractedly (during his "lost" years, from age twelve to age thirty) at Qumran and that it was from this apprenticeship that he ultimately came forth to initiate his own unique and fateful ministry. Regardless of whether this particular hypothesis is true, Jesus almost certainly knew the story of the Teacher of Righteousness, who had founded Qumran; and the evidence is unequivocal that he and his followers knew and often referred to certain religious books which the Essenes valued but which are not included in modern versions of the Bible.

The Essenes were deeply interested in spiritual healing; and in many respects in their community at Qumran they resembled the older Therapeutae of Greece and Egypt. Thus, reasons Potter, it is understandable that Jesus' ministry had from its inception a strong emphasis upon healing. And it was as healer and teacher and prophet, rather than as a god, that he first won popular acclaim and can still be most appropriately remembered and revered. The essence of Potter's argument on this score is summed up in the following paragraphs, which also climax and conclude his book as a whole:

The widely heralded and acclaimed "return" of religion and the churches has probably been due not so much to the attractions of theology, which interests lay people very little even when they understand it, but more likely to the new and growing fascination of the study of the psychology of personality, hence the quickened interest in the greatest personality of all time. Whether we approve of the trend or not, we are blind and deaf if we do not recognize that psychology is rapidly gaining on theology, if not superseding it, as the attraction, explanation, and dominating factor in modern religion.

And the reason why people the world over are so very much interested in the Qumran manuscripts, so dramatically brought to light, and why they will be for a long time asking keen questions about the finds, is the hope that somewhere in them there may be found or implied the secrets of personality development, perhaps learned by Jesus in these hidden and so-called apocryphal books and imparted by him to his disciples who so often "understood not the things which he spake unto them."

Those disciples and the theology-obsessed Church Fathers who followed them were so anxious to deify Jesus and build up a system of philosophical theology that would send their enemies and doctrinal opponents to hell, and would assure themselves front seats in heaven, that they tragically overlooked his real significance. They did admit that "he knew what was in man," and that he lamented their childish infatuation with miracles and the supernatural ("Except ye see miracles and wonders ye will not believe"), but they missed his big message—*that they could do the same things he did!* They missed, too, the psychosomatic character of his healings. Rather than think deeply and observe carefully what actually did take place, they preferred the easy explanation of the mentally lazy, and used the fuzzy blanket-word "god" to cover their ignorance.

The first-century followers of Jesus and the theologians and their successors can be excused to some extent for failing to perceive that he was no god come down from heaven, but rather a very great human being, ahead of his time in his intuitive understanding of his fellows and in his apparently instinctive knowledge of the technique of what we now call psychotherapy. They can be forgiven, for they had not studied psychology, as had the early followers of Gautama the Buddha, who preached salvation by the psychological suppression of vain desires. And it should be noted that the early disciples of the Buddha did not deify him, although he lived and died five centuries before Jesus.

But the present-day followers of Jesus, and modern Christian theologians, living in a day when the knowledge of the principles of psychology is available to almost anyone who cares to learn them, have no excuse for using the very limited and inadequate thought-forms of the Palestine people of two thousand years ago to explain the personality and character of this splendid leader and teacher of men, who was perceptive, keenly intelligent, sympathetic, comprehending all the vices, virtues, and motives of humans, a man who took the best he had read and thought, and interpreted it to humanity by embodying it in his own life.

He demonstrated truth, he incarnated righteousness; but that did not prove he was a supernatural being. It is Jesus the Man who understood men, whom men want to know and have always wanted to know. And the Scrolls from the Salty Sea fascinate us because they may throw some light on what he studied and thought and what his radiant personality really was before the theologians made a god out of him.[14]

I am aware that in some circles Dr. Potter's book is regarded as "highly unreliable," if not deliberately fraudulent. Or more moderately, the criticism is that many of his inferences are only conjectures, "not definitely proven." It is, I think, neither faulty logic nor questionable scholarship that really bothers Dr. Potter's critics but rather his unwillingness to accept *on faith* certain matters which are inherently far more improbable than anything which he himself suggests. The same persons who have the severest strictures for the Potter book accept "as gospel" New Testament and subsequent accounts of the Christian miracles and mysteries. I do not claim to be a technical scholar in this area and thus able authentically to evaluate the import and meaning of the contents of the Essene Library; but I find in Dr. Potter's book nothing that is clearly contradicted and much that is confirmed in such books as Wilson's *The Scrolls from the Dead Sea*, Davies' *The Meaning of the Dead Sea Scrolls*, Danielou's *Dead Sea Scrolls and Primitive Christianity*, and Gaster's *The Dead Sea Scriptures*. And there is certainly much in the contemporary scene to support the thesis that "psychology" is today on the offensive and "theology" on the defensive.[15]

------ ✳ ------

Written in much the same spirit as is Potter's book (though nearly a century earlier—it was published in 1863), Ernest Renan's *Life of Jesus* provides a different but related insight. As is well known, John the Baptist and Jesus were cousins and, what is less widely recognized, of approximately the same age; but John was more precocious than Jesus and was well established as a teacher and prophet when Jesus started his ministry. Both men were of the common people, and Jesus undoubtedly drew heavily upon John, in the beginning, for inspiration as well as method. But it was soon evident that something was emerging in the teachings of Jesus which was absent, or at best only nascent, in John. John was essentially apocalyptic in his approach, calling for repentance—"for the kingdom of heaven is at hand." A "great wrath" was to come, and people should prepare for it. Says Renan:

> Repentance, of which baptism was the type, the giving of alms, the reformation of habits, were in John's view the great means of preparation for the coming events, though we do not know exactly in what light he conceived them. It is, however, certain that he preached with much power against the same adversaries as Jesus, against rich priests, the Pharisees, the doctors, in one word against official Judaism; and that, like Jesus, he was specially welcomed by the despised classes. . . . It does not seem that he possessed even the germ of the great idea which led to the triumph of Jesus, the idea of a pure religion; but he powerfully served this idea in *substituting a private rite for the legal ceremonies which required priests*, as the Flagellants of the Middle Ages were the precursors of the Reformation, *by depriving the official clergy of the monopoly of the sacraments and of absolution.*[16]
>
> Jesus only wished to increase under John's protection; and thought himself obliged, in order to gain the multitude, to employ the external means which had given John such astonishing success. . . . Many other of John's expressions may be found repeated *verbatim* in the discourses of Jesus.[17]

Among such expressions was the declaration that "the kingdom of heaven is at hand." But it was so apparent that for Jesus this affirmation had another dimension. Renan expresses it this way:

> It seems also that his sojourn with John had, not so much by the influence of the Baptist, as by the natural progress of his own thought, considerably ripened his ideas on "the kingdom of heaven." His watchword, henceforth, is the "good tidings," the announcement that the kingdom of God is at hand. Jesus is no longer simply a delightful moralist, aspiring to express sublime lessons in short and lively aphorisms; he is the transcendent revolutionary, who essays to

renovate the world from its very basis, and to establish upon earth the idea which he had conceived. . . . This phrase, "kingdom of God," or "kingdom of heaven," was, as we have said, already long familiar to the Jews. But Jesus gave it a moral sense, a social application, which even the author of the Book of Daniel, in his apocalyptic enthusiasm, had scarcely dared to imagine.[18]

Thus a certain duality was emerging in the thought of Jesus. "The kingdom of heaven is at hand" continued to mean for him, as it had for John, that the end of the times was imminent; but it was also coming to mean that a richer, more abundant life is available, *here and now*, for anyone who will come into a new relationship with his brother and his neighbor. The way in which these two versions of "the kingdom" were merged in Jesus' own mind is suggested by Renan thus:

The revolution he wished to effect was always a moral revolution; but he had not yet begun to trust to the angels and the last trumpet for its execution. It was upon men and by the aid of men themselves that he wished to act. A visionary who had no other idea than the proximity of the last judgment, would not have had this care for the amelioration of man, and would not have given utterance to the finest moral teaching that humanity has received. Much vagueness no doubt tinged his ideas, and it was rather a noble feeling than a fixed design, that urged him to the sublime work which was realized by him, though in a very different manner to which he imagined.[19]

And then Renan adds the following analysis and appraisal:

That there may have been a contradiction between the belief in the approaching end of the world and the general moral system of Jesus, conceived in prospect of a permanent state of humanity . . . no one will attempt to deny. It was exactly this contradiction that insured the success of his work. The millenarian alone would have done nothing lasting; the moralist alone would have done nothing powerful. The millenarianist gave the impulse, the moralist insured the future. Hence Christianity united the two conditions of great success in this world, a revolutionary starting-point, and the possibility of continuous life. Everything which is needed to succeed ought to respond to these two wants; for the world seeks both to change and to last. Jesus, at the same time that he announced an unparalleled subversion in human affairs, proclaimed the principles upon which society has reposed for eighteen hundred years.[20]

In its apocalyptic sense, the claim that the kingdom of heaven, as the Last Judgment, was "at hand" was manifestly false. The world was not about to come to an end; and despite many similar prophecies during the intervening two thousand years, there is no reason to believe that we are even now "in the Last Days." Nor was this emphasis in any way originally or uniquely Christian. On this score the *Interpreter's Dictionary of the Bible* says that Apocalypticism is "a type of religious thought which apparently originated in Zoroastrianism" and was "mediated by Judaism to early Christianity." It was, it seems, a more or less routine (and now opprobrious) device which was used to call attention to and stress the urgency of any special message which was to be proclaimed. Hence, it was clearly the more "revolutionary" meaning which Jesus imparted to the imminence of "the kingdom of heaven" that gave his ministry unique appeal and his teaching such remarkable vitality.

When John the Baptist proclaimed that the kingdom of heaven was at hand, the implication was one of threat and warning: repent *or* be consumed in the fire to come! But Jesus had another vision, which implied a promise, a hope, or, as Renan says, "good tidings." The established Jewish religion had become oppressive, exploitative, and nonredemptive. And Jesus, the revolutionary, spoke *against* "the rich priests, the Pharisees, the doctors, in one word against official Judaism." And what he said, in effect, was this: "You do not have to follow all the prescribed rules and rituals to be saved. In order to inherit salvation, i.e., to find the good, the more abundant life, you do not need to make blood offerings or observe the hundreds of religious laws. The kingdom of heaven is available to you *now*, through a new and improved manner of relating to and dealing with your fellowmen. You can seek and find the kingdom directly, without the help of the professionals." Here was the "moral sense" and "social application" to which Renan refers. There were certainly intimations of this *revolt*, this *first* Reformation in the teachings and practices of the Essenes (and of John the Baptist); but only in Jesus of Nazareth did it find general appeal, cogency, and power. It will be our later thesis that the revolutionary slogan of Jesus is, today, dramatically relevant. Religious salvation and psychological recovery have again been taken out of the reach of individual human beings; and if ever humanity needed to hear the same Gospel—that the kingdom of heaven is indeed *at hand*, —it is *now*. Are we perhaps today entering what may be regarded as the *third* Reformation, which will involve, in certain important ways, a return to the goals and principles of the first?

Some readers may be inclined to feel that it is inappropriate and misleading to apply the term "revolutionary" to Jesus. When we think of his supreme emphasis on obedience, both in his teachings and in his own life, it does seem incongruous to attribute to him motives of sedition and rebellion. But an important distinction is in order here. If one were simply to say, "Jesus was in revolt against religion," this would be invalid or valid, according to one's interpretation of the word "religion." It would be invalid, and flagrantly so, if one interpreted religion to mean "true religion." This, as Jesus conceived it, was what he worked and ultimately died for. And in this sense he was by no means antireligious or anarchistic. But he was clearly and intransigently opposed to and in revolt against what he perceived to be a perversion and distortion of religion. In *this* context, the term "revolutionary" seems fully justified. (The similarity between Jesus and Martin Luther in this regard is obvious. Luther was not originally intent upon seceding from or destroying the Catholic Church, but rather upon reforming it from within. Like Jesus, he moved into a "revolutionary" role only when he found the established Church unwilling to consider his demands for change.) Let us not forget the famous temple scene:

> And they came to Jerusalem: and Jesus went into the temple, and began to cast out them that sold and bought of the moneychangers, and the seats of them that sold doves; and would not suffer that any man should carry any vessel through the temple. And he taught, saying unto them, is it not written, My house shall be called of all nations the house of prayer? but ye have made it a den of thieves. And the scribes and chief priests heard it, and sought how they might destroy him: for they feared him, because all the people were astonished at his doctrine.[21]
>
> And the Jews' passover was at hand, and Jesus went up to Jerusalem, and found in the temple those that sold oxen and sheep and doves, and the changers of money sitting: and when he had made a scourge of small cords, he drove them out of the temple, and the sheep, and the oxen: and poured out the changers' money, and overthrew the tables: and said unto them that sold doves, Take these things hence; make not my Father's house a house of merchandise.[22]

Also, we must not overlook the equally determined opposition of "the scribes and chief priests," and how they pondered ways to "destroy him," a destruction which they accomplished a few days later. The author of the article Money-Changer in the *Interpreter's Dictionary of the Bible* makes what is thus an odd observation when he says:

> Although the "money-changers in the temple" have become a familiar symbol of the sordid, especially of the profaning of religion by commercialism, the real meaning of this episode is by no means certain. . . . Evidently [Jesus] was not opposed to the maintenance of the temple and its sacrificial system.

Renan (see also the excerpts from Barclay in the following section) holds that Jesus *was* opposed, and implacably so, to the "sacrificial system."

He did not say, "The kingdom of heaven is in the temple." He said, "It is at hand, *within* you," a quality of life which each can achieve for himself.

Here is a first-rate enigma: why any scholar should hold that the explanation of Jesus' attack upon the money-changers "is by no means certain." If anything about Jesus' whole life is certain, the reason and rationale for this action would seem preeminently so. Yet the reforming, "revolutionary" theme is commonly denied, or at least deemphasized, as the following excerpt from the *Interpreter's Dictionary* concerning the "Kingdom of God, or heaven" will further indicate:

> These synonymous expressions represent an idea which is deeply rooted in the thought of the Old Testament, and which constitutes the central theme of the teaching of Jesus as recorded in the Synoptic gospels. . . . The Bible regards the kingly rule of God under three different aspects: as an eternal fact, as manifested upon earth in its acceptance by men, and as a consummation to be hoped for in the future. In the last of these aspects, the idea is an eschatological one. It is this eschatological aspect that predominates in the teaching of Jesus on the kingdom of God, and modern discussions of Christian eschatology have largely centered around the question of the interpretation of his teachings on this subject.[23]

Can it be that here is one of the major reasons for the futility and irrelevance of much contemporary theology? There is today, I venture to say, less interest on the part of ordinary men and women in the question of whether Jesus was or was not the long-awaited Messiah than there is in the question of what understanding of life and skill in interpersonal relations the teachings of this man can give us. Jesus felt that the Temple and its practices had become a barrier to existential wisdom and the good life; and why anyone should be mystified by his protest against its desecration is itself the greater mystery.

As Schweitzer[23a] and others have shown, Jesus was at times uncertain and vacillating with respect to the messianic and eschatological aspects of his ministry. On this score even the *Dictionary* article which has been cited says:

> Jesus expressly disclaimed any precise knowledge as to the time of the final consummation (Mark 13:32). . . . There is no saying of Jesus in which he explicitly connects the coming of the kingdom of God with his own death.[24]

(We may add that in the words accorded to Jesus in the New Testament, there is very little reference to the doctrine of the substitutionary atonement, as Paul would have us understand it. And such references as do appear could easily have gotten into the Synoptic Gospels and the Acts of the Apostles from the Epistles of Paul, which are commonly recognized as having been written before any of the rest of the New Testament.)

But in his conviction and role *as reformer*, Jesus never faltered. Paul seemed at first to think that the end of the times was imminent, only to admit his later uncertainty on this score. And the contemporary German theologian Rudolf Bultmann says:

> *The mythical eschatology* is untenable for the simple reason that the parousia of Christ never took place as the New Testament expected. History did not come to an end, and, as every school-boy knows, it will continue to run its course. If we believe that the world as we know it will come to an end in time, we expect the end to take the form of a natural catastrophe, not of a mythical event such as the New Testament expects.[25]

Yet some theologians and Biblical scholars would today have us believe that "it is the eschatological aspect that predominates in the teaching of Jesus on the kingdom of God." This is a very mistaken point of view so far as I can judge and serves only to mask and conceal the aspect of Jesus' life and ministry that has enduring significant and thus contemporary relevance. Again Dr. Bultmann:

> If the truth of the New Testament proclamation is to be preserved, the only way is to demythologize it. But our motive in so doing must not be to make the New Testament relevant to the modern world at all costs. The question is simply whether the New Testament message consists exclusively of mythology, or whether it actually demands the elimination of myth if it is to be understood as it is meant to be. . . .
>
> . . . Can the kerygma [message, teaching] be interpreted apart from mythology? Can we recover the truth of the kerygma for men who do not think in mythological terms without forfeiting its character as kerygma? [26]

It is my observation that modern man will not, cannot accept both Christian mythology and kerygma. The former, instead of being an aid, has become a barrier to the latter. But it is also my belief that to accept neither is calamitous! The only viable alternative is, precisely as Bultmann proposes, to eliminate the myth and keep the kerygma. Our immediate purpose, therefore, is to discover what the kerygma, as distinct from magic and myth, actually is.

------ ✳ ------

Because Ernest Renan, in his *Life of Jesus*, wrote as a secularist rather than as a believer, both he and his book have been subjected to persecution and neglect. Within five months after its original publication in France, *La Vie de Jésus* had sold 60,000 copies and was being translated into various foreign languages; yet Renan, for his pains, was dismissed from his professorship at the Collège de France, and his book is today commonly ignored on the grounds that it is fallacious and outmoded. Actually Renan had an uncanny appreciation of the Essenian influence upon Christianity long before the existence of the Dead Sea scrolls had even been suspected; and William Barclay, the eminent Scotch theologian, in his recently published book, *The Mind of Jesus*, substantiates (without once alluding to Renan) the latter's central thesis both generally and in particular. In the first chapter of his book Barclay says that Jesus "suddenly discovered that the whole paraphernalia of sacrifice was a vast irrelevance, and the whole apparatus of the law a barrier to God." [27] And in a chapter entitled "The Men Against Jesus," he paints almost exactly the same picture as does Renan. Here are some salient excerpts:

It is quite clear that under this system religion became the affair of the expert. Only the scribes knew the immense ramifications of the oral law; only the Pharisees could keep them. Obviously all this put true religion out of reach of the ordinary working man. He could not engage in the ordinary working activities of the world and keep the law. To keep the law was in itself a whole-time occupation. Religion in its higher reaches became the preserve of the expert and of the professional. . . .

Jesus' point of view was quite simple. He believed that human need takes precedence of any ritual, rule or regulation. . . .

Here was another head-on collision. The Pharisees narrowed the love of God until it included only themselves; Jesus widened the love of God until it reached out to all men, saints and sinner alike. . . .

It can be seen that the priests were a privileged body of men in a comparatively poor country, living a life of unexampled ease and luxury at the expense of the people. It is not in human nature that men should willingly abandon a way of life like that. . . .

Since the time of Josiah all local shrines had been forbidden, and the law was that sacrifice could be offered only at the Temple in Jerusalem, and only through a priest. The priest, therefore, stood between man and God. If a man sinned, and the right relationship to God was to be restored, sacrifice must be made, and that sacrifice could be made only through the priest. Seldom can any body of men have wielded such spiritual power.

All this was true of the priests—and yet one thing was abundantly and increasingly clear—*if Jesus was right, the priests were wrong.* If Jesus' view of religion was correct, then the priesthood and all its functions were a vast irrelevancy. There are not lacking signs in the religious history of Israel that many times there was a breach between prophet and priest. . . .

Here was the supreme challenge. Either Jesus had to go, or the whole sacrificial system had to go. Either the priesthood destroyed Jesus, or Jesus destroyed the priesthood. Beyond a doubt there were priests who loved the Temple service, and who through it sought devotedly to serve God; but, human nature being what it is, the vast majority of the priests must have seen in him a threat to their comfortable way of life, a menace to their spiritual supremacy, the assailant of their vested interests; and they decided that, before Jesus destroyed them, they must destroy him.

It was a queer tangle of human motives which hounded Jesus to the Cross. All the loveliness of his life mattered nothing. The Pharisees honestly and sincerely believed him to be a bad man and an evil influence on other men. The Sadducees wished only to remove a possible threat to their civil and political power and social standing. The priests were determined to eliminate a teacher whose teaching spelt the end of their perquisites and of their spiritual dictatorship. Jesus cut across blind and rigorous orthodoxy, political and social ambition, ritual and spiritual aristocracy; and so men came to the conclusion that he must die.[28]

Jesus was thus the implacable foe of legalism, ritual, and animal sacrifice; and although those who stood in opposition to him were physically victorious, his ideas and ideals have nevertheless shown an astonishing vitality. It would, however, be a mistake to suppose that the spirit of Jesus has enjoyed a continuously triumphant march down through the centuries. Almost immediately after Jesus' crucifixion, the Apostle Paul set to work trying to restore the logic of sacrifice by making of Jesus' own death a "blood offering" for the remission of human sin in general, provided only that the sinner profess *belief* in the system of "substitutionary atonement" which Paul promulgated. As we shall presently see, the movement which Jesus himself initiated managed to retain much of its original cast and vigor until the Dark Ages, i.e., the early Middle Ages, by which time a new system of sacraments had been elaborated; and by roughly 1200 A.D., a *reconstituted priesthood* had once more obtained absolute power over the remission of sins. Three hundred years later, the Church had become so indifferent and irrelevant to human need and so internally corrupt and so politically ambitious that when Luther in 1517 provided the spark, what we may call in our frame of reference the *second* Reformation flared into a great conflagration. The entrenched sacramentalism of the Medieval Church was seared by this fire but not destroyed; and Protestantism made the strategic error of trying to undercut this emphasis by stressing the possibility of confession of sins directly to God instead of through a human intermediary. As I have elsewhere indicated, all this has left large segments of the Christian world without clear and effective means of dealing with personal guilt and has encouraged the emergence of a new secular profession for "the care of souls" (which is what *psychiatry* literally means); and today some members of *this* profession are again claiming the exclusive right and ability to "treat" (do "therapy" with) persons thus afflicted.

Although, in terms of our over-all inquiry, many questions remain still unanswered, we can begin to discern certain recurrent patterns.

------ ✳ ------

Fortunately, the course of developments which we now wish to trace has already been admirably summarized by Dr. John T. McNeill in a book entitled *A History of the Cure of Souls*. McNeill makes certain general observations in the Preface of his book:

> The cure of souls is, then, the sustaining and curative treatment of persons in those matters that reach beyond the requirements of the animal life. . . .
>
> Yet the function of the healer of the soul is not less ancient than that of the physician of the body. In primitive societies both functions are commonly assumed by the same person. The *shaman* of American Indian or primitive Siberian tribes is at once healer, sorcerer, priest and teacher. . . .
>
> Socrates was, and wished to be, *iatros tēs psuchēs*, a healer of the soul. These Greek syllables have been recast to form the word "psychiatrist." But Socrates would hardly recognize the medical psychiatrist as a member of his fraternity. A scientific psychiatry indifferent to religion and philosophy is a new and strange phenomenon. Whatever may be the future importance of this new science, it is abundantly evident that the role of the religious physician of souls is not played out. In the stresses of the present century, his function seems, indeed, to be expanding. He stands in a long and honorable tradition, although, through the neglect of historians, the record of it has been largely concealed from him. The danger of obsession with the contemporary besets him.[29]

McNeill also alludes in a preliminary way to the matter which will be of greatest concern to us here, namely, "the changing philosophies of *the relation of the individual to the group* (or church)." [30] He says:

> New Testament Christianity, despite its intense group loyalty, unfailingly sought the spiritual vitality of the individual and achieved

a wholesome co-ordination of individual and group interests. . . .[31]

The Reformation, in its Lutheran, Reformed and Anglican branches, adopted this new orientation, and substituted for obligatory and exhaustive confession a voluntary confiding of sins and "griefs" to a minister or other suitable advisor, for relief and counsel. The favorite Reformation doctrine of the priesthood of all Christians encouraged mutual or group procedures in guidance. . . . Even in their stern and often unwholesomely authoritarian discipline, the Calvinist communions sought to employ the principle of the mutual cure of souls. Not without some loss and danger, but on the whole with great advantage, the Protestant churches have largely abandoned the legalism that has at times attended their methods, and are free to advance along new lines with the aid of modern scientific knowledge.[32]

Whenever it is suggested that psychopathology is mainly a function of loss on the part of an individual of his sociality or group affiliation and that psychotherapy, if meaningful and effective, is a means for the recovery thereof, the objection is almost certain to be raised (by both religionists and secularists, though for different reasons) that this conception is limited to Christian or Judeo-Christian cultures and therefore is not broadly human (universal) in its applicability. This is sheer ethnocentricism, as almost any competent work on comparative religion will indicate. And the generality of these principles is also clearly revealed by a book such as Paul Radin's *Primitive Religion* and by even a cursory examination of the Human Relations Area Files (originated at Yale University as the Cross-Cultural Index but now available in many other university libraries). McNeill himself finds in ancient Greece and in the Hindu, Buddhistic, Confucian, and Islamic religions many common denominators in "the cure of souls." We may therefore assume that we are here dealing with broadly human phenomena and not merely with the epiphenomena of a particular culture or value system.[33] However, since our immediate concern is a specific one, we shall restrict ourselves to the history of this problem in the Judeo-Christian tradition.

Although emphasis on the relation of man to God is by no means lacking in ancient Hebrew writings, each individual was given to understand that his identity and indeed his very being were intimately tied up with the history and life of his people (cf. Zborowski and Herzog's *Life Is with People*[34]). However, by the time of Jesus, creative prophecy had ceased and the life of the spirit had become dull, pedantic, and constricted. As we have seen, much of the thrust of Jesus' ministry was to release men and women from this bondage and open up for them the life more abundant. Jesus supplied the peculiar genius needed to give real impetus to this revolution, but there were pre-Christian stirrings of a similar kind. The

Essenes represented a definite protest against and break with the hardened, rigidified Jewish traditions; and McNeill indicates that there were other more or less independent efforts along these lines. For example:

> In their teaching on confession and repentance the rabbis also expressed a truly religious spirit. The day of Atonement was preceded by nine days of penitential preparation. But in addition to public repentance the rabbis stressed individual and inward penitence. The words of Numbers 5:6,7 were interpreted as requiring oral confession, along with restitution to the injured. . . . The rabbinical authority, S. Schechter, and the Jesuit scholar, J. Bonsirven, have called attention to the practice of confession of personal sins in late pre-Christian Judaism. Societies were formed whose members were pledged to a weekly confession.[35]

The centrality of the therapeutic emphasis in the ministry of Jesus and the fact of cultural continuity are both clearly brought out by the following excerpt from McNeill:

> It is increasingly recognized by scholars that most of the teachings of Jesus are substantially paralleled in the Wisdom and rabbinical literature. B. T. D. Smith, in a study of the parables of Jesus, points to many similarities of phrase and figure between the Talmud and the Gospels. . . . This scholar holds, too, that Jesus lived and taught as the rabbis, using the same methods of argument, and like them employing proverbs and parables. The word "discipline" applied to his followers is regarded as a technical term for the pupils of a rabbi. Gerhard Kittel had earlier remarked (in his study *Jesus als Seelsorger*) "He was not scribe and not rabbi, not teacher and master of wisdom; what men discovered in him was exactly this: healer of souls." [36]

And then McNeill provides a familiar "case history":

> Jesus' treatment of an unsocial and unintegrated individual in relation to the ethics of material gain is strikingly illustrated in the story of Zacchaeus (Luke 19:1-10). . . . We cannot know what confessions were made by this "malefactor of great wealth" in the liberating presence of Jesus, or how under his guidance a new course of action, the reverse of what had been habitual, was resolved upon. The private conference ends with Zacchaeus' declaration of intention to use his possessions for poor relief and in fourfold restitution of what he had fraudulently exacted. He who has been an exploiter becomes a benefactor of his fellow citizens, and realizes that he is identified with them. "Today salvation is come to this house. . . ." Here we have in another form the theme of the lost

sheep and the lost coin. The repentance of the sinner is the matter of importance.[37]

Although we perhaps think of Paul primarily as theologian and Founding Father, he too was interested in the ministry of healing. McNeill quotes Martin Schlunk as saying that Paul "possessed the gift of the cure of souls in outstanding measure and employed the art with wonderful mastery." [38] "Bear one another's burdens. . . . Live in harmony with one another. . . . None of us lives to himself. . . . Let everyone speak truth to his neighbor, for we are members one of another" are all phrases embodying, as McNeill puts it, "the emergence in early Christianity of a new dynamic for personal moral living, the releasing of power for a new therapy of souls with which nothing in the ancient world could compete." [39]

> It is far easier to fast twice a week than to share with others life's highest treasures. Yet the apostolic apprehension of the Christian cure of souls was not a vain dream. It was because many Christians —though perhaps a minority among them—faithfully adhered to these principles, that the Church emerged as a firmly knit organization. It was because they shared in these ways, and perpetuated by sharing, a new life in Christ, and effectively revealed it in their lives, that the Roman world failed to smother the Christian groups in its mass or crush them by its power, and that it finally turned to the Church for deliverance from its own political chaos. . . . Even today we have fresh practical lessons to learn from the Gospels and Epistles in the matter of the cure of souls.[40]

There is an extremely interesting paradox in the record of Jesus' therapeutic ministry, as it has come down to us. On the one hand, we have abundant evidence of the healing power of Jesus' teachings and personal example; but there is also recurrent reference to acts of exorcism on his part. Did Jesus think that his teachings were applicable to sane sinners (like Zacchaeus) but not to "insane" ones? Today, oddly, there are many who have in this respect apparently more faith than Jesus himself had. In response to the question "Did Jesus believe in demon possession?" Barclay says: "It is not in the least likely that the medical and scientific knowledge of Jesus was in any way in advance of his age; all the likelihood is that Jesus did so believe." [41] But suppose, as now seems likely, that many of the phenomena which were attributed to demon possession (and regarded as amenable to exorcism) are not "medical and scientific" but *moral*? One can then argue either that Jesus was not astute enough to see this, or that the demon-possession approach involved a subtle recognition of the moral aspect of the problem. In a paper entitled "A Neurosis of Demoniacal Possession in the Seventeenth Century," Freud said:

Despite the somatic ideology of the era of "exact" science, the demonological theory of these dark ages has in the long run justified itself. Cases of demoniacal possession correspond to the neuroses of the present day; in order to understand these latter we have once more had recourse to the conception of psychic forces. What in those days were thought to be evil spirits to us are base and evil wishes, the derivatives of impulses which have been rejected and repressed. In one respect only do we not subscribe to the explanation of these phenomena current in mediaeval times; we have abandoned the projection of them into the outer world, attributing their origin instead to the inner life of the patient in whom they manifest themselves.[42]

But again a correction is in order: it now seems that it is not "rejected and repressed" *evil* impulses or spirits that constitute the dynamic core of neurosis but rather the rejection and repression of conscience, which is to say *good* impulses, the *holy* spirit.[42a]

The Apostle Paul complicated matters still further for us. Although he continued to stress the parables and ethical teachings of Jesus, he reintroduced the idea of a "blood offering" for sin (which Jesus had tried so hard to eliminate); and he also retained and "elevated" the notion of exorcism in that now, instead of evil spirits being driven out of a possessed man into a herd of pigs, they were supposedly gathered up from all mankind and carried away by Christ in his death upon the cross. Various writers have called for a "purification" of Christianity, by which they mean, mainly, getting rid of the views and practices of the "cults and sects." Should we not instead perhaps reexamine much that has been regarded as central and most exalted in Christianity?

Now we come to a matter of special significance, the form and function of Christianity during the period of the primitive or apostolic Church. "In the early centuries," says McNeill, "two Greek words stand out in the vocabulary of Church discipline: *metanoia*, repentance, and *exomologesis*, confession":

> As far as Church discipline is concerned, the word *exomologesis* is of first importance. Before the middle of the second century confession was part of the Sunday services; whether this was a "general confession" or a personal confessing to one another as in James 5:16, is not indicated. In the *Didache* (*Teaching of the Twelve Apostles*, ca. 150) we read: "In church thou shalt confess thy transgressions, and thou shalt not betake thyself to prayer with an evil conscience. . . . On the Lord's day gather yourselves to-

gether and give thanks, having first confessed your transgressions.
. . ." Irenaeus some decades later tells of a deacon's wife who, having been victimized "in mind and body" by a magician, and rescued
from him, "spent her whole time in the exercise of confession
(*exomologesis*) weeping over and lamenting the defilement she had
undergone." This confession is evidently public; Irenaeus (ca. 180)
explicitly refers to confessions made "openly" in similar cases.[43]

Then we learn that penance, as well as confession, was commonly
made in public and was reputed to be highly efficacious:

> Tertullian furnishes explicit information on the penitential dis-
> cipline near the end of the second century. . . . He calls it "the dis-
> cipline of the prostration and humiliation of a man, requiring a
> behavior conducive to mercy." We confess our sins to God, and
> repentance arises from confession. But the confession is made before
> men. The penitent appears in sackcloth and ashes; he mourns over
> his sins, weeping and moaning day and night. He bows at the feet
> of the presbyters, kneels to "those who are dear to God," and urges
> all the brethren to intercede for him in prayer. Tertullian stresses
> the necessity of this remedial humiliation which even "wipes out
> eternal penalties," and lays the sinner low only to rise again. It is
> not explicitly said that the sins are declared by the penitent in this
> public act, but the use of the one word which signifies an unreserved
> confession makes this the more likely. It is also implied in other
> sections of the same work. He deplores the fact that too many
> shun or postpone exomologesis as a public self-exposure. To conceal
> their sin from men is not to conceal it from God. "Is it better," he
> asks, "to be damned in secret than to be absolved in public?" The
> shame of the discipline is more forbidding than the bodily hardship.
> But harsh as the remedy seems, it is not comparable to the hell-fire
> which it quenches for the penitent.[44]

Because so little is today generally known concerning the redemptive
("therapeutic") practices of the early Church, it is pertinent to explore
the evidence on this score somewhat further:

> Another feature in which a fundamental change occurred was the
> public exposure and humiliation of exomologesis. Tertullian, Origen
> and Ambrose seem to regard the public humiliation as its most
> dreaded feature. The private and secret confession of later days is an
> entirely different thing. It is possible that at an early period a private
> interview normally preceded the public act: but this cannot be
> adequately proved. What is explicitly requisite is the penitent's
> submission to open shame and his overt appeal to church officers
> and fellow members. Among the earliest to suggest private con-

fession is Origen who in his Homilies on Leviticus (ii), describing the laborious way of remission through penance, has the phrase: "When he does not blush to declare his sin to a priest of the Lord and to ask for the remedy." He cites the passage "Let him call for the elders of the church . . . he will be forgiven" (James 5:14-15). But while apparently here the process is initiated in private, it is continued in public. Origen, in accord with others of the Fathers, definitely demands a public confession, even of secret sins: "For sins of every kind are to be confessed and everything we do is to be made public. If we do anything secretly, if we commit any sin in word alone, or in the secrets of our thoughts, all must be published, all brought to light." The devil will reveal them otherwise: but if in this life we anticipate him and become our own accusers, we shall escape his wicked devices. "To utter forth our sin, merits the remission of sins." [45]

Here, it seems, is a particularly shrewd insight. Recently[46] I have advanced evidence for believing that psychoneurotic symptoms represent a compromise between (a) the energies of conscience which are trying to compel a sinful, duplicitous person to admit the truth about himself and (b) the energies of the ego, or conscious self, which are bent upon keeping this same truth carefully hidden. If the ego can be persuaded to change from a policy of concealment to one of admission, the struggle with the forces of conscience is terminated (this, surely, is the essence of "conversion"), and the ambiguous, half-intelligible, half-unintelligible actions known as symptoms subside and fade away. In the more colorful language of an earlier day, the foregoing references to the devil seem to be saying something similar.

Much more could be said to show the prevalence and general effectiveness of confession and penance in a public or at least quasi-public form (i.e., in small groups) during the first few centuries of the Christian era. But the thesis has perhaps already been sufficiently well established that *exomologesis* and *metanoia* were not merely incidental but central features of this new and powerful movement. Now we need only to add something on the severity of penance in those days, in contrast to its absence in Protestantism and its mere token form in modern Catholicism.

The Council of Ancyra (314), seeking to meet disorders induced by the persecutions that had just ceased, required of those who had readily apostatized that they spend one year as hearers, three years as kneelers, and two as co-standers. Amid numerous similar canons, bestial sins are penalized by a period among the weepers, here called the "storm-harried" since they were exposed to the weather as they stood without, begging the prayers of the worshippers. The Council of Nicea (325), at this point more severe than Ancyra, decreed that apostates should be restored after two years among the hearers, seven among the kneelers, and two among the co-standers. The Synod of Laodicea (of uncertain date) states the broad principle that sinners of various kinds who by "public confession and penance" have proved their repentance, shall, in consideration of the pity of God, be restored to communion "after a period of penance in proportion to their fall." . . . for adultery the period is fifteen years, four with the weepers, five with the hearers, four with the kneelers and two with the standers excluded from communion. Perjurers are subjected to ten years of penance, two, three, four and one, respectively, in the series of grades. . . . For homicide [Gregory of Nyssa, d. 398] commands a penance of twenty-seven years, nine years in each of the first three stations of penance.[47]

If these penitentials seem, by modern standards, unreasonably arduous, let it be noted that in the states which we today call mental illness the suffering is also severe and protracted. Could it have been more so in the life of the early Church? The supposition which we are here exploring is that in "mental disease" we are dealing with personal guilt which has been neither acknowledged nor expiated, in the *social* sense of these terms; and we know that such an affliction may last for years or even for a lifetime. The conditions imposed by the early Church for "the relief of conscience," though harsh, would seem eminently reasonable if they circumvented this inner confusion and travail which is today so common and so baffling.

------ ✳ ------

We are now in a position to examine and perhaps reappraise the system of sacramentalism which began to develop about 400 A.D. and which by 1200 A.D. had become more or less synonymous with Christianity. As McNeill has observed, every age suffers from "the danger of obsession with the contemporary"; and it is always easy—in the absence of a full knowledge of history—and tempting to assume that what is has always been and is therefore to be regarded as absolutely and eternally right. Special pains have been taken in the preceding sections to show that sacramentalism was not the central feature of the early Church and to show, also, that the early Church came into existence as a protest and rebellion against the prevalence of such a system in pre-Christian Judaism. Renan has already been quoted as saying that Jesus "powerfully served this idea in substituting a private rite [i.e., personal initiative and responsibility] for the legal ceremonies which required priests [and] by depriving the official clergy of the monopoly of the sacraments and of absolution." And Barclay also points out that in pre-Christian Judaism, the priest "stood between man and God. If a man sinned, and the right relationship to God was to be restored, sacrifice must be made, and that sacrifice could be made only through the priest. Seldom can any body of men have wielded such spiritual power. . . . Either Jesus had to go, or the whole sacrificial system had to go." Yet, irony of ironies, in the Holy Name of Christ a counterrevolution began in the early Middle Ages which was opposed to many of the basic values for which Jesus himself had lived and died! [48]

The situation in the middle of the fifth century is set forth by McNeill thus:

> Authorization of secret confession has been attributed to Pope Leo the Great (440-61), but his leadership in this direction is easily over-stated. We have seen that Sozomen, writing in the same period, describes the dramatic scene of public penance at Rome. Leo himself assumes that penance is public, and that it is not repeated—as had his predecessors Siricius and Innocent I. Innocent, however, gives large authority to priests to assign penance in accordance with the nature of the confession, and Leo similarly emphasizes the role of the priest in hearing confession and evaluating satisfaction. A letter which Leo wrote in 459 to the bishops of certain districts of Italy is his most striking utterance on the question. In this he condemns the practice—not otherwise attested and presumably local —of compelling penitents to read publicly a detailed confession. The use of this method he regards as an unauthorized innovation calculated to alienate penitents because it exposes them to danger from enemies who may seek to ruin them by legal action. It is sufficient to confess to God and to a priest who will intercede for them. . . .[49]

A familiar principle seems to be at work here. Rules, regulations, discipline arise as solutions to specific, persistent human problems. Always, they involve some element of inconvenience, sacrifice, "cost." But they are adopted because they represent the lesser of two evils. Now, by serving well its intended purpose (of averting the greater evil), all that remains experientially is the lesser evil, i.e., the inconvenience which a particular rule of discipline itself entails. Hence the tendency—when the original problem (greater evil) has been more or less forgotten—to turn against the solution itself (lesser evil). This seems to be what the Church was doing in the historical context described above. Full and radical redemption (from a condition of personal alienation and predisposition to madness) is manifestly costly, including, as it does, the risk (commonly overestimated, I believe, but real) that some persons will be so unprincipled as to use the penitent's self-disclosure as the basis for vilification or exploitation of some kind. Under the cloak of compassion and concern for the welfare of the penitent, the Church thus began a process which was ultimately (see later sections of this paper) to deprive millions of human beings of the true means of reconciliation and thus reexpose them to "Christian despair," "scrupulosity," "neurosis." The doctrine that it is "sufficient to confess to God and to a priest" slowly sapped the vitality of the lay movement which the early Church represented—and gave to the Church enormous new powers, which at first produced prosperity but ultimately resulted in ambiguity and weakness.

> Leo's indignation was perhaps as much due to the novel documentation of offenses, as to the publicity given to them in detail. It does not appear that Leo is forbidding all public confession, and the letter says nothing to alter the public character of penance itself as distinct from confession. Poschmann has shown that open confessions even of secret sins was still the rule. A contemporary of Leo, Maximus of Turin, reproves the sinner who "like a fox" conceals his sin, blushing to confess his wickedness "in the midst of the church." [50]

It will not be necessary for our purposes to follow in detail the course of events whereby confession was progressively sealed and transformed from a public into a strictly private (*secret*) act, involving only penitent and priest. Although this was clearly a retrogressive trend and represented a return to basically the same circumstances as those against which Jesus had led a successful revolution,[51] it is not difficult to see the factors which favored such a development: (1) the all too human resistance to the rigorous but effective demands of Christian discipline during the early centuries of the life of the church and a susceptibility to provisions which promised to be "just as good" but which made less strenuous demands upon the guilty individual; and (2) the greater control which members of the ecclesiastical hierarchy acquired when they began to administer absolution as a sacrament instead of its being sought and found as an improved quality of relationship with one's fellowmen. Or to put the matter succinctly, we may say that the sacramental system, as opposed to public (or quasi-public) confession and penance, offered the penitent a chance to *buy himself off* in private and the Church a chance to become rich and powerful. Again reference to McNeill is in order:

> The spirit of the harpy-like legacy hunters of pagan antiquity has never been extinguished, and cupidity found various expression in the medieval confessor. The practice of payments exacted by the confessor was later to be a subject of legislation and of frequent theme of literary satire. As in the Brahman codes, the requirement was discouraged but voluntary payments were often so eagerly welcomed as to become other than voluntary. H. C. Lea, who gives evidence on this matter, points to the fact that the *Beichtpfennig*, or penitent's fee to the confessor, reappeared in the Lutheran Church

and survived many regulations against it. In the Middle Ages it was not the gravest of the abuses that sprang from the conditions of penance. There is no escape from moral perils in the delicate relationship of the spiritual guide with his client's, save in his possession of the highest virtue.[52]

The progressive deterioration of the sacramental discipline in the Middle Ages is, however, associated less with the character of the confessors than with the practice of Indulgences which grew upon the Church from the beginning of the crusading era. A number of elements combined to produce the indulgence traffic. . . . Indulgences, or remissions of penalty due for confessed sins, were granted from this store of merit not, as Acquinas observes, annulling the penalty but providing to the sinner the means of paying it. The habitual use of commutations and money compositions in the penitentials made all too easy the commercializing of indulgences. . . . After Conscience [in Langland's satire, *Piers Plowman*] has aroused the king, who has sent Dread to frighten Liar, the pardoners take pity on Liar, wash him and put a gown on him, and send him out on Sundays "to give pardons by the pound"—for pennies. Chaucer's "gentil pardoner," straight from the Court of Rome, has a wallet full of pardons, and a bag full of diverting relics, from "oure lady veyl" to "pigges bones." With this equipment he gets more money in a day than the settled parson in two months. . . . There is little thought of true penitence in all this, but a growing spirit of cupidity which reached to the highest circles in the Church. Many of the popes had endeavored to resist the tide, but the Renaissance Papacy became immersed in it, and authorized papal agents contributed to the general deterioration and commercialization of indulgences, which, in the words of Gieseler, "completed the destruction of the ancient penitential system." [53]

The events of the Reformation (*second* Reformation, as we may call it) are sufficiently recent and sufficiently well known so that no extended discussion of it will be necessary here. The abuses of the sacramental system had become so widespread and so flagrant that popular resentment could no longer be restrained, and the unity of Western Christendom (the break with the Eastern Orthodox Church had already occurred) was violently ruptured. The Counter-Reformation brought some reforms in that part which remained loyal to the Roman papacy, but the sacramental system was retained, though subsequently administered with greater restraint and rectitude. The Protestant part soon split into many subdivisions, but one strategy was common to them all: they did not really abolish the sacrament of confession, penance, and priestly absolution but only transmuted it into confession of sins *directly to God*, repentance, and *divine* forgiveness. Thus, instead of reversing the determined trend of the medieval Church away from the early Church's emphasis upon public confession and penance and human reconciliation, the Reformers carried this trend still further, to its ultimate conclusion, and sealed the confession more tightly than even the Roman Catholic Church had previously ventured to do.

What the Reformers manifestly should have done (in the light of more than four centuries of subsequent history) was not to tighten the seal of confession but to have broken it and restored the vitality and liberating (therapeutic) power of the early Church. As we now see, the Protestant protest was really much less radical and thoroughgoing than is commonly assumed. It is today often said that the Reformation was "incomplete" and "must go on." Instead, it would perhaps be more appropriate to say that the Reformation was actually a continuation and extension of medieval Catholicism, whereas what was needed was, instead, an about-face and a return to and restoration of primitive, apostolic Christianity.

Since this is not a common way of thinking about the problem and since the distinction between absolution ("forgiveness") and reconciliation may also be a novel one for many persons, it will be useful at this point again to quote from McNeill:

> [In the late apostolic Church] the rite of reconciliation was performed normally by bishops only; infringements of this were not infrequent but were defended only on grounds of necessity. The imposition of the bishop's hands upon each penitent's head was a feature of the ancient *public reconciliation* rite. No extant liturgical materials of the Patristic era indicate the words used in reconciliation. A letter of Innocent I of about 416 indicates that it was customary at Rome to "grant remission" to penitents on the Thursday before Easter. The reference is to a *public reconciliation* of numerous penitents following the *public penance* to which our attention has been called. In the earliest extant formulations, *absolution* consists of a prayer rather than a declaration, and scholars are agreed that this had been so from the first. "We gather," says Msgr. Duchesne, "from the Life of St. Hilary of Arles (d. 447), that the bishop gave an address, laid his hands on the penitents, and recited a prayer." The view that *absolution is remission granted by the Church*, and "the act of the priest whereby in the sacrament of penance he frees man from sin" (*Catholic Encyclopedia*) was not expressed through the use of this deprecatory form. Some would say that the original imposition of hands "aimed to say" what was later expressed in the declaratory form, "I absolve thee" (Jungmann).

Some third century documents indicate that at the elevation of a bishop a prayer was offered that he might receive power to forgive sins. The *prayers of reconciliation*, however, imply no such power but appeal solely to the pardoning mercy of God. Morin found no exception to the "deprecative" type of absolution prayer *before the twelfth century*. . . . Gradually indicative forms were adopted. In the later Middle Ages the formulas included "I absolve thee," but this has regularly been preceded by a petition for divine absolution. The theological definition of the sacrament of penance advanced slowly, and was not completed until the Scholastic era. "The twelfth century," says Kenneth E. Krik, "witnessed the rapid development of *a sacramental theory of absolution*." . . . [54]

The requirement that every adult Christian "shall confess all his sins to his own priest" represents a long-time effort to render the local priest the principal administrator of penance. . . . There was a deplorable lack of watchful defense against the commercialization of penance—later the occasion of scandalous abuses.[55]

At a recent meeting of Roman Catholic and Protestant scholars, one of the former remarked, quite independently, that it is his opinion that scrupulosity, as it manifests itself today in members of the Catholic faith, first became common *in the twelfth century*. This priest went on to conjecture that the emergence of the phenomenon was correlated with and very probably caused by the transition from the medieval penitential system to the sacramental system now in force. Subsequently I have had occasion to talk with a Catholic bishop who related instances, personally known to him, in which Catholics who have confessed and been absolved and carried out the prescribed token penance have remained in emotional distress (scrupulous, "neurotic") until they voluntarily took upon themselves more serious penitential duties. Individual human beings, it seems, are often disposed to take their sins and guilt more seriously than does the Church itself.

Why, we may ask, did the Reformers choose the absolute sealing of confession in preference to a restoration of "the rite of public reconciliation"? Either of these procedures would have logically undercut the commercialism of penance. Why, then, did the Reformers advise penitents to have recourse directly to God, rather than revitalize the original emphasis of Jesus and his followers upon reconciliation of the erstwhile sinner with his fellowmen? Both procedures eliminate the need for intervention (mediation) by a priest and thus make it unnecessary to pay such a specialist. Why was the one procedure chosen and the other rejected?

The Protestant answer to this question has never, I believe, been clear and unequivocal (in fact, it would perhaps be fair to say that the question itself has rarely even been asked). Confession to another human being (minister or "Christian brother") has not been categorically forbidden in most Protestant circles. It has instead been regarded as strictly optional. One may resort to such a procedure if one wishes, but it is not obligatory, and certainly it is in no sense a sacrament. Belgum has recently examined several Protestant positions on this score.[56] Some Protestant leaders have experimented with group confession: witness Wesley's "class meetings." But the path of least resistance for the individual penitent has been that of confession and petition to God in silent prayer. And in emphasizing the primacy of man's relation to God, rather than to "mere man," the theologian has kept himself in the picture in a way which might otherwise not have been possible. Although "the Priesthood of all Believers" has been a Protestant ideal, the fact is that a professional priesthood (ministry) has been retained—or has retained itself—in a way which would almost certainly not have happened if the Reformation had produced a revival of primitive Christianity. Jesus, we recall, was in direct rebellion against the experts and the professionals. "The kingdom of God is *within you*," he maintained.

There is an interesting question concerning the position of the contemporary Roman Catholic Church on this score. It has a sealed confession in the sense of (*a*) requiring that admission of sin be made to a priest and of (*b*) obligating the priest not to reveal what has thus been told to him. But does the Church also require the penitent not to admit his sins *to others*, and not to make restitution over and beyond the prescribed penance (which is often a mere token)? Catholic laymen and parish priests with whom I have discussed this problem seem not to know the answer or give contradictory answers; and I have not consulted more authoritative sources on this score. But it would appear that there is a deep-seated ambiguity here. I doubt if the Church would dare take a definite stand *against* the type of personal openness which is under discussion in this paper. At the same time, I should think that, informally, it would almost certainly have to discourage participation in group therapy. Let us suppose (as could easily happen) that certain persons (i.e., the so-called scrupulous) who have failed to find solace for their sins in the sealed confession found such solace in a group. This experience would predispose such persons to conclude that the real power of deliverance lies, not in the confessional booth, but in a small social reference group.

Some of my Catholic friends think that the Church presently tries to solve this dilemma by saying that the basic concern of the Catholic religion lies in the sacraments. And since confession is a sacrament, it is not designed to make a person feel better psychologically but to rescue his immortal soul from the dangers of hell and purgatory. Thus the Church would seem to have withdrawn from the domain of psychotherapy (soul care) in this life and to be concerned with the soul's welfare only in the life to come. Yet this is not a position which the Church can very comfortably take, either. For in times past it has been deeply concerned with the state of a man's soul or psyche in *this* life; and it would probably scandalize a great many members of the Church today to think that this concern had been completely lost.

As indicated elsewhere[57] it seems probable that the Church has not adopted an official stand on this score precisely because of the deep ambiguity thus involved, and this is why individual Catholic writers are at liberty to take diametrically opposing stands concerning the psychological value of confession.[58] The position of Protestantism as to whether sinful man needs to confess and do penance before men or only before God is even more ambiguous and, by the same token, also more open to adaptive change. Since the concept and practice of human reconciliation has been replaced by essentially "vertical" procedures even more completely in Protestantism than in Catholicism, it would not be surprising if the revulsion against the latter and a recovery of the former would take place first in Protestantism.[58a]

------ ✳ ------

All of which brings us to the contemporary scene. As I have suggested on other occasions (and never been seriously challenged), Protestantism has left modern man with no satisfactory way of dealing with personal guilt, and it has so shaken Roman Catholicism as largely to deprive it, too, of such effectiveness as it may have possessed in this connection during the Middle Ages. Even though the Church had no particular right to the resulting revenues, pre-Reformation Catholics were at least provided an opportunity (even though a dubious one) to *pay* for their sins; and this functioned as a psychological advantage in many instances. After criticizing the medieval Church for its commercialization of penance, McNeill himself says of the medieval penitentials:

> We cannot doubt that they were instrumental in the recovery and rehabilitation of many who had made shipwreck of life, and in elevating and stabilizing the morals of many more. The experience of our ancestors under the guidance of confessors familiar with the [penitential] manuals must have helped to redeem them from superstition, inhumanity and vice, and to set their feet on the pathway of spiritual and moral advance.[59]

Besides the dubious right of the Church to profit from this traffic in human guilt and forgiveness, there were other fateful defects in the system. In a recent book[60] the point is made that the progressive sealing of confession, which was begun by the Roman Catholic Church and perfected by Protestantism, was in the end disastrous for the Church itself as a would-be self-perpetuating body. The authors point out that training in the art of reconciliation (or pastoral care) became exceedingly difficult when the confessional was sealed so tightly that the neophyte confessor could no longer discuss with a more experienced superior the problems encountered in the confessional and his attempt to deal with them. And when confession was still further sealed, as it was in the Protestant formula, all that was left for the shepherd of souls to know or do was to say to the guilt-ridden, soul-sick individual: "Go home and pray about your sins, and if you are properly contrite God will forgive you and you will be saved." Such a procedure requires no very special competence on the part of the spiritual advisor, and neither does he or anyone else learn anything from the transaction. As Professor Jaekle puts the matter in a recent personal letter: "It is impossible to teach or transmit skills and wisdom in a situation in which you have an absolute block of secrecy to contend with. And since the thirteenth century, and maybe even before, this has been the case with the sacrament of penance."[61]

Thus, when Sigmund Freud appeared on the scene and in effect said, "This kind of sickness can be scientifically studied and others can be objectively trained in its treatment," and when Carl Rogers also made it apparent that the behavior of the therapist himself can be empirically investigated (and thereby correctively modified), religious theory and practice were caught badly off guard. An effort has been made to recover some semblance of competence in this field by asking for "training" at the hands of the newly founded secular healing professions.

Sensing their strategic advantage in this situation, some psychiatrists set out to establish themselves as a new priestly elite in this field (just as Jewish priests had done at the time of Christ and Roman Catholic priests did in the Middle Ages). Let me cite only one of many exclusivistic claims which have thus been made during the last twenty or thirty years:

> For centuries the Western world has placed on the medical profession responsibility for the diagnosis and treatment of illness. Medical practice acts have been designed to protect the public from unqualified [!] practitioners and to define the special responsibilities assumed by those who practice the healing art. . . . Psychiatry is the medical speciality concerned with illness that has chiefly mental symptoms. . . . Psychotherapy is a form of medical treatment and does not form the basis for a separate profession. . . . When members of these [other] professions contribute to the diagnosis and treatment of illness, their professional contributions must be coordinated under medical responsibility.[62]

I think it is fair to say that this attempted *coup* or *putsch* did not, and will not now, succeed. On the basis of evaluation studies (conducted in many instances by psychiatrists), it has been shown that modern psychiatry has not proved itself effective to the degree that would warrant the ascription of power and authority ("responsibility") which it has been claiming; and since other professional groups (including psychology) have been competing for some of the same "business" which is available on the basis of private practice, there has been organized opposition to this maneuver, as well as resistance from lay sources. Elsewhere[63] I have brought together a collection of satires and criticisms by laymen aimed specifically at professionalism in this area; and laymen have further taken matters into their own hands by organizing their own therapeutic self-help groups.[64] This trend is still so new that it is impossible to be sure either of its inherent nature or of its destiny; but it is not a wholly implausible conjecture that it represents an attempt to recover the power of primitive Christianity, with its emphasis on personal redemption through social reconciliation and rehabilitation. If this perception of the situation is even remotely justified, we can properly refer to these developments as the *third* Reformation.

Somewhat facetiously but with more than a hint of seriousness, psychoanalysis has been called "the Jewish confessional." Would it be too wide of the mark to say that it has represented an attempt (in the guise of Science and Medicine) to reestablish, after two thousand years of Christian domination, the hegemony of the ancient Hebrew priesthood? It is relevant that Jones, Bakan, and Fromm have all documented the supposition that Freud was deeply motivated by a "messianic complex," which, if successful, would have delivered the Jew of much of his historic onus; and it is also well authenticated (see the same sources) that "The Committee," or Inner Circle, which Freud founded was secretly dedicated to the goal of fomenting psychoanalysis into a world-wide, cultural-ethical revolution. In any case, it must have been a source of wry satisfaction to more than one Jewish psychoanalyst to have Christians (Catholic and Protestant alike) resorting to them for psychological (spiritual) treatment and for instruction concerning the way of life ("problems of living"). That the revolution at which psychoanalysis rather clearly aimed is today losing momentum and is in imminent danger of grinding to a standstill is undoubtedly related to the growing willingness of psychiatrists and psychoanalysts to "enter into dialogue," in a conciliatory way, with theologians. As Boisen observes in a passage quoted near the outset of this paper, the last word concerning "spiritual healing" has certainly not been spoken for our time.[65]

------ ✳ ------

A recent issue of the *Journal of Religion and Health* contains two articles which present conflicting views concerning the Christianity-psychoanalysis relationship. In an article entitled "Medieval Medicine for Sin," George Christian Anderson (Director of the Academy of Religion and

Mental Health, which publishes the *Journal*) reviews the prescriptions of the medieval penitential manuals of the Catholic Church and undertakes to show that these are basically congruent with "new knowledge from psychiatry" and the "major goals of psychoanalysis." [66] More specifically:

> The healing ministry of penance was aimed at the reconstruction of personality, thus enabling the individual to have harmonious relations with his church, his fellowman, and God. This parallels an objective of modern psychiatry, which is to diminish anxiety and guilt so that one can live in harmonious relation with his social environment.
>
> Another similarity between penitential methods and those of modern psychotherapy relates to the importance of confession. Self-ventilation is regarded as a requisite in psychoanalysis.[67]

The other article to which I refer here, by Raymond E. Gibson,[68] begins thus:

> At present, one may surely say that Religion and psychiatry are, in a limited, undefined, and hesitant way, friends. But what kind of friendship is it? Is it a friendship on the order of the one between David and Jonathan . . . ? Or is it a friendship like that between Brutus and Caesar, where the one party, without denying the friendship, feels called by duty beyond it to kill the other for the good of the people?

In a recent study, the attitudes of twenty-five randomly selected metropolitan psychiatrists concerning religion are reported. Some of these are neutral or mildly conciliatory, but the majority of them run thus: "I have no religious beliefs, no religious affiliations. . . . I don't take it literally . . . I no longer have any truck with it. . . . I don't have the foggiest notion of what God is. . . . No need for religious affiliation. . . . Religion promotes regression to the patient's five-year-old conscience. . . . I am liable to see religion as one of a set of [causative] factors." [69]

And Walters, in a review of Report No. 48 on "Psychiatry and Religion: Some Steps Toward Mutual Understanding and Usefulness" by the Group for the Advancement of Psychiatry, points out that the position taken here is also highly ambiguous.[70] Although the report, according to Walters, "credits the psychiatrist with being eager to learn how to help his patient from *any* source, "including nonmedical ones such as . . . religion," it points out that he cannot overstep the boundaries of naturalism, for "it is not within the province of psychiatry to say anything about God's existence or about His activity in human life or history." Walters continues:

Indeed, this confident neutrality veers toward an atheistic premise as the report draws a contrast between the clergyman, who refers morality to a transcendental power, and the psychiatrist, who as a relativist approaches morality "without reference to divine authority." God is eliminated more decisively as the report goes on to declare that "sexuality is the basis, biologically derived, for the human experience of all . . . loving . . . call it love, *caritas, agape.*" . . . A reductive naturalism is invoked to explain religious experience. . . .

Even though the report maintains "we have no intention . . . of urging one system of psychology in preference to others," it uses the concepts of classical psychoanalysis to describe psychological processes without qualification or identification as elements of a sectarian system. Following its declaration of neutrality it devotes several pages to exposition of psychoanalytic theory. Offered ostensibly to "illustrate . . . the point that human psychology has much to learn from religion," the section nevertheless undertakes to demonstrate how psychoanalytic theory can "illustrate religious phenomena."

Here, surely, is sufficient evidence that, despite the benign and optimistic statements which one commonly hears today about "cooperation and harmony between psychiatry and religion," the objective reality is one of strain, mutual distrust, and dismay. I find it clarifying to think about this situation in terms of a Hegelian dialectic. Let Christianity be termed the original thesis; psychoanalysis appeared, around the turn of the present century, as a strident antithesis. For at least a decade now concerted efforts have been made to bring about a synthesis, along lines represented by the article by Anderson.[71] Such a synthesis, if fully consolidated, would be regressive. A radically different "integration" is possible, and in terms of broadly human benefit, decidedly preferable.[72]

------ ✳ ------

As the foregoing discussion indicates, the conflict between Christianity and psychoanalysis has two major dimensions. Christianity has been *normative and judgmental* in the sense of holding to the doctrine of the perfectability of man, as an ideal if not an attainable reality. Psychoanalysis, from the outset, has taken an antithetical position. The trouble with neurotic man, it insists, is that he has been taught to be *too good,* his superego (conscience) is excessively strict and severe; and the objective of therapy is to undo the effects of past training and reduce superego severity. By the same token, avoidance or prevention of this dread state calls for a ubiquitous reform in education and child rearing practices. All of which has involved an attack upon conventional standards and the encouragement of a pervasive philosophy of moral tolerance and permissiveness.

Christianity and psychoanalysis, at an early stage, thus came into mortal conflict; and in general it must be said that psychoanalysis has won! On the score of its traditional stand with regard to standards and norms, the Church has been pushed far back into a corner; and it is what Richard LaPiere has ironically called the *Freudian ethic* (which is really an anti-ethic) that is today being proclaimed most widely, not only in our college classrooms and in popular books and magazines but also by many pulpit ministers and pastoral counselors. What has happened to the *Judeo-Christian ethic?* By and large it has been discarded as "judgmental" and "moralistic," although there is today a new and growing interest in some quarters (including, incidentally, numerous state universities) in something called *values*, which seems to be merely a new term for an old reality, namely, the fact that without standards and a moral order of some sort, human beings and the social groups of which they are a part simply disintegrate.

The other major area of conflict between Christianity and psychoanalysis is this. Christianity, with its myths, mysteries, and miracles, has had extensive recourse to *supernaturalism*. With its strong identification with science, psychoanalysis has, by contrast, stressed *naturalism*. In this area, also, modern Christianity is very insecure and uncertain (cf. Bultmann's ambiguous proposal for the demythologization of religion); but I think it fair to say that here psychoanalysis has not pressed its attack with the same vigor and determination as in the first area of conflict, already cited. It is as if the analysts had said to themselves: "It is the moralistic stance of the church that does the greatest harm; and if we can get religious leaders to desist on this score, we will leave them to their folly in the area of their mythologies and metaphysics. Mind you, we ourselves will retain our own strictly scientific, naturalistic position. But we will not insist that the Christians give up their God, only that they modify their interpretation of him a bit so that he too (like us) is loving and permissive, rather than demanding and, when disobeyed, judgmental. After all, we can't ask the theologians to give up everything. If, after recanting on the score of common morality, they were also asked to abandon their metaphysics and supernaturalism, they would have *nothing* left. For the moment, at least, that would be asking too much."

By and large, Christianity has seemed to accept these terms from the psychoanalysts. Having been severely worsted in its earlier persecutions of Copernicus and Darwin, the Church is today afraid of science and is eager not to have any further trouble with it. Moreover, in addition to being afraid, the Church is also *guilty*. It knows that, in stressing form and liturgy and magic, it has seriously neglected and virtually deserted its ancient responsibility for the care and cure of souls (psychotherapy); and when a new secular profession springs up which is specifically dedicated to this task, the only honest thing the church can say is *mea culpa!*

How can we conceptualize this unhappy situation in a clear and simple manner? I find the following diagram useful on this score:

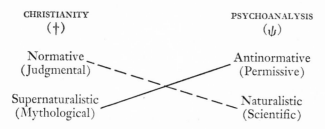

The "cooperation" or "friendship" which today exists between psychiatry and religion thus involves an uneasy truce which we here represent by the solid line: a sort of axis which is anchored at the one end in the antinormativism of psychoanalysis and at the other end in the supernaturalism of Chirstianity. A less defensible entente one can hardly imagine, but this is manifestly what we today have. The obvious alternative is a synthesis which (see dashed line) would instead stress the *normativism of Christianity* and the *naturalism of psychoanalysis* (and of science in general). But this, so far, has not had much appeal. Boisen, as we have seen, with his "belief in the perfectibility of man" and his "emphasis upon the empirical approach" (expressions which he himself has used in a recent letter to me to describe his position), was not able to compete with Freudianism and religious orthodoxy and so lost control of the pastoral counseling movement which he had founded. Renan and Potter, who are also normative (ethical) naturalists, remain in disfavor. Julian Huxley's book *Religion Without Revelation* seems to have attracted little attention. Erich Fromm is getting a hearing in some quarters. But as yet normative naturalism or naturalistic normativism, as proposed to the present anomalous and uneasy psychiatry-religion alliance, has not been widely accepted.

Does the preceding section of this chapter fairly and accurately portray the prevailing psychiatry-religion relationship? On the two or three occasions when I have presented this analysis to clergymen, there has been acute discomfort and numerous disclaimers. But in the article by Raymond E. Gibson which has already been cited, I find a clergyman, quite independently, appraising the situation in a strikingly similar way:

> To use technical language the philosophical and theological presuppositions of the religionists are theistic, idealistic; whereas the

philosophical presuppositions of psychiatry tend to be naturalistic, pragmatic, and realistic. When we speak about the nature of reality or the nature of man, religionists are driven toward a transcendental reference, psychiatrists are driven toward a naturalistic reference. The religionist is convinced that man can never be understood apart from his creatureliness and his relation to the divine. The psychiatrist, as a scientist, is driven to say that man is best known as a creature of nature; the psychiatrist is dubious of, indeed he cannot enter, at least scientifically, what is called the supernatural realm. The religionist may well lament the atheistic, or non-theistic position of the psychiatrist. The psychiatrist, for his part, has seen so many patients who, precisely because of their religious experiences, are, to modify Kierkegaard's phrase, "sick unto death." Whereas the religionist may say, with an imperialistic confidence, that "All men need religion," the psychiatrist can say, and document, that some—even many— who have found a religion, now need a doctor. Certainly so short a paper as this cannot probe into the diversity or complexity of this problem. It is mentioned here because it is as crucial as it is difficult. It is the question at present farthest from solution. Inevitably it will bear upon the whole dialogue between psychiatry and religion, if the two disciplines are to have a significant encounter or a lasting relationship.[73]

We can only concur when Gibson says that religionists are theistic (supernaturalistic) and, in their better moments, idealistic (normative) and that psychiatrists are naturalistic. But is it accurate to characterize psychiatrists as "pragmatic" and "realistic"? There is today good reason to suspect that Freud's conjectures concerning the nature and treatment of neurosis have very little justification in reality and that their widespread acceptance and application may yet turn out to be one of the most *unrealistic* things that has ever happened in Western civilization.[74] The fact that so many clergymen have been unable to see this flaw in psychoanalysis is a sad commentary on the extent to which they have lost their own historic moorings and confidence.

The disorientation and confusion of religious leadership is further indicated when Gibson says that many persons become patients "precisely because of their religious experiences." This, at best, is a half-truth. The perverse and pathogenic element in religion is not, as the analysts have insisted (and scores of clergymen have dutifully believed), religion's insistence upon high standards of conduct and personal rectitude. *No one*, I would hold, ever became neurotic by being *too good* by the standards of *any* great religion! The common virus of psychopathology lies in unacknowledged and unredeemed *sin*, which always involves palpable disloyalty and cheating with respect to one's social reference group. Religion "contributes" to neurosis, I would say, rather in offering to the faithful spuriously easy "metaphysical" (rather than psychosocially adequate) solutions to sin-engendered guilt. And here psychoanalysis, rather than functioning as a true corrective for religion, has made the even greater error of telling neurotics ("sinners") that their guilt is not only "forgiven" but was not real or justified in the first place. Psychoanalysis indicts religion as one of the "causative factors" in neurosis. A neuropsychiatrist says: "Judged by the duration of analysis, and by the reactions of originally healthy neophytes, the frivolous Viennese may have been in earnest when they defined psychoanalysis as that disease of which it fancies itself the cure." [75]

I would say, in final reference to the passage by Gibson, that the problem of finding the correct balance between religion and psychiatry is so difficult ("farthest from solution") by virtue of the fact that with respect to the normative-antinormative issue, religion has gone so far in *agreeing* with psychiatry. If theologians and clergymen had been able to hold their ground *here* and to give ground on the score of their supernaturalism, the present situation would, I believe, be a far more salubrious one.

------ ✳ ------

We are now faced by a final question: Why has the axis represented by the solid line in the diagram been generally favored over the alternative axis which is indicated by the dashed line? The prevailing emphasis on psychoanalytic permissiveness and religious supernaturalism has probably been maintained because both are readily salable commodities. Who would pay $30 an hour to lie on a couch and be told that he (or she) has been misbehaving and needs to "straighten up and fly right? This kind of counsel, however valid, can hardly be given away.

This then—its antinormative permissiveness—has been the commodity which psychoanalysis purveys. What is the stock in trade of religion? What, indeed, but its metaphysics! Who will support during their lifetime and leave legacies to an institution that emphasizes the naturalistic truth about human guilt and its resolution? But if men are offered an easy, miraculous salvation, what will they not give for that! Barclay refers to the *commercialism* that perverted and corrupted pre-Christian Judaism. McNeill speaks of the *commercialism* that perverted and corrupted the medieval Church. Can one honestly say that clergymen and psychiatrists are today *less* influenced by economic considerations?

Is it not suggestive that in a political and social order which has a planned economy, psychoanalysis and Christianity are both officially disapproved? Russian Communism, for all its shortcomings (and they are grievous), does not countenance either antinormativism or supernaturalism (our solid-line axis).[76] Instead, this political regime is highly normative (by its own lights) and also naturalistic (our dashed-line axis). The question is this: How long can we afford to permit the profit motive (or "free enterprise") to operate in clear opposition to the public interest? Many thoughtful observers are today saying that a *free* society, in order to avoid chaos, *must* have planning. And who could honestly maintain that psychoanalytic antinormativism and religious supernaturalism are to be rationally preferred over religious normativism and psychoanalytic (scientific) naturalism?

As we have seen, the practice of *public* confession and penance were the redemptive (therapeutic) measures which gave early Christianity its great vitality and historic momentum. In principle, there is nothing to prevent the revival of these same measures in our day; and I have elsewhere[77] presented evidence that such a development is in fact well under way. Furthermore, this emphasis upon man's basically *social* nature is thoroughly compatible with normative naturalism, as it has been defined in the growing emphasis on *milieu therapy* and *social psychiatry*, and not all religious leaders are blind to these new visions and endeavors. However, it would be unduly optimistic not to note that *economic* considerations presently push both psychiatrists and clergymen toward private practice, that is, toward the use of putative methods of resolving guilt which can be privately (i.e., "professionally") administered, rather than restorative experiences which are less easy to control and exploit because they are capable of being carried out directly, with mere relatives and friends.

Without explicitly conceding the common failure of "justification by faith" to bring solace to deeply guilty people, many Protestant groups are today beginning to look with new-found favor upon the practice of confession—but there will be a strong temptation for the professionals to advocate *private* confession. Here, for example, are Dr. Anderson's recent views on the subject:

> Protestants, too, are recognizing the value of confession as an essential factor in spiritual growth. A growing number of clergymen are aware of their unique role as spiritual counselors in serving the emotionally and mentally ill. Traditionally, spiritual counselors have always played an important role in the Christian church. Self-examination and confession are required, and the importance of penance and discipline in dealing with penitents is recognized. Traditionally, Protestants have shunned auricular confession, but today an increasing number of Protestant clergymen are suggesting confession to those who come to them with their difficulties. These confessions are often heard in the clergyman's study, or more often in the church at the altar or holy table. Many Protestant clergymen are using the forms of confession found in the Roman Catholic and Anglican churches.[78]

As we have already noted, Dr. Anderson draws much of his inspiration in this connection from the medieval Church, which hardly represents Christianity at its enlightened best. And he must also have been struck by the "sacrament" of "confession and penance" as they occur in the free association and free payment which are standard features of psychoanalysis. Is this the best the modern Church can do—merely ape medieval Catholicism and contemporary psychoanalysis? There is an infinitely brighter prospect, it would seem, which this chapter has attempted to delineate.

NOTES FOR CHAPTER 13

1 In the interim between the first completion of this chapter and its publication, the "death of God" movement has gathered momentum, and there have been other extraordinary developments as a result of the three sessions of the Second Vatican Council. A new journal (*Zygon*) has come into existence, under the inspiration and editorship of Profesor Ralph W. Burdoe of the Meadville Theological School (Chicago), which is specifically dedicated to the "yoking or harness of a team [science and religion] which must effectively pull together." Thus, parts of this chapter are dated—not as inaccurate but, rather, as incomplete. Systematic updating does not seem practical at this juncture, but a few new references have been inserted; and this footnote will remind the reader that events have recently been moving very rapidly—and, generally speaking, in the direction here predicted.

2 A. T. Boisen, "The Challenge to Our Seminaries," *Christian Work*, 1926, 120: 9.

3 *Ibid.*, p. 10.

4 A. T. Boisen, *The Exploration of the Inner World*, New York, Harper, 1936, pp. 243-244.

5 *Ibid.*, pp. 267-268.

6 *Ibid.*, p. 281.

7 Some readers who have been associated with pastoral counseling may feel it is inaccurate to say that this movement is predominantly Freudian and may hold that Carl Rogers instead has been the major influence. In the interests of clarity it should be noted (cf. my book *The Crisis in Psychiatry and Religion*, pp. 54, 164-165, and 193) that insofar as the *theory* of psychopathology is concerned, Rogers' position (until perhaps very recently—cf. his new book *On Becoming a Person*) has not been significantly different from that of Freud. Both held that the patient's life has been distorted and disturbed by the untoward impact of *other persons* (or "society" in general) and that it is in the special atmosphere of acceptance and permissiveness which therapy provides that new insights and behavior changes are most likely to emerge. Rogers took issue with Freud mainly in the matter of treatment techniques. Whereas Freud stressed *interpretation*, Rogers stressed *reflection*, i.e., he required the patient to make his own "interpretations," on the assumption that the therapist was thus less likely to foist a mistaken interpretation or "insight" on the client. Even with respect to technique, the two approaches had this in common, that they both encouraged the patient to verbalize his thoughts and feelings unreservedly,

the one by the rule of free association and the other by nondirectiveness.

8 Boisen, *Explorations of the Inner World*, p. 153.

9 *Ibid.*, p. 157.

10 *Ibid.*, pp. 166, 237.

11 *Ibid.*, p. 248. Italics added.

12 In the end, let us hope, we shall come through to a more coherent understanding of the situation than is as yet available. However, I do not wish at this juncture to exclude from consideration pertinent factors other than those already acknowledged. There was, as we have noted, the reality of Boisen's own emotional instability. And it is also reported that he was not very skillful in the detailed training and supervision of the students who came to work with him (a supposition which gains crediblity from the fact that Boisen's own program at Elgin State Hospital was ultimately disapproved by the very agency, namely, the Council for Clinical Training, which he himself had been instrumental in establishing). Could it have been that some intimation of these problems was involved in the 1936 collapse? Boisen's challenge to the Church to return to her ancient concern with the cure of souls also came into competition, in the 1930's, with the Social Gospel and later, in the 1940's, with Crisis Theology. However, it must be noted that during these very decades the pastoral counseling movement continued to grow and expand (cf. Niebuhr, Williams, and Gustafson, 1957), albeit now under the aegis of Freud and Rogers. No, I think it was basically Boisen's "ethical humanism" (which we shall later examine in a broader context) that was the major reason for the demise of his influence and program, with his personal instability and possible lack of didactic skill operating as decidedly secondary factors.

13 This is the title of the paperback version. The original title is *The Lost Years of Jesus*.

14 Charles Francis Potter, *The Lost Years of Jesus Revealed*, Crest Book, Greenwich, Conn., Fawcett Publications, 1963. Paperback.

15 For recent support of Potter's general position, see J. M. Allegro, "The Untold Story of the Dead Sea Scrolls," *Harper's Magazine*, 1966, 233: 46-54.

16 Ernest Renan, *Life of Jesus*, New York, Modern Library, n.d., p. 104. Italics added. By the term "private rite" I do not believe Renan means a secret rite. Rather, he seems to be implying something personal, i.e., something which the individual himself can do, on his own responsiblity and initiative, as opposed to something which, by virtue of special skill or ascribed role, can be done for one only by another person or persons. As we shall shortly see, the "rites" to which Christ's teaching most immediately and authentically led were essentially public—and were carried out by the individual himself (although, naturally, with the cooperation and encouragement of others).

17 *Ibid.*, p. 107.

18 *Ibid.*, pp. 111-112.

19 *Ibid.*, p. 114.

20 *Ibid.*, pp. 117-118.

21 Mark 11:15-18.

22 John 2:13-16.

23 George A. Buttrick (ed.), *Interpreter's Dictionary of the Bible*, 4 vols., Nashville, Tenn., Abingdon Press, 1962, Vol. III, p. 17.

23a Albert Schweitzer, *The Psychiatric Study of Jesus*, Boston, Beacon Press, 1950 (original German, 1913).

24 Buttrick, *op. cit.*, III, p. 23.

25 Rudolph Bultmann, *Kerygma and Myth*, New York, Harper & Row, 1963, p. 5.

26 *Ibid.*, pp. 10, 15.

27 William Barclay, *The Mind of Jesus*, New York, Harper and Row, 1961, p. 7.

28 *Ibid.*, pp. 154, 156, 158, 165, 166.

29 John T. McNeill, *A History of the Cure of Souls*, New York, Harper & Row, 1965 (1951), pp. vii-viii.

30 *Ibid.* Italics added.

31 *Ibid.*, p. ix.

32 *Ibid.*, p. ix.

33 O. H. Mowrer, *Identity and Community* (unpublished).

34 Mark Zborowski and Elizabeth Herzog, *Life Is with People*, New York, Schocken Books, n.d.

35 McNeill, *op. cit.*, p. 15.

36 *Ibid.*, p. 70.

37 *Ibid.*, p. 75.

38 *Ibid.*, p. 80.

39 *Ibid.*, p. 85.

40 *Ibid.*, pp. 86, 87.

41 Barclay, *op. cit.*, p. 74; see also W. K. L. Clark, *Concise Bible Commentary*, London, S.P.C.K., 1952.

42 S. Freud, "A Neurosis of Demoniacal Possession in the Seventeenth Century," *Collected Papers*, London, Hogarth Press, 1923, Vol. IV, pp. 436-472.

42a O. H. Mowrer, *The Crisis in Psychiatry and Religion*, Princeton, N. J., Van Nostrand, 1961.

43 McNeill, *op. cit.*, pp. 90, 91.

44 *Ibid.*, pp. 91-92.

45 *Ibid.*, p. 94. For a similar interpretation of the history of the Early Church, see two Catholic writers: Bertrand Kurtscheid, *The Seal of Confession*, St. Louis, Herder, 1927; and Bernhard Poschmann, *Penance and the Anointing of the Sick*, New York, Herder & Herder, 1964.

46 O. H. Mowrer, *The New Group Therapy*, Chap. 11; see also O. H. Mowrer, "Payment or Repayment? The Problem of Private Practice," 1963.

47 McNeill, *op. cit.*, p. 97.

48 For a literary treatment of this same remarkable phenomenon, the reader is referred to Dostoyevsky's "The Grand Inquisitor," in *The Brothers Karamazov*.

49 McNeill, *op. cit.*, p. 98.

50 *Ibid.*, p. 99.

51 Lest there be any ambiguity concerning the similarity to which I am here pointing between official Judaism, at the time of Christ, and the medieval Church, let it be noted (*a*) that in the former era the remission of sins required an animal sacrifice (blood offering) which could be made "only at the Temple in Jerusalem, and only through a priest . . . seldom can any body of men have wielded such spiritual power"; and (*b*) that in the Middle Ages the remission of sins was likewise made to depend upon an

official rite which nurtured a "spiritual dictatorship" as absolute, grasping, and unredemptive as that which prevailed a millennium earlier. Only now the "sacrifice," instead of being an animal (which, after the blood was let, was taken home and eaten or sold by the priest), was money and real estate which, directly or indirectly, was extracted from the penitent as the price that was demanded for this monopolistic service. The abundant life or "kingdom of heaven" which Jesus, through his example and teachings, had offered to the common people as a free and readily available gift, was once again made into an ecclesiastical commodity.

52 McNeill, *op. cit.*, p. 130.
53 *Ibid.*, pp. 149-150.
54 *Ibid.*, p. 150.
55 *Ibid.*, pp. 134, 135.
56 D. Belgum, *Guilt: Where Psychology and Religion Meet*, Englewood Cliffs, N.J., Prentice-Hall, 1963. See particularly Chap. 5, What Was Available in the Churches.
57 Mowrer, *The Crisis in Psychiatry and Religion*.
58 Cf. Alfred Wilson, *Pardon and Peace*, New York, Sheed & Ward, 1954; and R. P. Vaughn, "Mental Illness Among Religious," *Review for Religious*, 1959, 18: 25-26.
58a In the light of the many unprecedented actions taken by the Second Vatican Council, it is now an open question whether radical change is most likely to come in Protestantism or in Catholicism.
59 McNeill, *op. cit.*, p. 135.
60 William A. Clebsch and Charles R. Jaekle, *Pastoral Care in Historical Perspective*, Englewood Cliffs, N.J., Prentice-Hall, 1964.
61 In a passage cited earlier, Boisen similarly complains about the traditional inadequacy of the training of ministers in the cure of souls; and others have undoubtedly made equally pointed observations on this score. But I confess it was not until my recent meeting with Professor Clebsch and Jaekle that the full impact of this situation became clear to me. I am much indebted for this insight to these two gentlemen.
62 American Psychiatric Association, *Mailpouch*, October 1954, pp. 1-2.
63 O. H. Mowrer, *Morality and Mental Health*, Chicago, Rand McNally (in press).
64 *Ibid.*
65 Boisen, *loc. cit.*
66 George Christian Anderson, "Medieval Medicine for Sin," *Journal of Religion and Health*, 1963, 2: 164-5.
67 *Ibid.*, p. 163.
68 Raymond E. Gibson, "Psychiatry and Religion—What Kind of Friendship," *Journal of Religion and Health*, 1963 2: 143.
69 McCann, *The Churches and Mental Health*, New York, Basic Books, 1962; see especially Ch. xi, "Psychiatrists View the Clergy," pp. 197, 201.
70 O. S. Walters, in *Christian Century*, 1961, pp. 1556-8.
71 See note 66 above, and G. C. Anderson, *Man's Right to Be Human*, New York, Morrow, 1959.
72 Anderson, *loc. cit.*
73 Gibson, *loc. cit.*, pp. 148-149.
74 O. H. Mowrer, *New Evidence Concerning the Nature of Psychopathology* (to be published).

75 Warren S. McCulloch, "The Past of a Delusion," 1952, p. 3. Unpublished.
76 Cf. T. S. Szasz, *The Myth of Mental Illness*, New York, Harper, 1961.
77 O. H. Mowrer, *The New Group Therapy*, Princeton, N.J., Van Nostrand, 1964.
78 Anderson, *loc. cit.*, pp. 164-165.

QUESTIONS

1 Discuss the relationship between pastoral counseling and psychoanalysis, as Professor Mowrer views the problem. Can you list other possible areas of cooperation between the two disciplines?
2 Explain the author's view, which asserts that Protestantism is "a continuation and extension of medieval Catholicism," that it has no satisfactory way of dealing with the problem of personal guilt.
3 List some of the main objections of Mowrer against Freudian psychology. Give a brief but adequate critique of the author's position.
4 Is Mowrer's historical interpretation of Christianity, in its relation to the cure of souls, a sound view of its development? Whether your answer is negative or affirmative, state the defense of your position.
5 Is there some validity to Mowrer's charge that psychiatrists have deliberately set out to establish themselves as a new priestly class in the dimension of personal existence?

SUGGESTED READINGS

D. Belgum, *Guilt: Where Psychology and Religion Meet*, Englewood Cliffs, N.J., Prentice-Hall, 1963.

A. T. Boisen, *The Exploration of the Inner World*, New York, Harper, 1936.

Erich Fromm, *Sigmund Freud's Mission*, New York, Harper, 1959.

J. T. McNeill, *A History of the Cure of Souls*, New York, Harper, 1951.

O. H. Mowrer, *The Crisis in Psychiatry and Religion*, Princeton, N.J., Van Nostrand, 1961.

C. R. Rogers, *On Becoming a Person*, Boston, Houghton Mifflin, 1961.

T. S. Szasz, *The Myth of Mental Illness*, New York, Harper, 1961.

14 *Edward Norbeck*

Anthropological Views of Religion

Since its beginning as a scholarly discipline approximately a century ago, anthropology has included religion among its subjects of interest. Assumptions underlying anthropological research have expectably changed as the field has expanded, and subfields of specialization have developed that proceed from differing and sometimes conflicting viewpoints. Modern anthropological thought may be described as forming several major currents. Despite apparent diversity, however, much is held in common.

Anthropology is "the study of man," but for most anthropologists this definition has not meant the study of man as a biological organism. Only physical anthropologists concern themselves principally with the physical aspects of man, and their research has not directly concerned the subject of religion. To the vast majority of anthropologists, the study of man has meant the study of culture, the trait which sets man apart as unique among living things. Social anthropologists focus attention on social structure and social relationships, and their views of culture may differ in various respects from those of their more numerous colleagues, the cultural anthropologists and archeologists. There is agreement, however, that what is distinctively human is cultural, and it is through the study of culture that most anthropologists have sought understanding of human behavior.

To understand views of religion held by anthropologists, it is nevertheless important to be aware of certain anthropological views of man as a biological form. Anthropologists characteristically look upon all living varieties and races of man as being sufficiently similar that for most pur-

414

poses of study the human organism may be omitted from consideration as irrelevant. These words do not mean to imply that anthropologists believe all races are precisely alike in hereditary qualities—a statement which is manifestly untrue—and they do not imply that scientific proof has been given of uniformity of intellectual capabilities—a question which present techniques of investigation are unable to settle. Much evidence has shown, however, that the members of any race may have any culture, given the social opportunity, and that confusion has been the only result of recourse to putatively innate differences in attempts to understand differences in the religions and cultures of the societies and races of the world. Ideas such as "primitive mentality" and notions concerning innate inferiority and superiority of the races have been set aside in the study of culture as being false or undemonstrated and, for many purposes, irrelevant. In seeking to explain differences and similarities among cultures of the world, anthropologists look principally to culture itself and to its relationship to the physical environment. Reference to human biological traits is, of course, necessary for certain purposes—e.g., attempts to understand individual rather than racial or societal differences in personality, religiosity, and the like—but most research in anthropology has centered on modes rather than individual variations.

The general objective of cultural anthropology may be described as an attempt to understand the nature of culture, the relationships among its distinguishable elements, its manner of growth and change, and its effects upon man, its creator. To reach these goals, anthropologists observe and compare ways of life of both primitive and civilized societies, noting similarities and differences and seeking to explain them. These words imply a basic assumption that culture—the man-made part of the universe that includes ideas, sentiments, skills, knowledge, and objects—constitutes a scientifically valid category of phenomena amenable to objective observation that will lead to the formulation of scientific generalizations. As an element of culture, religion is then also regarded as an invention of man subject to scientific scrutiny.

Anthropological research and thinking on the subject of religion have, expectably, in other ways followed general trends of anthropological development. The main trends of anthropological theory have followed a complex and intertwining course of formulation, rejection, modification, expansion, and, sometimes, revival of theories, of which only the barest outlines will be given here.

When anthropology took form as a recognized branch of study during the nineteenth century, the prevailing theoretical orientation was evolutionist. I refer here to cultural evolution, which developed through its own channels independently from theories of biological evolution. Following the European discovery of the New World and Asia, accounts of the customs of foreign peoples presented an apparent picture of great and bewildering variety. But closer examination also showed remarkable similarities of custom among peoples living in areas separated by great distances and physical barriers that made the spread of ideas and objects through contact seem improbable. Similar or essentially identical beliefs and practices of supernaturalism appeared again and again among geographically far-flung societies, and it was possible to classify the whole range of beliefs and practices under a small number of headings. All peoples were seen to have religion, beliefs in souls and other spiritual entities, magic, and rites that bore many close resemblances.

The earliest anthropological attempts to account for these and other cultural similarities and differences were evolutionist; that is, they were guided by the theoretical assumption that culture, as a distinctive category of phenomena with properties and behavior peculiar to its class, followed a definable course of progressive development or evolution. Societies were classified on the basis of cultural traits into several stages in a serial order from simple to complex. Attempts were also made to explain the evolutionary processes leading from one stage to another, and these gave emphasis to technologic-economic innovations allowing increased control over the resources of nature as the forces most powerful in shaping social organization, molding ideologies, and leading to cultural change and growth.[1]

Evolutionism prevailed until about the beginning of the twentieth century, when a strong current of opposition arose toward it. The early decades of the twentieth century were given over principally to the gathering of facts. During this time much field research among primitive societies was conducted that resulted in many descriptive monographs. Although the groundwork leading to later theoretical formulations may be traced to this period, interpretive accounts published during this time consisted chiefly of inferences concerning the diffusion of traits of culture from one society to another.

During the 1930's the current of opinion turned again to emphasize interpretation rather than mere collection of data. Growing awareness of developments in the related fields of sociology, psychology, social psychology, and psychiatry stimulated the formulation of theoretical foundations that then emerged, and anthropology owes much to these disciplines. At this time the point of view called functionalism arose, and it has since continued to hold a prominent position in anthropology. Functionalism, its roots traceable in part to sociology, may be described briefly as the study of culture, or for many social anthropologists, of society as dynamic systems. Culture—either in a generalized sense or any individual culture— is looked upon as a unit composed of functionally interrelated parts so that change in any important part leads to adjustive changes in other parts. To gain an adequate understanding of the whole or any part of the whole, it is necessary to examine the relationships of the constituent parts.

As the years have passed since the emergence of functionalism, anthropological usages of the term "function," from which this point of view takes its name, have become varied, but all in one way or another concern relationships and look upon culture or society as systemic units.[2] Dependent upon the interests and views of the scholars concerned, the function of an element of culture might mean the "contribution" it makes to the maintenance—or as a negative function, to the disruption—of society or of the psychological integration of the individual. Thus, for example, religion has often been interpreted as contributing to the maintenance of society by creating social solidarity through joint rituals, common beliefs, and support of socially important rules of interpersonal behavior. For the individual, religion is held to serve a positive function of providing psychological assurance in various ways. Certain religious beliefs and acts might be seen as negatively functional—examples are food taboos that inhibit the efficient economic use of resources of nature, and religious teachings that instill fear—but, as we shall see, negative functions of religion have received little attention. The function of an element of culture might also refer to the hypothesized human needs it is held to serve. Some anthropologists have objected to the teleological implications of these points of view and have given their attention to deducing functional relationships or covariations between elements of culture—for example, the relationships between economic systems and social structure—without direct regard to their supportive or disruptive effects for society and the individual, or to human needs that they might fulfill.

Two additional major trends of anthropological theory and research developed about the time of the emergence of functionalism or shortly afterwards. One of these has been called *personality and culture*. Under this loosely fitting title are grouped various lines of anthropological research derived in part from psychology and psychiatry that center on the relationship between human personality and culture.[3] Much of this research has aimed to delineate modal personalities for different societies, subsocieties, and social classes and to deduce the cultural factors which determine the characteristic behavior or personality. These studies are also functionalist in the sense that they concern functional relationships, and they have often employed "functionalist" theories. Their interpretations of religion have most frequently concerned the role of religion in relation to culturally induced anxieties and in meeting psychic needs.

Cultural evolutionism, employing the same general ideas as those of the early anthropologists, revived shortly after the appearance of research in personality and culture.[4] Here again, the approach is functionalist in the sense that the evolutionary view also sees culture as a dynamic system. Evolutionists attempt to formulate a scheme of the sequential development of culture in general, whereas functionalists center upon the dynamic relationships of individual cultures or societies at fixed points in time and have given little attention to broad-scale comparison and generalization.[5]

All of the categories of anthropological research we have mentioned —evolutionism, descriptive ethnography, studies of cultural diffusion, functionalism, and personality and culture studies—have included the subject of religion. Anthropologists engaged in these various avenues of research have sometimes expressed conflicting viewpoints, and professional journals have carried heated arguments over matters of theory. Yet it is possible to see important points of agreement on fundamental issues among even those who have seemed in strongest opposition to one another.

From the evolutionists of the nineteenth century to contemporary ethnologists of all theoretical persuasions, anthropologists have regarded culture as man's mode of adjustment to the universe, his way of meeting the competition of other living forms and of ensuring the perpetuation of his species. Culture is the adaptive device that has made the species *Homo sapiens* successful, and it is functionally analogous with adjustive physical changes of biological evolution. As a part of culture, religion has been correspondingly seen as a technique of adjustment, in the biological sense, that has had value for survival.

The early evolutionists devoted much effort to attempts to formulate developmental schemes of religion proceeding from various hypothetical beginnings to a culmination in monotheism. These hypothesized sequences of development were discarded by later anthropologists because they were seen to represent ethnocentric viewpoints or to disagree with the facts as reported by field ethnologists, and attempts to deduce the ultimate origins of religion were abandoned as unscientific speculation. What interests us, however, is the similar view of the role of religion held by the early evolutionists and their modern successors, evolutionist and non-evolutionist.

The noted British anthropologist Edward Burnett Tylor, who has often been called the father of anthropology, presented a hypothesis of the evolutionary development of religion beginning with simple animism and belief in spiritual beings and proceeding finally to monotheism.[6] Pondering the circumstances that might have given birth to the idea of animism, he interpreted it as a cognitive attempt on the part of prehistoric man to explain the differences between life and death, sleep and wakefulness, and states of unconsciousness and normality. The idea of souls or spirits separable from the body—so Tylor thought—was suggested to early man by the experiences he underwent while dreaming or unconscious. Once primitive man had formulated the idea of spirits, he extended it to the whole universe, attributing spirits to phenomena of both the animate and inanimate worlds as explanations of their properties and behavior. Tylor regarded the invention of the idea of animism as an intellectual achievement, a crude philosophy that had adjustive value because it not only explained the unknown but also, through these explanations, suggested courses of action to be taken to bring recovery of normal states of being. Acts such as prayer, worship, and the making of offerings he regarded as techniques to assure well-being and success.

Sir James G. Frazer, one of the few anthropologists writing in the early twentieth century who held evolutionary viewpoints, similarly saw both magic and religion as tools of man.[7] Frazer thought that the earliest human beings had only magic and that religion arose later to displace it. Although he viewed religion and magic as functionally alike, he made a clear distinction between them on the basis of the attitudes they involved: magic rested upon the belief that man exercises control over the supernatural by means of certain mechanical procedures; religion implied ideas of the control of man by supernatural powers, and religious behavior correspondingly consisted of worship, prayer, and other forms of propitiation. In Frazer's view, magic was rational but fallacious, the pseudo-science of primeval man by means of which he sought to control the universe for his own purposes. When man finally observed that the mechanical acts of magic failed to achieve desired goals, he formulated a new interpretation of the nature of the universe and began to engage in religious behavior to reach the very objectives for which he had formerly employed magic.

Other theorists concerned with the origin and evolution of religion viewed the creation of gods and other beliefs of supernaturalism and the establishment of religious acts as emotional rather than witting intellectual responses of man to his environment.[8] Emotional states of awe, reverence, fear, and tension were variously seen as inspired by natural phenomena, the hazards of life, or the conditions of social living, and these states were held to have led to the creation of religious beliefs and acts as mechanisms for relieving tensions and binding people socially.

Although modern anthropologists do not concern themselves with the questions of the origins of religion, the problems of religion that hold their interest are approached from a viewpoint resembling that of their predecessors. Religion is regarded as the creation of man that has arisen, by whatever psychological processes, from man's experiences of daily life and serves for him various functions. It constitutes an attempt to formulate symbolic answers to questions and problems that confront man. Gods, demons, evil spirits, witches, souls, taboos and other supernatural sanctions governing behavior, rites at critical times during the lifespan, mythology, and other religious beliefs and acts are seen as the casting into concrete and comprehensible form of the fears, hopes, wishes, dreams, and animosities of man. Once man has put his problems in these forms, he can deal with them by acts analogous with those of his ordinary experience with objects of nature and with his fellowmen. Man has then created gods and religion in his own image and in the image of the world of his experience, and his religious beliefs and acts are functional responses to circumstances of life.

As the foregoing sentences imply, religion is regarded not as the mainspring of cultural or social life but rather as a derivative of more fundamental factors, especially ways of gaining a livelihood and the closely associated manner of ordering society. As simple examples of the correlation between religion and other aspects of culture, we may note that the religions of agricultural people lack gods of the sea but include prominently acts and supernatural beings relating to agriculture, and that the traditional Christian conception of God as a father is congruous with the familial organization of Christian societies but, as we shall later see, is incongruous in various other societies and does not exist in their beliefs. These words do not intend to say that religion is held to be wholly passive or that it lacks importance. Once religious beliefs and practices have taken form, they have a particular tenacity because of the emotional value surrounding them, and they too exert influence on social organization, technology, economics, and other aspects of culture. To gain a full understanding of religion, one must look especially to the more fundamental aspects of culture, but to understand economics and social organization one must also look to religion and its effects upon them.

Much of the foregoing may be restated in another way. Man and only man is capable of the kind of thought and action called religion, quite as he is capable of speech and other forms of symbolic behavior. For many years, anthropology has given little attention to the neurological basis of the capacity for creating religion or culture in general, and this capacity is assumed to be essentially the same for all societies and races of man. Instead, anthropologists have tried to understand the significance of religion in human life, the factors that have molded it into its particular forms, and the roles it plays in the total culture. Religious beliefs and practices are seen as principally derivative in form and content from other aspects of the cultural systems of which they are a part, and as playing important adjustive or supportive roles for the individual, the society, and the culture. In order to understand the roles and at the same time the distinctive forms of individual religions, anthropologists have examined religion in its relationship to other aspects of culture and in its total cultural context.

Consider the anthropological interpretation of the nature of moral codes and the relationship between religion and morality. Although popular Western thought and some Western theologians speak of moral absolutes and define religion as a moral code, anthropologists have not done so. Their acquaintance with foreign cultures has revealed highly variable conceptions of morality and many societies in which morality and religion bear essentially no relationship. Yet rules of proper behavior for men in their relations with other men, and means to ensure the enforcement of these rules, exist in all societies, as they must if the societies and the human species are to survive. Conceptions of morality and immorality are seen by anthropologists to arise from the circumstances of daily living, and for this reason they differ from society to society and change as ways of life otherwise undergo change. Murder, incest, and adultery—to cite only a few universal offenses against propriety—are variously defined, and these definitions may be seen as congruent with the ways of life of the peoples concerned. Enforcement of moral codes comes through numerous sanctions that are given varying emphases and are often exercised jointly. Like legal and other secular sanctions, religious sanctions vary in importance from society to society and may exert great or little force toward conformance with rules of behavior. When conformance with certain rules of behavior is vital to the successful continuation of society, multiple and powerful sanctions are commonly imposed and these frequently (but by no means always) include the religious.[9]

------ ✳ ------

A question arises that we have so far skirted. How do anthropologists define religion? The definition of religion has long been a problem, in part because of the difficulty encountered in setting magic apart from religion. Frazer's distinction, to which we have already referred, was often criticized by later anthropologists who observed that acts of magic and religion, as he defined them, were often interwoven into a single ceremony. Most contemporary anthropologists have failed to define religion explicitly, but inference drawn from examination of their writings reveals an implicit definition of religion as ideas and acts of supernaturalism. They have sometimes distinguished magic from religion according to two concepts of supernatural power said to underlie the acts of magic and religion. According to this view, magic involves the idea of an impersonal force residing in certain objects or acts, or everywhere in the universe, available for man's use if he learns the techniques for acquiring and employing it. Religion involves an underlying conception of power as the attribute of sentient supernatural beings which control the universe. The two conceptions commonly co-exist, although one may greatly overshadow the other, and the observable acts of magic and religion are held to derive from them.[10] Since the time of Frazer many other proposals have been made of suitable criteria for distinguishing magic from religion, but none of these has met with common acceptance. Included among them is the concept of a polar continuum based upon an elaborate set of traits representing a summary of major distinguishing characteristics that have been employed in anthropological writings. This polar classification includes, as traits more closely related to the magical than the religious pole, concrete specificity of goals (as opposed to generalized goals); a manipulative attitude (rather than supplication and propitiation); a professional-client relationship (versus relationships of shepherd-flock or prophet-follower); individual ends (versus group ends); the employment of magic only for instrumental ends (whereas religious acts tend to be ends in themselves); and impersonality and a lesser degree of emotion in magic.[11] Whether or not magic and religion are distinguished from each other in anthropological writings, however, both are looked upon as supernaturalistic devices of adjustment that are congruent with the culture as a whole. Functionally they are seen to be very similar and interpretation of both has proceeded along lines that are essentially alike.

A growing trend has recently become evident among anthropologists (and also among sociologists and some sectors of the general public) to define religion in terms that make no reference to supernaturalism but instead identify it as a set of values, often called "ultimate" values, about which people have strong emotional feelings. Thus all human beings, including agnostics, atheists, and Russians, may be credited with religion. This definition may be seen as a modification of one of the traits used by various earlier scholars to characterize religion. I refer here to the dichotomy between the sacred and the profane, a distinction that has in the past been criticized because of the difficulty it imposes in setting apart religion from other behavior that has not conventionally been called religion but which evokes emotional states difficult to distinguish from those brought forth by the sacred. Examples that have often been cited are attitudes toward national flags and national anthems.

The definition of religion as a set of ultimate values that may or may not include ideas of supernaturalism seems also to be a reflection of changing cultural circumstances in our own society, part of a trend of change that has often been called the secularization of religion. A tendency toward the disappearance of supernaturalism from religion has long been evident in our own society and shows no signs of diminishing. It is probably accurate to state that certain modern creeds customarily called religions quite lack ideas of supernaturalism although they retain many of the functions ascribed to supernaturalistic faiths. Formulating a definition of religion suitable to embrace all ideologies and acts that have been called religion will doubtless be a difficult task, and it appears likely that anthropology will long continue to employ supernaturalism as a useful working definition, at least when discussing primitive societies.

------ ✳ ------

No matter how anthropologists may define religion, they characteristically see it as much more than a set of abstract ideas and beliefs. It is also a system of ordered social interaction, not only between man and supernatural beings but—what is more important to the anthropologist—

also between man and his fellow human beings. In contrast with theologians, who until recent years gave little attention to the observable acts of religion, anthropologists have made them a focus of study. The identity of the performers and participants in religious acts, the relationships among them, the nature of their acts, the values expressed in myths and rites, and the occasions upon which myths are told and rites are performed are all regarded as information vital to the understanding of religion. From observations of these matters, inferences are drawn regarding the roles of religion that are not otherwise readily obvious.

The roles of a common set of beliefs and of joint ritual as social binders, for example, are doubtless readily apparent to educated citizens of modern civilizations. These and many other inferred roles of religion have not been apparent to members of historically known primitive society and, as seems evident from the quantity of anthropological and sociological writings on this subject, they have probably not been apparent to mankind in general during most of human history. Reasons for the existence of religious beliefs and acts, as these are comprehended by the average man, are regarded by anthropologists as inadequate or even valueless to provide an adequate understanding of the beliefs and acts. The origin of supernaturalistic beliefs and acts is ordinarily unknown or they are held to be of divine inspiration. The intended effects and explicitly comprehended reasons for the performance of rites, as they are expressed by the ordinary members of society, consist of the unquestioning pursuit of custom as the proper and often the only way to ensure well-being and to reach specific goals such as abundant crops, successful hunting and fishing, and recovery from illness.

Explanations of this kind—sometimes called by anthropologists and sociologists "explicit functions" of religion—are clearly inadequate to account for either differences or similarities of rite and belief found throughout the world. Anthropological attempts to interpret religion have therefore been directed strongly toward deducing its unintended effects or implicit functions. With this objective in mind anthropologists observe the identity and characteristics of religious performers and the nature and occasions for their performances. For the same reason, consideration is given to social and economic organization and other elements of culture and their relationship to religion.

Again, it is useful to illustrate by examples of specific studies. Cross-cultural comparison made it clear long ago that human beings tend to give social attention to events of importance to the group or in the lives of individual members of society. Birth, maturity, marriage, death, planting, harvesting, the beginning and end of seasonal activities such as hunting, fishing, and the gathering of wild foods, serious illnesses, the birth, accession, and death of rulers, and other important events are marked by special social activities. In most societies and during most of man's history, these observances have been conducted under a religious mantle that has given the events a special weight. These rites were interpreted by scholars as forms of social approval and official announcements of changes in the statuses and relationships of members of society that served, among other things, to ease the individual through his transition and to promote social solidarity through joint action.[12] Other rites were seen as dramatic assurances of success in economic and other activities and as palliatives for anxieties variously derived. Sometimes the rites were seen to contain as integral elements statements of important rules of behavior that were thus given supernatural sanction.

Interpretations of societally and individually supportive and integrative functions such as these met with general acceptance among anthropologists, but they left unanswered many questions concerning the particular form that rites assumed in different societies, and reasons for the presence or absence and relative degrees of elaboration of particular types of rites. Why, for example, should coming-of-age ceremonies be observed in one society and not in another, and why should coming of age and marriage be minor events in some societies but in others the occasions for grand religious ceremonies? Why should the Ghost Dance Religion, a movement promising salvation that swept through many American Indian societies in the late nineteenth century, have been so unimportant among the Indians of Nevada who invented it? The obvious answers to questions of this kind lie in the relative social importance of the events upon which ritual centers, but why the events are important or unimportant has often not been obvious. In attempts to answer questions such as these the study of religion in its cultural context has been important, and as progress has been made in studies directed primarily toward social organization, economics, and other aspects of culture, it has contributed to the understanding of religion.

In some societies, for example, there is no abrupt transition from social immaturity to maturity, no sharp change in privilege and obligation that marks physical maturation. This is a circumstance that may be seen as congruent with a lack of coming-of-age ritual. Only detailed examination of the cultures in question, however, can provide information of this kind.

Studies of social structure have revealed that enduring ties of marriage may be relatively unimportant in societies socially organized on the basis of kinship traced through female lines. Study centered principally upon economics has, in turn, indicated that the custom of tracing descent matrilineally depends primarily upon the existence of subsistence technologies that enhance the position of females by favoring uxorilocal residence; that is, residence of a married couple near or with the relatives of the bride. Matrilineal societies consist of a number of distinct social groups composed of women, their brothers, and the women's offspring of both sexes. In these societies adult males are frequently charged with economic and other responsibilities for their sisters and their sisters' children. A husband belongs to a matrilineal kin group within the society different from that of his wife, and his most important social affiliation is with this organization of relatives rather than with his wife and children. It is not surprising that "God the Father" and various other religious conceptions of European society have no place in the religious beliefs of societies thus organized.

Since women and children are both socially identified and economically supported through their own matrilineal kin, it is also unsurprising that in matrilineal societies marriage tends to lack sanction by elaborate weddings and that divorce is simple and relatively common. But exceptions to these general trends also exist, and understanding of the exceptions has been gained by examination of social and economic circumstances. Among the matrilineal Bemba of Northern Rhodesia, for example, ritual for girls who reach the age marking the borderline of adulthood is elaborate and includes many events sanctioning marriage, which immediately follows coming of age. This circumstance has been interpreted as due in part to the fact that local economic conditions make the family of husband, wife, and children vitally important.[13]

As the preceding paragraphs suggest, one of the important matters for anthropological observation has been sources of strain in social systems and other conditions of life. Matrilineal societies impose strains upon the relations between husband and wife by emphasizing the importance of ties with matrilineal kin at the expense of those between spouses, and this is reflected in ritual surrounding marriage.[14] In these societies, brothers sometimes compete with each other for the social prestige they derive from the privilege of economically supporting and holding authority over their sisters and their sisters' children, and the antagonism and hostility of the competing brothers may find controlled expression in ritual acts or even through witchcraft and black magic. Each of the various ways of organizing people into groups necessary for providing subsistence, protection, and well-being has its own problems of stress arising from the nature of the social roles to which individuals are assigned. The interests of the individual never wholly coincide with those of the group, and relationships that create circumstances of potentially severe conflict and strain are hedged with alleviating devices of various kinds, including taboos, acts of ritual, and religious sanctions applying to behavior toward kin and other members of society.

Human beings are also, of course, exposed to many other potential sources of anxiety, including those imposed by neighboring societies, and their cultural environment may often be described as including various foreign cultures. Consideration of both internal cultural circumstances and relations with neighboring cultures has often been important in trying to understand the religious movements that have arisen among primitive societies during the past several centuries. Primitive peoples whose existence and ways of life have been threatened by contact with European culture have frequently turned for salvation to new or heightened religious activity. The general sources of their stress are readily evident, but understanding of particular points of strain that come through conflict of native and foreign custom has required closer inspection. Questions concerning the forms of religious movements in particular societies and the relative intensities of movements that have spread from one society to another have required examination of both native and European cultures.

We may use as a brief example the Ghost Dance Religion,[15] one of the most important of the many religious movements arising among Indians of the United States since the coming of the white man. Threatened with extinction during the late nineteenth century and demoralized by loss of their old culture without satisfactory adjustment to the new ways imposed upon them, dozens of tribes of the Great Plains and Far West accepted the Ghost Dance Religion as a means of salvation. Arising in Nevada, the religion spread widely and took distinctive local forms. Among tribes suffering much distress, it was accepted with varying degrees of enthusiasm by many, though it was rejected by others. Among Indians of the Great Plains, the religion was feverishly accepted. It held less importance or none among tribes occupying Nevada, even though it arose in that region, and was rejected by the Pueblo Indian tribes of the nearby southwestern United States.

Probable reasons for its weak development among the Indians of Nevada may be inferred from examination of their cultural conditions. Living in a physical environment poor in natural resources, the Indians of Nevada were few, forming small groups that were loosely organized and widely dispersed and came together only rarely in numbers larger than 15 to 35 persons. Lacking social solidarity and powerful chiefs, they also lacked effective channels for the spread and development of the new religion. Since the Indians presented no truly serious threat to white travelers and settlers, they were given little attention by the white men. Unlike surviving Indians in many other areas of the United States, few were then placed on reservations that might serve to concentrate and unite them. Supernaturalistic revelations such as those which inspired the Ghost Dance Religion among one of their tribes were not rare or truly remarkable; many men had them. There is no question but that conditions of life were deplorable for the Indians of Nevada; but, compared with circumstances in the Great Plains, they had been deplorable before the coming of the white man.

Among tribes of the Great Plains, the state of crisis doubtless seemed far more urgent by comparison with their former circumstances of relative comfort and plenty. These tribes lived in much larger and more highly organized groups that had powerful leaders, circumstances that provided better ground for development of the cult activities. Their native religious beliefs also gave special value to revelations, and the singing and dancing of the Ghost Dance found among them established precedents. The Pueblo Indian tribes had also suffered from contacts with the white man, but much in their native way of life differed from customs of the Indians of Nevada and of the Great Plains. Revelations were not a part of their indigenous religion, and an ethic proscribing extravagant expression of emotions also made the frenzied dancing of Ghost Dance ritual unattractive to them.

The anthropological study of witchcraft has also concerned sources of stress in human relationships. In all societies in which it has been observed, witchcraft describes patterns; that is, the social relationships of persons accused of witchcraft and those who regard themselves as bewitched are distinctive and stressful. Examination of the social roles that their societies require the bewitched and those accused of witchery to play with respect to each other has been helpful in understanding the sources of ill-feeling between them. Witchcraft has commonly received anthropological interpretation as a channel for the expression of hostile feelings and repressed desires which people use when other safety valves are prohibited or too costly. Witchcraft is then seen to have positive functional value, an interpretation to which we shall return for further remarks.

Value as a safety valve is not the only positive effect of witchcraft that anthropologists have seen. Beliefs and practices of witchcraft have also been held to operate as mechanisms of social control, resembling in their operation supernatural sanctions for ethical or moral behavior.[16] Witches and those bewitched are ordinarily persons who in one way or another fail to meet social norms. Witches are commonly antisocial people who fail to conform with ideals of behavior, and the bewitched are those whose behavior is similar or who stand out in the group in some way that incites the dislike or envy of witches. Fear of either the consequences of bewitchment or the accusation of performing witchcraft and subsequent temporal and supernatural punishment are held to serve as strong sanctions for social conformance—and thus witchcraft is seen also to have positive value in maintaining ideals of proper behavior.

Anthropological interpretations of antisocial or seemingly antisocial rites of another kind have similarly viewed them as having social value.[17] These rites are institutionalized practices, conducted on fixed occasions, which permit and sometimes require obscenity, lewdness, adultery, incest, open expressions of hostility toward others, and the violations of other norms of behavior that are highly valued and at other times strictly observed. Among various societies of sub-Saharan Africa, for example, native custom during great annual festivals included the temporary suspension of many rules of behavior. People were allowed to indulge in otherwise forbidden sexual acts, to express directly any feelings of resentment or hostility they harbored for others, and to violate many other important rules of conduct. Similar customs were, of course, once common in Europe and they have existed in a great many societies of both the civilized and primitive worlds. These institutions have been interpreted as safety valves which, in the cultural contexts of the particular societies in which they are found, are held to have positive functional value for the individual and society as socially controlled channels for the expression of hostilities and frustrations that, if continually repressed, would be harmful.

These and other interpretations of the role of religion as a safety valve have often seemed illuminating, but as some critics within the ranks of anthropology have observed, they are open to question. Negative effects of these customs seem obvious, but objective techniques for weighing positive against negative are lacking. Our examples relating to stress are intended in part to point up a problem of functional analysis in anthropology: the danger of falling into value judgments. We shall add that many anthropologists have avoided the danger by avoiding interpretations of the kinds in question.

------- ❋ ------

Our examples and discussion also serve to illustrate a view—perhaps it is better called a bias—that appears to be implicitly held by most anthropologists. We have noted that anthropologists presenting interpretations of the role of religion have labored hardest to deduce its unintended effects and especially to formulate hypotheses concerning supportive rather than disruptive functions. Little attention has been devoted to negative effects even when these seem readily apparent. Probably no anthropologist would hold that witchcraft, for example, lacks negative effects, but anthropological writings on the subject are devoted principally to hypotheses concerning its positive functional value.[18] It seems reasonable to state that most anthropologists concerned with the interpretation of religion have proceeded on the assumption that within the context of the total culture in which any religion exists, the most significant functions of religion are socially and individually positive rather than negative. We may say anthropologists take for granted that the benefits of religion outweigh its harmful effects. Reference to the relative importance of positive and negative effects has been made only seldom, and in these instances discussion has usually been limited to specific beliefs and practices rather than to any total religious complex or to religion in a generic sense. (As an interesting contrast, we may note that anthropologists of the Soviet Union—if the few available examples of their writings on this subject are indicative—see the functions of religion as strongly negative.) [19]

The avoidance by anthropologists of published references to negative functions of religion is perhaps in part a reflection of Western attitudes toward religion. Although anthropologists have always maintained an interest in the subject, few have made it a field of specialization. Popular works on anthropological subjects, writings intended for the general reader, have become fairly abundant, but they include few books on religion that go beyond mere description. Anthropology has produced little writing on the religions of our own society. This seeming oversight is doubtless in part a reflection of the traditional anthropological interest in primitive societies; yet recent years have brought an increasing tendency among anthropologists to study aspects other than religion of modern industrial societies. The scientific study of religion has not been truly popular in any of the social sciences and it has not flourished in any other scholarly field. The first journal devoted to the scientific study of religion made a belated appearance in 1961 as the organ of a scholarly society organized only a few years earlier. [20]

Anthropological writings on the subject of religion have been scholarly writings, and their authors have found immunity from charges of unorthodoxy and subversiveness by publishing through channels little used by any persons except tolerant or like-minded colleagues. Although the controversial position that the subject holds in our society has doubtless inhibited anthropological emphasis on publications concerning religion, it seems doubtful whether this circumstance has had strong influence on anthropological thought regarding the negative function of religion. As we have already noted, the majority of anthropologists appear to assume that the functions of religion are predominantly positive. Although most anthropologists have no personal religious convictions, they have rarely been debunkers of religion in their personal lives and have never taken this position in their published works. And anthropological concern with religion entirely ignores the question of the scientific or objective validity of religious dogma as being irrelevant to its objectives of study.

Anthropologists have also avoided judgments on the relative inferiority and superiority of particular religions. Characteristically, they are committed to a viewpoint of cultural relativism with respect to judgments of this kind. It is not difficult to see this circumstance as congruent with the common anthropological view that any cultural system consists of elements in at least fairly compatible relations with one another, although individual cultural traits of one system may be incongruent or dysfunctional in another system.

This chapter is not the proper place for a detailed appraisal of progress, weaknesses, and failures in the anthropological study of religion. Some reference to these matters is, however, useful to point up characteristic anthropological views.

Descriptive accounts have provided much information on foreign religions and have prevented anthropologists from approaching the study of religion ethnocentrically on the basis of their knowledge of Christianity, Judaism, and other great religions of the world. These accounts have also revealed fundamental similarities in all religions. Over and over again, basically similar ideas and practices appear in varying combinations and with varying emphases. The anthropologist sees differences in the religions of primitive and civilized societies, but usually sees the similarities as being more outstanding than the differences and—given a definition of religion as supernaturalism—makes no sharp distinction between primitive and civilized religions. Although he employs the expression "primitive religion," he is usually careful to explain that it is a term of convenience denoting the religions of people of simple culture. The striking world-wide similarities in religion have been seen in part to derive from the essential identity of the innate traits and capabilities of man; in part from the diffusion of culture from one people to another; and in most significant part because similar conditions of culture in general have led to similar religious results. It seems reasonable to state that the anthropological examination of religious beliefs and practices in their total cultural contexts has yielded illuminating and plausible observations regarding the role of religion. They leave no doubt of the alliance of religion with the rest of culture. Religion has often provided support for the social and political structure, the economic system, and secular values important in maintaining social order; and for the individual human being it has provided psychological bolstering in various ways.

Although many anthropological writings have emphasized the value of religion for society and the individual, they have not maintained that it consistently gives blanket support to the culture as a whole or to the psychic well-being of the individual, or that it is the most effective or only mechanism for doing so. Secular counterparts exist for many beliefs and associated acts of supernaturalism. A general trend of religious change that anthropologists noted long ago—and today seldom discuss because it seems commonplace—is a decline in the scope of religion that has accompanied cultural growth and elaboration. In primitive society, religion may be said to enter importantly into most aspects of human life, performing many roles for which it has become unsuited in modern, civilized society and for which civilized society often provides secular institutions and devices.[21] Obvious secular displacements for beliefs and associated acts of supernaturalism of primitive society and our own society in the past that have commonly been called religion include modern theories of disease and medical practices, psychotherapy, psychiatric concepts, and scientific interpretations of the nature of the universe.

We have noted that the specific hypotheses of the evolution of religion advanced by nineteenth-century anthropologists have long been regarded as obsolete. No detailed scheme of religious evolution has yet been offered by modern cultural evolutionists. Formulating such a scheme seems possible, however, and it is congruent with the view that culture comprises a dynamic system of functionally related parts that change in accommodation to alterations, however induced, in any important aspect of the whole. Just as evolution occurs in technologic, economic, and social systems, so it occurs in the religious realm. Preliminary attempts at the modern formulation of statements of religious evolution have been made, and these involve a division of culture into the major categories: technologic-economic, social, and ideological.[22] Among these, the ideological aspects, including both naturalistic and supernaturalistic philosophies, are seen to serve vital, supportive roles, but their form and content are derived principally from the more fundamental technologic-economic and social components. These are ideas that agree fairly well with those of anthropological functionalism. The major issue over which functionalists and evolutionists differ is the evolution of culture. Functionalists do not seek to formulate statements of cultural evolution, and they may deny that the formulation of scientifically valid generalizations concerning cultural evolution is possible.

Although no generally accepted scheme of religious evolution has emerged, anthropological study has made it clear that religion is not immutable, that it changes to accord with other changes in culture. Once instituted, religious beliefs and practices may in turn exert considerable influence on other aspects of culture, inhibiting or spurring change and development. Cultural changes in our own society have led to a changing conception of religion. They have also produced many subcultures with correspondingly diverse conceptions of religion.

------ ✳ ------

A recent development worthy of note in the anthropological study of religion is a revival of interest in religious symbolism. Early studies of religion sometimes strongly emphasized the value of attention to the symbolic significance of ritual objects and acts, and of mythology. The French sociologist Emile Durkheim, whose writings exerted strong influence in the formation of the views and methods of anthropological functionalism, stressed the importance of studying symbolism as a key to understanding both the genesis of religion and its functional significance.[23] He held that the intrinsic nature of sacred things was unimportant; the important issue was to understand what these things symbolized. In

Durkheim's view, religion symbolized society, and society was the "soul of religion." Only society, he contended, could evoke the attitude of sacredness which he used as a primary characteristic to set the religious apart from the nonreligious. Religious beliefs and sentiments of a society were symbolic representations of the unity of the society, and this unity was upheld by common beliefs and periodic joint ritual in which the most important values of the society were expressed. Although some of Durkheim's theories concerning religion were discarded, his ideas of the functions of religion as a social binder were carried forward by later sociologists and by anthropologists, and as various earlier passages of this paper indicate, are thoroughly alive today. Durkheim's dictum concerning the value of the study of symbolism received less attention. Part of the neglect of the study of symbolism may have been the result of diversion by the success of studies, also stemming in part from Durkheim, that sought to understand religion as a system of action and social interaction among its participants. Study centering upon religious symbolism became regarded as less exciting and less fruitful than other approaches. Contemporary anthropologists are more and more inclined to think that knowledge of symbolism is not only interesting in itself but may also be vital to permit certain functional interpretations of religion.

As an example we may take studies such as we have already discussed that offer interpretations of ritual acts as socially regulated channels for the relatively harmless expression of hostile feelings. Whatever its significance might be for the psychologist or psychiatrist, symbolic behavior in ritual that involves on the part of the performers no awareness of feelings of conflict or of the expression of hostility through the acts does not permit the cultural anthropologist to interpret the behavior as a safety valve.[24] Knowledge of what the acts signify to the actors is of vital importance. Although much valuable information of this kind has been irretrievably lost by the extinction of countless native customs during the past century, it is encouraging to note that recent research by anthropologists has returned to an interest in symbolism.[25]

------ ✳ ------

In prevailing anthropological views, man is looked upon as a form of life which, rather than being a special creation, emerged on the earth by the same general processes of biological evolution as other living forms. All living varieties of man compose a single species and, so far as is known, differ from each other in hereditary qualities in no way that significantly influences the nature of their culture. Most relevant to our discussion here is the anthropological assumption that all races and peoples have basic psychic unity, and that there is "uniformity in the operations of the human mind under similar conditions of society." [26]

Man is unique among living things as the only form that creates and is capable of creating culture. By means of culture he ensures his survival and perpetuation. Distinctively human traits are cultural traits, and the traits of personality that distinguish representatives of one society from those of other societies are reflections of differing cultures. Culture is an adaptive mechanism that fills human needs for survival. The various logically distinguishable spheres of culture take forms that are mutually compatible and derive in varying part from each other. Anthropology looks upon culture as a dynamic system and seeks to understand the relationship of its parts, to determine which are the more fundamental and which the largely derivative elements, and thus to comprehend the processes by which culture grows and changes.

In attempting to reach these goals of understanding, anthropology gives attention to religion as an outstanding element of culture existing in all societies, and various assumptions about culture in general have correspondingly referred also to religion. Religion is a creation of man, a useful fabrication serving multiple functions, that takes variable forms dependent upon particular cultural circumstances. Religion is seen as part of a larger whole of secular and religious ideology and associated acts that take their form and content from more fundamental aspects of culture and serve important supportive roles, often through providing a rationale for a society's way of life. Although basically derived from other elements of culture, religion also exerts influence upon social, technologic-economic, and other spheres of culture. In order to understand its forms and functions, religion, like all other elements of culture, must be studied in cultural context. Holding these views of the nature of man and culture, anthropologists have expectably been unconcerned with the question of the truth of religious dogma and questions concerning the relative superiority or inferiority of particular religious complexes.

In the anthropological study of religion, a major problem, growing rather than diminishing as religious ideologies and practices of the world have undergone change during the past century, is the formulation of an adequate, scientifically useful definition of religion. The problem is not unique to anthropology but common to all scholarly fields concerned with the scientific study of religion. A wealth of data useful for solving this problem and for other comparative studies has become available as the result of anthropological field research. The modest beginnings of a comparative, scientific study of religion have been made, and it seems reasonable to think that the future will see much progress along this line in which anthropology will be only one of many contributors.

The preceding pages have sometimes called attention to weaknesses and deficiencies in the anthropological study of religion. This course of action has been followed with the aim of providing illumination on the viewpoints of anthropology, and does not intend to imply a negative appraisal.

The anthropological approach also has strengths. It seems justifiable to state that the anthropological view of religion as one of the elements of the system called culture has contributed to our understanding of the nature of religion. From the standpoint of future progress in the scientific study of religion by all disciplines of study, an outstanding contribution of anthropology is the broad knowledge of religions of the world that it has provided. Perhaps it is not immodest to state that this constitutes a unique contribution, a body of data valuable as a safeguard against ethnocentric reasoning and vitally important for the comparative study of religion by scholars in other fields.

NOTES FOR CHAPTER 14

1   See E. B. Tylor, *Primitive Culture*, 3rd ed., New York, 1889; and L. H. Morgan, *Ancient Society*, New York, 1877.
2   Expositions of functionalist points of view and examples of functionalist analysis are available in the writings of E. E. Evans-Pritchard, Emile Durkheim, Max Gluckman, Bronislaw Malinowski, S. F. Nadel, A. R. Radcliffe-Brown, and A. I. Richards. For a detailed exposition and critique see especially R. K. Merton, *Social Theory and Social Structure*, Glencoe, Ill., The Free Press, 1949.
3   See J. J. Honigmann, *Culture and Personality*, New York, Harper, 1954; and A. F. C. Wallace, *Culture and Personality*, New York, Random House, 1961.
4   See L. A. White, *The Science of Culture*, New York, Farrar, Straus, 1949; and *The Evolution of Culture*, New York, McGraw-Hill, 1959.
5   See, for example, E. E. Evans-Pritchard, *Nuer Religion*, Oxford, Clarendon Press, 1956.
6   E. B. Tylor, *Primitive Culture*.
7   J. G. Frazer, *The Golden Bough*, abridged, New York, Macmillan, 1922.
8   See W. J. Goode, *Religion Among the Primitives*, Glencoe, Ill., The Free Press, 1951, Appendix II; and Edward Norbeck, *Religion in Primitive Society*, New York, Harper, 1961, Chap. 2, for lengthier summaries and discussions of theories of the origin of religion.
9   See Edward Norbeck, *Religion in Primitive Society*, Chap. 10. For a rare example of the close identification of religion and morality in a simple primitive culture, see R. F. Fortune, *Manus Religion*, Philadelphia, Memoirs of the American Philosophical Society, Vol. 3, 1935.
10 For an elaboration of these views see Edward Norbeck, *Religion in Primitive Society*, Chap. 3.
11 See W. J. Goode, *Religion Among the Primitives*, pp. 53-54, for a summary of various criteria used by anthropologists to distinguish magic and religion.
12 See Arnold van Gennep, *Les Rites de Passage*, Paris, 1909.
13 A. I. Richards, *Chisungu*, New York, Grove Press, 1956.
14 For a discussion of the nature of matrilineal societies, see David M. Schneider and Kathleen Gough, eds., *Matrilineal Kinship*, Los Angeles and Berkeley, University of California Press, 1961.
15 See Edward Norbeck, *Religion in Primitive Society*, Chap. 13.

16 See B. B. Whiting, *Paiute Sorcery*, Viking Fund Publications in Anthropology, No. 15, New York, Viking Fund, 1950.

17 See Max Gluckman, *Rituals of Rebellion in South-East Africa*, Manchester, Manchester University Press, 1954; and Edward Norbeck, "African Rituals of Conflict," *American Anthropologist*, Vol. 65, No. 6, 1963.

18 See, for example, Clyde Kluckhohn, *Navaho Witchcraft*, Papers of the Peabody Museum of American Archeology and Ethnology, Vol. 22, No. 2, 1944.

19 See, for example, E. F. Murav'ev and I. V. Dmitriev, and I. Kryvelev, "Concreteness in the Study and Overcoming of the Vestiges of Religion," *Soviet Anthropology and Archeology*, Vol. 1, No. 2 (Fall 1962), pp. 3-10.

20 *Journal for the Scientific Study of Religion*, New Haven, Conn.

21 On this subject with respect to religious institutions as safety valves in primitive society, see, for example, Stanley Diamond, "The Search for the Primitive," in I. Goldston (ed.), *Man's Image in Medicine and Anthropology*, New York, International Universities Press, 1963.

22 See, for example, L. A. White, *The Evolution of Culture*.

23 Emile Durkheim, *Les Formes élémentaires de la vie réligieuse; le système totémique en Australie*, Paris, 1912.

24 See S. F. Nadel, *Nupe Religion*, Glencoe, Ill., The Free Press, 1954, p. 108; and Edward Norbeck, "African Rituals of Conflict," *American Anthropologist*, Vol. 64, No. 3, Part 1 (1962), pp. 463-485.

25 See, for example, V. W. Turner, *Ndembu Divination: Its Symbolism and Techniques*, Rhodes-Livingstone Papers 31, Manchester, Manchester University Press, 1961.

26 L. H. Morgan, *Ancient Society*, vi.

QUESTIONS

1 Discuss the early cultural evolutionist point of view toward religion. What topics within the range of religious phenomena were of special interest to them?

2 Give a critical account of the method that was used by early anthropologists in the study of religion, particularly of the cultural evolutionists.

3 Summarize the functionalist approach to religion. What is the relation of religion to culture from the functional perspective?

4 To what extent is the phenomenon of religion viewed as a distinctive experience by the modern anthropologist?

5 Discuss the author's view of religion as a safety valve.

SUGGESTED READINGS

J. G. Frazer, *The Golden Bough: A Study in Magic and Religion*, abridged, one-vol. ed., New York, Macmillan, 1922 (12-vol. ed., London, Macmillan, 1911-1915).

Walter Goldschmidt, *Man's Way*, New York, Holt, 1959.

Bronislaw Malinowski, *Magic, Science and Religion and Other Essays*, Glencoe, Ill., The Free Press, 1948.

Edward Norbeck, *Religion in Primitive Society*, New York, Harper and Row, 1961.

E. B. Tylor, *Primitive Culture*, 2 vols., 3rd American ed., New York, Holt, 1889 (first published 1871).

15 *Glanville Downey*

Religion in the Historian's Perspective

Religions in History: Paganism and Christianity For the historian who wishes to observe the function of religion in the life of a people and to evaluate the role of religion in history, the Hellenistic world in the era of the early Church provides material of special interest. The contrast between the pagan beliefs and the new Christian faith is especially instructive. The people of the Graeco-Roman world had many ways in which to seek satisfaction for their religious needs—in the formal cults of the Olympic gods, in the mystery cults, in the worship of deities such as Isis who came from outside classical lands, or in the various philosophical systems then current. These religions were closely allied with classical art and culture; Libanius of Antioch, one of the great pagan teachers, wrote that "literature and the worship of the gods are twin sisters."

But such religions, by their very nature, were primarily private matters, answering the personal needs of individuals, and there was no one belief which was capable of serving as a unifying force and source of spiritual strength among the people as a whole or of developing into a dominant and guiding factor in the history of the state. The Roman state cult, consisting of the formal worship of the goddess Rome and the emperor, was primarily an expression of political loyalty and had little or no connection with religious feeling. When the early Christians were persecuted for refusing to join in this cult, it was because their refusal constituted political disloyalty.

436

Christianity came into the world as a new thing in many ways, destined to play a role in private and public life such as no other religion had played in Western history. For the historical student, the significance of Christianity in human life and in history can be studied with special advantage in the contrast between paganism and Christianity. A study of the processes of the growth of the new faith brings out the unique qualities of Christianity and shows how it was in time to affect the whole history of the world. Christianity offered a new basis for morality and brought the news and the personal experience of a God who created, loved, and redeemed humanity, a God who through Christ and the Holy Spirit was at work in every individual, a God to whom every individual could have immediate access in prayer.

Christianity found a response both in the natural religious instinct and in the philosophical interests of the time. It created a new basis for human solidarity and brotherhood such as had never previously existed on so broad a scale. It offered salvation through a personal Savior, and forgiveness of sin. It freed men from the fear of death, of chance, and of demons. The individual learned that his own soul had value in the sight of God and that he had his own place in the world, into which he was sent by God for a purpose. Men learned that they needed each other and that they could find freedom by forgetting themselves and serving one another.

As such a teaching spread, it was bound to put men's individual lives on a new basis. Indeed one of the main reasons for the spread of Christianity was the example of the personal lives of its followers. In this way the Church, though only gradually and in the face of opposition, began to count as a factor in the life of the Roman Empire. In time, with the conversion of the Emperor Constantine (A.D. 306-337)—later to become St. Constantine the Great in the Greek Church—the Church entered public life and thenceforward was a major factor in the history of the Empire.

Christianity now began to play a part not only in the personal lives of its followers but in affairs of the state, through the public action of the bishops and the high officials of the government. Beginning with Constantine, legislation was modified in keeping with Christian teaching. Penalties were mitigated, and the legal conception of the family began to reflect Christian morality. At the same time the Church began to offer to everyone, both Christian and pagan, social services, relief of the poor, and medical care such as the pagan government had never thought it necessary to provide.

Gradually the tone of life in the Empire changed. Paganism slowly lost its following. Indeed, when the Emperor Julian (A.D. 361-363) tried to revive paganism, he paid Christianity the compliment of trying to imitate its institutions, but there was no living energy in paganism of this variety. Christianity in due course became the national religion of the Empire, and the Orthodox Church became the national Church. While there were inevitably different degrees of personal faith and religious observance, the national character of the Church, led by the emperor and the imperial family, created an atmosphere in which all aspects of life and all mundane activities were thought of as being—at least nominally—lived and carried out under religious auspices.

Such, then, is the setting for our present study. In the matter of personal and public religion, scholars today live in a world that is in many ways different; and when we study the ancient world it is not easy to rid ourselves of the results of our own training and of the effects of our social, political, and religious environment. Thus when as historians we analyze the role of religion in history, we inevitably approach it from the viewpoint of our own religious situation. The varieties of religious experience among historians are reflected in the varieties of history that they write. The problems connected with the history of Christianity in the Later Roman Empire and its continuation, the Byzantine Empire, offer fruitful opportunities to observe the role of religion in private and public life, to study the perspective of historians on religion as a factor in history, and to examine examples of the methodology of studies of this theme.

Religion Among Historical Factors: The Problem of the Decline and Fall of the Roman Empire When Edward Gibbon (1737-1794) came to write the concluding chapter of *The History of the Decline and Fall of the Roman Empire*, he visualized the story, as he looked back on it, as "the triumph of barbarism and religion." [1] The resounding success of his book on its publication (1776-1788) shows that Gibbon represented what at that time was thought to be the intellectual point of view of a well-educated and intelligent gentleman.

The modern descendant of Gibbon lives in a different world, with a different outlook and with some historical documents that were not yet available in the eighteenth century; and the historians of today no longer see a "decline and fall." Today the process seems rather to have been a transition and a transformation. Gibbon's view of history has itself become a historical phenomenon, so that a British historian writing in 1945 comments that "St. Augustine looked at Roman history from the point of view of an early Christian; Tillemont, from that of a seventeenth-century Frenchman; Gibbon, from that of an eighteenth-century Englishman; Mommsen, from that of a nineteenth-century German." [2]

It was only natural for Gibbon's phrase to become famous as a typical, if dogmatic, pronouncement, of one of the most distinguished writers of the Age of Reason.[3] The historian leaves no doubt as to what he thinks of Christianity as a force in history, and the elaborate rhetoric of his day afforded Gibbon ample opportunity for the calculated condemnation of the Church. The picture of Christianity which he develops is in reality a picture of what early Christianity seemed like to a man of Gibbon's background and temperament. Gibbon would not doubt that his picture corresponded to the truth, but as we read his chapters today, in the light of the work of subsequent historians, we perceive how much of the picture represents personal prejudice and literary effect.

The tenor of Gibbon's conception of his task as recorder of the history of a Christian people is indicated by one of his summaries of the role of Christianity in the life of the Empire:

> As the happiness of a future life is the great object of religion, we may hear, without surprise or scandal, that the introduction, or at least the abuse, of Christianity had some influence on the decline and fall of the Roman empire. The clergy successfully preached the doctrines of patience and pusillanimity; the active virtues of society were discouraged; and the last remains of the military spirit were buried in the cloister; a large portion of public and private wealth was consecrated to the specious demands of charity and devotion; and the soldiers' pay was lavished on the useless multitudes of both sexes, who could only plead the merits of abstinence and chastity. Faith, zeal, curiosity, and the more earthly passions of malice and ambition kindled the flame of theological discord; the church, and even the state, were distracted by religious factions, whose conflicts were sometimes bloody, and always implacable; the attention of the emperors was diverted from camps to synods; the Roman world was oppressed by a new spirit of tyranny; and the persecuted sects became the secret enemies of their country.[4]

The modern reader cannot avoid the thought that under the writer's hand the stately turn of phrase was studied for its own sake, and that opportunity for rhetorical effect helped shape judgment.

To many readers today, the famous coupling of barbarism and Christianity stands as the complete summary of Gibbon's understanding of the "decline and fall." When our own understanding of the historical process has changed so significantly, it is inevitable that such a phrase will be remembered and quoted when other details of Gibbon's work are no longer familiar. Yet the historian assigned other causes for the phenomenon of the disappearance of the old world. In his concluding chapter, Gibbon listed "four principal causes of the ruin of Rome, which continued to operate for a period of more than a thousand years."[5] The first was "the injuries of time and nature," such as hurricanes, earthquakes, fires, and inundations, causing physical damage to the cities and their monuments which could not be wholly repaired. Going on to his second cause, Gibbon writes,

> The crowd of writers of every nation, who impute the destruction of the Roman monuments to the Goths and the Christians, have

neglected to inquire how far they were animated by an hostile principle, and how far they possessed the means and the leisure to satiate their enmity. In the preceding volumes of this History, I have described the triumph of barbarism and religion; and I can only resume, in a few words, their real or imaginary connexion with the ruin of ancient Rome.[6]

The third reason, on the historian's mind, was "the use and abuse of the materials." [7] "The barbarian conquerors of Rome usurped in a moment the toil and treasure of successive ages," as they destroyed precious works of art and carried off the gold and silver money and art objects which formed the wealth of the Empire. "Whatever had escaped the Goths and Vandals was pillaged by the Greek tyrants," that is, by the Byzantine emperors. Gibbon concludes, "I have reserved for the last the most potent and forcible cause of destruction, the domestic hostilities of the Romans themselves," in the form of "frequent seditions" and "private war, which violated with impunity the laws of the Code and the Gospel." [8]

Such is the context in which an eminent historian of the eighteenth century placed religion as a force in history; but with the progress of scholarship, Gibbon's judgments on Christianity, and on the other forces at work in the late antique world, have been overtaken by the researches of the succeeding generations of scholars who have in their turn found themselves drawn to the same problem. The change in scholars' minds since Gibbon's day is illustrated by the title of an important modern study of the subject, published by the French historian Ferdinand Lot in 1927, *The End of the Ancient World and the Beginnings of the Middle Ages*.[9] What was once viewed as decline and fall is now seen as end and beginning; and where such alteration has occurred, we are curious to know what has happened to the views that Gibbon immortalized in his splendid prose. What place does religion find among other factors in history, in the eyes of Gibbon's successors?

What we find is that—as a modern student of the process has written —"the answers to this problem themselves form a commentary upon the ages that proposed them." [10]

It is not surprising, for example, to discover that some historians since Gibbon's day have been much more concerned with economic factors than the gentleman of the eighteenth century was. The problems of the modern world are reflected in the views of Vladimir G. Simkhovitch (1916) and of Ellsworth Huntington (1917), who respectively attributed the collapse of the Empire to the consequences of soil exhaustion and of climatic change.[11] Explanations based on racial factors—a subject of special significance for some modern writers—have been offered by scholars who saw the Empire's decline resulting from the dying out of the governing aristocracy, from the effect of the influx of Greek and Oriental slaves (inferior in character to the Romans), and from the effect of the dilution of Roman blood with alien elements.[12] Rostovtzeff, a bourgeois émigré from Russia, viewed the decline as a result of the social revolution through which the higher classes were absorbed by the lower orders, and the culture of the cities—which were the centers of civilization—declined as a result of the rising of the peasants against the city folk.[13] The contrary view, of Marx and his followers, is well known—namely, that the Empire's social structure, based as it was on slavery, was naturally unable to survive and was replaced by the feudal economy.

Other explanations represent the special academic interests of their authors. A British scholar found that the Roman administrative system never gave the people an effective voice in the government.[14] Several scholars believed that the Empire died because its industrial production was never adequately organized.[15] Another expert concluded that the secret of the Empire's fall was the decline in population and the consequent manpower shortage, as a result of which economic and political life could not be properly maintained.[16] Corruption of the bureaucracy is emphasized by another writer, who finds here the reason why the government was unable to keep up its responsibilities.[17]

Among all these theories it is difficult to make a choice, and some of the most experienced and prudent historians have concluded that the whole process involved in the end of the ancient world is composed of "a complex of interacting causes which the historian disentangles at his peril." [18]

As we read these proposed solutions of the problem, what seems to have become of the religious factor? Have the practical, secular aspects of the question so occupied scholars' attention that they have nothing to say for the Church, either favorable or unfavorable? If Christianity is no longer linked with barbarism as a cause for the "decline," many scholars either say nothing about religion as a factor in the process or content themselves with pointing out the more unattractive features of the Church's life and work.[19]

But if "religion" seems to have ceased to interest scholars, at least for a time, as a factor in the "decline," its companion, "barbarism," remained very prominent, and in the nineteenth century scholarly opinion leaned strongly to the view that it was the barbarian invasions that provided the true explanation of the end of the Roman world.[20] Later this theory gave way in popularity to the view that it was the expansion of Islam in the seventh century that disrupted the Roman world and brought its way of life to an end.[21]

Yet there has recently been a change. Professor Momigliano of London, who is well known as a distinguished "secular historian" and thus cannot be accused of professional bias in favor of Christianity as a church historian might be, has published an essay which brings a new spirit to the subject.[22]

Momigliano points out, very justly, that modern historians who have concluded that the Old Roman Empire came to an end as the result of social changes in the Roman world have in fact left out of account the most important social change of all, namely the rise of Christianity. To anyone familiar with the ancient sources, it is evident that the spread of the Christian way of living produced an alteration in the society of the Empire which is at least as important as any of the secular factors that have usually been adduced. Church historians have of course been well aware of the role of the Church in the latter days of the Old Empire, but to historians who happened to be either indifferent to Christianity or biased against it, the arguments of modern theologians would carry little weight. Yet as Momigliano points out,[23] "What Gibbon saw as merely destructive power must be understood on its own terms of *Civitas dei*— a new commonwealth of men for men. Christianity produced a new style of life, created new loyalties, gave people new ambitions and new satisfactions." In this sense, the triumph of Christianity has a direct relation with the end of the Roman Empire—though not the relation that Gibbon detected.

Momigliano looks at both sides of the picture where Gibbon's attention was concentrated on one:

> Much can be said about the internal conflicts, the worldly ambitions, the intolerance of the Church. Yet the conclusion remains that while the political organization of the empire became increasingly rigid, unimaginative, and unsuccessful, the Church was mobile and resilient and provided space for those whom the State was unable to absorb. The bishops were the centers of large voluntary organizations. They founded and controlled charitable institutions. They defended their flocks against the state officials. When the military situation of the empire grew worse, they often organized armed resistance against the barbarians. It seems to me impossible to deny that the prosperity of the Church was both a consequence and a cause of the decline of the state. People escaped from the state into the Church and weakened the state by giving their best to the Church. This is a situation which in its turn requires analysis and explanation. But its primary importance cannot be overlooked. The best men were working for the Church, not for the State.[24]

Indeed, the judgment of this modern historian should be read alongside the passages quoted above from his eighteenth-century predecessor:

> The superiority of Christianity over paganism in dynamism and efficiency was already evident in the fourth century. The Christians

could adapt themselves better to the new political and social situation and deal more efficiently with the barbarians. A closer analysis of the relations between pagans and Christians in the fourth century is therefore the necessary presupposition for any further study of the decline of the Roman empire.[25]

It is true that the modern student of the classical world has advantages which Gibbon lacked—better libraries, improved texts and translations, bibliographies, handbooks, and evidence from papyri and inscriptions not yet discovered in Gibbon's day. More historians are now at work, and a scholar today has the researches of his colleagues at his disposal.

Yet all our new knowledge has not changed the significance of the sources that were available in Gibbon's time, but has only added to them and confirmed them. When we read a Gibbon and a Momigliano together, we realize that it is not the evidence that has changed, but the historians. The contrast is striking. Gibbon viewed the Church as a religious phenomenon which had deleterious effects on social and political life. Scholars today have come to understand that the Church was not solely a religious factor in the history of the ancient world, but that by its own inherent power it came to be an active and fruitful social and political force. What we see in Gibbon as a hostility to Christianity based upon rationalism or atheism probably represented, to Gibbon himself, a personal conviction that stood in place of a personal religion. Yet a view such as Gibbon's—and we must recall that this perspective is not unique with him—helps us to realize more clearly what the true insight of the historian in these matters must be. We must also distinguish the good in Gibbon's work which is not affected by his antireligious bias. He had a breadth of vision, a grasp of the movement of history, and an insistence on meticulous accuracy that make his work in many ways a great book in spite of its well known defects.

The Interpretation of Motive in the Problem of the Conversion of Constantine the Great The problem of the "decline and fall" is a famous lesson in methodology, but it involves so many subsidiary problems that a full analysis would take us too far from our present purpose. Instead we may turn to another notable crux of ancient history, the conversion to Christianity of the Emperor Constantine the Great. Here we shall be able to study, in terms of a single episode and a limited body of evidence, an interplay of religious and secular factors which illustrate admirably the significance of the historian's perspective on religion.

Among the pivotal events in the history of Europe, the conversion of the Emperor Constantine (A.D. 306-337) is epoch-making in several senses. Not only did this conversion set the history of the Roman Empire and its direct descendants, the modern states of Europe and the Slavic world, in a new direction. It also created a new type of ruler, the Christian Roman Emperor, the prototype of rulers in Europe and the Slavic countries, a few of whose political descendants are still heads of states. If Christianity changed men's religious lives and social lives, it also, when adopted by Constantine and his imperial successors, brought a new conception of the state and of the state's structure and functions. When Constantine became a follower of Christ, the Roman Empire ceased to be the pagan Roman Empire, dependent for its prosperity upon the favor of the traditional gods, and became a new Christian Roman Empire which represented the kingdom of God on earth ruled by a Roman emperor who was the servant of Christ and the vicegerent of God on earth. Not every pagan in the Empire was converted instantly as soon as the emperor's new faith became known; but the life of the Empire was started on a new course from which the Western Middle Ages and Byzantium in time emerged.

Historically the conversion of Constantine provides the student with an admirable opportunity to analyze motivations and forces which sometimes seem personal, sometimes impersonal. The event marked the close of one of the most troubled and perilous periods of Roman history. In the third century the empire faced a growing weight of problems with which it found itself increasingly unable to deal. It is a challenge to the historian to try to disentangle the processes and the problems and assign due importance to each. Decrease of population; manpower shortage; difficulties in the supply of basic materials; the effects of inflation which was permitted by the government; strain on the machinery of the government and inability of an inadequate army to resist the growing pressure on the Rhine, Danube, and Persian frontiers of barbarians that sought living space within the Empire—cause and effect are difficult to distinguish. The lands of the great Empire were not producing enough men, enough food, and enough raw materials and manufactured goods to support the civilian population, the government, and the army. The emperor's task had become so difficult and the armies so influential, that there was a whole succession of rivals who occupied the throne for a few years in turn and then were overthrown.

The crisis was solved by the reforms devised by a succession of able emperors—Aurelian (270-275), Diocletian (284-305), and Constantine the Great (306-337). These able military men saw that the Empire was no longer able to live by means of its traditional political forms. They proceeded to transform it into an authoritarian state in which the emperor became a remote and powerful figure, on the pattern of the Persian monarch, at the head of a vastly strengthened army and bureaucracy. The whole economy, including agriculture, manufacture, and trade, was brought under government control.[26] In some aspects of both public and private life, the Roman Empire began to resemble some of the authoritarian states of the twentieth century.

The future Emperor Constantine grew up during this period of reorganization and recovery. Son of an able general who became governor of Britain under Diocletian, Constantine early saw the chance to make himself a place in the struggle for power that inevitably took place among the regional commanders among whom Diocletian had divided the administration of the Empire in an effort to give the eastern and western divisions greater stability under closer supervision than was possible for a single emperor.

It was in the course of his fight to displace his rivals that Constantine's conversion to Christianity is said to have taken place, and it is around this conversion—its sincerity, its motives, its spiritual nature—that our present problem revolves. Here a religious event had a tremendous impact on history. But the religious event was linked with other elements or influences of specifically secular nature—political rivalry, family intrigues, military struggles—all culminating in the desperate efforts of the few men at the top to destroy their rivals, the winner to become the sole ruler of the Roman world. How can the historian, viewing Constantine's ultimate success and its results, assign their true roles to the religious and the political springs of action?

The story of the conversion may be told briefly.[27] The background is the Great Persecution of the Christians by Diocletian, and the struggles for power, after Diocletian's abdication, of the Tetrarchs—the "four rulers" of the eastern and western divisions of the Empire whom Diocletian had left as his heirs. The details of the struggle cannot be reviewed here; but Christianity was becoming sufficiently important as an element in the state to make it necessary for the political rivals to take into account the question of how the Christians within their territories were to be treated, and how far they might hope for their support. In some regions there was persecution of Christians; in other regions there was an effort to conciliate them. Among the landmarks in this complex history were two edicts issued by two of the rival emperors, Galerius and Licinius, in 311 and 313 respectively. The first gave the Christians legal recognition in a part of the Empire; the second granted freedom of religious belief, in effect announcing the toleration of Christianity.

It was in the year between these two edicts that Christianity appeared as an element in the policy of Constantine. Constantine had some acquaintance with Christianity, since his mother, Helena (later St. Helena), was a Christian and other members of his family were followers of the cult. Constantine himself, like most of his peers, was probably a monotheist, believing in a supreme power ruling the universe; but he was also of course accustomed to the idea of the deification of the emperor, a well-known political device introduced in the Hellenistic period in an effort to bring political stability in a world composed of many nations and tongues. The chief gods of Olympus—Zeus, Apollo, Hercules and so on—were thought of as the patrons and protectors of the rulers.

In 312 the fighting among the rivals had brought Constantine to the point where, being in control of the Rhine frontier, he felt himself strong enough to set out for Rome to dislodge his rival Maxentius, who was in control of the city and was the leading contender for the rule of the West.

The army reached the neighborhood of the Milvian Bridge, outside of Rome. There—it was recorded by a contemporary historian, Lactantius, a Christian—just before dawn on October 28 Constantine had a dream "in which he was bidden to mark on the shields of his men the sublime sign of God and thus engage the enemy." The sign was the *chi rho* monogram representing the first two letters of the name of Christ in Greek. Constantine ordered the monogram to be placed on the shields and his army met the enemy and was victorious.

Such is the contemporary account of the circumstances of Constantine's conversion. Militarily, it was a surprising victory, one which Constantine might not necessarily have expected. Constantine himself declared in an inscription set up in Rome soon after his victory that the control of Rome had been won with divine help, through power coming to him from God.

A later tradition, recorded by the famous Christian historian Eusebius in his life of Constantine, published after the emperor's death, describes a daytime vision that appeared to Constantine while he was marching through Gaul on the way to Italy. This was a vision of the cross, seen against the afternoon sun. The cross bore the inscription: BY THIS CONQUER. Unlike the account of the dream at the Milvian Bridge, the vision of the cross is not recorded in any contemporary source, though Eusebius asserts that the emperor himself, "long after the event," described the vision to him on oath.

The remainder of the story can be told very briefly. Constantine's conversion was the beginning of a "bright new era" for the Church, which now emerged as a recognized factor in the life of the Empire. Christianity became a favored and protected religion. In time, when he had assured his position as sole emperor, Constantine founded his new capital Constantinople—"Constantine's City"—in a location much better adapted than that of Rome to the current administrative needs of the Empire; moreover it was to be a Christian capital, the first city in the classical world to be founded as a Christian metropolis.[28] The furtherance of the Christian faith became a matter of imperial concern, for Constantine (and his theological advisers) believed that the safety and prosperity of the state depended upon the maintenance of religious harmony and orthodox belief among the subjects. The Christian Emperor, in the new political theory worked out by the scholar-bishop Eusebius, was the vicegerent of God on earth, responsible for the spiritual as well as the material welfare of his people, and conducting his office under the guidance of the Holy Spirit.

The Christian sources seem unequivocal in their account of the emperor's conversion. Constantine, they declare, became a pious Christian, grateful to God for his victory, filled with zeal to spread the faith to which he had been brought by the direct intervention of the Deity. The emperor built churches everywhere in the Empire and his mother made the pilgrimage to the Holy Land, found the True Cross, and identified and adorned the sacred sites. With divine help, the Church had achieved the triumph for which it was destined.

The official picture of the first Christian emperor seemed to be firmly established. Yet there is other evidence which has given some scholars reason to doubt that Constantine's conversion was a sincere one, as it was represented in Christian sources. This evidence comes from several quarters. The emperor did not at once give up his official participation in the pagan cults that had been associated with the imperial office. The Roman emperor had been by long tradition *pontifex maximus*, the chief priest of the ancient state cult; and Constantine after his supposed conversion did not resign this office. Paganism continued prominent elsewhere. When Diocletian had sought to provide a religious basis for his new organization of the state, the eastern and western emperors and their assistants, the Caesars, had been placed under the protection of the most powerful gods; and thus Constantine had had as his patrons, first Hercules, then Apollo. The rulers' allegiance to their divine patrons was commemorated on the imperial coinage—a powerful medium of imperial propaganda—by the representation of the head of the deity and the head of the ruler, accompanied by suitable mottoes; and Constantine's association with Apollo on the coins continued long after his ostensible conversion to Christianity. Roman imperial coins were quick to reflect any new ideological concepts or public ideals that the rulers wished to put before their subjects and new developments in imperial propaganda are easily identified; yet the traces of Christian symbolism which one would expect to find on the coins after Constantine's conversion are sporadic and inconspicuous, and clearly marked Christian motifs only appear a number of years after the battle of the Milvian Bridge. Indeed the emperor waited for his deathbed to be baptized, though this was a not uncommon procedure at a time when it was believed that sins committed after baptism might not be forgiven.

It must have been evident in antiquity that Constantine would have had to proceed cautiously in the degree and kind of recognition given to

Christianity, for many of the high officials of the imperial court and the army continued to be pagans, and it was obvious that the whole empire was not going to be converted to Christianity overnight. The emperor even if he was the supreme ruler had to be prudent in a matter in which personal feelings were so strong; and it might be impolitic to remove all ties with official paganism at once.

In the face of this apparently conflicting evidence, the historian may feel that it is not easy to know what Constantine's conversion really meant. When an imperial conversion was connected, even if only chronologically, with major political disorder, and when the conversion was declared, at the time, to have contributed to the material success of the personage who was converted, the historian is bound to scrutinize the evidence carefully. Our review of the modern theories explaining the decline of the Roman Empire might prepare us to find that here again there is a whole gamut of opinions concerning the religious factor. Indeed, the distinguished British scholar Norman H. Baynes remarks in his summary of the problem that "the representations attempted by modern scholars of the convictions and aims of Constantine have been so diverse that at times it is hard to believe that it is one and the same emperor that they are seeking to portray." [29]

One would expect that Gibbon would interpret Constantine's conversion in purely materialistic terms. The emperor's adoption of Christianity could only, to Gibbon's mind, represent an effort to enlist the aid of the Christians in his struggle for power. The historian writes:

> the enemies of Constantine have imputed to interested motives the alliance which he insensibly contracted with the Catholic church, and which apparently contributed to the success of his ambition. In the beginning of the fourth century, the Christians still bore a very inadequate proportion to the inhabitants of the empire; but among a degenerate people, who viewed the change of masters with the indifference of slaves, the spirit and union of a religious party might assist the popular leader to whose service, from a principle of conscience, they had devoted their lives and fortunes. . . . The counsels of princes are more frequently influenced by views of temporal advantage than by considerations of abstract and speculative truth. . . . [Thus] the piercing eye of ambition and avarice soon discovered that the profession of Christianity might contribute to the interest of the present, as well as of a future, life.[30]

That the conversion might represent a significant personal religious experience is a notion that a historian such as Gibbon would not take into account and certainly would not credit. But as Baynes goes on, after having written the observation quoted above:

As students of history we protest energetically that a man can only be rightly understood against the background of his world, that he can only be fairly judged in the light of the standards and the values of the society in which he lived; and then, having formulated the principle, we straightway forget it. We write our biographies in terms of the thought of our own day and impose upon another age the standards with which we are familiar.[31]

Thus it is not surprising to find, as Baynes points out, Jakob Burckhardt, the well-known Swiss writer of the middle of the nineteenth century who published a popular volume on the Age of Constantine, opening his account of Constantine and the Christian Church with these words:

In the case of a man of genius, whose ambition and love of power refuse to him a moment's peace, there can be no question of Christianity or paganism, of conscious religion or irreligion. Such a man even when he persuades himself that he has his place in an ecclesiastical community is essentially *un*religious.[32]

Burckhardt goes on to say that Eusebius, because he gives us a picture of the emperor's conversion as a deep and sincere experience, "is the first historian of antiquity who is thoroughly dishonest."

Not all historians have been as limited in their views as Gibbon and Burckhardt. As was to be expected, the Swiss writer's pronouncement brought a reaction. For a contemporary historian, Theodor Keim,[33] the primary force in Constantine's policy and in his personal development was the religious factor, though this historian believed that Constantine as a practical man of affairs and statesman did not allow his personal religious inclination to become a conviction until he was satisfied that his public adoption of Christianity was practical and desirable. For Keim, Constantine's greatness stemmed from his combination of religious and political qualities.

However, there has been a return in some circles to the view that Constantine's action was purely political in motivation.[34] One of the leading representatives of this point of view was the German historian Otto Seeck, one of the distinguished authorities on the history of the Later Roman Empire, whose work was marked by what Norman H. Baynes, a moderate and judicious scholar, called a "passionate hatred of Christianity." Here we can perceive another variant in the treatment of the problem. Seeck portrayed Constantine as an honest man in the matter of his religion and devoted to his faith; but the historian's own evident scorn for Christianity, as Baynes points out, makes the resulting picture essentially false.

Another explanation is advanced by other scholars, such as the French historian Duruy and the Italian scholar Salvatorelli,[35] who interpreted the continued appearance of pagan coin types, and other evidences of paganism, following Constantine's supposed conversion, to mean that the emperor was trying to evolve a new type of religious syncretism; it would unite all of his subjects, of all shades of personal belief, in the worship of a single supreme divinity who would stand above all the historic cults and so bring them together and provide a focus of unity which could not otherwise be obtained.

Finally, there are a number of scholars who like Baynes,[36] believe that the key to the problem lies in the documents on religious affairs and the business of the Church, written by Constantine himself, that are quoted in Eusebius' biography of the emperor. Their having been preserved in a work which was admittedly tendentious has meant to some critics that these imperial letters and edicts can only be forgeries composed by Eusebius or others to support the historian's exaggerated picture of the emperor's piety. Most of the scholars who doubt the sincerity of Constantine's conversion have left these documents out of account or have cited them as examples of the way in which Constantine's supposed conversion was used as propaganda by Christian partisans. On the other hand, Baynes and those of like mind have been convinced that the tone of the letters, as expressions of Constantine's personal religious conviction and concern for the Church, is such that they can only be genuine. Baynes sums up the impression that these documents made on him and others:

> The letters and edicts of Constantine are not the writings of one who was merely a philosophical monotheist whose faith was derived from the religious syncretism of his day—a faith into which Christianity had been absorbed. . . . The emperor has definitely identified himself with Christianity, with the Christian Church and the Christian creed. Further, here is a sovereign with the conviction of a personal mission entrusted to him by the Christian God—a mission which imposes duties; it is a charge he cannot escape, if he would. In the third place, in Constantine's thought the prosperity of the Roman state is intimately, one may, I think, say necessarily, linked to the cause of unity within the Catholic Church. If God is to do his part, the emperor and the Christian Church must render to him in return . . . the loyalty of concord. . . . Constantine's vision was that of a Roman Empire sustained by a Christian God and founded on an orthodox faith.[37]

Admittedly, this was to some extent at least a subjective judgment, one opinion among others. For a time this view had to stand on its own merits; and then, quite unexpectedly, it was vindicated in the most decisive fashion possible.

The vindication occurred in a form which placed it beyond any question, through the publication of a Greek papyrus in the collection of the British Museum.[38] This papyrus is in fact a copy of a part of Constantine's official public letter addressed to the people of the provinces after his defeat of his rival Licinius (September 18, 324), which removed the last bar to his accession as sole ruler.

The condition of our sources for ancient history being what it is, it is not often that scholars are presented with a contemporary document—papyrus, inscription or coin—which brings new evidence in a long-standing problem. In this case, the contribution of the papyrus is dramatic, for this fragmentary sheet contains enough of the imperial letter to prove that it corresponds verbatim with the letter as quoted in Eusebius' life of Constantine. It is demonstrated that Eusebius used an official document and transcribed it exactly. The further significance of the discovery is of basic importance for the critical estimate of Eusebius' book, for this confirmation implies that the other documents Eusebius quotes are genuine.

Thus we can now be sure that we possess first-hand evidence, from Constantine's own pen, of the nature of his personal religious feeling. The intuition of the scholars who saw Constantine's conversion as a genuine religious experience, the mainspring of his political action, is confirmed.

Our investigation has dealt with the inner mind of an individual and with personal motives which are capable—whether justly or unjustly—of being challenged. But while the personality and the thoughts of Constantine form the key to our problem, the historian must take into account other types of evidence; and here the problem of the conversion of Constantine offers us another kind of lesson in methodology.

The special experience of his own generation gives the historian interests and sympathies that his predecessors could not have. The historians who lived during World War II began to view the problems of ancient history with insights based on their observation of the war and the changes that followed it. It is in such a context that the distinguished British historian A. H. M. Jones has made a study of "The Social Background of the Struggle Between Paganism and Christianity" in the fourth century.[39] In the age of Constantine, the social and economic changes consequent on the thoroughgoing political transformation affected all classes of society, and as Professor Jones points out, the toleration and then protection of Christianity coincided with an alteration in the structure of society. Men of the middle and lower classes were enabled to rise to positions of public responsibility and power which previously would not have been open to them.[40] It was precisely in the middle and lower classes that Christianity had had its strength before the time of Constantine, while the opposition to the new faith had been centered in the aristocracy. Thus Constantine and his successors, in their efforts to encourage the spread of

Christianity, had less opposition from the aristocracy, combined with more support from a new nobility and a new governing class whose rise, they knew, had been a result of the rise of the Constantinian house. Professor Jones concludes:

> It may be claimed that the social changes of the third and fourth centuries were an important factor in the triumph of Christianity in the empire as a whole. When Constantine staked his faith on the god of the Christians in 312, he was on all human calculations making a very rash venture. Christians were on any reckoning a small minority, particularly in the West, where the struggle with Maxentius was to take place, and they mostly belonged to classes which were politically and militarily negligible, the manual workers, shopkeepers, merchants, and lesser decurions [senators] of the towns and the clerks of the civil service. The army was overwhelmingly pagan. The senate was pagan. So too in all probability was the bulk of the provincial and municipal aristocracy, and the majority of higher administration, drawn as they were from the army and the curial [senatorial] class. By making himself the champion of Christianity, Constantine can hardly have hoped to win for himself any useful support, and might reasonably have feared to provoke antagonism in many important quarters; and this is incidentally to my mind an important piece of circumstantial evidence in favor of the view that Constantine's conversion was not a calculated political move, but, as he himself consistently proclaimed in his public pronouncements, the fruit of a genuine if crude conviction that the Highest Divinity, who had chosen him as his servant, was a more potent giver of victory than the old gods.[41]

Professor Jones' words show how modern scholarship has been able to bring new insights to the problem of the conversion of Constantine. We may go on to another episode which will show us how the true significance of a religious element in a political problem has only lately come to be understood after a period of misinterpretation.

Religion as a Political Problem: Better known to many students of his-
The Pagan Revival of Julian tory even than Constantine is the Emperor Julian the Apostate (341-363), the
gentle, bookish emperor, last prince of the Constantinian house, who attempted to restore paganism and suppress Christianity and died a soldier's death in Persia at the age of thirty-one. In his day a hero to pagans and a monster to Christians, Julian in the Middle Ages became a legend.

Julian's career was so dramatic that it might seem that for the historian there was no question as to the sources of Julian's religious policy; obviously his impulse sprang from the religious and cultural opposition to

Christianity on the part of the pagans, who were still strong in the Empire. Julian's effort, in the eyes of his contemporaries as well as of some modern students, simply brought out the unattractive character of Christianity by contrast with the pagan way of life. For us, comparison with the views of historians in the case of Constantine is illuminating. Whereas in the problem of the emperor's conversion, some historians looked entirely to political factors and disregarded the religious element, in the case of Julian, the opposite has been true, for many historians have accepted the religious motive as the obvious cause of Julian's policy and have not gone beyond this to the secular evidence.

But in the past fifty years there has been a major change of focus in the scholarship on Julian, which has put his career in a new light and has provided an instructive demonstration of methodology. Several specialists have produced studies of aspects of Julian's reign which previously had not been investigated in detail. One of the most important contributions was made by the Belgian scholar J. Bidez, who by a study of the emperor's preserved letters was able to date the correspondence more accurately than had been done before and thus was able to show that there was a significant chronological development in the emperor's policy with regard to paganism such as scholars had not suspected.[42] Studies of Julian's legislative and administrative policy by the German scholar W. Ensslin and the Italian savant R. Andreotti[43] have shown Julian's minute concern with all aspects of the functioning of the government and have demonstrated that as a ruler and lawgiver he was not preoccupied solely or even chiefly with the religious question. Investigation of the economic situation of the Empire has shown the hitherto unsuspected importance of economic factors—inflation, difficulties with the currency, a local famine and price spiral at Antioch—which had a strong effect on Julian's policy.[44] A recent study has changed our understanding of Julian's ideas on the political basis of the imperial office.[45]

From the individual contributions of these scholars, each following a lead suggested by his own specialty, quite a different view of Julian's policy—and one that does greater justice to the emperor himself—has emerged.[46] The emperor is no longer automatically called Julian the Apostate; some scholars write of him as Julian the Philosopher. While it is true that the restoration of paganism and the suppression of Christianity were a major preoccupation of Julian's, much more was involved than simply religious strife. Julian had in fact made the mistake that some political leaders—and some historians—have always made, of attaching to a religious issue other factors which are not necessarily or essentially a part of it.

When Julian became emperor—he was not yet thirty years old—he found himself faced with difficult problems. Originally a Christian, as a member of the Constantinian house, at the age of six he had seen the murder of his father and all his immediate relatives (except for a half-brother, Gallus), who were killed by order of Constantine's sons to prevent them from becoming rivals for the throne after the death of Constantine. With this memory of the Christian imperial house in his mind, Julian during an introspective and bookish adolescence secretly became a pagan; and when he became emperor, the public questions he found himself faced with could only represent, to his mind, the results of forty years of the rule of the Christian dynasty of Constantine and his sons.

The problems were serious. Constantine's extensive building program, plus the expenses of domestic and foreign wars, had produced an inflation, encouraged by the government, which as always bore hardest on the poor and the middle class. Gold and silver for the coinage were scarce, since they were being used to make jewelry and luxury goods. Constantine's measures to control the economy and regulate production had caused difficulties, especially in the commerce and public services of the local municipalities. The bureaucracy which had been growing under the Constantinian system was—at least people claimed—responsible for deterioration in the administration of justice. Moreover, Christianity was threatening the traditional educational system, based on the literature of the great age of classical Greece. Not only social life but careers in public life and in the civil service were based upon the training offered by this well-tried curriculum; and if the Christians threatened to suppress the course of study because some of the reading matter was immoral, the whole of society seemed endangered.

For Julian and his pagan friends, all these hardships and dangers were associated with Christianity. The state was in peril because the Christian dynasty had put an end to the worship of the traditional gods of Rome, the divine guardians upon whose good will the safety and prosperity of the Empire had depended. It was because these gods no longer received their accustomed worship that the government and the people were suffering hardships. Julian and many others believed that Constantine and his sons had been attempting to set up a state church dominated by the imperial house. The tensions within the Church resulting from the Arian controversy—the first of the great theological controversies over the nature of Christ—showed that Christianity was a source of social and religious instability. For the pagans, Christianity was a religion of bad citizenship, while Hellenism was a religion of good citizenship.[47]

Julian's effort to restore Hellenism ended with his sudden death after only twenty months as emperor. Perhaps his hopes could never have been realized even if he had had a longer time in power. Seen from the point of view of our present study, the episode has a remarkably modern air. Religious differences or attacks on personal religious belief or attempts to enforce a form of belief are notoriously potent in stirring up popular feeling. The historian encounters such episodes throughout the history of

Western civilization. In such a case the historian must beware lest the presence of a heated religious quarrel distract his attention from other evidence which may show that other factors are at work as well as the religious problem. It is the historian's task to seek to distinguish the true religious issue from the antagonisms and passions—social, nationalistic, racial, political—that can cluster about it. So also the historian must be alert to the efforts of demagogues to use a religious issue as a cover for their own political purposes.[48] To simplify a passage in history by seeing it entirely in terms of a religious problem is to do as much injustice to religion as a factor in history as it is to go to the other extreme and minimize the religious element.

Religion and the Foundations of the State: Another historical problem
The Durability of the Byzantine Empire raised by the advent of
Christianity was the question of the relation of Christianity to classical culture.

For the first Christians, classical philosophy, as representing "the tradition of men," was equated with "vain deceit." [49] Pagan culture, with its sensual art and literature, represented an immoral way of life that the Christian must have nothing to do with.

But pagan culture had developed a humanistic tradition in education on which society, in the world to which Christianity came, was based. The purpose of this education was the training of the individual for life and the development of human character. Though pagan art and literature presented human life in what to a Christian seemed carnal terms, there were also pagan writers who treated ethics and morality in noble fashion. Eventually some Christian teachers, themselves schooled originally in the classical curriculum, were able to show that the best elements in classical culture could be taken over into Christian culture and used with profit within the framework of Christian faith.[50] Here was the foundation of the new Christian classical civilization, which, with the new Christian political theory, forms the basis for modern European and American civilization.

While Constantine had to deal primarily with the political aspect of the religious question, Julian's problems showed the importance of cultural unity as one of the bases of political unity. A society divided into hostile camps over its educational and intellectual premises could not constitute a happy people. The final settlement of the cultural question, in the fourth to the sixth centuries, produced the brilliant civilization of Byzantium through which the classical Greek heritage was preserved for modern times.

But the civilization of Byzantium, reaching its characteristic form in the reign of Justinian (527-565), was much more than simply a cultural achievement.[51] It was a union into one organic and dynamic whole of religion, politics, and culture, forming a unity that gave the Byzantine state a characteristic strength that the Western world at the same period lacked. The Byzantine emperor, as secular head of the Church and vicegerent of God on earth, united in his sacred person two centers of loyalty, the political and the religious allegiances. Political fidelity and religious faith lent each other support and strength, and the emperor's subjects could feel that there was no conflict in the obedience they were expected to render to Caesar and to God since the emperor represented both spheres of the life of the Empire.

What was it that enabled the Church to play such a role in the life of the Empire and in the lives of its subjects? What were the special ingredients of the religious element in this unity of religion with culture and politics which in some other historical contexts has been so badly fragmented?

First, the Church was a church of the people—a national Church. To be a Greek of the Byzantine Empire was to be a member of the Orthodox Church. On occasion there might be heresy and schism, as there always had been throughout the history of Christianity; but there was only one Orthodox Church, from which heretics and schismatics separated themselves; and the heretics and schismatics could claim to represent the true Church of the people.

Again, one of the great strengths of the Church in the Byzantine Empire was that it supported and preserved the ancient cultural heritage of the Greek people. The Church was the patron of education and learning.[52] The leading theologians and teachers of the Church having seen the value, for Christian instruction, of the Greek classical achievement, this heritage was preserved and nurtured as a source of patriotic pride in the great past of the Greek people. Through its literature, the historic accomplishment of classical Greece was preserved as one of the foundation stones of the Christian Byzantine Empire. All through their education and their culture, the people of Byzantium were continually reminded of the greatness of their forebears. Christian professors expounded the works of Plato and Aristotle; Plato indeed came so close to Christian teaching that he was regarded as a divinely sent forerunner of Christianity.[53] Thus the Church, by making the cultural tradition and the patriotic tradition of its people a part of itself, identified itself with *all* of the national history and the national life. Going beyond the Christian tradition as such, the Church showed that the framework of Christian faith and thought was large enough to include the whole life of humanity.

But it would be false to visualize the Church reaching out of its own sphere to take into itself the intellectual and political life of its people. The Church was in fact a natural part of the whole life of the people, and it is this characteristic of life in the Byzantine world that made the Christian faith an essential factor in the history of that epoch. The Church was regarded by everyone as concerned with all aspects of the life of its people. With its sacraments—Baptism, Confirmation, Confession, Holy Communion, Marriage, Holy Unction (a healing service)—it cared for the faithful from birth to death.

This care was not confined to the sacraments. The Church was concerned with its people's activities, activities that in other cultures might be thought of as mundane. There was a service for the blessing of a new house. There were prayers to be said by a priest at the cleaning out of a well that had been contaminated by the dead body of an animal. There were official prayers for the crops and the fields. Not only were there prayers for the mother as she gave birth to a child; there were prayers for the neighboring women who came to assist. The great service of Holy Communion, the central service of the Church, brought together all of its members on an equal footing, emperor with fisherman, bishop with farmer, all united both visibly and spiritually in the one Body of Christ. The celebration of the Holy Communion, repeated by successive generations and throughout the Empire, was a corporate act of all the Byzantine people. The Greek creed, recited at the communion, began with the declaration "We believe . . ." not "I believe . . ." as in the creeds of the West. In such a service the individual found his meaning in his corporate membership in his church and his state. In the same way the state took its meaning from its members.

The universal character of the communion was proclaimed by its language. Prayers were said for all classes of people within the Empire and the local community, for clergy and laity alike, from the imperial family to the janitors of the local church. The officiating bishop or priest prayed "for the peace of the whole world . . . for all the clergy and people . . . for this city and every city and land." The God who was worshiped and praised was the "great king over all the earth . . . maker of heaven and earth and of all things visible and invisible." [54]

Thus the people of Byzantium possessed three sources of strength for their lives and their work—the historic national heritage, the imperial government, and the Orthodox Church. The Church joined with the state in providing for its people a daily resource and a historic heritage. Church, state, and people formed an ongoing, living body, rooted in a great past, finding in history a source of strength for the present and a secure basis of expectation for the future. Byzantine religious and intellectual life were permeated by a sense of the presentness of the past.[55]

Historians have sought to explain how it was that the Byzantine Empire survived the attacks of the barbarians for so long while the western half of the empire was giving way before the pressure of the same migratory nations. How was it that Constantinople remained the most brilliant city in the world while Rome, pillaged by the Huns and the Vandals, was little more than a historic ruin?

Some scholars have been coming to the conclusion that the answer lies in the unity of religion, culture, and politics that gave the Byzantine people a unique self-consciousness. In their democratic Church and its traditions of education and nationalism the people had a resource such as not all states in history have had. The culture and the religion produced visible results in preserving the physical strength of the Byzantine state; they were, for example, powerful enough to draw into the Byzantine world outside nations such as the Armenians, who eagerly sought to make themselves a part of the Christian Hellenic tradition. On such a basis the state was continually able to renew itself and maintain its sovereignty in the face of outside attacks. It seems certain that without the Orthodox Church as the center of its people's lives the Byzantine state could not have preserved itself as long as it did.[56] Here the Greek people developed the resources that enabled them to preserve their identity after the Turks finally overran the Empire and captured Constantinople (1453). Under the Turkish domination, the Orthodox Church was the political as well as the spiritual leader of its people, and the Greek War of Independence (1821-1828) was prepared and led by the Church.

Here the historical student may find an example of a national religion which served as a resource for its people in all aspects of their lives, not just a formal faith such as the ancient Roman state had been. Though we do not know that he was writing with this area of history in mind, we may be reminded of William Temple's observation that "it is a great mistake to suppose that God is only, or even chiefly, concerned with religion." [57]

But would every historian be prepared to acknowledge that the Church was one of the main sources of the political durability of the Byzantine Empire? What historical role would the economic historian or the Marxist historian or the historian like Spengler or Toynbee who sees history as a series of cycles assign to the Byzantine Church? What would be the action of chance or contingency that some historians might find in Byzantine history? Surely in so long and so varied a history there must be many factors that might have played decisive parts. The strength of the Byzantine military establishment, the remarkably effective diplomatic methods of the Byzantine government, the efficiency of the civil service, the appearance of a number of able rulers—these reasons and others connected with them can be offered to account for the durability of the Byzantine Empire, independently of any consideration of the role of the Church. Can we find the secret of the Empire by weighing the relative merits of various historical factors? Does the answer lie in the nature of the evidence, or in the view the historian takes of it?

Christianity and History   Before we can assess the significance and the function of religion as a phenomenon of history, and before we can consider the methodology of the historian in dealing with religion as a factor in history, we must look at the historian himself. If religion in the life of a people and a state is to be the subject matter, it is essential to establish not only the way the historian will approach his material, but what manner of man the historian himself will be.

Herbert Butterfield, the British historian and student of historiography, has observed [58] that "one of the most fundamental of the differences between people must be the question whether they believe in God or not; for on that depends their whole interpretation of the universe and of history—on that depends their answer to so many other questions." This statement would certainly be acceptable both to historians who are personally religious (as Professor Butterfield is) and to those who are not. It is obvious that the universe and the history of mankind mean different things to pagan Greeks and to Jews, to Christians and to rationalists. History can be made a technical exercise, an academic science in which events and processes are dispassionately studied by an expert schooled in impartiality, and their various aspects—economic, political, social, cultural, military—are isolated and assessed.[59] The "scientific" school of history, of which the famous German historian Leopold von Ranke was the founder and great exemplar, believed that it is possible for the historian to view the facts without prejudice and to analyze them into their true components. The possible effects of chance or of the unpredictable emergence of a great man such as Alexander the Great, Caesar, or Napoleon can be identified and weighed. Indeed, with Thomas Carlyle, we might be led to view history as a collection of innumerable biographies.

Again, what may seem to be mechanical sequences of events can be traced, their only relationship that of antecedent and consequence, the events repeating themselves over and over again, though with varying patterns. Or the historian may think he sees "a fortuitous string of occurrences, affected by chances of a thousand kinds." [60] Phenomena may be claimed as the result of the social struggle or of class warfare. The role of the Church may be described (in the words of Marx) as the purveyor of religion as the opiate of the masses. The historian who sees religion in this light will admit that in this sense religion is a factor in history; but to him it will not normally be (as it may be to other historians) the factor that controls other factors.

We have seen enough to be able to understand why Allan Nevins has written

there are as many different schools and theories of history as the schools of philosophy, medicine and painting. . . . Every strongly individual historian sets up his own standards, and few historians of the first rank will admit that a different conception of historical aims is as good as their own. . . . It may be confidently affirmed that no important history has yet appeared that did not reveal some bias, and that in the greatest of histories the element of partiality is strong.[61]

If this is true, there will be, to begin with, a general division among historians, that is, a division between the historians who believe that God is active in history and those who do not. There are distinguished names on both sides. The belief that there is a judgment of God involved in the processes of history, and that man can learn from it and be guided by it, is the basis of the historical scholarship which evolved in the Judeo-Christian tradition.[62] The writers of the books of the Old Testament, and the early Christian historians—men like Eusebius of Caesarea, to name only one of the best known—all tried to demonstrate that the history of their world was a reflection of the self-revelation of God and of the dealings of God with men. Thus, for some historians—that is, for those whose personal experience had led them to this belief—there is only one answer possible to the question whether God is active in history.

But if one school of historians sees history in the light of man's knowledge of God, another school claims that it is truer to see history in the light of man's knowledge of man. If then one cannot believe that God is active in history, what are the mainsprings of history? The historian must find his own answer. Professor Butterfield has sketched a vivid picture of the results that the possible choices open up:

> The liberal, the Jesuit, the Fascist, the Communist, and all the rest may sail away with their militant versions of history, howling at one another across the interstellar spaces, all claiming that theirs is the absolute version, and admitting no place even for an academic history that shall be a bridge between them.[63]

When any school of historians rejects the views of another school concerning the role of religion in history, the arguments are necessarily conditioned by the religious views of the dissenting scholars. An experienced and well-known historian contemplates the Christian interpretation of history in these terms:

> The triumph of Christianity over paganism brought with it sweeping changes in the conceptions of historical writing and in the ideas which guided it. Pagan culture was at least formally rejected as a product of the Devil. The historical writings of the pagans were held in far less esteem than the holy writings of the Jews which were embodied in the Old Testament, even though the major part of the Old Testament was far inferior as history to the works of the better

pagan histories. Likewise, the Christian debased reason, which had held so important a place in the mental life of the Greeks, and elevated faith to a predominant position. Credulity, especially with respect to the supernatural, became a major intellectual, as well as a spiritual, virtue.[64]

Another historian, H. P. Rickman,[65] claims that it is necessary to distinguish between the Christian view and what he regards as the real significance of the observed phenomena of history. If the Christian (Mr. Rickman writes) believes "that God rules the world, and that history is the unfolding of the divine plan," this belief "must be distinguished from the conviction that we can understand the individual events of history in terms of that plan." If (as this scholar observes) "Christians believe that God moves in a mysterious way, that his will is, to some extent at least, inscrutable, that revelation appeals to faith rather than to reason and that it reveals the inner meaning of all events rather than the connection between particular ones," then man still has to supply his own interpretation of the nexus of some events. So, Mr. Rickman concludes, "we can ask whether a conception of divine providence is relevant and illuminating in historical research."

To such an argument, the Christian historian would reply in the words of William Temple:

God's action in guiding the world is not constant in a mechanical sense; rather its constancy, as that of all personal action, is found in its infinite adjustability to present conditions. . . . Among the conditions are the attitudes adopted by, and the situations created by, the relatively free acts of finite intelligences like ourselves.[66]

The Christian historian cannot make his interpretation of history a mechanical one. If the Christian believes that man exists and has meaning only in terms of the nature of God, then history has to be viewed in terms of the nature of God. Within this perspective it is possible to believe that on occasion history reflects human failure to maintain the integrity of the image of God which is man's true nature. But this human failure does not affect the conviction that man's true nature, and the true goal of his action, is a reflection of the divine nature. If history does not always seem to the observer to exhibit the process that God's purpose ought to follow, this does not mean that the purpose does not still exist and that it will not be worked out.

Within the belief in a divine government of the universe, the Christian historian is able to recognize the action and influence of such elements as social, political, and economic forces and at the same time see the movement of history in a Christian context. If materialistic historians disagree —as for example in the case of the causes of the decline of the ancient world—Christian historians can use the materialistic evidence and subsume it under the Christian explanation of history.

The question always seems to come back to the historian himself. The verdict of the investigator depends as much upon what the investigator brings to his study of the facts as upon the facts themselves. Some historians will have had an assurance of the hand of God in their own personal experience, others will not.[67] The Christian historian believes that given the ability to distinguish between the hand of God and the hand of man in history, it is possible to present a consistent and meaningful picture of the past. The historians who do not accept this basis of history have to rely on their own personal judgment—and their readers find themselves compelled to make judgments of what is set before them. We have seen enough in the present study to realize that among historians who do not accept the Christian viewpoint there cannot always be unanimity. One motive or another, one force or another, always has to be selected as the decisive element and the true causation.

So it would seem that in our culture there are bound to be two kinds of historians, those who see a divine power at work in secular history and those who do not. So long as such a dichotomy can exist, there will be two kinds of history written; and it is for the critical reader to seek the gift of discernment.

NOTES FOR CHAPTER 15

1 Gibbon, *Decline and Fall of the Roman Empire*, edited by J. B. Bury, London, 1897-1902, Chap. LXXI, printed in Volume VII, p. 308.

2 T. M. Knox, writing in the introduction to R. G. Collingwood's *The Idea of History*, Oxford, 1946, p. xii.

3 Of course Gibbon was not alone, in the eighteenth century, in his anti-Christian position; Montesquieu and Voltaire are well-known examples of similar views. See A. Momigliano, "Christianity and the Decline of the Roman Empire," in A. Momigliano (ed.), *The Conflict between Paganism and Christianity in the Fourth Century*, Oxford, 1963, p. 3. A detailed account of Gibbon's position with regard to Christianity has been provided by Shelby T. McCloy, *Gibbon's Antagonism to Christianity and the Discussions That It Has Provoked*, Chapel Hill, N.C., 1933.

4 Gibbon, *op. cit.*, IV, pp. 162 f. in Bury's edition.

5 *Ibid.*, VII, pp. 305-325.

6 *Ibid.*, p. 308.

7 *Ibid.*, p. 310.

8 *Ibid.*, p. 313.

9 F. Lot, *La Fin du monde antique et le début du Moyen Age*, Paris, 1927; 2nd, 1951, translated into English in 1931 (London). See the edition in the Harper Torchbook series, edited by G. Downey (New York, 1961), with introduction and bibliography by the editor summarizing work that has been done on the subject since the original publication of Lot's work.

10 F. W. Walbank, *The Decline of the Roman Empire in the West*, London, 1946, p. 1. For summaries of the modern views on the end of the ancient

world, upon which the account given here is based, see Downey's introduction to the Harper Torchbook edition of Lot's work (cited in note 9) and the essay by Momigliano cited in note 3.

11 Simkhovitch's article, originally published in *Political Science Quarterly*, XXXI (1961), pp. 201-243, is reprinted in the same scholar's book *Towards the Understanding of Jesus*, New York, 1937, pp. 84-139. Huntington's theory is advanced in his paper "Climatic Change and Agricultural Exhaustion as Elements in the Fall of Rome," *Quarterly Journal of Economics*, XXXI (1917), pp. 173-208.

12 See O. Seeck, *Geschichte des Untergangs der antiken Welt*, Vol. I, ed. 4, Berlin, 1921, pp. 369-370; Tenney Frank, "Race Mixture in the Roman Empire," *American Historical Review*, XXI (1916), pp. 689-708; M. P. Nilsson, *Imperial Rome*, London, 1926, pp. 317-367.

13 Rostovtzeff, *The Social and Economic History of the Roman Empire*, 2nd ed., revised by P. M. Fraser, Oxford, 1957, p. 534; see also Momigliano's essay (cited in note 3), p. 5.

14 W. E. Heitland, *The Roman Fate: An Essay in Interpretation*, Cambridge, England, 1922; *Iterum; or a Further Discussion of the Roman Fate*, Cambridge, England, 1925; *Last Words on the Roman Municipalities*, Cambridge, England, 1928.

15 This theory is discussed by Rostovtzeff, *op. cit.* (note 13), pp. 348 ff., 537 f.

16 A. E. R. Boak, *Manpower Shortage and the Fall of the Roman Empire in the West*, Ann Arbor, Mich., 1955.

17 George R. Monks, "The Administration of the Privy Purse; an Inquiry into Official Corruption and the Fall of the Roman Empire," *Speculum*, XXXII (1957), pp. 748-779.

18 These are the concluding words of A. H. M. Jones in his lecture "The Decline and Fall of the Roman Empire," published in *History*, October 1955, pp. 209-226. This is one of the studies which offer the most valuable insights into the problem. See also Rostovtzeff, *op. cit.* (note 13), p. 541, and F. Lot, *The End of the Ancient World and the Beginnings of the Middle Ages*, New York, Harper, 1961, p. 236 (cf. p. xv).

19 See for example Lot, *op. cit.*, pp. 47-54.

20 See Momigliano, *op. cit.*, pp. 3 f.

21 This is the famous theory of Henri Pirenne; see Momigliano, *op. cit.*, pp. 4 f.

22 Momigliano, *loc. cit.*

23 Momigliano, *op. cit.*, p. 6.

24 Momigliano, *op. cit.*, pp. 10 f.

25 Momigliano, *op. cit.*, pp. 14-16.

26 For a detailed account of the process which is sketched here in the briefest terms, see the *Cambridge Ancient History*, Vol. XII (1939), *The Imperial Crisis and Recovery*, A.D. *193-324*.

27 For details and references to the sources, see the chapter "Constantine" by N. H. Baynes in *Cambridge Ancient History*, XII, pp. 678-699, and the same scholar's detailed examination of the problem of the sources in his "Constantine the Great and the Christian Church," *Proceedings of the British Academy*, XV, 1929.

28 On Constantinople as the Christian capital of the empire, see G. Downey, *Constantinople in the Age of Justinian*, Norman, Okla., 1960.

29 N. H. Baynes, *Constantine the Great and the Christian Church*, p. 4.

30 Gibbon, *op. cit.*, II, pp. 293, 297, 311.

31 Baynes, *loc. cit.*

32 The translation is that of Baynes, *loc. cit.* Burckhardt's book was first published in 1853. See the English translation by Moses Hadas, *The Age of Constantine the Great*, New York, 1949, where the passage quoted above occurs on p. 292. Professor Hadas in his Foreword (pp. 7-9) defends Burckhardt against his critics as follows: "Burckhardt was indeed a pioneer in the humanist reaction against the microscopic but unimaginative history of the 'scientific' historians, though his wide and deep erudition, aside from his imagination and taste, entitle him to a distinguished place even among the scientific historians. . . . Surely *Constantine* communicates not only a more intelligible but also a more valid picture of events, their nexus and their relevance than does the parallel twelfth volume of the sober *Cambridge Ancient History* (1939), which represents the latest technical knowledge, presented by a panel of the world's best specialists." Hadas notes the criticism Burckhardt makes of Eusebius: "Scholars jealous for the fair name of Church figures have criticized Burckhardt severely on this point. All that may be said is that Burckhardt knew his authors thoroughly (he was a student of Protestant theology before he became a historian and art critic) and also knew men and affairs; it is tolerably certain that none of the objections which were subsequently adduced to his views would have persuaded him to alter them essentially."

33 Theodor Keim, *Der Übertritt Konstantins des Grossen zum Christentum*, Zürich, 1862, cited by Baynes, *op. cit.*, p. 34.

34 See the theories of Schwartz and Brieger described by Baynes, *op. cit.*, pp. 36 f.

35 See Baynes, *op. cit.*, pp. 34-36.

36 See Baynes, *op. cit.*, pp. 38 f.

37 Baynes, *op. cit.*, pp. 29 f.

38 See A. H. M. Jones, "Notes on the Genuineness of the Constantinian Documents in Eusebius' Life of Constantine," *Journal of Ecclesiastical History*, V (1954), pp. 196-200.

39 A. H. M. Jones, "The Social Background of the Struggle Between Paganism and Christianity," in Momigliano, *The Conflict between Paganism and Christianity*, pp. 17-37.

40 A. H. M. Jones, *loc. cit.*, p. 37.

41 *Ibid.*, pp. 33 f.

42 J. Bidez, *La Vie de l'Empereur Julien*, Paris, 1930.

43 W. Ensslin, "Kaiser Julians Gesetzgebungswerk und Reichsverwaltung," *Klio*, XVIII (1923), pp. 104-199; R. Andreotti, "L'Opera legislativa ed amministrativa dell'Imperatore Giuliano," *Nuova Rivista Stoica*, XIV (1930), pp. 342-383, together with the same scholar's monograph *Il Regno dell'Imperatore Giuliano*, Bologna, 1936.

44 See G. Downey, *A History of Antioch in Syria from Seleucus to the Arab Conquest*, Princeton, 1961, pp. 380 ff.

45 See F. Dvornik, "The Emperor Julian's 'Reactionary' Ideas on Kingship," *Late Classical and Mediaeval Studies in Honor of A. M. Friend, Jr.*, Princeton, 1955, pp. 71-81.

46 For an extended discussion, see G. Downey, "Julian and Justinian and the Unity of Faith and Culture," *Church History*, XXVIII No. 4 (1959), pp. 3-13.

47 The phraseology is borrowed from C. N. Cochrane, *Christianity and Classical Culture*, 2nd ed., Oxford, 1944, p. 285.

48 In the period we are studying, an example of this problem in method is provided by the Monophysite heresy—one of the great heresies concerning the divine-human nature of Christ—in the fifth and sixth centuries. See A. H. M. Jones, "Were Ancient Heresies National or Social Movements in Disguise?" *Journal of Theological Studies*, New Series, X (1959), pp. 380-398.

49 Colossians 2:8.

50 See the account of this process by Werner Jaeger, one of the most experienced and sensitive students of the subject, in his last book, *Early Christianity and Greek Paideia*, Cambridge, 1961.

51 On the process sketched here, in which the cultural and religious development joined with the Christian political theory to produce the characteristic political, cultural and religious unity of the Byzantine Empire, see three studies by the present writer, *Constantinople in the Age of Justinian*, Norman, 1960; *Antioch in the Age of Theodosius the Great*, Norman, 1962; and *Gaza in the Early Sixth Century*, Norman, 1963.

52 See for example J. M. Hussey, *Church and Learning in the Byzantine Empire, 867-1185*, Oxford, 1937.

53 Plato's significance here is made very clear in the striking collection of the passages from his writings collected and translated by Adam Fox, *Plato and the Christians*, London, 1957. See also William Temple, *Plato and Christianity*, London, 1916.

54 On this aspect of the communion service, see further Downey, *Gaza in the Early Sixth Century*, pp. 157-159.

55 See G. Downey, "The Byzantine Church and the Presentness of the Past," *Theology Today*, XV (1958), pp. 84-99.

56 See Norman H. Baynes, *Byzantine Studies and Other Essays*, London, 1955, pp. 1-96.

57 William Temple, *The Hope of a New World*, London, 1941, p. 70.

58 Herbert Butterfield, *Christianity and History*, London, 1949, p. 113.

59 *Ibid.*, p. 22.

60 Allan Nevins, *The Gateway to History*, revised ed., Garden City, N.Y., Anchor Books, 1962, p. 50.

61 *Ibid.*, pp. 39, 41, 54.

62 In addition to Butterfield, *Christianity and History*, see R. L. P. Milburn, *Early Christian Interpretations of History*, London, 1954; D. S. Wallace-Hadrill. *Eusebius of Caesarea*, London, 1960; R. G. Collingwood, *The Idea of History*, Oxford, 1946, reprinted as a Galaxy Book, 1961; William Temple, Lecture XVII, "The Meaning of History," in *Nature, Man and God*, London, 1934, pp. 427-451.

63 Butterfield, *Christianity and History*, p. 23.

64 The quotation is from the opening of the chapter entitled "Early Christian Historical Writing" in Harry Elmer Barnes, *A History of Historical Writing*, 2nd ed., revised, New York, Dover Publications, 1962, p. 41. Following this passage, Barnes quotes the judgment of James T. Shotwell, *An Introduction to the History of History*, New York, 1922, pp. 284-286, who writes in sarcastic terms of the Christian historians, concluding that "it was . . . a calamity for historiography that the new standards won the day. . . . A well-nigh insurmountable obstacle was erected to scientific inquiry, one which has at least taken almost nineteen centuries to sur-

mount." The curious student will note that in the revised edition of Shot-well's work, published under the title of *The History of History*, New York, 1939, the passage has been extensively rewritten (Vol. I, p. 332). This new edition is not mentioned in the reprint of Barnes' work.

65 H. P. Rickman, writing in the introduction to *Pattern and Meaning in History: Thoughts on History and Society by Wilhelm Dilthey*, New York, Harper Torchbooks, 1962, pp. 27 ff.
66 William Temple, *Nature, Man and God*, p. 313.
67 Cf. Butterfield, *Christianity and History*, p. 107.

QUESTIONS

1 How far is it possible for a historian to be impartial when dealing with a controversial issue, especially an issue involving religion?
2 Do you believe that the writing of history is an art or a science?
3 Why is it said that every new generation of historians must write its own version of the history of the Graeco-Roman world?
4 Can a historian, writing of a period of history in which religion played a major part, be more objective if he is not himself committed to the religion involved?
5 Is it possible or desirable to write secular history without taking into account religious factors, or to write ecclesiastical history without taking into account secular factors?

SUGGESTED READINGS

Allan Nevins, *The Gateway to History*, New, revised ed., Anchor Books, Garden City, N.Y., Doubleday, 1962.

Herbert Butterfield, *Christianity and History*, London, Bell, 1949, and reprinted.

R. G. Collingwood, *The Idea of History*, New York, Oxford University Press, 1946, and reprinted.

R. L. P. Milburn, *Early Christian Interpretations of History* (The Bampton Lectures, 1952), London, Black, 1954.

George A. Buttrick, *Christ and History*, New York and Nashville, Abingdon Press, 1963. This book appeared after the present chapter was written.

16 *Walter G. Muelder*

Religious Frontiers in Political and Economic Responsibility

Religion runs the whole gamut of human life. Being personal, it is both private and social, for man is a socius with a private center. Religion is both a response to man's total environment and an exploration into its frontiers. It is both conservative and liberal, or even radical. It may defend the status quo or it may take the initiative against entrenched wrong. Religion may be fanatically zealous for custom, law, and tradition. It may be sacrificially compassionate, universally inclusive, and humbly redemptive. It may be profoundly inward, reflective, mystical, or it may be attached to externals. Religion participates in the polarities of life. It may be passionately ethical and seek the radical transformation of culture. It may seek a state of tranquility above all the ambiguities of good and evil.

Whatever its form, religion expresses an attitude toward what is ultimate. It is life in its ultimate dimension facing the facts and issues of mortality, meaning, frustration, good and evil, estrangement, reconciliation, reality. James B. Pratt once defined religion as the "serious and social attitude of individuals or communities toward the power or powers which they conceive as having ultimate control over their interests and destinies." [1] This definition will be very useful in considering religious frontiers in political and economic responsibility. It will be particularly helpful to view this definition in a functional way. In sociology of religion a functional method is particularly fruitful in providing a descriptive background for religious ethics. J. Milton Yinger, for example, stresses the active aspect of a functional approach when he notes that religion can be "defined as a system of beliefs and practices by means of which a group of people struggles with these ultimate problems of human life. It is the refusal to capitulate to death, to give up in the face of frustration, to allow hostility to tear apart one's human associations." [2] Religion is human life in its ultimate context struggling for meaning and responding to its various levels of personal, social and natural environment.

In defining religion so broadly have we perhaps confused it with culture as a whole? Religion has a twofold relationship to culture. In its visible institutional aspects religion may be viewed as one segment of culture alongside others such as the family, the economic order, political organization, aesthetic expression, systems of communication, and the like. On this level synagogues and churches, temples and mosques exist alongside local and state governments, schools, museums, stores, factories, airports, and the like. These institutions compete with and reinforce each other, depending on situations and circumstances.

Religion has a second and more profound relationship to culture. It is a dimension of each of the other major aspects of culture, whether or not this dimension is institutionally expressed or even acknowledged. Plowing a field, harvesting a crop, hunting game, rearing a family, governing a clan —these are all religious. It is a commonplace in studies of primitive or preliterate societies to note how religion pervades all parts of culture. Hardly anything is done without some explicit reference to religious practices. All significant portions of culture are related to the ultimate questions noted above. They express a struggle for the meaning of life.

It is for this reason that religion has historically had a basic function in aiding social integration. Social order requires a largely self-enforcing value scheme to give it unity. There is need for a "myth structure" along with specified approved means and ends. As persons and groups struggle for scarce values there must be developed within personality and within groups a structure of meaning and value to control them in the midst of the peak loads of frustration, hostility, and disappointment and to point the way for reconciliation and the release of creative resources. Religion and ethics merge as functional prerequisites in society.

In the economic struggle for scarce values the "rules of the game" do not always appear to be religious in a visible institutional sense, but they are nevertheless profoundly expressive of what a group believes to matter most. So too in the political sphere, where external coercion or force seems to be dominant and seems to grow with the size and mobility of the society, political enforcement must rely on the self-enforcing sources of order. For example, how is political authority to be made legitimate? Behind economic and political institutions are issues of the goals of society, both individual and shared. Then too, there are assumptions about man's basic nature and tendencies in the way government is structured. Moreover, there are problems of priorities among the values and claims of all citizens who participate in striving for interests or rights.

Culture is an interacting whole. Just as religion pervades the whole of culture so do the economic and the political dimensions. Churches, for example, have economic needs and they have government. Government and economic order, we may say, are ubiquitous. For this very reason the question of economic and political responsibility is finally one of religious ethics. Religious institutions, for their part, must struggle with their own economic and political natures.

The social forms of religion are many. In the foregoing paragraphs no value judgment has been made, approving any one way of religious expression and disapproving another. In the subsequent discussion, however, the normative dimension will be faced. Functionally speaking there is need to emphasize only one fact more. So-called secular or nonreligious answers to the ultimate issues of life may function as religious responses to them. These may be "bad" religion from a normative point of view, but no one can completely evade the ultimate dimension of any aspect of culture. Speaking normatively and descriptively, one may set up his own gods in the place of the true determiner of destiny. Thus atheistic communism or a nationalistic racism or a scientific ideology may serve as rival faiths.

The values and norms of religion, economics, and politics interpenetrate. In a rapidly changing world the frontiers of responsibility change accordingly. Rights and duties must then be redefined. A useful doorway into the complex issues of the relation of religion to economic and political responsibility is through the institution of property. What is property? Who should own and use what? How should material goods be produced and who should establish the rules of the game? Should the economic order be independent or autonomous? Should the political order set the rules of the economic game? What does religion have to say about a responsible society?

Property is perhaps the most comprehensive term which can be used to indicate and describe "every possible interest which the party (agent) can have." Property is complex: control of man over things, possession of things, the right of a claim to control, possess, or use something scarce, the permanence of a claim, the interrelationships of persons making claims or having rights. Property has to do with many things: personal property of the most private sort, or real estate, land, natural resources, and other material objects. It has also to do with faith or credit, with the value of time, privilege, reputation, and many other intangible values. In all cases the chief characteristic of property is control of scarce values, material or immaterial, either for the purposes of use or for power. Control may be by individuals or by groups or through institutions. Property is not primarily a relation of individual persons to material things but of rightful claims of persons on each other with respect to something scarce. So-called private property turns out upon inspection to be a social affair with political, ethical, and religious dimensions. Property inheres not in a thing but in relationships to that thing. These relationships are those of persons-in-community. Any individual property claim is part of an interdependent system of claims in a constantly changing society. One illustration may suffice. My property right to the food on my plate is my right, ethically speaking, to consume it. As food it is a means in the pursuit of physical well-being. As property it is a claim in relation to other people for exclusive use, or to consume it. Property is an instrumental value. The economic order as a whole exists for the purpose of satisfying human needs through means that have to be produced or distributed or both.

Private property is not a right that exists outside society. It is a claim that is made in society and must be evaluated in terms of the goals of society and of basic human rights. A right we may define as a moral claim of the person on the community for some value which is essential to the actualizing of personality, i.e., for the satisfaction of some common need in human nature. Property rights, then, have to do with moral claims of members of a community on each other, or of groups of persons on other groups, with respect to scarce instrumental values.[3]

The community makes property rights effective by defining them legally. Legal property rights are dependent on government. As R. M. MacIver has so well pointed out these rights as legal "exist only because government recognizes and protects them. A particular government may do little more than uphold an already established system of rights but in the longer perspective *it is government that creates property*. Property is not wealth or possessions, but the right to control, to exploit, to use or to enjoy wealth or possessions."[4] Behind the legal rights stand moral rights and these are related to the basic needs of interdependent persons. Society exists for the welfare of persons, and persons realize themselves in community. Both the plurality of persons and their solidarity must be affirmed, thus raising the question of freedom in relation to justice. The community as a whole must always reserve the right to modify the mode of property holding since it exercises through government a direct organizing function in social life. Legal "private" property is very much a social action subject to continual review.

The concept of property is closely related to the idea of freedom. The two concepts are similar in complexity and in being interpersonal. In social relations freedom is always a combination of restraints and liberties. It is not sufficient to say that "my" freedom stops where "yours" begins. It is more adequate to recognize, for example, that my freedom to exercise a property right is combined with a restraint on someone else's liberty with respect to that particular claim. When, to cite another example, the Wagner Act states that workers are free to join unions of their own choosing, this liberty is linked with a restraint on the management from interfering with such union activity. Laws which protect workers from unnecessary hazards in mines and factories make freedom for health possible, but they put a restraint on the liberty of managers and owners to do as they formerly pleased. How should the community determine what combination of restraints and liberties makes for the right kind of freedom? This question cannot be answered apart from an analysis of the various rights or ends which ought to be acknowledged. The answer requires also an evaluation of priorities among the various freedoms which are sought. Stated in religious and ethical terms, these are the questions, "What are the chief ends of man?" and "What is the chief end of man?" When those questions have been answered, it is possible to analyze what combination of liberties and restraints in the economic and political realm make for the fullest freedom of man.

We shall come one step closer to the identification of certain frontier issues by defining what is meant by a responsible society. The definition which will be used comes from the Amsterdam Assembly of the World Council of Churches (1948) and has been the working "middle axiom" of that portion of the ecumenical movement which is composed of Orthodox and Protestant churches. A social-ethics perspective representative of the Roman Catholic Church will be cited later. A middle axiom is a general ethical concept which provides guidelines and norms for ethical evaluation and action, but which is not as abstract or general as are ultimate theological principles on the one hand nor as specific and concrete as prescriptions in empirical decisions on the other hand. The middle axiom called the "idea of the responsible society" is an inclusive norm that unifies and relates a number of ideals and norms which are sometimes considered separately.

What is this idea? The Amsterdam Assembly said:

> Man is created and called to be a free being, responsible to God and his neighbor. Any tendencies in State and society depriving man of the possibility of acting responsibly are a denial of God's intention for man and his work of salvation. A responsible society is one where freedom is the freedom of men who acknowledge freedom and public order, and where those who hold political authority or economic power are responsible for its exercise to God and the people whose welfare is affected by it." [5]

A number of crucial themes in contemporary world society converge in this definition: (1) the role of religious norms in a just and free society, particularly the creative purposes of God and his concern for personal and social salvation; (2) the conception of man, his dignity, rights, and self-realization in community with others; (3) the nature, authority, and scope of the modern state and its functions in relation to the community; (4) the interpenetration of the political, economic, and social spheres of society; (5) the tension or polarity of such ideals as equality, freedom, and justice in both economic and political life and as inherent in the idea of responsibility; (6) the accountability of power groups within nations; (7) the responsibility of persons to domestic and international orders of freedom and justice as well as to God, the source of persons and community; and (8) the responsibilities of nations to one another and to the future of human welfare.

This definition was supplemented by a commentary paragraph which has affinities to recent papal encyclicals and to the spirit that animates the United Nations Declaration of Human Rights and Freedoms:

> Man must never be made a mere means for political or economic ends. Man is not made for the State but the State for man. Man is not made for production, but production for man. For a society to be responsible under modern conditions it is required that the people have freedom to control, to criticize and to change their governments, that power be made responsible by law and tradition, and be distributed as widely as possible through the whole community. It is required that economic justice and provision of equality of opportunity be established for all the members of society.[6]

The idea of the responsible society and this supplementary commentary are relevant to a great many frontiers in the present period of rapid social change when the common destiny of mankind is increasingly acknowledged. One of these frontiers is the unity of mankind which transcends the boundaries of organized world religions. As a valid middle axiom, the responsible society must apply to both Christian and non-Christian communities, nations, and cultures. World religions claim to be universal in their truth-claims about God, reality, and the human predicament. It is, nevertheless, a dilemmatic fact that religions and cultures with universal ideals are rooted in and accommodated to institutions and social systems which are limited in space, time, and function. While Christianity is in fact a world religion, some non-Christian religions like Buddhism and Hinduism are experiencing a resurgence and renewal and are making general claims. Whatever may have been their social linkages or cultural limitations in the pre-atomic or colonial period of modern history, these religions are asserting, along with Judaism and Christianity, their sanctions for universal rights and freedoms. They acknowledge not only change but the appropriateness of purposive change and seek participation in an era drawing heavily on scientific method and technology. All of these religions are challenged to help develop a global self-enforcing ethos which will undergird the world civilization and world community now emerging. Meanwhile the world religions are engaging each other in new ways; their supporting cultures are purposively being changed, some in a revolutionary way; and they are in conflict with each other on many important issues. The situation is very complex and the dilemmas are very real.

The frontiers of world religions are not only external, but they are institutionally internal. Universal ideals at the official level may be tied to memberships that are parochial in outlook. Judaism, Roman Catholicism, and Protestantism have universal goals and values, on the one hand, but they also have theological ethics that express the claims of specialized religious bodies. Their ideals are universal in form but not necessarily in function or effect. Practically speaking, they make world-wide assertions and demands on mankind, but do not seem to make an effective universal demand upon the churches, temples, and synagogues within whose life the ethic is formulated. Thus there is an internal institutional frontier in the major world religions.

A practicing adherence to the idea of a responsible society will be acutely more urgent as the spotlight of world communication exposes the gap between ethical and theological claims, on the one hand, and the functioning loyalties of individuals and groups, on the other hand.

The idea of the responsible society, though it represents the culmination of ethical reflection in many Christian churches on social questions, is not dependent entirely on appeals to Biblical revelation. Similarly the social teachings of the Roman Catholic Church as reflected in papal encyclicals during the past seventy years, more particularly in the late Pope John XXIII's *Mater et Magistra* and *Pacem in Terris*, appeals not only to dogma and tradition but equally to the moral natural law. In the case of *Pacem in Terris* the encyclical is specifically addressed to all mankind, not simply to the faithful in the church. Pope John XXIII takes note of the Universal Declaration of Rights and Freedoms and points out the position stated by Pope Pius XII in 1941: "to safeguard the inviolable rights of the human person, and to facilitate the fulfillment of his duties, should be the essential office of every public authority."

The ecumenical movement both in the World Council of Churches and in the Roman Catholic Church recognizes a view of the state which may be called "secular" or "neutral" and emphasizes the positive role of government in promoting the common good. These positions raise the further question of how a religiously sanctioned ethic will fulfill its proper role in such a state.

What are the traits of a secular society in relation to a secular state? Professor D. L. Munby, a British economist who is active in the ecumenical movement, identifies six characteristics of such a society.[7] (1) Such a society does not commit itself as a whole to any particular view of the cosmos or man's status in it. (2) It is pluralistic, not sacral. (3) It is tolerant in that it does not "attempt to enforce belief or to limit the expression of belief." On the other hand it tries "to set bounds to the natural persecuting tendencies of human nature." (4) Although such a society recognizes the need for common aims, its organizations and institutions have limited goals. (5) Not having any overall aim, other than that of assisting its members to achieve their aims, it has the function of making these as concordant with each other as possible. (6) "A secular society is a society without official images." The reason behind all these points is the value of respect for men. The limits here stated are not proposed in blindness to the fact "that men do not require organizations and social groupings to enable them to fulfill themselves, but because [of the belief] that society as such exists for men, and not vice versa." [8]

Such goals are difficult to pursue when it is acknowledged in many parts of the world, not least in the newer nations, that the state must take a strong and positive leadership role in nation building, in developing the economy, and in protecting the general welfare. Pope John XXIII concurred in a view often stated by Protestant and Orthodox Christian leaders in Asia, Africa, and Europe that governmental authorities should give wholehearted and careful attention to both the social and economic progress of citizens, assisting in the development of the productive system and of such essential services as the building of roads, transportation, communications, water supply, housing, public health, education, facilitation of the practice of religion, and recreational facilities. To these must be added insurance systems made available to citizens in case of misfortune and exceptional responsibilities, training for employment and placement services, protection of workers in their proper organizational privileges, and encouragement of cultural growth.

In such a political and economic development the state would be officially and actually "separate" from the church or organized religion in the sense of being "neutral" and "secular." However, it is difficult to see how a state so deeply involved in welfare, laudable as that is, would be free of common aims and images.

Is religion, as a consequence of these world-wide developments, to be in a position of bowing itself out of the picture after uniting for the purpose of affirming personal and social rights and duties? Does a "neutral" state and a "secular" society mean the withering away of religion? Or does one of the essential functions of religion come to fulfillment in the idea of the responsible society so that religion becomes thereby effectively world-wide? Can churches serve to animate culture with an ethos of dignity for man and of responsibility to God without institutionally pressing their claims upon government? How can a "neutral" state be rooted and grounded in a religious ethos?

These questions may be restated in terms of the relation of law to ethics. On November 11, 1962, Chief Justice Warren stated in a speech at the Jewish Theological Seminary of America in New York City that law cannot exist without ethics: "In civilized life, law floats in a sea of ethics. Each is indispensable to civilization. Without law, we should be at the mercy of the least scrupulous; without ethics, law could not exist." World civilization requires world law and world law requires world ethics. World ethics requires an ethos, a myth structure, a self-enforcing complex of meanings and values that hold society together. It is often acknowledged that law cannot evoke a nonexistent ethic or one that has become uncouth, obsolete, or irrelevant. Such an ethos and such an ethic must be appropriate to a pluralistic and highly interdependent world society, segments of which are at very different stages of social development and developing rapidly but at different gradients of growth.

The significance of the idea of the responsible society and of the social principles of the papal encyclicals with respect to economic and political institutions is noteworthy in contrast to the assumptions and shibboleths about American society that have dominated its past. America has tried to manage with an individualistic ethic which gives false images of the actual ethical situation. The United States is not any longer (and never fully was) an individualistic society thriving on a Puritan ethic of thrift and nonindulgence. America is corporate in structure with many collective enterprises of both a private and public and quasi-public character. Its economic order is not free enterprise with predominant free competition easily open to initiative of the single individual. It is characteristically a society dominated by mass corporate structures and administered prices. Ethically it is less and less "inner directed," with persons effectively expressing or creating their own moral climate and acknowledging Biblical and Puritan virtues as their own. It is more and more "other directed," with people failing to achieve genuine or mature autonomy (that is, responsible interdependence) and subject to pressures of the mass structures that are capable of wide ranges of overt or subtle manipulation. Banks (the earlier symbols of thrift) join producers and retailers in collusion with the agencies of mass communication, as evidenced by radio and television commercials, in promulgating an ethic of indulgence, status seeking, superficial achievement, and waste, with a complete leveling of values and no criteria of priorities. Deodorants, in fact, get more promotion than higher education. Cigarette advertising still lacks warnings about its proved health hazards. In this whole field those who hold economic power have not yet been made responsible to the people whose welfare is affected by it. The anonymity of money tends to homogenize all market values.

The problem of moving from a society dominated by eighteenth-century ideals and goals of individualism, through one in which the "gospel of wealth" perverted and supplanted the "Protestant ethic," and to one of social responsibility is not simply that of overcoming a few excesses along the way. There is evidence of widespread anomie and corruption in many spheres of society. Anomie is a condition of normlessness with respect to the ends of life and the means by which they are reached. When success or "getting there" is more important than how one gets there, the controlling rules of the game break down and deviant behavior becomes widespread. The two most effective forces in producing anomie are pecuniary standards and militarism. "Get the money" and "force is the only language they understand" are slogans and attitudes calculated to encourage the breakdown of responsible discipline of life and rational faith in settling conflicts. Corruption follows on the heels of anomie and is one of its major symptoms.

In a case book of "The Corrupt Society" drawn up by Fred J. Cook[9] the dimensions of this problem include ordinary citizens, law enforcers, judges, respectable businessmen, publishers, civil servants, leading church members, professional men, and so on. What makes the problem so serious is not just the widespread range of crime or its total amount but the apparent lack of ethics and moral fiber. A study of 1700 business executives showed that four out of seven stated that businessmen would violate a code of ethics whenever they thought they could get away with it. Cook recounts the following: the pressure a Negro janitor was under after honestly returning a large sum of money he had found; the case of the GE price-fix and organization ethics of the men involved; the common swindles of supermarket packaging and its thieving calculation which begets more fraud; robbery in highway contracting as in the Worcester scandal; white-collar crime in defaulting and embezzlement; organized theft by policemen; jungle ethics among corporations; the looting of government by business; the use of prostitution in sales promotion; cheating in sports and on television, as in the Van Doren case; and the widespread involvements of business, governmental, and ordinary people in the Billie Sol Estes phoney empire.

American society will not move beyond this morass of corruption and normlessness until the major goal-setters, opinion-formers, and decision-makers accept the responsible society as a frontier to be conquered. From the perspective of religious ethics this means the reintegration of norms and values at a higher level than heretofore. The agents of this higher integration must for the most part be the laymen and laywomen who participate on Sundays in corporate worship and during the week share policy making in the midst of secular ambiguities. Where so much of a burden is placed on motives of self-interest, it is doubtful whether self-regulation by business groups apart from political control will suffice to meet the temptations and strains of the economy.

Perhaps no more fundamental structural and functional challenge to the economic order confronts American life than the technological revolution called automation. Automation is not an entirely new phenomenon but is now widespread and penetrates deeply into economic life. The economic order is not simply an enlarged market place; it is economic life and it is a social system related to all phases of human existence. Automation is the end point of the technological revolution symbolized by the assembly line and by mechanical specialization and displacement of manpower. On the one hand, automation is the goal of technology by making the machine rather than man a slave. On the other hand, full automation means the end of industry as a social system. Herein resides its threat to the destinies of many workers, their families, their concept of work, their vocational self-respect, their trades unions, their on-the-job functional social relationships. Even more, the very existence of certain towns and cities is involved. Automation as a technological goal, therefore, conflicts with the economic and human goals of the industrial order viewed as a social system. Genuine economic goals are, like all values, *of*, *by*, and *for* persons. When economic leadership is not able to reorganize its social system for the benefit of persons whose welfare is affected by the power of the decision-makers for automation, the struggle for human dignity is transferred to the decision-making process in the political sphere. Workers and other citizens then naturally turn to the political order to redefine property use and power. The ground rules of an automated American civilization become the concern of all phases of the culture.

Some of the human and social dimensions of automation will illustrate a problem which is highly complex. It is ironical that the extent of the labor problem arising from automation is worked out on computers that displace labor. The United States Census in 1960 was able to do with fifty statisticians the tabulations that required four thousand one hundred statisticians in 1950. This is an interesting parable. We are told by automats that we are in an age of automation. And the correlations of consequences are calculated by computers.

Those who are displaced by automation and other advanced technology are mainly the unskilled: the farm laborer, the manufacturing operators, the routine clerical workers. A heavy toll falls and will increasingly fall on those with limited educational backgrounds. At the moment there is a particularly distressing displacement of the middle-aged, with serious consequences in family life. One of the reasons that people in middle age find it so hard to get jobs is not that they lack experience or particular skills, but that they lack the basic elementary education that is required for reemployment in today's economic system. When one recalls that people at age fifty or older have a reasonable expectation of living to age seventy-five, one can imaginatively anticipate something of the potential human tragedy that lies before millions upon millions of workers and their dependents who lose jobs at that time of life.

Acute as are the problems of disemployment among the middle-aged members of the labor force, the younger end of the age continuum presents a serious prospect as well. Indeed, Secretary Wirtz has observed that every month a larger proportion of the unemployed is among younger workers and among workers of minority groups. One of the most vulnerable groups comprises the dropouts from the nation's secondary schools because they are young and unskilled and lack the foundations in education to master the prerequisites of an increasingly scientific and technological society. Unless a sound cooperative program shared by management, government, schools, churches, and welfare agencies is provided, the dropout may become a person who will never have had a responsible job, or even any job, in his lifetime. The number of such young people is already counted in millions, those with a minority or color status having an additional handicap. The plight of youth is tied to that of middle age. When displaced middle-aged workers are effectively retrained and/or transferred with appropriate adjustments in their welfare claims to other jobs, the burden of unemployment is shifted to the backs of youth because they have no seniority, no priority in industry, and no tenure. Unless the economy expands significantly, the more society does for the displaced adult worker, the more vulnerable does the position of youth become. In such a complex interdependent situation that cuts across the generations, it grows ever clearer that an individualistic success ethic cannot bear the strain of modern life. Only an ethic which teaches men to bear each other's burdens and to establish institutions appropriate to freedom, justice, welfare, and mutual respect can carry the load of full responsibility demanded by the times.

The relation of religion to the economic and political responsibilities for the job victims of automation and the dropouts in the youth sector of the labor market should not be overlooked. Churches and synagogues have for a long time been increasingly middle-class institutions. They develop with the social drift because being voluntary societies, they attract the people who can support them and who have a sense of group congeniality. Churches, despite their ideals and formal Christian allegiances, tend to become clubs of like-minded people. Surveys consistently show that the educational level of the church members is rising and that the proportion of members who are blue-collar workers is declining relatively to white-collar workers and to the total number of blue-collar workers. Peer group acceptance is an important factor in maintaining a youth group in a local church or synagogue; and where the group as a whole is college-minded, the dropout from high school tends to become a dropout from the church. Thus, despite their ideals, churches and synagogues are caught in a social dilemma.

Problems attending automation are increased by the rapid growth in population, called the "population explosion" because of its scope and impact. This is a world-wide phenomenon occasioned at the present time mostly by the drop in mortality rates as a consequence of the control of disease, the improvement of sanitation, and the removal of a few of the greatest hazards to life expectancy. Population control is an explosive ethical issue among religious groups. Roman Catholics stress more the need for efficient productivity in the economy than birth control and view the latter within narrow limits. It is difficult to find an ecumenical consensus among all non-Roman Catholics. However, there is growing consensus on the ethical approach to questions such as "How many children?" and "At what intervals?" Responsible parenthood begins with responsible marriage. If it is granted that it is moral for Christians to employ means to prevent an individual act of sexual intercourse from resulting in conception, there would seem to be no moral distinctions among the means now known and practiced, provided that such means are acceptable to the consciences of both husband and wife and do neither physical nor emotional harm.

While religious groups are wrestling with the spiritual and ethical questions of family life in relation to population control, the social crisis occasioned by the population explosion becomes more serious every year. Throughout the world two out of three families are underfed. There is a widening disparity in living standards between the industrialized nations and the emerging nations. This disparity has not only economic but political consequences. Peace is threatened. Some economic authorities point out that there is simply not enough capital available to provide facilities to keep up with unchecked population growth in the under-developed countries. Political authorities have insisted that disarmament is almost a side issue so long as the specter of overpopulation stalks the earth. Standards of living have a direct bearing on political tension and both therefore depend in part on the rate of population increase. Programs of birth control are increasingly questions of governmental policy in adult education and health programs. They have direct bearing on agri-cultural development since, thus far, per capita food production has not exceeded, and may be dropping behind, the rate of population growth. Religion, economic life, and governmental policy must continue to be engaged in a dialogue of responsibility in behalf of population control.

In addition to the problems already indicated we must turn to what has been called the "military-industrial complex." Towards the end of his last term in office, President Eisenhower said:

> We have been compelled to create a permanent armaments industry of vast proportion. Add to this, three and a half million men and women are directly engaged in the defense establishment. We an-nually spend on military security alone more than the net income of all United States corporations. . . . Now this conjunction of an immense military establishment and a large arms industry is new in the American experience. The total influence—economic, political,

even spiritual—is felt in every city, every statehouse, every office of the Federal Government. We recognize the imperative need for this development. Yet we must not fail to comprehend its grave implications. Our toil, resources and livelihood are all involved; so is the very structure of our society. . . . In the councils of Government, we must guard against the acquisition of unwarranted influence, whether sought or unsought, by the military-industrial complex. The potential for the disastrous rise of misplaced power exists and will persist. We must never let the weight of this combination endanger our liberties or democratic processes.

The phenomenon to which President Eisenhower referred is sometimes called polemically *the warfare state*.[10] The term "complex" in the phrase "military-industrial complex" has a certain conspiratorial overtone. It is probably not ethically fruitful to treat the "complex" as a problem either of formal or informal conspiracy. There are, indeed, many military-industrial-governmental linkages in the web of contracts, deals, and political processes involved. Retired generals in considerable number are actually in the employ of large corporations possessing and seeking defense contracts. In individual cases this fact may warrant investigation. But the more basic fact of a changing ethos and way of life in America constitutes the chief frontier inviting ethical analysis and policy reconstruction.

Social institutions, including churches and universities, are in the course of years bound to be conformed to their environments unless they sustain a vigorous initiative and renewal of spiritual independence. The chronic perpetuation of a military-industrial complex constitutes a major crisis for all the segments of culture. Workers, management, researchers, students, families, communities are heavily subsidized by the defense budget of the federal government through contracts. Such living affects attitudes, thoughts, value systems. There is the spiritual concern that "public policy could itself become the captive of a scientific-technological elite." For the nation as a whole some authorities estimate that between one-quarter and one-third of all economic activity hinges upon military spending. Self-interest in military spending, Cook says, has become a national disease. Senator Ralph E. Flanders of Vermont voiced a concern regarding the effects of present trends on the ethos of American life. He said on the floor of the Senate: "It is not only that we are sacrificing to defense our standards of living and the free independence of our economic life. . . . We are sacrificing our freedom itself. We are being forced to shift the American way of life into patterns of the garrison state." [11]

The issues just cited have important involvements for the theme of national and world disarmament. Some have raised the question whether, all things being equal, the nation can now risk disarmament for fear of

depression and widespread unemployment. According to the United
States Arms Control and Disarmament Agency,

> The defense program absorbs nearly a tenth of the total United States
> production of goods and services and employs, directly and indi-
> rectly, a like percentage of the labor force. . . . In some industries
> dependence on defense employment is quite high. Approximately
> 95 per cent of the employment in aircraft and missiles, 60 per cent
> in ship and boat building, and 40 per cent of the employment in
> radio and communications equipment is dependent on defense ex-
> penditures. . . . Defense expenditures are particularly important in
> precisely those industries, notably the electronics and aerospace
> industries, that have shown the most rapid pattern of growth and
> technological innovation and provided a large share of the support
> for research and development. The defense program now finances
> about half of all industrial research and development and one-fourth
> of all pure research.[12]

Taken as merely a proportion of the total economy, the defense industry
would not seem of itself to be able to plummet the nation into a depression should disarmament come suddenly, but the combined economic
and political pressures involved in a program of disarmament—particularly from those areas most dramatically affected—raise serious questions
about any program for major disarmament in the foreseeable future.

With the question of disarmament we are directly engaged in international policies and responsibilities. There are not only the facts of distrust, of rival ideologies, of conflicts of economic systems, and of balances
of power. There are also the wide discrepancies in economic development,
standards of living, and resources in land, know-how, and manpower.
The close connection between economic and political life within a nation
affects the gap between the rich nations and the poor nations. Moreover,
the fact that vast numbers of people as in Mainland China are not politically part of the United Nations raises additional frontier problems. Mankind as a unit of cooperation and as bound together in a common destiny
lays upon the social conscience of the well-favored and affluent some
major obligations. The complacency of the affluent individual or group
in the face of interdependence and the possibility of human alleviation is
morally serious. The great immorality is to have the practical possibility
of common human betterment, such as wiping out abject poverty and
much disease and ignorance, and then failing to develop a social and
technical environment in which man can really be free and peaceful.

No one can predetermine or even envision the precise forms of the
economic and political institutions that would be appropriate for an environment in which persons would be truly free. Nevertheless, since law
rests on ethics and ethics is rooted in ethos, it is instructive to note some

of the basic value strivings that are emerging along with the new world civilization.

(1) For the new nations, under the leadership and guidance of the United Nations, there is a growing conviction that immorality attaches to acts of outside intervention or satellite imperialism.

(2) Countries undergoing rapid social change and newly emerging as autonomous nations deserve to manifest their own traits, drawing on traditions rich in cultural value and distinctive in quality, thus adding to pluralism and diversity in the context of world-wide interdependence.

(3) Economically developed nations must give disinterested aid through loans and capital investment, resisting the temptation to impose their own way of life while sharing assistance. There is a growing consensus in the United Nations that highly developed states must not turn the situation that prevails in less developed nations to their own aggrandizement be it economic or political.

(4) The Universal Declaration of Rights and Freedoms is an important cluster of goals and norms for guiding the constitutional and institutional growth of nations.

(5) Many of the Agencies of the United Nations are slowly and steadily building codes and policies which create a field of values. Here may be cited in addition to the Commission on Human Rights, and Food and Agriculture Organization, the World Health Organization, the International Labor Organization, and so on.

(6) There is an almost universal connection of racial equality and demand for freedom and justice. Few are willing to defend racist doctrines, even when they practice racist privileges.

(7) Almost everywhere is a groundswell of democratic values in the sense that the theme of a people's century is widely pervasive.

(8) Then there is also, despite the violence and revolutionary turmoil, a common hunger for peace and the belief that all peoples as a whole wish peace. Even the majority of statesmen accept the folly of general war. Hope for disarmament and eager demand for cessation of nuclear testing belong to this aspect of the ethos.

(9) Underlying these aspirations, fears, hopes, and revolutionary actions there is a common new attitude towards life. The future is viewed as not immutably fixed. Social structures are not subject to an objective fate. History yields in part to purposive change. Man's critical thoughts and disciplined actions make a difference. Human nature itself is adaptable. Socially and personally man can be reborn.

(10) Since so much is possible, people are determined to get out of the clutches of poverty, ignorance, disease, and exploitation. It is as if the whole of mankind were forging a common social creed which would put science and technology to work for personal and social betterment. Science—at least faith in science—is one of the basic ingredients of the

new international ethos. It carries with it revolutionizing attitudes towards nature, man, and problem solving generally.

(11) Governments are putting youth and adults to work mastering the elements of science and technology in many fields; but as a consequence the people are steadily growing in their conviction that the state exists as an agency for the welfare of the people and that advances in wealth and productivity should be widely shared with the people.

(12) The increasing tempo of world-wide communications occasions cooperative approaches to major cultural values. Music, art, dance, and the theater are global in their appeal and are creating people-to-people appreciation. Respect for diversity of cultural expression is united with understanding of what is common or universal in the arts.

(13) With all these trends towards a common ethos there is a deeper understanding, despite all evidences of evil, of the place and worth of man. There are unsolved problems of human togetherness which hang over the present generation with appalling menace. Yet the famous Chinese proverb applies: "If you plant for one year, plant rice. If you plant for ten years, plant trees. If you plant for a hundred years, plant men."

Religious leaders are concerned with the fact that the ethos which may be patterned out of such elements as have just been cited will be superficially secular. Secular democracy and economic progress by themselves do not satisfy a person's deepest longing for participation in community. They are, accordingly, threatened by traditional community ties of culture, religion, caste, and the like which in many places still give men and women a sense of belonging. Moreover, democracy and economic progress are still suspect in large parts of the non-Western world as Western cultural aggression. Such responses are capable of endangering both new nationhood and its proper economic goals. In any case, democracy must in large part be grown from below and there is a serious danger if so-called democratic principles and policies are forced on newly nationalized countries. Imported or imposed "democratic" governments are likely not to be representative of their people. There is, therefore, a paradox or dilemma. For the more the masses of people express their own present beliefs, values, and customs, the more family-centered, tribally divided, and tribally directed the new nations become. A people's revolution does not guarantee a Western-type democracy. Thus, many of the non-Western nations have to grow the forest all at once. They are challenged to telescope into decades or even less the economic, intellectual, political, and social revolutions which extended over centuries in the West. There is, of course, no defensible reason for demanding that the sequence or design of revolution should duplicate that of the West. In any case the revolutions are following distinctive national and situational complexities. Western democracies can learn much about the ethos of democracy from this fact. Religious leaders, for their part, are challenged to reexamine what is thought to be transient and what is permanent in social ethics and what are the absolutes which should be the reference points for the relative and the existential.

The issues which have been discussed in this chapter raise leading questions both for religious groups and for economic and political leaders and institutions. By formulating some of these problems we can summarize the frontier areas of religion in relation to political and economic responsibility. In the first place, religious leaders come from diverse Christian and non-Christian traditions. Leaders in the World Council of Churches are asking what the theological significance is of the fact that Christians with differing theologies can often agree among themselves and with non-Christians on concrete social problems and on objectives of social action. Closely related to this question is that of the authority of the Bible and of other sacred books for social ethics. How should this authority be expressed? What does it mean to say that God is at work in history today and that history has a center of meaning? How are the secular forces at work in society today related to the religious person's obedience to God? Is technical competence part of that obedience? Can the Christian conception of love, or any religious ethic of love, make use of moral laws or principles in order to be translated into political or economic decision? How is love related to the idea of the responsible society? Since, domestically, Americans live in a pluralistic society and since internationally mankind is composed of a plurality of nations and cultures, are there limits of compatibility of ethical practices with Christian love or any other religious ethic of love? How does a religious ethic effectively address itself to the ethos of society and how to visible institutional structures?

The idea of the responsible society has been offered above as the "middle axiom" or practical norm which can relate religious ethics to economic and political problems. Does this idea need to be expanded or otherwise modified in its essential ingredients?

Turning to economic frontiers we note that economic development has become a passionate concern of all nations, rich and poor. Every aspect of life is involved: work and leisure, villages and cities, tribal groups and regions, the structure of nations and their relations to each other. Old standards break down and new ones take their place. What are the purposes of economic growth? What concern should religious people have for the spiritual effects of economic change? Are there priorities of economic growth? Should automation be automatic or should it be planned in terms of personal, spiritual and social priorities? What are the demonic factors in technological development? From the standpoint of responsibility and obedience what does it mean for a person to be an obedient steward before God in a situation of unprecedented growth in technological and economic power? What is the economic responsibility of the strong for the weak? What is the difference between being a steward and being an exploiter? How is responsible social policy formed to express stewardship, when the agent is a large corporation or a nation? For Christians scientific development is often regarded as a sharing in understanding creation and technology as sharing in creation itself, though in ever so modest a way. These forms of sharing may lead to considering man's role in social redemption as well as in creation—in the will to sacrifice for overcoming injustice and in compassion leading to reconciliation. In obedient stewardship there is included a sense of responsibility for future generations with special respect, for example, to nuclear radiation, insecticides, the use of certain fertilizers, pollution of lakes and rivers, and the conservation of resources.

Finally, there are the issues of responsible government in a revolutionary age when world peace is not a luxury but a necessity; when in the aftermath of colonialism there is a lack of coherence between constitutional freedom and social change; when rival ideologies are associated with technologically successful, powerful, and productive states; when the power of government is growing in all forms of nation-states; and when there is developing integration between the national and international order. After the signing of a nuclear test-ban treaty, what are the next steps towards general disarmament? What means can be envisioned for regulating the use of force in the service of international order and justice and for providing alternative means of international change and adjustment? What policies should govern the transition from Cold War coexistence to cooperation? Many religious leaders are convinced that only a world organization that includes all nations can be an adequate vehicle for responsible world political order. Once this is achieved, are those persons right who like Grenville Clark and Louis B. Sohn, contend that there can be "no peace without law" and that this cannot be ensured by a continued arms race, by an indefinite "balance of terror," but only by universal and complete national disarmament together with the establishment of institutions on the world level which correspond to those that maintain law and order within local communities and nations? [13] These authors stress an effective system of enforceable world law in the limited field of war prevention; world law in constitutional and statutory form with appropriate penalties for violation; world judicial tribunals to interpret and apply the world law; a permanent world police force; complete disarmament of all nations; and effective world machinery to mitigate the vast disparities in the economic conditions of various regions of the world.[14] This plan contemplates that virtually the whole world shall accept permanent membership in a revised charter of the United Nations.

These proposals, like those sometimes made by ecumenical bodies, frankly question whether the nation-state is and can be an ultimate goal or only a stage in political development. Though it must probably be granted that unified nation-states may be essential in the transition from colonialism and in the task of nation building, current experience of interdependence points quickly beyond them as solitary sovereign entities to regional cooperation or federalism. How in an ethical perspective should one evaluate the fading of the national "mythos" in the Western world and the emergence of supranational constitutional forms? What are the implications for political order of the Common Market? What should be the goals of larger regional forms of political structure in eastern Europe, in the Arab world, in the Far East, and in Africa? Some see the regional institutions and organizations as necessary and useful political developments toward inclusive world order through international institutions.

Within the framework of a dependable pattern of responsible international government the question arises of the place and validity of national culture, religious, ethnic and linguistic groups, minority groups, and the interacting great civilizations of the world. We have already noted the values of cultural pluralism. Undoubtedly the great religions of mankind will play important roles in assisting in the dialogue among the plural elements just noted. The dialogues among the religions may perhaps be the most basic communication of all, if religious freedom is to be an ingredient in the emerging ethos of world community. If world law must rest on a sea of ethics, then religion, politics and economics have to explore their common frontiers of responsibility together.

------ ✳ ------

The preceding discussion has been primarily a statement of the idea of the responsible society and a number of applications of that "middle axiom" to contemporary frontier situations. In the second part of this chapter we must consider more fully the theoretical foundations of responsibility in terms of theology, the behavioral sciences, and ethics. The discussion will deal with responsiveness as fact and norm, with the theological context of responsibility, with levels of responsive communication, with conflict and the sense of common human destiny, with cultural pluralism and ethical relativism, and with the relation of responsibility to the basic requirements of economic and political order.

Religion, we have noted, is a response and a quest. It is a response to the power or powers which have ultimate control over man's destiny. It is also a quest—a quest for realization or for the achievement of goals. Human life is purposive. In the fulfillment of his quests man enlists the aid of the "Determiner of Destiny." Man prays. God in his goodness and power has the last word. The famous epigram states it: Man proposes, God disposes.

God's governance may be thought of in terms of law. The laws of nature as described by science are often viewed as the habits of God's acting. They are structural aspects of his providence. Yet laws are not only predictable patterns in the physical and biological realm; they are also conceived as principles or ultimate norms in the ethical or spiritual realm. They are objective structures in his goodness. The idea of God in relation to man is not conceived only in terms of ends or goals, so that man's purposes are viewed in relation to God's purposes, and not conceived only as law whereby man is viewed in relation to the orderly patterns of nature or as obedient or disobedient to the moral and spiritual laws of God; it is conceived also in terms of love and acceptance, with faith and trust understood as reconciling man's estrangement or alienation from God. In this sense the ideas of God responding to man and man responding to God include the other relations of goals and laws, but transcend them in more comprehensive and deeper attitudes. The supreme goal, the ultimate law, and the loving response are philosophical and theological conceptions which give orientation to the ways theology handles the problems of responsibility in the frontiers of economic and political life. This portion of this chapter will expound this theoretical context of responsibility and the responsible society.

The idea of responsibility roots in the basic idea and fact of personal responsiveness. Man is a being who responds. This means that he does more than just react. The whole of him is involved in his most significant responses. Viewed normatively, response involves responsibility. Man recognizes that he is accountable for his responses.

Personal response is both person-to-person, person-to-group, and group-to-group. All of these types of responsiveness are complex. Moreover, man responds to God, the ground of all responsiveness and responsibility. His responses at each level affect those at the other levels. Human life is interpersonal. Interpersonal responsiveness is triadic because while it involves two or more selves, it does so with respect to a third, some object in nature (thing, law, process) or some goal (value, end, norm). The third may also be another person. Nature and community provide a context for responsiveness.

Earlier in this chapter we noted this triadic situation when analyzing property, and we shall note it again when discussing the relation of theology to the economic and political orders. Property is not simply a person's relation to a thing which is scarce. Property is a person in relation to a community in a whole system of claims and standards with respect to that scarce thing. The responsive relationship does not stop with such a triad, however. There is an extensive community of interpretation and evaluation spread out in space and time to which an appeal is made. In the background of all interpretation and evaluation are theories, traditions, and persons who symbolize the historical norms of right relationships. Each tradition has its historical authority figures to which implicitly or explicitly the appeal is made, the silent listeners to the dialogue of responsiveness. Depending on the subject under consideration such figures might cluster around Moses, Jeremiah, Jesus, or Paul; or might include Milton, Locke, Jefferson, or Kennedy; or again, Adam Smith, Marx, Veblen, or Keynes. What such representatives of the community of interpretation signify can be symbolized through rational abstraction in phrases or figures of speech or statements of principle. Moses may symbolize the Torah, Jefferson the democratic faith, Marx the critique of capitalism, and so on.

In the widest context of responsiveness is the idea of God. The cosmic context of response, quest, and law is the divine community, a divine milieu in which persons live and move and have their being. H. Richard Niebuhr has recently stated this same point:

> To the monotheistic believer for whom all responses to his companions are interrelated with his response to God as the ultimate person, the ultimate cause, the center of universal community, there seem to be indications in the whole of the responsive, accountable life of man of a movement of self-judgment and self-guidance which cannot come to rest until it makes its reference to a universal order and a universal community, which that other represents and makes his cause.[15]

In Pierre Teilhard de Chardin's thought as expressed in *The Phenomenon of Man* and *The Divine Milieu*, this man-society-nature-God context is presented in terms of cosmic evolution.

Response as interpretation connotes an element of freedom. Since man's selfhood is reflexive by nature and his response to others is inherently interpretative, self-transcendence provides a degree of freedom. This freedom may in fact be quite limited in some persons at all times and in all persons under certain conditions, but it is inherent in personhood. Mutual self-transcendence applies to the God-man relation as well as to human relationships.

According to this view God does not force man's compliance with his will, but rather seeks to reconcile man to himself by self-giving love. Since God is the ground of the inclusive ultimate community wherein persons are valued, it follows that freedom, justice, welfare, and security are interlocked, for they are basic aspects of individual and social existence. As values or goals freedom, justice, and the common good may be abstracted from the interpersonal situation and considered separately. But taken together in polar tension with each other they coherently point the way to that important axiom, the responsible society, already considered above. The idea of the responsible society must of necessity include the idea of God not only because as a matter of faith God is creator and redeemer of man, but because, as H. R. Niebuhr says: "The process of self-transcendence or of reference to the third beyond each third does not come to rest until the total community of being has been involved." [16]

Response as interpretation involving God must recognize levels of community. We may express the relation of person and community in terms describing the various levels of communication. Communication leads to action, either of cooperation or of conflict. E. S. Brightman has summarized the levels of interpersonal relations as follows:

> (1) the level of mere causation—receptivity or action without awareness of the other persons affecting us or being affected by us; (2) the level of sympathy and antipathy—liking and disliking what others communicate to us; (3) the level of understanding—where the person or group is properly interpreted, yet perhaps all the more disliked; and (4) the level of love.[17]

This highest level of developing love presupposes and rationally criticizes all lower levels of interpersonal interaction. It envisions as an axiological goal a society of persons related in creative cooperation, mutual respect, loving devotion to truth, and the highest possible attainment of the experience of God. Such a society is both solidaristic and pluralistic. Both normative community and personal integrity are acknowledged in it.

Such a view is in contrast with a view that regards man's existence as acting within a hostile environment. An important segment of contemporary existential philosophy rejects the idea of a divine milieu. It is, indeed, frankly atheistic. Such a view has been stated by Sartre but also by Camus. The latter stresses the absurdity of man's hopes and fears, his feverish quests on an earth that cares nothing for him, within a space of years that is predetermined no matter what he does. Yet Camus's "absurdism" lead him to affirm that only love, justice, and unity matter. Though believing that this world has no superior meaning, he somehow knows that something in it, man, has meaning because he is the being who insists on having meaning. He goes so far as to insist that there has been no true work of art that has not in the end added to the personal freedom of everyone who has known and loved it. But one must press the question to both Sartre and Camus whether the part can have meaning unless the whole has meaning. Is not the connection between art and science close enough to insist that meaning is relevant to the farthest ventures of man?

There are undoubtedly persons, groups, and cultures that live in hostile and frustrating environments. They experience an estrangement which is often very deep. Nevertheless these responses, however justified they may be, are historical rather than necessitated by the nature of things. They are not ultimate. But because they are historical, ethics has a task and provides groups, nations, subcultures, and cultures with a challenge. In

Christianity the ultimate environment is conceived as being friendly, not hostile to human good. God is understood as giving to man a ministry of reconciliation. The historical realities of hostility are not denied, but man is given a vocation to break down the walls of hostility and to respond in creative ways. He is "called" by the One who is all-including to develop an inclusive perspective and concern. In Christianity the community which has this as a special vocation is the Church. Existence is not ultimately hostile, but historical existence is socially precarious, ambiguous, and fraught with tremendous danger.

One of the responses that a considerable number of persons are now making to threats to the very existence of common life is an increasing awareness of their common human destiny. Though God is creator and sustainer of the universe, he does not snatch men out of the evil consequences of forces which they set in motion. It is possible for mankind to destroy itself. Reliance on material wealth and on the power of unlimited wanton destruction causes some men to live anxiously and desperately. Though faced with the prospect of a common destiny in death, there is also the possibility of a society that will have banished hunger, want, ignorance, and disease. The responses of man are not assured.

A Biblical figure of speech identifies these alternative possible responses as follows: "Behold I set before you life and death! Therefore choose life." The response to God includes a goal and obedience to a command. But the command presupposes the freedom to choose death. Man is accountable in that he bears the consequences which follow quite objectively from his decisions. Therefore response becomes responsibility both toward God and toward fellowman.

The idea of a common human destiny points not only to the fateful consequences of man's choices with respect to such risks as nuclear war, but also to less dramatic facts.

Mankind is now the center of cooperation. This cooperation may be either unintended or purposive. Once it is recognized that for good or ill the whole human family constitutes an interacting whole, this fact has important involvements for religion and ethics. In God's purpose the essential unity of mankind means that men and women have an ultimate mutual dependence and a common need for world-wide cooperation.

There is no longer any human society that is completely cut off or unaffected by others. The causal chain of influence is continuous. Social cause and effect are not equally felt in all times and places, but no culture or nation lives to itself alone. Mankind has become a unit of intended or unintended cooperation. In popular religious parlance this truth is sometimes stated thus: Science, technology, and business have made mankind a neighborhood; the problem is to make it a brotherhood. If not fully a brotherhood, then perhaps at least a responsible society!

The idea of a common human destiny and the demonstrable fact of mankind as a unit of cooperation involve the confluence of national and cultural histories in an emerging history of civilization as a whole. This means that the idea of responsibility in political and economic affairs must be not only sociological but also historical. Cultures and nations have traditions. They have histories which developed in some cases in relative isolation from each other. They are unities of meaning and value which are threatened by other historical wholes. Modern life draws these national histories out of their introverted pasts and challenges them to find new unities in a larger common history. New nations have been born. Older nations are changing. In many Western countries the integrative development of national unity over the centuries has created in various nation-states a sense of common purpose and of civic responsibility and has led to stable legal structures of authority. In many new non-Western countries the creation of loyalty to the nation and the emergence of the nation as a functional community is now under way. Simultaneously both Western and non-Western worlds are involved in a new history-making civilization with its frontiers of responsibility.

Many societies that previously have been closed are now open. Such transitions are fraught with anxieties and confusion. Old norms and standards change and there is a strong feeling of anomie, normlessness. As old patterns of culture and institutions dissolve, individuals and groups, families and tribes, feel lost. They do not know how to respond or how to interpret what is right or good and what is wrong or evil. Their culture— that which man has created as his environment in relation to his ultimate environment—needs new normative reference points. In the period when the rules of the game are obscure this anomie makes for some moral confusion and social and personal disintegration.

In the developing countries there is powerfully felt need for new national identity. This often means that the slogan of freedom embraces the nation, but not personal liberty. It often also means a revival of the cultural heritage in the interest of group identity and national self-consciousness. Even racial factors are sometimes appealed to. Taking Africa as an example, some writers stress the need of the "African personality" and hold that a "national and regional cultural revival thus precedes a higher and truer internationalism because it will include African culture and civilization on an equal basis with that of other parts of the world." [18]

Cultural pluralism is a fact and presents the problem of relativism. The fact of cultural relativism should be distinguished from the theory of ethical relativism. The former does not necessarily imply the latter. Cultural relativism, or more properly cultural relativity, refers to the fact that cultures and nations are integrated in terms of dominant clusters of meaning and value. In such social systems operating as wholes the various parts are interacting and any major change in one part of culture entails changes in other parts. The parts are relative to the whole. Beliefs, practices, and culture patterns are understandable only when viewed in the whole system and get their inner significance from the myth structure in which they participate. An external view of cultural wholes has some value, but an internal interpretation is necessary to grasp fully the relativities of the cultural situation. Ethical relativism is another matter. This theory questions or rejects the idea, because of cultural relativity that there are any objective ethical norms universally valid and binding. The first view respects personality by requiring that human behavior can be appreciated by understanding the cultural whole in which it interacts. The latter throws doubt on the value of personality itself as an ethical norm.

A view that sees God as the ground of inclusive human community and universal responsibility is not inherently inconsistent with recognition of a diverse number of culture patterns, of distinctive national histories, and even of unique tribal practices.

How then is man to transcend the relativism that seems predetermined by cultural diversity and relativity? Are there cross-cultural norms? A number of anthropologists are convinced that such is the case. Man responds to his environment along relatively constant theme lines. Although diversity and variety abound in cultural patterns, they are classifiable in terms of cultural prerequisites, i.e., they can be categorized by types of functions which are common to all cultures. They correspond to recurring themes in man's adjustments and adaptations. Details of belief and practice are relative or subordinate to the larger functions which they express. Basic cultural problems are met by similar basic institutional responses. In the basic institutions of society man plays, as it were, a great many variations on a limited number of themes. To the behavioral scientist and the ethicist the continuity of these themes from culture to culture is more significant than the less fundamental discontinuity of cultural expression. This truth is recognized in the popular expression that human nature is fundamentally the same the world over.

As there are certain stable and constitutive elements in personality so there are constants also in society. Person and society are not fundamentally antagonistic ideas but rather involve each other. Internal to the self is a structure and a content which tends to represent the values of the group, and over against it, though internal to the same self, is a self-conscious self-transcendence which makes rational creative initiative possible. Though culture is a whole (wholes) the individual person should not be conceived as having only a passive or inert status in the process of cultural development. In communication among persons and between persons and the physical environment, norms have a significant function. Norms influence the perception of things and the quality of interpersonal interaction. Some norms are not bound by local community existence and there is evidence for the objectivity of values (norms) in cultural transcendence. The possibility of transcultural norms rests on the capacity of man for self-transcendence and on the postulate of his dignity even amidst cultural relativity, for the person is the valuer of all values. His worth is presupposed in all value criticism.

A comparison of the problems and turmoil in the new and developing nations, as well as a review of the Western world during the past four centuries, shows that they tend to be much more alike than overt conflict within the nations or among them might at first indicate. As various nations or cultures come into contact and even conflict with each other, the problems of communication become acute. Conflicts are often reinforced by ideologies which in the interests of rival states and economic systems may be fiercely antagonistic. Yet these conflicts are largely instrumental to common goal strivings. The determination to relieve the burden of poverty through industrialization is one such goal. And this process means the application of technology which in turn rests on the pervasive penetration of the nations by science. This and other elements in an emerging world ethos were noted in the first part of this chapter. In such a situation an international ethos, perceived theologically, develops in the direction of universality. But its concrete elements cannot be deduced from some ultimate norm or law. An international ethos, while acknowledging ideal ends, must emerge from all the groups which participate significantly in world society. No one nation, group of nations, economic society, or religious body can provide such an ethos for us. This fact does not, of course, prevent agencies like the Church or the General Assembly of the United Nations from being the teachers and catalysts of universal rights and freedoms.

The concept of responsibility is a fruitful one in this context because it combines in a new gestalt historically compelling ideals and norms in religion and ethics and symbolizes as well insights of the behavioral sciences. Goals or ends, laws and rights, virtues and conscience are subsumed under the idea of the responsible society. An ethic of responsibility stresses not only a subjective reaction to acts, events, persons, and institutions, but also the interpretation of these things at the level of rational critical response. In a world of conflict and communication it views culture and society as an interacting whole of interpretation. It recognizes that a response is often an anticipation of the way a policy or proposal will be interpreted. Moreover, it views this process as an ongoing one and therefore anticipates historical consequences, realizing that the new situation will be composed both of objective factors and interpretations. It is a realistic view that acknowledges interpretation itself as a causal factor. Yet responsibility does not founder in a sea of ethical relativity. The idea of the responsible society as an ethical norm affirms that all responses are accountable to the source of all ultimate norms, to the ongoing order of responsiveness, and to the persons affected by any and every pattern of power and authority.

The status of the idea of the responsible society is that of a middle axiom. It is not as abstract as the ultimate ideals of theology and it is not as specific as the programs of political and economic action. Though God be truth, righteousness, and love, it is not possible to obey much norms in the sense of perfectly satisfying the divine imperative in them. On the other hand, it is not possible to know by a direct contemplation of these ideals just what concrete ends must be pursued in politics and economics. What is needed is an ethical gestalt that both acknowledges ultimate ideals and provides guidelines for choice and action in the here and now. Freedom and justice in relation to power and welfare have reference points of accountability to God and to the people affected by the organization of power and authority. All power and authority are acknowledged as stewardship under God, the ideals of freedom and justice are recognized as being in tension with each other, and their service to personality is emphasized. At the same time the idea of the responsible society does not prescribe what the program of specific duties and obligations is. It is thus not an external norm superimposed from without, but an emergent axiom inspired by the dialogue between the Church as a community of God's people and the competing ideologies of such systems as capitalism and communism. It does not prejudge the outcome in terms of the form of future world economy. Yet it presses inescapable ethical questions.

In the idea of the responsible society economic and political power and authority are primarily considered. In an era of rapid social change these are fundamental problem areas for all nations. With a statement on the relation of theology to the economic and political sciences we may therefore bring our discussion to a close. We have already noted in dealing with the problem of property that economic questions are often basically resolved in the context of political decision. Economic values are predominantly instrumental. The major theological tradition of the West regards man as a steward of the scarce values which he tends and enjoys. The creative and constructive use of natural resources and human invention are major issues in social ethics. In an era when for the first time in human history it is possible to wipe out poverty as a material fate, the obligation to think and act with economic responsibility is great. To do so requires both economic and political decision making.

What are the main tasks of the economic order? The main functions of an economic system may be divided into five categories:

(1) Fixing standards
(2) Organizing production

(3) Distribution
(4) Maintenance and progress
(5) Adjusting consumption to production

With respect to the first function there has to be a social decision in a complex society as to the relative importance of different uses of productive power, as to which wants are to be satisfied and which left unsatisfied, and to what extent anyone is to be satisfied at the expense of another. Whose wants and which wants are to be satisfied and in what degree?

In the second function of economy there are questions of the allocation of available productive forces and materials and the effective coordination of the various means of production into such groupings as will produce the greatest result. This involves the establishment of suitable institutions, agencies, and procedures. Such decisions depend in part on the ethical spirit of the economy and on the social goals of the nations.

Distribution, the third function, is related closely to the control of production and the decision for whom to produce. Where traditions of "private property," "free competition," and "contract" prevail, the emphases are different from systems where the stress is on sharing production as widely as possible. Here the questions of incentives and rewards will be predominant.

In the fourth function of an economy the problem arises of how much development a society can afford or is willing to undertake at the cost of sacrificing present values and what forms development shall take. How much shall be consumed now? How much shall be saved? Who shall carry the burdens? Who will get the benefits?

The fifth function of an economy is to adjust consumption to production within very short periods. Here the problems of crop failures, of interruptions in manufacturing, or crises in the economy are illustrative.

In all five of these functions there are decisions which involve ethical responses. Such decisions affect the national economy, the persons involved within it, and the whole international economy. These decisions are interlocked with those of politics and government. We have already considered this factor in discussing property above and shall note it again below.

There is no sacrosanct economic system. Though all systems have the five functions or categories just noted, the various nations and cultures are at different stages of economic development, have distinctive historical backgrounds, and are infused with different ideologies or goals. The "idea of the responsible society" was formulated with the recognition that neither "capitalism" nor "communism" fully satisfies a critical ethical analysis. The "kingdom of God" ideal can be identified with no particular economic system. And every system must be held accountable to serving the welfare of the persons affected by its various forms of power and property. All forms of economic life are ethically ambiguous and provisional.

Theological perspective on political order and hence on political science regards the problem of government as ubiquitous, as provisional, as decisive. Government is a function of all social groups. Good government depends on a sound moral firmament throughout culture. Political order is more a matter of integration than of domination, for force alone is never enough to hold a state together. In all constituted government behind any show or organization of force lies authority. Authority always includes the idea of legitimate power, and authority is responsive to the underlying social structure. The force which government exercises— and in the state the monopoly of violence is granted the government—is but an instrument of authority, vindicating the demands of an order which force alone never creates. In a theological perspective the ultimate source of justice is God; the state has the vocation of being its guarantor.

In a responsible society, as was noted in the first part of this chapter, freedom is the freedom of men who acknowledge responsibility to justice and public order, and where those who hold political authority or economic power are responsible for its exercise to God and the people whose welfare is affected by it. There are times when personal worth demands the struggle for freedom, justice, or equality. These ideal norms are in tension with each other. Some see behind the demand for justice the social domination of a coercive state; some see in freedom the threat of anarchy or individualism; some see in equality the liquidation of personal individuality and the leveling of all creative genius to the plane of dull mediocrity. But the healthy dialectic among these norms serves the enhancement of person and community.

In the present dynamic stage of world social development freedom is closely related to the newer forms of nationalism. Scholars contrast "self-satisfied" nationalism with "self-assertive" and "self-expressive" types of nationalism. The drive of modernizing nationalism in the new countries has distinctive goals: national independence; rapid economic development; the creation of a nation-state governed by a regime based on popular identification of leader, party, and people; regional federation where expedient; and nonalignment in international affairs. These goals often bear the slogans of democracy but the ideologies of most of these countries seldom mention the liberal pluralistic constitutional democracy as developed in many Western countries. The freedom of the group in its determination to achieve national identity often overlooks the personal liberty which has become a hallmark of rights and freedoms in the older democracies.

The state has been given important directive and formative power in the fields of economic and social development. The state alone has the power and authority under God to act as trustee for society as a whole. The idea of the state is not a static principle unbalancing the sovereignties of present nation states, but refers to the state as developing in relation to sound political order as well. It must help men to create a social, economic, and political order in which man can indeed be free. The idea of the responsible society, therefore, has passed beyond the stage of merely rejecting the ideologies of laissez-faire capitalism and totalitarian communism. It recognizes a global enterprise in which new and old nations alike are called to an inclusive responsibility. It takes account of the new emphasis on state initiative and international organization on the one hand and the importance of relative freedom in enterprise and the regulating role of the market on the other. It recognizes that all of the economies are today "mixed" as between "public" and "private" sectors and that in some sense all states are today "welfare" states. At the same time it stresses a sense of personal worth within the community which rejects an interpretation of man solely in terms of his social and political functions and emphasizes a fuller participation by the people in the life of society at the level where power is exercised.

Paradoxical as it may seem, social solidarity rightly conceived is markedly pluralistic. Interdependence, mutual aid, group discipline, and freedom belong in one concrete whole. Social ethics must therefore consider community as an organic pluralism. Personal freedom finds its highest expression in rational love, the person finding fulfillment in productive labor and brotherly responsibility and the community planning its life not only in terms of social minimums and common necessities, but in terms of safeguarding and enhancement of the freedom which is fully personal. The responsible community grounded in the divine love is conceived normatively as rational love and as a pluralistic organism making for the actualization of the person.

NOTES FOR CHAPTER 16

1 James Bissett Pratt, *The Religious Consciousness,* New York, Macmillan, 1920, p. 2.
2 J. Milton Yinger, *Religion, Society and the Individual,* New York, Macmillan, 1957, p. 9.
3 I have gone fully into this question in *Religion and Economic Responsibility,* Chap. 5, and in *Foundations of the Responsible Society,* Chap. 7.
4 Robert M. MacIver, *The Web of Government,* New York, Macmillan, 1948, p. 126.
5 Amsterdam Assembly, *The Church and the Disorder of Society,* New York, Harper, 1948, p. 192.
6 *Ibid.*
7 D. L. Munby, *The Idea of a Secular Society, and Its Significance for Christians,* New York, Oxford University Press, 1963, pp. 14-30.

8 *Ibid.*, p. 33.
9 Fred J. Cook. "The Corrupt Society," *The Nation*, June 1-8, 1963.
10 Fred J. Cook, *The Warfare State*, New York, Macmillan, 1962.
11 *Ibid.*, p. 24.
12 United States Arms Control and Disarmament Agency, "Economic Impacts of Disarmament," *Economic Series 1*, January 1962, pp. 3-4.
13 Grenville Clark and Louis B. Sohn, *World Peace Through World Law*, Cambridge, Mass., Harvard University Press, 1962, p. XV.
14 *Ibid.*, pp. XV-XVI.
15 H. R. Niebuhr, *The Responsible Self*, New York, Harper and Row, 1963, pp. 86-87.
16 *Ibid.*, p. 87.
17 E. S. Brightman, "Personalistic Metaphysics of the Self: Its Distinctive Features," Chap. XV of Radhakrishan, *Festschrift*, p. 4.
18 See Paul E. Sigmund, Jr. (ed.), *The Ideologies of the Developing Nations*, New York, Praeger, 1963, p. 33.

QUESTIONS

1 What are the component elements in the idea of the responsible society?
2 How does the definition of property reflect the theory of responsiveness developed in the chapter and how should it be related to the main functions of the economic order?
3 Analyze in detail the dilemmas of the "military-industrial complex" from the perspective of the norms of the responsible society, such as freedom, justice, control of power, authority, personal welfare, and the like.
4 Criticize the optimism expressed in outlining the emergence of a possible international ethos.
5 If you reject the idea of the responsible society as a "middle axiom," what alternative would you propose to resolve the major problem with which the chapter wrestles?

SUGGESTED READINGS

Walter G. Muelder, *Religion and Economic Responsibility.*
————, *Foundations of the Responsible Society*, New York and Nashville, Abingdon, 1959.
D. L. Munby, *The Idea of a Secular Society, and Its Significance for Christians*, New York, Oxford University Press, 1963.
H. R. Niebuhr, *The Responsible Self*, New York, Harper and Row, 1963.
Robert M. MacIver, *The Web of Government*, New York, Macmillan, 1948.

NAME INDEX

TOPIC INDEX

Materialism, 26
Military-industrial complex, 480
Moral fallacy, 68
Motivations of religion, 341 f.

Naturalism, and religion, 57-76
Neo-scholastic tradition, 113-45
Noncontradiction, law of, 85 f.

Paganism and Christianity, 436 f.
Person (man), 23, 24, 212, 328, 420, 432, 487
Person-to-person relationship, 21, 489
Personality and culture, 417 f.
Phenomenology, and religion, 17-213
Philia, 207 f.
Philosophy, uses of, 151, 152
  as approach to religion, 3-8
Primitive religions, 343 f.
Private property, 495
Process Philosophy, and religion, 246-68
Projectionism, 309-16
Property, 469 f.
Protestant ethics, 475
Psychoanalysis, and Christianity, 369-413
Purity of heart, 209 f.

Realism, and religion, 77-112
  definition, 88
  theory of knowledge, 78 ff.
Receptiveness, 9
Relativism, cultural, 491 f.
Religion, as conserver of social values,

345 f.
  evidence in, 74
  goal, 11
  supernatural, 64
Responsibility, 493 f.
  of society, 475 f., 497

Salvation, 180 f.
Secularism, 324 f.
Self-identity, 21 f., 24
Self-transcendence, 333 f.
  as transcendental ego, 185 f.
Social solidarity, 497
Socioeconomic views, of religion, 467-98
Spiritualism, 26
Supernatural religion, 64, 74

Technology, and religion, 358 f.
Truth, 18, 32

Unification of life, 10

Values, 355 f.
  as universal ethics, 66, 360 f.
  special truths of, 75
Verification, 139 f.
Vienna circle, 221

Will, 6, 30
Wisdom, 8

Zen Buddhism, 305-9